The American Revolutionary Series

BRITISH ACCOUNTS

OF THE

AMERICAN REVOLUTION

*The American Revolutionary Series
is published in cooperation with
The Boston Public Library*

The Naval Biography of Great Britain:
Consisting of Historical Memoirs of Those Officers of the British Navy Who Distinguished Themselves During the Reign of His Majesty George III

By
JAMES RALFE

VOLUME IV

With a New Introduction and Preface by
GEORGE ATHAN BILLIAS

GREGG PRESS
Boston 1972

This is a complete photographic reprint of a work
first published in London by Whitmore & Fenn in 1828.
Reproduced from original copies in The New York Public Library,
Astor, Lenox and Tilden Foundations.

First Gregg Press edition published 1972.

Printed on permanent/durable acid-free paper in
The United States of America.

Library of Congress Cataloging in Publication Data

Ralfe, James, fl. 1820-1829.
 The naval biography of Great Britain.

 (American Revolutionary series. British accounts of
the American Revolution)
 Reprint of the 1928 ed.
 1. Great Britain. Navy—Biography. 2. Great
Britain—History, Naval—18th century. 3. United
States—History—Revolution—Naval operations.
I. Title. II. Series: American Revolutionary series.
III. Series: British accounts of the American Revolu-
tion.
DA87.1.A1R35 1972   359'.092'2 [B]   72-10833
ISBN 0-8398-1773-8

THE

NAVAL BIOGRAPHY

OF

GREAT BRITAIN:

CONSISTING OF

HISTORICAL MEMOIRS

OF

THOSE OFFICERS OF THE BRITISH NAVY

WHO DISTINGUISHED THEMSELVES DURING THE REIGN
OF HIS MAJESTY GEORGE III.

By J. RALFE.

IN FOUR VOLUMES.

VOL. IV.

LONDON:

PUBLISHED BY WHITMORE & FENN, CHARING-CROSS.

Printed by L. Harrison, 5, Prince's-street, Leicester-square.

1828.

Engraved by J.W. Cook, from a Miniature in the possession of Lady Otway.

Sir Robert Walter Otway

Rear Admiral, K.C.B.

𝔑𝔞𝔳𝔞𝔩 𝔅𝔦𝔬𝔤𝔯𝔞𝔭𝔥𝔶

OF

GREAT BRITAIN.

___

HISTORICAL MEMOIRS OF
ADMIRAL SIR ROBERT WALLER OTWAY, K.C.B.

CICERO is said to have recommended Pompey to the Romans for their general on three accounts: first, because he was a man of courage; secondly, because he was a man of genius; and, thirdly, because he was fortunate. These reasons appear to have operated on the minds of the Lords of the Admiralty in selecting Admiral Otway for the chief command in South America; for though it is not very probable that his courage will be called forth in battle, yet, owing to the complicated and important interests he will have to attend to, his political courage (which is quite as essential) will have many opportunities to display itself, and without which his genius would not avail: these qualifications, joined to that good fortune which has ever accompanied him, cannot fail of being attended with an increased personal reputation, as well as with great public advantage.

The family of Otway is of great antiquity, and has for several centuries been situated at Middleton and Ingmire-Hall, in the county of Westmoreland. During the civil wars, one of the male branches embraced the cause of Cromwell, and followed him to Ireland. As a reward for his fidelity and services, a considerable property was settled upon him. This property was certainly acquired by the sword, but the same may be said of most of the estates in that country: it still remains in the possession of his family, and is known by the name of Castle Otway. The father of the admiral was Cooke Otway, Esq. who married the sister of Sir Robert Waller, Bart. and niece of Sir Robert Jocelyn, Bart. of

Hyde-Hall, Hertfordshire, who was afterwards Lord Chancellor of Ireland, and subsequently created Baron Newport and Viscount Jocelyn. But though he is thus highly connected, we may safely and confidently say, that he owes nothing to family interest or influence; that he has attained every step in the service without their aid and assistance, and is entirely indebted to his own merit and exertions for the rank he now holds. His inclination to the naval service appears to have been in direct opposition to the views of his father, who being an officer of dragoons, and people generally have a predilection in favour of their own profession, wished him to enter the army, offering to purchase him a cornetcy: but the inducement was not sufficient to change his resolution; and his firmness having overcome all remonstrance, he was permitted to follow his own inclination. In 1784, at the age of thirteen, he embarked as a midshipman on board the Elizabeth of 74 guns, commanded by the late Sir Robert Kingsmill; and in the following year he removed to the Phaeton frigate, in which he proceeded to the Mediterranean, where he remained for three years. He was then appointed to the Blonde, and sailed to Jamaica, where he became a practical seaman, being able to steer, reef, or heave the lead, with any man in the ship. In 1793 he was promoted to the rank of lieutenant by Admiral Affleck, then a Lord of the Admiralty, who was well acquainted with his zeal and talents, having witnessed both during the three years he commanded at Jamaica. On his promotion to a lieutenancy, he was appointed to the Falcon brig; but in the following year he was removed to the Impregnable of 98 guns, bearing the flag of Rear-Admiral Caldwell, with whom he shared in the laurels acquired in the actions with the French fleet on the 28th and 29th May, and 1st June, 1794. It seldom occurs on such occasions that officers of the rank and station of Mr. Otway, that of a junior lieutenant, have opportunities particularly to distinguish themselves; perhaps more occur than are embraced: but it fell to the lot of Lieutenant Otway to render a most important service on this occasion. Seeing the fore-top-sail-yard was shot away in the slings during the action, he immediately went aloft, and, with the aid of Mr. Charles Dashwood*, lashed it to the cap, whereby the ship was enabled to wear in pursuit of the enemy. It is these instances which prove the activity of an officer, and also his genius; and so well pleased was the admiral with him for performing this essential service (without which the top-sail could not have been

* The present Captain Sir Charles Dashwood.

again set), that he took him by the hand and returned him thanks publicly on the quarter-deck.

The favourable opinion which the admiral had formed of Lieutenant Otway's abilities did not terminate with the expression of his thanks, but on the first lieutenant being promoted on account of the battle, he offered to appoint him to that situation. This proposal, however, Lieutenant Otway, with singular modesty, declined, alledging that he was on the best of terms with his messmates; and that being placed so suddenly over the heads of several *old officers* might possibly create jealousies, and prove detrimental to the service*. We record this anecdote with pride and satisfaction; it affords a proof of his good sense and disinterestedness; it could not fail of placing him upon still better terms with his brother officers; and if such motives and conduct were always duly appreciated by those " in authority," they would be attended with the most important and beneficial results. The rear-admiral acknowledged the justness of Lieutenant Otway's observation, but declared, that in the event of his flag being shifted into any other ship, he *should be* his first lieutenant. This actually happened a few weeks afterwards, when the admiral removed into the Majestic of 74 guns, accompanied only by his captain, secretary, and Lieutenant Otway, and was ordered to the West Indies, with four sail of the line, in pursuit of a French squadron. He was also appointed commander-in-chief of the Leeward Island station; and Lieutenant Otway there received fresh marks of the admiral's confidence and esteem, by being appointed to command the Thorn† sloop of war of 16 guns, with the rank of commander.

The West India Islands were at this time in a deplorable condition; most of them had lately been conquered by Sir John Jervis, but two of them, Guadaloupe and St. Lucia, had been retaken by a French force under Victor Hughes; and all of them were ripe for a revolt in favour of the new doctrines of the rights of man. Materials are always more or less ready for combustion in colonies where a few whites hold a multitude of negroes in slavery. These favourable circumstances were seized by the French commander with the greatest avidity, and the slaves were incited to revolt by the allurement of liberty, so congenial to the heart of man. A communication was opened with the discontented at St.

* Marshall.

† Captain Brenton says that she was one of the wretchedest little vessels that ever bore the name. She was, however, a very fine vessel of her class.

Pierre, Martinique; and agreeably to a plan concerted between them and Victor Hughes, a large schooner was fitted out at Guadaloupe, having on board two commissioners and thirty-six officers, many of whom composed the staff of Victor Hughes, charged with orders from him to land at Martinique, and distribute proclamations, to endeavour to excite the whole colony to revolt, and to commence by setting fire to the town of St. Pierre. Owing to the vigilance of Captain Otway, however, this plan was frustrated, by the capture of the vessel and her incendiary cargo; an event which was considered of so much importance by the French royalists on the island, and gave them so much satisfaction, that they presented Captain Otway with a gold-hilted sword of 200 guineas value, to mark their high sense of the service rendered to them.

Captain Otway continued to cruise round the island, and on the 25th May, 1795, fell in with, in the night, the French national corvette Le Courier of 18 guns and 119 men. The crew of the Thorn was at the time extremely sickly, and was reduced to 80 hands, men and boys. This circumstance, however, did not prevent Captain Otway from bringing her to action: the enemy fought with spirit and vigour, and twice attempted to board the Thorn, but was each time defeated with loss. At last, after an action of thirty-five minutes, the enemy was obliged to surrender to an opponent every way inferior, except in skill and gallantry. On this occasion Captain Otway and 5 men were wounded; but Le Courier had 7 men killed and 20 wounded, being nearly one-fourth of her whole number. A curious circumstance also attended the capture of this vessel: from the first it became evident that she intended to attempt boarding the Thorn; and on the following morning it was observed that she had slung a stink-pot filled with combustibles to the fore-yard, with the intention of dropping it on the deck of the Thorn when she came along side, and which on its explosion was expected to so intimidate the Thorn's crew that she would be easily carried. By one of those fortunate circumstances, however, which appear to have attended Captain Otway, the enemy's fore-yard was shot in the slings, and the vile plan which the enemy had prepared was rendered useless.

From Martinique the services of Captain Otway were transferred to St. Vincent, which was in a dreadful state of insurrection. Here, " in co-operation with the army, he made an attack upon Owia, which was surprised and taken by the Thorn and a party of soldiers belonging to the 60th regiment. He afterwards landed his crew, and, in conjunction with a detachment of troops, stormed the strong fort of Château Bellair, the loss of which obliged the enemy to retire into the interior of the island. Captain Otway on this occasion received a slight wound, and had 25 of his men killed and wounded*." The activity of Captain Otway was never more particulary manifested than at this period ; he was present in every scene of danger, and his attention was directed to every vulnerable point : but the island being placed in comparative security, and having received the unanimous thanks of the House of Assembly for his exertions and important services, he proceeded to the Island of Grenada, where his conduct became equally conspicuous and praiseworthy. His merits and services having attracted the attention of Sir John Laforey, who had succeeded Admiral Caldwell in the chief command, he promoted him to post-rank in the Matilda; but in consequence of a change at the Admiralty, and his commission as commander not having been confirmed, he was ordered by the new Board to go back from being captain of the Matilda, to his former situation as lieutenant of the Majestic ! However, upon a representation of the circumstance by Sir John Laforey†, Lord Spencer immediately confirmed his appoint-

* Marshall.

† The following is an extract from his letter addressed to Evan Nepean, Esq. dated H. M. S. Majestic, Martinico, October 1, 1795:

" Upon this occasion, I cannot dispense with doing justice to the Captains Vaughan and Otway, by a representation to their lordships of their merits. Upon my arrival here, the former, who commanded the Matilda, and the latter the Thorn sloop, were recommended to my notice in very strong terms by both the commanders-in-chief, for their great activity, diligence, and exertions in their line of duty. Captain Vaughan had been remarkably active in several instances in the station he was sent upon. Captain Otway has particular and signal services to speak for him : for one, I will beg leave to refer to Vice-Admiral Caldwell's letter to you, sir, dated at Spithead, the 29th July, 1795, which I have seen published, giving an account of his having captured a French ship of war, called Le Courier National, of 18 9 and 6-pounders and 119 men, by boarding her. He has had a present of a gold-hilted sword made to him by the legislature of this island, for his activity and vigilance in the protection of it, when stationed here. The highest encomiums of him have been transmitted to me from the legislature of St. Vincent during their distresses, where I had sent him for their protection ; and he has obtained my approbation of his gallant and spirited conduct there in more instances than one, particularly when there was a necessity for forcing a strong post the enemy possessed, and the landforce was not sufficient ; he landed with his men, and led the way to the attack, when the opposition was so great that the private men of the troops could not be induced by their officers to advance. I knew nothing of either of these gentlemen when I came here ; but on account of their merit, I removed Captain Vaughan to the Alarm, a larger frigate, and gave post to Captain Otway in the Matilda."

ment of post-rank, October 30, 1795, and he succeeded Captain Warren in the command of the Mermaid of 32 guns. In this vessel he was destined to add to his reputation and increase the glory of his country.

Being off Labaye, in company with the Favourite sloop of war, commanded by Captain (now Admiral Sir James) Athol Wood, and observing that some English troops were pent up in a block-house, from whence communication with the shipping was entirely cut off by the enemy, who had erected a battery in a position that enabled them to scour the beach, and thereby prevent supplies being sent to the garrison, Captain Otway instantly landed with a party of seamen and the marines of both vessels, under the cover of whose fire he stormed the battery and levelled it with the ground. Soon after this affair, several thousands of troops arrived, and were disembarked in the vicinity of Labaye, under the superintendence of Captain Wood, and were very shortly in action with the rear of the enemy's army. At this critical moment two French vessels, under English colours, arrived at Labaye with a considerable reinforcement of troops from St. Lucia. The general commanding the British troops immediately decided upon re-embarking, and communicated his intentions to Captain Otway, who seeing, however, that the carrying of such a measure into effect would be attended with the total loss of the island, *refused to comply*, saying that he had landed the troops there at great risk*, by the general's desire, and that they must now *fight it out, as he would not embark a man*. Having taken upon himself a most awful responsibility, he galloped up to a height on which were posted some field-pieces under the command of an artillery-officer, ordered their fire to be opened on the enemy's vessels, and by that means compelled them to cut their cables and stand out to sea, with the soldiers still on board. They were pursued with great promptitude by Captain Wood, but escaped in consequence of the Favourite unfortunately losing her fore-top-mast. A general attack was now made by the British troops, led on by Brigadier-General Campbell, the second in command, who charged the enemy on Pilot-Hill and gained a most decisive victory. Thus did the promptitude and energy of Captain Otway preserve the island under the dominion of Great Britain; and thus we see the benefit resulting from the firmness, resolution, and intrepidity of one man.

Seeing that the island was in a state of security, Captain Otway sailed

* The Ponsborn East-Indiaman was lost that night, in consequence of being detained after landing the soldiers embarked in her.

on a cruise off Guadaloupe; and on the 8th August, 1796, La Vengeance frigate, mounting 52 guns, was ordered to sea by Victor Hughes, for the express purpose of either capturing or sinking the Mermaid. The ships accordingly met about noon, an action ensued, and, after a sharp contest, which continued till half-past three p. m. the enemy's fire was nearly silenced, and Captain Otway had every prospect of capturing his colossal opponent; but it suddenly fell a dead calm, and baffled all his manoeuvres. The action was witnessed from the shore, and Victor Hughes, to prevent the disgrace attending the loss of his ship, immediately ordered all the boats from the shore to her assistance, and by them she was towed in under the battery of Basseterre, which during the action kept firing occasionally at the Mermaid. Exasperated at being thus defeated in his design, Victor Hughes first broke the French captain's sword, for what he termed his cowardly conduct, and then deprived some hundreds of English prisoners of water during the day, for having cheered upon seeing from their prison the result of the action! In this contest, the enemy's ship suffered considerably in her hull, sails, and rigging, and had 29 men killed and wounded; whilst the Mermaid had not a man hurt; and although she was much cut up in her sails and rigging, came out of action with all her spars, the fore-top-gallant-mast excepted, in perfect order. Such intrepidity as was here displayed should always be crowned with success; but the greatest degree of human bravery, joined to the utmost perfection of naval skill and discipline, cannot always command it.

" In the month of April 1797, the Mermaid, in company with the Hermione and Quebec frigates, had a smart affair with the forts at Jean Rebel, St. Domingo, and succeeded in cutting out twelve sail of merchantmen. Captain Otway soon after exchanged into the Ceres of 32 guns, the boats of which ship captured La Mutine French privateer of 18 guns and 90 men, lying at anchor in a creek at Porto Rico, and drove on shore and burnt another vessel of the same name and force. The party which boarded the latter was headed by Captain Otway, whose coxswain received a musket-ball when by his side and in the act of jumping on board. Early in 1798 he was cruising in the gulf of Mexico, under the orders of Sir Hyde Parker, by whom the Ceres and Trent were sent in chase of a guada-costa, near the Havannah. Unfortunately, they both ran aground, of which the Spaniard took advantage and placed himself in a position to annoy the Trent very much; which being perceived by Captain Otway, he threw himself into one of the boats sent from the squadron to their assistance, and, followed by five others, attacked, carried, and burnt the enemy's vessel, which mounted 6 long 24-pounders and 4 smaller guns, and bore the broad pendant of a commodore of flotilla. On this occasion Captain Otway had another narrow escape; Lieutenant Walker of the Thames, a most gallant officer, being badly wounded when about to board the enemy, and close to his gallant leader. The Ceres was almost immediately afterwards got afloat, and assisted in extricating the Trent from her very dangerous situation. The commander of the latter dying soon afterwards, she was given to Captain Otway, as a reward for his very great exertions in saving so fine a ship*.

" At the commencement of 1799, the Trent appeared off St. Juan, the capital of Porto Rico, which induced the Spanish governor to send orders overland for a schooner then lying in a small harbour on the south side, to reland her cargo, and to be dismantled. Soon after these directions had been given, the Trent accidentally went to that side of the island, and discovered the schooner moored close to a battery of 6 24-pounders. Captain Otway got hold of a negro on the coast, to whom he gave 100 dollars for shewing him a landing-place at some distance from the battery. The same night he landed a party of seamen and marines, and marching into the rear of the enemy, took them by surprise, at a moment when they were watching the movements of the Trent, with their guns loaded and primed. The battery was immediately destroyed, and the sails, rudder, and cargo of the schooner brought down from a house half a mile in the interior, reshipped, and the prize sent off for Jamaica by daylight the next morning. This service was performed with the loss of only one man killed on the part of the British; about twenty of the enemy were put to the sword in the battery. A few weeks after this affair (March 30), as Captain Otway was again reconnoitring on the south side of Porto Rico, accompanied by the Sparrow cutter, he discovered L'Alexandre and Le Revenge, French privateers of 18 guns, and a Spanish brig of 10 guns, and some coasting vessels, at anchor under a small battery within the *Dead Man's Chest*. The enemy's guns on shore were soon silenced by the Trent, and her boats sent under cover of the Sparrow to attack the vessels. On their approach, each of the privateers hoisted the bloody (red) flag, as an indication that no quarter would be given; notwithstanding which the boats resolutely

* The Trent was one of the first frigates built of fir; she sailed remarkably well, was rated at 36 guns, and carried 18-pounders on her main-deck.

pushed on, and after a smart action carried the whole, without losing a man; whilst the enemy had no less than 50 killed, wounded, and drowned*."

Captain Otway afterwards proceeded off the Spanish Main, and being about fifteen leagues to the northward of Laguira, on the 7th July, 1799, received information that the Hermione, whose crew had mutinied, and murdered the captain and officers, was lying in that port under the protection of the batteries, when he, having long wished to discover the place of their retreat, instantly formed the resolution of cutting her out. For this purpose the barge and large cutter were prepared, and manned with volunteers. Captain Otway and his junior lieutenant, Thomas Ussher†, went in the barge, and Mr. Maccleverty, the master, in the cutter. About one o'clock p. m. they left the ship, and after a fatiguing row of *nine hours*, a light was seen on shore, and shortly afterwards a fishing-boat was fallen in with, out of which a pilot was taken, and they proceeded for the harbour. At one o'clock a. m. the boats, with their oars muffled, entered the anchorage, and rowed through the shipping; but had the mortification to find that the Hermione was not there. Observing a vessel, apparently a corvette, which the pilot informed him had lately arrived from Spain, Captain Otway ordered the cutter to board her on the larboard bow, whilst the barge should board her on the larboard quarter. On arriving close upon her quarter, a musket was thrust out of one of the portholes and discharged, the shot from which passed close along Captain Otway's cheek, and its force knocked him backwards; but he recovered himself in time to prevent any return of the fire, lest it should serve to alarm the other ships and batteries. The men jumped instantly on board; those who resisted were cut down to a man, and she was carried in the most gallant manner, and in a style that left no doubt as to the result had she been the object of their visit, the Hermione herself. The cable having been cut, the prize was taken in tow; but the alarm having by some means been given, drums were heard in every direction of the town, and the batteries soon after opened a heavy fire on the ship and boats. The wind now died away, and little progress could be made; but as the smoke from the guns did not rise, the ship was consequently concealed, and but few shots took effect. By break of day she was clear of the batteries, and the Trent was eagerly looked for by the exhausted boats' crews; but as the sun rose, a flotilla of gun-boats was observed

---

* Marshall.   † Now a post-captain.

coming out of the habour in pursuit. To contend against such a superiority would have been useless; but the urgency and difficulty of the
situation afforded Captain Otway a fine opportunity to display that presence of mind and coolness of judgment, which distinguish him in all
sudden and dangerous emergencies, and which form such peculiar traits in
his character. From a fatiguing row of sixteen hours, the boats' crews
could with difficulty keep the tow-rope taught; the Trent was not in sight,
a dead calm existed, and Captain Otway's sole object was now to save his
brave fellows from falling into the hands of the enemy, who was rapidly
approaching with an overwhelming force. The accomplishment of this
all-desirable end now rested on his genius; and with the utmost com-
posure he ordered Lieutenant Ussher, who was on board the prize, to
have two of the 12-pounders treble shotted, and point them down the
main-hatchway; to keep double sentinels upon the prisoners confined in
the cabins; and upon the gun-boats arriving within grape-range, to fire
the guns, take to his boat, and abandon the prize. These directions
were strictly followed, and on the coming up of the enemy they found
full employment in saving their countrymen from going down with the
sinking vessel; by which means Captain Otway and his brave companions
effected their escape without farther molestation.

Captain Otway continued to command the Trent till September 1800,
when he sailed for England with the flag of Sir Hyde Parker, having
served in the West Indies for nearly six years, during most unhealthy
seasons, when the mortality was almost beyond conception, and when
very few remained on the station who could avoid doing so. During
that period he is supposed to have captured or destroyed two hundred
of the enemy's privateers and merchantmen (as great, if not a greater
number, than ever fell to the lot of one individual), mounting in the
whole above 500 guns; and besides these services, he assisted at the
sieges of Morne Fortuné in St. Lucia and Fort Matilda in Guadaloupe.
For such meritorious conduct, the thanks of the Admiralty were three
times communicated to him through the respective admirals under whom
he served.

Shortly after his arrival in England, Captain Otway, in the most handsome and disinterested manner, gave up the command of one of the
finest frigates in the service, in which, if he had remained, no doubt
several thousands of pounds would have been added to his private fortune; but, as honour with him was always superior to riches, he preferred

the offer that was made to him of an appointment to the Royal George, bearing the flag of his friend Sir Hyde Parker, and removed with him into the London on his being appointed to command the fleet destined to act against the Northern Confederacy. The fleet sailed from England in March 1801, and on their arrival in the Categat the fleet was brought to, when a consultation took place between the flag-officers, captain of the fleet, and some of the senior captains, as to the best means of carrying into effect the object of the expedition; and it was at last decided that it should be by the Belt.

In narrating this circumstance, and the subsequent change in the mode of attack, Mr. Southey has attributed it to the strong and forcible representations of the captain of the fleet. It is not with a view to lower the character of Sir W. Domett, or to detract from the well-earned fame of Sir Hyde Parker, that we allude to that event; but solely with a view of stating the particulars as they occurred, and of giving the credit to him who really deserved it. Captain Otway was not present at the consultation, but after it had broken up, and Nelson and the other officers had gone on board their respective ships, the signal was made for the fleet to make sail, and the Edgar was actually leading through the Belt, when Captain Otway came to a knowledge of the measure which had been decided on. Though he was still a very young post-captain, his comprehensive mind instantly told him, that if such measures were persevered in, the whole object of the expedition would be defeated; that the going round to Copenhagen by the tedious passage of the Belt would be attended with difficulties which would never be surmounted by even the energies of British seamen, as the whole of the guns and heavy stores belonging to the line-of-battle ships must have been taken out, to enable them to pass the " Grounds" in going to Copenhagen by that route. His situation was extremely delicate, the plan had been decided on by all the sages of the fleet, but with such a conviction on his mind, Captain Otway determined on laying his opinion before the commander-in-chief. Fortunately his intimacy with Sir Hyde Parker greatly facilitated this desirable object, and it was equally fortunate that Sir Hyde Parker was not a man to persevere in an error when pointed out, because he had formed a resolution to follow a particular line of conduct. The interview almost instantly took place, and Sir Hyde as soon became convinced that he was not taking the shortest route to victory, which was as speedily acknowledged by Sir W. Domett. *The fleet was again brought to*, and

Captain Otway was sent to apprise Lord Nelson of the reasons. On going on board the St. George, he was immediately introduced to Lord Nelson, and, on explaining to his lordship the alteration that had been made in the route, he exclaimed, " I don't care a d—n by which passage we go, so that we fight them." He determined to return with Captain Otway to the commander-in-chief, and, in consequence of the wind blowing fresh, was hoisted out in one of the boats, and on his arrival on board the London, every thing was finally arranged agreeably to the plan suggested by Captain Otway.

The particulars relating to the attack on the Danish fleet before Copenhagen we have detailed in the Memoirs of Sir Hyde Parker and of Lord Nelson. Owing to the London not forming part of the division ordered to engage the enemy, there appeared at the commencement of the battle but little probability of Captain Otway taking any share in it: yet he became one of the principal actors; and we will venture to say, that his services on that occasion were equal to those of any other officer employed, Lord Nelson's alone excepted. The early part of the action was viewed by him at a distance; it was an anxious period, and must have been mortifying to all those who, like himself, possessed an ardent desire to signalize themselves in such a contest. When Sir Hyde saw the critical situation of the squadron under Nelson, it became a question between him and the captain of the fleet whether he should make the signal to leave off action; but as that measure was strongly opposed by Captain Otway, it was determined that the captain of the fleet should proceed to Lord Nelson to ascertain the situation of affairs: he went below to adjust some part of his dress, but, whilst he was so doing, Captain Otway solicited and obtained leave from Sir Hyde Parker to execute the intended mission. At this moment a boat was passing the London; she was instantly hailed, and Captain Otway pushed off in her, with that promptness and alacrity which are congenial with his whole conduct and character. The boat had on board a ship's hawser coiled up, but Captain Otway would not wait to have it discharged, and in that dangerous vehicle passed through the enemy's fire to the Elephant. Had a shot struck her, she must have sunk like a stone, but Captain Otway fortunately reached his destination in safety; but before he got on board, the signal to leave off action was made: it was, however, disregarded by Nelson, and, as Captain Otway had *verbal authority from Sir Hyde Parker that the battle should continue if he saw there was a probability of success,* the action was continued till the enemy submitted ; and Captain Otway had thus the opportunity of being present at that most interesting and important event. His exertions, however, did not terminate with the fight: on the 2d April he displayed his activity and courage; and on the 3d he became equally celebrated for judgment and presence of mind. But before we narrate his conduct on that occasion, we shall insert the particulars of the circumstance alluded to, from Clarke and M'Arthur's *Life of Nelson.* They say, " Finding that one of the line-of-battle ships, the Zealand, which had struck the last, and was under the protection of the *Trekroner,* had refused to acknowledge herself to be a captured ship, and made some quibble about the colours and not the pendant having been hauled down, his lordship ordered one of our brigs to approach her, and proceeded in his gig to one of the enemy's ships which were within that battery, in order to communicate with the commodore, whose flag was still flying on board the Elephanten. When he got along side, he found it to be his old acquaintance Muller, whom he had known in the West Indies. He invited himself on board, and acted with so much ability and politeness towards his friend and the officers assembled, that he not only explained and gained the point in dispute about the Zealand, but left the ship as much admired by his enemies, as he had long been by those who were his intimate friends in his own fleet."—This account is followed by Mr. Southey, who, in addition, says, that " it was a brig and three long boats that Nelson ordered upon this service ; and that when he had gained the point with the commodore, through his own dexterity and urbanity, the men from the boats lashed a cable round the Zealand's bowsprit, and the gunvessel towed her away." Now whatever merit belonged to this enterprise (and certainly it was merit of the very highest order), *it is due to Captain Otway, and to him alone.* It was performed by him and a single boat's crew ; and we will venture to affirm, that it stands unparalleled in naval history. In the first place, we have to observe, that *it was the Holstein, and not the Zealand,* which was the object in dispute: two officers had been sent to demand and get possession of her, *but had failed.* Lord Nelson then wrote a note to Sir Hyde Parker, stating that the Holstein had struck her colours in the action, but that when she was some hours after attempted to be taken possession of, the Danish captain refused to surrender, under the subterfuge that his *pendant was still flying;* and actually fired musketry (it being nearly dark) at the boats that were ordered to take possession of her. His lordship then proposed that she should be peremptorily demanded; and concluded by saying, " You had better send Otway on this delicate affair."

Such a mark of his lordship's opinion of Captain Otway's judgment and abilities could not fail of being highly gratifying to his feelings: to be chosen to perform an important duty is at all times flattering; but to be selected to perform that which others with equal means had been unable to achieve, is the highest gratification that an heroic spirit can desire. Having obtained Sir Hyde Parker's permission to adopt and follow his own plan for the capture or recovery of the Holstein, Captain Otway instantly went on board the Eling schooner, Lieutenant Peek, hoisted a flag of truce, and anchored off the bow of the enemy's ship, which was at anchor within pistol-shot of one of the Crown batteries. Her pendant was still flying, though her colours were down, and she was preparing to warp into the arsenal. Seeing there was not a moment to be lost, Captain Otway immediately pushed along side of her in the Eling's boat, having ordered the coxswain (a bold and determined character) to take the opportunity, while he was claiming the ship from the surviving officers, *to proceed, unperceived if possible, through the main chains, into the main-top, haul down the pendant, and convey it into the boat.* Strange as this may appear, it was accomplished to the very letter, the attention of the whole crew being directed towards Captain Otway, who was standing on the quarter-deck demanding possession of the ship, which they still refused to give up, but referred him to their commodore, who was on board a two-decker close by in the arsenal; making use of their former plea, that the pendant (though it was then in the Eling's boat) *was still flying.* Thus far successful in his object, and his situation being such as, in the event of a discovery, would not have been a very pleasant one, Captain Otway gladly embraced the offer of a reference to the commodore. He accordingly proceeded to his ship in one of the Danish boats and accompanied by a Danish officer, having ordered the Eling's boat, containing the pendant, to return to the schooner. Finding on his arrival that the commodore spoke English very fluently, Captain Otway immediately entered on the object of his visit, and demanded that the ship should be given up. He was met with the old objection, that her colours had been shot away in the action, and that she had not surrendered; as a proof of which he said her pendant still remained flying. But this argument had been effectually removed, and Captain Otway replied, " I believe, sir, you are even mistaken on that point." With the utmost confidence the commodore requested him to walk to the stern-gallery (as they could not see the Holstein from the quarter-deck), saying, " I will soon convince you that it is you who are mistaken, and not I." However, on arriving at the stern-gallery, and seeing that the pendant was actually down, he expressed the utmost astonishment, but was constrained to acknowledge that she was a lawful prize, *and sent an order by the Danish officer who had accompanied Captain Otway for her delivery!* Captain Otway then hailed the Eling schooner, and desired Lieutenant Peek to take possession of the Holstein, to cut her cable (the wind being off the land), and make the signal to the fleet for immediate assistance. The Harpy brig instantly slipped her cable, and towed the prize up to the British fleet. During this transaction Lord Nelson, who was rowing round the prizes, accompanied by Captain Hardy, learned that Captain Otway was on board the Danish commodore's ship, and seized the opportunity of following him, in order, as he said, to look round him, in the event of a renewal of hostilities. The arrival of a flag of truce was reported to the commodore whilst himself and Captain Otway were taking some refreshment (the latter not having had any since the preceding day), and Captain Otway was informed that the officer in the boat wished to speak to him. On going upon deck, he was equally pleased and surprised to find that the officer in the boat was Lord Nelson: he was immediately invited on board, when both chiefs recognised each other, having both commanded frigates in the West Indies at the same time. An interesting conversation immediately ensued, and the parties afterwards separated, mutually pleased and satisfied. Such are the particulars of Captain Otway's conduct on that memorable occasion, and will for ever stamp his name as an active, brave, and judicious officer. He was immediately afterwards sent home with Sir Hyde Parker's dispatches; but his stay in England was but short: he again returned to the London, and remained in the Baltic till every appearance of hostility was removed. He subsequently commanded the Edgar of 74 guns, in which, after serving some time with the Channel fleet, he was sent, with several others, to the West Indies, from whence he returned to England after the conclusion of the war. On the renewal of hostilities in 1803 he was appointed to the Culloden of 74 guns; but ill health and a severe domestic calamity prevented him from joining her. His next appointment was to the Montagu, in which he was employed in the Channel.

In 1805, when the gallant and veteran Cornwallis made a dash at the enemy's fleet close in with Brest harbour, Captain Otway was one of his supporters, and on that occasion poured a well-directed fire into the Alexandre, a French 80-gun ship, killing and wounding many of her men. The Montagu had her gaff disabled, and sustained some damage in her sails and rigging, but had not a man hurt. Captain Otway was subsequently detached to the West Indies, under the orders of Sir Richard Strachan, in pursuit of a French squadron, and whilst on that service encountered a most tremendous hurricane. In 1807 he went to the Mediterranean; and in February 1808, under his able direction, the troops under Colonel Robertson evacuated Scylla, a fortified rock in the Faro of Messina, the garrison of which was embarked, under a smart fire from the enemy, on the Calabrian shore. He was afterwards intrusted with the command of a squadron employed in co-operating with the Spaniards on the coast of Catalonia; and received the thanks of the Junta of Gerona for the assistance afforded by him during the siege of that city, at which he was present, and for taking possession of the fortress of Rosas, by which the French troops were compelled to retire from Castalon, a town of some importance, situated five miles from the coast. Soon after this event, Captain Otway was appointed to the Malta of 80 guns, off Toulon, which ship he paid off at Plymouth in December 1808. In May following, he obtained the command of the Ajax; and towards the latter end of the year he escorted a large fleet of merchantmen to the Mediterranean. During the greater part of the winter he cruised, with a squadron under his orders, off the Island of Sardinia, and made many captures. He was afterwards employed in blockading Toulon, forming part of the in-shore squadron. On the 20th July, 1810, the Warspite, Conqueror, and Ajax, with the Euryalus frigate and Sheerwater brig, were all the force which the enemy could discover from the heights, and their squadron of six sail of the line and four frigates came out to attack them. Our ships lay nearly becalmed; and the Sheerwater, in obedience to a signal from the senior officer to close, had got much too near the French squadron. Captain Otway, being the sternmost of the British line and the nearest to the enemy, perceived that the Sheerwater must inevitably be taken unless some effort were made to save her. By a singular coincidence, the French 80-gun ship which led their line was also called the Ajax; she approached with a fine breeze from the land, and studding-sails set, whilst the British squadron had little wind. As she opened her fire on the Sheerwater, the British Ajax *put her helm down, came completely round, and interposed between the French ship and the English brig,* which received three broadsides without sustaining the least injury, although the enemy was within half-gun-shot. The moment the French admiral saw the Ajax in-stays, and that the Conqueror and Warspite followed her example, he put about, and with his squadron returned to Toulon*. Thus ended this little skirmish, in which no British ship was engaged but the Ajax. In the beginning of the following year Captain Otway was detached off the coast of Italy, and in March received instructions to intercept three French frigates which had escaped from Toulon to the eastward. He immediately pushed through the straits of Bonifacio, and directed the Unité frigate to go round by Cape Corse. On rejoining her off Elba, he was informed that she had been chased by the enemy's frigates, and that they were working through the Piombino passage. All sail was instantly made in that direction, and on the following morning they were discovered a little to windward. From the short distance they were from the land, one of them only, the Dromedaire, of 800 tons, but mounting only 20 guns, was captured. She was laden with 15,000 shot and shells and 90 tons of gunpowder, bound to Corfu. The others effected their escape by running into Porto Ferrajo.

Captain Otway's health had now become so much impaired, through the fatigues of long and indefatigable service, as to compel him to retire for a time from the active duties of his profession. He accordingly obtained permission to exchange into the Cumberland of 74 guns, the command of which ship he resigned on his arrival in England, the latter end of 1811. From that period he remained on shore until May 1813, when he was again appointed to the Ajax, and in her he joined the Channel fleet. During the ensuing autumn he was employed in covering the siege of St. Sebastian; and in March 1814, captured off Scilly a fine French corvette of 16 guns, 24-pounders. In the month of June he convoyed a squadron of transports from Bourdeaux to Quebec, having on board 5000 troops destined to reinforce the English army in Canada. Previous to his return to England, he visited Lake Champlain, and assisted in equipping the flotilla there†. In June 1814, he was advanced to the rank of rear-admiral; and in 1818, succeeded Sir W. J. Hope as commander-in-chief on the Leith station. One of the greatest tokens of

* Brenton.   † Marshall.

respect for public characters is the presentation to them, by respectable corporations, of the freedom of their cities; they are emblems of their approbation and gratitude, and a recollection of them serves to cheer and animate in the arduous and dangerous duties of professional service. These marks of respect Admiral Otway received: a short time before he hauled down his flag, he was presented with the freedom of the city of Edinburgh, and was entertained at a public dinner given by the noblemen and gentlemen of the club in St. Andrew's-square, as a testimony of their respect and esteem for his public character. In the beginning of 1826 he was offered the chief command in the East Indies, which, however, he declined; but shortly afterwards he was offered, and accepted, the chief command on the South American station (the duties of which he is now discharging), and in the month of June was nominated a Knight Commander of the Bath.

During his professional career, Admiral Otway has been at least *one hundred* times engaged with the enemies of his country. He has been an actor in scenes which every one would have been proud to share in, and has displayed talents which those who felt they possessed them in an equal degree, would have been, as he was, delighted with the opportunities of displaying them. If we possessed no other knowledge of his merits than that his undertakings have always succeeded, it would be sufficient for all fair and honourable argument in contending that he is deserving of those marks of honour and distinction which have been conferred upon him; but we possess the most indubitable proofs of his qualifications, in the opinions of all those under whom he served, some of which we shall here insert. The following is an extract of a letter from Captain George Bowen, who was captain of the Carnatic, in the gulf of Mexico, and witnessed Captain Otway's conduct in destroying the Spanish guada-costa, and saving the Trent and Ceres from being wrecked. In alluding to this circumstance, he says, " Those ships (without any flattery or compliment) would never have got off the shoal had it not been for your prompt and personal courage and seamanship. I sent you all my boats from the Carnatic (Bagot had all the other boats of the fleet, being the senior officer), and took the liberty of suggesting to you, by one of the lieutenants I sent, that as long as the Spanish gunboat's heavy 32-pound stern-chasers bore on the direction where the boats were towing out the anchors and cables, it would be impossible to save either of the frigates; and also, that I observed from the mast-head, in the offing, that large detachments of cavalry were coming in all directions to protect the gun-vessel on shore. Upon your being informed of these circumstances by the lieutenant, you took your own and the Carnatic's boats, gallantly rowed up to the gun-boat, boarded and set her on fire; then got off your own frigate, by being able to lay out the anchor and cables, and then heaved off Bagot's fine new frigate by yours, which, upon his death shortly after, you had given to you as a reward for *being the sole cause of saving both ships*."

The following is a copy of a letter from Admiral Cornwallis to Admiral Holloway, dated Ville de Paris, off Brest, respecting the attack made on the French fleet:

" DEAR HOLLOWAY,—It was a pleasing struggle the other day between Otway and Strachan: you will believe I was not in a hurry to put an end to such honourable zeal, happy, if we could have done any thing, to have had two such men at hand. Perhaps, now the French are likely to be employed some other way, they will let their navy rest again. They have been uncommonly bold of late."

The following is an extract of a letter from Admiral Cornwallis to Admiral Otway, dated January 1815:

" I remember with much pleasure your services when under my command, and most particularly your anxious zeal and struggle for the point of honour with Sir R. Strachan, which I very much admired, at the time the enemy had ventured out of the harbour, but continued under their batteries near Brest. I can, I am sure, with the greatest truth say, that *there is no officer whose services I should have preferred either as a captain or an admiral.*

(Signed,)   " W. CORNWALLIS."

The opinion of Earl St. Vincent is too important to be omitted: it is as follows:

" DEAR SIR,—I have great pride and pleasure in bearing testimony to the correctness of your conduct in the Channel fleet, in the Montagu and Royal George; and I perfectly well remember the remark I made upon the good condition of the masts and yards and furniture of the first named, when she rejoined after an uncommonly long cruise in the Bay, at a period when I had cause to complain of the number of masts and yards crippled by neglect and unskilful management; and I can with confidence declare, that when you arrived with the account of the impression made upon the floating and other batteries at Copenhagen, THE KING WOULD HAVE BEEN ADVISED TO CONFER SOME MARK OF DISTINCTION ON YOU, had not the ill state of his Majesty's health prevented it. I do farther declare, that in my judgment there is not an officer in his Majesty's navy of greater zeal and promise than Rear-Admiral Otway; and I foretel, that, *if justice is done him*, he will rival all the heroes of the last two wars.

(Signed,)   " St. Vincent."

A no less honourable testimony is borne him in the following extract of a letter from Captain Ussher, who was one of his lieutenants on board the Trent, and who, at the time of writing it, was travelling on the Continent with the Duke of Clarence. " I took the liberty," he says, " of mentioning to his Royal Highness the manœuvre by which you prevented the enemy off Toulon from capturing the Euryalus and Sheerwater, which his Royal Highness did not seem to have known. I also took the liberty of mentioning that it was a circumstance very little known, that when you commanded frigates, you *never suffered the boats to go away on service of great danger without accompanying them*, which the public knew nothing about, as you always preferred giving the credit of those enterprises to your officers. I likewise mentioned your having gone into Laguira, with a determination to bring out or destroy the Hermione. I can assure you his Royal Highness listened with great attention; and I told him, besides, that *there was but one feeling respecting you in the service**."

---

* We have also received a letter from Captain Ussher, of which the following is an extract, dated November 1826:

" I am most anxious to add my testimony to that of others in stating the meritorious and gallant services of my friend Sir R. Otway, when I was lieutenant of the Trent. In a national point of view it is right to do so, for it is right that services and activity like his should be recorded as examples to the service. He is, in my humble opinion, one of the best seamen in the service, certainly that I ever sailed under, and as undoubtedly the most active. It is also most true of him, that he had courage to execute whatever his head planned, however daring might be the attempt. There was also so much method in his manner of carrying on the service, that his officers and men, though in a constant state of activity, had perhaps as much leisure as any other ship's company, and no one was more attentive to the comfort of both officers and men. I may also mention that the Trent was considered the most perfect man of war in the West Indies, and always ready to go into action in five minutes: there was no unnecessary display on board of polished bolts or nail-heads; but every rope and spar was in its place, and the decks constantly kept clear. When at sea, and after the men had been exercised at quarters, the captain visited every gun, and saw that it was ready and in order; after which inspection not a rope-yarn or chip was to be seen at or near any of the guns. With respect to nerve and presence of mind (without which no man should enter the naval service) in real danger, no man possessed more; as an extraordinary instance of which I may state the following: When cruising off the coast of South America, I was ordered by Captain Otway (it being my watch on deck) to reconnoitre Laguira, and to stand well in for that purpose. As I

In February 1815, Admiral Otway received an address from those gentlemen, that were resident in London, who had witnessed his meritorious exertions in St. Vincent during that most perilous period, 1795 and 1796. In this address, which was signed by Sir William John

knew what ' stand well in' meant, I stood within gun-shot of the town ; but the wind dying suddenly away, I went down and acquainted the captain of the circumstance, who, coming upon deck, and perceiving our critical situation, and that we should be exposed to a heavy fire from the batteries, it instantly occurred to him, that, having some Spanish prisoners on board, it would be a good opportunity to exchange them; and he instantly hoisted a flag of truce for that purpose. But at that moment a boat was observed coming from the shore, and on arriving along side, Captain Otway was acquainted that an aide-de-camp of the governor and several people of distinction were in her, and that they had come to demand the surrender of the ship, considering her to be so near the batteries as to render useless any attempt to get away. He civilly invited them on board the Trent, and then sent a boat off to the governor, to say, that if a shot was fired at the Trent, he would hang every Spaniard at the yard-arms, and blow the town about his ears. To make it appear that he was in earnest, he instantly began reeving yard-ropes and clearing for action, which so intimidated the governor, that he quietly replied, he would give him twenty-four hours to get from under the batteries. Thus, by his promptitude, energy, and readiness, did we escape a Spanish prison.

"When we were cruising off the coast of Porto Rico, with the Sparrow cutter under his orders, looking out for vessels expected along shore, Lieutenant Wiley of the Sparrow came on board for orders, and to know how near the shore he was to keep; when the captain told him he expected the Sparrow would always be at night *on the wash of the surf*. In this respect he always set a noble example himself, and it was a matter of perfect indifference to him whether it was a lee or weather shore; wherever the enemy was expected there was the Trent, with leads-man in the chains and anchors ready. With regard to sending boats on service, if the duty to be performed was considered dangerous, he generally went himself (as a volunteer), unless the situation of the ship required him to remain on board ; and he several times did me the honour to come in the boat, advising, but not commanding.

"When the mutiny that broke out in the ships at the Nore was heard of, he ordered the ship's company on deck, told them what had happened, and then said, that in every ship there were some black sheep: if there were any in the Trent he warned them to be aware, as he would, on the least symptom of mutiny, put the ringleader to death; but assured them that he had no reason, nor ever had, to suspect any one of any such intention. In short, he spoke to them more like a father offering advice and warning them of danger.

"I must also mention the following circumstance: When cruising in company with another frigate, and dining with her captain, a boy came into the cabin and told the captain, that in ten minutes the men would rise in mutiny, and carry the ship into an enemy's port. The case was most difficult and urgent; but Captain Otway, with his usual presence of mind, recommended him to send the boy to the carpenter, and desire him quietly to turn the cocks, let water into the ship, then report a leek was sprung, and order instantly all hands to the pumps. This was immediately carried into effect, and from the information of the boy, the principal ringleaders were seized, and the ship saved."

Struth, Knt. and six other gentlemen who were formerly members of the Council at St. Vincent, they stated, " We who have witnessed your conduct both on land and sea, can testify to it in repeated acts of personal bravery and gallantry. We could state various instances in which we consider your claim to particular and distinguished notice as an officer as undisputed. We should not hesitate to recapitulate the instances alluded to, and only omit to mention them in delicacy to your own feelings; but should it ever be necessary, we pledge ourselves to the proofs of your well-earned title to every dignity that valour can deserve or honour bestow on the defenders of the country. Were the whole of the surviving inhabitants of that disastrous period here with us, we are confident there would not be a dissenting voice to the sentiments we express, and the attachment we profess towards you; on the contrary, we are persuaded there would be but one unanimous suffrage to your unqualified deserts."

It would be injustice to the feelings of Lord Egremont, as well as to the character of Admiral Otway, to omit the sentiments of his lordship as delivered in the House of Lords, April 20, 1815, when speaking of naval courts-martial. " I must observe," he said, " that in the circumstances of these trials, the mind of man cannot suggest the possibility of any undue bias in the members*; and in addition to this, I have the secret pledge of their integrity in the high character and known honour of a particular friend of my own, Admiral Otway (the president of Captain Brown's court-martial), an officer who has fought five-and-twenty battles, is honourable in his profession, and beloved in society; and of whom it is impossible for me, or any man who knows him, to speak but in the highest terms of esteem, affection, and respect."

Honourable as these testimonials are in favour of Admiral Otway, placing him as they do in the most interesting light, a still higher testimony was borne him by those brave men with whom he shared every danger and privation. " A party of the Trent's crew being on shore at Portsmouth, returning stores, the master-attendant of the dock-yard asked, ' *How they liked their captain?*' when one of them replied, ' *He was a man who never deceived his crew; for if any man deserved a couple of dozen, and he promised them, they were sure to get them.*' Another of them said, ' *The captain always slept with one eye open, and looked out for them all; and made the officers do their duty as well*

---

* We cannot agree with his lordship in this opinion.

as the men*.' " This anecdote may be put on a par with the story related of Germanicus, who, being desirous of obtaining some mark of the
esteem of his legions before a battle, is described by Tacitus " listening
in disguise to the discourse of a soldier, and wrapped up in the fruition
of his glory, whilst with an undisguised sincerity they praised his noble
mien, his affability, valour, and success in war." What a spur and encouragement does this afford still to proceed in the same steps, those
steps which have brought him such renown and given such universal
satisfaction!

English sailors, like the ancient Roman soldiers, are more partial to
those officers who share in all their dangers, who keep them strict to
their duty, who do not suffer any idlers about the ship, but who do not
introduce any unnecessary severity (no polishing of shot or stanchions),
than they are to those who are lax in their discipline, and more free in
their manners and conduct. The respect which seamen have for those
officers who keep up a system of regularity, founded on justice, is greatly
increased, and settles into the firmest confidence, when they find that
they are *practical seamen.* This was the case with Admiral Otway, who
never ordered either officers or men to do that which he could not do
himself.

On his appointment to the chief command in South America, Admiral
Otway received a letter from the Duke of Clarence, dated Bushy, February 19, from which the following is an extract:

" The appointment to the command in South America is, I trust, acceptable to
you. Under the very. extraordinary situation of those countries off which
you will have to cruise, the command cannot fail being interesting; and I rejoice
that so cool and valuable an officer as yourself has been selected for this singular
and especial purpose. The duchess unites with me in every kind wish towards
Mrs. but I trust shortly *Lady*, Otway, to whom I beg to be particularly remembered.   (Signed,)   " WILLIAM."

We have now stated the opinion of the prince, the peer, the merchant,
the admiral, the captain, the lieutenant, and the private seaman, in favour
of Admiral Otway, all proving that he possesses the happy art of maintaining his authority, and gaining the esteem and confidence of those he
commanded, as well as of those he obeyed; and that the officers and
seamen who served under him obeyed him as much through inclination
as a sense of duty. Notwithstanding all these favourable and flattering

* Marshall.

circumstances, he is perfectly free from the least taint of vanity, but possesses that just and reasonable modesty which sets off every other qualification, which heightens every virtue that accompanies it, and, " like the shades in a painting, raises and rounds every feature, and makes the colours more beautiful, though not so glaring as they would be without it."

In this sketch of Sir Robert's life we have confined ourselves to his public character; but the same degree of admiration might be excited in his favour by a description of his private conduct, did it accord with the plan of the work. He is one of the fortunate few who have no enemies, no detractors, none who will advance a hint or insinuation to his disparagement; the natural consequence of an even temper of soul, and an orderly tenor of actions founded on justice and honour. He possesses all the frankness and affability of the naval character, joined to the more refined habits of a private gentleman; to which must be added the most generous, disinterested, and independent principles. Since his first introduction to the navy, he has displayed the utmost industry of body and vigilance of mind; he has lived in familiarity with dangers; and when riding among shoals with little more water than the ship drew, which made others nervous and splenetic, he was found cool and cheerful, regardless of personal considerations, and thinking only of those means by which he could enhance the honour and reputation of his country. Thus has life risen to him until he has attained his present elevated rank and situation, which, as they are the reward of his own merit and exertions, and were obtained without solicitation, are perfectly unenvied.

Sir Robert married, in 1801, the eldest daughter of Admiral Holloway; a lady equally distinguished for mental and personal qualifications, as well as amiableness of manners and disposition, and by whom he has a large family.

HISTORICAL MEMOIRS OF
ADMIRAL ROSS DONNELLY*.

EVERY Englishman must feel gratified at the splendid achievements of the British army, whose heroic deeds terminated in the fatal overthrow of the greatest conqueror the world ever saw, and who had vowed destruction to the only country that set limits to his command: but, without the smallest wish or intention to lessen their merits, we may safely assert that those triumphs, and that result, would never have occurred without the previous triumphs of the navy. For a long period, the fleets of England formed the only barrier to the encroachments of the enemy; it was the navy alone which prevented those destroying hordes which were arrayed opposite to her shores from invading the country during the most eventful periods of British history. " In that tremendous conflict, they quelled the haughty and overbearing spirit of revolutionary France in fierce combat upon the Atlantic; chased and defeated her on her western and southern shores; overwhelmed her fleet off the shores of Egypt, and drove her from the Archipelago; forced the passage of the Dardanelles; destroyed the walls and navy of piratical Algiers, and gave the law from the Nile to the Straits of Gibraltar; overthrew and nearly destroyed the combined navies of France and Spain on the shore of Cadiz; dissolved the Northern Confederacy before the walls of Copenhagen, amidst the slaughter and ruin of the Danes and their defences; rode triumphant through the Baltic; defeated in obstinate battle the valiant Hollanders on their own shores; wrested the sceptres of both the Indies from the powers of Europe; and performed many other memorable and deathless exploits recorded in the page of history."

Justice, therefore, requires that if any preference be given, it should be to the navy; at all events, that both services should be placed on a level: but had this been the case, the subject of this Memoir would not have been without an honorary medal. For the battle of Waterloo, every individual engaged in it was presented with a medal to commemorate the victory: but this is never done in the navy to any one under the rank of post-captain; a rule which would be " more honoured in the

* From MARSHALL's *Biography.*

breach than the observance." Another circumstance is worthy of observation: most of those regiments which distinguished themselves in any particular battle have such circumstance inscribed on their colours. Why should not the same plan be adopted with the ensigns of those men of war which stood the brunt of those deadly contests which took place in a war of a quarter of a century, and whose flags were upheld with a brilliancy which has no parallel in history? Then should we see them emblazoned with the 12th of April, the 1st of June, St. Vincent, Camperdown, the Nile, Copenhagen, and Trafalgar; which could not fail to remind their crews of the heroic deeds of their countrymen, and stimulate them to rival their renown.

Admiral Donnelly, a son of the late Dr. Donnelly, entered the naval service early in the American war, and was employed in a battery during the siege of Charlestown in 1780. Some time after the capture of the place, he had the misfortune, when in charge of a prize, to be taken prisoner by the enemy, who inhumanly turned him adrift with his crew in an open boat, without sails or provisions; and in that helpless condition he was left to find his way to Trepassey, where he arrived, in a state of exhaustion, after a laborious pull of two days and a night. In the following year he was promoted by Rear-Admiral Edwards to the rank of lieutenant, in the Morning Star of 16 guns, on the Newfoundland station; from which vessel he removed into the Cygnet sloop of war as first lieutenant. His next appointment was to the Mediator of 44 guns, commanded by Captain Luttrell, with whom he continued till that ship was put out of commission, at the end of the war in 1783. He subsequently served as mate of an East-Indiaman, in which capacity he continued from 1785 till the commencement of the war with France in 1793, when he was appointed first lieutenant of the Montagu of 74 guns, commanded by Captain James Montagu, who fell in the glorious battle of the 1st June*, on which memorable day Lieutenant Donnelly particularly distinguished himself, as will be seen by the following extract from Earl Howe's public letter relative to that event:

* Much has been said by various writers on naval subjects of the manner in which the French fleet was manned; but no mention has been made of the inefficient state of the British ships when they first put to sea to meet the republicans. An idea thereof may be formed from the circumstance of the Montagu having joined the grand fleet with only 13 men, including the quarter-masters, able to take the helm, seven in one watch and six in the other. The captain of her fore-top had only been fifteen months at sea. The Ramillies was equally destitute of able seamen, and many others nearly so.

" Special notice is also due to the Captains Nicholls of the Royal Sovereign and Hope of the Bellerophon, who became charged with, and well conducted those ships, when the wounded flag-officers under whom they respectively served were no longer able to remain at their posts; and to the Lieutenants Monkton of the Marlborough and Donnelly of the Montagu, in similar situations."

Previous to her breaking through the enemy's line, the Montagu, then under the direction of Lieutenant Donnelly, was the next ship to the Royal George, bearing the flag of the late Lord Bridport, from whom he subsequently received the following letter:

PORTSMOUTH, *June* 18, 1794.

SIR,—I acquaint you that I have transmitted to Lord Chatham your letter, and have given my opinion to his lordship on your just claim to promotion, which I shall rejoice to see fulfilled. As Lord Chatham is expected here every day, and the king will certainly visit his fleet about the 29th, I have reason to suppose that some promotion will take place, in which I hope you will be included.

(Signed,)   ALEXANDER HOOD.

That the claim alluded to would have been backed by the testimony of Captain Montagu, had he survived the combat, may be inferred from the contents of a letter written by the present Sir G. Montagu to Lieutenant Donnelly, dated the same as the above:

DEAR SIR,—I have taken the liberty of begging your acceptance of a sword belonging to my late poor brother; it will remind you of a man, who at all times spoke of you in the highest terms of regard and approbation.

(Signed,)   G. MONTAGU.

Unfortunately for Lieutenant Donnelly, the same liberality in rewarding merit which has been subsequently evinced, was not displayed at that period; and, notwithstanding the expectations raised by the subjoined reply of Lord Howe to an application in his favour by the Earl of Tankerville, he did not obtain post-rank till June 1795.

PORTSMOUTH, *July* 2, 1794.

MY LORD,—I can now have the satisfaction of being able to assure your lordship, that your wishes in favour of Lieutenant Donnelly will be accomplished. His meritorious conduct in the direction of the Montagu, on the fall of her late commander, has not needed any interference of mine for obtaining the promotion he will gain*.   (Signed,)   HOWE.

* At the general promotion which followed, Mr. Donnelly and all the other first lieutenants of the fleet were made commanders, and took rank according to their seniority as lieutenants.

During the remainder of the war Captain Donnelly commanded in succession the Pegasus and Maidstone frigates; the former employed in the North Sea, the latter principally on the Jamaica station. In the Pegasus, carrying 28 long 9-pounders and 120 men, he fell in with the Dutch brigs of war, the Echo and De Gier, of 20 Dutch 12's and 140 men each, and after an arduous chase, during which his ship struck on East Friezeland, drove them both on shore to the eastward of the Texel. This circumstance is alluded to in the following letter, which he received from Admiral Duncan shortly after his victory over the Dutch fleet off Camperdown:

My dear Sir,—I am very sorry I have not had the pleasure of meeting, as I have a great deal to say to you. You are much mistaken in thinking you are forgot. In a conversation I had to day with Lord Spencer, he mentioned you as a great favourite of his, and am sure I joined most heartily in saying you are also of mine. In short, I have a favour to ask of you, and hope you will not refuse me. Should Hope not be able to go to sea, will you be my captain? I am to have the Tigre. I leave town to-morrow, and shall be back from Sheerness (where his Majesty is to be) on Tuesday next. As to the brigs, I shall only say, that Admiral de Winter states they were both lost; and have no doubt the matter, as respects the head-money, will be cleared up.

I have been hurrying about so from place to place that I have not heard a word from Lady Duncan since my arrival in port; but I have seen letters from her, and I assure you she never forgets your attention to her. Many thanks for your kind congratulations, which are most acceptable, as I am sure they are sincere. Believe me, with truth and esteem, 	Yours, &c.

	Duncan.

On the 30th November, 1796, exactly two years and a half after Lord Howe's action, each of the captains mentioned in his lordship's letter were ordered to be presented with a gold medal, to be worn with their uniforms, in commemoration of the victory they had assisted in achieving. Captain Donnelly's application for that honourable badge of distinction was replied to as follows:

Sir,—You will, I am sure, do me the justice to believe that I entertain a very good opinion of your merits and services; but it will really be impossible for me to comply with the request conveyed to me in your letter of yesterday, the medals having been limited by his Majesty's express command to those admirals and post-captains only who are mentioned in the letter from Earl Howe to the Admiralty relative to those actions, including the captains of the several admirals who were honoured with the gold chain. As you were not a post-captain at the time of the action, you will perceive that this line must necessarily exclude you from the distinction at present conferred*. (Signed,) SPENCER.

Previous to his leaving the Maidstone, Captain Donnelly was voted a handsome piece of plate by the merchants concerned in the Oporto trade, for his zealous exertions in protecting a large homeward-bound fleet, and bringing it in safety to England, at a time when the enemy's privateers were very numerous, both in the Bay of Biscay and the Channel. This token of their gratitude, however, he refused to accept; stating that, although a French frigate had hovered about the convoy, which was also surrounded during the passage by privateers, he had no opportunity of fighting in defence of their property; and he must therefore decline, as he had done before on a somewhat similar occasion, receiving any honorary reward for the bare performance of his duty: a sentiment in which we do not join; for if an officer succeeds in the object he has to achieve, either by his skill and manœuvres, his knowledge of seamanship, or his valour in the fight, he is entitled to reward as much in the one case as the other. The fleet consisted of 120 sail, on board of which the British factory at Oporto, apprehensive of Portugal being invaded by the French, had shipped no less than 32,000 pipes of Port wine, the largest quantity ever imported at one time into England. Captain Donnelly's zeal for the service induced him on this occasion to take the Netley schooner from her station; and, instead of being censured for so doing, he had the gratification to receive the thanks of Lord St. Vincent, who then presided at the Admiralty.

Towards the latter end of 1801 Captain Donnelly was removed into the Narcissus of 32 guns, and ordered to carry out the Algerine ambassador and his suite, with a great number of valuable presents for the Dey of Algiers, by whom he was presented with a handsome sabre. From Algiers he proceeded to Malta, and thence to the Archipelago, where he made an astronomical survey of all the principal islands. Whilst on that service he discovered a piratical galley in the act of boarding an English merchant-ship off Miconi, and immediately made sail in chase of the marauders, who rowed off with amazing swiftness to the Great Delphos, where they disembarked and posted themselves advantageously behind rocks, and from thence kept up a heavy fire of musketry, by

* The first lieutenants of captains killed in subsequent general actions have had post-rank and the gold medal immediately conferred upon them.

which one man was killed on board the Narcissus. The galley having been sunk by a broadside from the ship, Captain Donnelly landed a party of seamen, and succeeded in securing thirty-six of the pirates, whom he placed at the disposal of Lord Elgin, the British ambassador, who, with his family and suite, was then on board the Narcissus. The galley, on being weighed and brought along side, proved to be as long as the frigate, and had a very singular appearance, her hull, masts, sails, colours, and every thing about her, being black. She was handed over to the Miconians, and the specie found on board her, about 1000 piasters, given to the widow of the seaman who was slain. The capitan pacha, then at Constantinople, on hearing of the capture, sent Captain Donnelly a valuable Damascus sabre ; and it is said that he afterwards refused to liberate the principal corsair, although a sum equal to 10,000*l.* stirling was offered for his ransom*.

We next find Captain Donnelly with a broad pendant at Alexandria ; and he appears to have been there, making preparations for the embarkation of the British troops, at the time when Colonel Sebastiani arrived from Toulon to make a political and military survey of Egypt, the report of which, when published in the *Moniteur* by order of the First Consul, produced those angry discussions between Great Britain and France which terminated in a declaration of war between those countries. After the evacuation of Alexandria†, Captain Donnelly escorted General Stuart's army, and a number of French soldiers who had been taken prisoners during the late campaigns in that quarter, to Malta. From thence he proceeded with the latter to Toulon ; and subsequently visited Palermo, where he gave an elegant ball and supper to the King of the Two Sicilies, his family and court ; and he also convoyed the present King of Sardinia from Cagliari to Naples.

The Narcissus happening to be at Genoa when intelligence arrived of the British minister having left Paris, Captain Donnelly, eagerly seizing the opportunity that presented itself of evincing his zeal for the public service, issued orders for the vessels belonging to English merchants immediately to depart, and in several instances compelled their commanders to get under weigh and quit the harbour, contrary to their inclinations,

* The sabre alluded to was given by Captain Donnelly to the Prince of Orange three days before the battle of Waterloo, and is the same that his Serene Highness fought with on that memorable day.

† Captain Donnelly and the present Lord Beresford were the last persons who left the Egyptian shore.

thereby saving a large sum to the underwriters. He then went to Leghorn (where he found the Active frigate, Captain Danvers), adopted similar measures, and by his prompt and spirited conduct prevented property to an immense amount from falling into the hands of the enemy. It is here worthy of remark, that a French 74 and four frigates were then lying in Porto Ferrajo, and although they saw him pass on his way to Malta with the vessels he had thus rescued from impending danger, they made no effort to obstruct him; although there can be no doubt that they were aware of the rupture which had taken place, one of their frigates having been chased into that port a day or two before by the Narcissus. On the 8th July, 1803, being off Sardinia, he fell in with, and, after a pursuit of twenty-four hours, captured L'Alcion, a French corvette of 16 guns and 96 men, returning from Alexandria, where she had been on a particular mission. He was subsequently intrusted by Lord Nelson with the command of a squadron of frigates employed in watching the port of Toulon; and so high an opinion did his lordship entertain of Captain Donnelly's abilities, both as an officer and a seaman, that he placed his own relative, the present Captain B. W. Suckling, and several other young gentlemen in whose welfare he felt an interest, under his immediate care*.

In July 1804, Captain Donnelly sent the boats of his squadron to destroy about a dozen of the enemy's cutters lying at la Vadour, in Hieres Bay, which service was gallantly executed under a tremendous fire of great guns and musketry, as well from the vessels as from a battery and the houses of the town, close to which they were hauled in, and well secured by hawsers from their keels to the shore. Previous to Captain Donnelly's departure for the Mediterranean, he was employed on several missions to the Barbary States, and succeeded in obtaining the liberation of several English merchantmen that had been carried into Tunis and Algiers by the corsairs. He afterwards accompanied the expedition sent against the Cape of Good Hope, under the orders of Sir Home Popham and Sir David Baird. During the passage the Narcissus was detached to procure intelligence, and proceeding on that service, captured a French privateer of 12 guns and 70 men; retook a large English

* Among the gentlemen on the quarter-deck of the Narcissus at that period were, the sons of Lord Duncan, Sir Hyde Parker, Admiral Holloway, and Sir Thomas Troubridge. In writing to the last distinguished officer, March 17, 1804, Lord Nelson said, " *Your son cannot be any where so well placed as with Donnelly.*"

Guineaman, mounting 22 guns, laden with rum, tobacco, staves, ivory, &c.; and drove on shore a ship of 32 24-pounders and 250 men, having on board the ordnance of a French frigate which had been wrecked in Table Bay. After the subjugation of the Cape, Captain Donnelly proceeded with Sir Home Popham and General Beresford to the Rio de la Plata, from whence he returned to England with those officers' dispatches relative to the capture of Buenos-Ayres, and specie to the amount of 1,086,208 dollars, found in the treasury of that place. In his official letter, Sir Home said, " Captain Donnelly, who did me the favour of requesting I would go up the river in the Narcissus, and to whom, from his rank, no specific service could be assigned in our small scale of operations, applied himself on every occasion where he could promote the objects of the expedition; and as he is charged with this dispatch, I take the liberty of recommending him to their lordships' protection, under a full conviction that they will obtain through him every information which they have a right to expect from an officer of great intelligence and long meritorious service." General Beresford expressed himself to the following effect : " I halted two hours on the field, to rest the troops and to make arrangements for taking with us the enemy's guns, and our own, which had now, by the exertions of Captain Donnelly, been extricated from the bog. He had accidentally landed, and accompanied the troops on seeing them advance to the enemy. I am much indebted to him for his voluntary assistance." After the performance of this service he returned to the transports, all of which, together with the Encounter gun-brig, were at that time lying aground off Point Quelmey à Pouichin, where the army had been landed, and by great exertions succeeded in getting them afloat, and in removing them to secure anchorage.

Immediately on his arrival in England, Captain Donnelly was appointed to the Ardent of 64 guns, and ordered to escort a reinforcement of troops, commanded by Sir Samuel Auchmuty, to the river la Plata, where they formed a junction with Admiral Stirling, off Maldonada, in January 1807. During the siege and storming of Monte-Video, Captain Donnelly commanded the brigade of seamen and marines landed from the squadron to co-operate with the army; and the assistance rendered by him in transporting the battering train, ammunition, and provisions from the place of debarkation, a distance of seven miles, along a heavy sandy road, erecting batteries, &c. was acknowledged by General Auchmuty and the naval commander-in-chief, with whose dispatches he was again intrusted, and was joined in the thanks of both Houses of Parliament.

Subsequent to this event, Captain Donnelly brought an action in the Court of Common Pleas against Sir Home Popham, to recover a sum which he had paid to him in error. In the distribution of prize-money, he had allowed Sir Home the share of a flag-officer having the power of appointing a captain under him; but he afterwards found that Sir Home had only the temporary rank of commodore, and no authority to appoint his captain; consequently his proper share was much less than had been calculated at. The judge was of opinion that Captain Donnelly had established his claim; and the jury accordingly returned a verdict for him of 2004*l.* 17*s.* 3*d.* the sum overpaid.

In 1808 Captain Donnelly was appointed to the Invincible of 74 guns, and towards the close of the year served off Cadiz, under the orders of Admiral Purvis, by whom he was deputed, with 200 men, to fit out the Spanish fleet at the Caraccas; which service, notwithstanding the sad disorder in which he found the ships, and the reluctance with which the Spaniards consented to such a measure, he performed by means of very extraordinary exertions in the short space of eight days; and thus saved them from falling into the hands of the French, who were endeavouring to obtain possession of them. From the Cadiz station he proceeded to the Mediterranean, and joined Lord Collingwood off Toulon at the commencement of 1810; but was soon after compelled, in consequence of a cataract, to resign the command of the Invincible. This disease continued about two years, and prevented him from going afloat during that period. Immediately on his recovery, he applied for employment, and had the gratification of receiving an appointment, by return of post, to the Devonshire, a new ship of 74 guns; but the termination of hostilities prevented him from proceeding to sea. In June 1814 he was advanced to the rank of rear-admiral, and in May 1825 to that of vice-admiral.

HISTORICAL MEMOIRS OF

ADMIRAL SIR WILLIAM CHARLES FAHIE, K.C.B.

IF actions speak the man, we shall be fully justified in simply narrating the services of Admiral Fahie, who, during a period of nearly fifty years, has been indefatigably employed in the faithful discharge of his professional duties and the active services of his country, whose rights he has asserted with equal spirit and ability; and who has shared in the glory arising from eight general actions with the fleets of the enemy, twice in the reduction of all the French islands in the Caribbean Sea, also in the reduction of other islands and fortresses, and in encounters with single ships.

Sir William is descended from a respectable Irish family, whose name was formerly spelt Offahie, and is the same mentioned by Keating, in his *History of Ireland*, as an ancient Milesian family. His grandfather became one of the earliest colonists of the Island of St. Christopher, where he settled on a considerable estate, and where Sir William was born, being the youngest son of the Hon. John Fahie, who died Judge of the Vice-Admiralty Court of that island. Having made choice of a naval life, and having been previously borne on the books of the Deal Castle, he embarked on board the Seaford, under the late Sir John Colpoys, in August 1777, at that great crisis of the war between England and her American colonies when it became more and more evident that France and Spain would soon be the enemies of Great Britain. In the Seaford he continued to serve on the Leeward Island station till July 1778, when he proceeded to England, and was employed in the Channel till the November following. He then removed, with his friend Captain Colpoys, to the Royal George, was attached to the Channel fleet, and continued on that station till October 1779. In that month he was removed to the Sandwich, the flag-ship of Sir George Rodney, with whom he proceeded to the relief of Gibraltar, and was of course present at the defeat of the Spanish squadron under Langara. The relief of Gibraltar being effected, he sailed to the West Indies, and was in the actions of the 17th April, and 15th and 19th May, 1780, with the French fleet under the Count de Guichen.

In August 1780, Mr. Fahie was appointed a lieutenant of the Russell of 74 guns; and on the 28th April, 1781, was again in action with the French fleet off Martinique*. In January 1782, he was in the fleet under Sir Samuel Hood at St. Kitt's, and of course in the encounters which took place with the enemy's fleet on that occasion. Having volunteered his services, in consequence of his local knowledge of the island, he was twice dispatched by Sir Samuel Hood † to communicate with the garrison of Brimstone-Hill, for the purpose of ascertaining their state and the possibility of affording them relief. On his second landing he found, on approching Brimstone-Hill, that terms of capitulation had been that evening agreed on; and before he could regain the part of the island off which the fleet lay, it had sailed : his situation then became precarious, but having promptly determined to throw himself on the generosity of the French general, the Marquis de Bouillie, he was by him permitted to depart in a flag of truce without exchange ; when he rejoined the Russell at the Island of St. Lucia, and resumed his situation on board of her. He soon after rose to be her first lieutenant, and in that situation served in the actions of the 9th and 12th April, 1782, which decided the fate of the war with France and Spain‡. After that action, Lieutenant Fahie was removed to the Ville de Paris, and in that ship he continued till the following August, when he was removed to the Sibylle, and sailed to the coast of America. In October, he exchanged into the Tartar and returned to Jamaica, where he continued to be employed until the conclusion of the war in 1783, when he rejoined his family at St. Kitt's.

On the occasion of the armament in 1790, Lieutenant Fahie lost no time in returning to England and offering his services, and was appointed first lieutenant of the Martin ; but on the termination of the dispute which had called forth that armament, he returned again to his family, with whom he remained till the commencement of the war in 1793 ; soon after which he was appointed to the Zebra, commanded by Captain Faulknor, and went out first lieutenant of her to that station where he passed so great a portion of his life, where by the zealous discharge of his duty he had received his first commission, and where he was to be again engaged in active services and to obtain farther promotion. We first find him at the attack of Martinique, where the Zebra was employed in covering the landing of the troops in the Bay of Galleons ; after which

---

* See *Memoir of Lord* Hood.   † *London Gazette.*

‡ See *Memoir of Sir* James Saumarez.

he assisted at the attack of St. Pierre's, and subsequently in storming (with Captain Faulknor) Fort St. Louis in the Bay of Port Royal, which led to the surrender of the whole island*. His conduct on these occasions attracted the notice of Sir John Jervis, who removed him into his flag-ship (the Boyne), in which he served at the reduction of St. Lucia and Guadaloupe. The latter and most important of those islands was subsequently retaken by a French force under Victor Hughes; and in the attempt to recover it, Lieutenant Fahie was employed in command of the boats of the squadron, to make demonstrations under the enemy's batteries for the purpose of drawing their attention from the approaches making by our troops; and he also commanded a detachment of seamen landed at the post of Gozier. His long and zealous services now met with their reward, by his promotion, on the 5th August, 1794, to the

* In 1791, a small republican force from France made an attempt to get possession of Martinique; but having been repulsed by the royalists, who were then predominant in the island, they went to St. Kitt's, where, with the permission of the governor, they replenished their store of water and provisions to enable them to recross the Atlantic. During this operation several soldiers escaped from the transports, and professing themselves to be royalists at heart, were allowed to conceal themselves in different parts of the island till the ships had sailed. Among this number, a soldier of the name of Pierre found shelter on the premises of Mrs. Fahie, the mother of Lieutenant Fahie: he was himself absent at the time from the island, but returning soon after, and landing at night, he was surprised the next morning to see a strapping fellow in the full decoration of the national uniform. His mother soon appeared and explained the circumstance, adding, that Pierre assured her that he was *un bon royalist*, and would die for his king, and only solicited her present protection till he could find a passage to a neighbouring island, where he would work at his trade and await better times. But Lieutenant Fahie soon discovered that Pierre, though disgusted with the restraint and hardships he had recently undergone, was still in principle and feeling a rank republican, and that his mother had been imposed upon: this he represented to her; but her humanity had been excited, and Pierre's renewed protestations of fidelity to his king secured to him a further continuance in his good quarters and of his good cheer. His intended removal to the neighbouring island, in order to work at his trade and await better times, was postponed under various pretences from time to time; till, hearing of the excesses committed in France, and foreseeing to what they would lead, Lieutenant Fahie said jokingly to his mother, " Madam, you are feeding that fellow here; we shall soon be at war with France, and he will one day have a shot at my head." Such an idea, once awakened in Mrs. Fahie's mind, led to the immediate dismissal of Pierre. At the storming of Fort Louis, while Lieutenant Fahie was pushing on at the head of a party of the Zebra's crew, to dislodge a guard drawn up apparently to oppose him, he was surprised to hear himself loudly called by name, and to see at the same instant a soldier at his feet, begging protection from the British cutlasses that were brandishing around him: it was Pierre, who had been many hours that morning verifying his (Lieutenant Fahie's) nearly forgotten prediction.

rank of commander, and appointment to the Woolwich, armed *en flute*, but employed as a cruiser. In this ship he continued till December 1795, when he obtained post-rank in the Perdrix of 22 guns, in which he sailed on various cruises among the Leeward Islands. On the 7th December, 1798, he was informed that a French ship was cruising off the Virgin Gorda, and he immediately used every exertion to get to windward of that island; but from foul weather this was not accomplished until the 10th, when his perseverance met with its due reward. At daylight the following day he discovered the object of his search; all sail was immediately made in chase, which continued sixteen hours, when he came up with, and after an action of forty minutes captured, L'Arme d'Italie, a French private ship of war of 18 guns and 117 men, six of whom were killed and five wounded, without any loss on his part.

Captain Fahie continued on the same station, in the command of the Perdrix, till May, when he sailed for England with a large convoy, and was paid off in August 1799. During the short peace which intervened between 1801 and 1803, Captain Fahie took the opportunity of returning to his family at St. Kitt's, when he was called up as a member of his Majesty's Council, by his connection with Lord Lavington, the then governor. On the renewal of hostilities he hastened back to England, and was appointed, in September 1804, to the Hyæna of 28 guns, and again proceeded to the Leeward Islands, having in charge a valuable convoy, the whole of which reached their destination in safety. In January 1805 he removed into the Amelia frigate, and in February 1806 he joined Sir John Duckworth, soon after his action off St. Domingo, and assisted in burning the Imperial and Diomede, which had been driven ashore. In the month of March following he removed to the Ethalion; and in the summer of 1806 he was ordered to escort a very numerous convoy from Tortola, and having seen it in safety to the chops of the Channel, he immediately returned to Barbadoes. In December 1807, he accompanied the expedition under Sir Alexander Cochrane and General Bowyer against the Danish islands, and was intrusted with the summons to the governor of St. Thomas to surrender that island. Terms having been agreed upon, Captain Fahie and General Shipley were sent with a similar message to the governor of St. Croix, which was attended with similar success.

In November 1808, Captain Fahie was appointed to the command of the Belleisle of 74 guns; in this ship he was actively engaged in the

operations which were commenced early in the following year (1809),
under Sir Alexander Cochrane and General Beckwith, against the
Island of Martinique. In February, the Æolus, Gloire, Cherub, and
Swinger were placed under his orders by Sir Alexander Cochrane : with
this force, and some transports having on board a division of the army
under the command of Major-General Maitland, he proceeded to Marins
Bay, and landed the troops in Ance-Seron. In the performance of this
service he met the approbation and thanks of both the commanders-in-
chief, as well as being included in the vote of thanks passed by the two
Houses of Parliament. In the following month of March he removed to
the Pompée of 80 guns, and formed one of the squadron employed, in
the conjunct expedition under Rear-Admiral Sir Alexander Cochrane
and Major-General Maitland, against the Saints (a cluster of islands belonging to France and situated close to Guadaloupe), where an enemy's
squadron of three sail of the line and two frigates had recently arrived
from France. As there are three passages, one to the N. E. another to
the N. W. and the third to the S. W. by either of which the enemy
could escape from the anchorage, the difficulty of watching them was increased considerably. Captain Fahie was stationed off the N. W. and
to enable him the more effectually to watch the motions of the enemy,
some small vessels were placed more in shore, under the orders of Captain Cameron of the Hazard. At half-past nine p. m. of the 14th April,
Captain Fahie observed the signal from the Hazard that the enemy had
put to sea; and at forty-nine minutes after nine, the Lower Saint bearing
E. about a mile and a half, he distinctly saw them coming down, closely
followed by the Hazard and others of the in-shore squadron. At ten
o'clock he closed up with the sternmost ship of the enemy, and endeavoured to stop her by the discharge of two broadsides; but being under
press of sail and a strong breeze, steering W. S. W. she succeeded in
crossing him without returning his fire. Now commenced an anxious
pursuit, which was increased by the weak and debilitated state of Captain
Fahie's body, through long and severe illness arising from the climate ;
but his mind partook not of his bodily weakness; he ordered a chair to
be placed on the quarter-deck, and there, regardless of all personal considerations, he continued during the whole chase and till the surrender
of the enemy. But such was his weakness, that he was prevented from
sinking under the fatigue by the aid of strong stimulants, which of themselves were highly injurious to his disorder, but which were administered

to him by his own desire, he being regardless of the consequences arising therefrom. Shortly after ten o'clock, the Neptune (bearing the admiral's flag) joined in the pursuit, several other ships of the British squadron being in sight. The chase continued during the whole night of the 14th, and so close was the Pompée to the enemy's ships, that she occasionally received and returned their fire. At daylight on the following morning (the 15th) the only British ships near the Pompée were the Neptune and Recruit brig, commanded by Captain Napier, whose conduct throughout that day excited the admiration of all who witnessed his gallant perseverance in keeping within the range of the enemy's stern chasers, and frequently annoying them with his own fire. The enemy's ships of three sail of the line being ahead to the westward about three miles, during the day of the 15th, as the wind freshened the Pompée was enabled occasionally to near and exchange shot with them. At eight p. m. on the 15th, the enemy's ships separated, two of them steering W.N.W. the third N.W. Captain Fahie followed the latter, she being much the nearest to him; but at the same time made the prescribed signal, pointing out to Sir Alexander Cochrane the course taken by the other two, and continued the chase with unremitted ardour during the night. At daylight on the morning of the 16th he had the satisfaction to find that he had rather gained on the chase: at this time the Neptune was still in sight astern on the S. E. quarter, and two frigates on the starboard quarter, bearing N. E. about four or five miles from the Pompée, which proved to be the Latona and Castor. At five p. m. the Neptune was lost sight of from the mast-head of the Pompée, but the Latona and Castor had joined her. Captain Fahie's exertions to close with the enemy continued unremitted, and just before sunset the high land of Porto Rico was seen bearing N. N. E. eight or nine leagues distant; the night closed in extremely dark, and as he drew in with the land he was baffled with light and variable winds from the northward and westward, but, fortunately, the chase was never for a moment lost sight of. At half-past three o'clock on the morning of the 17th, the Castor succeeded in getting within gun-shot, and opened a smart fire, which was immediately returned by the enemy, who, in yawing to bring his guns to bear, gave the Pompée an opportunity to range up on his larboard beam and bring him to a close and decisive action. In this position they continued hotly engaged till twenty minutes past five, when both ships being nearly wrecks and within their own lengths of each other, the enemy lowered his top-sails and surrendered. At that moment the only ships seen from the Pompée were the Latona and Castor. The captured ship was immediately taken possession of by Lieutenant Bone, first of the Pompée, and proved to be the Hautpoult of 74 guns, commanded by Captain Amand le Duc, Chevalier of the Legion of Honour, with a crew of 680 men, between 80 and 90 of whom were killed or wounded, including several officers. The Pompée had her boatswain and 8 seamen killed and 30 wounded, including among this latter number Captain Fahie, the first lieutenant, Bone, and Lieutenant C. E. Atkins, royal marines; the Castor had one man killed and six wounded. The greatest praise is due to Captain Fahie for the zeal and perseverance with which he continued this chase during three nights and two days, and which was at last crowned by his capture of the enemy after a severe action of an hour and a half, in which he proved that his valour was equal to his professional abilities. In speaking of this event Sir Alexander Cochrane said, " I should not render justice to that excellent officer were I to withhold the praise due to him for his unremitted attention during so long and arduous a pursuit, and his taking such advantages of the enemy's situation as they occasionally occurred."

We have now only to notice the claim that was made by the Polyphemus and Tweed to share in this capture; but as that has been fully done in the answer given by Captain Fahie to the allegations exhibited on the part of those ships in the Court of Appeal, we content ourselves with leaving our readers to form their opinion of that claim from a perusal of the document*.

* " On the night of the 14th April, 1809, at about half-past nine o'clock, then cruising off the Islands of the Saints in the West Indies, I commenced a chase in his Majesty's ship Pompée, of three sail of the enemy's line-of-battle ships, which had about an hour before escaped from the harbour of those islands. His Majesty's ship the Neptune, bearing the flag of Rear-Admiral Sir Alexander Cochrane, K. B. soon after joined me, and several other of his Majesty's ships, part of the squadron under the orders of the said Admiral Cochrane, were in sight. The chase continued during the night of the 14th, and I occasionally received and returned the enemy's fire.

" At daylight of the 15th April there was no other of his Majesty's ships near his Majesty's ship the Pompée under my command but his Majesty's ship the Neptune and the Recruit brig; but several other of the said squadron under the command of Admiral Cochrane were in sight in the N. E. quarter, at different distances, standing after us. The enemy's squadron of three sail of the line were ahead to the westward, about three miles distance, steering under all sail W.S.W. During the day of the 15th I occasionally fired at, and was fired at by, the enemy's sternmost ship: at eight o'clock p. m. of the 15th,

On the 1st August Captain Fahie was appointed to the ship which had been the reward of his valour, and which was added to the British

the enemy's ships separated on different courses, two of them steering about W.N.W. and the third N.W. ½ W. I followed the latter, being much the nearest to me, making at the same time the prescribed signal to Admiral Cochrane, to point out the course steered by the other two. I continued this pursuit during the night of the 15th.

" At daylight on the morning of the 16th of April, I had rather gained on the enemy: his Majesty's ship the Neptune was in sight astern, in the S. E. quarter, and two frigates on the starboard quarter, bearing N. E. about four or five miles from me; but there was *no other* of his Majesty's ships in sight. The two frigates above alluded to proved to be his Majesty's ships the Latona and Castor. At about five o'clock p. m. of the 16th, his Majesty's ship the Neptune was lost sight of from the mast-head of the Pompée; the Latona and Castor continued in company, but there was *no other* of his Majesty's ships in sight. When the night closed in on the 16th April, I found that I had neared the enemy's ships considerably; his Majesty's ships Latona and Castor had also closed nearer to the Pompée; but at the close of *this day* there was *no other* of his Majesty's ships or vessels in sight from the Pompée's mast-head. The chase continued all this night of the 16th, and until about half-past three o'clock a. m. of the 17th April, when I ranged up on the enemy's larboard beam and commenced a close action with her. At this time *no other* of his Majesty's ships or vessels was seen from the Pompée but the Latona and Castor. The night was extremely dark; the action continued until about a quarter-past five o'clock a. m. of the 17th April, when the enemy's ship struck: the day had just dawned, but the atmosphere was much clouded by the heavy smoke arising from such a continued fire. At the moment of the enemy's surrender, or during the continuance of the action, *no other* of his Majesty's ships or vessels but the Latona and Castor was seen from the Pompée; and I do verily believe that no others were seen from the enemy's ship. When the French captain was brought along side a prisoner, and I was standing on the quarter-deck, near the starboard gangway, ready to receive him, two ships were pointed out to me to the westward and leeward of us: my first impression was that they were the enemy's other two ships; and on the French captain coming on the quarter-deck and delivering his sword, pointing to those ships, I said, " Sir, I believe those are your ships ?" We both looked at them for a moment, when he answered, " No, they are not." I also at the instant saw that one was much larger than the other, and was assured that they were English. Those ships proved to be his Majesty's ships Polyphemus and Tweed; they were, I think, standing on a wind on the starboard tack, about five or six miles to leeward of us. About this moment, as the smoke had dispersed, several others of his Majesty's ships, being part of Sir Alexander Cochrane's squadron, were discovered in different quarters, the nearest of them about four or five miles distant. This action commenced in the night, and terminated just as the day had broke; the firing therefore served as a beacon to all ships within the distance of the visible horizon, and attracted them towards the scene of action, without a possibility of their being seen by the ships engaged.

" If the claims of his Majesty's ships the Tweed and Polyphemus are to be decided by the exertions their captains made to close in the action, there can be no doubt of their being fully entitled to share; for, as gallant officers, those captains undoubtedly exerted themselves to do their duty. But if their claims are to be decided on the principle of

navy under the name of the Abercrombie. On the 2d of the same month Sir Alexander Cochrane sailed with several ships of his squadron for Halifax, where he continued till the November following, leaving Captain Fahie, with a broad pendant, in the command of the ships and vessels remaining on the Windward Island station. On the attack of Guadaloupe, in January 1810, he was intrusted with the superintendence of the debarkation of the grand division of the army at St. Mary's, which being effected without opposition, he was further charged with the duty of keeping up a communication with the division on its march along the eastern part of the island and supplying it with provisions: for this purpose he removed from his own ship to the Ringdove brig, commanded by Captain Dowers. When the troops reached and halted at Trois Rivières, Captain Fahie landed, and, placing himself in personal communication with the general, Sir George Beckwith, remained at that post superintending the landing there of such supplies of provisions and other stores as were required to enable the division to cross Morne Palmiste and to advance to the attack of the enemy's principal position, and where the French general, Ernouf, commanded in person. These duties being accomplished, and the division having quitted Trois Rivières, Captain Fahie proceeded round to the road of Basseterre, where Sir Alexander Cochrane's flag and the other ships of the squadron having assembled, he was ordered by the admiral to land with a detachment of two hundred marines and occupy the town of Basseterre

any assistance afforded by them to his Majesty's ship the Pompée during the action, whether that assistance be constructive or otherwise, then I deny their right to share: for I do solemnly declare, that I did not see them until the period already stated; and I do verily believe that they were not, or *could not* have been, seen from the enemy's ship, which was close along side of us, either before the commencement of the action, during the action, or at the moment of her surrender. It appears by the allegations given in by the Polyphemus and Tweed, ' that they got up to the squadron, by which the Pompée and captured ship were *then* surrounded, at about half-past nine o'clock a. m. of the 17th April:' this was four hours and a quarter after the action had ceased, during the whole of which time they were progressing towards us under a press of sail, while we were also drifting towards them. This fact shews at once the distance they must have been from us even at the termination of the action, and the consequent impossibility of their being seen by us or the enemy, engaged as we were in the night; or even some time after the day had broke, enveloped as we still continued to be in smoke.

" The circumstance of the Polyphemus and Tweed having been ordered to receive part of the French prisoners gives them no claim to a share of the prize; it was a point of duty which they were ordered by a superior officer to execute.

(Signed,) " WILLIAM CHARLES FAHIE, *Captain.*"

(which the municipality had offered to deliver up), and upon his arrival before the place, to demand possession of Fort Matilda: this was accordingly done, but the officer commanding refused to surrender the fortress; and the next day General Ernouf offered to capitulate, and terms were soon agreed to, on which the whole island surrendered. On the termination of this service, Captain Fahie received the thanks of the admiral and general. The following is a copy of a letter from Sir George Beckwith to Captain Fahie, dated February 8, 1810:

DEAR SIR,—I have the honour to acknowledge the receipt of your obliging letter of this date (four o'clock), and am extremely sensible of your indefatigable exertions, the effects of which go to the security of no less an object than the health of the army and the consequent safety of the whole West India Islands. The health of British troops in this climate is as brittle as a china vase, and forty-eight hours in wet weather may save or shake the health of many thousands of men : I am therefore most anxious, as you may well perceive, to snatch the corps from the perils of their present position by separating them in as far as I dare, and spreading them throughout the Archipelago. To your exertions in the embarkation, and the admiral's kindness in assisting me in carrying my views into effect, the king's service is greatly indebted ; and I am availing myself of every means in my power, through the medium of the schooners in my possession, to withdraw the flank companies from hence, whose regiments have not been employed in the present expedition. On this particular point I desired Mr. Matthew King to communicate the details to you ; although these companies will, as I understand, be embarked in the boats of the vessels.

(Signed,) GEORGE BECKWITH.

The professional character of Captain Fahie had now attained a considerable degree of reputation, and the capture of Guadaloupe being completed, he was ordered by Sir Alexander Cochrane to hoist a commodore's pendant, and to proceed with a small squadron, accompanied by a body of troops under Brigadier-General Harcourt, against the Dutch Islands of St. Martin and St. Eustatius. He arrived off the first of these islands on the 14th February: the governor was immediately summoned to surrender ; but, replying in evasive terms, the troops were landed, accompanied by Commodore Fahie, who was anxious to afford every facility and assistance to the general, and determined to remain by his side until the final accomplishment of the service intrusted to them. As soon as the troops began to take a forward position, a message was sent by the governor, expressive of his desire to enter into terms of capitulation: commissioners were accordingly appointed, and at noon of the 15th articles were agreed to, which were to be ratified by the governor in three hours; but, before the expiration of that time, the Dutch commissioners returned, and solicited to be allowed till eight o'clock on the following morning: this was granted, on their positive assurance that they would be prepared at that hour to put the British troops in possession of the principal fort. At nine o'clock therefore on the following morning General Harcourt, accompanied by Commodore Fahie, marched towards the town of Philipsburg, the seamen drawing the howitzers over the hills, and every measure having been taken for an immediate attack, should it have been found necessary; but on their march, to their great surprise, they were informed that the governor had refused to ratify the articles, and preferred to surrender at discretion: this was confirmed shortly after by the appearance of the governor, who surrendered himself and his garrison as prisoners of war. The French quarter of the island having also surrendered on the same terms as those granted at Guadaloupe, and the measures necessary for the regulation and government of the whole island having been completed and adopted by the 20th, the commodore and general proceeded to the Island of St. Eustatius, which submitted without opposition; an event which finally expelled the flags of France and Holland from the Antilles*.

In June 1810, Captain Fahie quitted the West Indies, with two sail of the line under his command and in charge of a most valuable convoy, with the whole of which he reached England in the month of August following. As the Abercrombie had been captured and commissioned

---

* The following is an extract from the general orders of Sir George Beckwith, dated February 26, 1810:

" The commander of the forces has the highest satisfaction in announcing to the army, that, by the surrender of St. Eustatius on the 21st instant, the power of France is extinguished in the West Indies, and the assurances held forth after the last campaign completely fulfilled on this occasion. It will be a pleasing reflection to the troops employed by his Majesty in this part of the world, and that for the first time in the annals of the British empire, that such an event has been produced by their honourable exertions in the service of their country. The commander of the forces returns his thanks in this public manner to Brigadier-General Harcourt, for his judicious and temperate conduct at the reduction of St. Martin's and St. Eustatius, and to Brigadier Skinner, the officers, and troops employed on those different operations, so accelerated as they have been by the cordial and able co-operation of the navy, under the command of Commodore Fahie, supported by the captains, officers, and seamen under his orders†."

† See also Sir Alexander Cochrane's dispatches.

abroad, she was found to require some repairs and alteration of her interior arrangement; this occupied some time, and she was not ready for sea till the end of November. Early in the next month (December) he was ordered to Lisbon with part of a battalion of marines, to join the squadron of twelve sail of the line under Admiral the Hon. Sir George Berkeley, K. B. On this service he continued while the British army, commanded by Lord Wellington, remained in the lines of Torres Vedras: the enemy in the front having broken up early in May 1811, and retreated from Portugal, it was no longer necessary to keep so large a squadron in the Tagus; Captain Fahie was then ordered back to England in charge of a convoy of transports and merchant-ships, with which he arrived at Spithead in June. From this period to February 1814, he was employed in the Channel service, during which he was twice left in the command of the British squadron in Basque roads, blockading the enemy's ships off Isle d'Aix. In February 1814, the Abercrombie, being found defective, was paid off. In June of that year he was made a colonel of marines; and in January 1815, he was again called into active service, and appointed to the command of the Malta of 80 guns, in which, on the escape of Buonaparte from Elba, he was ordered to Gibraltar to await there the arrival of Lord Exmouth, commander-in-chief of the fleet about to be formed in the Mediterranean. Having joined his lordship early in April, he proceeded with him to Genoa, and from thence to Naples, from whence he was detached with a squadron to co-operate with the Austrian army in the reduction of the fortress of Gaieta: on this service he was employed from the 24th May till the 8th August following, when the garrison surrendered. During the whole of that time, the personal exertions of Captain Fahie were highly conspicuous, and secured to him the thanks of Lord Exmouth " for the persevering zeal and gallantry displayed throughout the whole of that arduous service;" and from Baron Lauer, commanding the Austrian troops, for " vigorously seconding his views and facilitating all the operations of the siege." The King of the Two Sicilies presented him with the insignia of a Commander of the Order of St. Ferdinand and of Merit, and also his thanks for the services rendered by him and the squadron under his command, which were communicated in a letter from Sir William A'Court, the British minister at the court of Naples, of which the following is a copy:

NAPLES, *August* 15, 1815.

SIR,—I have the greatest satisfaction in conveying to you and your officers, on the part of this government, its sincere thanks for your very great and unremitted exertions during the arduous service in which you have been engaged before the fortress of Gaieta. As a mark of the high sense which his Neapolitan Majesty entertains of your personal services, I have the pleasure to inform you, that he has been graciously pleased to confer upon you the Cross of Commander of the Royal Order of St. Ferdinand and of Merit. His Majesty has charged me to say, that he has the greatest satisfaction in offering to you this proof of his esteem.   (Signed,)   W. A'COURT.

The following is an extract of a dispatch from Sir William A'Court to Lord Castlereagh: " I have been particularly charged to mention to your lordship the high sense that is entertained of the services of Captain Fahie, commanding the squadron of his Majesty's ships employed in the blockade. I have also been informed by the Count de Sauran, that he considered it as a duty incumbent upon him to draw the Emperor of Austria's attention to the zealous exertions of this meritorious officer."

On the 12th August, 1819, he was advanced to the rank of rear-admiral; and in January 1820, he was appointed commander-in-chief on the Leeward Island station: he sailed from Plymouth April 7th, and reached Barbadoes May 14th, when he superseded Commodore Huskisson. He continued on that station till November 3, 1821, when he proceeded to Halifax by orders from the Admiralty, and relieved Vice-Admiral Griffith Colpoys in the command on that station, where he continued till August 1824; at which time he was relieved by Rear-Admiral Willoughby Lake, and returned to England, striking his flag on the 7th of the following month. In the October following he at last obtained that mark of distinction, the being nominated a Knight Commander of the Bath, which his whole career so fully and justly entitled him to. Why he did not obtain this reward for his long, active, and, we may add, important services sooner, it would be useless and perhaps invidious to inquire, seeing that many had that order conferred upon them whose claims were, to say the least, not superior to his: that Sir William did not quietly submit to be thus passed over and unjustly neglected, but that he, on the contrary, asserted on all proper occasions his claims with a manly and independent spirit, we have reason to know. Such honours and rewards are looked upon by some with apparent contempt; but whatever may be said against them, we contend that they help to raise emulation, cherish merit, and inspire those who are in the path to attain them with an ambition which promotes the public good. The Romans abounded with those honorary rewards which, without conferring influence or riches, give only place and distinction to the possessor: such is the nature of the Order of the Bath, in the conferring of which the utmost care and impartiality should always be observed, since it is to be considered as a mark of public approbation for actions performed, and that the most honourable and sensitive minds are the most invigorated by applause and depressed by unmerited neglect.

Sir William married, first, Elizabeth Renie Heyliger, daughter of William Heyliger, Esq. of St. Eustatius; and, secondly, Mary Esther Harvey, daughter of the Hon. Augustus William Harvey, Member of his Majesty's Council of Bermuda.

HISTORICAL MEMOIRS OF

CAPTAIN ALEXANDER HOOD.

WE have already recorded the services of two members of the Hood family, who attained, by their perseverance and courage, the highest rank in their profession; both of whom were celebrated in the times in which they lived for naval achievements and the exhibition of talents useful to themselves and beneficial to their country; and though they were duly rewarded by their sovereign with titles and honours, they were still more distinguished for their virtues and abilities than for their rank and situation, the latter being outshone by the lustre of the former.

It is generally admitted, that of all the passions to which human nature is subject, there is none so beneficial to society as emulation; it is example which excites courage and animates that spirit which is innate in almost every breast, and by which men are led into a participation of noble daring, brave adventure, and gallant achievement. It was the example of his illustrious relations which early called the attention of Captain Alexander Hood to the sea service; and, indulging the natural bent of his disposition, he entered that profession under the protection of his relation, who afterwards attained the title of Lord Bridport. The father of the distinguished individual who is the subject of this Memoir was Samuel Hood, Esq. formerly of Mosterton, Dorsetshire, whose father, Alexander, was elder brother of the Rev. Samuel Hood, vicar of Butleigh, Somersetshire, who was the progenitor of Viscounts Hood and Bridport: he left three sons, Arthur, Alexander, and Samuel, all of whom devoted their lives to the service of their country and in support of its liberties. Arthur, who was lieutenant of the Pomona, perished in a hurricane on the Leeward Island station, in 1775, with that ship and her whole crew; Samuel, the younger brother of the three, died of the fever of the country whilst commander-in-chief on the East India station; and Alexander, the second brother, was born April 23, 1758: his first voyage was made with that distinguished officer, Captain James Cook, whom he accompanied in the Endeavour during that voyage of discovery round the world which began in the year 1772 and terminated in 1775. The various occurrences which took place in the course of a voyage which will ever reflect honour on the nation at large, and immortalize those who conducted it, were well calculated to form the mind of an aspirant for naval fame. It was a school in which some of the first naval characters were formed; and a better one could not be devised to train a young mariner to the various duties of his perilous profession. In addition to the rough encounters of storm and tempest, so necessary to accustom the practical seaman to his duty, the many great difficulties they had to surmount during the course of a three years' navigation in unknown seas, when the ordinary means of precaution were often of no avail, were lessons that could not fail of forming a young mind to deeds of hardihood; whilst the constancy displayed in pursuing his object by the great character who conducted the expedition, was well calculated to inspire his followers with a due sense of the importance of that first of naval virtues—perseverance*.

In the beginning of the American war, which commenced shortly after his return from the Southern Ocean, Mr. Hood was placed under the command of Lord Howe. After serving some time on the American station as midshipman, he obtained the first step in the service, and on the 14th March, 1780, was appointed to command the Ranger cutter. Lieutenant Hood remained actively employed on this station for some time, and was then ordered to join the fleet in the West Indies under Sir George Rodney. Shortly after her arrival in the West Indies, the Ranger was put on the establishment of a sloop of war, by the name of the Pigmy, and on the 17th May, 1781, Lieutenant Hood was ordered to continue in the command of her, with the advanced rank of master and commander; but he retained this command only for a short period, as on the 26th July following he was posted into the Barfleur, bearing the flag of his relation, Sir Samuel (afterwards Lord) Hood, with whom he served in the action off St. Kitt's; but on the 4th February, 1782, he was removed to the command of the Champion, a situation more suitable to his youth and activity of disposition. In the actions of the 9th and 12th April the Champion acted as repeater, and, after the last great contest, was dispatched with a squadron towards the Mona Passage in quest of the flying enemy, when two 64's and a frigate were captured, and the Ceres of 18 guns retaken, the latter of which struck to the Champion.

Shortly after the arrival of the fleet at Port Royal, Captain Hood was appointed to L'Aimable of 32 guns, one of the ships captured in the

* Naval Chronicle.

Mona Passage; in her he remained until the termination of the war, actively employed in various services, in which he acquired much credit and the universal esteem of his brother officers, who looked upon him as a young man of great promise. On the ratification of the treaty of peace he returned to Europe, and was paid off 29th July, 1783. In 1790 he was appointed to the Hebe frigate, which was paid off in 1792; but in the following year he was reappointed to that ship, and continued to command her till July 1794, when he was promoted to command the Audacious line-of-battle ship, and remained in her about twelve months. Captain Hood's strength of body had never been equal to the energies of his mind, and a constitution naturally weak was so shook at this period, as to compel him reluctantly to quit his command, that he might prolong a life destined to be devoted to the service of his country*. His health being re-established, he again cheerfully came forward, and was appointed, in January 1797, to command the Ville de Paris; but in the following month he was removed to the Mars of 74 guns, and attached to the Channel fleet. Hitherto Captain Hood had not been so fortunate as to distinguish himself by any action of *éclât:* an event was now, however, approaching which fully developed the resources of his mind, and which, in the sequel, clothed his memory with a splendour that has commanded the applause of the present generation, and will secure the admiration of posterity. The Channel fleet, under Lord Bridport, was cruising off the coast of France; and on the evening of the 20th April, the Mars, with the Ramillies and Jason frigate, was directed by signal to look out ahead of the fleet during the ensuing night. On the following morning, the wind being to the S. W. a French lugger was discovered examining a Swedish brig to windward, which was chased; following this pursuit, the Mars distinguished a line-of-battle ship running before the wind for Brest. Information of this circumstance having been immediately given to the commander-in-chief by signal, the Ramillies and Jason frigate were directed to join the Mars in chase; but the line-of-battle ship outsailed the frigate. About half-past six p.m. the Ramillies carried away her fore-top-mast, and, losing way, left the Mars singly to continue the chase: this accident called forth the characteristic and simultaneous feeling of British sailors, which for a considerable period had, to their disgrace and the imminent danger of the country, remained dormant.

* *Naval Chronicle.*

Mutiny having broken out through the Channel and other fleets, the crew of the Mars was composed of more than the usual number of quota or pressed men, and was during that eventful period extremely violent; nor were they in a settled state even after the ship had put to sea. The instant, however, the Ramillies sustained the loss before-mentioned, and was observed by the crew of the Mars to fall astern, they cheered, expressive of their joy that the distinguished honour of engaging the enemy single handed was now their fortunate lot. Those of the ship's company who had been most turbulent came aft, shewed their contrition to Captain Hood for past conduct, told him how gratified they were by the opportunity now afforded of testifying their devotion to their king and country, their attachment to him, and their wish to wipe away the stigma that had attached to them previously as British sailors; and they now impatiently desired to be laid along side the enemy. The Penmarks bore E. S. E. distant nine or ten leagues: the utmost exertions being made by the crew of the Mars to accelerate her sailing, she gained considerably at every tack on the chase; and the enemy perceiving that she was a ship of the line, hauled her wind, but being unable to escape in that direction, again bore up and ran till the strength of the tide compelled her to anchor off the entrance of the Passage du Raz. Night now closed in, and the enemy was lost sight of—a circumstance which occasioned the greatest anxiety in the mind of Captain Hood; to which may be added the extreme intricacy and great danger of the navigation, which was at the time but little known. Having ascertained from the pilot the impracticability of the enemy passing through the passage in the then state of the tide, he ordered his ship to be steered in the direction of the enemy, regardless of all considerations of danger. The chase was shortly after discovered by her lights at anchor, when Captain Hood determined to cross the hawse of the enemy, pour his larboard broadside into her bows, and then bring her to close quarters with his starboard guns. On approaching the object of attack, Captain Hood perceived that the rapidity of the tide would prevent this admirable plan; ranging therefore as much ahead of the Hercule as the tide permitted, and receiving from that ship, at a quarter-past nine, a broadside, he instantly laid the enemy on board. Such a moment was not to be lost; and Lieutenant Ford, and the men under his command on the forecastle, immediately lashed the Mars to the enemy's cathead: in the collision many of the lower-deck ports were carried away: the ships remained in such close contact that some of the muzzles of the guns were actually in the enemy's ports, whilst others were fired from within board, there not being room to run them out. In this situation the French maintained a most bloody conflict with determined bravery, but the rapid and destructive fire from the lower-decks of the Mars, commanded by Second Lieutenant (now Captain John) Bowker*, with the assistance of Lieutenant Bowden, succeeded at length in silencing the lower-deck guns of the enemy. Lieutenant (now Captain George) Argles, who was alone in the command of the main-deck, notwithstanding he was much annoyed by combustibles, which maimed many of his men and severely wounded himself in the right shoulder, not only refused to quit the deck, but, by the most persevering conduct, overcame the opposite quarter. The numerous soldiery of the Hercule gave her a great advantage; they were placed on the poop, quarter-deck, gangway, and forecastle, and caused great slaughter, especially amongst the marines of the Mars, at whose head the gallant Captain White fell: his death, however, was nobly avenged by his subalterns, Lieutenants Tate, Epworth, and Hawkins. In this part of the action Lieutenant Ford received a contusion on the head, which subsequently occasioned his death. Under the fire of their musketry, the enemy then attempted to board the Mars from their fore-chains, but were nobly repulsed by Welch the boatswain and those under him. Orders were then given to board the Hercule, when Lieutenants Bowker, Bowden, and Mr. Southey, with many others, rushed from the ports of the Mars into those of the Hercule; the latter officer†, whilst between the ships, received a severe wound: others boarded from the main-chains, and at this moment of the action Captain Hood fell mortally wounded by a musket-ball fired from the rigging; but his brave officers and crew, after a sanguinary contest hand to hand, obliged their enemy to surrender. The chaplain, Mr. (now Dr.) Morgan, received the sword of the French captain, and conveyed it to his brave and expiring commander, who, on being taken below, evinced great regret that he had been moved from his post The dying hero, although unable to express his joy at the sight of the trophy, evidently recognised it, and grasping it with inward satisfaction, closed his eyes for ever.

The superior seamanship which the commander of the Mars evinced

* This excellent officer has on many similar trying occasions merited the warmest admiration from officers of distinction in the service.

† Brother of the Poet Laureate, a brave officer, and since a captain in the navy.

in the pursuit of the enemy, the manner in which he laid him on board, the undaunted courage, combined with the greatest coolness and presence of mind, which he exhibited, cheered with ardour his officers and men; whilst his personal bravery in the hottest fire animated them, and infused into their minds that enthusiasm which is the sure presage of glorious victory. L'Hercule being on fire in three places, it was only by the unwearied exertions of the boarders, whose situation was at one time extremely dangerous, that the devouring element was got under.

Shortly after L'Hercule had struck, the Jason (which had not, on account of the darkness of the night, been seen during the action,) came up, when it was thought necessary to report to her captain the state of the two ships. The officers being either wounded or fully occupied in securing the prize, the chaplain, the Rev. Mr. Morgan*, volunteered to go on board the frigate for that purpose. The night being dark, and the tide very strong, the bowman missed the rope thrown from that ship; they were consequently placed in a situation of much peril, being in danger, if they escaped the sunken rocks, of going ashore on the French coast, when a prison would have been their sure destiny. By great good fortune, Mr. Morgan at length reached the frigate, and communicated his message to Captain Stirling, whose lieutenant had already been dispatched to render every possible assistance to the Mars and her prize, which he did in securing the safety of the two ships, whose sides were in many places driven in. The masts, yards, and rigging of either ship were but little damaged. The killed and missing on board the Mars amounted to 30, and the wounded to 60. The French officers stated their loss in killed and wounded to be 290; but it is believed that it exceeded that number.

Thus fell, at the age of forty, the gallant Captain Hood, whose life had been employed in the service of his country from early youth; whilst the sacrifice of it in the defence of all that was dear to the nation has tended to exalt its glory. He was as beloved by his brother officers in life, as by them in death he was deplored. In the words of one of the crew, "no ship had ever a better or more able captain." His public cha-

* This gentleman was present in the Alfred at Lord Howe's victory on the 1st June, and in Lord Hotham's action he was on board the Bombay Castle. He has subsequently filled the situation of chaplain and secretary to Sir Charles Cotton; and for his meritorious and long services was appointed, without interest, application, or solicitation, to the chaplainship of the dockyard at Portsmouth, which he now holds.

racter will be upheld by his conduct, whilst in private life his amiable and unassuming manners endeared him to all who had the pleasure of his acquaintance. With an excellent understanding, he possessed a diffidence which concealed his abilities from the world in general. It was only in the private circle of his friends that he displayed those engaging qualities that adorn and cheer the social hour. As a husband, father, and friend, his conduct was indeed estimable.

The lot of those who fall in the arms of victory is, perhaps, in many respects an enviable one; they live in the memory of their grateful country to the end of time, and often escape the regrets and mortifications incident to a change of popular feeling. In the case of this brave officer, however, neither public monumental reward, nor the usual pension to the widow and family, was awarded. The meed of valour should be distributed with an equal hand; reward should be the certain consequence of victory. The man who honourably dies in the defence of his country should have some distinguishing trophy raised to perpetuate his fame. But what was omitted by his country has not been forgotten by his own family, who have erected an elegant Gothic monument to his memory in the parish church of Butleigh, Somersetshire. His widow, the only child of John Periam, Esq. of the Middle Temple, and of Wootton in the before-named parish, still resides upon her estate there, which has been held by her ancestors for many generations. His son inherited a baronetcy from Sir Samuel Hood, his uncle, and is now Sir Alexander Hood: he represents the elder branch of the Hood family.

HISTORICAL MEMOIRS OF

ADMIRAL SIR SAMUEL HOOD, BART. G.C.B.

IT but rarely falls to the lot of any family to have more than one of its members distinguished for talents and courage, and to be advanced to rank and honours through their own intrinsic abilities: that of the Hoods is, however, an exception. Of the two cousins of Sir Samuel Hood (Viscounts Hood and Bridport), and of his two brothers (Arthur and Alexander), mention has already been made*; and of them nothing more honourable can be added, than that as they were employed, so they ended their days in the service of their country. *" Dulce et decorum est pro patriâ mori."* Thus connected it is not surprising that the examples of his noble relatives should have roused the highest spirit of emulation in his mind, and, being once excited, that it should have arrived to that degree of enthusiasm which it attained, and which induced him to contemn all dangers and difficulties in the accomplishment of his laudable ambition. He was the youngest of three sons, and was born in November 1762, and about the age of fourteen commenced his naval career as a midshipman on board the Courageux, then commanded by Captain S. (afterwards Lord) Hood†. He remained in that ship and the Robust, commanded by Captain A. Hood (afterwards Lord Bridport), till 1779, and in the latter ship was present at the action between Admiral Keppel and Count d'Orvilliers. Having removed into the Lively sloop, he assisted, in 1780, in capturing La Duchesse de Chartres, a French privateer.

At the latter end of the year 1780 (in which Mr. Hood was placed on board the Barfleur, bearing the flag of Admiral S. Hood,) he sailed to the West Indies, and served as acting-lieutenant and lieutenant till the 31st January, 1782. During that period he was in the battle with De Grasse off Martinique in April 1781, in the engagement off the Chesapeake in September following, and in the actions between the two fleets at St. Kitt's on the 25th and 26th January, 1782. In five days after this last event, Mr. Hood was promoted to the rank of commander, and appointed to the Renard sloop; an appointment which took place when he had scarcely passed his twentieth year. His appointment was, however,

---

* Page 48.   † *Naval Chronicle.*

rather nominal than real, as at that period the Renard was lying as a convalescent ship at Antigua; and he therefore remained as a volunteer on board the Barfleur, and was consequently in the actions of the 9th and 12th April. That ship was afterwards detached in pursuit of the enemy, and was present at the capture of two sail of the line in the Mona Passage. This was the last action in which he was concerned during the war; and it would be unjust to dismiss this part of the subject without observing, that he must and did derive ample experience and profit from the situation in which he had been placed. Acting under the immediate eye of his relation and such a distinguished commander-in-chief, he could not fail to acquire a portion of his skill, and imbibe a feeling of emulation, which opened to him a prospect that produced the brightest and happiest results. Favoured by nature with an excellent constitution, a brave and martial spirit, Fortune seems to have indulged him with an opportunity of turning those advantages to the best account, and the tenour of his life proved that he availed himself of those opportunities to the utmost and put them to the best of uses*. Having returned to England, he took the opportunity, afforded by the termination of hostilities, of going to France, where he remained until the year 1785. On his return he was appointed to the Weazel sloop of war, in which he proceeded to Halifax. He was there employed in surveying the coasts and harbours on that station, where, for the vigilance and activity of his services, he was rewarded by the commander-in-chief with a post-captain's commission (dated 24th May, 1788), and appointed to the Thisbe frigate. He remained on that station till the latter end of 1789, when the Thisbe was ordered to England and paid off.

In May 1790 Captain Hood was appointed to the Juno frigate, in which he proceeded to Jamaica. Nothing particular occurred on this station till February 1791, when Captain Hood, in a manner the most honourable to his character as an officer and a man, had the satisfaction of saving the lives of three men from a wreck at sea. His ship was then lying in St. Anne's harbour, and in the height of a gale of wind, which increased to an absolute hurricane, a wreck was descried from the masthead, with three people upon it, over whom the waves broke with such unremitting violence, that it appeared scarcely possible to rescue them from their dreadful situation. The Juno's cutter and launch had been previously dispatched by Captain Hood to the assistance of a vessel in

* *Naval Chronicle.*

the offing, so that he had nothing but his own barge with which to attempt the preservation of his unfortunate fellow-creatures. From the apparently extreme danger, the crew evinced the greatest reluctance to descend into the barge, until Captain Hood undauntedly leaped in, exclaiming, " *I never gave an order to a sailor in my life which I was not ready to undertake and execute myself.*" The barge then pushed off, and, through the most determined perseverance, Captain Hood had the happiness of succeeding in his gallant and meritorious effort.

The officer who has forfeited the esteem of his men can never command their obedience with effect; but he who sets them an example of zeal, courage, and humanity, will be sure to conciliate the respect of his followers, and deserve and obtain the applause of his country. By his conduct on this occasion Captain Hood proved himself a veteran in noble daring, a veteran in humane feeling, and a veteran in the love and admiration of the public. So highly was the government of Jamaica impressed with a sense of the humane and adventurous conduct displayed by him on this occasion, that the House of Assembly unanimously voted the sum of 100 guineas for the purchase of a sword, to be presented to him as a testimony of respect which they entertained for his merit, his gallant and humane exertions. Having returned to England in the course of 1791, he was stationed in the Channel, between Dunnose and the Start; but in the autumn of that and the succeeding year he had the honour of attending upon their Majesties at Weymouth. This duty must have afforded him a pleasing relaxation from the toils of severe service; but a scene more animating, more congenial to the enterprising spirit of Captain Hood was on the eve of presenting itself. At the breaking out of the war in 1793 he was first employed in the Channel, where he captured several vessels and two privateers, and was ordered up the Mediterranean in the Juno, where he was very actively employed. Previous to the evacuation of Toulon he was dispatched to Malta, and on his return from thence, with supernumeraries for the fleet, being wholly unacquainted with the events which had occurred during his absence, he stood into Toulon harbour. His escape from thence may be regarded as one of those fortunate circumstances which history has but rarely an opportunity of recording; and in reading the following narrative of his proceedings, we cannot avoid regarding with applause and satisfaction the signal display of the most perfect presence of mind and promptitude of decision, the great and leading qualifications which were manifested on this occasion:

JUNO, BAY OF HIERES, Jan. 13, 1794.

On the 3d instant I left the Island of Malta, having on board 150 supernumeraries, 46 officers and private marines of his Majesty's ship Romney, the remainder Maltese, intended for the fleet. On the night of the 7th passed the south-west point of Sardinia, and steered a course for Toulon. On the 9th, about eleven a.m. made Cape Sicie, but found a current had set the ship some leagues to the westward of our expectation; hauled the wind, but it blowing hard from the eastward, with a strong lee current, we could but just fetch to the westward of the above cape. The wind and current continuing, we could not, till the evening of the 11th, get as far to the westward as Cape Sepet; having that evening, a little before ten o'clock, found the ship would be able to fetch into Toulon, I did not like to wait till morning, as we had been thrown to leeward before, and having so many men on board, I thought it my indispensable duty to get in as fast as possible. At ten I ordered the hands to be turned up to bring the ship to anchor, being then abreast of Cape Sepet, entering the outer harbour. Not having a pilot on board, nor any person acquainted with the port, I placed two midshipmen to look out, with night-glasses, for the fleet; but not discovering any ships until we got near the entrance of the inner harbour, I supposed they had moved up there in the eastern gale; at the same time seeing one vessel, with several other lights, which I imagined to be the fleet's. I entered the inner harbour under the top-sails only; but finding I could not weather a brig which lay a little way to the point called the Grand Tower, I ordered the fore-sail and driver to be set, to be ready to tack when on the other side of the brig. Soon after the brig hailed us, but I could not make out in what language: I supposed they wanted to make out what ship it was; I told them it was an English frigate, called the Juno: they answered, "Viva!" After asking in English and French for some time what brig she was, and where the British admiral lay, they appeared not to understand me, but called out, as we passed under their stern, "Luff! luff!" several times, which made me suppose there was shoal water near: the helm was instantly put a-lee, but we found the ship was on shore before she got head to wind. There being very little wind and perfectly smooth, I ordered the sails to be cleared up and handed: at this time a boat went from the brig to the town. Before the people were all off the yard, I found the ship went astern very fast by a flow of wind that came down the harbour: hoisted the driver and mizen-staysail, keeping the sheets to windward, that she might get farther from the shoal. The instant she lost her way, the bows being then in $\frac{1}{4}$ less 5, let go the best bower anchor, when she tended head to wind; the after-part of the keel was aground, and we could not move the rudder. I ordered the launch and cutter to be hoisted out, and the ketch-anchor, with two hawsers, to be put in them, to warp the ship farther off. By the time the boats were out, a boat came along side, after having been hailed, and, we thought, answered as if an officer had been in her. The people were all anxious to get out of her, two of whom appeared to be officers. One of them said, he came to inform me that it was the regulation of the port, and the commanding officer's orders, that I must go into another branch of the harbour, to perform ten days' quarantine. I kept asking him where Lord Hood's ship lay; but his not giving any satisfactory answer, and one of the midshipmen having at that instant said " they wore national cockades," I looked at one of their hats more stedfastly, and, by the moonlight, clearly distinguished the three colours. Perceiving they were suspected, and on my questioning them again about Lord Hood, one of them said, " Soyez tranquille, les Anglois sont des braves gens, nous les traitons bien; l'amiral Anglois est sorti il y a quelque tems." It may be more easily conceived than any words can express what I felt at the moment. The circumstance of our situation was of course known throughout the ship in an instant; and, saying we were all prisoners, the officers soon got near enough to know our situation. At the same time, a flow of wind coming down the harbour, Lieutenant Webly*, third lieutenant of the ship, said to me, " I believe, sir, we shall be able to fetch out, if we can get her under sail." I immediately perceived we should have a chance of saving the ship, or at least if we did not, we ought not to lose his Majesty's ship without some contention. I ordered every person to their respective stations, and the Frenchmen to be sent below: they perceiving some bustle, two or three of them began to draw their sabres, on which I ordered some of the marines to take the half-pikes and force them below, which was done. I then ordered all the Maltese between decks, that we might not have confusion with too many men. I believe in an instant such a change in people was never seen: every officer and man was at his duty; and I do think, *within three minutes*, every sail in the ship was set, and the yards braced ready for casting. The steady and active assistance of Lieutenant Turner and all the officers prevented any confusion from arising in our critical situation. As soon as the cable was tought, I ordered it to be cut, and had the great good fortune to see the ship start from the shore the moment the sails were filled; a favourable flaw of wind coming at the same time, got good way on her, and we had every prospect of getting out, if the forts did not disable us. To prevent being retarded by the boats, I ordered them to be cut adrift, as also the French boat. The moment the brig saw us begin to loose sails, we could plainly perceive she was getting her guns ready, and we also saw lights upon all the batteries. When we had shot far enough for the brig's guns to bear on us, which was not more than three ship's-lengths, she began to fire, and also a fort a little on the

---

* Now Captain Webly Parry.

I 2

starboard bow, and soon after all of them, on both sides, as they could bring their guns to bear. As soon as the sails were well trimmed, I beat to quarters to get the guns ready, but not with the intention of firing till we were sure of getting out. When we got abreast of the centre part of the land of Cape Sepet, I was much afraid we should have been obliged to make a tack; but as we drew near the shore and were ready, she came up two points, and just weathered the cape. As we passed very close along that shore, the batteries kept up as brisk a fire as the wetness of the weather would permit. When I could afford to keep the ship a little from the wind, I ordered some guns to be fired at a battery that had just opened abreast of us, which quieted them a little; we then stopped firing till we could keep her away with the wind abaft the beam, when, for a few minutes, we kept up a very brisk firing on the last battery we had to pass, and which I believe must otherwise have done us great damage. At half-past twelve, being out of reach of their shot, the firing ceased. Fortunately we had no person hurt; some shots cut the sails, part of the standing and running rigging was shot away, and two French 36-pound shots struck the hull, which is all the damage the ship sustained.

Such was the issue of this extraordinary escape, in which both the vigilance and skill of British naval officers were conspicuously displayed, and in which the men executed their orders with equal alacrity and success, and with a calm intrepidity that presaged the most fortunate result. For a short time the ship appeared irrecoverably lost; but her critical situation served only to stimulate their energies and undaunted spirit, and the termination of their exertions proved how obstacles and dangers are to be overcome by talents and perseverance.

In the month of February Captain Hood proceeded to Corsica, under the orders of Commodore Linzee, and was employed in the Bay of St. Fiorenzo in covering the debarkation of the troops under the command of General Dundas. On the following day the Juno was employed in cannonading the tower of Mortella; and though the attempt to reduce it at that moment was not successful, the bravery of the assailants was not less conspicuous, and Captain Hood accordingly received the thanks of Commodore Linzee. Having removed into the Aigle frigate, Captain Hood assisted at the capture of Calvi; and so highly meritorious were his services considered, that he received the thanks of the commander-in-chief. He was subsequently ordered up the Archipelago with a small squadron, for the purpose of protecting the trade, and also to blockade a squadron of the enemy's frigates, of equal force, at Smyrna; and for the unwearied activity and diligence which he displayed while on this station, he received an address of thanks from the Levant Company, which was conveyed to him in the most flattering terms. He also received a similar address from the British factory at Smyrna*, for the essential services he had rendered to them.

In April 1796, Captain Hood was appointed to the Zealous of 74 guns, and during that year was employed under Sir John Jervis off Toulon. In the early part of 1797 he was off Cadiz; and in the summer of that year he was with Lord H. Nelson at Teneriffe, where, by his spirited and judicious conduct in effecting the return of the British troops and seamen from that disastrous attack, he had the satisfaction of endearing himself to his great and gallant commander. After Admiral Nelson had been wounded and carried to his ship, and all the boats had been either sunk by the dreadful fire from the batteries or swamped in the surf, Captain Hood and Sir Thomas Troubridge found themselves in the heart of the town of Santa Cruz, at the head of a few seamen and marines armed with pikes, but surrounded by some thousands of Spaniards. As daylight approached, their situation became most cri-

---

* The following is a copy, dated Smyrna, Dec. 2, 1795:

"Sir,—Impressed as we are with the liveliest sense of gratitude towards you for the innumerable benefits which we have derived in our trade and persons from your protection, during the time you have been in these seas, we should do the greatest violence to our feelings, and justly incur the imputation of a want of this sentiment, if we were to suppress the expression of it: permit us therefore to offer you our warmest acknowledgments for the very effectual and satisfactory manner in which you have accomplished the object for which you were sent by the commander-in-chief in the Mediterranean, and your very condescending and obliging attention to every request of ours, consistent with your duty; and to assure you that we shall consider ourselves as peculiarly bound to retain a deep and grateful sense of the important benefits which we are indebted to you for; benefits which have been extended in a great measure to every foreign nation here, who speak in the highest terms of admiration of the propriety and dignity which have marked your conduct, and which form such a striking contrast to that of our enemies here, that even the Turks themselves, who are partial to the French, join in the general applause, and have received so favourable an impression from it of our national character, that we assume no small degree of pride to ourselves from the circumstance. To superior merit like yours no commendations of ours can confer additional lustre; we therefore confine ourselves to mere matter of fact in the particulars, and shall content ourselves with assuring you, that you will ever have a place in the admiration and affection of the British factory, every individual of which would deem himself happy in the occasion of giving you proofs of those sentiments, and of our regret that you should have experienced so many inconveniences from the necessity of being unconnected with the shore; this regret being considerably heightened by that circumstance having put it out of our power to shew you personally that respect and those attentions which you are so much entitled to from us."

tical; and in this extremity Captain Hood was sent with a flag of truce
to the governor of the citadel, on being introduced to whom, he said,
" I am come, sir, from the commanding officer of the British troops and
seamen, now within your walls, and in possession of the principal *strutto*,
to say, that as we are disappointed in the object which we came for (alluding to specie), provided you will furnish us with boats, those we came
in being all lost, we will return peaceably to our ships; but should any
means be taken to molest or retard us, we will fire your town in different
places, and force our way out of it at the point of the bayonet." Taking
out his watch, he added, " I am directed to give you ten minutes to
consider of this offer." The governor was astonished at the proposal,
made with such confidence on the part of the men whom he conceived
to be already in his power. He observed, that *he thought they were his
prisoners; but as it was not so, he should hold a council with his officers, and let the British commander know the result in an hour.* To
this Captain Hood coolly replied, that *he was limited to a second, and
that his friends were anxiously awaiting his return, to recommence hostilities, should not the demands be complied with.* He was about to take
his leave, when the governor, alarmed at the probable consequences of
driving Englishmen to extremity, acceded to the proposal. He accordingly provided boats, and sent all the English off to their ships, where
they had ceased to be expected, laden with fruit and various other refreshments. The conduct of the Spanish governor was indeed eminently
noble and generous: previous to the embarkation of the invaders, he
furnished them with rations of wine and biscuit, and gave orders that
such of the British as had been wounded should be received into the
hospital. He also intimated to Admiral Nelson that he was at liberty to
send on shore and purchase whatever necessaries the squadron might
be in need of, whilst it remained off the island*.

Captain Hood was afterwards employed in blockading the port of
Rochefort, from whence he was recalled and ordered up the Mediterranean to reinforce the squadron under Admiral Nelson. On the memorable 1st of August, Captain Hood, having the look-out, was the first
who discovered the French fleet in the Bay of Aboukir, and was ordered
by signal to reconnoitre their position. When Admiral Nelson, about
six in the evening, arrived off the Bay of Shoals, he hove to, and hailed
Captain Hood, to ask him, *what he thought of attacking the enemy that*

* *Naval Chronicle.*

night. His answer was, "*We have now eleven fathoms' water, and if the admiral will give me leave, I will lead in, making known my soundings by signal, and bring the van ship of the enemy to action.*" Late as it was, the firmness of the answer decided the admiral, who said, "*Go on, and I wish you success.*" During this conversation, the Goliath passed, and took the lead, which she kept; but not bringing up along side the first ship, went on to engage the second. On this, Captain Hood exclaimed to his officers, "*Thank God, my friend Foley has left me the van ship.*" He soon after took such a position on the bow of Le Guerrier, the ship in question, as to shoot away all her masts, and effect her capture in twelve minutes from the time that the Zealous commenced her fire. This was achieved without the loss of a man, or the slightest injury to Captain Hood's ship. He was afterwards engaged with others of the enemy's ships, and on the following morning pursued the four French ships which made their escape, until called off by signal. For the services which Captain Hood rendered in this glorious and important engagement, he was subsequently honoured with the thanks of Parliament, and was also presented with a sword by the city of London.

On the return of Admiral Nelson to Naples, Captain Hood was left in command of the British squadron on the coast of Egypt, and was particularly employed in blockading the port of Alexandria. He also contributed, in a material degree, to the interests of the country, by his amicable communications with all the pachas and governors under the Grand Seignior, and particularly with Jezzar, Pacha of Acre, whose friendship he succeeded in acquiring. While on this station, Captain Hood took and destroyed upwards of thirty of the neutral transports which had carried the enemy's troops to Egypt; and, as an honorary reward for his services, was presented by the Grand Seignior with a handsome snuff-box set with diamonds. In the month of February 1799, he joined Lord Nelson at Palermo, and was employed in reducing his Sicilian Majesty's subjects to obedience, and in driving the French out of the kingdom of Naples. At Salerno, with only 40 marines belonging to the Zealous, he kept in check 3000 men, who were attacking that place, until the few Neapolitans that had taken up arms had time to escape. The enemy attempted to surround the little band of Neapolitan royalists; but, favoured by the exertions of Captain Hood, they had the good fortune to effect a retreat, with the loss of only two killed, nine wounded, and six prisoners. Twice also Captain Hood drove the French out of

Salerno by the fire of the Zealous. He was afterwards employed on shore at Naples, in taking charge of Castel Nuovo, and kept the city perfectly quiet during the siege of St. Elmo and Capua, until the periods of their reduction. His Sicilian Majesty acknowledged these services by presenting him with a snuff-box enriched with diamonds, and at the same time conferring upon him the rank of Commander of the Order of St. Ferdinand and of Merit.

In the month of May 1800, the Zealous was paid off, and Captain Hood was appointed to the Courageux of 74 guns, in which he was for some time actively employed in the Channel fleet. The Courageux afterwards formed part of a detached squadron under Sir J. B. Warren at Ferrol and Vigo, until January 1801; at which period Captain Hood removed into the Venerable of 74 guns, in which he was employed in the Channel service till April, when he escorted a valuable fleet of East Indiamen beyond the Cape de Verdes. On his return he joined Sir J. Saumarez off Cadiz, and after making some captures on that station, was in the action of the 6th July off Algeziras. This action was not of the most fortunate description; but, as we have observed in the Memoir of Sir James Saumarez, the failure was attributable to causes which no prudence could foresee, nor valour could controul. Sir James, in his official account, said, " I had previously directed Captain Hood in the Venerable, from his experience and knowledge of the anchorage, to lead the squadron, which he executed with his accustomed gallantry; and although it was not intended he should anchor, he found himself under the necessity so to do from the wind's failing (a circumstance so much to be apprehended in this country), and from which circumstance I have to regret the want of success in this well-intended enterprise." Sir James also observes, " My thanks are particularly due to all the captains, officers, and men under my command; and although their endeavours have not been crowned with success, I trust the thousands of spectators from his Majesty's garrison, and also the surrounding coast, will do justice to their valour and intrepidity, which were not to be checked by the fire from the numerous batteries, however formidable, that surround Algeziras." On this occasion the Venerable sustained a loss of 8 killed and 25 wounded. The Venerable accompanied Sir James in his pursuit of the combined squadron on the 12th, which continued the whole of that night, and during which two sail of the line were burnt, and one captured*. In his dispatch of the 13th, Sir James says, " It blew excessively hard till daylight, and in the morning the only ships in company were the Venerable and Thames, ahead of the Cæsar, and one of the French ships, at some distance from them, standing towards the coast of Conil, besides the Spencer, astern, coming up. All the ships immediately made sail with a fresh breeze; but as we approached, the wind suddenly failing, the Venerable was alone able to bring her to action, which Captain Hood did in the most gallant manner, and nearly silenced the French ship, when his main-mast, which had been before wounded, was unfor- tunately shot away, and it coming nearly calm, the enemy's ship was enabled to get off, without any possibility of following her. The highest praise is due to Captain Hood, the officers and men of the Venerable, for their spirit and gallantry in the action, which entitled them to better success." In his letter of the following day he said, " Captain Hood's merits are held in too high estimation to receive additional lustre from any praises I can bestow; but I only do justice to my own feelings when I observe, that in no instance have I known superior bravery to that displayed by him on this occasion†." For this service Captain Hood not only received the thanks of Sir J. Saumarez, but also of the British Parliament. The Venerable having been repaired, returned to England, and on the signing of the preliminaries of peace, she was paid off.

* See *Memoirs of Sir J. SAUMAREZ and Sir R. KEATS.*

† The following is an extract of Captain Hood's official letter on the occasion : "You must have observed my giving chase to an enemy's line-of-battle ship this morning at daybreak: at seven she hoisted French colours, and I could perceive her to be an 80-gun ship; at half-past, being within point-blank shot, the enemy commenced firing his stern chase-guns, which I did not return for fear of retarding our progress, until the light and baffling airs threw the two ships broadside-to, within musket-shot, when a steady and warm conflict was kept up for an hour and a half, and we had closed within pistol-shot, the enemy principally directing his fire to our masts and rigging. I had at this time the misfortune to perceive the main-mast fall overboard, the fore and mizen-masts nearly in the same state, and since gone: the ship being near the shore close to the castle of Saucti Petri, the enemy escaped. It was with much difficulty I was enabled to get the Venerable off, her cables and anchors all disabled; and it was only by the great exertions of the Thames, with the boats you sent me, she was saved, after being on shore some time. I shall have no occasion to comment on the bravery of the officers and ship's company in this action, who had, with much patience and perseverance, suffered great fatigue by their exertions to get the ship to sea, and not 500 men able to go to quarters."

In his official letter Captain Hood stated his loss to be 18 killed and 87 wounded; but in a memorial which he subsequently presented to the king, he stated his loss to be 30 killed and 100 wounded.

The services of Captain Hood were, however, too valuable and important for him to be permitted a long enjoyment of repose. In the month
of October 1802, he was appointed a joint commissioner for the government of the Island of Trinidad; and on the death of Rear-Admiral
Totty, he was appointed commander-in-chief on the Leeward Island
station, with the rank of commodore. The state of inactivity to which
he was reduced by the signature of peace was but of short duration,
and, on the eve of a renewal of hostilities, orders were sent out to Commodore Hood to take measures for acting hostilely against the enemy;
and not only to act hostilely on the first notice, but to intercept all supplies that were proceeding to the colonies of the enemy; and we may
safely assert, that these orders were duly observed and fulfilled by Commodore Hood. His first operations were against the Island of St. Lucia,
before which, with the troops under General Grinfield, he appeared on
the 21st June; the troops were immediately landed, and at four o'clock
in the morning of the 22d Morne Fortunée was carried by storm, which
placed the colony in their possession. No time was lost in embarking
the troops and conveying them to Tobago, which was taken possession
of on the 30th of the same month, and 1200 of the enemy's troops were
made prisoners. Within the period of three months Demerara, Isse-
quibo, and Berbice were added to the colonies of England; and on the
4th May, 1804, Surinam shared the same fate. In addition to which,
the Island of Martinique was reduced to great distress; and, owing to the
activity of his cruisers and the judicious dispositions which he made, a
vast number of the enemy's merchantmen, together with several privateers, fell into his possession. For these signal and important services
his Majesty was pleased to bestow upon him the Order of the Bath,
with which he was invested in the West Indies, and on which occasion
he was addressed by Lord Lavington as follows:

" Commodore Sir Samuel Hood, after the honour which you have this
day received by command of his Majesty, no eulogy from me of those services which have so meritoriously obtained it, can enhance its value or deserve your acceptance. But I cannot repress the expression of my own gratification in being delegated by my sovereign to administer a mark of royal
favour to a gallant officer, the very name of whose family occurs in no
page of our naval history without circumstances of celebrity and distinction. There wants no herald to proclaim the well-known, well-earned
reputation of the two veteran chiefs of it who are now enjoying an

honourable repose from danger and fatigue, under the shade of those honours which the services of their past lives have so eminently merited. But your nearest and ever-to-be-lamented relative has secured to himself a place in the temple of Fame paramount to all the ranks and titles which princes can confer, and which the King of Kings alone can bestow—the glory of sealing with his blood, in the arms of victory, a life spent in, and devoted to, the service of his king and country. May this period of renown, if ever it be destined for you, although the ultimate ambition of patriots and of heroes, be far, far distant, for the sake of the country, for the sake of every other object which is dear to you! May your conduct, of which the harbour of Toulon and the bay of Aboukir were witnesses, be only the presages of future trophies and still more splendid achievements! And may you, in the mean time, after a safe and prosperous voyage, experience that auspicious reception from our gracious sovereign which the best of masters will feel to be due to a brave and faithful servant!"

In February 1805 an enemy's squadron, much superior to that under Sir Samuel Hood, made its appearance in the West Indies; upon the information of which he immediately collected his scattered ships, threw reinforcements of troops into those islands most likely to be attacked, and put them in the best possible state of defence. Being superseded in this command by Admiral Cochrane, he shortly after left the station; but the whole of his regulations had so effectually preserved the British trade from capture, that previous to his departure the warmest acknowledgments for his services were presented to him from the merchants and inhabitants of Barbadoes and other islands, who testified their high approbation of his zealous conduct by the most flattering addresses and the presentation of a service of plate. He also greatly annoyed the commerce of the enemy; and one means of his advantageously doing so was, by having conceived and executed the laborious task of fortifying the Diamond Rock, an occurrence that will ever stamp his name as a skilful engineer.

Shortly after his arrival in England, he was made a colonel of marines, and was subsequently appointed to the Centaur, and placed under the orders of Earl St. Vincent, who gave him the command of seven sail of the line, with some other vessels, to watch the motions of the enemy off Rochefort. On the morning of the 25th September, after four months' perseverance in this service, he had the good fortune to fall in with a squadron of the enemy, consisting of five large frigates and two corvettes, full of troops, and succeed in capturing four of the frigates *; but in the action he received a shot in the right elbow, which reduced him to the necessity of having his arm amputated. For his conduct on this occasion, and in consideration of losing his arm and of his former numerous services, his Majesty was graciously pleased to grant him a pension of 500*l.* per annum. In July 1807, and having the rank of commodore, he accompanied the fleet under Admiral Gambier against Copenhagen. In October he was advanced to the rank of rear-admiral of the Blue, and shortly after hoisted his flag on board the Centaur at Portsmouth, when he sailed, with a force under General Beresford, for the purpose of taking possession of the Island of Madeira, which was done without opposition†. On his return from thence he was appointed second in command of the Baltic fleet, where, in conjunction with Captain Byam Martin of the Impiacable, he was highly distinguished in engaging the rear of the Russian fleet, and in the capture of the Sewolod of 74 guns ‡; and it is here only necessary to insert an extract from Sir Samuel's official letter on that subject:

" The line-of-battle ship engaged by the Implacable having fallen to leeward, grounded on a shoal at the entrance of the port (Rogerswich). There being then some swell, I had a hope she must have been destroyed; but the wind moderating towards the evening, she appeared to ride at anchor, and exertions were made to repair her damage. At sunset, finding the swell abated, and that boats were sent from the Russian fleet to tow her into port, I directed Captain Webley to stand in and endeavour to cut her off: this was executed in a manner that must ever reflect the highest honour on Captain Webley, the officers and ship's company of the Centaur, for their valour and perseverance in the support of my orders. The boats had made considerable progress, and the enemy's ship was just entering the port, when we had the good fortune to lay her on board. Her bowsprit taking the Centaur's fore-rigging, she swept along with her bow grazing the muzzles of our guns, which was the only signal for their discharge, and the enemy's bows were driven in by this raking fire. When the bowsprit came to the mizen-rigging, I ordered it to be lashed: this was performed in a most steady manner by the exertions of Captain Webley, Lieutenant Lawless, Mr. Strode the master, and other brave men, under a heavy fire from the enemy's musketry, by which Lieutenant Lawless was severely wounded. The ship being in six fathoms'

---

* See *Memoir of Sir* R. Lee.

† The Factory of the island presented him with a sword valued at 100 guineas.

‡ See *Memoir of Sir* Byam Martin.

water, I had a hope I should be able to tow her out in that position; but an anchor had been let go from her unknown to us, which made it impossible to effect it. At this period much valour was displayed on both sides, and several attempts made to board by her bowsprit; but nothing could withstand the cool and determined manner of the marines, under Captain Bailey and the other officers, as well as the fire from our stern chase-guns, and in less than half an hour she was obliged to surrender. On this occasion I again received the greatest aid from Captain Martin, who anchored his ship in a position to heave the Centaur off, after the prize had grounded; which was fortunately effected at the moment two of the enemy's ships were seen under sail standing towards us, but retreated as they saw the ships extricated from this difficulty. The prize proved to be the Sewolod of 74 guns. She had so much water in her, and being fast on shore, after taking out the prisoners and wounded men, I was obliged to give orders for her being burnt; which service was completely effected under the direction of Lieutenant Biddulph of this ship*."

The conduct of Sir Samuel Hood was so highly gratifying to his Swedish Majesty (with whose fleet he was acting), that on the receipt of the intelligence and the Russian flag, which Sir Samuel had forwarded to him, he immediately wrote him the following letter:

SIR,—Lieutenant Thompson delivered to me, on the 1st of this month, your letter of the 28th of August, with the papers inclosed, and the Russian pendant which was flying on board the Sewolod when she was captured by you on the 26th. I cannot sufficiently express to you the satisfaction with which I have been informed of your gallant conduct, as well as that of the officers and crews under your command, against the common enemy; and though your principles, and the honours you had already previously acquired in war, assured me of the new laurels you would obtain if occasion permitted, your success in this instance is attributable to your great exertions, zeal, and honourable endeavours; so that you have acquired a double right to my distinguished esteem. I have therefore resolved to send to your sovereign the pendant you have offered me, because it was captured by his own man of war; and I shall seize the opportunity to ask his Britannic Majesty's leave for you, and the principal officers under your command, to receive the proofs of my respect.   (Signed,)   GUSTAF ADOLPHUS.

As a mark of his Majesty's approbation, Sir Samuel was created a Grand Cross of the Swedish Order of the Sword. Neither were his own countrymen backward in shewing their respect for his character: he was presented with the freedom of the cities of Exeter, Glasgow, and Edinburgh, and of the corporation of the Trinity-House at Leith.

* See Plate in *Naval Chronology*, vol. II. p. 88.

Towards the close of the season Sir Samuel returned to England, and in the beginning of 1809 we find him superintending the embarkation of the British army at Corunna; which service he executed with so much satisfaction, that he received the thanks of the British Parliament. He afterwards proceeded to the Mediterranean, and in the course of that year, his Majesty, taking into consideration the long, active, and important services of Sir Samuel Hood, was pleased to grant him the dignity of a baronet. At the expiration of his command in the Mediterranean, he was appointed to the chief command in the East Indies. In June 1814 he was advanced to the rank of vice-admiral of the Red; but neither on this last station, nor that of the Mediterranean, do we find that any circumstance occurred in which he could exercise his skill and gallantry. In January 1815 he was nominated a Grand Cross of the Bath, an honour which he did not live to enjoy, having died at Madras on the 24th December, 1814, after an illness of three days. Every public respect was paid to his obsequies, his remains being attended to the tomb by all the high official characters of the place.

Sir Samuel Hood had raised himself so high in public estimation by the number and importance of his actions and the benefit of his services; had shewn himself so admirable in the conduct of every enterprise in which he had been engaged; was still so young in years, so unbroken in spirit, and had so thoroughly gained the enthusiastic admiration, as well as entire confidence, of every man in his profession, that his loss was considered a great and severe misfortune to the country. He possessed in a peculiar degree the qualifications which form a great commander; to the calmest and most accurate judgment, he added a presence of mind and a rapidity of perception, under every change of situation, that enabled him to turn every event which arose, even out of unforeseen difficulties and dangers, to the purpose he had in view. In common with Nelson, he was anxious and impatient while there remained a doubt that the foe could be grappled with; but when the battle raged, his intrepidity, his coolness, and the precision with which all his orders were given, begot a confidence that was uniformly attended by victory. It was, however, not only on those great and trying occasions that he proved himself one of the best of officers, he was eminently skilled in every branch of his profession, whether scientific or practical. He was intimately versed in astronomy, as connected with navigation and geography; in ship-building, in fortification, and in all the branches of mechanical philosophy. He studied, without any exception, the language, laws, and customs of every country he visited. His strong natural taste for scientific inquiry, and unbounded curiosity to see every thing with his own eyes, were kept in perpetual action by the belief that those acquisitions of knowledge might one day be useful to his country: that they proved to be so, we hope this statement of his services sufficiently testifies. His memory, like that of Nelson's, with whom he acted in some of his most trying and glorious days, will for ever be held sacred in that profession to which he devoted nearly forty years of his life. The unaffected modesty and simplicity of one who filled so great a space in public admiration, was not the least remarkable part of his character. He had the rare felicity, even to his latest years, to preserve undiminished the vivacity of youth, and that taste for simple pleasure which so seldom survives a mixed and active intercourse with the world. The charm which this happy feeling communicated to his conversation and society is said to have had something in it irresistibly pleasing, and that he was consequently no less the delight of his friends than the pride of his country. With a mind of this temper, we may easily imagine the warmth of all his domestic feelings. He was perhaps one of the few men who, in dying, would scarcely have wished to change any circumstance of his public or private life.

Sir Samuel married, in November 1804, Mary, eldest daughter of Lord Seaforth, by his wife, the daughter of Dr. Proby, Dean of Lichfield. He was succeeded in his title and property by his nephew, Sir Alexander Hood, Knight, now Baronet, son of Captain Alexander Hood, who was killed on board the Mars.

HISTORICAL MEMOIRS OF

ADMIRAL SIR CHARLES ROWLEY, K.C.B.

THE family of Rowley has long been distinguished in the naval annals of Britain; but few families have had better success, or met with greater attention and advancement; and though they possessed considerable interest and influence, the most fastidious cannot find fault with their promotion, or say that the rewards bestowed upon them were given to unworthy objects.

Sir Charles is the grandson of Admiral Sir William Rowley, K. B. and fourth son of Vice-Admiral Sir Joshua Rowley, Baronet, and brother to Admiral Bartholomew Rowley. He was born in the month of December 1770; and having made choice of a naval life, made his first voyage, in 1785, on board the Thisbe, commanded by Commodore Sawyer, with whom he sailed to Newfoundland. In the following year he removed to the Pegasus, then under the command of his Royal Highness the Duke of Clarence, with whom he remained till 1789, and with him visited all the West India Islands. In that year he was promoted to a lieutenancy, and to command the Trepassey cutter on the Newfoundland station, by Admiral Milbanke. In the following year he joined the Orion, Captain Duckworth; and on the Russian armament being paid off, he was appointed to the Niger, Captain Keats, in which ship he was employed in the Channel. At the commencement of the war in 1793, he was appointed to the London, fitting for his Royal Highness the Duke of Clarence; but, unfortunately, the royal duke did not again go to sea, and in 1794 the London was paid off. Lieutenant Rowley was then appointed to the Resolution, bearing the flag of Admiral Murray, commander-in-chief on the Halifax station, by whom, in the latter part of the year, he was made acting-captain of the Hussar frigate. He was then employed in cruising, and succeeded in making several captures. Early in 1795 he was made a commander in the Lynx sloop, and in August following obtained post-rank in the Raison, captured by Captains Cochrane and Beresford. He afterwards received acting orders for the Cleopatra, in which he was employed during the winter, when several of the enemy's merchantmen and privateers, and also the *armée en flute*

Aurore, mounting 24 guns, from Martinique to Bourdeaux, were captured. In 1796 Captain Rowley was reappointed to the Hussar, and returned to England, when he was appointed by Lord Spencer to command the Unité of 36 guns. He was then attached to the Channel fleet, and after serving for some months as repeater, he was detached, with Captain Stopford, on a cruise along the French coast, when he captured La Brunette of 16 guns, assisted at the capture of the Indian of similar force, and several other vessels. He continued to command the Unité, on different stations and on different services, till 1798, when he was obliged to resign the command from ill health.

In 1800 Captain Rowley joined the Prince of 98 guns, bearing the flag of Sir Charles Cotton, off Brest, acting *pro tempore;* and early in the following year he was appointed to the Boadicea, the boats of which, in company with those of the Fisguard and Diamond, cut out the Spanish ship of war Neptuna of 20 guns, and a gun-boat carrying a 32-pounder, from under the batteries of Corunna. Captain Rowley continued in the command of the Boadicea till 1803, when she was paid off; but in the following year he was appointed to the Ruby of 64 guns, and employed off the Texel, under the orders of Admiral Thornbrough. He afterwards joined the squadron under Sir John Ord off Cadiz, and was subsequently attached to the Channel fleet till October 1805. From the Ruby he removed into the Eagle of 74 guns, and in the month of December sailed with a convoy for Gibraltar. Having joined Lord Collingwood off Cadiz, he was detached, on the 7th March, 1806, to Palermo, and on his arrival assumed the command of the squadron allotted for the protection of Sicily. He consequently adopted every method for the security of that island, and cruised himself off the west end for the annoyance of the enemy's trade. But on the 21st April, Rear-Admiral Sir Sidney Smith arrived, and having taken the command of the squadron, directed Captain Rowley, by order dated the 11th May, to take the Intrepid under his command, and make an attack on the Island of Capri. The manner in which that order was executed will be best seen from the following extract from Sir Sidney Smith's official letter:

" That brave officer (Captain Rowley) placed his ship most judiciously, nor did he open his fire till she was secured, and his distance marked by the effect of musketry on his quarter-deck, where the first-lieutenant, J. Crawley, fell wounded, a marine was killed, and six or seven wounded. An hour's fire from both decks of the Eagle, between nine and ten o'clock, with that of two Neapolitan mortar-boats, drove the enemy from the vineyard within their walls; the marines were then landed, and gallantly led by Captain Bunce. The seamen in like manner, under Lieutenant Morrell of the Eagle and Lieutenant Redding of the Pompée, mounted the steps, for such was their road (headed by the officers), nearest to the narrow pass by which they could alone ascend. Lieutenant Carroll had then an opportunity of particularly distinguishing himself. Captain Stannus, commanding the Athenian's marines, gallantly pressing forward, gained the heights, and the French commander fell by his hand. This event being known, the enemy beat a parley, and the island was surrendered, on terms which were agreed to and signed by Captain Rowley."

The vicinity of this island to the city of Naples, and the means it afforded of annoying the enemy, rendered it an object of importance to them, and one which they would no doubt seize the first opportunity of retaking. The greatest attention was therefore directed to its preservation, and the Eagle was employed in cruising in the bay, taking every method of distressing the enemy by means of gun-boats and ships' boats, and keeping the coast in a constant state of alarm. Captain Rowley was then engaged in a close correspondence with Mr. Elliott, Sir John Acton, and Sir Sidney Smith, on the affairs of the enemy, and on the best and most effectual means to be taken for the benefit of the common cause. At this period the fortress of Gaeta, the most important in the kingdom of Naples, was closely besieged by the French, and Captain Rowley proceeded thither to decide upon the best means for its preservation. The Eagle arrived off that place on the 17th July, when Captain Rowley immediately landed; but on examining the different breaches, under fire of the enemy, he received a severe contusion from the bursting of a shell. He, however, suggested the repair of certain works, and directed the Sicilian flotilla to fire on the enemy's line during the night, in the middle of which Colonel Hotz, the Neapolitan commander, entered into a capitulation with the French general, and surrendered the fortress, without the knowledge or concurrence of the English. Seeing that there was now nothing further to be done, Captain Rowley received the garrison on board the British men of war and Sicilian vessels, and conveyed them to Palermo. In March 1807 he again became the senior officer on the coast of Sicily and its vicinity, and a strict communication was opened between him, Lord Collingwood, General Fox, and Sir William Drummond, on the means best adapted to harass the enemy and divert his attention from the invasion of Sicily. In the prosecution of this service, which was most effectually performed, Captain Rowley displayed the greatest zeal and ability, till August 1807, when he was relieved by the arrival of Rear-Admiral Thornbrough. After remaining some time longer on that station, he joined the fleet under Lord Collingwood; and in August 1808, he was selected by him to take the command of a small squadron, and make an attack upon the town of Marseilles, with a view of trying the effect of Congreve's rockets, under the impression that they would fly over the town and set fire to the shipping. But the impracticability of so doing soon became apparent, and the object was relinquished.

The defects of the Eagle now being very great, and rendering it indispensable that she should return to England, Captain Rowley was ordered to return, and arrived in Cawsand Bay 28th December. The Eagle afterwards proceeded to Portsmouth, and having been docked and refitted, sailed, with the squadron under Sir Joseph Yorke, off the Western Isles. On her return she was employed in the Walcheren expedition; and whilst so employed, the Eagle, with several other ships, got on shore; but owing to the great exertions and professional skill of Captain Rowley, she was extricated from her perilous situation: the damages, however, which she received rendered her return to England necessary, when Captain Rowley, ever anxious to promote the good of the service and to render the utmost assistance, suggested the idea of receiving as many wounded officers and men of the army as the ship could conveniently take; and, for their greater accommodation, gave up possession of his own cabin, by which several valuable lives were saved to the country. The Eagle having been repaired, Captain Rowley was ordered in July 1810 to join Rear-Admiral Pickmore at Portsmouth, and from thence proceeded with him for Cadiz; from whence he was dispatched to Carthagena, with the Spanish Generals Elio and Blake, and money for the Catalonian army. In addition to which, Captain Rowley was charged with another and more important mission, the removing a Spanish line-of-battle ship, two frigates, and the stores in the arsenal of Carthagena, to Mahon; an object which it appears was not accomplished till after a great deal of correspondence with the captain-general, and then only in part: the two frigates being considered unseaworthy, remained; but the ship of the line and some of the stores were safely conveyed to their destination, and Captain Rowley joined the fleet off Toulon. In January

1811 he was appointed by Admiral Sir Charles Cotton to the command of the squadron in the Adriatic, and entered upon the duties thereof by relieving Captain Eyre of the Magnificent, on the 2d April. At this period the enemy held the Island of Corfu, and either possessed or influenced all the ports (except those which belonged to Ali Pacha) on either side of the Adriatic. The necessity of having some post or place of rendezvous for the ships employed in the upper part of the Adriatic soon suggested itself to the mind of Captain Rowley, coupled with the advantages that would arise if an *entrepôt* could be established from which British goods might be sent to the surrounding countries; and the small Island of Lissa appearing to possess the requisite capabilities for both these objects, it was pointed out to the commanders-in-chief of the army and navy, who, coinciding in opinion with Captain Rowley, an English garrison was placed on it, and it became of considerable importance both in a maritime and commercial point of view. At this period there was considerable activity displayed on this station; many of the enemy's vessels put to sea, and the whole coast required strict attention on the part of Sir Charles and the squadron under his command, to prevent them from becoming extremely injurious to the commerce of England. But the utmost diligence and assiduity being used, their perseverance was rewarded by a number of prizes, a mere list of which will be sufficient to prove the judicious disposition of his force, and the zeal manifested by the whole: On the 27th July the Active and Acorn captured a convoy of twenty-eight sail and three gun-boats. On the 27th November the Eagle discovered three French ships, to which she immediately gave chase, one of which soon after separated and effected her escape into Ancona. Captain Rowley continued in pursuit of the other two till half-past seven p. m. when he came up with and captured La Corceyre, pierced for 40 guns, but mounting only 28, with 300 tons of wheat and a quantity of military stores, destined for Corfu. Owing to the darkness of the night, however, her consort, the Uranie of 40 guns, effected her escape. On the following day the Alceste, Active, and Unité engaged the French frigates Pauline and Pomone, and Persanne store-ship, and captured the two latter. On the 14th and 21st January, 1812, the Eagle was unfortunately struck by lightning: on the first of those days ten men were wounded; but on the latter day, though the main-mast was on fire for ten minutes, there was fortunately no one hurt. On the 22d February, 1812, the Victorious and Weazel captured the

French ship Rivoli of 74 guns.   The Weazel at the same time engaged three French brigs, one of which blew up in the action, when the other two made sail and got clear off.   In the month of April the boats of the Eagle and Alceste, under Lieutenant Cannon of the former, cut out a merchant-brig from Rovigno; and on the following day took and destroyed the remainder of a convoy which had taken shelter in a creek near the town of Orsera.

The Eagle had now been at sea for fourteen months without any intermission, and it became necessary that she should proceed to Malta to refit.   That object being accomplished, Captain Rowley returned to his station, and resumed those active operations which had distinguished his previous command.   On the 19th, 20th, and 22d July the boats of the Eagle, with three gun-boats previously captured, with 20 soldiers of the 35th regiment and 10 marines, the whole under Lieutenant Cannon, were successively in action with the enemy, and in which they stormed the battery of Cape Ceste, embarked the guns, blew up the works, and captured a gun-boat.   In the evening of the 16th September, being off Cape Maistro, the three barges were dispatched, under Lieutenant Cannon, to intercept the enemy's coasting trade.   On the following morning a convoy of twenty-three sail, carrying an 8 or 6-pounder, with two gun-boats, were perceived standing towards Goro, and which, on the approach of the barges, drew up in line of battle under cover of a 4-gun battery, the beach being lined with armed people; the two gun-boats advanced in front.   The largest of those vessels became the first object of Lieutenant Cannon, and having succeeded in carrying her, he turned her guns against her consort, which was also speedily captured, when the whole attention of the British party was directed against the convoy, and twenty-one became the reward of the victors; but as the whole could not be manned, six were burnt, and the remainder carried off in triumph. Unfortunately, however, in the execution of this well-conducted enterprise, Lieutenant Cannon was mortally wounded, and died on the 22d.

Thus did Captain Rowley continue to harass the enemy, in the same regular manner and with undeviating success, till the arrival of Rear-Admiral Fremantle, when he became under his orders.   On this occasion Captain Rowley received the following letter from Sir Edward Pellew, commander-in-chief in the Mediterranean, dated August 1812:

DEAR SIR,—It having become necessary, from various causes, to increase the force employed in the Adriatic, and provide against the growing strength of the enemy in that quarter, I have directed Rear-Admiral Fremantle to continue in the command of the ships employed on that station, receiving from you all standing and unexecuted orders relative thereto in your possession ; and he is directed to take you under his orders accordingly.   I should not do justice to your constant and zealous exertion, or to my own feelings, if I did not convey to you the sense I entertain of your judgment and services, by requesting you to accept my best thanks for your continued attention to the various duties of your command. I most sincerely wish it had been rewarded to your utmost expectation ; and I still flatter myself that you will be afforded an opportunity of obtaining distinguished laurels before the campaign is terminated.

(Signed,)   P<small>ELLEW</small>.

The attention of the rear-admiral having been directed to Fiume, from its great commercial importance and military strength, being defended by four batteries mounting heavy guns, he determined to make an attack upon it ; and accordingly, on the evening of July 2, he anchored off that city with the following squadron : Milford, Elizabeth, Eagle, Bacchante, and Haughty gun-brig.   On the following morning the squadron weighed with a light breeze from the S. W. but from the wind shifting, and the tide running out of the river, the Eagle and Haughty were the only two that could fetch in.   The Eagle anchored close to the second battery, which she soon silenced.   Upon this being communicated to the admiral by telegraph, the signal was made to storm, when Captain Rowley, leading in his gig the first detachment of marines, took possession of the fort and hoisted the British colours.   Captain Hoste, with the marines of the Milford, now landed, and took and spiked the guns of the first battery, after which he proceeded to join Captain Rowley in the pursuit of the enemy.   Captain Rowley, determining to lose no time, had left a party of seamen to turn the guns of the second battery against the block-house, and then boldly dashed through the town at the head of his marines (commanded by Lieutenant Lloyd) and a gig's crew, in all about 88 men.   Although greatly annoyed by the enemy's musketry from the windows of the houses, and a field-piece in the centre of the great street, yet such was the firmness of the marines and seamen, that the enemy retreated before them, drawing the field-piece until they came to the square.   Here they fell back upon their main body, consisting of between 400 and 500 men, a few horse, and four field-pieces.   This force Captain Rowley gallantly charged with the bayonet, and drove it before him over the bridge out of the town; whilst Captain Markland, in command of the boats, each with a carronade, opened upon another part of it. The field-pieces and many prisoners fell into the possession of Captain Rowley, and he was then joined by Captain Hoste, who had succeeded in driving the enemy from the other parts of the town. Ninety vessels were captured; but more than half of them were returned to their owners. Thirteen, laden with oil, powder, and merchandise, were sent to Lissa, and the rest destroyed. The guns on the batteries were rendered useless; 8 brass 18-pounders, 500 stand of arms, and 200 barrels of powder were carried off; the whole of which was accomplished with the loss of one marine killed, Lieutenant Lloyd, R.M. and five men wounded. On the 5th the squadron proceeded against Porto del Ré, which suffered the same fate, and without loss to the assailants. The whole of these proceedings, and the individual conduct of the officers and men employed, gave such satisfaction to Rear-Admiral Fremantle, that he immediately after issued the following orders:

" Rear-Admiral Fremantle requests Captain Rowley will communicate to the officers and company of the ship he commands, that he never witnessed more zeal, greater attention, or such steady, sober conduct, as that of the companies under his orders during the whole of their arduous services at Fiume and Porto del Ré, and that he shall feel highly gratified in representing it to the commander-in-chief."

On the 7th July, 1813, the fortress of Farasina, mounting 5 18-pounders, was attacked by the Eagle, totally destroyed, and all the stores, &c. burnt. On the 2d August, whilst sailing along the coast of Istria, in company with the Bacchante, a convoy of twenty-one sail was discovered in the harbour of Rovigno: Captain Hoste was ordered to lead in; a fire was opened on the batteries, and on their being abandoned by the enemy, the boats' crews of both ships, with the marines under Captain Hoste, were landed, who drove the enemy out of the town, destroyed the batteries and defences, and brought out the vessels.

The Austrian troops being now, with the aid of the British squadron, in possession of all the principal forts and places on the coasts of Istria and Dalmatia, it was determined, by Admiral Fremantle and Count Nugent, to make an attack upon Trieste. The admiral collected his squadron at Fiume; but Captain Rowley was directed to proceed to Lissa, and thence to Zante, to collect such British troops and arms as could be spared, and to rejoin the admiral at Fiume. On his arrival, however, at the latter place, the squadron had sailed; but he found the following letter waiting for him:

" DEAR SIR,—By a letter I have just received, I am of opinion that this place must be taken by a regular siege : as I know no man more able or more willing to undertake the management than yourself, I beg you will not lose a moment in joining me here [Trieste]."

Captain Rowley accordingly proceeded thither, and having joined the admiral, landed to direct the operations. Every movement was conducted with his usual zeal, and drew forth repeated encomiums from the admiral. On the 22d October he wrote as follows: " I am quite delighted with you, and all you have done;" and on the 24th he said, " Your arrangements are all so good that I have only to know them to approve." The utmost difficulties, however, continued to oppose themselves, and doubts began to be entertained as to the practicability of taking the place with the means possessed by the besiegers; but Captain Rowley at last succeeded in advancing a long 32-pounder, which had been dragged through vineyards for more than a mile, under a galling fire, within a few yards of the Shanza, a strong building, which stood on a hill, with a wall fourteen feet high surrounding it. On firing the first shot from the 32-pounder, the ground gave way, and the gun fell six feet below the platform. " It was fine (said the admiral in his official letter) to see Captain Rowley and his men get a triangle above the work, and the heavy gun with its carriage run up to its place again, in the midst of a shower of grape and musketry, which did considerable mischief, and occasioned severe loss to our brave men." The perseverance of Captain Rowley was, however, crowned with success; the enemy surrendered the Shanza, and the men were made prisoners. In the course of the night and the following day, six or nine of the Eagle's 32-pounders were planted in the Shanza and turned upon the castle. This battery, with the addition of others, obliged the enemy to ask terms of capitulation, which were accepted by the general and admiral, and Trieste was taken possession of by the besieging army. The place was extremely strong; mounted forty-five large guns, forty mortars, and four howitzers, and was defended by above 800 Frenchmen. The number of vessels found in the harbour amounted to fifty. The whole of Captain Rowley's conduct having so decidedly merited the approbation of Admiral Fremantle, he intrusted him with the command of an expedition, in conjunction with the Austrian troops under Count Nugent, to act against the enemy in the north of Italy, the troops being disembarked at the mouths of the Po. In this latter service the abilities of Captain Rowley were called

into action to the fullest extent, and, aided by the bravery of his followers, were attended with the most complete success.

The following extracts from Count Nugent's dispatch to Lord Bathurst will, however, best explain the important objects gained, and the
great credit due to Captain Rowley:

" Your lordship has had a regular account of my proceedings until the fall
of Trieste, which terminated the operations in Illyria. Admiral Fremantle and
myself being convinced that the most useful manner of employing the means at
our disposal would be a landing in the rear of the enemy's army, this expedition was resolved upon; and the admiral's presence being necessary upon the
Illyrian coast, he destined Captain Charles Rowley for the naval part of it, which
consisted of two ships of the line and one brig, besides two British and nine
Austrian transports, with some small vessels. The disposable British and Austrian troops, to the amount of 2,300, were accordingly embarked. The 8th November the castle of Trieste was given up, and the day following the expedition
sailed for the mouths of the Po. The season of the year, the want of harbours
on the enemy's coast, and the bad state of some of the transports, made the
whole enterprise very hazardous : Commodore Rowley, however, found a safe
position in the Bay of Goro, where we anchored on the 14th. The enemy had
strong forts at the two extremities of the bay : we began to land in the night ;
the enemy came with the greater part of the garrisons of the forts to attack our
van, which charged him with such rapidity that he was overthrown, and nearly
the whole garrison of the fort of Solano made prisoners. The reserve having
in the mean time landed, I was enabled to follow up this advantage, and the fort
of Solano was taken, with four guns and a gun-boat. The fort of Goro, with
five guns, capitulated ; that of Magna Vacca was abandoned by the enemy.
This action was highly creditable to the troops and seamen, and particularly to
the judicious dispositions of Commodore Rowley.

" On the 17th I marched towards Ferrara, and reached that place on the 18th.
In the mean time Commodore Rowley extended along the coast, and sent Captain
Moresby with a small expedition to the mouths of the Po, by which the enemy's
forts there were taken and destroyed. He fitted out gun-boats with great celerity, and sent them, under the command of Lieutenant Hotham, up the Po, to
act in conjunction with the land-force. On the 20th Major Birnstill passed the
Po, attacked Rovigo, and made 100 prisoners. The enemy was forced to
abandon the Lower Adige, by which our communication with the Austrian army
was opened, and Venice completely blockaded. In consequence, the enemy resolved to make a general attack upon the troops under my command. One division, under General Pino, advanced from Bologna to attack Ferrara ; another

advanced between the Adige; and a third, from Ravenna, towards Comacchio.
After an obstinate action, the enemy was repulsed at Ferrara with considerable
loss, leaving 300 dead.   In the mean time the enemy's column from Ravenna
had passed the Primaro, and attacked Comacchio and the fort of Magna Vacca,
threatening to cut us off from the ships; but by the good measures taken by
Commodore Rowley this was prevented: he detached Captain Moresby to dis-
engage the fort of Magna Vacca, which he accomplished with great bravery.
The inhabitants of Comacchio took up arms, and, being assisted by Captain
Rowley, the enemy was stopped, and I had time to march against him.   I immediately left Ferrara, and reached Comacchio on the 29th.   As soon as the fortifications, and other measures for the security of our position, were completed,
and 1200 men, which were in march from the army, had arrived, I resolved to
attack the enemy, and pass the Po di Primaro, a large and rapid river, on which
he was posted.   This was effected, on the 6th December, by the bravery of the
troops and the extraordinary exertions of the navy; Commodore Rowley having
brought the boats, necessary for the passage, through the swamps, and then had
them dragged over-land, under the enemy's fire, into the Po.   Ravenna was taken
the following day, and the enemy retreated with considerable loss.   Owing to
the orders I had received from the commander-in-chief, nothing was undertaken
for some time, and the interval was employed to put Comacchio and all our
positions in the best state of defence.   As soon as I was allowed to act, I resolved
to undertake a grand attack upon the enemy's positions at Forli and Cervia.   This
was executed on the 26th December; the enemy's corps at Forli was completely
destroyed, the position at Cervia forced and seven guns taken.   The fort of
Cesenatrio, containing 200 men and seven guns, was besieged, and surrendered
on the 9th January.   This enterprise terminated the operations on the coast,
which were the more creditable to the troops and navy, as the enemy had a very
great superiority against us.   His loss in the different actions surpassed our
whole force.   We took 1350 prisoners and seventy-one pieces of cannon, besides
ammunition, stores of every kind, and a considerable part of the provisions
destined for Venice.

    " Your lordship will perceive by the above narrative the important services
which Captain Rowley has rendered.   Besides having conducted, with the greatest
ability, the naval part of the expedition, under the most difficult circumstances,
and maintained his station in the worst season on the coast, deemed before impracticable, he directed the defensive measures on shore during my operations
upon Ferrara, and, by repulsing the enemy, prevented my being cut off.   Without the activity and resolution he displayed in bringing boats into the Po di Primaro, I should not have been able to pass that river, nor could I have moved in
a country so intersected with canals and rivers if it had not been for the assist-

ance given me by him. I consider it my duty to bring to your lordship's knowledge these circumstances, confident that the services of this distinguished officer will meet with deserved reward."

This was the case, and Count Nugent's own sovereign, the Emperor of Austria, set the example, by conferring upon him the Order of Maria Theresa, which was communicated to him by Admiral Fremantle in the following terms:

TRIESTE, *Feb.* 20, 1814.

DEAR SIR,—I have the honour of inclosing the copy of a letter from Marshal Belgrade, wherein you will read that his Imperial Majesty the Emperor of Austria has been graciously pleased to confer on you the Order of Maria Theresa. It affords me infinite satisfaction in conveying this proof of his Imperial Majesty's approbation of your services, as it affords me the opportunity of expressing how well merited it has been by you, as well as how much I feel I am indebted for the same honour to your support, advice, zeal, and gallantry, on all occasions during the time I have commanded in the Adriatic.

Hostilities having ceased, Captain Rowley returned to England, when he had the honour of being placed under the command of his Royal Highness the Duke of Clarence, in one of the ships selected to accompany the king and royal family of France upon their return to that kingdom; and in June 1814 he was advanced to the rank of rear-admiral. In January 1815 he was nominated a K.C.B.; and in the same year was appointed to the chief command in the Medway. Towards the end of 1820 he was appointed to the chief command at Jamaica, and in May 1825 was made vice-admiral of the Blue.

Sir Charles married Elizabeth, daughter of the late Admiral Sir Richard King, Bart. by whom he has several children.

HISTORICAL MEMOIRS OF

ADMIRAL SIR CHARLES BRISBANE, K.C.B.

SIR CHARLES BRISBANE is descended from a very ancient family, which settled at Bishopton, in the shire of Renfrew, in the reign of Robert II. He is the fourth son of the late Admiral Brisbane, and entered the naval service the latter end of 1779, when he was only ten years of age, on board the Alcide of 74 guns, commanded by his father, with whom he sailed, under the orders of Sir George Rodney, to the relief of Gibraltar, and of course witnessed the capture of the Caraccas fleet and the defeat of the Spanish squadron under Langara. The first object of the expedition having been accomplished, the Alcide proceeded with Sir George to the West Indies; but as she was shortly after ordered to return to England, Captain Brisbane, knowing that the West India station would shortly become the theatre of the most active operations, and that it would consequently be the most desirable for youth, placed his son on board the Hercules, Captain Savage, with whom he fought on the 12th April, 1782, and by his conduct gained the approbation and lasting esteem of his commander. In that action he gave an earnest of his future conduct, which he sealed with his blood, having received a severe wound in his back, which nearly rendered him incapable of further service; but notwithstanding the severity of his wound, and the great pain arising therefrom, the moment it was dressed he returned to his post, where he continued till the termination of the contest. So highly pleased was Captain Savage with his behaviour, that he furnished him with a certificate, which was subsequently the means of his obtaining a lieutenancy. In 1784 he was placed on board the Thorn, Captain Lechmere; and having cruised a short time in that vessel, he was removed to the Druid, in which he was employed for three years cruising against smugglers. In 1787 he was placed on board the Powerful, and afterwards removed to the Adamant, which bore the flag of Sir Richard Hughes, with whom he sailed to Halifax, where he was appointed acting-lieutenant of the Weazel, and in which he returned to England. But notwithstanding this favourable circumstance, and the notice of his commander-in-chief, he failed in getting his commission confirmed. Thus disappointed, but not disheartened, he again sought employment as a midshipman, and was placed on board the Colossus, Captain H. C. Christian. In 1790 he removed into the Brunswick, bearing the flag of Sir Hyde Parker; and towards the close of that year he obtained a lieutenant's commission: but it is said that, even at that period so difficult was it to obtain promotion, he would not have succeeded but for Captain Savage's certificate.

In 1791 Lieutenant Brisbane was appointed to the Spitfire, and in 1793 to the Meleager frigate, Captain Tyler, and proceeded to the Mediterranean. An active period of operations was now about to take place, which opened an extensive field for exertion; and the zeal exhibited by him on all occasions gained for him the approbation of his admiral and the reward due to his merit and abilities. During the first operations at Toulon, he was employed in landing the cannon, ammunition, and stores; and his conduct on these occasions having attracted the attention of his superiors, he was removed to the Britannia, the flag-ship of Admiral Hotham. In a few days afterwards he was appointed by Lord Hood to command Fort Pomet, one of the advanced and most dangerous posts in the neighbourhood of Toulon. He assisted in repulsing the French at Fort Mulgrave in November; and after being engaged in various skirmishes on the heights of Pharon, he remained at Fort Pomet till it was found necessary to evacuate Toulon. He was then ordered to evacuate the fort; but, although the French troops were advancing in great numbers, and not more than two musket-shots' distance, he stopped to set fire to a train which communicated with five hundred barrels of powder, and which, in exploding, blew the fort to atoms. He then, amidst many dangers and difficulties, effected his retreat in safety. Shortly after the evacuation of Toulon, Lieutenant Brisbane proceeded with the squadron to Corsica, and, with 100 men belonging to the Britannia, landed at Fiorenzo. He was afterwards engaged in storming Conventional Hill, was present and assisted at the capture of two French frigates, and went through all the extensive variety of service in which Lord Nelson was at that period engaged. Like him he was employed afloat and ashore; like him he was selected to command a battery at Bastia; and like him he received a dangerous wound in the head, which nearly deprived him of the sight of his left eye. In consequence of the dangerous nature of his wound, he was obliged to be conveyed on board the Alcide, where he was confined for six weeks, at the expiration of which time he returned to the Britannia. Soon after he had rejoined that ship off Toulon, five French ships of the line assembled in the outer harbour, and he then proposed a plan to Lord Hood to burn them. The plan was accepted, the Tarleton fitted as a fire-ship expressly for the purpose, and the command given to Lieutenant Brisbane. *But in the evening, when the plan was to be put into execution, the enemy's fleet came out, and Lord Hood found it necessary to retire.* Lieutenant Brisbane was consequently prevented from carrying it into effect; but Lord Hood was so well pleased at the manifestation of his abilities and the practicability of his plan, that he was rewarded for his zeal and assiduity by being promoted to the rank of commander in the Tarleton.

Throughout the whole of this article we have closely adhered to the particulars as recorded by Sir Charles Brisbane in a memorial which he presented to his Majesty. The last circumstance which we have narrated is differently related by naval historians, who have stated, that when Lieutenant Brisbane proposed his plan the enemy was in Gourjean Bay, whither he had been chased by the British fleet; and that when the fire-ships under the command of Lieutenants Miller and Brisbane approached the bay, they found the enemy so strongly posted, and so well protected by strong batteries, that they were obliged to abandon the attempt as impracticable.

Captain Brisbane was afterwards employed in blockading the French fleet in Gourjean Bay, and subsequently in protecting the trade between Bastia and Leghorn: in the prosecution of that service he made several captures. He was also present at Admiral Hotham's action with the French fleet in March 1795; and was shortly afterwards removed to the Moselle sloop, in which he was employed, under Captain Macnamara of the Southampton, in watching the port of Genoa. After the arrival of Sir John Jervis in the Mediterranean, Captain Brisbane was ordered to Gibraltar, from whence he was ordered by Admiral Mann to Barbadoes, with two troop-ships. On his passage he fell in with a Dutch squadron, and conceiving it of more importance to watch the motions of the enemy than to proceed on his original destination, he sent the troop-ships forwards, and followed the Dutch squadron till he ascertained they were going to the Cape of Good Hope; he then made sail, and communicated the intelligence to the commander-in-chief on that station. Preparations were of course made for the reception of the enemy, and the whole were subsequently captured in Saldana Bay, at which Captain

Brisbane assisted.   For his conduct, attention, and exertion in conveying this inteHigence, Sir George Keith Elphinstone promoted him to
post-rank in the Dutch admiral's ship Dordrecht; and what was still
more satisfactory to his feelings, proving as it did the propriety of his
conduct, Sir John Jervis, on being made acquainted with the circumstance, sent him a commission for the Nemesis frigate; and the Lords of
the Admiralty returned him their thanks.   On the arrival of Admiral
Pringle, who was appointed to command at the Cape, Captain Brisbane
was appointed to command L'Oiseau frigate, and ordered on a cruise off
the Rio de la Plata; he there fell in with two Spanish frigates, with
which he had a sharp contest, and, as he stated in his memorial to the
king, notwithstanding their great superiority of force, succeeded in
beating them off.   Another version has, however, been given of this affair; it is as follows:

  " At daylight on the morning of the 20th May, 1797, the Oiseau,
standing on the starboard tack, with the wind at about south by west,
discovered, and immediately chased, a strange sail bearing south-west by
west, distant about three or four leagues.   At half-past seven a. m. a second sail made her appearance astern of the first.   At half-past nine a.m.
the leading ship, now seen to be a frigate, hauled up her main-sail and
took in her top-gallant-sails, and in another quarter of an hour fired a
gun to leeward and hoisted Spanish colours.   The Oiseau, who had now
approached within gun-shot, hoisted English colours and discharged her
broadside in return.   Perceiving, however, that the other ship, a frigate
also, was coming up fast under a heavy press of canvas, the Oiseau
made all sail from two opponents, either of which had the appearance
of being at least equal to herself.   At three-quarters past two p. m. the
headmost of the two Spanish frigates, finding that a longer chase would
separate her from her consort, shortened sail and hauled to the wind;
thus destroying the hope entertained by the Oiseau of bringing one of
the frigates to action without interruption by the other."

  The Oiseau having returned to the Cape, Captain Brisbane was again
removed to the Dordrecht, and ordered to St. Helena with a convoy.
Shortly after his arrival at that island, intelligence was received of the
general mutiny in the fleet at Spithead in 1797; upon learning which
the crew of the Dordrecht manifested symptoms of the most violent insubordination, rose upon their officers, and threatened them with instant
destruction: but by great exertions on the part of Captain Brisbane,

aided by his officers, he fortunately succeeded in quelling the dangerous spirit which existed. He seized one of the ringleaders, placed a halter about his neck, and was apparently proceeding to immediate execution, but at the moment when the culprit expected to be turned off, the captain relaxed from the threatened infliction of justice; he pardoned the offender, but solemnly declared, that if he again evinced the least disobedience, the yard-arm should inevitably be his portion. This prompt and decisive measure on the part of Captain Brisbane shook the guilty resolution of the mutineers, and by his continued firmness he succeeded in reducing them to a proper sense of duty. The same mutiny which existed at Spithead, at the Nore, in the fleet before Cadiz, and at St. Helena, also found its way to the Cape, where it broke out with great violence; and Captain Brisbane was sent for expressly to return and resume the command of the Tremendous, the crew of that ship having risen upon their officers and sent them on shore. The whole was, however, fortunately suppressed, and Captain Brisbane continued with Admiral Pringle till 1798, when he returned with him to England in the Crescent. He was afterwards appointed to the Doris, attached to the Channel fleet, and intrusted by Admiral Cornwallis with the command of a squadron of frigates, to watch the French fleet in Brest harbour. Whilst so employed, he seized an opportunity of rowing round and reconnoitring the enemy's ships, for the purpose of ascertaining the best mode of effecting their destruction; and finding it practicable, he proposed a plan to Admiral Cornwallis for burning them: the admiral accepted the plan, but it was not carried into execution in consequence of some difficulty arising in the appointment of officers. Under his plan and arrangement, the boats of the Doris, Boileau, and Uranie succeeded in cutting out the French national ship La Chevrette from Camaret Bay; an enterprise which was remarkable for the gallantry and intrepidity of the assailants.

In 1802 Captain Brisbane was appointed to the Trent of 36 guns, and sailed to the West Indies, where he successively removed, first, into the Sans Pareil of 80 guns, and secondly, into the Goliath of 74 guns. At the recommencement of the war in 1803, he was employed in watching the operations of the enemy in that quarter, and assisted at the capture of the Mignonne corvette of 16 guns. He then returned to England with a convoy; but during the passage he encountered a severe hurricane, in which the Goliath was in imminent danger of foundering, and in which above twenty of the convoy were dismasted or otherwise damaged. But notwithstanding this circumstance, owing to the perseverance of Captain Brisbane and his great exertions, the whole were carried safely into port. The Goliath having been repaired, Captain Brisbane was ordered off Rochefort; and whilst he commanded that ship he had the misfortune to break two of his ribs and dislocate his arm, by the breaking of the man-rope as he was stepping over the ship's side.

In the beginning of 1805 Captain Brisbane was appointed to the Arethusa frigate, and again proceeded with a convoy to the West Indies: in his passage he fell in with a French squadron of five sail of the line and three frigates; but by a prompt execution of signals the whole convoy effected their escape. He was afterwards employed in cruising off the Havannah, where he captured several small vessels; but early in 1806 the Arethusa unfortunately ran ashore among the Colonados, and it was not until twelve hours of severe and unremitting labour, in the course of which all her guns were thrown overboard, that she was got off and cleared from danger. Immediately after this accident a circumstance occurred which served to place the dauntless bravery of the Arethusa's crew in the most conspicuous light. In working up to the Havannah, she fell in with a Spanish line-of-battle ship, but, though without a gun, Captain Brisbane turned his ship's company up, told them it was his determination to lay the enemy on board, and that in the attempt to carry her they should be led by the officers. Three cheers from the men proved their hearty approval of the enterprise, and all possible sail was carried in pursuit of the enemy; but before the plan could be put into execution, the chase had sought safety under the guns of the Moro Castle*. Captain Brisbane now returned to Jamaica, and having supplied himself with fresh guns, he resumed his station off the Havannah. A dangerous fever, however, having broken out in the Arethusa, he was obliged to run down to Bermuda for the recovery of the health of his crew; and as soon as they were in a convalescent state, he returned to the Havannah, with the Anson, Captain Lydiard, under his orders; and at daylight on the morning of the 23d August, 1806, he discovered the Pomona Spanish frigate of 38 guns off the Moro Castle. He immediately made the signal to Captain Lydiard, communicating his intention to lay the enemy on board the moment he should come up with her; but he was prevented from putting this design into execution by the Po-

* *Naval Chronicle.*

mona bearing up, and coming to an anchor within pistol-shot of a castle mounting sixteen 36-pounders, where she was joined by twelve gun-boats from the Havannah. Supported, however, by the Anson, Captain Brisbane ran along side the enemy, and came to an anchor in one foot more water than the ship drew. The action immediately became general, and in thirty-five minutes the Pomona struck her colours; three of the gun-boats were blown up, six sunk, and three wrecked upon the breakers. During the action the castle, by firing red-hot shot, set fire to the Arethusa, but the flames were speedily extinguished; and the castle itself, which contained a quantity of specie belonging to the King of Spain, landed from the Pomona, soon afterwards blew up with a tremendous explosion*.

In this contest Captain Brisbane was wounded in the knees; but, although he suffered excruciating pain, he refused to quit the deck till Victory had proclaimed herself in favour of the British flag. Vice-Admiral Dacres, in his letter to the Admiralty announcing the capture of the Pomona, justly observed, that " the success which attended this bold enterprise Captain Brisbane was entitled to, for the promptness and decision with which he anchored in shoal water to attack a force of such magnitude." The prize having been carried to Jamaica, and the Arethusa refitted, three other frigates, the Latona, Anson, and Fisguard, were likewise placed under his orders, with which he was directed to reconnoitre the Island of Curaçoa. Having arrived off the island, it was determined to attempt carrying it by a *coup-de-main*, which was put into execution early in the morning of the 1st January, 1807. The harbour was defended by regular fortifications of two tiers of guns, Fort Amsterdam alone mounting 66 pieces of cannon; the entrance only fifty fathoms wide, athwart which was the Dutch frigate Hatslar of 36 guns, and Surinam of 22 guns, with two large schooners of war, a chain of forts on Miselbourg height, and that almost impregnable fortress, Fort Republique, within the distance of grape-shot, enfilading the whole harbour. Notwithstanding these formidable defences, Captain Brisbane, having hoisted a flag of truce, led the squadron, closely followed by the Latona, into the harbour, and came to an anchor in such a position as to enfilade the principal street. With the jib-boom of the Arethusa over the town-wall, Captain Brisbane wrote the following note to the governor:

* See Plate in Ralfe's *Naval Chronology*.

" The British squadron is here to protect, and not conquer you ; to preserve to you your lives, liberty, and property. If a shot is fired at any one of my squadron after this summons, I shall immediately storm your batteries. You have five minutes to accede to this determination."

No notice being taken of this communication, " a severe and destructive cannonade ensued : the frigate, sloop, and schooners were carried by boarding ; the lower forts, the citadel and town of Amsterdam, by storm ; all of which by seven o'clock were in our possession. For humanity's sake, I granted a capitulation, and at ten o'clock the British flag was hoisted in Fort Republique*." In his memorial to the king, Captain Brisbane stated that he was the first who boarded the Dutch frigate, and himself hauled down the colours ; that he then landed with twenty-four men, stormed Fort Amsterdam, which was defended by 275 men, and there also had the honour to strike the enemy's colours. The gallantry displayed throughout the whole of these proceedings excited the surprise of Admiral Dacres, the commander-in-chief, who expressed his feelings in the following terms :

" Whilst I contemplate the immense strength of the harbour of Amsterdam, and the superior force contained in its different batteries, opposed to the entrance of the frigates, I know not how sufficiently to admire the decision of Captain Brisbane in attempting the harbour, and the determined bravery and conduct displayed by himself, the other captains, and all the officers and men under his command : it is another strong instance of the cool and determined bravery of British seamen."

Immediately after the capitulation, Captain Brisbane assumed, *pro tempore*, the functions of governor of the island, and commenced disarming the militia, which amounted to about twelve hundred men, and to administer to the inhabitants, who amounted to thirty thousand, the oath of allegiance to his Britannic Majesty. He was afterwards superseded in the command of the island by the arrival of Sir James Cockburn, appointed by his Majesty. He then resumed the command of the Arethusa, which he retained till the autumn of 1808, when he was appointed to the Blake of 74 guns, and shortly afterwards to the government of the Island of St.Vincent. For their gallant and judicious conduct in the capture of Curaçoa, his Majesty presented each of the captains with a

* Official letter.

gold medal, and conferred the honour of knighthood on Captains Wood and Brisbane; and as a further mark of royal approbation, Captain Brisbane was granted an honourable augmentation, with supporters, to his arms. In January 1815 he was nominated a K.C.B. and in August 1819 was made a rear-admiral.

Sir Charles married Sarah, one of the daughters and coheiresses of the late Sir James Patey, Knight, and has several children.

HISTORICAL MEMOIRS OF
ADMIRAL GEORGE PARKER.

THERE are but few names better known to the readers of naval history than that of Parker; several members of that family have repeatedly distinguished themselves both in the naval and military service of their country during a long series of years, embracing the last ten reigns, and the services of some of them have already been recorded in this work.

The subject of the present Memoir is the nephew of Admiral Sir Peter Parker, Bart. who attained the distinguished honour of being admiral of the fleet, and is descended from the Rev. Dr. Parker, who was Archbishop of Canterbury in the reign of Queen Elizabeth. Having selected a naval life as the one most congenial to his thoughts and inclinations, he entered the service under the patronage of his uncle, and by him was promoted to the rank of lieutenant on the 13th March, 1782, and having served through the whole of the American war, was paid off at the termination of hostilities. In 1786 he was appointed lieutenant of the Wasp sloop of war, stationed in the Downs, and served on board that vessel till 1788, when he was removed to the Phœnix frigate, commanded by Captain George Byron. In the following year he sailed for the East Indies with the squadron under the command of the Hon. W. Cornwallis. Hostilities having broken out with Tippoo Saib, the Phœnix was actively employed in co-operating with the army under General Sir Robert Abercrombie; the boats were in constant requisition, and the greater part of the officers and men were employed on shore till Sir Robert Abercrombie ascended the Ghauts, to join the army under the command of Lord Cornwallis, at the siege of Seringapatam. Captain Byron having been shortly after obliged to resign the command of the Phœnix on account of ill health and to return to England, he was succeeded in the Phœnix by Captain R. J. Strachan; and Mr. Parker having risen to be first lieutenant, served in that capacity during the action with, and capture of, La Resolue French frigate*, and was afterwards sent to England with the commodore's dispatches. This event

* See *Memoir of Sir* R. STRACHAN.

took place previous to any declaration of war against the French nation, but arose out of the " right of searching neutral vessels."

In October 1792, Lieutenant Parker was appointed first of the Crescent frigate, mounting 36 guns, commanded by Captain (now Admiral Sir James) Saumarez; and war having been declared against the French republic the beginning of the following year, they were employed cruising in the Channel, and in the month of October fell in with and captured La Réunion French frigate, mounting 40 guns, after an action of upwards of two hours' duration. For his conduct on this occasion Lieutenant Parker was promoted to the rank of commander, and in the month of November was appointed to the Albicore sloop, and was employed in the North Sea till April 1795, when he was appointed to post-rank, and to command the Squirrel of 20 guns. He was then again attached to the North-Sea squadron under the orders of Admiral Duncan, and continued with him till towards the end of 1796, when he was removed to the Santa Margaretta of 36 guns, and placed under the orders of Admiral Kingsmill on the Irish station. This was in every point of view an important command as connected with the protection of British commerce: the enemy's cruisers and privateers frequently made their appearance, and several of them fell into the hands of Captain Parker. He was also frequently employed in protecting convoys, and received a letter of thanks from their masters and owners, transmitted through the Admiralty, for his care and attention to them; and the Board of Admiralty were also pleased to express their approbation of his conduct on those occasions.

In 1798 the Santa Margaretta was ordered to the West Indies, and Captain Parker remained on that station for about eighteen months, cruising against the enemy, and succeeded in capturing several of their merchant-ships and privateers*. He was then ordered to England with a large convoy, and notwithstanding the number of the enemy's cruisers, the whole arrived in perfect safety. From that period to the latter end of 1801 Captain Parker was employed in convoying the trade to Quebec, the Mediterranean, and in accompanying East India ships past the Canary Islands. He then proceeded to Jamaica, and continued on that station during the

* The following were amongst those captured by Captain Parker during the time he commanded the Santa Margaretta: L'Ardour of 16 guns, pierced for 20, and 147 men; La Victorine of 16 guns and 82 men; Sau Francisco of 14 guns and 53 men; and Le Quatorze Juillet of 14 guns and 65 men.

remainder of the war, when he was obliged to resign the command of the Santa Margaretta on account of ill health, and returned to England in the hope of obtaining a restoration. After the recommencement of hostilities, having sufficiently recovered, he was appointed, in 1804, to the Argo frigate of 44 guns, on the North-Sea station; in the following year he was removed to the Stately of 64 guns, and again ordered to the North-Sea, under the command of Admiral Russell, employed in blockading the enemy's squadron in the Texel. Having been intrusted with the command of three sail of the line, he was ordered to the Baltic on a particular service, where he was to be joined by a frigate and some sloops of war: he sailed from Yarmouth in the month of January 1808, and after a voyage which could not be otherwise at that season of the year than attended with great danger and difficulty, he reached Gottenburg, where he was shortly after frozen up. In the month of March, having received information that the enemy was on the alert, and that the Baltic was free from ice, he caused the squadron under his command to be cut out of the ice, and by main force got them to sea, as well as a large convoy of merchant-ships bound to England. He then proceeded to the entrance of the Sound; and having received information of the enemy's movements, he made the necessary division of his squadron, and proceeded himself, in company with the Nassau, in quest of the Danish ship Prince Christian Frederick of 74 guns, which he had the good fortune to fall in with on the 22d March. At forty minutes past seven p. m. the Nassau, Captain Campbell, got up with the enemy and commenced action; and in a few minutes afterwards the Stately closed, when a running fight was commenced, and continued till half-past nine, the enemy standing towards the shore. Being now within two cables' length of the shore of Zealand, the enemy struck his colours; but before the first lieutenant of the Stately, who took possession of the prize, could cut away her anchor, she grounded. The Stately immediately brought up within a cable's length of her, and the remaining part of the night was employed in removing the prisoners. On the following day, seeing that the Danes were preparing their artillery on the coast, that the wind was blowing strong on shore, and a good deal of sea running, Captain Parker determined on destroying the prize, rather than risk the loss of any part of his squadron in the attempt to get her off: she was accordingly set on fire, and shortly afterwards blew up. During the action the enemy's ship suffered considerable damage, and had 55 men killed and

88 wounded. The two British ships also sustained considerable loss, the Stately having had 32 men killed and wounded, and the Nassau 18 killed and wounded. After repairing the damages sustained in action, Captain Parker returned to Gottenburg with the Nassau, and there landed the prisoners. He was afterwards succeeded in the command by Rear-Admiral Sir Samuel Hood, who expressed his entire approbation of all the arrangements made by Captain Parker and the able conduct he had manifested on every occasion. The crews of the Stately and Nassau having become very sickly, those ships were ordered to England, and in the month of April arrived in Yarmouth roads. As a mark of the approbation of the Lords of the Admiralty of the professional duty displayed by Captain Parker, they promoted his first lieutenant to the rank of commander, and those midshipmen who had passed their examination to the rank of lieutenants. He was himself appointed to the Aboukir of 74 guns, attached to the North-Sea fleet, and in that ship served in the Walcheren expedition. In that expedition but few officers had any opportunity to distinguish themselves, except by undergoing fatigue and hard service, without any of those cheering and gratifying circumstances usually attendant on professional employment. It reflected no honour on the country, and was productive of no kind of benefit to those employed in it.

Captain Parker continued attached to the North-Sea fleet till 1812, when he was ordered to the Mediterranean, where he served under the command of Sir Edward Pellew. The war had, however, now long assumed an entirely military appearance; there were but few objects left for the navy to gain, and but few duties to perform, except watching the enemy's ports. Captain Parker was stationed off Toulon, and though the enemy occasionally got under weigh, and gave their opponents some expectation that they intended to put to sea and try the event of a battle, they invariably hauled their wind on arriving nearly within gun-shot distance. Having been thus employed till the latter end of 1813, Captain Parker exchanged into the Bombay and returned to England. In June 1814 he was promoted to the rank of rear-admiral, and in May 1825 to that of vice-admiral.

HISTORICAL MEMOIRS OF

Admiral Sir JOHN POO BERESFORD, Bart. K.C.B.

THE name of Beresford stands recorded amongst those distinguished officers of the British navy who have obtained the lasting gratitude of their country. Having made choice of a naval life, Sir John entered the service under the patronage of Lord Longford, who, in 1782, placed his name on the books of the Alexander, and also those of the Carnatic. In the following year he removed to the Winchelsea frigate, commanded by Captain Farnham, with whom he sailed to the Newfoundland station, where he continued for three years, and where a circumstance of an interesting and extraordinary nature occurred. Having landed on service, a thick fog came on, and he missed the road, when he wandered about for fifty-two hours without any thing to eat, and was given up for lost by the ship's company. At the end of that time he was, however, enabled to make his appearance, and was received by his companions with those marks of pleasure and delight which betokened the high estimation in which he was then held. Notwithstanding he was reduced to the greatest privations, he never lost his spirits; neither did his sufferings diminish that zeal and determination with which he commenced his career. On his return to England he was placed on board the Ganges, Sir Roger Curtis, in which he remained four months, and then removed to the Maidstone frigate, Captain Newcome, in which he proceeded to the West Indies, where he continued till he had completed the probationary period of his service. He now visited his native country, and having passed his examination, was placed as acting-lieutenant on board the Trusty of 50 guns, bearing the flag of that distinguished and truly honourable officer, Sir John Laforey, with whom he again proceeded to the West Indies. In 1791 he was promoted to a lieutenancy, and appointed to the Lapwing, commanded by the Hon. Captain Curzon, then in the Mediterranean. He sailed from England in the Romney, bearing the flag of Admiral Goodall, and joined his ship at Gibraltar. He subsequently proceeded to Genoa, and was at the court of Turin when the express arrived announcing the invasion of the King of Sardinia's territories by the French troops. When Nice was taken possession of by the enemy he was sent across the country, and intrusted by his captain with a secret mission to the British consul in that city, to ascertain whether the English residents were well treated by the troops of the Convention, and to consult with him on the best means of removing all the English families in the neighbourhood. In the accomplishment of this desirable object he ran great personal risks, on account of the violent spirit of the times, and the open insurrection which then existed through all parts of the country; he was obliged to assume the character of a peasant and to wear the national cockade, to protect himself from violence. He, however, could not effect his return without applying to the commander, General Byron, who granted him an escort to the water-side. He then introduced himself to Lucien Buonaparte, the commissary-general of the French army, who also treated him with great kindness, and through his means the Lapwing was supplied with fresh beef and provisions. She was afterwards ordered to England with a convoy, but was eleven weeks on her passage from Gibraltar; and, after her arrival, was for a short time attached to the fleet under Lord Howe as repeater. He was afterwards ordered to Ostend, to assist in the operations then going on in that quarter; and was subsequently placed, with Captain Curzon, in the Pallas frigate, in which he again joined the Channel fleet.

In 1794 he joined the Resolution, bearing the flag of Admiral Murray, and sailed with him to North America. On their passage they fell in with a French convoy, of which they captured thirty-two sail. After their arrival he was placed on board the Cleopatra frigate as acting-captain, and proceeded to New-York with Admiral Murray, who hoisted his flag on board the Cleopatra; after which he was sent to Bermuda, to ascertain whether it were possible to make that place an eligible anchorage for his fleet. This object he accomplished with his usual zeal; and from the information he derived from Lieutenant Hurd, who, with great skill and perseverance, had completed a survey of the islands, he was enabled to make the most favourable report; and that station has since proved of the most essential advantage to the interests of England. In November 1794 he succeeded Captain Penrose in the command of the Lynx sloop; and on the 20th of that month left the Chesapeake with a convoy for Halifax. But shortly afterwards three French ships, of 24 guns each, were observed standing for the convoy. Signal to wear was immediately made, and Captain Beresford, after a partial action of two hours with the enemy, anchored the Lynx and convoy in perfect safety within the Capes.   After his arrival at Halifax he was ordered, in company with the Thisbe, Captain Oakes Hardy, to cruise along the coast of America; during which they received intelligence of two ships of war, supposed to be enemies, being within about twelve leagues of their then station.   All sail was immediately made in the direction pointed out, and on the 23d December, at eleven a. m. two strange sail were discovered, one riding at anchor and the other aground; the latter of which made the signal for immediate assistance, and proved to be the Thetis frigate, Captain the Hon. Alexander Cochrane; the former, the Cleopatra, Captain Penrose.   Captain Beresford immediately ran the Lynx in, and came to an anchor in three fathoms, when every means was taken to preserve the Thetis; but as neither the Cleopatra nor Thisbe could approach near enough to render assistance, the object in view became one of great difficulty and fatigue.   The ensuing six days were employed in lightening the Thetis; a work of great labour, and which was often interrupted by the freshness of the breeze, and the Lynx being obliged to haul off into deeper water.   On the 29th, however, the Lynx was run in shore, brought to an anchor abreast of the Thetis, and cables run out to heave her off, which was at last happily accomplished, and the Thetis again floated, after being aground for ten days.   During the whole of this time the conduct of Captain Beresford was highly exemplary, his zeal and perseverance were indefatigable, and through their united exertions only could such a result have taken place.   The judicious conduct of Captain Beresford was duly reported to Admiral Murray by Captain Cochrane, who acknowledged that to the skilful and unwearied exertions of Captain Beresford, whose ship was placed in the most dangerous position, was the preservation of the Thetis to be attributed.   He was afterwards ordered to the Bahama Islands for the purpose of making various arrangements connected with the service; and on the 2d March captured La Cocarde Nationale French privateer of 14 guns, recaptured a valuable Jamaica ship, and was the means of preventing three others from falling into the enemy's possession.   The favourable reports transmitted to Admiral Murray of the conduct of Captain Beresford in protecting the convoy off the Chesapeake, and in saving the Thetis from destruction, gained him the approbation of the admiral, who appointed him acting-captain of the Hussar frigate.   He was then placed under the orders of Captain Cochrane, and again proceeded off the Chesapeake, for the purpose of intercepting some French store-ships then lying in Hampton roads.   On their arrival off Cape Henry on the 17th May, five sail were discovered in the S. E. standing to the N. W. and which, on the approach of the Thetis and Hussar, formed into a line of battle. About half-past ten a. m. the enemy hoisted their colours, and shortly afterwards Captain Beresford was directed by signal to attack the two van ships; which order he obeyed with the utmost alacrity, carrying his ship nobly into action, received the fire of the centre ship in passing, and brought up between the two headmost ships in such a position as to bring his guns to bear upon the quarter of one and the bows of the other; whilst Captain Cochrane brought up against the centre or largest ship. By eleven o'clock Captain Beresford beat his two opponents out of the line, and they crowded all sail to the S. E.; he then hauled round, and brought the two rearmost ships to action, which, together with the one opposed to the Thetis, hauled down their colours about three quarters past eleven. But notwithstanding this act of submission, the two rear ships crowded all sail, and endeavoured to effect their escape: they were, however, pursued by Captain Beresford, and one of them, the Raison, was secured; but the other succeeded in getting off. The Raison was pierced for 24, but mounted only 18 guns; and the Prevoyante, which struck to the Thetis, was pierced for 60, but mounted only 24 guns: she was originally intended for a ship of the line, and had ten lower-deck ports. For his conduct on this occasion Captain Beresford received the thanks of the commander-in-chief, which were communicated to him by the following letter from Captain Cochrane:

THETIS, 6th June, 1795.

SIR,—I have the greatest satisfaction in conveying to you Rear-Admiral Murray's approbation of the conduct of the officers and ships' companies belonging to the ships under our command on the 17th ult. in the engagement with the French ships off the Chesapeake; and I have the more pleasure in doing so as his sentiments with respect to your conduct in so handsomely leading into action, and subsequent thereto, are perfectly congenial with my own. I have therefore only to request that you and the officers and ship's company of the Hussar will permit me to add my best thanks to those of the admiral.

During his previous cruises Captain Beresford was so extremely fortunate in capturing or destroying the armed ships and privateers of the enemy, that the committee for encouraging the capture of French armed vessels seized this occasion to vote him a piece of plate of the value of one hundred guineas, as a token of their approbation of his active and vigilant conduct, and as an acknowledgment that through his laudable exertions the commerce of the country had been greatly benefited. On the arrival of Captain Beresford with the two prizes at Halifax, Captain Wemyss was found there waiting the arrival of the Hussar, having been sent from England to take the command of that ship. The two prizes having been repaired and purchased for the British navy, Admiral Murray immediately appointed Captain Beresford to the Prevoyante, which he manned at his own expense as a 40-gun frigate, and sailed on a cruise, which was attended with his usual success, by the capture of many of the enemy's vessels. He was also ordered off Block Island with the Thetis and Hussar, to watch three of the enemy's ships in New-London; but although the Thetis and Hussar were driven from the station by the violence of the weather, Captain Beresford was enabled to remain, and for three months in the midst of winter did he persevere, in spite of every obstacle, to observe the enemy's ships, and during that time he succeeded in capturing several neutral vessels with the enemy's property on board. Having commanded the Prevoyante for about six months he returned to Halifax, and had the mortification to find that he was again superseded, by orders from England, by Captain Wemyss, and removed to the Raison of 24 guns. Admiral Murray, however, strongly remonstrated against this proceeding; and Captain Beresford was advised to return to England, to personally explain the particulars of his situation to the Lords of the Admiralty. This step he, however, declined, with the observation, that he thought himself bound to obey their lordships' order, and to do his best to equip the Raison. But mortifying as was the circumstance which deprived him of the command of the Prevoyante, after the great expense he had been at in equipping her, and the trouble he had had in organizing her crew, which had now arrived at a high state of discipline, it was increased by an order which prevented him from removing a single individual from her to the Raison, though the latter was also to be fitted out at his own expense. Being afterwards at Boston, he was ordered to take on board 200,000l. and proceed to Halifax. On the 25th August, at one o'clock p. m. an American ship, with masts and naval stores, bound for Brest, was taken possession of by the second lieutenant and sixteen men; shortly after which a large ship was observed coming down under a press of sail, which was supposed to be the Asia, Captain Murray, and was at first taken but little notice of; but as she did not answer the private signal, she was of course concluded to be an enemy: the officer and boat's crew were consequently recalled, and the prize abandoned, at which time the enemy had arrived nearly within gun-shot. From the immense disparity of force which existed, Captain Beresford could have no great inclination to bring him to action; he therefore made all sail, ordering two 6-pounders to be brought aft on the quarter-deck, and two 9-pounders into the cabin, for stern-chasers. About half-past seven the Raison had but little wind, but the enemy brought up a breeze, and having arrived in her wake, a running fight took place, which continued for several hours, when the enemy hauled his wind, and the weather being thick, was lost sight of. In order to secure the weather-gage, in case of again falling in with him, the Raison was hauled to the eastward; and about seven a. m. her opponent was observed to be close upon her larboard quarter. The little Raison was then hailed to strike, but the discharge of her broadside was the reply, when a sharp and close action commenced, which continued for one hour and three quarters, the vessels at times touching each other; and to give an idea of the disproportion of the combatants, it is only necessary to observe, that the enemy's main-yard locked with the top-gallant cross-trees of the Raison: notwithstanding which, the energy and gallantry of Captain Beresford and his little crew proved superior to their opponents, and they were prevented from boarding the enemy only by the height of his deck. At the end of that time a well-directed broadside was poured into the enemy, and he dropped astern; a thick fog then came on, and he was entirely lost sight of. The Raison was, however, kept in nearly the same situation for forty hours, when the fog cleared away, but no enemy was to be seen. Several neutral vessels were, however, in sight, some of whom were spoken to, and though they had heard the firing, they had seen nothing of the enemy. In this action, which may be classed among the first of the defensive kind, the Raison suffered considerably in her masts, sails, and rigging, but had only 14 men killed and wounded. Captain Beresford then proceeded to Boston, and afterwards received from the British consul at Philadelphia the following letter:

DEAR SIR,—We have not, until these few days past, had any sort of intelligence which could fix with any degree of precision the size of the French ship of war which you so gallantly engaged in his Majesty's ship La Raison, under your command. By a paragraph published in many of the American newspapers, it appears that your enemy was no less than a French 50-gun ship. This, and another action between the Pelican sloop and La Medée French frigate, furnish two of the most splendid instances of the prowess of our navy recorded in the history of any age, and impress upon our minds a full confidence in that natural security which this national bulwark must continue to afford us, whilst his Majesty's naval commanders vie with each other in such glorious achievements.

(Signed,) P. Bond.

The British consul at Boston afterwards ascertained from the French consul, that the enemy's ship was the Vengeance, mounting 52 guns; that she was one of Admiral Richery's squadron, which he expected there with dispatches, but that she never arrived: a circumstance which adds weight to the intelligence which was afterwards conveyed to Captain Beresford by Captain Mc Kellar, who was then a prisoner in France, that the Vengeance, shortly after the action, sunk, in consequence of the Raison's shot having riddled her between wind and water; but that she had been previously fallen in with by the French frigate La Concorde, which removed the whole of the crew*.

In March 1797, Captain Beresford had another opportunity to display that zeal and intrepidity which he had invariably shewn on every trying occasion. Being on a cruise off the Bahamas on the 17th, about six a. m. two strange sail, which proved to be Spanish, a ship and a brig, were discovered: all sail was immediately made in chase, which was continued the whole day, and towards night the Raison was disguised with hammock-clothes and two tier of lanterns. About midnight, having approached within gun-shot, a gun was fired to bring them to, which, however, they returned. About half-past twelve, having arrived within hail, the enemy asked, " What ship?" and was answered, " The British 64-gun ship Raisonable." Feeling the necessity of adopting decisive measures, Captain Beresford ran along side the largest, and ordered her to strike; but on her refusing to comply, an action commenced, which was soon terminated by the surrender of the enemy's ship, and by the other running on the rocks, where she was lost. Both were richly laden, and bound to Vera Cruz. The one captured proved to be his Catholic Majesty's ship St. Louis, pierced for 50 guns, and mounting 26. Great as was the merit attending this action, it did not terminate with the capture of the enemy. The action took place in the most intricate and dangerous passage of the Little Isaac, and at the moment the enemy struck his colours both ships were within pistol-shot of the rocks, with the wind at E. N. E. As in this extremity, through a moment's hesitation, or the

---

* We have been informed that the enemy afterwards named another ship, a *rasée* of similar force, the Vengeance.

slightest unskilful management, the Raison and her prize might have shared the fate of the third ship, Captain Beresford hooked the prize under her fore-chains with his starboard anchor, and thus by a most skilful manœuvre hauled her round, by which means both were saved. He afterwards continued his cruise and captured several of the enemy's vessels, amongst which was a valuable Spanish brig of 16 guns. He subsequently fell in with a Spanish frigate, to which he gave chase, and continued it for eleven hours almost within gun-shot; but the enemy at last effected his escape by superior sailing. She was afterwards chased by several ships belonging to the fleet under Earl St. Vincent, but succeeded in getting into Cadiz. She mounted 44 guns, and had on board property to the amount of 1,500,000*l*. He was shortly afterwards placed in charge of a convoy and returned to England, when he was paid off.

In the following year Captain Beresford was, at a moment's notice, appointed to the Unité frigate, and ordered to the West Indies. After his arrival, he became under the orders of that excellent officer, Lord Hugh Seymour, and was senior officer of frigates at the capture of Surinam. He was then sent, with the Amphitrite, Captain Ekins, under his orders, to reconnoitre the fortifications erecting on the Devil's Islands, near Cayenne. Seeing on his arrival a favourable opportunity to make a dash at them, he made the signal to prepare for action; and having stood between the two southernmost, hauled round the point, when, about half-past eleven, the guns from the battery opened a smart fire. Both frigates immediately opened their broadsides, and their boats were sent to effect a landing. About one o'clock the batteries were silenced, the enemy deserting their guns; the boats' crews attacked them in their rear, and having defeated them, took possession of the forts, both of which were dismantled, the magazines destroyed, and the guns conveyed on board the frigates. Had the islands been fortified as laid down in the French surveys, they most likely would not have been so easily captured; but even in that case, the coolness with which both ships were anchored under a heavy fire, the method pursued, with two such commanders and such excellent ships' companies, there would have been no fear as to the issue of the contest.

Captain Beresford* was afterwards detached on a cruise off Basseterre, and perceiving a large French corvette close to the shore, he determined,

---

* During the time that he commanded the Unité, finding on several occasions that she did not steer well, he had the rudder actually unshipped at sea and lengthened; a thing which, we believe, was never before attempted.

if possible, to surprise her and cut her out. Accordingly, in the night, the boats being manned, he placed himself at their head, and, accompanied by Lieutenant Black, dashed at the enemy. The corvette was soon boarded and the enemy driven out of her; but the alarm was given, and all the batteries immediately began firing. Notwithstanding the object of attack had been carried in the highest style, every effort to bring her out proved impracticable; she was actually chained to the fort, and he was reluctantly compelled to abandon her. In January 1800 he proceeded off Cumana, where some French vessels had taken shelter, and seeing that they were not inclined to come out, he therefore frequently annoyed the place by attacking the batteries and alarming the inhabitants, till the governor obliged the French to put to sea, when they were of course captured. In all his cruises he had been remarkably fortunate in protecting the commerce of England, and in distressing that of her enemies by the capture of their merchant-ships and armed vessels. But few officers ever made a greater number of prizes; and he now returned to Martinique, in company with twenty-two vessels, and although they were not of much value in themselves, they were of sufficient importance to prove his zeal and activity in the discharge of his professional duties. He was then removed by Lord Hugh Seymour to the command of the Diana of 36 guns, and in that ship was senior officer of frigates under Sir John Duckworth, when he took possession of the Danish and Swedish Islands of St. Martin, St. Bartholomew, St. Thomas, St. John, Santa Cruz, and all their dependencies. He was afterwards stationed at Santa Cruz and St. Thomas, for the protection of those islands, and to reconcile the inhabitants to the government of England, and by his mild and impartial conduct so gained their good opinion that they offered to present him with a service of plate; but the acceptance of which he thought proper to decline.

During the whole career of Captain Beresford he had experienced no interval of repose; it had been a continued series of fatiguing service, without relaxation, and a great part of it in the burning climate of the West Indies. He, however, now returned to England, in charge of a large and valuable convoy amounting to 200 sail, the whole of which arrived perfectly safe; and preliminaries of peace being shortly after signed, he resigned the command of the Diana. On the renewal of the war in 1803 his services were, however, again called for; he was appointed to the Virginia frigate, which he soon got ready for sea, and was then ordered to Copenhagen on a particular service. On his return from thence, he was directed to take the command of the squadron off Goree, and he there closely blockaded the flotilla which was intended to join that at Boulogne. During the six months that he here remained constantly at sea, the weather was so extremely boisterous, that the Virginia became quite unfit for farther service, and he consequently returned into port. In August 1804 he was ordered to take his passage in the Revolutionaire, Captain Hotham, for the American station, and take the command of the Cambrian frigate. He shortly afterwards sailed on a cruise, and that success which had hitherto followed him still attended his operations; and he captured so many of the enemy's armed ships and privateers as to call forth the particular thanks of Sir Andrew Mitchell, the commander-in-chief. On the death of that distinguished officer, Captain Beresford became the commander-in-chief on that important station: he of course followed the orders and instructions of the Admiralty to that lamented admiral, stationed himself at Halifax, in order to correspond with the British authorities in the United States, and so judiciously disposed the whole squadron under his command, that the intercourse of the enemy's vessels with that part of the American coast embraced within his orders was nearly cut off; scarcely a vessel could effect her entrance. Many prizes were consequently made ; at the same time the trade of England was so well protected, that not a single vessel, either merchant or national, fell into the hands of the enemy. He consequently received the entire approbation of the Board of Admiralty ; and the merchants of Halifax and Nova Scotia, justly appreciating the whole of his conduct, his immediate attention to every mercantile application, his promptness in rendering every possible assistance, and his decisive measures in promoting the commercial interests of their country, voted him the following address, dated Halifax, August 4, 1806 :

" Your command of his Majesty's ships on this station having terminated by the arrival of the Hon. Vice-Admiral Berkeley, the merchants of Halifax would be inexcusable were they to omit testifying the high sense they entertain of your uniform attention to their interests and convenience. Witnesses as they have been of the early traits of your honourable professional career, it was with unfeigned satisfaction they contemplated your return to this station ; and while they have with pleasure seen the squadron devoted to your care, and directed with uncommon vigilance to the annoyance of his Majesty's enemies, they bear testimony with frankness to your uniform exertions to promote the commerce and fisheries of this province. They have on all occasions applied to you, sir, with confidence where their interests have been concerned, and your compliance with their requests has been rendered more grateful by the readiness with which they have been granted, and by that pleasing urbanity of manners for which you are so justly distinguished. In this mutual intercourse of confidence and regard, the utmost harmony has been invariably preserved between the inhabitants and the naval forces; the best interests of the province have been promoted, and its merchants enabled to forward large supplies of fish and lumber to his Majesty's colonies in the West Indies.

" The expressions of regard conveyed to you on this occasion are not the commonplace language of complaisance; they flow from the hearts of men who feel grateful for your attention; who contemplate with solicitude your future glory and prosperity; who wish you all the honours our beloved sovereign can bestow, and who are satisfied, if occasions present themselves, that you will continue to deserve them."

Shortly after the arrival of Admiral Berkeley, Captain Beresford was detached in search of a French squadron which was expected on the American coast. Off the Chesapeake he fell in with a strong squadron of ships of the line under Sir J. Warren, who had approached much too near the shore: Captain Beresford, who from long experience was well acquainted with every part of the coast, pointed out to the admiral the danger his ships were exposed to in their then situation; they were immediately put upon the other tack, and scarcely had this been accomplished, than its propriety was verified. The wind changed to S. E. and blew with such violence that it was with the utmost difficulty they were saved; and had they remained on the contrary tack, their destruction would have been inevitable. He then returned to Halifax, to inform Admiral Berkeley of Sir John Warren's squadron being in search of the enemy expected in that quarter; and he was then dispatched towards the Western Islands, in quest of two frigates that had escaped from Guadaloupe. These he had not the good fortune to fall in with, but he captured three other vessels, with which he arrived at Bermuda. He was then ordered to England with secret dispatches from Admiral Berkeley; and after his arrival, as the Cambrian was in want of a thorough repair, he was placed in the command of the Hero; but that ship being found on examination to be unfit for service, he was appointed to the Theseus of 74 guns, and placed under the orders of Lord Gardner in the Channel. He was subsequently detached under the orders of that indefatigable officer, Sir Richard King, off Ferrol, to blockade the enemy's force in that harbour, where they continued for eight months without going into port. He was then intrusted with the command of three sail of the line and sixteen smaller vessels, to blockade the port of l'Orient, which contained four sail of the line and five frigates, all with top-sail-yards hoisted; and having watched them for upwards of five months, on the 21st February, 1809, when reconnoitring the port, after some very stormy weather, and at the moment they were expected to put to sea, another French squadron of eight sail of the line (one of three decks), two frigates, and a brig, were perceived in the N. E. steering for the British squadron, then standing to the E. S. E. This new enemy had escaped from Brest, through the Passage du Raz, and only wanted to be joined by the l'Orient squadron to proceed to the West Indies, for the purpose of relieving the Island of Martinique, at that time blockaded by Admiral Cochrane. To prevent a junction without an action appeared almost impossible; and to engage such superior numbers, under such peculiar circumstances, not justifiable. That, however, which is rash in one instance, becomes prudent in another; and Captain Beresford, perceiving the enemy to be in chase of him, instantly determined on his measures, and to assume a bold front. He tacked his squadron to the W. N. W. himself leading, and kept them in such a position as indicated an intention to harass the enemy's rear. Intimidated by this bold manœuvre, the French admiral hauled his wind, and went off l'Orient, followed by Captain Beresford, who having at this critical moment been joined by the Revenge, in the face of the enemy provisioned his squadron from that ship, they having been for some time on short allowance, and were reduced to two days' bread. Perceiving that the enemy were running along shore for Basque roads, without having effected their junction with the l'Orient ships, he immediately followed them, and effected a junction with the squadron under Admiral Stopford. A few days after the enemy had anchored, the Jean Bart, one of their line-of-battle ships, tailed upon the shore, which was not more than a cable's length from her, and was lost; whereupon Captain Beresford, having examined their position, was induced to write to Admiral Moorsom, private secretary to Lord Mulgrave, to inform his lordship that the enemy's squadron could be attacked with advantage by fire-ships, and, if not totally destroyed, at least so crippled as to render it unfit for service.

This communication we find was laid before Lord Mulgrave three weeks before any other proposition having the same object in view. On the arrival of Lord Gambier plans were submitted to him, and fire-ships ordered to be fitted under the direction of the captain of the fleet, Sir Harry Neale, who, in conjunction with Captain Beresford, undertook to conduct them against the enemy. This plan was afterwards adopted by the Admiralty, and carried into effect by Lord Cochrane. On the following day the Theseus was sent in to assist in the destruction of the enemy, and rendered every assistance in her power to accomplish that object. Captain Beresford was afterwards sent to England with duplicates of Lord Gambier's dispatches, and also with 600 prisoners taken on that occasion. Early in 1810 the Theseus was paid off, and Captain Beresford was appointed to the Poictiers, in which he joined the Channel fleet, and for four months was senior officer off Brest. He was afterwards dispatched to Lisbon, and placed under the orders of Admiral Berkeley. On the retreat of the French army from Santarem, he was ordered to obey the directions of Admiral Sir Thomas Williams, whom he accompanied with six hundred boats up the river, to assist the operations of the British army under Lord Wellington; by which means 16,000 men, under the command of Lord Hill, were conveyed across the Tagus in twenty-four hours! Shortly afterwards the Poictiers was ordered to England with a convoy of forty sail of merchant-ships, all of which arrived safe. In 1811 he was acting under the orders of Admiral Young in the North Sea, and covered the blockade of the Texel with three sail of the line and a frigate, consisting of the Poictiers, the Theseus, Captain Prowse, Defiance, Captain Ragget, and Desirée, Captain Farquhar. At one period the enemy, whose force consisted of five sail of the line, manifested every disposition to put to sea, which was encouraged by Captain Beresford, who endeavoured by all the means in his power to induce them to come out, and for three days offered them battle; but though they came to the outer anchorage, nothing could tempt them to venture farther, and they then returned to their former anchorage.

In 1812 Captain Beresford was ordered to America with a squadron under the command of Sir John Warren, in consequence of hostilities with the United States and his great knowledge of the American coast. They arrived at Halifax in September following, from whence he was sent to Bermuda, with orders to capture any vessels belonging to the United States. On the 28th October he captured the American sloop of war Wasp, of 20 guns, and recaptured the British brig Frolic, her prize, by which means the Frolic's convoy were saved and conveyed into Bermuda for protection. He afterwards proceeded on a cruise off the Chesapeake with a small squadron under his orders, and captured several armed vessels and letters of marque. In January 1813 he returned to Bermuda, and Admiral Warren having shortly after arrived, he was ordered to hoist a commodore's pendant. In the following month he proceeded with five sail of the line under Admiral Cockburn to the Chesapeake, from whence he was ordered to blockade the Delaware with a squadron of small vessels. On this service he remained four months, and during the whole of that period not a single vessel escaped him either in attempting to go in or to come out; and he obliged the enemy to supply his squadron with fresh beef and provisions, as the price of his forbearance in not making any attack upon their towns. Amongst the ships captured was a valuable East Indiaman, the Montesquieu. Having been relieved in that command, he returned to Bermuda, and from thence was directed to go off New-York, and to cruise as far as the banks of Newfoundland. In this cruise he again succeeded in capturing several of the enemy's armed ships, and retook many of their prizes, with which he returned to Halifax. In the month of November he was ordered to England with a large convoy, and having conducted them safe to the Downs, proceeded to Chatham, where he was paid off. He was shortly afterwards appointed to the Royal Sovereign yacht, and in the month of March 1814 was ordered to Dover, to carry into effect one of the most important events recorded in the history of England. By the persevering energies of the British army and navy, the power of Buonaparte was dissolved; he was obliged to abdicate the throne, and Captain Beresford was selected to convey Louis XVIII. to his paternal dominions. On the 23d April the Board of Admiralty hoisted their flag on board the yacht, when the Prince Regent, the King of France, the Duke de Bourbon, with their suites, went on board, where they remained till the following day, when the Prince Regent having taken leave of his most Christian Majesty (whose standard was afterwards hoisted on board the yacht), a royal salute was fired, and the yacht started for Calais, where his Majesty was landed in two hours and twenty minutes, under the protection of the British flag, and the chief command of his Royal Highness the Duke of Clarence, who had hoisted his flag as admiral of the fleet.

In May following Captain Beresford was created a baronet of Great Britain, and in the month of June was advanced to the rank of rear-admiral. About the same period he and Sir Edmund Nagle had the honour of kissing hands on being appointed *naval aides-de-camp* to his Royal Highness the Prince Regent, then on a visit with the Allied Sovereigns to the fleet at Portsmouth. In September following he was ordered to hoist his flag in the Duncan, and proceed with a convoy to Rio de Janeiro, where he arrived in the month of December. He was then placed at the disposal of the Prince Regent of Portugal, who was expected to proceed to Lisbon with his whole family on board Sir John's squadron. On the 1st February, 1815, the Prince Regent, with two young princes, paid a visit to Sir John, and after dining with him on board the Duncan, departed under a royal salute. In the month of April, however, the prince informed Sir John that it was not his intention to return to Lisbon, and that he was of course at liberty to return to England. He then conferred upon him the Order of the Tower and Sword, placing his own ribbon on Sir John's shoulder; after which, having taken leave, Sir John returned to England, and arrived at Spithead on the 14th June. In August 1819 he was made a K. C. B. and in 1820 he was appointed commander-in-chief at Leith: whilst on this station, he had the gratification to witness the enthusiastic and truly loyal reception given by the people of Scotland to his Majesty George IV. who is the only monarch who has visited that part of the empire for several generations; and in May 1825 he was advanced to the rank of vice-admiral of the Blue.

Sir John married, first, in 1809, Miss Molloy, daughter of Captain Molloy, R. N. by whom he had issue one son, born 1st March, 1811. That lady having died at Bermuda in 1813, Sir John married, secondly, in August 1815, Harriet, daughter and coheiress of Henry Pierse of Bedale, Yorkshire, Esq. M. P. By that lady, who died in February 1825, in the 35th year of her age, Sir John had five children, three girls and two boys.

HISTORICAL MEMOIRS OF
ADMIRAL WILLIAM PROWSE, C. B.

ALTHOUGH there are many instances in the army and navy of individuals who, from the most humble situations, have risen to high rank and honours in the service, and who have obtained their elevation by their own merits, it has not hitherto fallen to our lot to record the services of one who rose from so humble a station as the gentleman who is the subject of this Memoir. His career, however, furnishes a proof that he was not only a brave and skilful officer, but that obscurity of birth and lowness of condition are not the smallest impediments in the British service to a man possessing the necessary requisites for the formation of a good officer. It has been said that he was originally impressed into the navy; but this we rather think is a mistake: he was, however, an able seaman for several years, and served as such on board the Dublin from the 13th November, 1771, to the 24th February, 1776; and again as an able seaman on board the Albion from the 1st November, 1776, to the 21st December, 1781. In this latter ship he served for a considerable period in the West Indies, and was in Admiral Byron's action off Grenada; and also in the actions of Sir George Rodney on the 17th April, 15th and 19th May, 1782; on which latter occasions the Albion suffered severely*, and amongst the wounded was W. Prowse, who was struck by a large splinter on the head. Thus for ten years did he perform the duties of a common seaman; but his conduct was always strict and exemplary, which, joined to a good deal of mildness of manners, procured him the friendship of his officers, and on the 22d December he was removed to the Atlas as midshipman and master's mate. He was now in the highroad of preferment, and on the 13th April following was promoted to the rank of lieutenant, and appointed to the Cyclops; but although he continued in that vessel till the 1st March, 1784, the conclusion of the war stopped for a time his farther advancement.

In the armament of 1787, Lieutenant Prowse was appointed to the Bellona; but in two months afterwards he was paid off, and remained

* See *Memoir of Sir* GEORGE BOWYER.

unemployed till the 23d February, 1790, when he was appointed to the Barfleur, which he retained till the 30th September, when he was removed to the Stately; but on the 20th November that ship was also put out of commission. In August 1791 he was appointed to the Duke, bearing the flag of Lord Hood; and in January 1793 removed to the Prince, bearing the flag of his old friend, Admiral Bowyer, with whom, in December following, he removed to the Barfleur as signal-lieutenant; and in 1794 was in the actions of the 28th and 29th May and 1st June. On the last grand day Admiral Bowyer lost a leg, and Lieutenant Prowse was severely wounded in the thigh by a large shot, which tore away a considerable portion of the flesh, after having disabled the gun he was in the act of pointing. In August following he was appointed first lieutenant of the Theseus, Captain Calder; and in November 1795, he accompanied Sir John Jervis to the Mediterranean, on board the Lively frigate, of which he was a supernumerary lieutenant. On their arrival on that station he was appointed to the Victory, and continued in that ship till the 20th October, 1796, when he was promoted to the rank of commander in the Raven sloop of war, and in that vessel acted as repeater in the memorable action of the 14th February, off Cape St. Vincent; shortly after which he was promoted by Sir John Jervis to post-rank in the Salvador del Mundo, which commission was confirmed by the Admiralty, and he continued in command of that vessel till November 1797. In August 1800 he was appointed flag-captain to Sir Robert Calder, which situation he retained till April 1802. On the 4th August following he was appointed to the Sirius frigate, in which he was variously employed in the Channel; was afterwards attached to the squadron under Sir R. Calder off Ferrol, and in the action with the combined fleet on the 22d July, 1805, he had five men killed and wounded. Previous to the actual commencement of the action the Sirius, being the weathermost frigate, passed along the whole of the enemy's line from van to rear, and signaled the exact number of their fleet; she afterwards fetched into the enemy's wake, and it was owing to the near and bold approach of Captain Prowse to the Sirène frigate, which had a rich galleon in tow (the latter of which he had determined to attempt carrying by boarding under favour of the thick and hazy weather which existed), that occasioned the French admiral to wear his whole fleet in succession; and when Captain Prowse was preparing to carry his plan into execution, he discovered, through the fog, the enemy's van ship approaching on his lee bow. By this movement the Sirius was herself in danger of being captured; and abandoning his object of attack, Captain Prowse bore up to pass to leeward of the combined fleet, some of which fired into the Sirius, and immediately afterwards the action became general.

Captain Prowse afterwards became under the orders of Lord Nelson, and was employed in closely watching the combined fleet in Cadiz. On the last day of his lordship's life, he and Captain Blackwood were for several hours with him on board the Victory, bore down with him to attack the combined fleet, and when the enemy's shot began to fly about their heads, after an affectionate farewell, they departed to their respective ships, and to carry some verbal messages to the vessels in the rear. On the death of that great leader, Captain Prowse continued under the command of Lord Collingwood, was employed by him on various services in the Mediterranean, and by his zeal, assiduity, and strictness of conduct, gained the admiration and lasting friendship of that celebrated admiral. It was not, however, till April 1806, that Captain Prowse had an opportunity of signalizing himself by any detached or separate operation; he had been in several general actions with fleets, but not one in which he had commanded: his abilities in that respect were, however, now put to the test. Being on a cruise to the eastward of Civita Vecchia, on the 17th April, at two p. m. he received intelligence that a strong French flotilla was to have sailed from thence that morning, bound to Naples: such a moment was not to be lost, and he immediately crowded all sail in that direction. About a quarter-past four he obtained a sight of the enemy, whose force consisted of one ship, a corvette of 18 long 12-pounders and a 36-pound carronade, bearing a commodore's pendant; one of 18 long 9-pounders and 2 36-pound carronades, two of 12 long 9-pounders, one of 12 long 18-pounders and 2 68-pounders, and four smaller vessels, each of 4 long 4-pounders and 1 36-pound carronade; altogether mounting 97 guns, drawn up near a dangerous shoal, and about two leagues from the mouth of the Tiber. Without a moment's loss of time Captain Prowse dashed at the enemy, who awaited the attack with the utmost confidence, relying upon his superiority of force and compact position to gain him the victory. But Fortune favours the brave; and Captain Prowse, having reserved his fire till within pistol-shot, about sunset opened both his broadsides, directing his particular attention to the commodore, and continued very hotly engaged for two hours, the

Sirius completely surrounded, when the French commodore struck his colours, and was taken possession of. It was now nine o'clock, and owing to the smoothness of the water, the enemy had been enabled to bring all their guns into play, by which the Sirius had suffered considerably, and was prevented from pursuing her success any farther; a circumstance particularly regretted by Captain Prowse, as several others of the enemy were greatly damaged, and, had it been daylight, would no doubt have fallen into his possession. In this very brilliant affair the Sirius had one officer (the captain's nephew) and eight men killed and twenty wounded. Captain Prowse continued in command of the Sirius till May 1808, and effected the capture of several small vessels of the enemy.

In March 1810, he was appointed to the Theseus of 74 guns, and attached to the North-Sea squadron, and served under the orders of Sir John Beresford in blockading the enemy's force in the Texel. On the 23d December, 1813, he resigned the command of the Theseus, and did not again go to sea.

In June 1815, he was nominated a Commander of the Bath; in August 1819, he was made a colonel of marines; and in July 1821, was advanced to the rank of rear-admiral.

Such was the career of Admiral Prowse, who, during his eventful life, was in *eight general actions* with the fleets of the enemy, besides those partial engagements on the 28th and 29th May, 1794, and assisted at the capture of thirty-two sail of the line; participated in the thanks of Parliament voted on three separate occasions, and was honoured with three donations from the Patriotic Fund, one of which, an elegant vase, was presented on account of the merit displayed by him in his action with the French flotilla off the mouth of the Tiber; and as a farther mark of their admiration, the sum of 360*l.* was at the same time directed to be distributed among his wounded officers and men.

HISTORICAL MEMOIRS OF

ADMIRAL RICHARD HUSSEY MOUBRAY, C.B.

THE family of Moubray is of Norman extraction, and is descended from Roger de Moubray, a follower of the fortunes of William the Conqueror: his descendants appear in the history of Scotland so early as the reign of Alexander II.; the name of Philip de Moubray (who possessed a considerable extent of land in Edinburghshire and Fifeshire) is a witness to some charters of that monarch; and Sir David Moubray, Knight, of Barnbougall, was one of the hostages sent to England for the ransom of King James I. who was detained eighteen years a prisoner in England, and who returned in 1423*. In 1511 Sir John Moubray, Knight, of Barnbougall, having a daughter, but no son, conveyed during his lifetime the property of Cockairney, in the county of Fife (where the charter is preserved), to his father's brother, William, grandson of the above-mentioned David; and from William is descended, in a direct and uninterrupted male line, the present proprietor of Cockairney, Lieutenant-Colonel Sir Robert Moubray, Knight, the only and elder brother of Admiral Richard Hussey Moubray, the subject of the present Memoir, both being the sons of the late Robert Moubray of Cockairney, M.D. by his wife Arabella, youngest daughter of Thomas Hussey, Esq. of Wrexham, and sister to the late Lady Bickerton, mother of the present Admiral Sir Richard Bickerton.

Admiral Moubray was born at Plymouth, March 16, 1776; and being destined for the naval service, his name was placed on the books of the Sibyl, commanded by his relation, Captain Bickerton. In 1789 he was placed as a midshipman on board the Impregnable, bearing the flag of the late Admiral Sir Richard Bickerton, and in the following year formed part of the fleet under Lord Howe. In 1791 he removed to the Pegasus, Captain Domett, on the Newfoundland station; and in the following year was employed on board the Andromeda, Captain Salisbury, cruising in the Channel, and in attending on his late Majesty at Weymouth, having the Earl of Chatham and the Lords of the Admiralty on board. In November he removed to the Europa of 50 guns, bearing the broad pendant of Commodore Ford, appointed commander-in-chief at Jamaica;

* Nesbitt's and Douglas's Heraldry.

and after his arrival on that station, removed to the Serpent sloop, in which he was employed at the Bahama Islands; but on the commencement of hostilities in 1793 he joined the Europa, and became a participator in all the operations in St. Domingo in the latter part of that year and at the beginning of 1794, particularly at the capture of Jeremie and Cape Nicholas Mole. Immediately after which he was appointed to a lieutenancy, and in April was removed to the Magicienne, Captain G. Martin; but in May following he was made acting-captain of the Iphigenia, in which he was employed before Port-au-Prince in attacking batteries and making demonstrations with detachments of the 22d regiment and royals under Colonel Handfield; so that in three months he was a midshipman and a captain of a frigate!

Captain F. Gardner having been appointed to the Iphigenia, Lieutenant Moubray rejoined the Europa as first lieutenant; and Port-au-Prince having fallen before their united exertions, he was appointed, June 9th, to command the Fly sloop of war, and to convey Captain B. S. Rowley of the Penelope and Lieutenant-Colonel Whitelock with the dispatches of the two commanders-in-chief, announcing the fall of that important place, and the capture of about sixty large vessels laden with the produce of the island. The Fly having been refitted, he was employed in convoying transports to Helvoetsluys; and on the 4th December he received a letter from the Duke of York, dated at the Hague, requesting a ship of war might be in immediate readiness to convey him to England. He instantly got under weigh to save the tide, there not being sufficient depth to pass over the sands at low water, and was soon after joined by the Prince of Orange packet, with his royal highness on board, and conveyed him to England, for which he received the approbation of the Lords of the Admiralty. He was afterwards ordered to Plymouth, and in January 1795 he there assisted in taking possession of the Dutch squadron, then on its way to the Cape of Good Hope.

Captain Moubray was afterwards employed, under the orders of Captain Drury, in convoying to and from Gibraltar. In November following he was appointed acting-captain of the Magicienne, and was employed in Channel service and convoying ships from Lisbon; after which he rejoined the Fly, was again employed in protecting convoys and cruising in the Channel, in which he captured several vessels, amongst which was Le Furet French privateer. In April 1797 he was promoted to post-rank, though only twenty-one years of age. He then served, with permission of the Admiralty, as a volunteer on board the Ramillies and Terrible, commanded by the present Sir Richard Bickerton, till the latter was promoted to a flag in February 1799.

In October 1801, Captain Moubray was appointed to the Maidstone frigate; and in April 1802, was ordered to the Mediterranean with dispatches, announcing the ratification of the treaty of peace. In November following he conveyed the Russian ambassador, the Chevalier d'Italinsky, from Naples to Constantinople, and had the honour to receive from the grand vizier a valuable pelisse. This, however, was not the only attention paid to him, as he was permitted, though contrary to the usual custom of the Porte, to pass through the Bosphorus to Buguderé, to be near the British ambassador, Lord Elgin, who had there taken up a temporary residence to avoid the plague, then raging at Constantinople. Trifling as this may appear, it was considered as a great mark of respect on the part of the Sublime Porte, and which, joined to a little circumstance that afterwards occurred, served to prove the gratitude of the Turkish government for the support which they had received during the war from Great Britain. Lord Elgin having taken his departure on board the Diana, Captain Maling, for England, owing to some informality on passing the fortresses in the Dardanelles, was not saluted with the usual number of guns; which he represented in a dispatch to the Capitan Pacha at Constantinople, under whom all the maritime fortresses and defences are placed, and who immediately on the receipt of it requested a conference with Captain Moubray. This accordingly took place, when his highness stated, that it had given him much pain to find the governors of the castles in the Dardanelles had so neglected their duty; that he was anxious to make all the reparation in his power, and to shew the utmost respect to the representative of his Britannic Majesty; and as the Maidstone was to sail in a few days, requested Captain Moubray would receive the salutes which were due to the ambassador. At the same time he read an order, or firman, which he had prepared, addressed to the governors of the different castles in the Dardanelles, directing them, in very peremptory terms, to fire the salutes; and which, on the passing of the Maidstone, were fired accordingly. Captain Moubray was also intrusted by the Grand Signior with three valuable swords, as presents to his Majesty, the Prince of Wales, and the Duke of York. After remaining about a fortnight at Malta, Captain Moubray proceeded to Gibraltar, and was there lying when

Lord Nelson arrived in the Amphion, with intelligence of the war having been renewed.   On the following day both frigates proceeded to the Mediterranean, and off Cape de Gatte captured two merchant-vessels. On the 11th June the Hon. Hugh Elliott, minister to the court of Naples, and who had taken his passage from England in the Amphion, removed to the Maidstone, when the two frigates separated, Lord Nelson proceeding to Malta, and the Maidstone for Naples.   On the following day Captain Moubray captured a French armed brig, carrying 8 4-pounders, formerly an English packet, conveying a collection of antiquities (made under the direction of the Duke de Choiseul Gouffier in various parts of Greece) from Athens to l'Orient.   Having landed Mr. Elliott at Naples, and received dispatches for Lord Nelson, Captain Moubray joined his lordship off Naples on his way to Toulon, and was stationed off Cape Sepet, to watch the motions of the enemy.   On the 1st August he was removed to the Active of 38 guns; but was still employed watching the enemy, and continued on that service, almost without intermission, till November 1804, when he repaired to Malta to refit, not having been in any port, except for water, for eighteen months.

In January 1805, he rejoined Lord Nelson off Toulon, by whom he was left watching the enemy, with the Seahorse, Captain the Hon. Courtenay Boyle, under his orders, whilst the fleet proceeded to the Madalina Islands, from whence his lordship intended to return on the 17th, either by the route of Cape Corse or straits of Bonifacio.   On the morning of the 18th, at daylight, a detachment of the enemy's fleet was observed from the Active and Seahorse about five or six leagues off the land, evidently having sailed during the night, with the intention of surrounding the two English frigates.   The enemy now made sail in chase, which was continued for several hours, but in the afternoon they stood back towards Toulon.   The two frigates now hauled their wind, and stood after the enemy, keeping sight of them until dark, when they were close in with Porquerolle.   At ten p. m. it then blowing so hard from the N. W. that the two frigates were under close-reefed main-top-sail and stay-sails, with their heads off the shore, the enemy's fleet was discovered coming towards them under a press of sail.   The Active and Seahorse were immediately put before the wind, and sail made as quickly as possible from them, but scarcely in time to prevent their headmost ships from getting within gun-shot.   The enemy now steered south, going at the rate of ten or eleven knots; and as they would at that rate pass the

straits of Bonifacio before daylight, both frigates pushed for the Madalina Islands, to apprise Lord Nelson of the circumstance; which was
communicated to him by signal at half-past one p. m. on the 19th. He
immediately got under weigh, and proceeded through the narrow channel
between the small Island of Biche and Sardinia, the way being led by
the Active, to the southward, concluding, from the course the enemy was
steering when last seen, that he was bound to the southward of the island:
but strong southerly winds prevented the British squadron from making
much progress; and the enemy, having had one ship of the line crippled
and several others damaged, returned to Toulon. In the mean time Lord
Nelson, fancying that they were gone to Egypt, proceeded thither, and it
was not till the 15th March that he again arrived off Toulon; and having
looked into the harbour, proceeded to the gulf of Palma, leaving Captain
Moubray, with the Phœbe, Hon. Captain Capel, to watch the enemy's
fleet. On the 29th March the French admiral again put to sea, and was
discovered from the mast-heads of both frigates about nine a. m. on the
morning of the 31st, in the N. W. steering S. S. W. with light and variable winds. In the course of the day the frigates were enabled to near
the enemy, so as to see their top-gallant-sails from the deck. On the
preceding day the Active examined a Ragusan vessel from Smyrna to
Marseilles, which had passed through the British fleet two days before
off the south part of Sardinia, Lord Nelson having gone to Pulla to
complete water. In the afternoon this Ragusan was observed from the
Active to pass through the enemy's fleet (bearing N. W. by W. six or
seven leagues, on the starboard tack, with the wind at W. N. W), by
which she was brought-to and examined. At dark the Phœbe was dispatched by Captain Moubray to Pulla, to apprise Lord Nelson of the
enemy's situation; whilst the Active, during the night, endeavoured to
close with the enemy's fleet; but at daylight the following morning
Captain Moubray had the mortification to find that the enemy were not
in sight, they having, as it afterwards appeared, in consequence of the
intelligence obtained from the Ragusan, tacked during the night to the
northward: but supposing, from the variable state of the wind, that the
enemy were to the westward of him, Captain Moubray, for three days,
continued his search of them, when finding it ineffectual, he steered
for the south point of Sardinia, where he joined Lord Nelson. Intelligence having at last been obtained that the French had passed the
Straits, Captain Moubray was dispatched to England, with orders to

communicate with the commanders-in-chief of the Channel fleet and at Cork.

On the 19th May Captain Moubray arrived at Plymouth, and received the approbation of the Admiralty for his perseverance and activity. The Active having been docked and new-coppered, he was ordered to the coast of Norway, as senior officer of a small squadron employed on that station: but in the following October he was removed to Cork, under the orders of Lord Gardner; and whilst employed on that station fell in with, on the 17th December, in lat. 45 deg. 10 min. and long. 14 deg. 30. min. the Arethusa, Captain C. Brisbane, on his passage to the West Indies with a valuable convoy, but which had been dispersed the day before in consequence of being chased by a French squadron of five ships of the line and three frigates, which were then in sight. The Arethusa now proceeded to collect her convoy, and the Active to keep sight of the enemy, steering westward; but the French squadron having obtained a breeze whilst the Active was nearly becalmed, she lost sight of them in the evening. Having fallen in with a brig from Newfoundland to Lisbon, Captain Moubray dispatched by her a letter to the British minister at Lisbon, informing him of the enemy's course; and having now obtained the breeze, continued his pursuit of the enemy, whom he again obtained a sight of on the 25th, in lat. 44 deg. 30 min. long. 24 deg. W. on the larboard tack, and with the wind at W. N. W. Having approached to within five or six miles of them during the day, and concluding from their course that they were steering for Ireland, he, after dark, proceeded for Ushant, to inform the commander-in-chief of the Channel fleet. He afterwards resumed his station off the Irish coast, captured a beautiful fast-sailing schooner letter of marque, and eight vessels laden with Prussian property. In June 1806 he was ordered to the Mediterranean with a convoy, and was afterwards employed in watching the port of Cadiz. In November following he was detached, under the orders of Sir T. Louis, to the Dardanelles; and on the 3d January, 1807, received on board the Russian ambassador, the Count d'Italinsky, and conveyed him to Malta. On approaching Valette he fell in with the squadron under Sir J. T. Duckworth, by whom he was dispatched with letters to the English ambassador at Constantinople, but found him on board the Canopus at Tenedos. He afterwards had the satisfaction to save a great many of the crew of the unfortunate Ajax, which was destroyed by fire on the night of the 14th February, being so near her at the time she took fire as to hear Captain Blackwood, before the flames burst out, calling for the Active's boats, which were instantly sent to her assistance. He afterwards accompanied the squadron through the Dardanelles, acted under the immediate orders of Sir Sidney Smith, and in the destruction of a part of the Turkish fleet secured to himself the approbation of the commander-in-chief, who, in his official letter, said, " The terms of approbation in which the rear-admiral relates the conduct of Captains Dacres, Talbot, Harvey, and Moubray, which, from my being under the necessity of passing the point of Pesquies before the van could anchor, he had a greater opportunity of observing than I could, cannot but be highly flattering; but I was a more immediate witness to the able and officer-like conduct which Captain Moubray displayed, in obedience to my signal, by destroying a frigate with which he had been more particularly engaged, having driven her on shore on the European side, after she had been forced to cut her cables from under the fire of the Pompée and Thunderer." She was then boarded by boats from the Active, a train laid to her magazine, and entirely destroyed*. This was not the only service performed on this expedition by Captain Moubray : circumstances rendering it impracticable for Sir Sidney Smith, at the moment, effectually to destroy the formidable battery at Point Pesquies, he directed Captain Moubray to remain there for that purpose ; and which was fully and meritoriously performed under his directions. The Turks appeared in great force on the heights above the batteries, and occasionally charged, with cavalry and infantry, the party of sailors and marines he had landed under the direction of Lieutenant (now Captain) Carroll; but the enemy was driven back by the fire of the Active, which was kept under sail for that purpose, and by which means the party on shore was enabled completely to destroy the fortifications.

* The boats of the Active, with the last of the prisoners, were about two cables' length distance when she blew up ; and we may here mention a little anecdote, to the honour of the Turkish captains (for each Turkish ship of war has two) : They had been informed by the agents of France that all prisoners would be put to death by the English, but were agreeably surprised, on going on board the Active, to find the erroneousness of that assertion ; and much more so on the senior captain being allowed to land in the night, to procure boats to convey his companions, on giving his promise to return the following night. He kept his word ; and, on again going on board the Active, held out his hand (which had been shot through on landing, being taken for an enemy),and said to Captain Moubray, " I trust you will now have reason to think a Turk is a man of honour." On their being sent on shore, Captain Moubray returned the captains their scimeters.

On repassing the Dardanelles, the Active received a granite-shot, weighing 800 pounds and measuring six feet six inches in circumference; which passed through her side two feet above the water, and lodged on the orlop-deck, close to the magazine-scuttle, without injuring a man. The aperture made by it was so wide, that Captain Moubray, on looking over the side, saw two of his crew thrusting their heads through at the same moment. Had there been a necessity for hauling to the wind on the opposite tack, she must have gone down. To shew still farther the extent of the damage done by this shot, we may observe, that, after the arrival of the Active at Malta, the Count d'Italinsky, a man of very large stature, on going on board to visit Captain Moubray, was led by curiosity to examine the hole made by it in the starboard bow, and actually entered the ship through it from the boat!

Having been refitted, Captain Moubray was employed in the blockade of Corfu, on which service he captured several vessels, amongst which was one containing the library of the French general, Donzelot, appointed governor of Corfu, and who narrowly escaped capture in another vessel in company. This capture became the means of establishing a perfect good understanding between the English squadron on that station and the new French governor; and as such conduct always tends to alleviate the miseries of war, it is with pleasure we record it. Having no wish to make war on private property, and having proved to the world his professional abilities, Captain Moubray seized the earliest opportunity to restore the books and other property to General Donzelot, and thus give his enemy a proof of his clemency and liberality. Subsequent events proved that this generosity had its proper effect on the mind of General Donzelot, who handsomely acknowledged, by letter, his sense of the obligation, and who always afterwards had a seat set apart at his table for any English officer who might happen to be a prisoner on the island. It is these little circumstances which prove the characters of men; and of Admiral Moubray we may here observe, that his professional career has proved that he is not more admirable for his courage, than for his application of it; that he was modest and generous in success, and that he never failed to let fall the arm of conquest to extend the hand of consolation.

It being an object of importance with Napoleon to strengthen Corfu, General Donzelot, a man of great attainments, was selected by the emperor to command there and superintend the immense fortifications to be erected on the island, the blockade of which became of the utmost importance, and was diligently maintained by the squadron under the command of Captain T. Harvey.   In February 1808, two French squadrons appeared at the outer entrance of the Adriatic, one of which was seen by Captain Moubray off Corfu on the 18th, intelligence of which he sent, on the following day, to Lord Collingwood at Syracuse; and on the 21st, the Standard in company, another squadron of five ships of the line was observed near the gulf of Taranto.   As these ships had evidently eluded the watchfulness of Lord Collingwood, from whom no intelligence was received, Captain Harvey, on the 23d, proceeded to Syracuse to apprise him of the enemy's situation, leaving the Active to watch their movements. On the following day the Porcupine, Captain H. Duncan, joined the Active, and continued with her till the 12th March, when she was dispatched by Captain Moubray to Lord Collingwood, to say that the enemy had put into Corfu.   During the whole period that these two vessels continued to watch the enemy, the weather was generally very boisterous, and the French squadron was driven from off Corfu, where it was first seen, to the southward, as far as Cape Spartivento, so that the frigates were occasionally separated; but not a day passed without their seeing either one squadron or the other, which proved to be those from Rochefort and Toulon, but which had not joined till they put into Corfu. On the 23d March the Standard rejoined the Active, and on the 26th they captured the Italian brig of war Friedland, mounting 18 guns, and bearing the broad pendant of Commodore Paolucci, commander-in-chief of the Italian navy. Captain Moubray continued on this service till the following August, during which time several captures were made by the Active; he was then appointed to the Montagu, which he joined off Toulon.   In May 1809, he was detached, under the orders of Captain Hargood of the Northumberland, to the Adriatic, where and off Corfu he remained till January 1811.   In March 1810 he was employed in the siege and capture of the Island of St. Maura, under Captain Eyre and General Oswald.   The forces destined for the expedition assembled at Zante, near which island, owing to the ignorance of the pilot, the Montagu got upon the shoal, now marked in the charts Montagu shoal, and knocked her rudder off, which prevented her from proceeding with the squadron, which sailed on the 21st, on the evening of which day the troops were landed at St. Maura: " but," says Captain Eyre in his official letter, " Captain Moubray having, by the greatest exertions, rehung his rudder at Zante, lost not a moment afterwards in following us, and rejoined me on the 30th. On her arrival two of her lower-deck guns were landed, and 100 of her seamen, to do duty on shore. I, at the same time, directed Captain Moubray to superintend all the operations that were going forward, that no assistance which the ships could give might be omitted. On the 7th April I left the transports under the care of the Montagu, and proceeded to the opposite side of the island, where our batteries opened the following morning." The two guns landed from the Montagu (32-pounders) were drawn with much difficulty, under the direction of Captain Moubray, the distance of four or five miles, to a spot chosen by himself and Colonel (now Sir Hudson) Lowe, where a battery was erected, and, although at the distance of a mile from the fortress, the guns, from taking the bastion opposed to the advanced batteries in flank, did considerable execution, and greatly tended to the reduction of the fortress, which capitulated on the 15th; Captain Moubray and Colonel Lowe having been authorized by the general and Captain Eyre to treat with the enemy and to sign the articles of capitulation*."

* The following is a copy of the articles, dated 16th April, 1810 :

1. La garnison de la forteresse de St. Maura evacuera cette forteresse avec les honneurs de la guerre, les armes et le bagage, pour monter abord des batimens Anglais, pour être conduits dans le port de Trieste ou Ancone, appartenant à sa Majesté l'Empereur Napoleon.

Answer.—The garrison shall march out with the honours of war, and after laying down their arms, shall be embarked on board transports, to be conveyed to such ports of his Britannic Majesty's dominions as may be found most expedient. The officers shall be permitted to return to Italy on their parole of not serving until exchanged. The officers shall preserve their swords.

2. La garnison sortira par la porte d'Epire et l'embarquera au port Nicolo.

Ans.—Granted.

3. Au moment que la garnison sortira la porte d'Amamich sera occupé par les troupes de S. M. B.

Ans.—The gates of the fortress shall be given up to the British troops as soon as the capitulation is signed and ratified.

4. Les non-combatants seront rendus à Corfou.—*Ans.* Granted.

5. Les malades et blessés resteront dans la place, pour être conduit ensuite à Corfou. Ils sont recommendés à la générosité au gouvernement Anglais.—*Ans.* Granted.

6. Les officiers et troupes auxiliaires de quelque nation que ce soit suivront le sort de la garnison.—*Ans.* Granted.

7. Les malles et portemanteaux des officiers et les havresacs des soldats seront respectés.

Ans.—All private property shall be respected ; but at the same time all private debts and obligations towards the inhabitants or others must be satisfied.

All public property of every description, money, magazines, provisions, guns, ammu-

In his official dispatch Captain Eyre paid a well-deserved compliment to Captain Moubray, in the following terms: " Though the part which the ships could take, from the peculiar situation of the place, was very limited, yet I am sure you will readily believe, from the known character of the captains I had the honour to have under my command, that the greatest zeal and anxiety were shewn by them to do every thing that was possible. The assistance I received from Captain Moubray, and his unremitting attention to every piece of duty that was going forward, demand my warmest acknowledgments."

The Montagu being ordered to England, Captain Moubray exchanged, in February 1811, to the Repulse, and remained in the Mediterranean, chiefly off Toulon, till January 1814. During this period the Repulse was employed, almost without intermission, with the in-shore squadron, a most anxious service, and was frequently engaged with the enemy's batteries. At the latter end of May 1812, when an attempt was made by a detachment of Sir Edward Pellew's fleet to take the town of Ciotat by a *coup-de-main*, and thereby gain possession of the shipping lying in the mole of that place, the Repulse was attached to the squadron under the orders of Rear-Admiral Hallowell, and selected to conduct the boats to the coast, cover the landing of the marines intended for that service, and then attack the sea-defences. The boats reached the point of debarkation on the 1st June; but the wind unfortunately failed before the whole of the squadron could enter the bay, and the enemy being alarmed, the enterprise was necessarily abandoned. On the 2d May, 1813, being off Morjean with the Volontaire, Undaunted, and Redwing, the enemy was observed to be actively employed in preparations for remounting cannon on the batteries; and viewing the importance of the situation as a place of protection to the coasting trade, Captain Moubray landed 100 marines of the Repulse, in conjunction with those from the frigates, for the purpose of destroying the works; while the boats should bring out such vessels as were in the harbour, covered by the fire

nition, and plans of the engineers and artillery departments, shall be delivered up to officers charged to receive them, in the same state as they now actually exist; and the officers charged to receive them are to enter the fortress at the same time with the troops who take possession of the gates, by whom sentries are to be furnished until the embarkation of the garrison takes place.

(Signed,)   R. H. MOUBRAY.

H. LOWE, *Lieut.-Col. Com.*

CAMUS, *le Général de Br.*

of the Redwing and launches. The marines, under Captain Innis, having driven the enemy's armed force to the heights, kept them in check till the boats had secured the vessels in the harbour and destroyed the batteries, which was accompanied with the loss of two killed and four wounded. In the month of August another very gallant affair was performed by the boats of the Repulse and Aigle. Having chased some vessels into Vernezza, in the gulf of Genoa, it was found necessary, in order to get at them, to take possession of the town, which was accomplished by anchoring the ships close to it and landing the marines, who drove the enemy out of it, and not only prevented them from re-entering it, but also kept in check a considerable body of troops who hastened to its relief from the neighbourhood, until the vessels were completely destroyed, which was accompanied without any loss to the victors. In February 1814 Captain Moubray sailed from Malta with a convoy for England; and hostilities having terminated, the Repulse was paid off in June, and Captain Moubray retired on half-pay, after a long, zealous, and constant employment, during the last thirteen years of which, mostly on foreign service, he was never absent from his duty for a single day, even on leave; an instance of persistency which we believe is almost unparalleled in the profession. That his services were active, diligent, and praiseworthy, the foregoing narrative perhaps sufficiently proves; but the two following extracts of letters from Sir J. T. Duckworth will on that point be more satisfactory:

ROYAL GEORGE, *Nov.* 7, 1808.

MY DEAR SIR,—I anxiously hope, after our separation, that your great services were rewarded by some good luck; and I now add another hope, that you may have an equal opportunity in the Montagu to display your professional abilities and gallantry, as you did under my eye in the Dardanelles.

ROYAL GEORGE, *March* 7, 1809.

The Brest squadron got out on the 21st ult. the l'Orient on the 22d at night, and the Rochefort, it is said, on the 24th; but where they are gone to I know not, though I encourage a hope that we shall meet; and it would be a pleasure to have you of our party, as your services I have seen and admired.

In June 1815 Captain Moubray was nominated a Companion of the Bath, and in July 1821 was made a rear-admiral. He was married, in January 1815, to Emma, fifth daughter of William Hobson, Esq. of Markfield, Middlesex; and has four children, three daughters and one son.

HISTORICAL MEMOIRS OF
ADMIRAL HENRY DIGBY, C.B.

HOW fortunate it is for society that men will, for the sake of fame, spurn the lap of ease and retirement, and embrace a life of toil and adventure in search of events and circumstances, which not only increase their own, but also their country's honour and reputation! In the prosecution of such designs the noblest attributes of man are called into action, and a display of them places their country under a debt of gratitude which should never be forgotten, neither should those who have risked every thing in her defence go unrewarded. It has been asserted, that " whatever industry and enterprise men have at any time displayed, has originated in the bosom of pain, of want, or of necessity." But if an instance were required as a proof of the falsity of this position, it may be found in the life and conduct of Admiral Digby, who is the eldest son of the late Hon. and Rev. William Digby, dean of Durham, vicar of Coles-Hill, a chaplain in ordinary to the king, and canon of Christ Church. Having made choice of a naval life, he went to sea, in 1784, with Admiral Innes, on board the Europa, with whom he proceeded to Jamaica, where he remained for two years, when he returned to England. He afterwards served with those excellent officers, Commodore Elliot and Sir Erasmus Gower, on the Newfoundland station until the end of 1788, when he was removed to the Racehorse sloop, and employed in the North Sea and on the coast of Scotland, cruising against smugglers, till the spring of 1790. Subsequently he served with the late Sir Thomas Pasley in the Bellerophon, until he had completed the probationary period of his service, when he was promoted, in October of that year, to be lieutenant of the Lion, commanded by the Hon. Seymour Finch, and sailed with Admiral Cornish to the West Indies. In 1793 he was appointed to the Eurydice, and was employed in Channel service. In 1794 he was removed to the Pallas; and in the following year had the satisfaction, in the jolly-boat, of saving several of the crew belonging to the Boyne, when she was burnt at Spithead. In August 1795 he was appointed to command the Incendiary fire-ship, and accompanied the expedition to Quiberon Bay. He was afterwards employed on detached service in the Channel, and was subsequently under the orders of Lord H. Seymour and Sir A. Gardner.

In October 1796 Captain Digby was sent on a secret expedition, with troops, &c. off the Texel, under the orders of Sir R. Bickerton; but the service was stopped by the decision of a council of war held on board Admiral Duncan's ship, the Venerable. In December following he was promoted to post-rank, and to command the Aurora, in which he sailed with a convoy to Lisbon, on which station he remained, under the orders of Lord St. Vincent, for the protection of the British trade and annoyance of the enemy, principally on the north coast of Spain; and the following list of ships captured or destroyed is sufficient to prove the activity and perseverance with which he executed his orders: Forty-eight merchant-ships, the French privateer Neptune of 14 guns, St. Blas of 8 guns*, La Marie Anne of 14 guns, L'Aigle of 14 guns, L'Espeigle of 14 guns, L'Aventure of 10 guns, L'Egalité corvette of 20 guns, and the Velos Aragonesa, pierced for 30 guns (in which were three of the mutineers of the Hermione), the whole mounting 124 guns, and having on board 744 men.

In October 1798 Captain Digby was appointed to the Leviathan, and assisted at the capture of Minorca under Sir J. T. Duckworth. In March 1799 he removed to the Alchmene, and was again employed in cruising against the enemy, which was attended with his usual success. On the 3d April he cut out, from under a fort near Malaga, Le Depit of 8 guns; and on the 26th June, after three days' chase in light winds and sweeping off Corvo, he captured La Courageux, mounting 28 guns, with a complement of 253 men. On the 18th June the boats of the Alchmene cut out from the harbour of Vivero, La Felicidad, pierced for 22 guns, and a ship of 400 tons burden, both laden with ship-timber and iron for Ferrol. On the 1st July he captured Les Deux Amis of 6 guns; and on the 16th and 17th of October, being in company with the Naïad, Triton, and Ethalion, captured the two Spanish frigates Thetis and Santa Brigida, both with valuable cargoes from Vera Cruz, and for which the English captains received upwards of 40,000l. each. Besides the above vessels, Captain Digby captured, during the time he commanded the Alchmene, about twenty merchant-vessels. In 1801 he was appointed to the Re-

* This vessel was Spanish, and it was judged by Lord St. Vincent politically expedient to give her up, being taken too near a fort on the coast of Portugal.

sistance, and ordered to Quebec with a convoy, and remained on that station during the remainder of the war.

In September 1805 Captain Digby was appointed to the Africa of 64 guns, and ordered to join Lord Nelson off Cadiz without a moment's delay; and he joined him a few days previous to the battle of Trafalgar. " The Africa having had the misfortune to lose sight of the fleet during the night, was, when the firing commenced, broad upon the Victory's larboard beam, and nearly abreast of the van ship of the combined line. Seeing her danger, Lord Nelson ordered the Africa's signal to be thrown out to make all possible sail. The intention of this signal appears to have been misunderstood, and instead of using means to run his ship out of danger, Captain Digby set every sail he could spread to hasten her into it. Passing along and exchanging broadsides in succession with the ships of the combined van, the Africa, with much less injury done to her than might have been expected, bore down ahead of the Santissima Trinidad. Meeting no return to her fire, and seeing no colours hoisted on board the latter, Captain Digby concluded that the four-decker had surrendered, and sent Lieutenant John Smith in a boat to take possession. Upon the lieutenant's reaching the quarter-deck, and asking an officer, who advanced to meet him, whether or not the Santissima had surrendered, the Spaniard replied, ' Non, non!' pointing at the same time to one Spanish and four French sail of the line then passing to windward. As, for want of masts, the Santissima was settling fast to windward of the two fleets, and he had only a boat's crew with him, Lieutenant Smith quitted the Spanish ship (the crew of which singularly enough permitted him to do so) and returned on board the Africa," which then pushed on into the thickest of the fire, and, in the most gallant manner, brought up along side the French ship Intrepide, and, in spite of the superiority of force to which she was opposed, maintained the contest for three quarters of an hour, when the Orion coming to her assistance, the Frenchman struck his colours and was taken possession of. In this brilliant action the Africa sustained great loss, having had her main-top-sail-yard shot away, and her bowsprit and three lower-masts so badly wounded, that none of the latter could afterwards stand. Her remaining masts and yards were also more or less injured, her rigging and sails cut to pieces, and her hull, besides other serious damage, had received several shot between wind and water. Her loss in men amounted to 18 killed, 20 severely and 24 slightly wounded, which, considering that her complement was only 490 men and boys, and that Captain Digby had voluntarily engaged so superior a force, proves, that although but a 64, the Africa had performed as gallant a part as any in the British line*. Captain Digby accordingly participated in Lord Collingwood's public testimony of high approbation of the meritorious services and conduct displayed by the officers, seamen, and marines on this occasion, and likewise in the thanks of both Houses of Parliament. He was also presented by his Majesty with a gold medal, to commemorate the victory. But notwithstanding all these favourable circumstances, the foul tongue of envy and slander could not remain silent; and whether it arose from the signal made by the Victory, which we have noticed above, we cannot say, but it was currently reported that Lord Nelson had expressed great dissatisfaction at the conduct pursued by Captain Digby. We are happy, however, in having it in our power fully and satisfactorily to contradict this report, and on the authority of one whose opinion cannot be gainsaid:

PUTNEY, *June 27, 1815.*

MY DEAR DIGBY,—On my arrival here last night, I found your letter of the 21st instant, and I cannot sufficiently express my surprise at hearing that a captain of the navy had informed you, that Lord Nelson was displeased with your conduct on the 21st October. I beg to assure you, that Lord Nelson *expressed great satisfaction at the gallant manner in which you passed the enemy's line; and I assure you he appeared most fully satisfied with the conduct of the Africa.* I shall be most happy personally to contradict the report, if you will inform me of the captain's name who conveyed it to you.

I remain yours most sincerely,

T. M. HARDY.

In 1815 Captain Digby was nominated a Companion of the Bath, and in 1819 was advanced to the rank of rear-admiral. He married, in March 1806, Jane Elizabeth, relict of Charles Viscount Andover (son of the Earl of Suffolk) and daughter of T. W. Coke, Esq. M. P. for Norfolk: by that lady he has two sons and one daughter.

---

* James.

HISTORICAL MEMOIRS OF

Admiral Sir EDWARD HAMILTON, Bart. K.C.B.

ADDISON, in his treatise on the Love of Fame, says, that the soul, considered abstractedly from the passions, is of a remiss and sedentary nature, slow in its resolves, and languishing in its execution. That the use of the passions is to put it upon action, to awaken the understanding, and make the whole man more vigorous and attentive in the prosecution of his designs. As this is the end of the passions in general, so is it particularly of ambition, which pushes the soul to such actions as are apt to procure honour and reputation to the actor. We may farther observe, that men of the greatest abilities are most fired with this passion; and that, on the contrary, mean and narrow minds are the least actuated by it. Were this not the case, were the desire of fame not very strong, the difficulty of obtaining it, and the danger of losing it even when obtained, would be sufficient to deter an ordinary man from such a pursuit. In a general sense, how few there are who are furnished with abilities to recommend their actions to the admiration of the world, and to distinguish themselves from the rest of mankind! and, in a military sense, how few there are who are furnished with opportunities to signalize themselves and render their names celebrated, even if possessing every personal requisite! Happily for the subject of this Memoir, Fortune threw in his way at least one such opportunity, and the manner in which it was seized by him was sufficient to render his name illustrious among the illustrious, and to secure to his memory a niche in the temple of Fame.

The distinguished subject of this Memoir is the second son of the late Captain Sir John Hamilton, Bart.* and brother to the present Vice-

---

* Sir John Hamilton served under Sir Hugh Palliser on the Newfoundland station during five years, when he commanded the Zephyr and Merlin sloops, from the year 1764 to 1769. He was continued in employment at home until the year 1775, when he was sent to Quebec in the Lizard frigate, with money and clothing for the troops in America, which place, on his arrival, finding besieged, he held a council of war, and formed a battalion of seamen of his own ship's company and of the Hound sloop, and, in conjunction with the military, defended and protected the place. In the spring of 1766 he returned to England, received the thanks of the House of Commons, and

Admiral Sir Charles Hamilton, Bart. He was born on the 12th March, 1772, and may be truly called a son of Neptune, since at the age of seven (in the year 1779) he first went to sea with his father, who then commanded the Hector of 74 guns, and served on board that ship, and the Ramillies, Captain J. Moutray, in the West Indies, till 1781, during which he was in one general action with the French fleet with Admiral Cornwallis, and experienced the dreadful hurricane of 1780. On the return of peace he was sent to complete his education at the Royal Grammar-School at Guildford, where he continued during two years. In 1786 he joined the Standard of 64 guns at Plymouth, and in the spring of 1787 removed to the Calypso of 16 guns, commanded by the late Sir William Mitchell, K.C.B. (who was impressed into the British navy by Sir John Hamilton about the year 1776), and in that sloop proceeded to the Jamaica station. Returning at the end of three years, he served, during the Spanish armament, on board the Melampus frigate, commanded by Captain C. M. Pole, stationed in the Channel. In the Russian armament he served on board the Victory, under the auspices of Lord Hood. When this armament was dismantled, Mr. Hamilton went over to the University of Caen, in Lower Normandy, and afterterwards travelled through part of France, visiting all the seaports along the coast. Soon after his return to England, he went to Portugal, and visited all the ports in that kingdom. While he was thus acquiring a competent knowledge of foreign languages, he did not omit making such nautical observations as might, on a future emergency, be of essential benefit to himself and his country. At the commencement of the war in 1793, he returned to England, and was placed on board the Queen Charlotte, bearing the flag of Lord Howe; and in a short time after was appointed to a lieutenancy in the Dido frigate, commanded by his brother. In the same year (1793) the Dido being ordered to cruise in the North Sea, while off the coast of Norway she fell in with a French brig privateer, mounting 13 guns and carrying 45 men. To elude the Dido's pursuit, the privateer ran ashore beyond the reach of her guns. Sir Charles Hamilton, confiding in that arduous spirit of enterprise which

on the 6th July, in the same year, was created a Baronet of Great Britain. He was at the same time appointed to a guard-ship at Portsmouth, which command he held till 1778, when, after serving in Admiral Keppel's action, he was ordered to the West Indies; but the climate so impaired his health, that he survived but two years, leaving two sons, Charles and Edward.

his brother had on several occasions manifested, sent him, with a boat's crew consisting of only eight men, to take possession of the privateer. After a trivial opposition, Lieutenant Hamilton boarded the enemy's brig and took possession of her, just in time to prevent her taking fire from the combustibles kindled by the enemy as they quitted her. At this moment he could not resist giving way to that manly impulse of vengeance which the base attempt of burning a subdued vessel excited in his mind: he therefore instantly landed on a strange and rugged coast, followed by his brave boat's crew, and, after some resistance and struggle, made thirteen men belonging to the privateer prisoners of war, and conveyed them on board the Dido. In this stage of his services it is unnecessary to make any comments on those dawnings of undaunted spirit and enterprise, which gave indications of what his mind, when enlightened by more mature and practical knowledge, might one day judiciously plan, and successfully put into execution; but the following is an extraordinary circumstance: Lieutenant Hamilton was put on board the prize, which proved to be the Vrai Patriot, and, with two midshipmen and twenty men, ordered to cruise off the Naze of Norway till the winter set in, with a view of watching the entrance of the Sleeve. A few days after his arrival off the Naze, the Nimble cutter left one of the ports on the coast, manned with volunteers from some English vessels there, for the express purpose of capturing the Vrai Patriot, not knowing that she had been captured by the Dido. On her approach she fired her bow guns, when Lieutenant Hamilton hove-to and hoisted the French colours under the English at the main-top-gallant-mast-head: the firing was, however, repeated, when he immediately lowered his topsails, thinking this would have the desired effect; but so convinced was the commander of the Nimble that he was firing at an enemy, that he ran along side, and, without attempting to ascertain what she was, or to listen to Lieutenant Hamilton, who was standing on the gunwale, fired his starboard broadside; then went ahead, wore round, fired a second broadside into the Vrai Patriot; then tacked, brought up along side, and hailed to know who and what she was, and whether she had struck, desiring a boat might be immediately sent on board! Lieutenant Hamilton immediately went on board the Nimble, found all hands at quarters, two of her 12-pound carronades dismounted, two of her men wounded, one with his arm blown to atoms from the bursting of a seven-barrelled gun, and her commander in the greatest possible agitation. On being convinced of his mistake, he was ready to fall on his knees, begged Lieutenant Hamilton would take no notice of it, and offered every assistance in refitting the Vrai Patriot, which had her fore-top-gallant-mast shot away, the sails and rigging much damaged, a twelve-pound shot-hole between wind and water, and about twenty shot in the hull. Fortunately not a man was hurt, owing principally to the precaution taken by Lieutenant Hamilton, who, on the first commencement of the firing, sent the crew below, and seizing the helm himself, steered her during the whole time, and whilst so employed, a double-headed shot struck the fore-part of the wheel, and nearly carried away both his legs. Strange as it may appear, the whole of the proceedings took place at three o'clock p.m. of a fine clear day.

Having continued off the Naze till the autumn, Lieutenant Hamilton proceeded to the river, and having delivered up the prize to the agents in London, rejoined the Dido as second lieutenant, and proceeded in her with convoy to Cadiz and the Mediterranean. On arriving off Majorca, information was received of the evacuation of Toulon by Lord Hood, when the Dido proceeded with her convoy to Leghorn. She was then ordered to blockade the port of Calvi, and Lieutenant Hamilton was occasionally sent in with boats during night to cut off any of the small vessels bringing provisions, which the frigate, being obliged to keep at a greater distance, could not prevent entering. Whilst so employed, one morning, just at the break of day, he was hailed from the shore by some people pretending to be English prisoners, who called out, " Venez à terre, nous sommes des prisoniers Anglois." But his only reply was, " If you are English prisoners, why don't you speak English ?" and seeing that they were armed and within gunshot, he pulled from the shore, but they did not attempt to fire. Shortly afterwards he was ordered to land with 50 seamen from the Dido, 50 from the Aimable, and two 18-pound guns, to lay siege to a martello tower, called Garalatta, a strong position held by the French near Calvi. In this service he was assisted occasionally by the Corsicans. After much labour and difficulty, he succeeded in dragging the guns up a very steep and rough hill, and having mounted them on a battery within point-blank shot of the enemy's works, kept up an incessant fire for nine days, when the enemy capitulated, on condition of being sent to Toulon. As a reward for his great exertions and meritorious services on this occasion, Lord Hood immediately appointed him to the Victory, the flag-ship. He was then sent on shore, under the

orders of Captain Nelson, and was employed during the nights in erecting batteries and mounting guns near the fortifications of Calvi.   On this
service Captain Sericole, R. N. was killed, Nelson lost an eye, Lieutenant
Moutray of the Victory died from fatigue, and Lieutenant Hamilton was
then left acting senior officer, though Nelson, confined to his tent, still
gave all the necessary orders and directions relative to the siege; during
which time Lieutenant Hamilton lodged with him in the same tent, and
for his conduct received the thanks of Nelson, and also of the commander-in-chief.   In consequence of the rapid routine of promotion of
the other lieutenants, Hamilton became first of the Victory on the 7th
of October in the same year.   His advancement to the rank of commander did not, however, take place so soon as he had reason to expect,
on account of Lord Hood's return to England.   It was expected to have
taken place on their arrival at Gibraltar, but Lord Hood did not like to
remove Captain W. Brisbane, who was the son of an old officer, and had
been appointed, on a vacancy, by Admiral Cosby: Lieutenant Hamilton
therefore returned to England as first of the Victory, and continued in
that situation till May 1795, without once putting his foot on shore, except on Chrismas-day, when he dined with his captain, and returned to
the Victory before the gun fired.   He refitted his ship and took her to
St. Helen's; but when on the point of sailing, all his expectations were
blasted by the hauling down of Lord Hood's flag, in consequence of
some misunderstanding between him and the First Lord of the Admiralty*.   After this unexpected event, Lieutenant Hamilton had the mortification to find himself reduced to a junior lieutenant of the Victory,
she being ordered to the Mediterranean as a private ship†.

In the Mediterranean he continued serving in the Victory as junior
lieutenant, first under Admiral Linzee, and then under Admiral Man, in
the action with the French fleet on the 13th July, 1795, when that ship,
and a few others of the van division, bore the brunt of the action, as the
centre and rear could not get up, owing to calms and baffling winds.   On
this occasion Lieutenant Hamilton experienced a second diappointment
in his promotion. On intelligence of the action reaching England, Lord

* It has since been usual to promote all first lieutenants of flag-ships on the hauling
down of the flag.

† It is here necessary to observe, that admirals in chief may give rank to junior lieutenants on board their own ships without distinction of seniority; but in other ships
lieutenants must take rank according to the dates of their commissions.

Spencer, conceiving that he still held the situation of first lieutenant of the Victory, which led into action and was chiefly engaged on that occasion, directed Admiral Hotham to promote the first lieutenant of the Victory, without mentioning his name ; and the first lieutenant was promoted accordingly: but on his lordship being made acquainted with the circumstance, he sent out directions by Sir John Jervis, who was ordered to take the command of the fleet, to promote Lieutenant Hamilton on the first vacancy; which took place in January 1796, when he was appointed to the Comet fire-ship. In that vessel he captured two privateers and several merchant-ships; was also employed at the evacuation of Leghorn, when he received on board several English and emigrant families, brought away all the English vessels, and as much of their property as could be saved from the shortness of the notice; for the French army entering the place, began firing on the Comet before she could get clear of the anchorage. At the evacuation of Corsica his services were equally useful and important, as well as on the first division quitting Porto Ferrajo, when he proceeded down the Mediterranean to join the admiral at Gibraltar. In December following he was dispatched, at a moment's notice, to the West Indies, to inform Admirals Harvey and Parker of a French squadron having sailed from Europe, supposed for that hemisphere. On this occasion he was limited as to the time in which he was to rejoin Sir John Jervis at Lisbon, and in consequence did not chase out of his course. Having accomplished the object of his mission, and on his return from Cape Nicholas Mole, he fell in with, in the night, some Spanish galleons from the Havannah, with several millions of money on board : this circumstance he communicated to Lord St. Vincent on rejoining him, which he did within the prescribed time, at Lisbon, and there found the British fleet, after the action of the 14th February, when his lordship said, " Ha, Hamilton, you are a d—d unlucky fellow! had you been with us on the 14th, you would have burnt the Santissima Trinidad. I know you would have done it, and you would have had the gold chain. But never mind, you shall have your promotion; the San Josef of 120 guns will be vacant in a day or two, and I will promote you into her." This took place in a few days, and was the reward for the great exertion and successful manner in which he had executed his orders across the Atlantic; but Captain Hamilton preferring a more active service, and not wishing to return to England, exchanged with Captain Charles Stuart of the Surprise, a 24-gun corvette, which had been captured a short time before. In the month of April he was dispatched with a large convoy to Newfoundland, and having arrived with them all safe, was sent on a cruise of eight weeks. On his return, he was directed by Admiral Waldegrave to take charge of a large convoy for England; but on his arrival he had the mortification to find that, though he had been promoted to post-rank in the month of March, his commission was not confirmed till June, which occasioned him a loss of three months' rank.

In the spring of 1798, having been refitted, the Surprise was rated as a 28-gun frigate, and placed under the orders of Captain Lawford, to watch the motions of the enemy on the coast of Dunkirk. But in the following autumn, having volunteered his services for employment in the West Indies, Captain Hamilton was ordered thither in charge of a large convoy, and, after seeing them in safety to the different islands, to place himself under the orders of Sir Hyde Parker on the Jamaica station. From this period until the 20th January, 1800, when he quitted the station, he was constantly employed in the most active and hazardous services: he captured, burnt, sunk, or destroyed more than eighty of the enemy's armed vessels and merchant-ships; and notwithstanding prize-property does not always sell to the best advantage, particularly in the West Indies, those vessels and cargoes which he preserved sold for 200,000*l.* on which the charges for law and other expenses amounted to the enormous rate of 33 per cent.! At one time he chased a privateer and her prize into Lagoon, on the north side of Cuba, and having brought-to off the port, sent the boats in under his first lieutenant to bring them out. On approaching the entrance, the boats were repeatedly fired at by two guns landed from the privateer; and Captain Hamilton perceiving, in consequence, a hesitation on the part of the officer to make the attack, ordered the ship to stand into the harbour, and, passing the boats, silenced the battery, entered the port, and captured the privateer and her prize, and also a Spanish schooner; but the wind, which blew directly into the harbour, continuing in that direction, he was prevented from sailing out, neither could he beat nor warp out, in consequence of the extreme narrowness of the harbour, and for two days and a night remained in that situation. Seeing the difficulties under which the Surprise lay, the enemy took courage, remanned the battery, and with the addition of a considerable quantity of musketry, kept up a continual fire within pistol-shot; but as she was fortunately warped up to the entrance of the harbour, under the height on which the enemy had placed their guns, which could not be sufficiently depressed to bear upon her hull, she escaped without any material damage, except in the masts and rigging. In the middle of the second night the land wind having sprung up, the Surprise and her three prizes left the harbour.

His achievement, however, in cutting out, with the boats of his ship and a chosen band of 100 men, the Hermione from the harbour of Porto Cavallo, though surrounded with 200 pieces of cannon mounted on the batteries, stands at the head of desperate enterprises, and is nearly unparalleled in naval annals, as combining the most judicious disposition of attack with the most daring gallantry. The Hermione was formerly a British vessel, commanded by Captain Pigot, the crew of which, in September 1797, had mutinied, murdered the captain and officers, and carried the ship into La Guira, where she was fitted out by the Spanish authorities, and employed in cruising against the English. In October 1799, Captain Hamilton was ordered by Sir Hyde Parker to cruise between the Island of Aruba and Cape St. Romain for the ship in question, which, from information he had received, was expected to sail for the Havannah through that channel. He immediately proceeded off Porto Cavallo, and there had the gratification to find the Hermione lying at the entrance of the port, moored between two very strong batteries, so that it became necessary to proceed with a great deal of precaution; two days were consequently spent in reconnoitring, when Captain Hamilton, having arranged his plan, successfully carried it into execution. The dishonourable circumstances which threw the ship into the possession of the Spaniards, the miserable and lamented fate of her officers, were strong inducements for him to make every effort in his power for her recovery; indeed the honour of his country and the glory of the British navy, as he himself emphatically expressed it, prompted him to make the attempt. The whole crew were animated on the occasion with an eagerness and zeal which raised them apparently almost superior to men; and a well-timed harangue made to them by their captain, contributed to increase it to so great a height, that many instances occurred of pecuniary offers being made by those who were ordered to remain with the ship, on condition of their exchanging stations with such as had been selected to make the attack.

It has been thought by many persons that in boarding the Hermione, Captain Hamilton succeeded in surprising that vessel, and thereby made an easy capture of her; but the following will prove the erroneousness of this opinion: Every thing being arranged, on the night of the 24th October the boats pushed off from the ship, and on arriving within sight of the Hermione, were discovered by the guard-boats at the distance of three-quarters of a mile, and the discharge of their bow-guns and small-arms raised general alarm; and on arriving up with them, two of the English boats stopped to engage them, instead of closely following the boat under Captain Hamilton. The enemy had therefore time to prepare for the encounter; and at that moment, as was afterwards ascertained, those on board the Hermione supposed they were about to be attacked by two frigates, from seeing firing in two directions, and on the boat rowing under the Hermione's bows, her bow and forecastle-guns were all discharged, but fortunately without effect. On crossing the cut-water, the sternfast of a boat at the buoy leading to the forecastle of the Hermione got between the rudder and the stern-post of Captain Hamilton's boat; upon which the coxswain exclaimed, " Sir, the boat's aground!"— " Why, you d—d fool," said Captain Hamilton, " how can the boat be aground and the frigate afloat?" The rudder was immediately after unshipped, and the boat went along side the ship under the starboard bow. Fearing any farther delay, and notwithstanding the other boats had not arrived, Captain Hamilton determined to board where he was— the fore-part of the fore-chains and under the cat-head, although the part which he had originally fixed on was the starboard gangway, which was considered the post of danger. He was the first who attempted to mount the enemy's ship, but having unfortunately got upon the shank of her best bower anchor, which had been weighed that day and was covered with wet mud, both his feet slipped, and his pistol went off in his hand; but he fortunately held on with the lanyards of the fore-mast shrouds, and recovered himself, though with two broken shins. Owing to this accident, he was only second or third on the enemy's forecastle, where he found the fore-sail stretched across, with yard-ropes attached ready to bring it to the yard, and which afforded an excellent screen for the boarders. The moment Captain Hamilton stepped on the forecastle, one of his men fell by his side, wounded by a musket-shot. On advancing to the gangway, the main-deck came into view, with lanterns alight fore and aft, with all the men at their quarters, firing their great guns, still supposing that two frigates were advancing. He now advanced aft on the starboard gangway, with an intention of getting to the general rendezvous, the quarter-deck, and had almost reached it when a tremendous opposition took place, and he was driven back to the forecastle, with several of his men wounded, himself in two places, the knee and thigh : a stand was here made, and the conflict continued without intermission. Had the enemy possessed a few bayonets fixed, the contest might have had a different termination, but fortunately they had not one, and after discharging their muskets, were too closely pressed to reload them, and were consequently obliged to make use of their but-ends. But Captain Hamilton's party, having a few pikes, possessed a great advantage over the enemy, whose front ranks, as they advanced, were in succession either killed or wounded, whilst some jumped overboard, and others down on the main-deck, to avoid a similar fate. Finding that he could not advance on the starboard gangway, and astonished that none of the other boats had yet come to his assistance, and expecting to be overpowered, Captain Hamilton left the break of the gangway in charge of Mr. Maxwell, the gunner, with strict orders to hold it with his party to the last extremity, while he himself went in search of assistance. Seeing some one leaning over the larboard bow, Captain Hamilton hastened up to him, and found it to be Mr. M'Mullin, the surgeon, who was encouraging his boat's crew to board*. Having assembled about a dozen

* It may seem strange that Mr. M'Mullin, a surgeon, should be in such a situation, or that he should have been allowed to proceed on such a service : it was not the intention of Captain Hamilton that he should ; but hearing the names of those called over who were to be of the party, and finding his own omitted, he sent into the cabin, and requested to speak to the captain. This was of course granted ; and on entering, he said, " I find, Captain Hamilton, that my name is not in the list: I hope no conduct of mine has given occasion for this omission ; and I have only to say, that if you will not allow me to accompany you on this occasion, I will immediately blow my brains out, for which purpose I have pistols ready loaded." He had frequently been on boat service, and Captain Hamilton, knowing his resolute character, said, " My dear M'Mullin, you know I have the very highest opinion of you ; that I think you as brave as a lion ; but having no other medical man on board, and fearing we may have too much occasion for your services afterwards, I could not with justice or propriety allow you to go on such a desperate service. Finding you are resolved, and knowing your character too well to think you would make use of an empty threat, I must consent against my own inclination. I must, however, impose one condition on you, which is, that you do not quit the boat you go in till all the boarders are out of her." To this he promised compliance ; but, instead of adhering to it, was the first on the enemy's deck, and was calling to his men *to follow him* when first discovered by Captain Hamilton, who, at this critical period, when assistance was so essentially necessary, thinking it was some one not inclined to do his duty to the utmost, actually pricked him behind with his dirk, before he dis-

of this party, Captain Hamilton placed himself at their head, advanced along the larboard gangway, and gained possession of the quarter-deck, after a severe conflict. But in the eagerness of pursuit, the whole party, forgetting the original orders to rendezvous on the quarter-deck, advanced to follow the beaten party on the starboard gangway, leaving Captain Hamilton with one wounded sailor on the quarter-deck, where he was immediately attacked by four Spaniards, whom he kept at bay, retreating backwards from the binnacle till he came to the coil of the fore-braces, where he made a stand, and was struck by the foremost on the left temple with the but-end of a brass-bound musket, which broke over his head and knocked him half across the deck. Some of his followers soon came to his assistance, and both parties now supporting each other, the enemy was placed between two fires, and the slaughter was consequently great: so closely pressed were they, that many of them jumped overboard to escape that death which they saw awaited them on the deck, whilst most of their officers and comrades fled down the after-ladder. The quarter-deck being now secured, the lieutenant of marines, M. de la Tour du Pin, at that moment boarded, with about a dozen men, on the larboard gangway, from the black cutter under the command of the second lieutenant of the Surprise; and as the enemy was forming a strong force on the main-deck, it became necessary to act against him with promptitude and vigour: the marines having discharged their muskets down the hatchway, immediately after, with bayonets fixed, and accompanied by Mr. M'Mullin and his party, descended the ladder, made a charge upon the enemy, and very soon had fifty prisoners in the captain's cabin. The enemy now formed a strong party under the forecastle, from which there were no means of dislodging them but by firing at them till they surrendered. At this moment Captain Hamilton was informed by one of the men, who understood Spanish, that the enemy were determined to blow the ship up, and were gone down to the magazine for that purpose; and wished him, on that account, to give no quarter. But instead of complying with this request, Captain Hamilton (who was so severely wounded as to render it impossible for him to leave the quarter-deck) ordered all those who had surrendered to be placed

covered who and what he was; but on his turning round and saying that he could not get his men up, the captain begged his pardon, reminded him of the orders he had given him, and then joined him in calling to the men in very peremptory language, when they came over the bow.

in the cabin, with a guard at each side of the deck, and steps were taken for securing the ship. By the original directions, the first lieutenant, in the launch, was to cut the bower cable of the Hermione, and the carpenter, in the jolly-boat, to cut the stern cable, and then both to go ahead and take the ship in tow, men having been ordered to loose the fore and main-top-sails. These orders being executed, and the ship under sail, the batteries on shore, seeing that she had been carried, began a most furious cannonade; but as she was changing her station by the aid of the wind, sails, and boats, no great deal of mischief occurred, owing to the lightness of the wind, which prevented the smoke from rising: several shot, however, struck the ship, one of which, a 24-pounder, went through her under-water, and the leak was with difficulty kept under; and one grape-shot, nearly spent, struck Captain Hamilton on the leg, when in conversation with Mr. M'Mullin, which fell between his feet, and was picked up by the doctor, who exclaimed, " By Jasus, captain, if that gun had had a few more grains of powder, I should just have had to cut your leg off!" During the whole of this time the contest continued on board: the enemy last of all retreated to between-decks, and continued firing till their ammunition was expended; then, and not till then, did they cry for quarter, after a dreadful slaughter, having had 119 killed and 97 wounded. As soon as the Hermione was a little advanced out of the harbour, all hands were required to the pumps and to secure the main-mast, both the stays having been shot away, and the ship making much water: the launch was immediately placed along side from towing, every thing taken out of her, all the prisoners in the cabin placed in her, and she was veered astern in tow; by which means the danger of a rising was lessened, and the whole force of the English on board, about fifty, were engaged in securing the ship, trimming sails, and pumping water. At noon, having brought-to an American schooner bound to Porto Cavallo, the prisoners were put on board of her to be landed.

Such are the particulars of this remarkable and desperate contest, a contest which undoubtedly stands at the head of boat-enterprises; and yet it is scarcely to be believed, that, in a conflict of such a nature, the loss of the assailants was only one officer killed and twelve officers and men wounded. Amongst the latter number was Captain Hamilton, who was wounded in six places, the principal one being on the temple with the but-end of the musket; he also received a severe wound with a sabre on the left thigh, one on the right thigh with a pike, one on the shin-bone with a grape-shot, one finger was much cut, and his loins dreadfully bruised. Next to Captain Hamilton, whose boat's crew successfully contended against the enemy for an hour and a half, the greatest merit was due to Mr. M'Mullin, who rendered the most essential service in taking the quarter-deck, and in going down the after-ladder with the marines to attack the enemy on the main-deck; and so convinced were the two lieutenants (both acting ones) of his useful and meritorious conduct, that they agreed that he should share prize-money with their class*; whilst the officers of the ward-room voted the gunner, Mr. Maxwell, a sword for his distinguished conduct on the occasion. The two lieutenants had nothing to do with the fighting part, owing in a great degree to their falling in with, and being delayed by, the guard-boats: not a man got on board the Hermione from the first lieutenant's boat till after she had been taken in tow, and none from the second lieutenant's until after the quarter-deck was taken possession of: both of their commissions were, however, confirmed. What is here said about those two boats applies also to the red cutter under the command of the boatswain, and the jolly-boat under the direction of the carpenter.

We cannot omit to point out one peculiar feature belonging to this distinguished service—the accession of glory it produced to the country: for if we consider the difficulty of the attempt, we may safely say, that very few have been bolder; if we examine the disposition made to accomplish it, none could be conducted with more wisdom and energy; and it was, if possible, increased by the humanity shewn to the prisoners. It has often been asserted by the enemies of the country, that our naval exploits have been achieved by superiority of numbers, or experienced discipline and skill: here, however, was an instance which raised the glory of the navy, and which was effected by the naked valour of Britons, who killed and wounded more than double their own number of the enemy. In this respect the value and importance of the exploit was considerably augmented; and in every point of view in which it can possibly be regarded, it challenges the most unqualified admiration. Although every individual was emulous and anxiously active to do his duty, it is on Captain Hamilton we must bestow the chief attention; and as generosity and humanity are generally allied to true courage and magnanimity, we cannot resist here giving a trait of his character in this

* He much wished to quit the profession, and to be made a lieutenant; but the admiral would not grant his request. He was afterwards killed in the Mediterranean.

respect. Previous to leaving the Surprise, he promised the men who accompanied him to give them a sum of money, to be divided amongst those who should most distinguish themselves, as a means of emulation; and finding about eight thousand dollars on board the Hermione, he, with the consent of his officers, distributed the whole of it to the most deserving, some of whom received three hundred dollars: thus setting a noble example of valour and generosity, which has ever its due influence on the minds and hearts of British seamen. It is said to be the most consummate virtue which shews that it is above pecuniary considerations when it has the best claim to them; and here is the captain of a frigate, who, forgetting all sober maxims of prudence*, with a noble generosity hazards the loss of life in cutting a prize out of a fortified harbour, scorning all benefit to himself, other than the glory of the act. Honour should always have greater weight than interest. Captain Hamilton's extraordinary gallantry and ability made a deep impression on the public mind† ; and the declared approbation of the sovereign and people followed in the most distinguished marks of favour, the highest boon which can be conferred on military men. His Majesty not only conferred upon him the honour of knighthood by letters patent, but ordered the naval gold medal of merit to be presented to him. The House of Assembly at Jamaica voted him 300*l.* for the purchase of a sword; the common council of London voted him the freedom of their city in a gold

* " Prudence, as it is always wanted, is without great difficulty obtained. It requires neither extensive view nor profound search; but forces itself, by spontaneous impulse, upon a mind neither great nor busy; neither engrossed by vast designs, nor distracted by multiplicity of attention. Prudence operates on life in the same manner as rules on composition; it produces vigilance rather than elevation; rather prevents loss than procures advantage; and often escapes miscarriages, but seldom reaches either power or honour. It quenches that ardour of enterprise by which every thing is done that can claim praise or admiration; and represses that generous temerity which often fails and often succeeds. Rules may obviate faults, but can never confer beauties; and prudence keeps life safe, but does not often make it great or happy. The world is not amazed with prodigies of excellence, but when wit tramples upon rules, and magnanimity breaks the chain of prudence."——JOHNSON.

† Soon after the exploit of the Hermione, one of the seamen belonging to Captain Hamilton's own boat, and who distinguished himself in boarding, was taken up as a deserter from the Swallow sloop, and tried by a court-martial. At his trial it appeared in evidence that he had saved Captain Hamilton's life when he had been knocked down on the quarter-deck and was without arms. The court, in considering the mitigating circumstances in favour of his character, thought proper to recommend him, and to get the sentence of three hundred lashes, ordered to be inflicted, remitted.

box of fifty guineas value; and the committee of Lloyd's voted him 100*l.*
for the purchase of a piece of plate.

In the month of April 1800, Sir Edward, returning to England in the
Jamaica packet for the re-establishment of his health and the cure of his
wounds, was unfortunately captured by a French privateer of 36 guns,
and carried into France. He was sent to Paris, where he was taken
notice of by Buonaparte; and after remaining there six weeks, was exchanged for six midshipmen. On the 25th of October following, being
the anniversary of cutting out the Hermione, Sir Edward, by special invitation, dined at the Mansion-House, when the chamberlain presented
him with the freedom of the city, and in an appropriate speech returned
him the thanks of the corporation for his conduct in an action, which, in
the emphatic language of his commander-in-chief, Sir Hyde Parker, "must
ever rank among the foremost of the gallant actions executed by our navy."

" About this period Earl Spencer, then at the head of the Admiralty,
in consideration of the number and severity of Sir Edward's wounds,
gave directions for a pension of 300*l.* per annum to be settled upon him
for life; but Sir Edward's near relative, the Marquis of Abercorn, persuaded him not to accept of it, stating as a reason, that he had already enriched himself by prize-money, and that it might be made an excuse for
not employing him actively. A short time after, Admiral Lord Hood,
who ever had the interest of the navy at heart, called at his former
lieutenant's house, and finding him at home, said, ' Sir Edward, I hear
you have refused a pension for your wounds, and in so doing I think you
have done an injustice to the service; for recollect, that other officers may
not have the good fortune which you have met with, and this will be a
precedent for refusing pensions to those who may be similarly wounded,
without losing a limb.' Sir Edward's reply was strictly in unison with his
well-known character: ' My lord, I have applied again for service, and I
am more desirous of putting into execution a plan which I have given in
to Lord Spencer, than of receiving a pension.' Here the conversation
ended, and his lordship took his leave. Shortly afterwards, in an interview with Lord Spencer, that nobleman offered Sir Edward an addition
to his armorial bearings, which he also declined. The earl then expressed his regret that Sir Edward's standing on the list of post-captains
would not admit of his soliciting higher honours for him. Sir Edward
was subsequently appointed to the Trent, a fine 36-gun frigate, in which
he occasionally commanded a small squadron employed in the blockade

of Havre de Grace, Cherbourg, and St. Maloe. Whilst on this service he captured and destroyed several of the enemy's privateers and mer-chantmen, and completely stopped the coasting trade on that part of the enemy's shores. On the 3d April, 1801, Sir Edward discovered a large ship, under the protection of two armed vessels, proceeding from Brehat to Plampoul, and immediately dispatched the Trent's boats to attack them. The armed vessels, after sustaining a severe conflict, supported by an incessant fire from five batteries, were driven on the rocks and de-stroyed. The ship was taken possession of in the most spirited manner, and found to be laden principally with corn. Two Frenchmen were lying dead on her decks, and several were drowned; the remainder ef-fected their escape. In the execution of this service, the Trent had but one man killed, who was her captain's coxswain. The only person wounded was Lieutenant Taite of the marines, who lost his right leg, and to whom, on the salvage-money for the recapture being paid, Sir Edward presented one hundred guineas (one moiety of his own share) for the purchase of a sword. With the other half he bought a chro-nometer for his first lieutenant, Mr. George Chamberlayne, who had conducted the enterprise, and presented it to him on the quarter-deck*." He also took and destroyed several other small privateers and coasting vessels, in the performance of which he ran very great risks by keeping so close in shore between the islands and the main, and was carried by the currents so near the forts, that on the clearing up of the fogs and thick weather, he was often within hail; but being perfectly acquainted with the French language, he was enabled to extricate himself.

It is now unfortunately our duty to notice a circumstance which oc-curred in January 1802, and which led to the temporary suspension of Sir Edward from the British navy. The following letter will explain the circumstance:

TRENT, at SPITHEAD, Jan. 17, 1802.

SIR,—In pursuance of your order of yesterday's date, we have been on board his Majesty's ship Trent, and have made a very minute and particular inquiry into the circumstances represented in the letter from the gunner of his Majesty's ship Trent to Evan Nepean, Esq. secretary to the Admiralty, bearing date the 11th January, 1802; and we find Sir Edward Hamilton, captain, had given very particular directions to the first lieutenant, on his going out of the ship on duty, Saturday, the 9th instant, at nine o'clock a. m. that the guns and carriages should

* Marshall.

U 2

be run in, washed, and cleaned; and, on returning on board, he found the guns and carriages on the quarter-deck not cleaned to his expectation; on which he reprimanded the gunner, and ordered him to be tied up in the main-rigging, with four men of his crew, where he remained about an hour; and on his application, the surgeon (who was then walking upon the quarter-deck) went to the captain, and the gunner was then taken down from the rigging. The surgeon reports, on the gunner being taken down, he fell into the arms of the man who cast him off. He appeared to be agitated with considerable tremor from cold; he also appeared to be faint, which the surgeon thought at the time to be feigned.

(Signed,)   A. MITCHELL,

To MARK MILLBANK, *Esq.*   C. M. POLE,

Admiral of the White, Commander-in-Chief, &c.   C. COLLINGWOOD.

A court-martial was consequently held to try him for the same; and Sir Edward, in his defence, said, that motives of humanity had often restricted him from bringing the gunner to a court-martial for repeated intoxication, as he had a family and was an old man. He then stated that he had been in his Majesty's service ever since he was seven years of age, during which time he had been concerned in many engagements with fleets, single ships, and several times on shore. He trusted therefore that as his whole life had been devoted to the service of his king and country, the honourable members of the court would be satisfied, that in his conduct on the 9th January he had not the least intention to hurt the gunner; but that the punishment was given in the heat of violent passion, in consequence of the gunner having disobeyed his orders. After witnesses had been heard for the defence, the court passed the following sentence:

" The court has maturely and considerately weighed the whole of the evidence, as well as Sir Edward Hamilton's defence, and are of opinion, that the charge has been proved, and therefore sentence him to be dismissed his Majesty's service;" which sentence was carried into execution.

It appears that the court-martial which thus dismissed the gallant Sir Edward Hamilton from the service was grounded on the report of a previous court of inquiry; but it is somewhat extraordinary, that Vice-Admiral Sir A. Mitchell, the president, and Rear-Admiral Collingwood, two of the officers who signed the report, should sit as members of the court-martial, although Sir Edward objected to their sitting as his judges, on account of their incompetency. A question therefore arose, whether the court-martial was legally constituted. It is laid down, on unquestionable authority, by writers on military law and naval courts-martial (namely, by Adye and Tytler on military law, and by M'Arthur on naval courts-martial), that the members composing a court of inquiry are incapacitated to sit as judges of a court-martial; on a similar principle as laid down by Blackstone, that the members of the grand jury are not competent to be empanneled into the subsequent petty jury on the same cause. So jealous is the law of the perfect impartiality of jurors, that it is allowed to be a good challenge, that the juror has been heard to give his opinion beforehand that the party is guilty. It is no good answer to say, as Mr. Williamson, in his *Elements of Military Arrangements*, observes, " that the members of a court of inquiry do not in reality decide upon the guilt or innocence of any party, but report only that there is matter for a judicial inquiry, and thus they cannot be said to prejudge the cause." It is a sufficient objection to their admissibility as jurors, that they do not come to try the issue with a free and unprejudiced mind; but, on the contrary, must involuntarily feel themselves under the bias of supporting a preconceived opinion*. But we cannot allow this subject to close here; we must endeavour to place the character of Sir Edward Hamilton in that clear point of view in which it ought to stand, and in which it does stand with all those who are fully acquainted with him and the particulars of that unfortunate affair.—On his appointment to the Trent in the autumn of 1800, he found a gunner belonging to her with whom he had every reason to be satisfied; but in about twelve months afterwards another one made his appearance, stating himself to be the gunner of the ship *by warrant*, and that he had been left behind sick at the hospital at Jamaica, on the return of the Trent from that station when commanded by Captain Otway. Under these circumstances he was of course allowed to resume his station; but it was very soon found that he was, from bodily as well as mental infirmity, incompetent to do the duty of a gunner on board any ship of war, arising from constant and excessive drunkenness; so that the captain was under the necessity of stopping his allowance of rum for some months. This, however, had not the desired effect; and in December 1801, the captain was determined to get rid of him, but, if possible, *without trying him by a court-martial.* The surgeon was consulted on the occasion, who, thinking he was a proper object for invaliding, his name was included in a list for a survey which was to take place in a

* *Naval Chronicle.*

short time on board the Trent. The day for the examination was fixed, and the officers appointed for the examination were going on board, when Mr. Scallon, the first lieutenant*, interceded with Sir Edward in favour of the gunner, by representing to him, that preliminaries of peace being signed, the ship would in all probability be paid off, in which case the gunner, who had served but a short time as a warrant-officer, would, if invalided, be deprived in ordinary of certain advantages, begged that his name might be erased from the list, and hoped that this mark of kindness would operate as an inducement for him to behave better during the short time they were expected to remain together. This was consented to by Sir Edward from the best of motives, and things continued in the same state till the 9th January, 1802, when, on his leaving the ship at nine a. m. on service, he gave particular directions that the carronades should be run in, the slides and carriages properly cleaned, and the double breechings examined, together with some other particulars respecting the guns, which had been much neglected by the gunner. On his return at noon, he was much surprised to find that *not one* of his orders had been attended to; but that the gunner had satisfied himself by throwing a few buckets of salt water over the guns, without even casting loose the double breechings and tackles, which not only did no good, but tended to rot and destroy the security of the guns: and we doubt not that similar carelessness was the cause of many misfortunes and disasters during the war; for the ropes being wetted in that position, of course they would not become dry during the day, which would naturally cause them to decay. Vexed and somewhat irritated at such neglect and inattention, he expressed his anger and surprise to the first lieutenant that his orders had not been obeyed, and desired him to place the gunner and his crew, four in number, in the main rigging, and then retired to his cabin. In about half an hour the surgeon, who had been walking on the quarter-deck, went to the captain, and informed him that the gunner had expressed his wish to be allowed to come down, as he was unable to stand the cold. Permission was no sooner asked than it was granted, and the gunner was taken down. In a few days afterwards the gunner, at the instigation of some others of his class, wrote for a court-martial to try Sir Edward for the act; and the consequence was, that three admirals, whose report we have inserted above, went on board the Trent to inquire into the circumstances. But in the mean time

* Now commander.

the gunner, conscious of the leniency which had been practised towards him, wrote to the Admiralty, acknowledging his general misconduct, and requested permission to withdraw his letter from the court-martial. But this the Board would not allow, and the result was as we have stated. Sir Edward was shortly after sent for by the First Lord of the Admiralty, Lord St. Vincent, who endeavoured to sooth his feelings by fine compliments, expressed his sorrow for the event, but said that *it was necessary at the moment;* promised that he should soon be reinstated, and that he should then have a frigate to cruise where he liked; but advised him in the mean time to keep himself quiet, and be easy as to the result. Keep himself quiet! Why, is it possible for any man of feeling and spirit to keep himself quiet under such circumstances? Instead of such a sentence being *necessary at that moment,* the time was, of all others, favourable to a mild consideration of the circumstance: preliminaries of peace had been signed; and, in fact, it was owing to this circumstance that the affair took place; for had it not been for that, the man would have been previously invalided and sent ashore. Sir Edward felt the harshness of the sentence, and replied to his lordship that he could not, under existing circumstances, accept of another command; that he had served too zealously, and could not expect any pleasure or satisfaction by again serving under the then administration of affairs; but requested permission, on being restored, to accept a flag in the Russian navy. When his lordship replied, " No; never will I advise his Majesty to grant you any such permission." The conference then terminated; and in the month of June following, his Majesty restored Sir Edward to his rank and station in the British navy. We must, however, here observe, that previous to his being reinstated, the form of the memorial he was to present to his Majesty was sent to him from the Admiralty, beginning with a clause, *that he did not intend to call in question the legality of the court-martial by which he had been tried;* a clear proof of the view taken of it by the legal advisers of the Board.

It is the farthest from our wish or inclination to defend any act of tyranny or oppression by whomsoever committed; but there are some errors and imperfections, which, though attended with fatal consequences, are still often viewed with respect, or at least every allowance is made for them; and though they may be condemned by the severe moralist, the more moderate and considerate will not only regret the circumstance, but endeavour to palliate its enormity. We do not mean to assert, that Sir

Edward was perfectly justifiable in the step he took to punish the gunner; but it is very clear that it was not done wantonly; that it was done in a moment of irritation, caused by the man's neglect of duty, and formed no part of Sir Edward's general conduct or character: on the contrary, we confidently believe that it was entirely owing tò his forbearance and leniency to that individual that the misfortune happened. Had he been of a harsh and arbitrary disposition, he would never have taken the trouble for months together to reclaim him, but would have had him tried by a court-martial, and dismissed the ship at once. Is it any wonder then that he should, after all his lenity and delay of punishment for repeated irregularities, on finding all his endeavours fail in their effect, and his orders neglected, so far forget himself as to take the punishment into his own hands? Plutarch says, " the weakness of human nature is such, that we can produce no excellence without some taint of imperfection, even in minds the best formed for virtue. The traces of occasional oversight and forgetfulness are frequently discovered in those individuals whose natures have been dashed with a gigantic sublimity; and Providence for the most part sets us upon a level, and observes a kind of proportion in its dispensations towards us. If it renders us eminent in one accomplishment, it generally leaves us defective in another, and seems careful rather of preserving us from meanness and deficiency, than in making us pure and perfect." There are, however, but few instances of imperfection more mortifying to our pride, than those incidental ones which occur in illustrious and distinguished characters: when we see that men whose actions have been the admiration of the world, or at whose nod and command nations have submitted to the yoke, who have been held up as the pageants of human greatness, but who were still subject to failings, we cannot wonder at the frailty manifested in the instance before us. It only behoves us to watch the advance of such passions with extreme care, and to check their progress with fortitude and perseverance.

One word with regard to the sentence passed upon Sir Edward. If it could have been proved, if it had been attempted to shew, that his conduct in that instance was of frequent occurrence, we should not complain of its severity; but when, on the contrary, his character for humanity was unimpeached and unimpeachable, that he should be dismissed the service for such an isolated act, proceeding, as it did, from the best of motives, was, we must say, a harsh, an unnecessary and excessive punishment. We have taken a considerable degree of pains to make ourselves acquainted with the particulars of this case and the general character of Sir Edward, and we cannot help thinking that a great share of blame attached itself to the first lieutenant of the Trent: in the absence of the captain, it was his duty to see the orders which he left on going out of the ship executed; and if he had done so, the circumstance would not of course have occurred. We think him also remiss in another point of view: from what we have heard of similar cases, it is very usual for the first lieutenant, or for the captain, when an admiral is on board, on receiving any such hasty orders for punishment, to delay it, and to put it off till the admiral's or captain's anger has abated; so that the individual escapes. Admiral Penrose, in his pamphlet on Corporal Punishment, mentions this particularly, and cites a strong case at page 18. Had Lieutenant Scallon acted with such discretion, we think we may safely say, that Sir Edward would never have inquired whether the punishment had been inflicted; at all events, it would not have taken place in an irregular manner.

From what we have heard, we also much doubt whether the sentence passed upon Sir Edward did not decrease that strict attention which had been paid by captains to the gunner's department; and was, consequently, the cause of some of those misfortunes which attended subsequent actions. We are amongst those who believe, that the whole prosperity of this country depends upon its naval superiority; and though we condemn all tyrannical, harsh, or unnecessary severity, we should be sorry to see captains deprived of that just and necessary power with which they are invested, or the good old discipline of the service relaxed or given up, especially upon any of the canting reasons which some have advanced.

Having now, we trust, placed this circumstance in a just and correct point of view, we have only to notice a few observations which we have heard respecting Sir Edward's general professional character, and a little anecdote, which places his character as a man in a very interesting light. His zeal for that service of which he is a member has been described to us as of an unbounded nature, equal to the most ardent passion; that the ships he commanded were never surpassed in their equipment either for manœuvring or fighting; and that he never left a ship without the regret of all belonging to her. That, during his services, he never called but one court-martial (on a boatswain for stealing canvas out of the ship on a foreign station); that he never parted with any officer whatever on account of quarrel or disagreement; and that fewer punishments took place on board the Surprise and Trent, during the time he commanded them, than in almost any other ships in the navy.

The little anecdote to which we have alluded is as follows: In the year 1800, Mr. Halford, who was then first lieutenant of the Arethusa, and had been presented with a pair of pistols by the ship's company, was dismissed the service by a court-martial, in consequence of a private quarrel with the third lieutenant, a very young lad, who had just been promoted. Taking a warm interest in the welfare of an old friend and messmate, Sir Edward, on hearing of his misfortune, immediately waited on the First Lord of the Admiralty (Lord Spencer), and represented Lieutenant Halford's case to his lordship; stated his merits as an officer, a seaman, and a gentleman, and offered to take him as his own first lieutenant, if his lordship would reinstate him in the service. Lord Spencer promised compliance with this disinterested act of friendship, on condition that Lieutenant Halford should procure a certificate of general good conduct from the captain of the Arethusa. But his pride and spirit were hurt, and he would not consent to ask a favour of one by whom he considered himself injured. Sir Edward's kind intentions were therefore unavailing; but Lieutenant Halford having afterwards procured an appointment to an East-India ship, and being deficient of the means necessary to fit himself out, applied to one who had so unequivocally proved himself his friend, and a hundred pounds was most generously placed at his disposal. He continued in India for ten years, when he died; but having by industry and perseverance acquired some property, his relatives, into whose hands it fell, having heard of the circumstance, begged Sir Edward to accept of the hundred pounds; and it was accordingly presented to him about the year 1815.

During the greater part of the last war Sir Edward commanded the Mary yacht. He was nominated a K. C. B. in January 1815; appointed to the Prince Regent yacht in the following December, and created a baronet of Great Britain, as a reward for his meritorious services, in December 1818. On the 19th July, 1821, he was advanced to the rank of rear-admiral. Sir Edward is a member of the University of Cambridge, being a Master of Arts belonging to Emanuel College. He married, in November 1804, a daughter of J. Macnamara, Esq. and niece of Rear-Admiral James Macnamara, by which lady he has issue two sons and two daughters.

HISTORICAL MEMOIRS OF
ADMIRAL JAMES WALKER, C. B.

WHOEVER attentively considers the naval history of England, particularly during the reign of George III. will perceive, that in proportion as her enemies increased, did she increase in her exertions; and not increase in her exertions only, but the genius and ability of her officers kept pace with her necessities. So that it was made manifest, that the acme of public difficulty is the crisis of public improvement; that a sense of danger inspires men with a zeal and enthusiasm which enable them to surmount the obstacles by which they are surrounded, and to perform actions which, under other circumstances, they would not contemplate. Neither the threats of the enemy, nor their superiority of numbers, have ever intimidated the British navy, the merits of whose officers are celebrated throughout the world. Amongst them the deeds of but few deserve to be more amply recorded than those of Admiral Walker, whose whole life has been devoted to the service of his country; and who has, upon every occasion, displayed so much zeal, ability, and science, as to acquire him the esteem and confidence of all those with whom he acted. He is descended, on his father's side, from the old and respectable family of the Walkers (Barons) of St. Fort, in Fifeshire, N.B.; and on that of his mother, from the ancient and noble family of Leslie, being grandson of Alexander the fifth Earl of Levin and Melville. He entered the navy in 1776 as a midshipman on board the Southampton frigate, Captain Garnier, in which ship he served during a period of five years, principally on the Jamaica and Channel stations. While in the West Indies he was frequently sent with her boats on the dangerous service of attacking and cutting out vessels from under the enemy's batteries, as well as performing other active duties. In 1780, the Southampton captured, off Portland, a French privateer of 18 guns and 80 men. Mr. Walker was sent on board to assist in removing the prisoners, after having accomplished which, he remained on board, in the hope of saving the ship by assisting in bailing and pumping, she being in danger of sinking, in consequence of having received two shots between wind and water; but notwithstanding all the efforts made to save her, she suddenly sunk, and Mr.

X 2

Walker was precipitated into the sea, and in the utmost danger of being carried down in the vortex: from this perilous situation he was providentially rescued by the boats coming to his assistance, but not until he had been in the water more than ten minutes. He afterwards sailed to the West Indies, and on the 18th of June, 1781, was promoted to the rank of lieutenant in the Princess Royal, a second rate, which soon afterwards sailed for England with a large convoy, which attempted the Windward passage; but after having been a month at sea, and finding it impracticable to accomplish that object, they returned to Jamaica, when, finding the Torbay 74 about to sail for North America, where Mr. Walker's uncle, the Hon. General Leslie, then was third in command, Mr. Walker exchanged into her, and served in her under Sir Samuel Hood during the splendid operations at St. Christopher's, and in the memorable engagement between Sir George B. Rodney and the Count de Grasse, April 12, 1782, on which latter occasion she had 10 men killed and 25 wounded. The Torbay was at that time commanded by that excellent officer and worthy man Captain Gidoin, from whom Mr. Walker experienced all the kindness of a father, and who retained for him during the whole of his life the warmest friendship. Mr. Walker was also under the particular patronage of Sir George Rodney, who was the intimate friend of his father, and was the third on his list for promotion when that gallant officer was superseded by the arrival of Admiral Pigott. In the month of October following, the Torbay, being on a cruise off the east end of Hispaniola, in company with the London of 98 guns and the Badger sloop, fell in with Le Scipion, a French 74, which stood towards them, and when at about two leagues distance, made the British private signal; but on its being answered, she tacked and made off under all sail, and it was not till after a most arduous chase, which lasted from ten in the morning until sunset, that they could bring her to close action: when that object was accomplished, the action was maintained with very great skill and bravery by the French commander, Monsieur Grimoire, who succeeded in clearing the Scipion from the London, which had got on board him, and made for the shore. The London, which had been considerably damaged in the action, and had suffered severely in killed and wounded, bore up in the night for Jamaica; and the Torbay and Badger followed up the enemy all night and until morn next day, when, as the Torbay was about to bring her to action, to avoid capture, she bore up and ran ashore in Samana Bay, where she was totally lost.

At the peace of 1783, the Torbay being paid off, Lieutenant Walker went to the Continent, and spent some years in France, Italy, and Germany. While at Vienna in 1787, he was informed by his friend, Sir Robert Murray Keith, then ambassador at that court, of the fitting out of the Dutch armament; and he lost no time in setting off for England, to solicit employment: but he met with an adventure on this journey which had nearly deprived the navy of his services for ever, and from which he narrowly escaped with his life. While travelling through the forest near to the town of Aschaffenbourg, the diligence was attacked by ten armed men, who fired into the carriage, demanding at the same time the money of the passengers. Lieutenant Walker rushed into the midst of them; but as he received no assistance from his fellow-travellers, it may easily be supposed he could not long resist so powerful a force as that opposed to him; and after being robbed, and, as the villains believed, murdered, they threw him into a ditch by the side of the road. But after a time he came to his senses, and attempted to get into the road again; but being perceived by one of the banditti, the wretch gave him a severe cut on the head with a sabre, and kicked him into the ditch again. In this condition he remained till the party rode off, after having robbed the diligence of 800*l.* which some farmers were sending to Aschaffenbourg to pay their rents, and which the banditti had got information of. He was then lifted into the diligence, his wounds tied up as well as they could be under such circumstances, and as soon as the party arrived at Aschaffenbourg, the passengers immediately gave notice to the authorities, of the place where the disaster had befallen them, and of the dangerous state in which a young British officer was lying in consequence of the spirited resistance he had made. On learning this, the authorities gave directions that Lieutenant Walker should be attended by the most skilful surgeons of the place, that every attention should be paid to him, and that he should stay as long as he conceived it necessary for the recovery of his health, without being at the slightest personal expense. His anxiety to reach England, however, made him resume his journey too soon, and he was obliged to remain ten days at Frankfort, on account of the wound in his head; and he had much difficulty in preventing the surgeons from trepanning him, but he declared he would rather die than suffer an operation that would prevent his following up a profession which he was enthusiastically attached to. Here he was waited upon by the lodge of Freemasons, who offered him any money he might require; and after accepting what he thought necessary for his journey, he proceeded to Mentz, where he was presented to the prince-bishop, who paid him every attention, and who, on Lieutenant Walker leaving the place, gave him a very handsome letter, describing the adventure that had detained him so long from his services at home, and speaking in high terms of his bravery on the occasion. An occurrence of the kind above-mentioned had not taken place for more than twelve years; and the search made after the robbers was so vigilant, that they were all taken, and two years afterwards Mr. Walker received half the money he had been robbed of. Upon his arrival in England, finding that tranquillity was restored in Holland, and that the sending out the armament was abandoned, he returned to the Continent. When the war broke out in 1788 between Russia and Turkey, he was offered the command of a ship belonging to the former power; but was obliged to decline it, as he could not obtain permission to accept of it from the British government.

In 1789 Lieutenant Walker was appointed to the Champion on the Scotch station, from which he removed to the Winchelsea; and on the breaking out of the war in 1793, he commissioned the Boyne of 98 guns, intended for the flag of Rear-Admiral Affleck. From the Boyne he was appointed to the Niger, which was one of the repeating frigates to the fleet under Earl Howe in the battle of the 1st of June, 1794; and Mr. Walker was soon after advanced to the rank of commander for his conduct as first-lieutenant and signal-officer on that glorious day. Immediately after his promotion to the rank of commander, he went as a volunteer with his late captain, the Hon. A. K. Legge, and his old messmate of the Niger, in the Latona. At Christmas, in the same year, he was appointed to act as captain of the Gibraltar, an 80-gun ship (under orders for the Mediterranean), when, unfortunately for him and to his great disappointment, just as he was setting out to join her, intelligence was received at the Admiralty, that the French fleet had put to sea in great force, which rendered it necessary to strengthen the grand fleet. The Gibraltar was consequently attached to it, and it was considered right that an older officer should be appointed to her: Captain Walker was, however, noted for the first vacant sloop of war, and soon after appointed to the Terror bomb. In the month of June following he was ordered to assume the temporary command of the Trusty of 50 guns, and to escort five sail of East Indiamen to a certain latitude, when, *after having seen them in safety*, he was to return to Spithead. For two or three days after he reached the prescribed latitude, the wind continuing at S. W. he did not consider his charge *in safety*, and consequently the *spirit of his orders* not completed : he therefore thought it his duty to continue with the Indiamen till the wind became more favourable; immediately after which he parted company, and proceeded towards England.   The next day he spoke a Dane from Cadiz, who acquainted him that about forty sail of English merchant-vessels had been lying there some time for want of convoy, and under heavy demurrage.   This information being confirmed shortly after by a Swede, also from that port, Captain Walker, conceiving that he would only be fulfilling his duty by protecting the commercial interests of his country, took upon himself to touch at Cadiz, and to take charge of all the British vessels lying there, amounting to thirty-three sail of merchantmen and three transports, the whole of which he convoyed in perfect safety to England.   Two memorials of the Spanish merchants residing in London, presented in favour of Captain Walker, stated the value of this fleet to amount to upwards of a million sterling, which, but for his active exertions, would have been left in great danger, *at a most critical time, when the Spaniards were negociating a peace with France.*   During the Trusty's stay at Cadiz, five of her officers were arrested by orders from the governor, for carrying money off to the ship on account of the merchants; and the Spanish government made such strong representations on the subject to the British ministry, that it was deemed politic to bring Captain Walker to a court-martial on his return to Portsmouth; and notwithstanding the very important service he had rendered to the mercantile interests of the country, it being found that he acted *without orders, he was broke !* Under the bitter feelings caused by this severe sentence, which cruelly cut him off from the service at the beginning of his career as a commander, he had the no small consolation in his misfortune of knowing, that the Lords Commissioners of the Admiralty duly appreciated the motives that had actuated his conduct, and warmly interested themselves in his favour; and by their directions he embarked for the West Indies in one of the ships belonging to the fleet of Admiral Christian.   The difficulties this fleet experienced during a succession of heavy gales for the space of six weeks, its consequent dispersion and return to Spithead, we have already noticed in the Memoir of his life.   After Captain Walker's return with this fleet, he was given to understand by the Admiralty, that his interests would be best answered by remaining at home; and in March 1797, he was reinstated in his rank of commander; the Spanish ambassador having received orders from his court to request of the British government that the whole transaction might be forgotten, and regarded as *non avenue.*

In the summer of 1797, while the mutiny raged at the Nore, he suggested a plan for attacking the Sandwich by means of the smasher guns invented by his relation, the late General Melville, and volunteered to conduct the enterprise in person. It so happened that a plan exactly similar had been adopted not an hour before by the Board of Admiralty; and Captain Walker was immediately appointed to the command of a division of gun-boats fitting at Woolwich for the purpose of acting against the mutineers, and being the first officer who arrived at his post, Sir Erasmus Gower handsomely offered him his choice out of upwards of thirty gun-vessels. He immediately took his command, and repaired to Gravesend; but before he arrived there the mutineers had surrendered at discretion. He was then appointed acting-captain of the Garland, and ordered to escort the trade bound to the Baltic as far as Elsinore. On his return from that service he was appointed to succeed his cousin, the Earl of Northesk, in the Monmouth of 64 guns, employed in the North Sea under the orders of Admiral Duncan.

When Captain Walker took the command of the Monmouth, he found her crew in a state of total insubordination, having been the most mutinous of all the ships at the Nore; and to any but an officer of more than common energy, the task of commanding such a crew, consisting of four hundred and twenty men (the Monmouth being seventy short of complement), would have been found very difficult; but by the efficacious system adopted by Captain Walker, and the determined resolution he displayed in adhering inflexibly to it, he had the satisfaction, in the course of a fortnight, to see his refractory crew restored to a perfect state of discipline and to a sense of their duty. On the memorable 11th October, 1797, when the Monmouth was bearing down on the enemy's fleet under all sail, Captain Walker turned the hands up, and addressed them in the following energetic words: " Now, my lads, you see your enemy; I shall lay you close aboard, and thus give you an opportunity of washing the stain off your characters in the blood of your foes. Go to your quarters and do *your duty!*" So well were the gallant captain's orders obeyed, that the Monmouth was closely engaged for an hour and a half with the Delft and Alkmaar, both of which were compelled to surrender. The latter was taken in tow immediately afterwards by the Monmouth; and notwithstanding the heavy gale that ensued, during which, while off the Hook of Holland, they could not weather the land on either tack for two days, Captain Walker never cast off his tow, but persevered in anxious charge of her, till he had the good fortune on the fifth day, the wind having providentially veered to the northward on the third, to anchor her in Yarmouth roads, but with all her masts gone, having made a great deal of water, and having been obliged to throw twenty-two of her guns overboard. The Delft, the other prize, was not so fortunate, she having, while in tow of the Veteran, foundered, and two hundred prisoners and two of our marines perished in her. For his gallant conduct in the battle off Camperdown, he was immediately confirmed in the rank of post-captain and the command of the Monmouth, whose loss on that glorious occasion was 5 men, including a lieutenant, killed, and 22 wounded; he was also honoured with the naval gold medal and the thanks of Parliament. On the 19th December following, Captain Walker assisted at the ceremony of depositing the colours taken from the enemy by Lords Howe, St. Vincent, Duncan, &c. in the cathedral of St. Paul. He subsequently commanded in succession the Veteran 64, Braakel 56, Prince George 98, Prince of the same force, and Isis of 50 guns. The Isis formed part of Lord Nelson's division in the sanguinary battle off Copenhagen, April 2, 1801, and was declared by the hero himself to have borne a most gallant and distinguished part in the desperate conflict; in the very heat of which Lord Nelson sailed past the Isis, took off his hat, waved it, and cried, " Well done, brave Walker ! go on as you have begun; nothing can be better." This he afterwards told Captain Walker, for he was too arduously engaged to be sensible of the honour done him at the time. The morning after the action, his lordship came along side the Isis; but on finding that Captain Walker was not on board (he having not half an hour before quitted his ship for the purpose of paying his respects and offering his congratulation to his lordship on the glorious results of the day), he begged the officers to excuse his ascending the ship, " being," as he jocosely said, " but a poor one-armed sailor;" but desired them to tell their captain that he left his ship expressly to offer him, his officers and ship's company, his warmest thanks for the gallant and decided part they had had in the glorious victory of the preceding day; and he farther desired, that the crew might be called upon deck and be informed of what he said. In this action the Isis was most warmly engaged for four hours and a half with two of the enemy's heaviest block-ships, moored about two cables' length from each other, and a battery of 14 guns and two howitzers in the interval between them, at the distance of about three cables' length. The loss she sustained, considering the smallness of her crew, was immense; it amounted to no less than 9 officers and 103 men killed and wounded.

In the ensuing summer Captain Walker obtained the command of the Tartar frigate, and was ordered to convoy a fleet of merchantmen to the Jamaica station, where he received a commission from the Admiralty, appointing him to the command of the Vanguard 74. On the renewal of hostilities in 1803, we find Captain Walker actively employed in the blockade of St. Domingo: while on that service, in company with a squadron under the orders of Captain Bayntun, he captured the Creole frigate of 44 guns, having on board the French general Morgan and 530 troops, bound to Port-au-Prince; and subsequently, in company with a squadron under the command of Captain Loring, he captured the Duquesne of 74 guns, bearing the broad pendant of Commodore Que-rangal: the latter had slipped out of Cape François during a heavy squall; but the weather soon moderating, she was discovered and imme-diately pursued by the squadron. After a chase of twenty hours Cap-tain Walker came up with her, and after a running fight of an hour and a half, during which he had two men killed, the mizen-top-sail and fore-top-gallant-yards shot away, as well as the fore-top-mast-studding-sail brought down, he ran the Vanguard close abreast of the Duquesne and compelled her to strike. After escorting his prize, and a French schooner of 16 guns and 60 men, which had been taken by the squa-dron near Port-au-Paix, to Jamaica, he was immediately sent by Admiral Sir John Duckworth upon a special service to Dessalines, the black general, at Gonaïves. This chief had openly declared his intention of attacking St. Marc, in the immediate neighbourhood, and of putting to death every white man in the place. To divert him from this sangui-nary project, Captain Walker engaged himself to summon St. Marc to surrender, provided Dessalines would, on his part, agree to allow the garrison to retreat to Cape Nicolo Mole without molesting them. This he having promised, Captain Walker accordingly sailed to St. Marc, and, on the 1st October, summoned it to surrender. On the following day the governor, General d'Henin, sent off an officer to treat with him; and a convention was accordingly entered into, by which the French gar-rison, the Papillon corvette, a transport-brig, and a schooner laden with ammunition, were surrendered to the Vanguard. The situation of the French soldiers was the most deplorable that can be conceived; they were literally reduced to skeletons, having long had nothing but horse-flesh to subsist upon*. Captain Walker having reason to doubt the good faith of Dessalines in his agreement respecting these unfortunate men, humanely took them all on board his own ship, as a sure way of securing them from his vengeance, and landed them in safety at Cape Nicolo Mole. Though highly gratifying to his feelings to have thus saved so many fellow-creatures from a cruel death, this act of humanity, however, proved a serious injury to Captain Walker in a pecuniary point of view; for, being in all 1100 men, and remaining on board the Vanguard, her prizes and boats, for eight days, his provisions were exhausted, and he was compelled to return to port for a supply at the critical moment when Cape François was about to surrender, thus losing prize-money to a considerable amount. However, during the fourteen weeks that he remained off that place, he had the satisfaction of considerably hastening so desirable an event, not only by his exertions in maintaining a most vigorous blockade, but by keeping up a constant correspondence with the black chiefs, and informing them of every occurrence at the Cape. In this place it may be apposite to observe, that while at St. Marc, he was so forcibly struck with the representations of General Dessalines as to the consequences resulting from the desertion of one of his chiefs with a body of 2000 men, which had taken possession of the plain near Cape François, and were by that means enabled to furnish the European French in the city with ground provisions and fruit, thereby materially adding to their resources and enabling them to protract their surrender; that, without hesitation, he took upon himself the responsibility of supplying him with powder, the total want of which Dessalines assured him had alone prevented him from attacking them. In consequence of this supply, General Christophe, the late Emperor of Hayti, then second in command of the blacks, took the field, routed the deserters, and hanged their leaders. It is beyond all question that this event accelerated the surrender of General Rochambeau at least six weeks or two months.

Captain Walker's next appointment was to the Duquesne, which ship, as already stated, he had taken. Soon after he took the command of her, he returned to England, having 160 officers and soldiers on board who

---

* See official letter, *Naval Chronology*, vol. I. p. 19.

had formerly belonged to General Moreau's army; and it is but justice to those officers and men to say, that, although Captain Walker had but 160 seamen in the Duquesne, a circumstance which made the utmost vigilance necessary and naturally caused him great anxiety, nothing could be more orderly and respectful than their conduct during a period of nearly three months that they continued on board. The Duquesne being in want of extensive repairs, was paid off soon after her arrival, and Captain Walker was appointed to the Thalia frigate at Deptford. When he reached the Nore, finding there was no immediate prospect of being manned, he proposed to the Admiralty to go to sea as he was, with the hope of falling in with the homeward-bound Greenlandmen and getting manned from them; which being approved of, he sailed for the North Seas, 120 men short of his complement. After cruising there three months, he was ordered to Spithead, where, being completely manned, was sent to the East Indies with treasure, and to convoy two valuable ships, which also carried treasure to Calcutta. This voyage was so safely and expeditiously made, that Captain Walker returned to Spithead the very day ten months that he had sailed from it. Although the season was far advanced, he was ordered to take two frigates under his command and protect a convoy to Quebec; from whence he could not sail on his return to England with a convoy until the 1st December, in consequence of heavy gales blowing up the river. Off the banks of Newfoundland so violent a gale of wind came on, that the Thalia ran twelve hundred and ten miles under bare poles in five days, during which she was pooped three times. A fortnight after his arrival at Spithead he was sent on the Guernsey station, under the command of Sir Edmund Nagle, when, being the senior captain, a squadron of three frigates and an 18-gun brig was put under his command, to watch the enemy's force in St. Malo. During the months of January and February he kept the sea on this dangerous coast, half of which time it blew so hard a gale from the eastward that the fore and mizen-top-sails were in. October following Captain Walker was appointed to the Bedford 74, in which ship he accompanied Sir W. Sidney Smith to Lisbon, and was by him selected to escort the royal family of Portugal to the Brazils, along with Commodore Moore, in the Marlborough, the London, and the Monarch. When off Madeira the fleet was dispersed by a heavy gale of wind; but two days after, the Bedford rejoined the two Portuguese line-of-battle ships in which the royal family were embarked, and was the only

English ship with them during thirteen weeks. The crews of the Portuguese ships having become sickly, the Prince Regent, by Captain Walker's advice, put into St. Salvador for refreshments. While there his royal highness determined upon reviving the military order of the Tower and Sword, that he might create Captain Walker a Knight-Commander, in consideration of his unremitted attention to the Portuguese fleet during a long and tempestuous voyage; and at a public breakfast, given by Captain Walker to the royal family and their court, his royal highness, immediately after having invested himself with the order, created Captain Walker a Knight-Commander of it; who thus stands the senior Knight-Commander of the Tower and Sword. Captain Walker accompanied the royal family to Rio Janeiro, and, during a residence of two years there, he had the honour of enjoying the friendship and entire confidence of the Prince Regent, who, upon his departure, testified the most affectionate regret at parting with him, and with his own hand presented to him his portrait, set with brilliants, and a valuable diamond ring; and gave him a letter, of which the following is a copy, to be presented to his Majesty George the Third, recommending, in the strongest terms, Captain Walker to his Majesty's consideration, as an officer who had proved himself worthy of his (the Prince Regent of Portugal's) highest esteem, from his uniform respect, kindness, and prudence during his residence at his court. It is difficult to account for this letter, and two others equally strong in favour of Captain Walker, not being followed by some marks of attention; but from whatever cause it arose, it is certain that Captain Walker derived no advantage from them.

Sir, my Brother and Cousin,—Knowing all the extent of the friendship and intimate connection which unites me to your Majesty, I cannot resist the feelings of my heart, which induce me to recommend to your Majesty Captain Walker of the Bedford, who is going to England into your Majesty's presence, and who has so highly distinguished himself in my service by his zeal and by his attachment to my person, having never separated himself from me during my voyage, which I shall not forget at any time; and it being my intention always to give him the most distinguished marks of my esteem, I flatter myself that your Majesty will be pleased that I address myself to you by this same able officer, who leaves so much regret behind him on account of his excellent conduct; and that in doing justice, I avail myself of the opportunity of assuring your Majesty again, how much I flatter myself every day more and more that our close alliance will make the happiness of our reciprocal subjects and the despair of our enemies.

I am, with the most perfect friendship, sir, my brother and cousin, your good brother and cousin,   JOHN.

RIO JANEIRO, *Jan.* 11, 1809.

Soon after Captain Walker's return to England he was sent, at his own request, to join the North-Sea fleet. While on that service, being in Hoazely Bay, under Admiral Ferrier, in company with three ships of the line, they, on the 20th January, 1814, experienced a heavy gale, accompanied with hazy weather and sleet: the Bedford rode out the night, but at eight next morning she parted; the sheet-anchor was immediately let go, but in snubbing it went, as did also the lee cable, thus leaving the ship in a most perilous situation and in momentary danger of running foul of the Cumberland; and had it not been for the superior skill displayed by him, both the Bedford and the Cumberland, with their crews, amounting to between 11 and 1200 men, must inevitably have perished. In this critical situation Captain Walker found the practice he had uniformly adopted, of stowing the jib close to the cap, prove of the most essential service; for, on being instantly set and standing, the ship wore almost clear of the Cumberland, but unfortunately not entirely so, the bowsprit of the Cumberland coming over the break of the Bedford's poop, by which it was carried away, and all her masts went in succession; the Bedford sustaining comparatively but little damage, and owing to her having fresh way, the ships fortunately separated. This happy escape from a situation that threatened utter destruction was hailed by the squadron, who had witnessed the accident, and were watching, in breathless apprehension, the consequences of it, with three cheers. Having got so happily clear of the Cumberland, Captain Walker had no alternative but to run for the Swin, the navigation of which was exceedingly difficult, owing to the extreme thickness of the weather, which did not allow of two buoys or beacons being seen at the same time, and to the rocky bank near the shore, which he had to pass. Here again the Bedford occupied the anxious attention of the squadron, for they dared hardly hope of her clearing those rocks; and so certain were the people on shore that the loss of the ship was inevitable, that they were seen running in crowds towards the sea with ropes, to be ready to give assistance in saving the lives of the crew;

but most providentially Captain Walker steered clear of this dangerous reef; upon witnessing which, the worthy admiral, in the impulse of his joy, threw up his hat in the air, and loudly cheered him. The weather having cleared up a little, allowed of two buoys being seen, which enabled Captain Walker to go on, and about four o'clock in the afternoon he had the satisfaction of anchoring in the Thames, in the Lower Hope, in safety, having thus escaped from a situation which, for a considerable time, threatened total destruction to his ship and all on board; and his anxiety and alarm were not a little increased by his having Mrs. Walker and two of his children with him. It is a curious coincidence, that, five days after this narrow escape from shipwreck, the two ships that had so nearly caused each other's destruction, cast anchor at the Nore at the same time: it is easy to conceive with what feelings of satisfaction they witnessed their mutual safety, and how cordial were the joyous huzzas with which the crews greeted each other in meeting. It was in consequence of the above-related accident, and Captain Walker's conviction of the unfitness and danger of Hoazely Bay as an anchorage, especially for men of war, that he addressed the following letter to Lord Melville:

H. M. S. Bedford, Sheerness, *Feb. 5*, 1814.

My Lord,—The imminent danger to which the Cumberland and Bedford were recently exposed in Hoazely Bay would imperiously induce me to intrude this letter on your lordship's important time, even were it not the indispensable duty of an old officer to convey to the head of his department whatever information he may have acquired from his observation and experience; and, as the object of this representation is one of vital importance, I most respectfully submit its utility to your lordship's decision. Hoazely Bay, by some fatality which might eventually have produced the most lamentable consequences, became, about three years ago, the rendezvous of that part of Admiral Young's fleet which periodically cruised off the Texel, and was supposed in the interval to complete their provisions and water while there. That most essential object is very often defeated by the severity of the weather and the heavy sea, inasmuch as the craft is frequently detained a week at a time in Harwich; nor, were they to reach this bay, could they with safety be brought along side: therefore the supply is most precarious, and we have not unfrequently put to sea without it. This important circumstance, joined to the physical disadvantages it labours under, makes it impossible to calculate upon the ships that are lying there as a disposable force on any emergency; and therefore I presume, in a military point of view, it is every way ineligible, because it does not realize the object. It has indeed been said, that since the obstruction to the road of Yarmouth, from its proximity to the coast of Holland, it was deemed the next best anchorage : I, however, beg leave to differ from those who hold this opinion, and will endeavour to shew, in the course of this letter, that all the objects proposed by that arrangement were attainable by going a few leagues to the westward. Hoazely Bay is in every way a most dangerous anchorage; in blowing or hazy weather, neither the egress nor ingress is safe; you have no kind of shelter with the wind from E. N. E. to W. S. W.; when it blows hard, the sea makes a breach over the Whiting, and when the Bedford parted, on the 20th ult. it was breaking into the head. The ground is loose and shingly, therefore does not hold; it is moreover full of broken or parted anchors and other wreck : you are thus left, in stress of weather, solely depending on your anchors, in bad ground, without shelter or sea-room, exposed to a heavy sea, which new cables even have not withstood. If an accident happens in the night, you are inevitably lost, because you cannot put to sea; if in the daytime, your safety alone depends upon the most prompt exertions, joined to your being able to see the buoys and beacons amidst surrounding dangers. I would a thousand times rather be at anchor in a gale of wind on the Dogger Bank than in Hoazely Bay. During the severe winter of 1798, when I commanded the Braakel 60-gun ship, I lay in Harwich harbour as a guard-ship, and I understood from the best informed seamen of the place, and which my own observation invariably confirmed, that the coasters and colliers never anchored in Hoazely Bay, but to stop tide in moderate weather; and that if it came on to blow fresh, either from the eastward or westward, if against them, they always ran into Harwich for shelter. I now, my lord, beg leave to draw your lordship's attention to the *Wallet*, which I am well acquainted with, from having lain in the Braakel six months in it, at the time of the threatened invasion, 1798. It is one of the very best of the few good harbours in England, not even excepting Spithead; it has sufficient depth of water, excellent holding ground, being mud and ooze; it is sheltered on thirty points of the compass at all times, and after ebb becomes a perfect bason, since the Gun-Fleet sand is then dry for many miles. The entrance, Goldermere's Gat, is two good turning miles wide : I occasionally, to exercise the men, worked through it, though my ship, I believe, was the worst sailer in the navy. This bay or harbour is, besides, sufficiently capacious to contain fifty sail of the line; and all kinds of supplies might regularly and promptly be had from Harwich in safety, almost in the worst weather, and anchors and cables even, were they wanted. The tower on the Naze forms so good a land-mark, that there is no kind of danger in running into it. I rode out some hard summer gales in it, and the only accident I had was, the arm of the anchor we rode by breaking, and which we recovered the next day. There is, I have heard, a traditionary story of Lord Dartmouth* having been caught in it, with an easterly wind, at the time of the Revolution, when King William sailed down the Channel, and which prevented his lordship following him. This may have operated to its prejudice; but I have not been able to find it mentioned, either in his life or any of the contemporary historians: besides, were it true, the difference in our ships and their appointments now would make us hold cheap what might have appeared insurmountable obstacles then. I do not think, *cæteris paribus*, two ships sailing at the same time, one from each place, for the Texel, with an easterly wind, there would be half a tide's difference in their arrival. After so providential an escape in Hoazely Bay, I felt it to be a duty I owe to the service to make the above statement to your lordship.

I have the honour to be, &c.

JAMES WALKER.

As soon as the Bedford's damages were repaired, she was sent to join Admiral Young in the Room-Pot; and in the distribution of his force, Captain Walker was appointed to command a division of pikemen, which it was supposed would be required. On the return of the fleet to England, after the capture of Paris, Captain Walker was ordered to accompany Admiral Scott to Flushing; and soon afterwards had the honour of being selected to accompany his Royal Highness the Duke of Clarence to Boulogne, for the purpose of bringing over the Emperor of Russia and the King of Prussia. On the Bedford's return from Boulogne, she made one of the grand fleet reviewed by his present Majesty in person, accompanied by the royal strangers. During this summer, Captain Walker went twice to Royan to bring over the army; and in September 1814 he was appointed to command a squadron, on board of which was embarked the advanced guard of the army sent against New-Orleans, under Major-General Keane. The naval and military forces employed in this disastrous expedition arrived off Chandeleur Islands on the 8th December, and the debarkation of the troops commenced on the 16th. From that period till the termination of the campaign, Captain Walker's situation was one of the most anxious and painful description. During the absence of Sir Alexander Cochrane and Rear-Admirals Malcolm and Codrington, who were with the army during the whole of the operations on shore, he was left in charge of the line-of-battle ships, which, on account of the shallow water, could not approach within one hundred miles of the scene of action; and the Bedford, after the failure of

* With a squadron.

the enterprise, was literally crowded with wounded soldiers for a very considerable period. We should here observe, that most of her officers and 150 of her best men were landed, to co-operate with the troops against New-Orleans.

Since the peace, Captain Walker has commanded the Albion, Queen, and Northumberland 74's: the latter he paid off on the 10th September, 1818. On the 19th July, 1821, he was promoted to the rank of rear-admiral, the promotion of that memorable day ending with him; and in May 1825 he was made rear-admiral of the White.

Rear-Admiral Walker has been twice married: his first wife was a daughter of the late Right Hon. General Sir John Irvine, K.B. His present lady is third daughter of Arnoldus Jones Skelton, Esq. of Branthwaite-Hall and Papcastle, Cumberland, first cousin to the late Marquis Cornwallis. He has three sons: the eldest, Melville, is a lieutenant in the 16th lancers, now in India, and one of the regiments employed at the taking of Bhurtpore; the second, Leven Charles Frederic, a lieutenant in the navy; and the youngest, Alexander Thomas Donaldson, a midshipman: both these young officers have already given fair promise of being a credit to the service, and worthy of the root from which they spring. The youngest has, upon two occasions in the West Indies, distinguished himself, and has been made honourable mention of to the admiral on the station.

We have thus, we believe, fully and truly stated the services of Admiral Walker, from which it will be seen that he has been fifty-one years in the navy, twenty-one of which he was a post-captain. During that time he was in five general actions with the enemy's fleets, besides those with detached squadrons and single ships. We wish we could add that he has been adequately rewarded for such a life of toil and adventure; but unfortunately his case adds one to that list which has been so cruelly neglected by the late First Lord of the Admiralty. It is true, that, in 1814, after assisting in conveying to the shores of England those crowned heads of Europe who had mainly contributed to the overthrow of Buonaparte, it was proposed to recommend him to the Prince Regent as deserving the honour of knighthood. This proposition, however, did not emanate from Lord Melville, but from the Royal Duke who now presides over the navy. It was, however, respectfully declined by Captain Walker, who felt assured, that, in the event of the Order of the Bath being extended, as was then fully expected, he should not fail to receive that which his merits deserved; but he was disappointed, as he received only a Companion's Order, though fourteen captains, junior to him in rank, were made Knights Commanders; the knowledge of which circumstance may serve as a guide to other officers in similar situations. That Admiral Walker is deserving of the higher order of knighthood, we suppose no one will dispute after reading the above statement of his services, and his not having received it can consequently be only attributed to that system of favouritism which has been so long indulged in, but which, we trust, has now been cut up by the roots. Hope and fear are the principal causes of action, and set in motion every principle of honour and activity. If men can hope that, by extraordinary exertion in the service of their country, by braving every danger, by risking their lives and subduing her enemies, they shall reap the rewards of their services and obtain the consummation of their desires, they will become her servants, and execute manfully and cheerfully the duties of their stations. But if, by narrow-minded and niggardly policy, cold-hearted and selfish principles, they are unjustly denied those honours to which they have a claim, an act of injustice is not only committed, but the country is deprived of the benefit of that extra exertion, to excite which honours and titles were invented. It is not by the mere pay that men are brought into that enthusiastic state of mind which leads them to prefer trouble to peace, hardships to ease, and dangers to security; it is a love of fame, of glory, of renown, and those designations which men have sought after in all ages; and to cultivate those feelings is the duty of those who (we are sure it is the inclination of him who now does) preside over the British navy.

In addition to what we have stated above relative to the professional life of Admiral Walker, we have to observe, that while he was at Sheerness and in command of the Northumberland, he, one night, at the head of his officers and men, was fortunately chiefly instrumental in saving the dock-yard from being entirely burnt, after an alarming fire had broken out; and his exertions were no less useful and extraordinary on another occasion, when a fire occurred in the town, and for a time raged with great fury.

We must mention another circumstance. To a pleasing cheerful disposition, Admiral Walker joins a true sense of honour and integrity of principle, rejoices in the happiness of those around him, and is always desirous of promoting any plan of innocent amusement. Whilst some strive only to make themselves feared and obeyed by their attempts to break down the independence of men's spirits by the aid of the cat-o'-nine-tails, he endeavoured to make himself respected, and to correct the errors of those about him, by lenity and goodness. That he succeeded, we have ample proof, as, during the time he commanded the Bedford, not a man was punished for *five months and three weeks;* during which time she was in the highest state of discipline, and her captain received a letter from his commander-in-chief, Sir William Young, complimenting him upon the circumstance, and acknowledging that the system of discipline which he had adopted was equally honourable to his professional and private character. The beneficial effects of it were still farther manifested by the conduct of the crew, which perhaps the following little anecdote will elucidate: When the ship was lying at Sheerness, the signal-man waited upon the captain, and, in the name of the ship's company, requested permission to go on shore, to order a play at the theatre on the second following day, that being the anniversary of the battle of Trafalgar; with a farther request that he would allow as many as possible of the crew to attend the representation. It was certainly a very delicate affair; it was putting their apparent good feelings to the trial; but Captain Walker, having the utmost confidence in them, and knowing that they had no complaints, promised compliance. A deputation was sent to the manager of the theatre, and *The English Fleet* ordered, with a representation of the battle. Some little difficulty was started on the part of the manager, on account of the shortness of the notice; when the spokesman replied, "What! you want more than two days to get up a mock thing like this, when we did the real business in two hours! None of your lubberly tricks here!" A promise of an audience of 3 or 400 sailors overcame all difficulties, and the representation accordingly took place. But what we wish particularly to point out is, that though, we believe, above two-thirds of the crew were allowed to go on shore at once, not a squabble or disturbance took place, and the whole, with the exception of six, were on board again the same night before twelve o'clock, and those six by eight o'clock the following morning.

HISTORICAL MEMOIRS OF
ADMIRAL SIR JAMES ATHOL WOOD, Knt. C.B.

SIR JAMES is the third son of the late Alexander Wood, Esq. of Perth, and brother of Sir Mark Wood, Bart. He was born in 1756, and engaged at a very early age in the naval service of his country. He first went to sea in 1772, was on board the Hunter sloop of war in 1774, and having sailed to North America, served on shore at the siege of Quebec in 1776. In the following year he served on board the Barfleur, Captain Milbanke, and having returned to England, was placed on board the Princess Royal, bearing the flag of Admiral Byron, and again sailed to North America in search of the French fleet under D'Estaing. On his arrival at New-York he was appointed by Lord Howe to be first lieutenant of the Renown, Captain Dawson, and was intrusted with the command of the Renown's tender, in which he captured so many prizes that the captain's share amounted to 11,000*l.* On one occasion, in boarding an American galley, he was severely wounded in two places, the head and body; in the latter with a pike, which had nearly proved fatal. He continued on that station about two years, during which he was in a great variety of service, both afloat and on shore, particularly at the siege of Charlestown in 1780, soon after the surrender of which he returned to England. He was shortly after placed as second lieutenant in the Anson, Captain Blair, and sailed to the West Indies, where he was in the memorable battle of the 12th of April. Owing to the death of Captain Blair, who was killed in the action, he was appointed first lieutenant of the Anson by Lord Rodney, whose son succeeded Captain Blair in the command of the ship. During the peace Lieutenant Wood passed two years in France, and in 1788 proceeded to the East Indies, from whence he returned in 1792, and went to the West Indies.

War having taken place between France and England, and Sir John Jervis having arrived with the British fleet at Barbadoes, Lieutenant Wood immediately tendered his services, which were as quickly accepted, and he was placed on board Sir John's ship, the Boyne. After the capture of Martinique, he was directed by Sir John to take charge of some cartel-ships, with prisoners on board, and convey them to St. Malo, where he unfortunately arrived during the sanguinary government of Robespierre. That tyrant, without any respect to the laws or common usages of nations, not only seized the ships, but threw Lieutenant Wood into prison. He was afterwards ordered to Paris*, and underwent an examination before the Comité de Salut Public, and was then sent to the Abbaye†: but after the death of Robespierre, whom he saw

* The following is a copy of the order:

Comité de Salut Public.
Bureau de la Surveillance Administrative et de la Police Générale.

Extrait des Registres du Comité de Salut Public de la Convention Nationale du 13 jour du mois Prairial, l'an 2 de la république Française une et indivisible.

Le Comité de Salut Public ordonne à l'agent national du district port Malo, département d'Isle en Vilaine, faire traduire sur-le-champ à Paris sous bonne garde un Anglais appellé Wood, détenu dans la maison d'arrêt Solidor, près port Malo.

Il rendra compte sous 10 jours de l'exécution de cet arrêté.

Signé en registre, Robespierre, B. Barrère, Couthon, Carnot C. A. Prieur, Collot d'Herbois, Billaud, Varenne R. Lindes.

Pour extrait, signé Carnot, Robespierre, Couthon.

Le présent extrait conforme à l'arrêté que reste par-devers moi. Port Malo, le 18 Prairial, l'an 2 de la république Française une et indivisible.   LASAUDRAYEJAU.

En vertu de l'ordre ci-dessus il est ordonné par nous, substitut de l'agent national du district de port Malo, département d'Isle en Vilaine, au citoyen Choppy le Couture, lieutenant de la gendarmerie en Solidor, de transférer de la maison d'arrêt du dit lieu à Paris Wood Anglais, sous sa responsabilité.

Port Malo, le 19 Prairial, l'an 2 de la république   LASAUDRAYEJAU.
Française une et indivisible.

Nous, substitut de l'agent national de port Malo, invitons le corps constitué de fournir au citoyen Choppy, officier de la gendarmerie, en vertu de l'ordre de l'autre part, une garde, en cas qu'il le requière, àfin d'éviter la fuite du dit Wood. Le 19 Prairial, l'an 2 de la republique Française une et indivisible.   LASAUDRAYEJAU.

Vu au bureau de la police militaire de Paris, le 27 Prairial, l'an 2 de la république Française une et indivisible.   RENAULT, *Sécrétaire de la Police Militaire.*

Vu au comité revolionère de la section de la Halle Bloix, pour lui servir de carte de 6 jours, ce 28 Prairial, l'an 2 de la république Française.

ABADIS, *Commissaire.*
COLLET, *Commissaire.*

† The following is a copy of the order:

Le citoyen gendarme auquel a été confié le nommé Wood Anglais, venant de port Malo, le déposera dans la maison d'arrêt dite l'Abbaye, où il sera écroué en sa qualité d'Anglais, ici conformément à l'article 4 de la loi du 19 Vendémaire.

Le commissaire des administrations civiles, police et tribunaux, HERMAN.

Ce 27 Prairial, l'an 2 de la république.

pass to the place of his execution, he was released on parole*, and returned to England; but not till he had used his utmost exertions in behalf of his unfortunate countrymen immured within the prisons of Paris, as appears by the following letter from General O'Hara (who was taken prisoner at Toulon†) to the Secretary of State for the War Department:

PARIS, PRISON DU DRENEUX, April 6, 1795.

SIR,—Give me leave to present to you Lieutenant Wood, of the royal navy, whose long confinement in a common gaol, where our acquaintance began, renders him highly deserving your protection, as *the unexampled severities he experienced* arose from his manly endeavours to oblige those faithless people to carry into execution the object of his mission to this country.

Lieutenant Wood will, I am fully persuaded, sir, have a farther claim to your good offices, when you are acquainted, that several English families, who had languished for several months in the prisons of this town, the mansions of despair and accumulated cruelties, are indebted to his friendly interference for their liberty; and that likewise the exchange of several officers of the royal navy has been, in a great measure, brought about by his unremitting exertions.

I trust, sir, you will have the goodness to forgive the liberty I take in endeavouring to contribute my feeble aid to be useful to an officer, whose sufferings have been so great, and fortunes so deeply wounded, from a spirited discharge of his duty.

<table>
<tr><td>Right Hon. H. DUNDAS.</td><td>(Signed,)</td><td>CHARLES O'HARA.</td></tr>
</table>

" Soon after his return to England, Lieutenant Wood was advanced to the rank of commander, and appointed to the Favorite sloop of war,

---

* The following is a copy of the order:

Extrait du registre des arrêtés du Comité de Salut Public de la Convention Nationale, du 2 mois, l'an troisième de la république Française une et indivisible.

Le Comité de Salut Public arrête que Athol Vood, officier parlementaire Anglais, et Helven, son homme de confiance, détenus au Luxembourg, seront élargis, et mis en liberté sur leur parole d'honneur.

La commission des administrations civiles, police et tribunaux, demeure chargée de l'execution du present arrêté.

Les membres du Comité de Salut Public, signé Cambacères, Pelet, A. Dumont, Carnot, Boissy, Marée, J. P. Charal, Prieur de la Marne.

Pour copie, conformée à l'original deposé au greffe de la maison d'arrêt du Luxembourg, de celle delivrée au citoyen Athol Vood, officier parlementaire Anglais, ce 30 Nivose, l'an 3 de la république Française une et indivisible.

DELAYADJEURIE, Greff.

† See *Memoir of* LORD HOOD.

in which, after cruising for some time in the Channel, he proceeded to the West Indies, where he arrived in time to assist in quelling the insurrections which had long raged in the Islands of St. Vincent and Grenada, and threatened the total destruction of those colonies*. Among the many instances of his activity and zeal while on that service, was the capture and destruction of three formidable French privateers in the course of one day. These vessels, which he fell in with in the gulf of Paria, had been long and but too successfully employed in carrying provisions to the insurgents of the latter island. Subsequent to this event, Captain Otway, the senior officer on that station, ordered the Favorite to cruise to windward of Grenada, where she fell in with three other armed vessels, chased them during a whole day in light variable winds, and at length came up with a ship mounting 16 guns, which struck without firing a shot; and Captain Wood by this means obtaining a knowledge of their private night-signal, was fortunate enough to get possession of her consorts before daylight. From this period no supplies were received by the brigands, for the only vessel that afterwards attempted to get over was taken in a most gallant manner by the boats of the Zebra sloop, under the directions of Lieutenant Senhouse. He was afterwards ordered by Captain Otway to cruise off Labay, and to attend the garrison of that place along shore in their retreat to Sauteur. At daylight on the morning of March 1, 1796, observing the enemy take possession of Pilot-Hill, the Favorite weighed and worked up through an intricate channel full of rocks and shoals, and anchored off Sauteur about 3 p.m. The insurgents were at that time bringing their heavy cannon forward by means of a string of mules, upwards of 100 in number, and at five o'clock made their appearance on the neighbouring heights. There being no other vessel than the Favorite and an armed transport then at that anchorage, Captain Wood immediately pressed two large sloops lying at Isle Ronde, moored them close to the beach, and before eight o'clock succeeded in bringing off all the troops and the followers of the army, the whole amounting to above 1100 men, whom he conveyed in safety to St. George's, where they were landed by daylight the next morning. Had any delay occurred in the embarkation, there can be no doubt that every man of them would have been massacred, as the port of Sauteur was not tenable against cannon, and the brigands gave no quarter. It is proper also to mention, that there is not depth of water in Labay for

* See *Memoir of Sir* R. Otway.

a ship of war to approach the shore near enough to fire her guns with effect; while she would, in attempting to do so, be a dead mark for the enemy's artillery placed on the adjacent heights; and that Pilot-Hill, after the destruction of the town, was no longer a post to be defended with any prospect of success, as the insurgents, being greatly superior in numbers, commanded every part of the shore, and the garrison could not protect their own landing-place, or even obtain a supply of water*."

For some time the capture of the Island of Trinidad formed a principal object in the mind of Captain Wood; he examined it closely and minutely, saw its vulnerable parts, and strongly represented to the commander-in-chief, Sir H. Christian, the propriety of making an attack upon it: but the command in the West Indies was at that time very precarious, and he was shortly after recalled. However, a few days previous to his departure for England, Captain Wood waited upon him, in company with Captain R. W. Otway, to entreat that he would, on his arrival, represent to the British government the ease and facility with which the island could be made a British colony.

In January 1797, Sir Ralph Abercrombie arrived on board the Arethusa in the West Indies, to assume the command of the troops in that quarter; and before the frigate cast anchor, Captain Wood went on board of her to congratulate the general on his arrival, and to point out to him the favourable opportunity he had to capture an island, with four sail of the line in its harbour, when the following conversation took place:

Sir Ralph. Well, Captain Wood, what's the news?—*Captain Wood.* Why, general, you have arrived at a most fortunate period: there is the finest island in the West Indies, with four sail of the line and a frigate, at your service in forty-eight hours, if you choose to go against it.—*Sir Ralph.* Poh! poh! Captain Wood, don't talk nonsense: come down below and give us the news. They then went into the cabin, when the general renewed the conversation by saying, " Are you in earnest, Captain Wood? What island is it?"—*Captain Wood.* I am glad you ask me in a serious manner, general: I am serious, and it is the Island of Trinidad. A long conversation then took place on this subject, all of which occurred in the presence of the present Earl of Hopetown, General F. Maitland, and others then belonging to the general's staff; and Sir Ralph concluded his observations by stating, that he would discuss the matter with the admiral immediately on his arrival at Port-Royal. At that

* Marshall.

moment the admiral was working up to leeward of Martinique, with his flag just above the horizon, and was expected at Port-Royal that evening. On the following day Captain Wood received directions from the admiral to inspect the defences of the island*; but he took the liberty to observe, that such a measure was unnecessary and only losing time, as he had a few days before made the necessary examination, and that he knew every part of it, with the position of the enemy's squadron, as well as if he was hovering over them. His orders were, however, peremptory: he accordingly proceeded thither, and then made the following report, dated January 13, 1797 :

SIR,—In pursuance of your secret orders of the 6th instant, I arrived with his Majesty's ship under my command off Trinidad at seven o'clock on the 8th inst. where I spoke an American who had left the gulf of Paria that morning. After receiving all the information that I could from him, I proceeded on to enter the first Boca ; hoisted out a small but very fast-sailing boat, which had been blacked like a canoe for this express purpose, and sent an intelligent officer in, with directions to post himself on a small island covered with a thick wood, and to haul the boat up into a small cove, where it would be impossible to see her either from the Spanish ships or the shore. The officer remained on the island until eight o'clock next morning.

There are three two-decked ships lying in Shagaramus Bay, not moored, no sails bent, nor top-gallant-yards across. The Spanish admiral, bearing a flag at the mizen, lies the inside ship : in fact, they are in their old position. The Favorite's boats rowed round them several times during the night; and it is my

---

* The following is a copy:

[*Secret.*]   *By* HENRY HARVEY, *Esq. Rear-Admiral of the Red, &c. &c.*

You are hereby required and directed to proceed, without a moment's loss of time, in his Majesty's sloop under your command, off the Island of Trinidada, and use your best endeavours to gain every possible intelligence respecting the Spanish squadron that were assembled in the gulf of Paria, of the number of their ships, strength, and position, and to collect the best information of the land force that may now be on that island.

And whereas his Majesty's ship Alarm, with the Victorieuse and Thorn sloops, are stationed off Grenada and Tobago, you are therefore to endeavour to fall in with either of them, in order to obtain such intelligence as they may be enabled to furnish you with on this occasion.

You are to use the utmost dispatch possible in performing the service hereby directed, and return again immediately to this bay.

Given on board the Prince of Wales, in Fort Royal Bay, Martinique, Jan. 6, 1796.

To Captain WOOD, *of his Majesty's*   HENRY HARVEY.
sloop Favorite.

opinion, that these ships might be boarded and carried by boats in the night, without the loss of a man, as they keep but a very indifferent look out.

On the east point of Parsangs Island, or Gaspar Grande, which forms the west entrance of Shagaramus Bay, there is a small battery of masonry, about twenty feet above the water's edge, where the enemy have four guns; and on the summit of the same island there is a look-out-house and some huts, with a flag-staff lately erected; but no works yet thrown up, nor any fortifications erected on the peninsula of Point Gourd, or the Island of Shagaramus, which com-pletely commands it, and also Trimbledaire Bay, and the carenage to the east-ward of it, where there is a most capital landing-place for troops.

There is also a two-decked ship of 80 guns and a frigate, that now lie seven or eight miles higher up the gulf, abreast of Port d'Espagne; but at such a dis-tance, that the guns could give them no protection in case of an attack. From the best information I have been able to procure, there are not more than 1000 land troops on the island, and not more than 600 of them fit to serve. From the local knowledge I have of this island, and all the information that I have suc-ceeded in obtaining, I have no doubt of its accuracy; and in the event of an expedition being undertaken against it, if you will permit me to have the honour of laying the Prince of Wales (the admiral's flag-ship) along side the Spanish admiral, and to pilot in your squadron, I will answer for the success of the en-terprise with my life. (Signed,) J. A. WOOD.

Captain Wood was shortly afterwards directed by the admiral to turn his attention to the mode of attack necessary to be adopted; and having fully considered the subject, drew out the following plan, which was sanctioned and approved of by both the admiral and general:

Secrecy and the utmost expedition are most earnestly recommended.

The squadron, with the transports and troops, ought to assemble at the Island of Curiaco. It would be proper to leave that island by three o'clock in the afternoon, that the transports and heavy-sailing ships might have time to clear the small islands and keys to the southward of it before dark. The squadron might then proceed under easy sail, in a S. E. by S. course, so as to arrive well to windward on the north side of Trinidad by two or three o'clock in the after-noon of next day. The squadron might then proceed as far as the westernmost point of the island, where it might be proper to detach a company of light troops to take possession of the bay and road of las Quebas, the only road that com-municates between the plantations on the north side of the island and the town of Port d'Espagne. This would effectually prevent the enemy from having any know-ledge of our arrival; or, if thought necessary, a large body of troops might be landed to take the enemy in the rear, to prevent the men landing from the ships, or to cut off their communication with the country. To prevent any alarm, the squadron should keep the coast close on board (as there is no danger that does not appear, and good anchorage every where along the shore), and under such sail as to arrive at the Bocas about nine o'clock in the evening. An attentive observer always knows by the appearance of the high hills whether there will be a good breeze or not during the night in the Bocas; but indeed it is seldom or ever calm in the Great Boca at this season of the year.

The squadron should proceed into the gulf through the Great or southernmost Boca. As soon as the gulf is entered, the sea is as smooth as a mill-pond; and it is most probable that a stretch of six or seven miles to the southward, and a tack of five or six miles to the northward, will enable the squadron to enter Shagaramus Bay, or to weather it. The troops ought to be immediately embarked in the boats, and an attack made on Gaspar Grande, where the enemy have erected a redoubt, surrounded with palisades, since last reconnoitred. Three hundred men would ensure complete success to this attack. The rest of the troops ought instantly to be landed in Trimbledaire Bay, and take possession of the neck of land which separates Point Gourd from the main, where there is nothing to oppose them. By having possession of Point Gourd and Gaspar Grande, the enemy's ships have no retreat or communication with the shore left them, and must fall into our hands: Point Gourd not only commands Shagaramus Bay but also Trimbledaire Bay, and is fifty yards higher than Gaspar Grande.

In case any black troops accompany the expedition, it might be proper to land them on the low marshy land to the southward of the town, as well to ensure abundant supplies of cattle, as to cut off all communication with the town and this quarter, from whence it draws its chief subsistence.

                              (Signed,)   J. A. Wood.

As the admiral at that time appeared to be undecided about attacking the island, Captain Wood took the opportunity of informing him, that the Spanish frigate was lying in such a position as afforded a favourable opportunity for attack, and that if he would reinforce the Favorite's crew with 200 men, he would engage to bring her out; but at the same time observed, that if the admiral did intend to proceed against the island, he would not advise any attempt to be made on the frigate, as it might put the enemy more on their guard respecting the island. Captain Wood's offer was then declined, and he was dispatched to the northward in search of the Vengeance of 74 guns; but during his absence the admiral ordered the Arethusa and Pelican to make an attack on the Spanish frigate; but the Pelican separated from the Arethusa, and as Captain Wolley was unacquainted with the place, he not only failed in the object, but was nearly come up with by one of the Spanish ships of the line.

The attack on the island having been successful, Captain Wood was directed to haul down the enemy's colours, and having done so, informed the admiral that he was ready to lay them at his feet; but the admiral desired him to keep them, observing that no one else had so great a claim to them; and at the same time promised particularly to mention him in his public letter. This, however, was not done; and Captain Wood, on his arrival in England, waited upon Lord Spencer respecting it, who informed him, that the admiral had done him ample justice in a private communication.

In 1797 Captain Wood was ordered to England in charge of a large convoy; and in 1798 was appointed to the Garland frigate, in which he sailed to the Cape of Good Hope; from whence he went with a small squadron on a cruise off the Mauritius, during which information was obtained that two French frigates, which had done much mischief on the Indian coasts, had proceeded for Madagascar. The squadron immediately followed in that direction, and off the south-east end of the island a large ship was seen at anchor. The Garland was immediately ordered to reconnoitre, and having arrived within a mile of the enemy, she struck on a pointed rock, fifteen feet under water, which unshipped her tiller, and water soon rushed on the main-deck through the midship-ports and the hawse-holes. In this critical situation it was with great difficulty that the boats could be got out, and the ship ran between two rocks before she went down. On seeing the Garland approaching, the enemy deserted their vessel and ran ashore, but perceiving the misfortune which had attended her, they again put off in their boats and endeavoured to regain possession of her, but were prevented by Captain Wood, who, by great exertions, had pulled for the enemy's ship, first reached and then effectually secured her. Instead of a frigate, the French ship proved to be a large merchantman, pierced for 24 guns. This circumstance proved of the most essential advantage to Captain Wood and the crew of the Garland, all of whom were saved, together with a great part of the rigging, stores, and provisions; and finding means to conciliate the minds of the natives, the whole of the Frenchmen were delivered up to him, and he was supplied with such provisions as he stood in need of during the time that he remained on the island. As the prize was by no means sufficient to transport the crews of both vessels to the Cape, Captain

Wood constructed one vessel of 15 tons, and had made considerable pro-gress in another, when, at the end of four months, the Star sloop of war arrived, sent by Admiral Christian, to ascertain the fate of the Garland and her crew: in that vessel the French prisoners were conveyed to the Cape, while the crew of the Garland proceeded thither in the prize*.

Captain Wood shortly afterwards returned to England, and in April 1802 was appointed to the Acasta frigate, in which he was employed in the Channel and Mediterranean during the remainder of the war, and the North Sea and at Guernsey during the peace. On the recommencement of hostilities he was placed under the orders of Admiral Cornwallis, off Brest. "In this dangerous and fatiguing service, he continued to be employed under that gallant admiral nearly two years, a part of which time he had the charge of the in-shore squadron appointed to watch the motions of the enemy. The dangers and difficulties of this service can be appreciated only by seamen: in the dreary winter months, embayed amongst rocks and shoals, during long nights, short days, and tempestu-ous weather, the inevitable fatigues and exertions are such as the most robust constitutions are seldom able successfully to encounter†." Captain Wood, however, made occasional cruises, in one of which he captured L'Avanture de Bourdeaux, a privateer mounting 20 guns, and retook three merchant-vessels, her prizes; a capture which was of the greatest consequence in a commercial view, as, during the chase, the Acasta passed through a fleet of West-Indiamen, several of which, from their having parted from their convoy, would no doubt have fallen into her possession. In November 1804 he was ordered to escort a valuable fleet of merchantmen to the West Indies, where he arrived in February 1805. Previous, however, to the arrival of the Acasta, Admiral Duckworth, the commander-in-chief on the station, heard of his being recalled, and had determined to return in the Acasta; for which purpose he super-seded Captain Wood in the command of that ship, and nominated him to the Hercule, in which it was then well known that Admiral Da-cres intended to hoist his flag: so that by this stretch of authority Cap-tain Wood was left without command, and obliged to return to England

---

* During his continuance at Madagascar, Captain Wood surveyed the coast from Fort Dauphine to St. Luce, and about three miles to the southward of the latter place, dis-covered an anchorage within the reef sufficient to contain a numerous fleet of line-of-battle ships.

† *Naval Chronicle.*

as a passenger on board his own ship! After his arrival he preferred several charges against Admiral Duckworth, who was brought to a court-martial; and though acquitted, the Lords of the Admiralty immediately adopted a regulation, to prevent, in future, any admiral on a foreign station from exercising his authority so much to the detriment of the public service. As we have in the *Naval Chronology** fully given the particulars as they were stated in the House of Commons, together with the opinions of the most eminent counsel on the subjects in dispute, it is unnecessary here to enter farther on the legality of the proceedings. Shortly after the sentence, Captain Wood was appointed in succession to the Uranie and Latona frigates; in the latter of which, after serving a short time in the Channel, he was again ordered to the West Indies with a convoy; and on his arrival at Jamaica, Admiral Dacres directed him to take the Anson under his command, and proceed to Curaçoa, with such other frigates as he might meet with on his passage; promising to send more particular directions for his proceedings when the ships were reported ready to sail. About this time the Arethusa appeared off Port-Royal, when the commander-in-chief made the signal for Captain Brisbane to enter the port; and he being the senior captain, was directed to take the Latona and Anson under his orders, and the orders intended for Captain Wood were transferred to him; nor could they have been given to a more zealous officer.

The three ships sailed from Jamaica the beginning of December, and, after a continuance of adverse winds and lee currents, arrived at the Island of Aruba, where they anchored for a short time, and where Captain Brisbane communicated his orders to the captains of the Anson and Latona; at the same time declaring that he would attack the Island of Curaçoa, if it was not surrendered on his sending in a flag summoning the governor to do so. He farther issued directions to the captains to get a bower-cable through the gunroom-port, and that it should be bent to a bower-anchor; that his intention was to send in a flag of truce by Captain Lidyard of the Anson, and that when the flag put off from the Anson, the other ships were to hoist out their boats and be in readiness to follow the Arethusa's motions; and that if the town was not surrendered, he should give the governor two hours' notice to get the women and children out of it; at the expiration of which time the Are-

* Vol. I. p. 107.

thusa, Latona, Anson, and Fisgard, the latter of which had just
joined, were to enter the harbour. Having made these arrangements,
Captain Brisbane asked Captain Wood whether he approved of the
plan. But the latter replied, with that plainness and freedom which
are characteristic of his whole conduct, that he did not by any means approve of it; and said it would be quite madness to give the enemy notice
of the determination to enter the harbour. He farther stated, that as
the admiral had directed a flag of truce to be sent in, the best way
would be to carry it in at the mast-head. This advice was not, however,
listened to by Captain Brisbane, who replied angrily, " that he did not
care whether his plan were approved of or not; but he should not alter it."
Convinced, however, of the futility of the scheme, Captain Wood lost
no opportunity of urging a different plan of attack, but in such a way
as to give the least offence possible : he represented to the commodore
that the enemy, having notice of their intentions, would get a chain
across the harbour, and that even an old ship or vessel would block the
passage. But the commodore answered this by saying, he would jump
over it. " I can jump as well as you," said Captain Wood, "but neither
of us can make our ships jump." Thus the matter stood till the 30th
December, when, after a long passage of a month from Jamaica, about
sunset the signal was made from the Latona for land in the north-east
quarter, which was known to be the Island of Curaçoa ; on which the
commodore made the signal to prepare to tack. This sufficiently indicated his intention to work up close under the lee of the island, and that
he was determined to adhere to his plan of attack and of sending in a
flag of truce. Captain Wood, however, determined to make one more
effort to induce him to alter it, being convinced that success could not
have attended it : he therefore made the signal to speak with the Arethusa, hastened on board that ship with his pilot (a very respectable and
well-informed man), and went down into the cabin with Captain Brisbane, when the subject was again fully canvassed ; and, after much
conversation, Captain Wood said, " Now, Brisbane, let us continue on
the tack we are now upon, stand over to the main land, where we shall
have a weather current, and work to windward all day to-morrow, and
where we cannot be seen from Curaçoa ; to-morrow night we may
stand over, fetch to windward of the harbour of Curaçoa, and be ready
to enter the harbour at daylight : we shall then find all the Dutchmen

drunk, and the town will be ours; for in all Calvinistic countries the last and first days of the year are the greatest rejoicing days; and you may ask my pilot, who is well acquainted with the fact, if it is not so." On which Captain Brisbane went aside to the pilot and had some conversation. He then returned to Captain Wood and said, " Why, your pilot says quite the contrary." Naturally irritated at such an assertion, Captain Wood upbraided the pilot for such conduct, alledging, though very unjustly, that he was adverse to going in: Mr. Brislake the pilot, however, said, " The commodore is only joking." When Captain Wood, again addressing the commodore, said, " Brisbane, this is too serious a matter to joke about; our reputation depends upon it, and if you adopt my plan I will insure you the island."—" Well, then," said Captain Brisbane, " it shall be so." They then shook hands, and the commodore said, " Wood, you never gave me any encouragement before."—" Nay," replied Captain Wood, " do not say I ever discouraged you : for, on the contrary, I always told you that I would lead or follow wherever you chose to go; but that I never approved of your plan." The island was now looked upon as taken, and they began some preliminary arrangements about the good things resulting therefrom : after some conversation about appointing Captain Wood governor, he strongly remonstrated against it, observing, " that he would not give up his ship for any government in his Majesty's gift, but should stick to the ' old main-top-bowling:' " but added, " if the commodore chose to make him vendue-master and naval officer, he would, if he kept them, give up one of them to Captain James Brisbane at the end of three years." This was agreed to ; the appointments afterwards took place, and every thing turned out according to their most sanguine expectations. At four o'clock in the morning on the 1st January, 1807, the commodore made the signal to bear up and sail large: only three of the ships obeyed the signal. At the dawn of morning they were about a mile or more from the fort, when the Anson shot up on the Latona's weather quarter, almost on board of her; when Captain Wood hailed and directed her captain to keep more open order, as it was not a time, going to enter a very narrow port, to get on board each other. The Anson then suddenly dropped astern, and became greatly out of her place; which was afterwards accounted for by her boats having at that moment broke adrift, and it of course took some time to pick them up: all the frigates had their boats in tow. The Arethusa and Latona pushed into the harbour, and in about half an hour silenced the Dutch frigate, the 20-gun ship, two schooners, as well as Fort Amsterdam, none of which dared to touch a gun afterwards. Fort Republic, situate on a commanding hill to the east, and about a mile distant from where the ships lay, and a fort on the west side of the harbour, still farther off, at about long random-shot distance, still continued their fire. When the Anson entered the harbour, *which was about half an hour after the Arethusa and Latona,* she ran on board the Latona, carried away that ship's driver-boom, swung round, and got on the rocks on the west side of the harbour, along side the Dutch 20-gun ship, with her head to Fort Amsterdam*, where she lay until the island surrendered. *An hour and eleven minutes after the Anson, the Fisgard at last made her appearance,* entered the harbour, and grounded on the rocks, on the larboard side, within the entrance. About this time Captain Brisbane landed, and was walking along the quay with 20 or 30 men, when he hailed Captain Wood, and asked if the Dutch frigate had struck? To which he replied, that the enemy had called for quarter; but their colours being foul, they could not get them down; and that he had directed an officer to take possession of her. However, on looking over the Latona's side, he found the officer had not put off; on which he directed Mr. Grint, now Captain Grint, to put off and take possession: he went on board accordingly, and manned the ship for Captain Brisbane; previous to which there had been no person on the deck of the Dutch frigate for a considerable time, as Captain Wood had ordered them all below; nor was there a single person upon the ramparts of the fort, except one black man, who had concealed himself under a gun. The rampart of the fort was about fifteen or twenty yards from the frigate's stern, and about fifteen or twenty feet high. Captain Brisbane landed with his boat's crew and entered the fort by a scaling-ladder, from whence he entered the Government-House, and the seamen and marines landed from all the ships on the quay abreast the Government-House. No resistance whatever was made from the fort. The black man that was under the gun where Captain Brisbane entered, fired his musket and ran away, but was shot by one of the Latona's men. About this time, the governor stopped along side the Latona, with a lady in the boat with him, and

* See annexed plan.

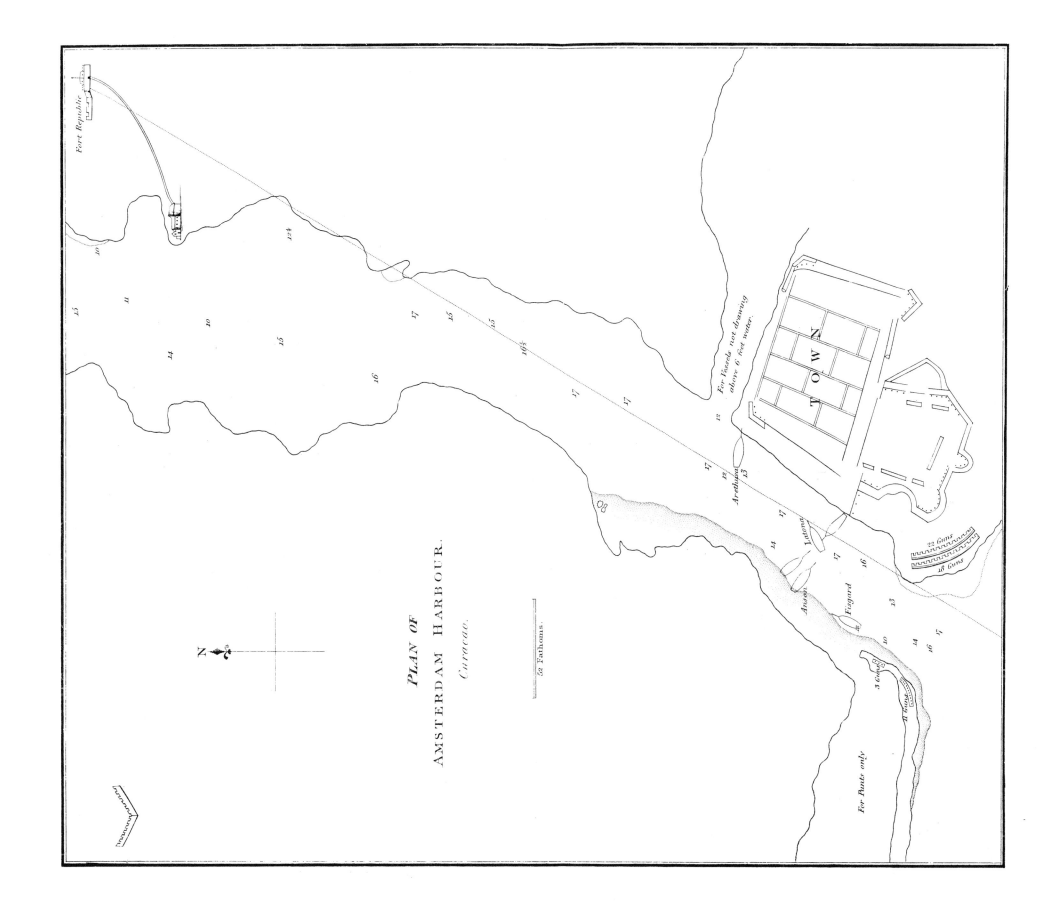

N

PLAN OF
AMSTERDAM HARBOUR.
Curacao.

52 Fathoms.

Fort Republic

For Vessels not drawing
above 6 feet water.

TOWN

Arethusa

22 Guns
18 Guns

Latona

Anson

Fisgard

For Punts only

3 Guns

4 Guns

was directed by Captain Wood to go on shore to the commodore, who was in the Government-House. Thither he accordingly repaired; and soon after Fort Republic, on receiving a messenger from the Government-House, ceased firing and hauled down the colours. About this time Captain Wood went on shore, ordered the seamen on board, and joined Captain Brisbane, when the following conversation took place: *Captain Wood.* Well, Brisbane, I wish you joy: did I not tell you how it would be?—*Captain Brisbane.* Ah, Fisgard! Fisgard!—*Captain Wood.* Brisbane, you have done what will do you immortal honour; let the fellow go to the d—l: let us have no rows; he is not worth your notice.—*Captain Brisbane.* Wood, I never loved a fellow so in my life as I did you to-day.—*Captain Wood.* For what?—*Captain Brisbane.* For what? why for lying aback under the fire of all these batteries, and allowing me to pass you.—*Captain Wood.* I did no more than my duty; for if I had not done so, I was fearful you would have gone on shore on the lee side of the harbour.—*Captain Brisbane.* Ah! but how few people would have done it!—*Captain Wood.* Well, if you think so much of it, mention it in your public letter.—*Captain Brisbane.* I will mention it particularly to the admiral.—*Captain Wood.* I could very easily have got in before you.—*Captain Brisbane.* If you had, I never should have forgiven you.—After some little conversation, Captain Wood asked what was the matter with the Arethusa, as she sailed worse than usual. He said his yards were braced too much up; when Captain Wood added, "I went in in the old style, 'trim as you go.'"—"Yes," said Captain Brisbane, "you went in like a seaman; and there is no difference between you and me, except that I stand a few before you on the list." We have been thus particular in stating this conversation in consequence of having heard reports propagated to the prejudice of Captain Wood—that his motive for lying aback was, that he was afraid to enter the harbour. Had he, however, not have done so, but had pushed ahead, even a cable's length farther, he would have been out of the line of fire of all the batteries which defended the harbour's mouth; a fact well known to all persons acquainted with the defences of Curaçoa.

Such are the particulars of the extraordinary attack and capture of the Island of Curaçoa; and the reader will perceive, on reference, how greatly they differ from the Histories of James and Brenton, both of whom ascribe the whole merit of the enterprise to Captain Brisbane.

But it is very clear that neither of them was acquainted with the particulars, as they both state, that the squadron entered the harbour in *close order*. Captain Brenton indeed says, that they entered in " the closest order," and " anchored in a style of grandeur and precision to which no words can do justice;" although, as we have already stated, only the Arethusa and Latona entered the harbour in close order, the Anson having been prevented doing so by an accident which threw her out for half an hour, when the principal part of the business was accomplished; and the Fisgard did not enter for one hour and eleven minutes after her, when nothing remained to be done. For his services on this occasion Captain Wood was, by desire of his Majesty, presented with a gold medal, and was also voted a sword by the committee of the Patriotic Fund.

Captain Wood was shortly after directed by Sir A. Cochrane to superintend the blockade of the Danish islands, which terminated in their surrender. He was afterwards appointed to the Captain of 74 guns, and assisted at the reduction of Martinique; after which he returned to England, when his Majesty conferred upon him the honour of knighthood. He was then appointed to the Neptune, a second rate, which he commanded in Channel service till 1810, when he joined the Pompée of 74 guns, and was again employed in Channel service, and in March 1812 fell in with a French squadron; before we enter upon the particulars of which, we shall insert the following extract from James's *Naval History:* " M. Allemand put to sea on the night of the 8th; and, but for his extraordinary good fortune, might, as we shall presently see, have terminated his cruise in Portsmouth or Plymouth, instead of Brest, whither, it appears, he was bound. On the 9th, at one p.m. when about seven leagues to the southward of the Penmarks, four French sail of the line and two corvettes were discovered by the 38-gun frigate Diana, Captain W. Ferris, but were lost sight of in the evening. On the 10th, however, at nine a.m. when close hauled on the starboard tack, with the wind at N.E. the Diana regained a sight of the French squadron, then on her weather bow, twelve or thirteen miles distant, steering the same course as herself, N. by W. The frigate continued sailing parallel with the French ships, to watch their manœuvres, until three p.m. when the 74-gun ship Pompée, Captain Sir J. A. Wood, joined company to leeward. At four p.m. Captain Ferris hove-to to communicate with his superior officer; and at 4 hours 30 minutes p.m. the British 74 and frigate filled and made all sail on the starboard tack,

Shortly afterwards the Diana, who still kept to windward of the Pompée, observed two vessels on her weather beam, to windward of the French squadron; the ships of which immediately bore up, under all sail, evidently to avoid them. These two vessels were the British 74-gun ships Tremendous, Captain Robert Campbell, and Poictiers, Captain John Poer Beresford, chasing the French squadron, which they had discovered since daylight, when cruising six or seven leagues W.S.W. of Ushant. At 11 a.m. Captain Campbell had detached the Poictiers in chase of a ship to the eastward, which proved to be the British 18-gun ship-sloop Myrtle, Captain Clement Sneyd; and whom Captain Beresford, on joining him at 1 p.m. sent to warn an English convoy, then seen in the N.E. standing to the westward, of the presence of an enemy's squadron. At 4 p.m. the Poictiers having rejoined the Tremendous, the two 74's resumed the chase of M. Allemand, and were descried by the Diana in the manner we have just related.

" As the French ships, when they bore up to avoid the Tremendous and Poictiers, *steered in a direction to cross the bows of the Diana and Pompée,* the two latter, at 6 hours 15 minutes p.m. tacked to the S.E. Soon afterwards the Diana lost sight of the Pompée in the S.S.E. and about the same time observed and answered the night-signal for an enemy made by her two friends to windward. The Pompée also observed the flashes of guns and rockets, which were the signals made by the Tremendous and Poictiers; but it does not appear that she answered them. Towards midnight the wind shifted to the N.N.W.; and at about thirty minutes past midnight, the Pompée suddenly discovered two ships in chase of her, in the S.E. The British 74 immediately bore up and made all sail, altering her course frequently to avoid her pursuers, one of whom got near enough to fire three or four shot at her. On this the Pompée started eighty tons of water, and then gained so rapidly upon the two supposed enemy's ships, that at daylight they were no longer to be seen. In the course of the forenoon of that day the Diana, and in the evening the Bulwark and Colossus, joined company with the Pompée; as on the following day did the Tonnant, Tremendous, and Poictiers. The two latter had lost sight of the French ships at dark on the 10th; but having again discovered them at daylight on the 11th, had chased them until two p.m. when foggy weather coming on, the Tremendous and Poictiers shortened sail, and hauled to the wind on the larboard tack.

"The account we have given of the escape of the French admiral from the Pompée, Tremendous, and Poictiers, although the only account to be seen in print, is far from being so full and clear as it might have been could we have gained a sight of the minutes of the court of inquiry, which it appears was held at Portsmouth on the subject. We turned to the Biography of Sir James Wood in the work of Mr. Marshall; but, although thirteen closely printed pages are devoted to an account of the rear-admiral's life, not a line is spared to throw some light on the proceedings of the Pompée in the spring of 1812."

Coupling the last sentence of this extract with the first, it appears clear that Mr. James wishes it to be believed that the escape of the French squadron was attributable to Sir James Wood; which appears to us somewhat odd, as he admits that he had not seen the minutes of the court of inquiry, or rather the court-martial, which was held to inquire into the particulars. His statement, moreover, though speciously drawn up, is not free from errors. According to the log of the Diana, when she first discovered the enemy's squadron, she was about seven or eight *miles* from the Penmarks, and not so many leagues. When she regained a sight of them on the 10th, the enemy were not steering the same course as herself; they were steering N.W. with the wind at E. by N. and she was steering S.E. by S. and she consequently tacked to observe them. Having lost sight of the Pompée, he says, the Diana " observed and answered the night-signal for an enemy made by her two friends to windward." The following is from the Diana's log: " At 6h. 30m. lost sight of the Pompée, bearing S.S.E.; observed the *strangers* to windward fire several guns and shew lights. 6.40. fired two rockets; at 7. fired two more; at 8. do. tacked ship; at 9.20. observed a light on the lee bow; 9.30. burnt two rockets, which were not answered." And this is what Mr. James calls " observing and answering the night-signal for an enemy." He also says, that " in the course of the forenoon of the 11th, the Diana, and in the evening the Bulwark and Colossus, joined company with the Pompée; as on the following day did the Tonnant, Tremendous, and Poictiers." The Diana, Bulwark, and Colossus did not, however, join the Pompée till the afternoon of the 12th, nor the others till the 13th. We must also observe, that the Poictiers was not commanded by Captain Beresford, but by Captain Samuel Jackson. So that it would really be difficult to find a paragraph of the same extent, containing so many errors as the one we have inserted above from Mr. James's work.

The affair having created some surprise and disappointment, Lord Keith was directed by the Lords of the Admiralty to make particular inquiries into it; and having done so, transmitted to their secretary a report respecting it, in which he stated, that he had

Called for attested copies of the logs of the ships named in the margin* between the 9th and 12th March, and had endeavoured to reconcile the various reports which they contain respecting the position of the different ships and those of the enemy at the same period; but in so doing had experienced such considerable difficulty from the inaccurate manner in which the logs had been kept, that it was impossible to place the enemy and the several ships of his Majesty in any reconcileable relative position; but transmitted two plans, the first of which, marked A, was prepared from the logs of the different ships by Captain Jackson, of his Majesty's ship San Josef; and the one marked B by Mr. Sidley, master of the fleet; and respecting which he says,

" In these plans the situation of his Majesty's ships, as well as that of the enemy, is given at six p.m. of the 10th and six a.m. of the 11th, and that of the Pompée is also laid down at midnight of the 10th; and their lordships will also observe, that as the two sketches do not materially differ, the ships seen by the Pompée at midnight, when she started her water, could not possibly have been those of the enemy which she observed at sunset; and that, in all probability, they were an outward-bound convoy, as appears to be admitted by Captain Sir J. A. Wood, in a letter which I have received from him, transmitting his log, a copy of which is inclosed.

" While, on the one hand, it is to be lamented that Captain Campbell did not at 4. 30. p.m. of the 10th, when he first saw the two strange sail, that no doubt were the Pompée and Diana, endeavour to approach nearer to them, or to form a junction with them, which, *as he was to windward, it is supposed he might have done without losing sight of the enemy's squadron*; it is, on the other hand, to be regretted that Captain Sir J. A. Wood did not tack and stand towards the two strange sail seen to windward from the Pompée before sunset, which, there is also no doubt, were the Tremendous and Poictiers; for if either of these measures had been adopted, signals might have been exchanged before the close of day, and a junction formed afterwards. What ships were so near the Pompée at midnight, it is impossible to say; for if the plans above-mentioned are correct, the distance is too great to have rendered it possible for them to have been ships of the French squadron. Sir James A. Wood indeed admits that he saw at least twelve or thirteen sail during the night making signals by flashes, &c. Of course they could not be the enemy's ships, but were in all probability vessels belonging

* Pompée, Diana, Tremendous, and Poictiers.

to one or more convoys. At six a.m. on the 11th, the Pompée saw three sail steering W.S.W. distant five or six miles ; but as the bearings are not mentioned in the log, their position cannot be accurately laid down in the plan. It could not have been difficult, however, to have ascertained what they were, if Sir J. A. Wood had steered towards them.

"The Tremendous, at the same hour, might, from her situation, have seen, and actually did see, six sail, though very distant, bearing west. These, no doubt, were the enemy's squadron, which were finally lost sight of at eleven a.m. As all his Majesty's ships outsailed those of the enemy, the latter might have been approached with little risk ; and it perhaps would have been more advisable if they had all continued to keep as near the enemy's squadron as it was possible to do with safety. It is so difficult, however, to judge at a distance how things may appear to those upon the spot, or how the same things may impress different men, that I feel great delicacy in hazarding these opinions ; for, although it would appear, under all the circumstances of the case, that events might have been more fortunate, I am persuaded that all the officers in question were actuated with the same degree of zeal to promote the general service of the country and their own honour."

In consequence of Lord Keith's report, a court-martial was ordered to be held, to inquire into the conduct of Sir James Wood, and also that of Captain Robert Campbell of the Tremendous ; and which, after hearing the evidence of the officers of the respective ships, came to the resolution, that "Sir James was blameable for tacking at 6.40. p.m. on the 10th March, before it was better ascertained that the enemy had wore and stood towards him ; for not tacking again to the northward when the flashes of the guns and the lights were discovered abaft the beam, and for not replying thereto ; and also for not reconnoitring the strangers reported to be seen on the morning of the 11th : but that such blame arose from erroneous impressions at the time, and not from any want of zeal for the good of his Majesty's service." Captain Campbell was fully acquitted.

In the course of this work we have repeatedly differed from the sentences of those courts-martial which we have had occasion to notice ; and, we believe, there are none from which we differ more than the one held upon the above occasion, which attributed blame to Sir James Wood. We have gone through the whole of the minutes, which are very voluminous, and it appears clear to us (and we hope to make it appear so to others), that so far from Sir James being blameable, he had scarcely a choice of conduct left, and that his duty pointed out that line of conduct which he did pursue.

Lord Keith, in his report, says, that " it is much to be regretted that Captain Campbell did not, at 4 h. 30 m. endeavour to approach the Pompée, as he was to windward, it is supposed, *which he might have done without losing sight of the enemy.*" A question was afterwards put to Captain Jackson at the court-martial to ascertain the fact, and he acknowledged it to be the case; and also that, if the Pompée had made any attempt to join the Tremendous, she must have increased her distance from the enemy, and consequently have lost sight of them. The court in their sentence, however, take no notice of this circumstance, but go at once to the time when the Pompée tacked to the S. E. to avoid the enemy. It is this moment of time which is the most important of the whole proceedings; and if we can clearly establish the fact, that the enemy did wear round in hopes of cutting off the Pompée and Diana, the conduct of Sir James must be fully justified. The court indeed admit, by the wording of their sentence, that they were in doubt whether the enemy did wear round; or, we should rather say, admit that they did wear round: their words are, that " Sir James was blameable for tacking at 6 h. 40 m. before it was *better ascertained* that the enemy had wore and stood towards him." Lord Keith, in his report, makes use of a very just observation, that " it is so difficult to judge at a distance how things may appear to those upon the spot, or how the same things may impress different men, that he felt great difficulty in hazarding any opinion on the subject." The opinion of the Pompée's officers must then surely be the best evidence respecting it; and with regard to that part of the question, Sir James Wood, in his defence, says,

" The enemy's ships were at sunset between eight and nine miles distant from the Pompée, which I estimate from their poops being seen from ours, and they bore N. by E. the Pompée then lying up N. by W. wind N. E. by E. and the Diana about two miles on our lee bow. At this time I observed the enemy's leading ship wearing round to the larboard tack, and setting his larboard fore-top-mast studding-sail. The Pompée was tacked before the close of day, and we stood close hauled to the S. E. and by E. on the larboard tack, with a view to prevent the enemy closing with us too soon, as well as to *shew the two strange ships to windward, in the event of their being friends, how we intended standing after dark, that they might be enabled to join us without being embarrassed by the enemy in this movement.* The necessary orders were given to get an additional number of shot up for the guns, and an additional proportion of powder filled, and the ship in every way prepared for action. It was a pitch-dark night, and no possibility of keeping sight of the enemy's ships at much greater distance than musket-shot when no lights were shewn. About half-past seven the reflection of the flashes of guns was reported to have been seen in the horizon. About this time a rocket was thrown up in the N. W. quarter, in the direction in which the Diana was last seen; and lights were reported to be visible at intervals, of more or less than half an hour, nearly in the direction in which the enemy was last seen during the whole of the first watch until seven bells, when I directed the bearings of the last light seen to be taken by compass, which was N. and by E. From the fatigue occasioned by being constantly on deck, with the exception of an hour at dinner, from morning of that day until within a few minutes of midnight, when it fell little wind, the ship then only going a little more than a knot, and the men at their quarters, I went into my cabin, and lay down on a couch with my clothes on, having previously given to the officer of the watch the strictest orders to sweep the horizon with the night-glass, particularly in that quarter where the enemy's lights were last seen; that the best possible look-out should be kept, and to inform me of the slightest alteration; and that every man should be kept at his quarters, as I had reason to believe that the lights seen at different intervals were those of the enemy, and that they appeared to me to near us, and if a good look-out was not kept, they would be along side of us before we saw them : but as there was but little wind, I did not think they could be up with us before daylight; but if the breeze freshened, I was to be immediately acquainted with it. A little after one bell, the lieutenant of the watch, who had just relieved the deck, informed me, that there were two large ships close to us to windward, which he believed to be the enemy. I instantly got upon deck, and with the night-glass perceived two large ships about musket-shot from us, before the weather beam; and on some person saying, that there were two more astern of them, visible with the naked eye, I pointed the glass, and distinctly saw them also in a line together, appearing to me to be a cable's length distant from each other, and about four cables' length astern of the two ahead of them. I thought that they did not see the Pompée, because they did not immediately alter their course. I directed the helm to be put up, with an intention to make sail large; but considering that some time must elapse before studding-sails could be set in a pitch-dark night, and with so superior a force near us, it occurred to me to be the best measure in this situation to wear round and haul to the wind on the starboard tack, more especially as the enemy appeared to have their larboard studding-sails set, and this movement would embarrass them in following us.

" As we hauled to the wind on the starboard tack, the breeze freshened, and I think about that time shifted to the northward. I could then perceive, from the weather and starboard gangway, the enemy's ships almost before the wind, two or three points on the weather quarter, appearing to wear round together after the Pompée; but by the time they got to the wind they were about a point on the Pompée's lee quarter. Here I beg leave to call the attention of the court, and ask if any convoy of merchant-ships would have wore round in this manner without signal, and have stood after a strange ship on a different tack to that on which they were standing before.

" After we had let our reefs out and set the royals, two or three sail were discovered on the weather quarter, and I could just perceive with the glass that they were square-rigged vessels; and as I took them for the enemy's frigates, or the ships seen to windward before dark, bearing down upon us, I edged away gradually. About this time two or three shot were fired at and over the Pompée; a dark cloud and drizzling rain coming on at the time, and the wind freshening, the royals were lowered: as we continued to edge away, we lost sight of them."

This statement of Sir James's was in the main corroborated by the evidence of the master and other officers; and he farther proved, that there was scarcely an officer or man on board that, at the moment, doubted they were in the presence of the enemy's squadron at midnight. That the enemy *could have wore round* and attacked the Pompée was proved by the evidence of Captain Ferris of the Diana, who said, " I continued standing to the northward till a little after six o'clock, when I observed the Pompée tack to the S. E; the enemy then bore about N. half E. or N. and by E. eight or nine miles; the Pompée S. E. about two miles, and the headmost of the ships to windward E. N. E. fourteen or fifteen miles. As the ships to windward were coming down, *and the enemy steering across our bows*, about W. and the Pompée still standing to the S. E. at dark I deemed it advisable to tack to the S. *to prevent our falling betwixt the ships that we knew to be the enemy's and the ships to windward, thereby precluding the possibility of escape.*" So that though Captain Ferris was so much nearer to the ships to windward than the Pompée, his doubts were so great as to their being friends, that he altered his course, because he would not come " betwixt them and those which he knew to be enemies." Being asked if he saw the enemy wear round and set larboard studding-sails, he said, " I did not observe them wear round, nor did I observe them, to the best of my knowledge, steering to the S. of W.; but somebody told me, that they thought the enemy *had larboard top-gallant studding-sails set*." The following question was also put: " At the time you saw the enemy steering across the bows of the Diana, supposing the Pompée and Diana had continued on the starboard tack, and the enemy had hauled up, steered for, and brought us to action, with their united force, were the ships to windward near enough to have rendered us assistance, until there was every reason to believe we should have been totally disabled by so superior a force and rendered unmanageable?" To which he replied, " My reason for hauling to the southward was to avoid the enemy, as by their hauling to the southward they would have fetched us with a leading wind; and had they brought us to action in that situation, I conceived, from the moderate state of the weather and the distance of the ships to windward, that we should have been considerably disabled by so superior a force, between the hours of dark and eight o'clock, before the ships to windward could have rendered us assistance."

That the enemy *did wear round* was fully proved by the evidence of Captain Jackson of the Poictiers, who stated, that " about half-past nine o'clock, being still in pursuit of the enemy, the night being extremely dark and squally, a light was discovered on the lee bow, which I was at first at some loss to ascertain whether it might be a light from the Tremendous or the enemy's squadron. A short time afterwards I found that the vessel which had the light was on the larboard tack. I immediately shortened sail and wore round after her, not then seeing the Tremendous, to ascertain whether that was she or not: I made the private signal, which was answered by the established distinguishing night-signal. Shortly afterwards the Tremendous made the signal to pass within hail; I ran down, and was hailed by Captain Campbell, *that he had just wore clear of the enemy, and that* HE BELIEVED THEY HAD PUT BEFORE THE WIND." By a reference to the logs of the Tremendous and Poictiers, it will be seen that the wind was then at N. E. and as they went before the wind, they must consequently have gone in the direction of the Pompée.

Having now, we trust, made it sufficiently clear that the enemy did wear round, and that sufficient evidence was offered to the court to prove it, it will be unnecessary to offer any observations on the second point on which the court thought Sir James was to blame—not tacking again to the northward—as, by his so doing, he would have wilfully placed his ship in jeopardy. We shall therefore dismiss this part of the question by supposing, that had he again tacked to the northward, and, as he most probably would, have fallen into the hands of the enemy, what would have been said of him? What would have been the sentence of the court which would have been held on him for the loss of his ship, when it was proved, that he had himself seen, and that other officers of the ship had seen, the enemy wear round after him?

The court also thought Sir James blameable " for not reconnoitring what the strangers reported to have been seen on the morning of the 11th were." This, however, we consider a most frivolous thing, and one which ought not to have been mentioned. Sir James was not on a cruise; he was proceeding under particular orders to join Sir Richard King in Quiberon Bay; and unless it can be asserted that he ought, under those circumstances, to chase every strange sail that he saw, he could not be to blame for not chasing those which were *reported to be seen* on the morning of the 11th. Sir James, however, proved, that though they were reported to be seen, before he could take their bearings the weather came on so thick that they were entirely lost sight of.

We shall only farther notice the following observation of Lord Keith respecting the plans which he forwarded to the Admiralty: " In these plans the situation of his Majesty's ships, as well as that of the enemy, is given at six p. m. of the 10th, and six a. m. of the 11th; and that of the Pompée is laid down at midnight of the 10th; and their lordships will observe, that *as the two sketches do not materially differ*, the ships seen by the Pompée at midnight, when she started her water, could not possibly have been those of the enemy which she saw at sunset, and that in all probability they were an outward-bound convoy, as appears to be admitted by Sir James Wood in a letter which I have received from him in transmitting his log." How Lord Keith could say that " the two sketches do not materially differ," we are at a loss to know, as we should think the most casual glance would be sufficient to discover the most essential differences. In the one marked A, which he said was drawn by Captain Jackson, it will be seen, that at six p. m. on the 10th of March the enemy's squadron, Pompée, Diana, and Tremendous are placed as standing to the N. W.; while the Poictiers, Myrtle, and convoy are steering a direct contrary course: but in the plan marked B, at the same moment of time, the enemy's squadron is still represented as standing to the N. W.; but the Pompée, Diana, Tremendous, Poictiers, Myrtle, and convoy are going to the W. N. W. The difference, however, is still greater in the second position. Both in A and B the enemy's squadron is described as standing to the S. W. at six a. m. on the 11th; but the Poictiers and Tremendous in A are placed right astern of them, standing to the N. W.; whilst in B they are placed nearly astern, but standing to the S. W. Whilst the difference in the positions of the Pompée is still more striking: in A she is represented on the starboard bow of the enemy, standing to the N. W. the same course as the Tremendous; but in B she is represented on the larboard quarter, at least sixty miles off, standing to the S. W. the same course as the enemy, Tremendous, and Poictiers. One of them indeed, B, bore its condemnation on the face of it; as it was there stated that " the Pompée and Tremendous are placed in the latitude and longitude agreeably to the courses and distance run by their logs;" and then adds, " it appears, on the 10th at noon, by the log of the Tremendous, she was in the latitude of 48 deg. 28 min. and longitude 6 deg. 4 min. W. Ushant S. E. by E. half E. by compass, distant ten miles. If Ushant was then seen, *there appears to be an error of forty miles in longitude.* The Poictiers, on the 10th at noon, was in latitude 48 deg. 4 min. N. longitude 6 deg. 21 min. in company with the Tremendous; and by her log Ushant bore N. 65 deg. E. distant 56 miles." What reliance can be placed on such documents? And yet these were submitted by Lord Keith to the Lords of the Admiralty, and by them laid before the court-martial. The fact is, they are both erroneous; it was impossible for any one to judge correctly from them; and we have heard that Sir Richard Bickerton, the president of the court-martial, than whom a more honourable man does not exist, stated, that the members of the court did not understand the position of the different ships. In the plan marked C we have endeavoured to trace the course of each ship, which, with the above observations, will, we have no doubt, sufficiently explain the whole of the circumstances.

Respecting the assertion made by Lord Keith, that Sir James had, in a letter to him, admitted that the ships he fell in with in the night were not the enemy's squadron, but an English convoy, we must insert the following satisfactory explanation made by Sir James in his defence:

" That it was possible, nay probable, and, independent of any other proof, is susceptible of mathematical demonstration, that the ships which got within gun-shot of the Pompée at midnight were unquestionably those of the enemy seen at sunset; because, from their position to windward, at the distance of no more than nine or ten miles when we stood close hauled on the larboard tack, having little

wind, and the enemy's ships bearing up after us with a press of sail, and bringing
down with them any occasional flaws and breezes, they could, under such circumstances, undoubtedly run, in about six hours' time, twenty-four miles for the
Pompée's eighteen, which is in the average proportion of four miles by the enemy
to three by the Pompée in an hour; and it is more than probable that they brought
with them a similar breeze to that mentioned in the evidence of Captain Jackson,
wherein he says, that he carried as much sail during the night as his masts would
bear. That these ships were no other than the enemy's will be proved from the
bearings of their lights at different intervals during the first watch; and this fact
is even corroborated by the evidence of Captain Ferris, who states, that when he
saw the enemy crossing his bow, he stood from three quarters of an hour to an
hour to the S. and E.; he then tacked, and stood until half-past nine to the
northward, and then tacked again to the S. E.; and in a short interval he saw a
light on the lee bow, which he supposed to be the Pompée's. The court will observe, that, in laying down these three different courses of the Diana till half-past
nine, it was impossible, from the distance, for her to have seen a light from
the Pompée, had she even shewn one: but the fact is, that the light then seen on
their lee bow could be no other than that of the enemy's bearing down after the
Pompée, steering about S. S. E. with the wind at N. E. and by E. As to the
opinion given by his lordship of all his Majesty's ships outsailing those of the
enemy, it has already appeared they did collectively; but there was a ship or two
of the enemy's squadron which sailed better than some of his Majesty's ships.
Were it even to be admitted or established by proof that the Pompée, after sunset and before starting her water, sailed in every way equal to, if not better, than
the enemy's ships, yet, with all deference to Lord Keith's opinion, it is possible
they might have approached us within gun-shot by midnight. This is the more
obvious in considering the relative bearings and distance of the one from the
other, and that the Pompée was close hauled on the larboard tack, and in the
trough of a N. E. swell; while the enemy's ships were sailing large, under a press
of sail, and had also the advantage of the first breeze which sprung up from windward, with a very favourable shift of wind to the northward and the swell abaft
the beam: this fact is confirmed by the Pompée's getting the breeze immediately
after the enemy's ships were discovered at midnight. In addition to what I have
just stated, it has occurred to me, that, notwithstanding the opinions given by Captain Jackson and other officers, of his Majesty's ships sailing better than the
enemy collectively, yet it must appear to this court, that such opinions are vague
and nugatory, as it does not appear by their evidence that they were nearer the
enemy in the evening than in the morning of the 10th, and while they were lying
to and running after other ships on various courses. Now, was it possible for

them at such a distance to see what sail the enemy set or shortened, or if his head-
sails might not have been aback or shivering to deceive them, as they appeared
to me to be at half-past six on the evening of the 10th, with a view to deceive us?
With respect to my having admitted, as Lord Keith has been pleased to say I did
in the letter I sent with my log, that in all probability the ships seen at midnight
were an outward-bound convoy, his lordship appears inadvertently to have drawn
such an inference from a single paragraph, of which, if compared by the court with
the contents of my letter, the true meaning will be perfectly obvious, and which, in
justice to myself, I shall now briefly explain.   After having detailed in the letter
alluded to the Pompée's proceedings from the time I first discovered the enemy
and strange ships, and described the position of the different ships subsequently
seen during the night and until daylight of the morning of the 11th March, I
concluded with these words: *' Judging from what I have since learned, I think
these ships were the two frigates and corvettes from Bourdeaux ; and for the same
reason,'* having a reference to the former words, *' from what I have since learned,
I also believe that the ships we fell in with after bearing up from the enemy were an
English convoy.'* The ships alluded to in the beginning of the paragraph were
those seen at daylight of the 11th March, which were immediately lost sight of
from fog and drizzling rain ; and as I never bore up from the enemy until an hour
and a half after midnight, it is obvious that the ships alluded to in the conclusion
of the above paragraph had a reference only to those seen on the weather quarter
at that time, and not to those on the lee quarter, that had been crowding all sail
after the Pompée for an hour before, and from which I bore away gradually.''

In addition to what is here stated we have only to observe, that, since
the termination of hostilities, Sir James has had opportunities of seeing
and conversing with some of the officers of the French squadron, who
fully confirmed his statement as to their having wore round, in the hopes
of capturing the Pompée, and that they most certainly would have succeeded had they not have obtained sight of the convoy at midnight,
which were taken for the blockading squadron, instead of merchant-ships,
upon which they bore away to the S. or S. S. W.

Sir James after the trial proceeded to the Mediterranean, where he
continued during the remainder of the war, and was left by Lord Exmouth in charge of a squadron off Catalonia, to prevent the enemy from
throwing supplies into Barcelona, and in 1815 to command the squadron
off Toulon and the coast of Provence.   In June 1815 he was nominated
a Companion of the Bath, and in July 1821 was made a rear-admiral.

HISTORICAL MEMOIRS OF

Admiral Sir WILLIAM SIDNEY SMITH, K.C.B.

IT has been said that there is something peculiarly gratifying to generous minds in perusing the professional services of our naval officers, in accompanying them through the paths of conquest and glory, in identifying ourselves with all their motives and conduct, and, without robbing them, fully participating in the fame acquired from their noble exertions; and that the biographer who undertakes to record their actions cannot fail to find his labours the labours of pleasure. Be this as it may in a general point of view, we approach the present subject with feelings of delight, pain, and anxiety; delight, that the exertions of one man have so greatly increased the stock of national glory; pain, that his exertions have been so inadequately rewarded; and anxiety, lest the reputation of the officer should suffer through the inability of the narrator.

Sir William Sidney Smith is the grandson of Captain Edward Smith, who commanded the Burford, and who was mortally wounded at the attack of la Guira in 1743, and son of Captain Smith, an officer in the army, who was aide-de-camp to Lord George Sackville during his campaign in Germany. He is also nephew to the late Lord Camelford, who married the sister of Sir Sidney's mother*. He was born in 1764, and entered the naval service in 1776 on board the Unicorn, commanded by the late Admiral Ford; he was also a short time on board the Lion with Captain Folkes, and from that ship removed to the Sandwich, bearing the flag of Sir George Rodney, with whom he proceeded to the West Indies, and acted as his aide-de-camp in the action of the 17th April and 15th and 19th May, 1780. He then served for a short time as a supernumerary lieutenant of the Greyhound, and on the 25th September was appointed fifth lieutenant of the Alcide, commanded by Captain C. Thompson, and was with him in the actions off Martinique in April 1781, the Chesapeake in September following, St. Kitt's in February 1782, and the actions of the 9th and 12th of April. Shortly after the last im-

---

* They were the daughters of a Mr. Pinkney Wilkinson, an opulent merchant; and as the marriage of his daughter with Captain Smith took place without his consent, he left the whole of his property to Lord Camelford.

portant day he was promoted by Sir George Rodney to the rank of commander in the Fury sloop, in which he succeeded in cutting out several vessels from under the batteries of St. Domingo. On the 7th May, 1783, he was advanced to the rank of post-captain in the Nemesis frigate; and hostilities having terminated, he returned to England in that vessel.

Universal peace now reigned throughout the states of Europe, and Captain Smith remained unemployed till 1788, when the probability of a war taking place between Russia and Sweden, he repaired to Stockholm, and afterwards became a volunteer in the Swedish navy. We regret that we are not able to give a detailed account of his services whilst so employed; but, says a gentleman, " from the frequent conversations I have had with him on that subject, his conduct there was marked with that energy and firmness which never deserted him on any occasion." It was here that that romantic spirit of enterprise which he possessed was fully displayed, which brought his character into general notice, and pointed him out as one who was likely to add to his country's honour and greatness. In the month of June 1790, a desperate battle took place between the Swedish and Russian fleets in the gulf of Wybourg, in which the Swedes lost seven ships of the line, three frigates, and twenty gallies. In this action he served on board the king's yacht, and rendered the greatest assistance by his advice and personal exertions. The Swedish fleet, under the Duke of Sudermania, had been previously lying in the harbour of Wybourg, blockaded both by sea and land by the enemy, who had erected batteries on all the islands to defend the passage; and it was fully expected that the Swedish admiral would be obliged to surrender. In this extremity Captain Smith volunteered his services to the king to carry a letter from his Majesty to the Swedish admiral, ordering him to put to sea at all events. With two gallies he reconnoitred the enemy's fleet, and observing some Dutch ships at anchor in the mouth of the harbour, he put the king's letter in a bladder, which he tied round him. In the headmost galley he entered the passage, followed by the other; but the enemy opening a brisk fire occasioned a calm: he then stripped off his clothes, leaped overboard in the smoke, and swam to the nearest Dutch ship, a distance of two miles, the master of which received him on board, and at night conveyed him to the Swedish admiral's ship. Having delivered his letter, he went on board a galley, and during the action which ensued sailed past the Russian batteries, and escaped without any accident. But for this heroic act of Captain Smith's, the whole of the Swedish fleet would have been taken, as Wybourg soon after surrendered. The loss sustained on this occasion was, however, fully retrieved shortly afterwards, when the King of Sweden commanded in person, assisted by the valour, intrepidity, and judgment of Captain Smith. The Russian admiral was defeated with the loss of nearly fifty vessels of various descriptions, taken or destroyed, and which led to a peace between the two powers. His services to the Swedish monarch did not go unrewarded, as he was made a Grand Cross of the Order of the Sword, the insignia of which was presented to him after his arrival by his own sovereign at St. James's. He afterwards proceeded to Turkey, and when his country became involved in a war with France in 1793, he was " travelling in the Levant for amusement and improvement, and chanced to be at Smyrna, where there was collected a number of English seamen out of employ, some saved from shipwreck, and others straggling along shore. Sir Sidney being intent on returning home, in obedience to the usual notice from the Admiralty, bethought himself of these men, as likely to be lost to their country at such a critical time, and with equal patriotism and humanity determined to reclaim them. He accordingly purchased one of the latteen-rigged small craft of the Archipelago, and fitted her out at his own expense, under the title of the Swallow tender, in which diminutive man of war, of between thirty and forty feet keel, he sailed down the Mediterranean in search of the British fleet, which he found at Toulon a short time before the evacuation*." Having delivered up his troublesome charge to the commander-in-chief, he was waiting, as a guest, with his old commander, Lord Hood, on board the Victory, for a passage to England, at the moment when it became necessary to decide upon the fate of the French fleet and arsenal, and also upon extricating the allied army, which was the principal object of solicitude, and absorbed almost the whole naval means of the British and Spanish squadrons. It was at this anxious moment that Sir Sidney volunteered to set fire to the enemy's ships and arsenal; a service generally considered as impracticable, owing to the slender means with which it could be attempted. The following is his own account of this important transaction:

* *Naval Chronicle.*

TOULON, *Dec.* 18, 1793.

MY LORD,—Agreeably to your lordship's order I proceeded with the Swallow tender, three English and three Spanish gun-boats, to the arsenal, and immediately began making the necessary preparations for burning the French ships and stores therein. We found the dock-gates well secured by the judicious arrangements of the governor, although the dock-yard people had already substituted the three-coloured cockade for the white one. I did not think it safe to attempt the securing any of them, considering the small force I had with me; and considering that a contest of any kind would occupy our whole attention, and prevent us from accomplishing our preparations. The galley-slaves, to the number of at least six hundred, shewed themselves jealous spectators of our operations; their disposition to oppose us was evident, and being unchained (which was unusual), rendered it necessary to keep a watchful eye on them. I accordingly restrained them on board the galley by pointing the guns of the Swallow tender and one of the gun-boats on them, in such a manner as to enfilade the quay on which they must land to come to us; assuring them, at the same time, that no harm should happen to them if they remained quiet. The enemy kept up a cross fire of shot and shells on the spot from Malbousquet and the neighbouring hills, which contributed to keep the galley-slaves in subjection, and operated in every respect favourably for us, by keeping the republican party in the town within their houses, while it occasioned little interruption to our work of preparing and placing combustible matter in the different storehouses and on board the ships, such was the steadiness of the few brave men I had under my command. A great multitude of the enemy continued to draw down the hill towards the dock-yard wall; and as the night closed in they came near enough to pour in an irregular though quick fire on us from the Boulargerie and the heights which overlook it. We kept them at bay by discharges of grape-shot from time to time, which prevented their coming so near us as to discover the insufficiency of our force. To repel a closer attack a gun-boat was stationed to flank the wall on the outside, and two field-pieces were placed within against the wicket usually frequented by the workmen, of whom we were particularly apprehensive. About eight o'clock I had the satisfaction to see Lieutenant Gore towing in the Vulcan fire-ship; Captain Hare, her commander, placed her, agreeably to my directions, in a most masterly manner across the tier of men of war, and the additional force of her guns and men diminished my apprehensions of the galley-slaves rising on us, as their murmurs and occasional tumultuous debates ceased entirely on her appearance; the only noise heard among them was the hammer knocking off their fetters, which humanity forbade my opposing, as they might thereby be more at liberty to save themselves on the conflagration taking place around them. In this situation we continued to wait most anxiously for the hour concerted with the governor for the inflammation of the trains. The moment the signal was made, we had the satisfaction to see the flames rise in every quarter. Lieutenant Tupper was charged with the burning of the general magazine, the pitch, tar, tallow, and oil storehouses, and succeeded most perfectly: the hemp-magazine was included in this blaze. It being nearly calm was unfavourable to the spreading of the flames; but two hundred and fifty barrels of tar, divided among the deals and other timber, ensured the rapid ignition of that whole quarter which Lieutenant Tupper had undertaken. The mast-house was equally well set on fire by Lieutenant Middleton of the Britannia. Lieutenant Pater of the Britannia continued in a most daring manner to brave the flames, in order to complete the work where the fire seemed to have caught imperfectly. I was obliged to call him off, lest his retreat should become impracticable: his situation was the more perilous, as the enemy's fire redoubled as soon as the amazing blaze of light rendered us distinct objects for their aim. Lieutenant Ironmonger of the Royals remained with the guard at the gate till the last, long after the Spanish guard was withdrawn, and was brought safely off by Captain Edge of the Alert, to whom I had confided the important service of closing our retreat and bringing off our detached parties, who were saved to a man. I was sorry to find myself deprived of the farther services of Captain Hare: he had performed that of placing his fire-ship to admiration, but was blown into the water and much scorched by the explosion of her priming when in the act of putting the match to it. Lieutenant Gore was also much burnt, and I was consequently deprived of him also, which I regretted the more, from the recollection of his bravery and activity in the warm service of Fort Mulgrave. Mr. Eales, midshipman, who was also with him on this occasion, deserves my praise for his conduct throughout this service. The guns of the fire-ship going off on both sides as they retreated in the direction that was given them towards those quarters from whence we were most apprehensive of the enemy forcing their way upon us, checked their career. Their shouts and republican songs, which we could hear distinctly, continued till they, as well as ourselves, were in a manner thunderstruck by the explosion of some thousand barrels of powder on board the Iris frigate, lying in the inner road without us, and which had been injudiciously set on fire by the Spanish boats on going off, instead of being sunk as ordered: the concussion of air and the shower of timber falling on fire were such as nearly to destroy the whole of us. Lieutenant Pater of the Britannia, with his whole boat's crew, nearly perished; the boat was blown to pieces, but the men were picked up alive. The Union gun-boat, which was nearest to the Iris, suffered considerably, Mr. Young being killed, with three men, and the vessel shaken to pieces. I had given it in charge to the Spanish officers to fire the ships in the basin before the town; but they returned, and reported that various obstacles had prevented them entering it. We attempted it together, as soon as we had completed the business in the arsenal; but were repulsed in our attempts to cut the boom by repeated volleys of musketry from the flag-ship and the wall of the Batterie Royale. The cannon of this battery had been spiked by the judicious precaution taken by the governor previous to the evacuation of the town. The rear of our column being by this time out of the eastern gate, the horrid cries of the poor inhabitants announced that the villanous part of the community had got the upper hand. Boats full of men, women, and children, pushed from the shore, even without oars, claiming our protection from the knife of the assassin by the most sacred of all ties—our professed friendship. We accordingly kept our station for the purpose of affording them an asylum. Many straggling Neapolitan soldiers, whose undisciplined conduct had separated them from the main body, were among the number thus driven into the water. We received them as more particularly belonging to us, repulsing their pursuers by our fire; nor did we quit the shore till we had received all who were there to claim our assistance. The failure of our attempt on the ships in the basin before the town, owing to the insufficiency of our force, made me regret that the Spanish gun-boats had been withdrawn from me to perform other service. The adjutants, Don Pedro Cotiella, Don Riguelme, and Don Truxillo, remained with me to the last; and I feel bound to bear testimony of the zeal and activity with which they performed the most essential services during the whole of this business, as far as the insufficiency of the force allowed, it being reduced by the retreat of the gun-boats to a single felucca and a mortar-boat, which had expended its ammunition, but contained thirty cutlasses. We now proceeded to burn the Hero and Themistocles, two 74-gun ships lying in the inner road. Our approach to them had hitherto been impracticable in boats, as the French prisoners who had been left in the latter ship were still in possession of her, and had shewn a determination to resist our attempt to come on board. The scene of conflagration around them, heightened by the late tremendous explosion, had, however, awakened their fears for their lives. Thinking this to be the case, I addressed them, expressing my readiness to land them in a place of safety if they would submit; and they most thankfully accepted the offer, shewing themselves to be completely intimidated, and very grateful for our humane intentions towards them in not attempting to burn them with the ship. It was necessary to proceed with precaution, as they were more numerous than ourselves. We at length completed their disembarkation, and then set her on fire. On this occasion I had nearly lost my valuable friend and assistant, Lieutenant Miller of the Windsor Castle, who had staid so long on board to ensure the fire taking, that it gained on him suddenly; and it was not without being much scorched and the risk of being suffocated, that we could approach the ship to take him in. Mr. Knight, midshipman, of the

Windsor Castle, who was in the boat with me, shewed much activity and address on this occasion, as well as firmness throughout the day. The explosion of a second powder-vessel, equally unexpected, and with a shock even greater than the first, again put us in the most imminent danger of perishing; and when it is considered that we were within the sphere of the falling timber, it is next to miraculous that not one piece of the many, while the water foamed around us, happened to touch either the Swallow or the three boats with me. Having now set fire to every thing within our reach, exhausted our combustible preparations, and our strength to such a degree, that the men absolutely dropped on the oars, we directed our course to join the fleet, running the gauntlet under a few ill-directed shot from the Forts Balagué and Aiguelette, now occupied by the enemy, but fortunately without loss of any kind. We proceeded to the place appointed for the embarkation of the troops, and took off as many as we could carry. It would be injustice to those officers whom I have omitted to name (from their not having been so immediately under my eye) if I did not acknowledge myself indebted to them all, for their extraordinary exertions in the execution of this great national object; the quickness with which the inflammation took effect on my signal, its extent and duration, are the best evidences that every officer and man was ready at his post, and firm under most perilous circumstances. We can ascertain that the fire extended to at least ten ships of the line; the loss of the general magazine, and of the quantity of pitch, tar, rosin, hemp, timber, cordage, and gunpowder, must considerably impede the equipment of the few ships that remain. I am sorry to have been obliged to leave any, but I hope your lordship will be satisfied that we did as much as our circumscribed means enabled us to do in a little time. (Signed,) W. S. SMITH.

Sir Sidney Smith returned to England with Lord Hood's dispatches; and in July 1794 was appointed to the Diamond frigate, in which he had frequent opportunities to distinguish himself, which were always embraced with his usual zeal, serving to display his own abilities and to annoy the enemies of his country. Having sailed with Sir John Warren off the French coast, they fell in with La Volontaire of 38 guns and two corvettes, the former of which the Diamond, being far ahead of the squadron, brought to action, and she was driven on shore, as were the two corvettes, and totally destroyed. In the next cruise they fell in with the Revolutionaire, which was brought to action by the Artois, and struck when the Diamond was in the act of laying her on board. On the 3d January, 1795, the Diamond was detached by Sir John Warren to reconnoitre the harbour of Brest, information having been received that the French fleet had sailed from that port. The wind being to the eastward, the Diamond was obliged to beat up, and about two p.m. observed three sail working up, which proved to be French men of war; shortly after which one of them anchored between Ushant and Brest. At five, the Diamond was also obliged to anchor within two miles of her, to wait for the flood tide. At eleven Sir Sidney again weighed and passed within half a mile of the French ship, which he distinctly observed to be of the line, much disabled, and under jury-masts. About two a.m. on the morning of the 4th, the Diamond was well up with the entrance of Brest harbour, where a frigate was lying at anchor; but the ebb tide making down before it was daylight, Sir Sidney was obliged to keep under sail to prevent getting to leeward or creating suspicion, and he continued standing across the harbour often within musket-shot of the enemy. At daylight he stood close in, and having satisfied himself that the French were at sea, he bore away to rejoin Sir John Warren. A corvette, which was coming out of Brest, hove-to and made a signal, which not being answered by the Diamond, she began making signals to two other ships, which immediately got under weigh. His situation now became critical, more especially as the line-of-battle ship had taken a position to cut off his retreat, and left him to his own resources, which were found amply sufficient. As there was no way of removing their alarm but by conduct which shewed he was perfectly undismayed, he bore down within hail of the line-of-battle ship, and perceiving her to have no upper-deck guns mounted, and to be very leaky, he began a conversation with the French captain, by accounting for his change of course in consequence of seeing his disabled state, and requesting to know if he could render him any assistance. He replied in the negative; that he had been dismasted in a heavy gale of wind, and had parted with the French fleet three days before. Some other conversation passed; and Sir Sidney, seeing that his presence of mind had prevented the other ships from pursuing him, crowded all sail and stood out to sea. He was afterwards placed under the orders of Sir Richard Strachan; and in May he assisted in capturing a convoy of the enemy's coasting vessels. He was then intrusted with the command of a small squadron, consisting of the Diamond, Syren, and Sibylle, with four gun-boats, with which he sailed from St. Helen's on the 1st July, and stretched over to the French coast. On going round Cape Barfleur two ships were discovered at anchor, and he immediately made sail towards them; soon after which an enemy's convoy was observed coming along shore within the Island of St. Marcou. The wind dying away, and the ebb tide making against him, he had the mortification to see the enemy's vessels drift with the tide under the batteries of la Hogue, without being able to approach them. At four a.m. July 4, a breeze sprung up with the first of the flood, and he then worked up towards the enemy, who were observed warping closer towards the batteries. About nine the action commenced, and continued for three-quarters of an hour, when, finding it impossible to get along side the enemy without grounding, he hauled off. He, however, continued on the enemy's coast harassing his trade, and in September fell in with a corvette of 22 guns, and, after a long chase, the enemy endeavoured to escape by running amongst a labyrinth of rocks; but the attempt proved fatal, as she struck on one of them, and after filling, fell over. The boats of the Diamond were immediately dispatched to her relief, by which the greater part of the crew were saved. In the following year he displayed his usual characteristic spirit of enterprise and valour, which were again rewarded with deserved success. Having in the month of March received information that a corvette of 16 guns, three luggers, four brigs, and two sloops, were in Herqui, he proceeded off that port, and having sounded the channel, found it very narrow and intricate, and the entrance defended by two batteries on a rocky promontory: notwithstanding which, having succeeded in obtaining a knowledge of their situation, and being joined by the Liberty brig and Aristocrat lugger, he determined to attack them without loss of time. The batteries having been stormed and carried, the Diamond and her two consorts then proceeded in to attack the vessels, all of which were completely destroyed.

In the following month the country was for some time deprived of his services, and of that unparalleled spirit of enterprise which Sir Sidney had manifested throughout his career. " Eager in the pursuit of that system of warfare which he had proved himself so complete a master of," and being at anchor on the 17th April in the outer road of Havre, he discovered in the inner harbour an armed lugger, the only remaining vessel which annoyed the English trade on this station; she mounted 10 guns, and was commanded by a bold enterprising captain. As Sir Sidney had established it as a point of honour that an enemy's vessel should not pass from one port to another, he determined to carry her in the night by means of his boats. After a contest of about ten minutes, she was carried; but during the action the cable was cut, and she drifted above the forts. The dawn of day discovered them to the enemy on shore, the signal of alarm was given, and they were soon attacked by an overwhelming force, consisting of a lugger, gun-boats, and other armed vessels, with which he contended for some time, but in the end was obliged to surrender, after having had four men killed and seven wounded.

Such was the issue of this daring attempt, respecting which Captain Brenton says, " Sir Sidney Smith, while cruising off Havre in the Diamond, went in his own boats to cut out *some* small vessels in the mouth of the Seine. He succeeded in boarding one of them; but whether this gallant officer, led by that spirit of enterprise for which he was so remarkable, landed and was taken prisoner, or whether his boats drifted so far up the river as to be unable to escape, has never been stated to the public: we believe the former account is correct; and are *confirmed in our suspicion from the very close and rigid confinement of that officer*, and which would not, under any other circumstance, have been justifiable or necessary*."

Captain Brenton appears to us to be the oddest reasoner we ever heard of: so because Sir Sidney was subjected to " very close and rigid confinement," he must have landed on the enemy's coast; and the inference is, that he had become a spy and deserved the treatment he experienced. Captain Brenton, however, appears to have forgotten that he had himself given a different account of the affair in the preceding volume of his work†, wherein he says, " On the 8th April Sir Sidney Smith, in the Diamond of 38 guns, while off Havre, went with his boats to cut out *a* French lugger; he succeeded in boarding her, but the flood tide setting in, *he was forced to anchor;* and during the night the cable being either cut by the prisoners or parted by accident, the vessel was *most carelessly allowed to drift up the Seine*, when she was retaken by some gun-boats." As these accounts are very different from each other, and also from the facts themselves, we shall insert the following statement, which was drawn up by Mr. Westley Wright, who was one of the party, and who has considered it under the three following heads:

" Ought a commander of a squadron to risk his own person on detached service? Was the capture of the Vengeur lugger an object of sufficient magnitude to authorize the attack in her own port? And, did the circumstances of her situation, wind, weather, and tides, afford a reasonable prospect of success in the attack?

" As to the first, it is answered, that in a squadron on service of peculiar activity and hazard, wherein much more is expected both of officers and men, this is usually required in the ordinary routine of cruising service. It is not only allowable, but it is the duty of a commander to be himself foremost wherever his presence may appear to be most necessary at the time; and to command by example, as well to inspire emulation and confidence, as to silence those *(some of whom are to be found in every body of men)* who hold language tending to discourage enterprise by magnifying the danger and diminishing the value of the object pursued; for it is impossible to answer such by argument, without entering into a debate that would be subversive of subordination and that prompt obedience which form the very essence of the naval strength of the country. A lieutenant might perhaps have been detached on this particular occasion, *had there been one on board fit for duty;* but the first lieutenant was gone home from Herqui with dispatches; the second lieutenant was sick; the third lieutenant had been ill, and kept watch from the necessity of the case, though unequal to any great exertion; the acting-lieutenant, though equal in courage to any service, was considered too young to command; the master, an excellent pilot, was better left in charge of the ship than detached. The squadron being extended along the coast from Jersey to Havre, the Diamond *was alone* on this eastern part of the station, having directed her course thither for the express purpose of intercepting privateers, of whose depredations information had been received both from the shore and from the Admiralty officially.

" As to the second question, this capture was of the more consequence as the squadron had so effectually blockaded the enemy's ports within the limits of the station for the past year, that no capture had been made by the enemy in the Channel during that time, till those recently announced; which had given our coasting trade such a degree of confidence that they frequently ventured without convoy. The Vengeur had been the most successful cruiser during the preceding week: this had been learned by the recapture of one of her prizes, whose prize-master represented her captain as very enterprising, and well acquainted with the English coast. She had narrowly escaped the Syren, who had chased her into Isigny river; at which time her light draught of water and superior sailing proved it to be impossible she could ever be captured otherwise than by being boarded during a calm by boats. She was discovered at anchor in the main road of Havre, evidently ready to start on a fresh cruise. The Diamond having been nearly four months at sea, her provisions and water were so much reduced that she was unable to remain off the port to watch the Vengeur, and there was no lugger in the squadron to perform this service. Add to this, a rendezvous was given for all the ships to meet off Cape Barfleur three days afterwards, for a particular and indispensable service, and two of the squadron were gone to Portsmouth to bring over the necessary supplies to that rendezvous; so that every thing prompted the necessity of not leaving this active cruiser at liberty to come out and commit new depredations during the forced absence of the squadron from the eastern extremity of the station; and, in short, of cutting her out at once, if possible.

" This leads to the third question, as to the prospect of success. The boarding a vessel of force by boats is reckoned so hazardous by naval officers as not to be attempted. The attacking party are necessarily obliged to row up under her fire, and must expect to meet a vigorous resistance from a greater number of men than they can bring to one point, who have, at the same time, the advantage of standing a few feet more elevated than the men in the boats : it is therefore advisable to choose a moment when she does not expect an attack, and to approach at least within musket-shot unseen, before the alarm occasions her fire to open. This moment offered, with every circumstance that could be wished. The security the lugger's people could not but feel, lying under the protection of several batteries, rendered it probable they would be unprepared, thinking an attack unlikely. The calmness of the weather was favourable to the approach of the boats, and the moon being obscured by clouds afforded a degree of light suitable to such an enterprise. The little air of wind there was being from the sea, occasioned the lugger to be to windward of any thing that might come out from Havre pier : it was necessary, however, to wait till the ebb was done, against which the boats could not pull to where she lay. A person not acquainted with the Havre tides will naturally ask, ' Why not go in with the last of the flood, and come out with the first of the ebb, taking the slack water for the operation of boarding ?' To obtain a conclusive answer to this question, it is necessary to consult the *Petit Neptune,* where the peculiarity of these tides is remarked and accounted for. The first of the ebb coming down the Seine meets the Channel flood and stops, making three hours slack water and full tide in Havre pier and basin : the first drain of the ebb tide in the inner road partakes of the direction of the flood still running with rapidity in the Channel, so that the muddy waters of the Seine are carried up to and round Cape la Heve; in which case the lugger, being cut from her anchors at the first of the ebb, in little wind, must have drifted under the new battery of Cape la Heve, and very slowly passed it : whereas the first of the flood setting southward, to fill the Toque and Dive rivers, and partaking of the direction of the Channel ebb, would carry her directly from all the batteries of Havre, when once clear of the pier tide. This moment was therefore chosen; and likewise because the two gun-boats, which had been ordered to follow the Diamond, and keep close in shore, were likely to be at that time off Dive. Every part of this calculation answered, except that of the arrival of the gun-boats, whose protection was looked for. One untoward circumstance happened, which was the cable being cut by the enemy during the contest, before the boats were ahead to tow, or the sails set to catch the light air of wind from the sea ; consequently the vessel remained longer in the partial tide setting round the pier-head than would have been the case had she been got under weigh properly, and this occasioned her to drift to leeward of the pier. It is evident she must otherwise have been so far to the windward of the pier in the stretch off as to keep the weather gage of whatever might come out of Havre on the alarm of the firing, at an equal distance to that she was to windward of at getting under weigh, which would have rendered her being cut off impossible. As it was, the capture was made without loss, the prize was brought from under the guns of Havre without molestation, and anchored on the Harfleur shore ; after which Sir Sidney put off to return to the Diamond in his boat, and had made considerable way when the enemy's vessels came out of Havre ; he then returned on board the lugger, determined to defend her, if possible, till the north-east tide made. The boat in which he was returning escaped afterwards, as did the launch ; so that if he could have considered his personal safety alone, and have deserted those whom it was his duty to encourage by his example and presence to such a degree of resistance as might extricate the whole party, he might have got off ; but after the first shot flight is out of the question for any man of honour, and particularly a commanding officer : the defence was prolonged while there was the smallest hope of extrication ; and if there had been more wind the lugger would have been brought out, having beat off the first assailants."

After a short stay at Havre Sir Sidney was conveyed to Paris, where he was thrown into prison, and " where the nature of his situation will be best understood by knowing that, among his *mitigations*, was the permission to walk occasionally in the court, and to enjoy the privilege of shaving himself;" but he was afterwards treated with less rigour. The means of escape appear to have constantly occupied his mind, and after several attempts had been made and failed, he was at last successful. From his own account, we extract the following :

" We were so far, however, from suffering ourselves to be discouraged, that we still continued to form new schemes for our deliverance; the keeper perceived it, and I was frequently so open as to acknowledge the fact. ' Commodore,' said he, ' your friends are desirous of liberating you, and they only do their duty ; I also am doing mine in watching you still more narrowly.' Though this keeper was a man of unparalleled severity, yet he never departed from the rules of civility and politeness; he treated all the prisoners with kindness, and even piqued himself on his generosity. Various proposals were made to him, but he rejected them all, watched us more closely, and preserved the profoundest silence. One day when I dined with him, he perceived that I fixed my attention on a window then partly open, and which looked upon the street. I saw his uneasiness, and it amused me: however, to put an end to it I said to him, laughing, ' I know what you are thinking of; but fear not: it is now three o'clock; I will make a truce with you till midnight; and I give you my word of honour, until that time, even were the doors open, I would not escape: when that hour is passed my promise is at an end, and we are enemies again.'—' Sir,' replied he, ' your word is a safer bond than my bolts or bars; till midnight therefore I am perfectly easy.' When we arose from the table he took me aside, and said, ' Commodore, the Boulevard is not far; if you are inclined to take the air there, I will conduct you.' My astonishment was extreme; nor could I conceive how this man, who appeared so uneasy, should thus suddenly persuade himself to make me such a proposal. I accepted it, however, and in the evening we went out: from that time forward this confidence always continued. Whenever I was desirous to enjoy perfect liberty, I offered him a suspension of arms till a certain hour: this my generous enemy never refused; but when the armistice was at an end his vigilance was unbounded. Every post was examined; and if the government ordered that I should be kept close, the order was enforced with the greatest care. Thus was I again forced to contrive and prepare for my escape, and he to treat me with the utmost rigour. This man had a very accurate idea of the obligations of honour: he often said to me, ' If you were under sentence of death, I would permit you to go out on your parole, because I should be certain of your return. Many very honest prisoners, and I myself among the rest, would not return in the like case; but an officer, and especially an officer of distinction, holds his honour dearer than his life: I know it to be a fact, commodore, and therefore I should be the less uneasy if you desired the gates to be always open.' My keeper was right: while I enjoyed my liberty, I endeavoured to lose sight of the idea of escape; and I should have been averse to employ for that object means that had occurred to my imagination during my hours of liberty. One day I received a letter containing matter of great importance, which I had the strongest desire immediately to read; but as the contents related to my intended deliverance, I asked leave to return to my room and break off the truce. The keeper, however, refused, saying, with a laugh, that he wanted to take some sleep; accordingly he lay down, and I postponed the reading of my letter to the evening.

" On the 4th September the rigour of my confinement was increased: the keeper, whose name was Lasme, was displaced; I was kept close prisoner, and, together with my liberty, lost the hopes of a peace which I had thought approaching. At this time, however, a proposal was made to me for my escape, which I adopted as a last resource. The plan was to have forged orders drawn up for my removal to another prison, and then to carry me off. A French gentleman, M. de Philipeaux, a man of equal intrepidity and generosity, offered to execute this enterprise. The order then being accurately imitated, and by means of a bribe the real stamp of the signature procured, nothing remained but to find men bold enough to put the plan in execution. Philipeaux and C. L. Oiseau would have eagerly undertaken it, but both being known, and even notorious at the Temple, it was absolutely necessary to employ others. Messrs. B. and L. therefore, both men of tried courage, accepted the offer with pleasure and alacrity. With this order they came to the Temple, B. in the dress of an adjutant, and L. as an officer. The keeper having perused the order, and attentively examined the minister's signature, went into another room, leaving my two deliverers for some time in the cruellest uncertainty and suspense; at length he returned, accompanied by the register (or *greffier*) of the prison, and ordered me to be called. When the register informed me of the orders of the Directory, I pretended to be very much concerned at it; but the adjutant assured me, in the most handsome manner, that the government were far from intending to aggravate my misfortunes, and that I should be very comfortable at the place whither he was ordered to conduct me. I expressed my gratitude to all the servants employed about the prison; and, as you may imagine, was not very long in packing up my clothes. At my return the register observed, that at least six men from the guard must accompany me; and the adjutant, without being in the least confounded, acquiesced in the justice of the remark, and gave orders for them to be called out; but on reflection, and remembering as it were the laws of chivalry and honour, he addressed me, saying, ' Commodore, you are an officer, and I am an officer also, your parole will be enough; give me that, and I have no need of an escort.' —' Sir,' replied I, ' if that is sufficient, I swear on the faith of an officer to accompany you whither you choose to conduct me.' Every one applauded this noble action; while I confess I had great difficulty to avoid smiling. The keeper now asked for a discharge, and the register gave the book to Mr. B. who boldly signed it with a proper flourish, ' L'Oger, adjutant-general.' Meanwhile I employed the attention of the turnkeys, and loaded them with favours, to prevent them from having time to reflect; nor indeed did they seem to have any other thought than their own advantage. The register and keeper accompanied us as far as the second court; and at length the last gate was opened, and we left them, after a long interchange of ceremony and politeness."

They instantly entered a hackney-coach, but they had not got a hundred paces before the man drove against a post and hurt a passenger, which drew a crowd of persons around them; they immediately quitted the coach, took their portmanteaus in their hands, and separated. Sir Sidney proceeded to Rouen, from thence to the coast, and having procured a boat, proceeded to sea, and was soon after picked up by the Argo frigate, Captain Bowen, and landed at Portsmouth*. For some time previously the British government had vainly endeavoured to effect the release of Sir Sidney; and the French captain, Bergeret, who had been taken prisoner by Sir E. Pellew, had been permitted to go to France on his parole in hopes of effecting an exchange; but not succeeding, he returned to England. His conduct throughout gave the highest satisfaction to the British government, and they now permitted him to return to France without any stipulation. " Sir Sidney was welcomed in England by the general congratulations of the people: his arrival was considered as a miracle, which few who heard of it knew how to believe. His sovereign received him with the warmest affection, and afforded him every mark of attention, not only by his behaviour at his public presentation, but by honouring him with an immediate and private interview at Buckingham-House."

In the month of June Sir Sidney was appointed to the Tigre of 80 guns, and his talents were duly appreciated by his being appointed to a separate command on the coast of Egypt, with the rank of commodore, and, in conjunction with his brother, joint minister plenipotentiary to the Ottoman Porte. He proceeded, in the first instance, to Constantinople, where he was received with the greatest respect and attention by the Turkish government. Having been informed of the enemy's progress and of their ultimate views, Sir Sidney left Constantinople on the 19th February, and arrived at Alexandria on the 3d March. Having relieved Captain Troubridge in the command, he steered for Acre, to consult with Djezzar Pacha for the defence of that place, the fortifications of which were in the most ruinous and dilapidated state, though much had been done by Captain Miller of the Theseus and Colonel

* Captain Brenton, in noticing the escape of Sir Sidney, says, " Facts have since come to our knowledge of the whole having been *contrived by the French government:* of this perhaps even Sir Sidney himself was at the time ignorant. The police of France was too vigilant and too avaricious to allow a victim to elude its grasp without a sufficient reason; and a bribe of three thousand pounds sent to *one of the Directory* by our own government unlocked the gates of the Temple and removed all obstruction to the sea-coast." No authority is, however, given for this assertion.

Philipeaux, who had been detached a few days previously. The Tigre anchored before Acre on the 15th, and on the 16th Sir Sidney landed to pay a visit to Djezzar. On the 17th the enemy's advanced guard was discovered at the foot of Mount Carmel, who, not expecting to find a naval force in Syria, took up their ground close to the water-side, and were consequently exposed to the fire of grape-shot from the boats which were immediately sent against them by Sir Sidney, and which put them to the rout the instant it opened against them, and obliged them to retire precipitately up the side of the mount. The main body of the army then proceeded by the road of Nazareth, and invested Acre to the east. As the enemy returned the fire opposed to them by musketry only, it was evident that they had not brought their cannon with them, and was therefore expected by sea; measures were in consequence taken to intercept it. On the 18th the enemy's vessels were observed from the Tigre coming round Mount Carmel, consisting of a corvette and seven sail of gun-vessels, which, on seeing the Tigre, began to haul off, but after a chase of three hours she came within gun-shot, and captured seven of the enemy*. They were laden with the battering train of artillery, ammunition, platform, &c. for the siege of Acre; and as those articles were particularly wanted for its defence, they were immediately landed, whilst the vessels themselves were manned from the ships, and employed in harassing the enemy's forts†. On the 20th March the enemy opened a trench about nine hundred feet from the east front, and pushed his works with so much rapidity, that on the ninth day he had twelve pieces of cannon and four mortars mounted, which played with such effect as to pierce the town, while a mine had been pushed on to blow up the counterscarp. The mine was sprung, but it made only a hole in the glacis, although the enemy thought the counterscarp injured. The ditch, which they badly reconnoitred, appeared of little depth, and an attempt was made to storm the place; but instead of finding every obstacle smoothed and levelled, they were stopped by a ditch of fifteen feet wide, which was scarcely half filled up by the rubbish

* Captain Brenton most erroneously states that they were captured by the Theseus, Captain Miller.

† Captain Brenton is very short in his account of the defence of Acre; and, though he acknowledges that it presents " some wonderful instances of courage and desperation," says, " the details would occupy too much of his time, and the reader would think himself ill requited for his trouble:" we shall see.

of the breach. On the 1st April they plunged into it, and with the aid of ladders climbed the breach, but found themselves separated by the counterscarp from the troops which were to support them, and they were obliged to retreat with a severe loss. During these operations, the ships under Sir S. Smith were forced out to sea by a heavy gale, except the Alliance and prize gun-boats. On his return, considerable apprehensions being entertained from the mine, a sortie was determined on, in which the British marines and seamen were to force their way into it, while the troops attacked the enemy's trenches on the left and right. This took place on the morning of the 7th, just before daylight; and though the impetuosity of the Turks prevented the enemy from being surprised, the party entered the mine with the pikemen, and not only verified its direction, but destroyed all that could be destroyed in its then state; but in so doing Major Oldfield of the marines, a brave and distinguished officer, was unfortunately killed*. In the course of the month of April the enemy continued their operations, and made two attempts to storm the place, but were each time driven back with loss. During the same period the garrison made several sorties, protected by the boats on their flanks, which were attended with successful results. On the 1st May the enemy, after a severe cannonade of several hours from thirty pieces of cannon, made a fourth attempt to mount the breach, which was then much widened, but was again repulsed with loss. The Tigre moored on one side, and the Theseus on the other, flanked the walls, whilst the gun-boats, launches, and other boats continued to flank the enemy's trenches, to their great annoyance; " and," said Sir Sidney, " nothing but desperation could induce them to make the sort of attempts they do, to mount a breach practicable only by means of scaling-ladders, under such a fire as we pour in upon them; and it is impossible to see the lives even of our enemies thus sacrificed, and so much bravery misapplied, without regret." The loss of the besieged was likewise great: Captain Wilmot was killed by a musket-ball, and Colonel Philipeaux fell a sacrifice to anxiety and fatigue. Two ravelins having

---

* His body was afterwards discovered at the mouth of one of the enemy's mines and at the foot of our works : some of his brave companions hooked him by the neck-cloth, as he lay dead, to draw him off; the enemy at the same time pierced him in the side with a halbert, and each party struggled for the body; the neck-cloth gave way, and the enemy succeeded in dragging him to their works: on the following day they buried him with the honours of war.

been completed by the besieged for the reception of cannon to flank the enemy's nearest approaches, distant only ten yards, they were attacked on the 1st May, and for five successive nights the enemy attempted to storm, but were each time driven back with immense slaughter. On the evening of the 7th and fifty-first day of the siege, a fleet of Turkish corvettes and transports, under Hassan Bey, arrived as a reinforcement to the garrison; the arrival of which was the signal to Buonaparte to make a vigorous and persevering assault, in hopes of getting possession of the town before the reinforcement could reach the garrison. The fire of the besiegers increased tenfold, while that of the besieged, especially the flanking fire from afloat, was attended with less effect than before, owing to the enemy having thrown up epaulements and traverses to protect them from it. The besiegers consequently gained ground, and made a lodgment on the second story of the north-east tower, the upper part being entirely battered down, and the ruins in the ditch forming the ascent by which they mounted. Daylight shewed the French standard on the outer angle of the tower, and the enemy covered themselves in the lodgment and the approach to it by two traverses across the ditch, which they had constructed under the fire that had been opposed to them during the whole night, and which were then seen composed of sand-bags, and the bodies of their dead built in with them, their bayonets only being visible above them. Hassan Bey's troops were then in the boats, but only half way in shore. " This," said Sir Sidney, " was a most critical point of the contest; an effort was necessary to preserve the place for a short time till their arrival. I accordingly landed the boats at the mole, and took the crews up to the beach, armed with pikes. The enthusiastic gratitude of the Turks, men, women, and children, at the sight of such a reinforcement, at such a time, is not to be described. Many fugitives returned with us to the breach, which we found defended by a few brave Turks, whose most destructive missile weapons were heavy stones, which, striking the assailants on the head, overthrew the foremost down the slope, and impeded the progress of the rest. A succession, however, ascended to the assault, the heap of ruins between the two parties serving as a breastwork for both, the muzzles of their muskets touching, and the spear-heads of their standards locked. Djezzar Pacha, hearing the English were on the breach, quitted his station, where, according to the Turkish custom, he was sitting to reward such as should bring him the heads of the enemy, and distributing musket-cartridges with his own hands. The energetic old man, coming behind us, pulled us down with violence, saying, if any harm happened to his English friends, all was lost. This amiable contest as to who should defend the breach occasioned a rush of Turks to the spot; and thus time was gained for the arrival of Hassan Bey's troops. I had now to combat the Pacha's repugnance to admitting any troops but his Albanians into the gardens of his seraglio, become a very important part, as occupying the terreplein of the rampart. There were not above two hundred of the original one thousand Albanians left alive. This was no time for debate, and I overruled his objections by introducing the Chifflic regiment of 1000 men, armed with bayonets, disciplined after the European method under Sultan Selim's own eye, and placed by his Imperial Majesty's express command at my disposal. The garrison, animated by the appearance of such a reinforcement, was now all on foot; and there being consequently enough to defend the breach, I proposed to the Pacha to get rid of the object of his jealously, by opening the gates to let them sally, and take the assailants in flank: he readily complied, and I gave directions to the colonel to get possession of the enemy's third parallel, or nearest trench, and there fortify himself by shifting the parapet outwards. This order being clearly understood, the gates were opened, and the Turks rushed out; but they were not equal to such a movement, and were driven back into the town with loss. Mr. Bray, however, as usual, protected the town-gates efficaciously with grape from the 68-pounders. The sortie had this good effect, that it obliged the enemy to expose themselves above their parapets, so that our flanking fire brought down numbers of them, and drew their force from the breach, so that the small number remaining on the lodgment were killed or dispersed by our few remaining hand-grenades, thrown by Mr. Savage, midshipman of the Theseus. The enemy began a new breach by an incessant fire directed to the southward of the lodgment, every shot knocking down whole sheets of wall, much less solid than that of the tower on which they had expended so much time and ammunition. The group of generals and aides-de-camp which the shells from the 68-pounders had frequently dispersed, were now assembled on Richard Cœur de Lion's Mount; Buonaparte was distinguishable in the centre of a semi-circle; his gesticulations indicated a renewal of attack, and his dispatching an aide-de-camp shewed that he waited only for a reinforcement. I gave directions for Hassan Bey's ships to take their station in shoal water to the southward, and made the Tigre's signal to weigh and join the Theseus to the northward. A little before sunset a massive column appeared advancing to the breach with a solemn step. The Pacha's idea was not to defend the breach this time, but rather to let a certain number of the enemy in, and then close with them, according to the Turkish mode of war. The column thus mounted the breach unmolested, and descended from the rampart into the Pacha's garden, where, in a very few minutes, the bravest and most advanced among them lay headless corpses; the sabre, with the addition of a dagger in the other hand, proving more than a match for the bayonet: the rest retreated precipitately. Buonaparte will, no doubt, renew the attack, the breach being, as above described, perfectly practicable for 50 men abreast: indeed the town is not, nor ever has been, defensible according to the rules of art, but according to every other rule it must and shall be defended; not that it is in itself worth defending, but we feel that it is by this breach Buonaparte means to march to farther conquests. It is on the issue of this contest that depends the opinion of the multitude of spectators on the surrounding hills, who wait only to see how it ends to join the victors; and with such a reinforcement for the execution of his known projects, Constantinople, and even Vienna, must feel the shock*."

Sir Sidney, however, did not wait till the termination of the conflict without endeavouring to gain over those who were then neutral; he wrote a circular to the princes and chiefs of the Christians of Mount Lebanon, recalling them to a sense of their duty, and engaging them to cut off the supplies to the French camp, requesting them to choose between the friendship of a Christian knight and that of an unprincipled renegado.

---

* Two attempts to assassinate Sir Sidney in the town having failed, a flag of truce was sent in by an Arab dervise, with a letter to the Pacha, proposing a cessation of arms, for the purpose of burying the dead bodies, the stench from which had become intolerable, and threatened the existence of every person on both sides. Many indeed in the garrison had died delirious, within a few hours after having been seized with the first symptoms of infection. It was therefore natural that the besieged should listen to the proposal, and be off their guard during the conference. While the answer was under consideration, a volley of shot and shells announced an assault, which, however, the garrison was ready to receive, and the assailants only contributed to increase the number of dead bodies. Sir Sidney rescued the Arab from the indignation of the Turks by conveying him on board the Tigre, whence he was sent back to the French general, with a message that must have made the army ashamed of having exposed itself to so well-merited a reproof.

This had the desired effect, and Buonaparte's career northward was effectually stopped. Another sally was then made by the Turks from Acre,
and possession obtained of the enemy's third parallel; after which the
French grenadiers absolutely refused to mount the breach any more
over the putrid bodies of their unburied companions, and the siege was
raised on the 20th May, the French army leaving behind them their
train of battering artillery. Sir Sidney then having afforded the Turks
such other assistance as lay in his power, proceeded to the islands in the
Archipelago to refit his little squadron, and then sailed to Constantinople,
to concert with the Ottoman Porte such measures as were necessary to
extirpate the French troops from Egypt. In the mean time Buonaparte
gained a complete victory over the Turks near Aboukir; at which moment Sir Sidney arrived in the bay, but was unable to render the smallest
assistance. Having received an accession of ships and troops from Constantinople towards the end of October, Sir Sidney proceeded to the Da-
mietta branch of the Nile, to draw the attention of the enemy to that
part, and favour the advance of the army under the Vizier on the side
of the desert : various operations were there carried on till the 1st
November, when the Turks, who had been landed, and had at first met
with great success in their encounters with the enemy, were totally
routed.

In the month of December 1799, proposals were made by General
Kleber for the evacuation of Egypt; and it being agreed that terms
should be entered into for that purpose, and that the conferences should
be held on board the Tigre, plenipotentiaries, duly authorized by the
Grand Vizier and General Kleber, repaired thither. The following day
the ship was blown out to sea, but the conferences were carried on: preliminary articles were signed on the 29th December, by which it was
agreed that the French army, with all its stores, artillery, baggage, &c.
should be permitted to return to France unmolested by the allied
powers. Upon Lord Keith's receiving the articles of the above convention, he wrote to the French general, informing him that he had received
*positive orders from his Majesty to consent to no capitulation with the
French army in Egypt, unless it laid down its arms and surrendered as
prisoners of war.* Hostilities immediately recommenced, and the French
troops, rendered desperate by their situation, fought with the most determined resolution, and obtained a great and decided victory over the
Turkish troops, in which thousands were killed and wounded.

The refusal to ratify the treaty entered into by Sir Sidney Smith afterwards became the object of debate in the House of Commons, where it was asserted that the minister was aware of the convention, and that Sir Sidney possessed a joint diplomatic power with his brother, the minister at Constantinople, and that it was a breach of good faith not to ratify its terms. The ministry, however, denied the power of Sir Sidney to conclude any such treaty, and also that they were in possession of a knowledge of the circumstances when they sent the order to Lord Keith; as a proof of which, they said, the moment they heard of it, they sent counter orders to Lord Keith to agree to it. Unfortunately, however, these orders arrived too late, hostilities had recommenced. Attempts were made by Sir Sidney to renew the negociation, which would have had a favourable termination, but at that moment General Kleber was assassinated, and his successor, Menou, refused the terms, and consequently the war continued. On the 1st March, 1801, a British army, under General Abercrombie, arrived off Alexandria, and, after various operations, obtained a complete victory over the French army on the 21st, in which the gallant Abercrombie was killed and Sir Sidney Smith was wounded. Similar terms to those which had been granted by Sir Sidney Smith to the French were again proposed and accepted, and the enemy were conveyed to the nearest ports of France*.

In September following Sir Sidney returned to England with dispatches relative to the campaign†. We must now notice the honours conferred upon the gallant hero of Acre for the extraordinary degree of skill and

---

* After the surrender of the French army Sir Sidney visited the holy city, where the following anecdote of Buonaparte was related to him by the superior of a convent: When General Dumas had advanced with a detachment of the French army within a few leagues of Jerusalem, he sent to his commander-in-chief for leave to make an attack upon that place. Buonaparte replied, that *" when he had taken Acre he would come in person and plant the tree of liberty in the very spot where Christ suffered; and that the first French soldier who fell in the attack should be buried in the Holy Sepulchre."* Sir Sidney was the first Christian who was suffered by the barbarians to go into Jerusalem armed, or even to enter in the dress of a Frank : his followers, and all who visited by his means, were allowed the same privilege.

† Previous to his return he partook of a grand entertainment given by the Capitan Pacha, who presented him with a valuable scimeter, and, what was considered of far greater consequence, one of his own silk flags ; a badge of distinction which claims from all Turkish admirals and others an equal respect with that which they owe to the Pacha, such as the ceremony of personally waiting upon him on their leaving and joining the fleet.

determination he had manifested in the defence of the place. The thanks of both Houses of Parliament were conferred upon him, and in such terms as made them doubly valuable. Lord Spencer, in proposing them, said, he had to notice an exploit which had never been surpassed—the defence of St. Jean d'Acre by Sir Sidney Smith. He had no occasion to impress upon their lordships a higher sense than they entertained, of the brilliancy, utility, and distinction of an achievement, in which a general of great celebrity and a veteran victorious army were, after a desperate and obstinate engagement, which lasted, almost without intermission, for sixty days, not only repulsed, but totally defeated by the gallantry and heroism of the British officer and the small number of troops under his command. He owned that it was not customary, nor did he think it had any precedent in the proceedings of Parliament, that so high an honour should be conferred for services which might be performed by a force so inconsiderable in point of numbers; but the splendour of such an exploit as defeating a veteran and well-appointed army, commanded by experienced generals, and which had overrun a great part of Europe, a fine portion of Africa, and attempted also the conquest of Asia, eclipsed all former examples, and should not be subjected to the rules of ordinary usage. He therefore moved, in full confidence of universal approbation, the thanks of the House to Captain Sir W. Sidney Smith and the British seamen under his command, for their gallant and successful defence of St. Jean d'Acre, against the desperate attack of the French army under the command of General BUONAPARTE.

Lord Hood said, he could not vote on the occasion without bearing his testimony to the skill and valour of Sir Sidney, which had been so conspicuously and brilliantly exerted when he had the honour and benefit of having him under his command. Had Sir Sidney been at the head of a more considerable force, there was every probability that not a Frenchman would have escaped.

Lord Grenville said, there never was a motion since he had had a seat in the House, to which he gave a more hearty concurrence and assent. That the circumstance of so eminent a service having been performed with so inconsiderable a force was, with him, an additional reason for affording that testimony of public gratitude. " By that gallant and unprecedented resistance, we behold the conqueror of Italy, the future Alexander, not only defeated and driven from the situation at which he had arrived, but also obliged to retreat, in disorder and confusion, to parts where it was not likely that he would find a shelter from the pursuit of British skill and intrepidity. How glorious did the whole appear when they looked to the contrast between the victor and the vanquished! Buonaparte's progress throughout the whole of his military career was marked with every trait of cruelty and treachery. Sir Sidney Smith, in defiance of every principle of humanity, and of all the acknowledged rules of war, had been long, with the most cool and cruel inflexibility, confined in a dungeon in the Temple, from which he was only rescued *by his own address and intrepidity.* But the French, from making him an exception from the general usages of war, had only manifested their sense of his value, and how much they were afraid of him. This hero, in the progress of events, was destined afterwards to oppose the enemy in a distant quarter, and, instead of indulging any sentiments of revenge or resentment against his former persecutors, yielded to the natural feelings of his heart, by interfering and saving the lives of a number of French prisoners*. Soon after this, when victorious in an obstinate contest, where he was but indifferently supported by the discipline of the native troops, or means of defence in the fortifications of the fortress, he generously and humanely lent his protecting aid to a body of miserable and wounded Frenchmen who implored his assistance, when the cruelty and obstinacy of their own general had devoted them to almost inevitable destruction."

In the House of Commons, Mr. Dundas (afterwards Lord Melville) said, a twelvemonth had not elapsed since this country felt some alarm on account of the probable destination of the French army in Egypt, an apprehension that was much allayed by the memorable and most glorious victory of Lord Nelson; but the power of that army was still farther reduced by the efforts of Sir Sidney Smith, who, with a handful of men, surprised a whole nation, who were his spectators, with the brilliancy of

* M. Delasalle, a second lieutenant of dragoons, serving under Buonaparte in Syria, has since published an account of his capture by the Arabs, of his being brought into Acre, and of his deliverance to Sir Sidney Smith, which does equal honour to the narrator and to the chivalrous humanity of his gallant enemy. After having spent four days in constant expectation of death from the Arabs, he was brought before Djezzar, when Sir Sidney interceded for his liberty, but in vain. He was committed to one of the dungeons which Djezzar had crowded with victims, and hourly expected his fate. But he was deceived; the unwearied generosity of his illustrious enemy at length subdued the tyrant's fierceness, and he was released, conducted on board the Tigre, and loaded with all the courtesy that RICHARD CŒUR DE LION could have shewn to a French knight.

his triumph, contesting for sixty days with an enterprising and intrepid general at the head of his whole army. This conduct of Sir Sidney was so surprising, he said, to him, that he hardly knew how to speak of it; that he had not recovered from the astonishment the account of the action had thrown him into. He had looked at it over and over again, and no view he had been able to take of it had quite recovered him from the surprise and amazement which the account of the matter gave him. However, so it was, and the merit of Sir Sidney Smith was the object of consideration, to praise or esteem whom too highly was quite impossible. He had heard that Sir Sidney Smith, who had his difficulties, had been sometimes lightly spoken of by some persons; but whoever they were, they were inconsiderate, and they might be left to their own inward shame if they did not recant. Be that as it might, the House he was confident agreed with him, that the conduct of Sir Sidney, for heroism and intrepidity and active exertion, was never surpassed on any occasion.

On his return to England, Sir Sidney was presented with the freedom of the city of London, and also a valuable sword; on which occasion the chamberlain addressed him as follows:

" I will not, sir, attempt a panegyric upon an action to which the first oratorical powers, in the most eloquent assemblies, have been confessed unequal; but I cannot help exulting on this happy occasion, at the vast acquisition national reputation acquired by your conduct at the head of a handful of Britons in repulsing him who has been justly styled the Alexander of the day, surrounded by a host of conquerors till then deemed invincible. By this splendid achievement you frustrated the designs of the foe on our East Indian territories, prevented the overthrow of the Ottoman power in Asia, the downfall of its throne in Europe, and prepared the way for that treaty of peace, which, it is devoutly to be wished, may long preserve the tranquillity of the universe, and promote friendship and good-will among all nations. It must be highly gratifying to every lover of his country, that this event should have happened on the very spot where a gallant English monarch formerly displayed such prodigies of valour, that a celebrated historian, in recording his actions, struck with the stupendous instances of prowess displayed by that heroic prince, suddenly exclaimed, ' Am I writing history or romance?' Had, sir, that historian survived to witness what has recently happened at St. Jean d'Acre, he would have exultingly resigned his doubts, and generously have confessed, that actions no less extraordinary than those performed by the gallant Cœur de Lion, have been achieved by Sir Sidney Smith*."

Shortly after the renewal of the war in 1803, Sir Sidney was appointed to the Antelope of 50 guns, and in the spring of the following year was stationed off the enemy's coast to watch the movements of his flotillas. In the month of May he intercepted a squadron of fifty-nine sail, which he engaged from four to eight o'clock; and though several of their vessels struck, he could secure only one, owing to the enemy keeping so close in shore that it was impossible to get possession of them†. In the spring of 1805 he was appointed a colonel of marines, and throughout that year continued cruising along the French and Dutch coasts, harassing the enemy, and displaying that zeal on every occasion which was characteristic of his whole conduct. On the 9th November he was advanced to the rank of rear-admiral, and in the following year hoisted his flag on board the Pompée of 80 guns, in which he sailed to the Mediterranean. Shortly after his arrival he was appointed to a command off the Italian coast, with a squadron of five sail of the line. With this force he began his operations by introducing

* In 1802 Sir Sidney was elected M.P. for the city of Rochester; and in January 1803 the king granted him permission to bear the following honourable augmentation to the armorial ensigns borne by his family: On the cheveron *a wreath of laurel, accompanied by two crosses Calvary;* and on a chief of augmentation, *the interior of an ancient fortification* in perspective, in the angle a breach; and on the sides of the said breach, the standard of the Ottoman empire, with the Union flag of Great Britain: for his crest, *the Imperial Ottoman chelengk, or plume of triumph, upon a turban;* in allusion to the highly honourable and distinguished decoration transmitted by the Turkish emperor to Sir Sidney Smith, in testimony of his esteem and in acknowledgment of his meritorious exertions in the defence of Acre; and the family crest, *a leopard's head, collared and lined, issuant out of an Oriental crown.* The said arms and crest to be borne by Sir W. Sidney Smith and his issue, together with the motto, "Cœur de Lion." And although the privilege of bearing supporters be limited to the peers of the realm, the knights of the different orders, and the proxies of princes of the blood royal at installation, except in such cases wherein, under particular circumstances, the king shall be pleased to grant his especial licence for the use thereof; his Majesty, in order to give a further testimony of his particular approbation of Sir Sidney Smith's services, was also graciously pleased to allow him to bear for supporters to his arms *a Tiger guardant, navally crowned, in his mouth a palm-branch,* being the symbol of victory, *supporting the Union flag of Great Britain,* with the inscription, "Jerusalem, 1799," *upon the cross of St. George; and a Lamb, murally crowned, in the mouth an olive-branch,* being the symbol of peace, *supporting the banner of Jerusalem.*

† See official letter and plate, Ralfe's *Naval Chronology,* vol. 1. p. 49.

into Gaeta supplies of stores and ammunition, which its garrison had been greatly in want of. He afterwards proceeded to the Bay of Naples, spreading such alarm along the coast, that the French conveyed, in haste, to Naples part of their battering train from the trenches before Gaeta, to protect the capital from insult. It happened at the moment that Sir Sidney came in sight of the capital the city was illuminated on account of Joseph Buonaparte being crowned King of Naples. It was in the power of Sir Sidney to have disturbed the festivity; but as the sufferers must have been the inhabitants of Naples, he humanely forbore, and made for the Island of Capri, of which he took possession. He then proceeded southward, giving the greatest annoyance to the enemy, obstructing by land, and intercepting by sea, their communication along the shore, so as to retard their operations against Gaeta. He afterwards proceeded to Palermo, and from the active turn and sanguine temperament of his mind, he was induced to enter with eagerness and alacrity into the projects of the court, and to second its views on Calabria. Finding him favourably inclined to second their schemes, and anxious to distinguish himself by some great exploit, his Sicilian Majesty invested him with the most ample authority in Calabria, constituting him viceroy in that province. But though active and indefatigable in the duties of his new department, he found there was no chance of producing an insurrection against the enemy unless aided by an English army. Sir John Stuart, the commander of the English troops, was therefore solicited by the court to assist in its operations on Calabria, who at last consented to land his army in that province, and commenced his operations by a splendid victory in the plains of Maida; a victory which would not have been gained without the assistance of the navy. It was not, however, attended with the advantages expected by the court of Palermo.

In January 1807 Sir Sidney was ordered to proceed to the Dardanelles* under the orders of Sir John Duckworth, and where the only

* Previously to his departure he received the insignia of the Order of St. Ferdinand and of Merit, and the following letter from the queen:

My very worthy and dear Admiral,—I cannot find sufficient expressions to convey the painful feelings which your departure (so very unforeseen) has caused both to me and among my whole family. I can only tell you that you are accompanied by our most sincere good wishes, and more particularly on my part by gratitude, that will only cease with my life, for all that you have done for us; and for what you would still have done for us, if every thing had not thwarted you, and cramped your zeal and enterprise. May you be as happy as my heart prays for! and may you continue, by fresh laurels,

service performed on that occasion was effected by the squadron under the command of Sir Sidney Smith*. " At a subsequent period Sir Sidney Smith's opinions were taken on certain points of important consideration; but if we may judge from his answers to a string of queries from the vice-admiral, bearing the date of the 27th February, it appears that he was consulted rather as to what might have been done, than with a view to any plan of operations in prospective. From the queries and answers alluded to, we learn that Sir Sidney did not conceive that it would have promoted his Majesty's service to cannonade the city of Constantinople on the arrival of the British squadron, there being reason to hope that the objects in question might be obtained by negociation: whereas immediate hostility would have precluded intercourse, and all possibility of amicable discussion and arrangement. For various causes, such as the circuitous eddies within the harbour, the prevalence of the northerly current of the Bosphorus, which, setting directly on the Seraglio point, would prevent a disabled ship from extricating herself, and the Turkish mode of warfare, every man being armed with a rifle, and skilful in using it, Sir Sidney was of opinion that it would not have been advisable to lead the squadron to the attack of the arsenal†." Although Sir Sidney Smith did not entirely coincide with Sir John Duckworth in his management of the expedition, he " was much more inclined to ascribe the original cause of its failure to the mismanagement of the ambassador, than to any error of the commander-in-chief. Indeed, from a private letter of Sir John Duckworth's to Sir Sidney Smith, a copy of which has by chance fallen in our way, it appears, that, even after their return to England, and at the very time of the public outcry respecting the failure of the expedition, a perfect harmony and general good feeling continued to be preserved between the two flag-officers. In the letter alluded to, Sir John expressed his happiness in having a man of his honour and character to bear him out in the representation of his not having had the power to destroy the Turkish fleet, or to effect a political change in the Turkish government‡.

both to augment your own glory and the number of the envious! I still cherish the hope of again seeing you in better times, and of giving you proofs of those sentiments which, at the present moment, I cannot express; but you will find, in all times and places (whatever may be the fate reserved for us), our hearts gratefully attached to you, even unto the grave.   (Signed,)   CHARLOTTE.

     * See *Memoir of Sir* JOHN DUCKWORTH.
     † *Naval Chronicle.*   ‡ *Ibid.*

In the month of June 1807 Sir Sidney returned to England, and shortly after struck his flag. In the month of October he was, however, appointed to command a squadron off the coast of Portugal, the government of which had, at the direction of Buonaparte, shut their ports against the commerce of England. On his arrival off the Tagus, he opened a communication with Lord Strangford, the British secretary of legation, who had endeavoured to persuade the royal family to migrate to their possessions in South America; but failing in the object, and as a French army was rapidly advancing on Lisbon, he now took refuge on board the admiral's ship, which he did on the 18th November, leaving Mr. Consul Gambier to do his best for the liberty of the factory; and an agent for prisoners of war was appointed, with the approbation of the Portuguese government. On the other hand, the admiral declared the Tagus, Setubal, and Oporto in a state of blockade; but in adopting hostile measures he did not neglect the powers of persuasion, and continued to cultivate an amicable correspondence with the ministry at Lisbon, tending to convince their wavering minds of the futility of such timid policy in averting the scourge of French invasion. At length, on the 25th November, his activity and perseverance were rewarded by receiving a notification from the minister of state, M. Aranjo, that the regent had resumed the intention to emigrate. In consequence of which hostilities were suspended, and the admiral sent the Confiance into the Tagus under a flag of truce, to convey those solemn pledges of safeguard adapted to the crisis, and which, from an officer of Sir Sidney Smith's chivalrous fame, could not fail to dispel doubt and fear. Lord Strangford, who was waiting on board the flag-ship for a conveyance to England, took the opportunity of accompanying Captain Yeo, to revisit Lisbon for the final settlement of affairs connected with his late mission, and to pay his respects to the court. Wind and tide would not allow the frigate to enter the Tagus till late in the evening of the 28th, so that it was near midnight when Captain Yeo and Lord Strangford reached the capital. They found the royal palace a solitude, the queen being already embarked, in consequence of General Junot having passed the Abrantes, and even pushed his patroles to the vicinity of the metropolis. During this time the admiral was waiting with such solicitude the issue of the mission by the Confiance, that he manned and armed a Spanish prize lugger, and on the 28th sent her in with a message to Captain Yeo, purporting that, under certain circumstances, he was to annul the flag of truce, and immediately act against the French, sending off pilots to the squadron, which Sir Sidney said he would bring in abreast of, or above the city, making a dash at the batteries with his marines *en passant;* and then, seconded by an indignant population, dispute every inch of ground with the invader, concluding with the peculiar emphasis of the defender of Acre—" Lisbon surely must be as defensible as Buenos Ayres." It was not, however, the fortune of the gallant knight to repeat the achievement of Palestine on that day, as on standing into Cascaës Bay on the morning of the 29th, daylight disclosed to his anxious eyes, the interesting sight of the Portuguese navy conducting a numerous fleet to place them under the convoy of that force, whose duty, but a few hours before, would have been to destroy instead of to protect. The weather was serene, and the spectacle of the meeting of the two fleets, under a reciprocal salute of 21 guns, magnificent beyond description. The admiral immediately went on board the ship bearing the royal standard of Portugal (then no longer flying on the continent of Europe), to pay homage due to the sovereign. His reception was marked by all the honours due to a British admiral, and by every distinction the individual merited, the interview taking place with a dignity suitable to the solemnity of the occasion. Having made every suitable arrangement, he placed the Portuguese squadron under the protection of Sir Graham Moore, who escorted them in safety to the Brazils. Thus was the house of Braganza rescued from the power of France by that warrior who had alone defeated her chief. The departure of the royal family of Portugal afforded a novel sight, a sight unparalleled in the page of history; a sovereign family voluntarily abandoning the conveniences, comforts, and luxuries of royalty, committing themselves to the care and confidence of an enemy, to court dangers unknown, on an element untried; proceeding to a distant clime, to throw themselves into the arms of a rude unpolished people, in order to save themselves from French friendship*. Such a step was worthy the character of the hero of Palestine, by whose exertions it had been accelerated. The light in which his conduct on this occasion was viewed at home, will be sufficiently evident from the subjoined extract of a letter from Mr. Secretary Pole, dated 28th December, 1807:

" Sir,—I lost no time in laying your dispatches, brought by Captain Yeo and by the Trafalgar letter of marque, before the Lords Commissioners of the Admi-

---

* *Naval Chronicle.*

ralty ; and I am commanded by their lordships to express their high approbation of your judicious and able conduct in the management of the service intrusted to your charge, and in the execution of the various orders you have received from time to time. Their lordships are strongly impressed with the propriety of the whole of your conduct towards the royal family of Portugal ; the respectful attention which you appear to have shewn to the illustrious house of Braganza has been in strict conformity to their lordships' wishes ; and they have directed me to express their complete satisfaction at the manner in which you have in this, as well as in every other respect, obeyed their instructions.''

In January 1808 Sir Sidney was, however, removed from this station, and appointed to the chief command in South America, where he rendered such essential services to the commercial and shipping interests of the United Kingdom, that he subsequently received the thanks of the committee of merchants trading to the Brazils. In the month of June he gave an elegant entertainment to the royal family and court on board his flag-ship, when the Prince Regent was pleased to create him a Knight Grand Cross of the Tower and Sword, and to present him with the standard of Portugal, to be borne as an augmentation to his coat of arms. In August 1809 he returned to England, and having struck his flag, was shortly after presented with the honorary decree of D.C.L. by the university of Oxford, and of M.A. by the university of Cambridge. In August 1811 he was presented with the freedom of the city of Edinburgh ; and in 1812 was appointed second in command of the Mediterranean fleet. In the following year the King of Sardinia and suite honoured him with a visit, and dined on board his flag-ship at Cagliari. From this station Sir Sidney returned to England at the conclusion of the war, and then received the freedom of the borough of Plymouth in a silver box. In January 1815 he was nominated a K.C.B. and was invested with the insignia of the order by the Duke of Wellington at the Elisée-Bourbon, in Paris ; the evacuated palace of that chieftain whose ambitious career he had first checked, and to which he had retired after his defeat by the Duke of Wellington at Waterloo. In July 1821 Sir Sidney was advanced to the rank of admiral of the Blue. He married, in October 1809, the widow of Sir George Rumbold, Bart.

From the above sketch of Sir Sidney's services, it will be seen that his character early passed its ordeal. His genius appears, from his earliest entrance into the service, to have been particularly adapted to the most arduous and desperate enterprises, and Fortune has in general favoured his undertakings. His uncommon rage for adventure and his eagerness to signalize himself led him to almost every part of the world where any service was to be performed or danger encountered. It may be mentioned as an extraordinary circumstance, that he went to the West Indies as a midshipman, passed through the campaigns with the gallant Rodney, and returned to England a post-captain before he had reached the age of manhood; and scarcely had he attained those years when, in ordinary cases, reason and reflection assume their sway over the human mind, than Europe with astonishment beheld him filling the situation of a personal friend and adviser to one of the most heroic, patriotic, and chivalrous of monarchs. The impetuosity which he evinced in battle, and the ardour with which he courted danger, excited such a degree of admiration, that his country formed the highest expectations from his abilities; and her enemies evinced the fear they entertained of his genius by their impotent malice and severe treatment when he fell into their power. Throughout the whole course of his career, or at least from the first moment he was intrusted with command, there was no scene of action in which he was employed in which he did not eminently display his courage and intrepidity. But, in estimating his warlike character, attention must be particularly paid to his conduct; first, at Toulon, where but for him the whole proceeding would have terminated in utter abortion; but for which he neither received honour nor reward of any description; the rules of the service even deprived him of a share of that prize-money which was acquired by his own exertions, presence of mind, and manly fortitude. Secondly, his attempt to cut out the Vengeur from Havre, where, though he failed and became a prisoner of war, though he was deprived of his liberty and for the time the chance of acquiring farther glory, the very attempt proved him to be worthy of command, and entitled him to the highest praise. He could not command success, but he proved that he deserved it. In his person the government of France was justly accused of unnecessary harshness and severity; but he fortunately escaped from the power of a foe who ought to have known how to reward and honour such determined and obstinate valour. Thirdly, at St. Jean d'Acre, where, with his limited means, he had to defend the place against a well-appointed army, commanded by the most successful generals of modern times; a place which in itself was not defensible by any rules or art of war, but that ardent spirit which led him to prefer a life of hardship and danger

to one of ease and tranquillity, was but the more stimulated to the in-
vention of means to surmount those difficulties to which he was opposed.
Knowing that " great actions are commonly transgressions of ordinary
rules," and as he wanted neither courage nor capacity, he proceeded
with such judgment and foresight, and adopted his means with such
discrimination and success, that, after a sixty days' continued contest, the
enemy was at last defeated, and Sir Sidney gained over the most distinguished warrior of the age that triumph which was never exceeded
in glory by any other achievement. This success, no doubt, was owing
to the valour of all concerned ; but it was chiefly to the sagacity, conduct,
and all-powerful resources of Sir Sidney that that desirable consummation was attributed. No one ever possessed more eminently the power
of inspiring their followers with sentiments similar to their own than he
did ; nor did any commander exhibit to his companions in the day of
battle more striking examples of those qualities which excite valour and
ensure success. His subsequent conduct in the Downs and Mediterranean was equally ardent, zealous, and persevering, although he was not
favoured with opportunities to distinguish himself in a manner equal to
the former part of his career.

The author of the *Naval Chronicle*, on comparing the services of Sir
Sidney Smith with those of Lord Exmouth, says, " I place them together
for this reason, that what Sir Sidney counselled and advised to be done,
his lordship, at the voice of his country, successfully and gloriously performed. That the Algerine piracy should have continued so long must
form matter of great astonishment to every reflecting mind ; but that a
subject so interesting to humanity, and to that chivalrous and ardent disposition which he is known to possess, should have, at the close of a long
and arduous contest, taken full possession of Sir Sidney's mind, all who
know him will readily be convinced was perfectly in unison with his noble
character. To him then is due the praise of having suggested the abolition
of Algerine piracy, not only to his own government, but to that of every
European power ; and whilst to Lord Exmouth belongs the merit of
having bravely and skilfully attacked and destroyed the ships and city
of Algiers, to Sir Sidney must be ascribed that of having pointed out its
necessity. Should those services be the last which these distinguished
officers may have of rendering to their country and to mankind, they
will be worthy of their former lives, which from their earliest youth were
directed to the pursuit of fame and honour, of which they have reaped

a noble harvest. The one was the first to shew to wondering Europe that the once mighty Emperor of France was not invincible; while the other was the first to strike a blow against republican colours, which he soon hauled down, and, at the close of a mighty warfare, returned from a most important command to abolish Christian slavery. Sweet must be the reflection arising from such noble and heroic actions to those who performed them; nor will the country be slow to recognise the merits of such defenders. Lord Exmouth, then, and Sir Sidney Smith have deserved well of their country; their career has been strongly and continually marked by a succession of eminent services, which, although they heve not led them to participate or gain any laurel in general actions with fleets of the enemy, have, nevertheless, secured them the approbation of their countrymen."

This comparison, however, breaks off at the most interesting point. Of " fame and honour both have certainly reaped a noble harvest," and the *country* has not been " slow to recognise the merits of such defenders:" but it cannot be said that both have been equally rewarded. At the termination of the war Sir Sidney was made a K.C.B.; Lord Exmouth was made a K.C.B. a peer of the realm, and had also a pension settled upon him. It surely cannot be maintained that Sir Sidney being made a Knight Commander of the Bath is a sufficient reward for the services performed by him. A writer in the *Naval Chronicle* says, " His services have been great, and their value of no common order; for, in my opinion, that value has been doubled by the air and character with which they have been charged. So great indeed, so characteristically great, have been his achievements, that we must in charity suppose our different administrations, under which they have been performed, despairing adequately to estimate them, have withheld the rewards which lesser merits might be understood to claim; and his country has long beheld, with mingled emotions of shame, anger, and indignation, the affronting neglect with which his brilliant character has been insulted." What we have already said respecting the services of Sir Sidney Smith, recording, as we have done, the high and favourable opinions of some of the most competent judges and distinguished characters the country can boast of, may perhaps be sufficient to portray his character and his claims to reward, yet we should be sorry to dismiss the subject without some few observations.

The life of a naval officer has always been considered as " a continued course of care and exertion to all those who build their fortunes on an honourable basis, or maintain character on noble and independent principles." During the whole career of Sir Sidney Smith, it is said that he sought honour and glory and titles from the most praiseworthy motives: that he sought distinction by means which should benefit his country— a display of reason, activity, industry, and zeal: that he was foremost in whatever he undertook, prompt in the conception of design, and rapid in the execution: that he ever maintained, that the most easy method of achieving an enterprise was by example, which inflames courage, unites passions, and impels a performance of duty; which raises hope, provokes emulation, makes the timid bold and the bold heroic. The laudable ambition to advance in reputation as we advance in life can only thus be prosecuted; but though by his heroic disposition of soul, the greatness of his courage, and the actual services rendered to the country, he has proved himself deserving of a title which might be handed down to posterity by his family, it has been most unjustly withheld. If, however, he should not leave behind him an hereditary title, he will leave behind him the records of his fame, and of as bright a character as ever adorned the page of history.

HISTORICAL MEMOIRS OF

ADMIRAL THOMAS BAKER, C. B.

THE sun, in its whole rotation, does not impart its light to a class of men who are more uniformly noble and manly than accomplished British seamen. " Courage is obviously a prime requisite in this profession. It has, of course, been cultivated and encouraged by it in high perfection. But courage, when it does not arise from animal insensibility, is connected with every generous virtue. The sailor has therefore been distinguished for openness, honour, truth, and liberality. To the solid virtues he has added the high polish of urbane and easy manners. His various commerce with the world has rubbed off those asperities and removed those prejudices which too often adhere to the virtuous recluse; and perhaps it is difficult to exhibit human nature in a more amiable and honourable light than it appears in the accomplished sailor; in the sailor fully prepared for his profession by a liberal education, and furnished, through the favourable circumstances of it, with all those qualities which render men generous in principle and agreeable in conversation." The personal character of each individual is generally subordinate to the national character; but what is here said generally may, with great truth and propriety, be said individually of Admiral Baker—high-minded, just, and disinterested, he pursued his career with a fearlessness and an intrepidity which at once portrayed his heroic nature.

The family of Admiral Baker has been long settled in the county of Kent; and several members of it have, at various times, been honoured by royal notice. Her Majesty Queen Anne granted them permission to add the trident to their arms; and George II. presented the grandfather of Admiral Baker with a ring, which has ever since been considered an heirloom. There have also been several of its members in the British navy, one of whom lies most honourably interred in Westminster Abbey.

Admiral Baker commenced his naval career on board the Dromedary, Captain Stone, on the 23d August, 1781. With some short intervals, he continued on board the Dromedary, Kite, Carnatic, and Hermione, till October 1785; he then remained unemployed till March 1788, when he joined the Dido, Captain Sandys, with whom he continued till

July 1790, when he removed to the Brisk, Captain Curzon. He afterwards served on board the Royal Sovereign, Dictator, Winchelsea, and Minerva till October 1792, when, being in the East Indies, he was promoted by Commodore Cornwallis to the rank of lieutenant, and removed to the Swan sloop, Captain Halsted. On the 22d October, 1793, he received an Admiralty commission as first lieutenant; and being in communication with Admiral Mac Bride, that distinguished officer was so pleased with his zeal and spirit, that, on the 21st December following, he appointed him to command the Lion armed cutter, which he retained till May 1794, and during that period, from her bad sailing, he had many narrow escapes of a French prison. He was then appointed to the Valiant armed lugger, and was charged with dispatches to the commander-in-chief in the West Indies; and in consequence of the great dispatch used by him on this occasion, he was promoted to the rank of commander by Lord Spencer, October 24, 1795, when he was appointed to the Ferret sloop of war; but owing to ill health he was unable to take the command. He then continued on half-pay till November 1796, when he was appointed to the Fairy, and was employed in the Downs and along the French coast watching the enemy's force in Dunkirk, and harassing their coasting trade. In June 1797 he attained post-rank in the Princess Royal, bearing the flag of Sir John Orde; but which situation he retained only a short time. In January 1799 he was appointed to the Nemesis frigate of 28 guns, in which success began to dawn upon him, and opportunities to distinguish himself, which he had long and anxiously wished for, were afforded him, and which he never failed to embrace and to push to the utmost extremity. During the whole of that year he was employed in the Downs and North Sea; and in the evening of the 12th January, 1800, he captured Le Renard French privateer of 14 guns.

In the ensuing summer Captain Baker was intrusted with the command of a small squadron, consisting of the Nemesis, Prevoyante (36), Terpsichore (32), Arrow (20), and Nile lugger. For some time disputes had arisen between the northern courts of Europe and that of St. James's as to the right of searching neutral ships—a right which Great Britain had ever maintained, and was, notwithstanding the multiplicity of foes with which she was surrounded, determined to maintain, regardless of all consequences. Information having been received that a Danish convoy was about to leave that kingdom, Captain Baker was directed to examine them, and if opposition was made to such a step, to use such force as might be necessary to carry that object into execution. On the 25th July, about noon, he observed a convoy, under the protection of a frigate, steering down the Channel, and he instantly made the signal for a general chase. A gun was then fired ahead of the convoy to bring them to; when the Danish frigate immediately hoisted an ensign and fired one gun. The Terpsichore, Captain Gage, was then directed to continue the chase and examine the strangers. The Terpsichore soon arrived up with the frigate, and Captain Gage informed her captain that he was ordered to board and examine the convoy; but was immediately answered that such conduct would be resisted by force. Captain Baker's permission was then asked by signal to commence action, as the only possible means of enforcing obedience to his orders. This permission, however, Captain Baker refused, till every circumstance that induced the Danish captain to resist should be explained to him. For this purpose he directed every ship of his squadron, by signal, not to engage the frigate, but to attend to the convoy. The Nemesis shortly after arrived within hail of the Danish frigate, when Captain Baker informed her commander, that he was determined to board and examine the convoy, and requested to know if he still persisted in his intention to oppose it. Being answered in the affirmative, Captain Baker apprised him that he was then lowering his boat for that purpose, and that if he should fire a single shot at her, he should consider it an act of hostility, and that he might prepare himself accordingly. The boat then put off, and as she was rowing for the convoy was fired at by the Danish frigate; a well-directed broadside from the Nemesis instantly followed, and a close action continued for a quarter of an hour, when, the Prevoyante and Arrow having joined in the action, and placed themselves in raking positions, the Danish captain hauled down his colours, and the firing ceased. His frigate and convoy were conveyed to the Downs, to await the decision of the British government.

Thus through Captain Baker was the naval superiority of Britain upheld; and it was thus made manifest to her enemies, and to the world in general, that she would not allow neutral powers to become the conveyers of the property of any state hostile to her interests and welfare; a most wise and judicious use of her maritime supremacy, which has proved itself the great barrier against universal empire, and which, if it be always as wisely directed, will prove itself sufficient to protect and uphold her pre-eminence against every possible combination.

Throughout the whole of this delicate affair, Captain Baker conducted himself with such coolness, firmness, and decision, as to obtain the full and entire approbation of the British government; and as a mark of their satisfaction he was, early in the following year, appointed to the Phœbe, a fine frigate of 36 guns. He was then attached to the Cork station, and continued on board the Phœbe till May 1802, when, hostilities having ceased, he resigned the command to travel with Prince William of Gloucester, and with him visited the courts of Sweden, Russia, and Denmark. On the renewal of the war in 1803, he returned to England, and was appointed in the month of April, by Lord St. Vincent, to command the Phœnix of 36 guns, when his activity became proverbial. He served under the orders of Admiral Cornwallis in the Channel, was employed cruising against the trade and armed ships of the enemy, and in all the various duties he was called upon to perform, he invariably received the thanks of that great and distinguished officer. One particular circumstance connected with that command we must not pass over. Being intrusted with the command of the squadron of frigates employed in shore, he observed the enemy's fleet take up a position in the Goullet passage in confident security. But his penetrating mind instantly saw their vulnerable point, and, with his usual zeal for the service, directly apprised Admiral Cornwallis of their situation, and of the apparent confidence with which they had taken it up; concluding his letter with the following observation: " But, with an easterly wind and a flood tide, perhaps you will think they are not so safe ;" which led to the almost immediate attack made upon them by that distinguished officer*. It was not, however, till August 1805 that he obtained for himself a never-fading laurel by the capture of the French frigate La Didon of 44 guns, after a close action of three hours. Being on a cruise, at five a.m. on the 10th of that month, a sail was discovered in the south-west, the wind being N.E. by E.; all sail was immediately made in chase, and about seven the stranger was clearly discovered to be an enemy's frigate, and whose captain, with great confidence and resolution, waited the approach of the Phœnix; a sufficient indication of his courage and of the severity of the approaching contest. At eight the enemy hoisted his colours, fired a gun to windward, and at a quarter before nine commenced a sharp fire on the Phœnix. To prevent the enemy's escape, Captain Baker determined to engage to leeward ; but

---

* See *Memoir of Admiral* CORNWALLIS.

the French captain appeared resolved to maintain his position, and managed his ship with such skill as to defeat every attempt made to accomplish it: three times did he fill his sails, wear, bring-to on the opposite tack, and discharge his broadside into the bows of his opponent. No other alternative being left, Captain Baker steered direct for the Didon, and by this measure the broadsides of both ships were brought to bear within pistol-shot distance, each pouring into the other an animated fire of round, grape, and musketry. After several manœuvres, which proved the French captain to be a most skilful officer, the two ships became foul of each other, the larboard bow of the Didon pressing against the starboard quarter of the Phœnix, and in such a position that not a gun could be brought to bear with effect, except a 36-pounder from the bows of the Didon, but which, owing to the destructive fire kept up by the marines of the Phœnix, was not discharged. In this extremity, Captain Baker determined to make an attempt to carry his opponent by boarding; but was met by such numbers of the enemy that he was obliged to act on the defensive, and the contest was continued by repeated discharges of musketry from both ships. With a mind ever fertile in expedients, always directed for the benefit of the service, Captain Baker had ordered the sill of the cabin-window next the quarter to be cut down, to serve as a port-hole in case of necessity: this precaution now proved of the most essential advantage; but before it could be brought into use some time elapsed, in consequence of the gunner having neglected to prepare tackle sufficiently long to transport the aftermost main-deck gun to that position: this was now superintended by Captain Baker, the enemy all the time pouring in a destructive fire of musketry through the cabin-window, so that scarcely an officer or man escaped without being killed or wounded. At length the gun was run out, and its important effects were soon visible; the Didon was swept from her larboard bow to the starboard quarter, and her deck covered with killed and wounded. Having been on board of each other for nearly three quarters of an hour, the Didon began to forereach; other guns were then instantly brought to bear, until it again became a yard-arm and yard-arm cannonade. The advantage was now evidently on the side of the Phœnix, which discharged upon an average three shot to two; but owing to the damages she had received, the Didon passed out of gun-shot, and the firing ceased. A short suspension then took place, which was employed by both parties in repairing and splicing their rigging. During this operation, the fore-mast of the Didon fell over her side, a circumstance which was received by the crew of the Phœnix with three cheers; and a light breeze having sprung up, Captain Baker bore down to renew the contest; but when he had taken his position, and was about to open his fire, the enemy declined all farther opposition and hauled down his colours. The loss of both ships was in proportion to the length and severity of the action: the Phœnix had 12 killed and 28 wounded. That of the enemy was much more severe, having had 27 killed and 44 wounded. Although the action was now over, and possession was taken of the enemy, the difficulties attending Captain Baker's situation had not ceased: the number of the prisoners exceeded the crew of the Phœnix, and required constant watching; both ships were considerably damaged and required refitting, which, with the small number of hands that could be spared, rendered it a work of great difficulty. This was no sooner accomplished, and the Didon taken in tow, than they fell in with the French fleet under M. Villeneuve. Captain Baker immediately bore up to the southward, chased by a division of the French fleet till sunset, at which time they were nearly within gun-shot, when the enemy stood back to their main body. Captain Baker now steered for Gibraltar, and having passed Lisbon in a thick fog, became alarmed by the ringing of bells and occasional discharges of guns in almost every direction. He now fortunately spoke the Euryalus, and learning from her that the sounds proceeded from the combined French and Spanish fleet steering for Cadiz, he again altered his course to the westward, and reached Plymouth in safety; where he had the gratification to receive from his commander-in-chief, the gallant Cornwallis, a letter of congratulation, dated September 1805, and from which the following is an extract:

" I have great satisfaction in the receipt of your letter, dated the 13th of last month, giving me the account of your having, in the ship you command, had the good fortune to fall in with the French frigate La Didon, of superior force; and after a severe conflict, ably supported by your officers and ship's company, captured the enemy's ship. The truly gallant conduct of yourself, and all under your command, must be manifest when I consider the stubborn resistance of the enemy. The event will ever redound to the honour of yourself, as well as the brave officers and men on board the Phœnix, and add a fresh laurel to the British navy."

Towards the end of October following Captain Baker was ordered to sea with sealed orders, which were not to be opened till his arrival in a certain latitude; but shortly after leaving Falmouth he spoke some neutral vessels, and was informed that a French squadron had been recently seen by them proceeding into the Bay of Biscay. Not doubting that this was the famous Rochefort squadron, which had eluded the pursuit of several English squadrons, and considering that it was of the utmost importance to ascertain their route, he determined to open his orders to ascertain their import, and found that they merely directed him to proceed one hundred leagues to the westward, and afterwards to cruise to the southward. Although his carrying those orders into execution was an object of the utmost importance to his personal interest, from the advantages which it promised him from prize-money, yet, ever actuated by a paramount sense of duty to his king and country, he did not hesitate to change the course of the Phœnix to go in quest of the enemy's squadron. He crossed the bay, and on the 2d November, in the latitude of Cape Finisterre, he discovered four sail standing W.N.W. which proved to be enemy's ships; and as they commenced a chase of the Phœnix, Captain Baker, aware that Sir Richard Strachan was cruising with a squadron off Ferroll, steered south, with the anxious hope of inducing the enemy to follow him until he should be able to communicate with Sir Richard. About three p.m. Captain Baker discovered four sail in the south, which were soon after discerned also by the enemy, who thereupon altered their course to the eastward. Not doubting that the ships to the southward were friends, Captain Baker covered the Phœnix with signals, fired signal-guns, and steered a south-easterly course; but it was not till 11 p.m. that he was enabled to ascertain to a certainty that they were English ships: he then passed under the stern of the Cæsar, and having informed Sir Richard of the enemy's situation, was ordered to hasten up the ships astern, whilst the Cæsar made all sail in pursuit of the enemy. Although it might have been expected that the Phœnix would have been sent ahead instead of astern, Captain Baker ran down to the leewardmost ship, and having delivered his orders, again crowded all sail in the direction of the enemy, passed the Cæsar on the evening of the 3d, and proceeded ahead to assist the Santa Margaretta, Captain Rathbone, in harassing the rear of the enemy, till the Cæsar and the other ships of the squadron could arrive up, when a general action took place, which terminated in the capture of the enemy's four ships.   On this occasion the Phœnix had two killed and four wounded.

Captain Baker continued in command of the Phœnix till the 17th November, when he was appointed to the command of that frigate (La Didon) which had been the reward of his valour and intrepidity; but he retained it only till the 24th December following, and was kept out of employment till the 23d May, 1806; he was then appointed to the Tribune of 38 guns, and attached to the Channel fleet.   On the 29th April, 1807, in company with the Iris, he destroyed the greater part of a convoy of thirty vessels, passing from Ferrol to Bilboa under the protection of several gun-boats*. During the time he commanded the Tribune

* We have been favoured with the following account of the action by an officer who was on board:

" On the 29th April, 1807, the wind W.S.W. we were standing in for the land about Ferrol; at 12 h. 5 m. p.m. observed the Iris between us and the land, with the signal flying for thirty sail of the enemy bearing east; at twenty-eight minutes after twelve we made the Iris' signal No. 1. to prepare for battle, doing the same ourselves, and making all possible sail in chase; at forty minutes past twelve made the signal No. 14. to the Iris to prepare to anchor with springs on her cables: by this time we plainly perceived the enemy, consisting of gun-vessels and merchantmen, to be steering along shore to the eastward (supposed bound to Bilboa).   On our nearer approach we discovered the enemy to take shelter in a bay, within a serf of rocks, two miles to the eastward of Cape Prior.   The wind then being light and baffling, Captain Baker thought it advisable, for the safety of the ships, and to prevent the escape of the enemy, to anchor; but previous to this made the Iris' signal, having a pilot on board, to lead through difficult navigation. About three, a breeze springing up from the W. N. W. we weighed: the Iris being to leeward was the first to weigh and bring the enemy to action; no time was lost by us in seconding her, and from our more judicious situation, I am happy to say, our fire proved much more effectual.   At twenty minutes past four Captain Tower asked leave, per signal, to anchor, which, for prudential motives, Captain Baker answered in the negative: three minutes after No 514. was made to the Iris to act discretionally.   During the whole of this time we were keeping up a most tremendous fire, beginning at the sternmost and running along the line of the enemy.   The Iris was without us.   No. 34. was then made to her, to engage the weather division of the enemy.   She still kept her position on our weather beam.   Various were the conjectures as to the cause of her so acting; at length, not perceiving her to have sustained any damage, her signal was made to bear up into our wake; this she did not do: the reason given by Captain Tower on his coming on board was, that he really did not like to fire at them, as they were not constantly keeping up a fire at us."

" *April* 30.

" Captain Baker being anxious to ascertain the number of vessels destroyed, also to assure himself whether or not any thing more could be done to effect the entire destruction of those still afloat, the wind being too light to trust the ship near enough to recon-

a circumstance occurred which we must not omit to mention, proving, as it does, his presence of mind in the hour of danger. Being at anchor off the coast of France, a fire was discovered in the gunner's store-room, and, owing to the thick volumes of smoke which arose, it was impossible to get at it: every moment the danger increased, and he was urged by the officers to abandon the ship; but instead of which he ordered the cable to be cut, put her before the wind, which was fortunately off shore, by which means she became cleared of the smoke, and by the greatest exertions of all on board she was saved from destruction. He afterwards had the command of the squadron off Bourdeaux, and continued in the command of the Tribune till the 19th April, 1808. On the 21st May following he was appointed to command the Vanguard, in which he was employed off the Isle of Hunen, and in sight of Copenhagen, till the close of the season, to protect the English and Swedish convoys passing up and down the Sound; and during that time scarcely a day passed in which he was not employed against the Danes, either in chasing their gun-boats or destroying some of their small convoys, which service was of the most essential consequence to the commerce of both England and Sweden. On one occasion the enemy appeared determined to rid themselves of so troublesome a neighbour, and sent out from

noitre, went himself in his barge for that purpose, accompanied by the boats of both ships well manned and armed. About a mile and a half from the beach on which most of the convoy were wrecked, Captain Baker lay on his oars, in order to take a full view of them: three vessels we perceived still afloat, the larger and outer one we supposed to be a gun-boat. Finding this to be the case, Captain Baker repeatedly observed to me, who was in the boat with him, that the most effectual method to destroy or bring them out would be under the cover of the Martial brig, then standing towards us: this idea was communicated to the officers commanding the different boats, and every arrangement made and perfectly understood. Many armed men were at this time assembled on the hill commanding the bay, and the officers, not being aware of their number, and fearing that more would be collected, urged Captain Baker not to delay for the Martial, then at some distance, with a very light air, but to dash in at once: this being repeated, and a desire added by the officer commanding the boats of the Iris, that Captain Baker would not himself go, caused him, it is my earnest belief, to make the attempt unaccompanied by the brig. He then pointed out to each officer the vessel they were to attack, meaning himself to cut out the one we supposed to be armed: however, on our going along side, an unremitted fire of musketry was kept up from the shore, so much so, that, after having cut her cables, and being in the act of towing her off, from the circumstance of her being moored by means unknown to us, we were obliged, after previously ordering all the other boats to retreat, to do so ourselves, in order to prevent a most dreadful slaughter, which must inevitably have followed had we persevered."

Copenhagen a large flotilla of gun-boats to attack the Vanguard, the time and weather appearing to favour the attempt. They were, however, beat off with considerable damage; but Sir Archibald Dickson, under whom he acted, being of opinion that the Vanguard was in some danger from the great number of the enemy's gun-boats, ordered Captain Baker to join him off Helsingborg, that they might be able mutually to assist each other; and he was employed under that indefatigable officer till the arrival of Sir T. Birtie, who hoisted his flag on board the Vanguard.

Having returned to England at the end of the season, Captain Baker solicited and obtained leave of absence, when he repaired to Sweden, where he remained for two years. On the 22d November, 1811, he was appointed to the Cumberland of 74 guns, and after being variously employed off the coast of Ireland, in the Channel, and in the North Sea, he sailed to the West Indies, in December 1812, with a convoy of seventy vessels. He remained in the West Indies till the month of May, when a convoy of 220 sail of vessels was placed under his protection, and with which he returned to England in perfect safety. The great care and attention manifested by Captain Baker on this occasion induced the masters of the ships from the port of London to present him with a service of plate, as a tribute of their respect and esteem. He was afterwards employed in the North Sea, and being, in the month of November, off the Texel, he became acquainted with the changes in the fortune of Buonaparte, and the consequent effect it had on the minds of the people, particularly on those of the Dutch. With a spirit ever active and alive to the interests of his country, Captain Baker could not regard with indifference so favourable an opportunity of displaying his devotion to her welfare: he entered into a communication with the governor of the Hague, and landed a body of marines for the protection of that place. In this service he was found when the Prince of Orange arrived to assume the sovereignty of his paternal dominions, and from whom he received the Order of Guillaume.

In June 1814 Captain Baker proceeded in the Cumberland to the Cape, with a convoy of vessels destined for the East Indies and the Brazils; and whilst on that station he proved the humanity of his disposition by giving vent to those feelings which do honour to human nature. On the 15th February, 1815, he detained a Portuguese vessel with a cargo of slaves and ivory. "Of all the distressing sights," said he, "I ever witnessed, none ever came to my knowledge of greater magnitude; in addition therefore to the fulfilment of a professional duty, by sending this vessel into port, I feel the greatest call, on the score of humanity, to make it a question of the law of nature and of nations, if so infamous a traffic, under all the circumstances of this cruel case, must be suffered to exist. This brig of 229 tons sailed on the 24th Jan. from Mazambique with 354 slaves, 13 of whom died on the passage of only twenty-two days; and there are now four more in their last agonies, with 37 sick, the whole being in the most deplorable state of naked confinement: added to which, the vessel is so leaky as to make, in moderate weather, twenty inches of water an hour, requiring every four hours one hour and a half's continual pumping. How it is possible that the master of any vessel, belonging to any nation, so circumstanced, could think of passing the Cape, or any friendly port, where he might ameliorate the lot of such unhappy creatures, must be left to the feelings of those who contemplate their profit in the human species, purchased at the average, as they were, of six pounds sterling each! Having provided for the temporary relief of these unhappy creatures by ordering the vessel into port, I feel, sir, that I have only done my duty; the question of her proceeding farther, I am happy to think, must now depend upon your better judgment." That no difficulty or delay might occur to the prejudice of those miserable beings on account of any pecuniary benefit likely to accrue to Captain Baker from her detention, he gave the prize-master the following order:

" If it be found upon your arrival at the Cape that there is cause to detain the brig, I consent to it only upon condition that the slaves are immediately provided for, landed, and taken care of; as it would totally defeat my purpose in sending her in, to have them endure their chains one day longer than is necessary for their comfort and the repair of the vessel. The object therefore of the ivory and other articles must not impede the sailing of this vessel; for if they cannot be decided upon at the same time that the case of the slaves is, I would rather forego any probable profits likely to arise from that source, than detain her."

Captain Baker continued at the Cape till the month of April 1815, when he returned to England in charge of another valuable convoy, and for his protection of which he was presented by the East India Company with a present of 300*l.* In August 1819 he was made a colonel of marines, and in July 1821 was promoted to the rank of rear-admiral.

We have thus plainly stated Admiral Baker's professional services, and in so doing have offered but few observations as we proceeded, in order that the whole might be collected under one view. Whoever provokes danger; whoever quits a peaceful retreat, where he might have slumbered in ease and safety, for peril and labour, to drive before a tempest, or to combat the enemies of his country; in short, whoever exposes his life for the good of others, is deserving of praise; and to withhold that portion of honour and reward which his merits deserve, is equally unjust and injurious. " Great is the pleasure attendant on exertion, and sweet the reward of applauding fellow-creatures when the exertion is virtuous and successful. But there is a great deal of unsuccessful exertion in the pursuit of fame; and many, after serving in pain and labour, reap only a harvest of disappointment." This is too often the case, and we regret exceedingly that the case of Admiral Baker should add another instance to the melancholy truth. During the greater part of his career, he was most actively employed; he neither wanted opportunities to exert himself, nor did he fail to embrace them as they occurred. He has had the farther good fortune not only never to have been the subject of the reproach, or even the complaint, of any one officer whatever, but to have acquired the esteem and regard of all. The first instance in which he had a particular opportunity of manifesting his zeal for the service by the faithful discharge of his duty, was in the case of the Danish convoy, when the enemies of his country sought to embroil her with the northern powers of Europe by the well-known expedient of sending a frigate with a fleet of merchantmen, and giving her captain orders to resist the right of search. On this occasion he was highly complimented by Mr. Pitt and Mr. Wyndham; the latter of whom acknowledged, at the Duke of Gloucester's, that he had obtained the praises of the whole of the king's cabinet. No war has produced a braver action than the one which terminated in the capture of the Didon; none was ever more bravely contested by the enemy; none was ever more skilfully conducted by the victor, or brought to a more triumphant conclusion. In spite of numbers, rate, or weight of metal, he acquired honour and renown; and that day's engagement will ever stand conspicuous among the many occasions on which the British flag has maintained its wonted superiority. This was quickly followed by his conduct previous to and during the action which terminated in the capture of four sail of the line by Sir Richard Strachan: to his penetrating genius, quick discernment, and enterprising spirit, joined to the most active personal exertions, his companions on that occasion have always ascribed the successful termination of that day. It was owing to his having disregarded all personal considerations of benefit, by relinquishing a cruise which promised to be attended with great pecuniary advantages, which enabled him to fall in with the enemy's squadron; and it was owing to his dexterity in expedients and skilful manœuvres by which he brought it into the power of Sir R. Strachan. His success in these three instances procured him the approbation of his superiors, was the subject of the most sanguine hopes of himself and family, and of the congratulations of his friends. Unfortunately, however, these hopes have proved chimerical; and in him we see an officer of undoubted merit, of great intellectual qualities, and whose exertions have been crowned with the most brilliant success, deprived of those honours and rewards which his whole life has been devoted to obtain; and, what is still more galling, which others have obtained without having so strong a claim. Why should this be? We have heard that he is considered too ambitious, too high-minded, and has sought those rewards as a matter of right, which should be granted only as a matter of grace and favour. Ambition, when properly directed, is praiseworthy; and we may say this of him, that, if he has ambition, it is of a noble and generous description, and has prompted him to raise himself and to obtain honours by laborious service, and to secure to himself advancement in his profession by a display of all those qualities which portray the distinguished officer. Notwithstanding these favourable and flattering circumstances, he has been not only disappointed in obtaining those honours to which he naturally looked forward from his own government, but has been refused permission to accept and wear that decoration which was presented to him by the King of Sweden, for services rendered to that nation! Hope has been repeatedly sounded in his ear, but has always avoided his grasp. Sir James Saumarez, Sir Edward Pellew, Sir Michael Seymour, and others were knighted for actions similar to the one which ended in the capture of La Didon, and he naturally expected the same honour would have been conferred upon him; but neither the First Lord (Barham) nor any member of the Board either thanked or congratulated him on the result of his action, or shewed him the smallest favour or attention beyond the cold letter of thanks usual on such occasions. Upon his making some application on the subject, he was informed that the institu-

tion of an order of merit was in the contemplation of the ministry, and
that he should have *the highest order that could be awarded to officers
of his class*. This was somewhat consolatory; but at the end of 1808,
finding no farther notice taken of it, he addressed Lord Mulgrave on
the subject, told him of the neglect that he had experienced, and trusted
that his lordship would lay the particulars of his case before the king,
in the hope that he might receive the only boon he ever looked forward
to—the honourable approbation of his Majesty. But his lordship coolly
replied, " I regret that you should conceive the merits of your action
with the Didon to have been overlooked by my predecessors; but I cannot
enter into any *retrospective view* of the circumstances which may have
guided their conduct on that occasion." Not enter into a retrospective
view! Why, is it ever too late to do an act of justice? It is never too
late to satisfy a noble mind, unless we fall into the error, that to be neglected is to be unworthy. How completely may any officer be rendered
hors de combat by such a cold answer to his grievances! According to
this doctrine, there is no hope of remuneration for neglected merit. But
let us suppose that he had failed in his duty, or done any thing repre-
hensible, would the same argument have shielded him from punishment,
or prevented him from being put upon the " yellow list?" Would not a
retrospective view have been then taken of all the circumstances? Justly indignant at such a mode of evading the subject, Captain Baker immediately
after addressed a letter to Lord Barham, stated the answer he had received from Lord Mulgrave, and requested that he would inform him
the reason, if any, why he had not received the same honorary reward
that had been bestowed upon others, and to which the following answer
was returned:

Barham-Court, 8th Feb. 1809.

Sir,—I have received your letter of the 6th, and can only say, that if Mr.
Pitt had lived a few weeks longer, a new military order would have been instituted,
which would have provided for all ranks of officers entitled to distinction.
Amongst those it certainly was my intention to have recommended you and
several others, who had highly distinguished themselves at home and abroad.
Whether or not this will now be instituted I cannot say ; but considering the num-
ber of those entitled to distinction, and the limited number of the present order,
I do not see how gentlemen can be rewarded without it.

As this new order was agreed upon, and which was known to Lord Mulgrave,
and possibly to the succeeding ministry, it naturally subsided on account of the

change that took place, and I had no opportunity of acting farther in it. Captain Lambert in the East Indies, as well as yourself, was particularly in my mind; but as no ribbons were then vacant, and it was especially intended by Mr. Pitt to reserve that of the Bath for ministers abroad, and provide for all ranks of the army and navy out of the new order, the whole in that case would have been provided for. This is all that occurs to me on the subject of your letter, and which I hope will prove satisfactory.

Very satisfactory certainly, when Captain Baker had received a short time before a letter from a particular friend, in which he stated, " I can venture again to repeat, that you had not any enemies at the Board; but you had unfortunately to deal with a man whose time of life and habits withdrew him wholly from the court and from his colleagues. *This, and this only, take my word for it, was the real cause of your disappointment.*"

On the appointment of Lord Melville to be First Lord of the Admiralty, Captain Baker again renewed his claim, enforced by the following letter from Sir Richard Strachan:

" My Lord,—Having been informed by Captain Baker of his Majesty's ship Cumberland, that he had presented a memorial of his services to your lordship, it gives me great pleasure to have the power of adding my testimony to that of the other officers with whom he has served. I have known Captain Baker several years ; he owes an early promotion to his zealous and active services. His gallant conduct as captain of the Phœnix when he took the Didon is too well known to require repeating ; but your lordship may not be so well informed respecting the skilful manner in which he diverted the course of the French squadron which escaped after the action off Trafalgar from getting into Rochefort, and brought it in chase of the Phœnix towards Cape Finisterre, where he knew a squadron of his Majesty's ships was cruising under my command : he joined me at night, with the French squadron close to him ; *and to his excellent management I attribute our having the opportunity of taking it.* As Captain Baker has since been constantly employed, his merits are known to your lordship ; I have therefore only to add, that I shall be much gratified if what I have stated should render him service."

This, however, was not attended with the desired success, and Captain Baker received from the gentleman above alluded to the following note :

" It was not till Saturday that Lord Melville spoke to me on your subject, which he did in the handsomest manner, feeling very much the awkwardness of your situation; but feeling, precisely as I have always told you, *that you were let through by a combination of circumstances which no one could have foreseen, and which most probably will never happen again*: but he feels also that he is the fourth in succession from the person who ought to have done your business; and though this will *not deter him from doing what he may judge to be proper, yet one must be aware that it will preclude him from acting so freely and independently as he might have done if no such impediment existed.*"

So, an injustice is acknowledged to have been committed in the first instance, and because committed, it is to be perpetuated! No one is to have spirit and independence enough to grant that remuneration and bestow that mark of distinction which all allow are due. But we will proceed a little farther. At length, in January 1815, came forth the extension of the Order of the Bath, which was to satisfy all claimants; but, in the first instance, Captain Baker's name was entirely omitted, which gave occasion to the Countess Baker to write to Lord Melville on the subject, when the following answer was returned:

ADMIRALTY, *Jan.* 7, 1815.

MADAM,—I had the honour to receive yesterday your letter of the 5th inst. on the subject of Captain Baker's claims *to that mark of distinction which he is desirous of obtaining*; and I can have no difficulty in assuring you, in reply, that it is not my intention that the services of Captain Baker should remain unregarded. (Signed,) MELVILLE.

Countess AUGUSTA BAKER.

Captain Baker's services did not remain entirely unregarded; but instead of his name being included " *in the highest order conferred on officers of his class,*" it was placed amongst the lowest; among the captors of privateers, and those who had fired a few shots at some of the enemy's flotillas; and this too whilst some who had scarcely ever seen a shot fired, had the higher order conferred upon them. That mind must be constituted of very strange materials which could decide upon conferring the highest honorary distinction upon those who had scarcely ever been in action, and the lesser one on him, who, by his conduct in battle, had fairly won the most honourable title. No one whose mind was not perverted by partiality and favouritism, or sunk in the most deplorable ignorance and stupidity, would so act, in defiance of honour, justice, and every noble feeling. Can such neglect as Admiral Baker has experienced be defended? Are not honours and distinctions the proper rewards of military men? They are in the gift of the sovereign, to whom all look up with hope and confidence of receiving the due reward of their exertions. It is this hope which keeps up their spirits to that heat and vigour which drive on the current of success, and by which they have achieved such astonishing exploits. We know it will be said, that the sovereign cannot act but by advice, and that those distinctions merely signify the favour of ministers and the political power of the party; that they are of no consequence to men of sterling merit; that they know their own value; and that the difference between them and the more favoured will always remain the same, however external distinctions may be misplaced and confounded. But it has been already answered, that " if this is so, every title, order, medal, or decoration of whatever sort, is a mere toy and plaything, which none but trifling minds can value, and which may be dispensed from henceforth to whomsoever will take them, without the least regret on the part of those who really deserve them." They will then cease to be sought after by the meritorious, and must be considered as badges of disgrace, rather than as symbols of distinguished conduct. Had it been Admiral Baker's lot not to have had opportunities to distinguish himself, he would not have been the subject of public notice and remark ; but, as it is, his very successes have been made the grounds, for those who are unacquainted with him, to conclude, by the navy at large to suspect, and by his friends to fear, that some circumstance to his prejudice exists, that is sufficient to divert the stream of the royal bounty, and prevent him from receiving that recompence he is entitled, from his conduct and exertions, to expect ; and the disappointment he has experienced has consequently left him in a situation the most painful to his feelings, and hurtful to his character as an officer and a man. We may, however, safely aver, that his mind is both great and noble ; that he is void of sordid desires and unworthy designs ; and that there is no individual more deserving of reward, nor one who would reflect back the honour conferred upon him with more brilliancy, than Admiral Baker, whose name will always stand associated with all that is lofty in spirit and noble in principle.

It has been said, that " time alone can decide the degree of estimation to which every man is entitled; the partialities or prejudices of contemporaries exalt or depress every virtue, heighten or palliate every fault, and represent every action in the light that is most favourable to their different purposes of panegyric or invective." And with respect to the capture of La Didon, Captain Brenton says, " It is singular, that for this action Captain Baker did not receive any particular mark of appro- bation; and shortly after greater events occupied the public mind and absorbed its whole attention. A small action, however brilliant, is un- fortunately timed if it come too near a great one; it is entirely eclipsed, and never recovers its true splendour." But this mode of reasoning on the unmerited treatment of the illustrious is calculated to damp the ardour of those who are panting with ambition, and to check in its pro- gress that thirst of glory and emulation from which great actions take their rise. It should be recollected by those who have the distribution of honours and rewards, that, in managing those great springs of human activity, natural courage, hope, and fear, nothing so damps men's alacrity as an idea that their exertions will go unrewarded; that nothing so quickens it as a confidence that their merits and services will be acknow- ledged, by having conferred upon them those honours which were in- vented as a means of encouraging and rewarding eminent abilities; and the approbation thereby imparted is no less grateful to the mind, than beauty is to the eyes, or harmony to the ears. And one of the greatest judges of the human mind has observed, that " when the prospect of reward has vanished, the zeal of enterprise will cease; for who will per- severe to cultivate the soil which he has, after long labour, discovered to be barren? He who hath pleased himself with anticipated praises, and expected that he should meet in every place with patronage or friend- ship, will soon remit his vigour when he finds, that those from whom he has a right to expect every thing, nothing can be hoped but cold civility, and that many refuse to own his excellence, lest they should be too justly expected to reward it. A man thus cut off from the prospect of that port to which his address had been employed to steer him, often abandons himself to chance and to the wind, and glides careless and idle down the current of life, without resolution to make another effort, till he is swallowed up by the gulph of mortality." It cannot therefore be object- ed to Admiral Baker, or any one else, that he has shewn an over-anxious solicitude to obtain that which he considered himself entitled to. He asserted his claim with spirit, with manfulness, with independence; and if it be said that he shewed too great an anxiety to obtain honours and titles, we say that those honours and titles are in themselves to be con- sidered as marks of approbation for actions performed; that generous minds are peculiarly sensible of ungenerous treatment; and that it is only such persons as are far above the common level who are thus affected with either of those extremes, as " in a thermometer it is only the purest and most sublimated spirit which is either contracted or dilated by the benignity or inclemency of the season." Fortunately, however, for Admiral Baker, fortunately for the profession to which he belongs, and by consequence the country in general, the administration of its naval affairs has devolved into the hands of one who is above all evasion and subterfuge, who knows how to appreciate honourable conduct and motives, and from whom consequently every thing that is just and proper may be hoped and expected.

Admiral Baker married the daughter of his Excellency Count Ruuth, one of the most ancient and noble families in the kingdom of Sweden: by that lady he has several children.

HISTORICAL MEMOIRS OF
ADMIRAL BENJAMIN WILLIAM PAGE.

THE blessings bestowed by Providence on the English nation have been strongly manifested in various ways—by that general prosperity which has attended her, and particularly by that host of naval heroes which has been bestowed upon her, by whose zealous pursuits in their profession their conduct has been attended with well-merited success. Some, however, have not been so conspicuously serviceable as others; and though the officer whose Memoirs, from his rank, we are here induced to give, may be classed amongst them, still he is one of the many who have proved, that a steady pursuit in the path of honour and glory in the service of their country is the road to fame and happiness.   He was born at Ipswich in 1765, and commenced his naval career in November 1778, on board the Superb of 74 guns, bearing the flag and under the patronage of Sir Edward Hughes (a friend of his father's), sailed with him to the East Indies, shared with him in all his hard-fought battles with the French fleet under De Suffrein*, and was twice wounded in thus defending the cause of his country. He continued on board the Superb as an active and favourite midshipman till the end of 1782, when he was made an acting-lieutenant of the Exeter at Bombay. On the latter ship being ordered home at the termination of hostilities, Sir Edward appointed Mr. Page lieutenant of the only sloop of war on the station, the Lizard, a French prize, of 18 8-pounders, as a mark of his friendship and approbation of the whole of his conduct, and to give him an opportunity, though so young, of doing all the duties of a first and only lieutenant; and in which he gave such general satisfaction as to induce Captain Courtenay, of the Eurydice frigate, to solicit his appointment to that ship as his only lieutenant. This took place on the 20th November, 1784; and thus was he, at the age of nineteen, and having only just completed his six years' servitude, confirmed a lieutenant, asked for, and appointed, first of a post-ship.

In the following year the Eurydice accompanied the admiral, in the Sultan, Captain Troubridge, to England, and both ships were paid off.

* See *Memoir of Sir* EDWARD HUGHES.

In 1786 Captain Peter Rainier being appointed to the Astrea frigate, and second in command at Jamaica, procured Lieutenant Page a commission as second lieutenant of that ship; and under the direction and able auspices of that respectable officer was Mr. Page completed in his professional knowledge.   On their return to England in 1790, Lieutenant Page was recommended by his friend and captain to Captain R. M. Sutton of the Minerva, and in three days afterwards sailed with him to the East Indies, where he was removed by Commodore Cornwallis to his own ship, the Crown, and returned with him to England in 1792.   In January 1793 he was appointed first lieutenant of the Suffolk of 74 guns, Captain Rainier, and served in the fleet under Lord Howe till May 1794, when Captain Rainier being appointed to the East India command, with the rank of commodore, he accompanied him to that station; and although they had forty-four ships under convoy, they sailed from Spithead to Madras without dropping an anchor, or procuring any other supplies than those which they received in England, and without experiencing any casualty or sickness; a circumstance so uncommon in those days as to be attributed to the good order of the Suffolk's crew, and the great attention of the commodore and his officers.   On this occasion the commodore had no captain under him to aid in the duties of the ship, but the Admiralty allowed a sixth or additional lieutenant; and Mr. Page, as her first lieutenant, was allowed the batta or pay of a commander, at the commodore's request to the Admiralty, till a captain was appointed.   In June 1795 the commodore was promoted to a flag-officer, and in August reduced the Dutch settlements in the Island of Ceylon.

In September 1795 Lieutenant Page was promoted to the rank of commander, and appointed to the Robart sloop of 18 guns; and on the 1st October, with a detachment of troops under Colonel Monson, he took possession of the Dutch factory of Molletive.   In January 1796 he sailed with the admiral and an expedition against the Molucca Islands, and, owing to his great knowledge of the Indian seas, was selected to head the fleet through the difficult passages leading to those islands, which he successfully accomplished; but previous to their capture he was sent back to Madras with important dispatches, and by this means was prevented from sharing in the large sums of prize-money arising therefrom, although he had been so greatly instrumental in their capture.   In December 1796 he escorted a valuable convoy of China traders from

Prince of Wales Island to Bombay; for which he received the thanks of both government and merchants, and a present from the latter of five hundred guineas; and a post vacancy having shortly after occurred by the death of Captain Newcome, he was appointed by Admiral Rainier to the Orpheus, which was confirmed by Lord Spencer. In consequence, however, of ill health, Captain Page was obliged to return to England, which prevented him for some time prosecuting his professional career; but on his restoration he was appointed by Lord Spencer, in January 1800, to the Inflexible of 64 guns: but for the purpose of enabling her to carry troops, her lower-deck guns were taken out, and her complement of men reduced to 350. He then sailed, under sealed orders, with fourteen other ships of war similarly fitted, and having altogether 5000 troops on board, to Minorca, where he joined Lord Keith, and afterwards proceeded with him to the blockade of Genoa; but having been sent to Leghorn on special service the day before its surrender, he was again disappointed of, and prevented from, sharing in the profits. On his return he was ordered to England with a convoy, and having called at Gibraltar and Lisbon, arrived safe at home, when Lord Spencer again ordered him to the Mediterranean, to convey part of the 42d Highland regiment, which he landed in Egypt on the 8th March, 1801, and was then employed in the blockade of Alexandria. On the surrender of Cairo he was ordered to convoy the French troops to Marseilles; but was not allowed to share in the spoils of the Egyptian campaign, in consequence of his not being able to return previous to its final close. Having taken on board the second in command of the British troops, Sir Eyre Coote, and the 3d regiment of guards, he returned to England, and was paid off in 1802. Lord Spencer, however, shortly afterwards appointed him to the Caroline of 36 guns, on the Irish station, where he remained till May 1803, when he suddenly received orders to sail to the East Indies: in one hour afterwards he left the Cove of Cork, having on board only the usual Irish cruisers' equipment, and reached his destination in 103 days, stopping only a few hours at Madeira for water and wine. In his passage he captured one French ship and detained two Dutch ships; the latter of which were, however, made droits of Admiralty, and a moiety only given to the captors. Captain Page's local knowledge of the Bay of Bengal, where he found himself senior officer, enabled him to convoy the Company's ships safely for several months, during which he captured two French privateers, one of

16 guns and the other of 26, from Europe, before they had made any captures ; and the merchants of Calcutta and Madras, to express their satisfaction of his prompt, zealous, and spirited services, sent from each settlement their public thanks and a present of five hundred guineas. He was then ordered by Admiral Rainier to take under his command the Grampus of 50 guns, Dedaigneuse of 38, and Dasher of 18, and protect a valuable convoy to and from China, it being expected that the French admiral, Linois, in the Marengo of 80 guns, with some frigates, would have made an attack upon them, as they had previously done on the East India fleet under Commodore Dance*.   In January 1805 Captain Page, with his convoy, returned to Prince of Wales Island ; and in the month of March was promoted by Admiral Rainier to his flag-ship, the Trident of 64 guns, with whom he returned to England, accompanied by forty-four ships, and having on board the present Duke of Wellington.   On their voyage they stopped at St. Helena, at which time, it is said, the duke first became aware of its strength and security, which ultimately led to its becoming the residence of Napoleon.   On the Trident being paid off in September, the Court of Directors of the East India Company presented Captain Page with their thanks and a present of five hundred guineas, for the great care and attention he had shewn to their interests ; thus making up the sum of two thousand guineas which he had received from the mercantile community for the manner of conducting convoys placed under his protection, and which, next to the destruction of the enemy's forces, is the most useful employment of a naval officer.

Captain Page afterwards received an appointment for the sea-fencibles, which he retained till the breaking up of that corps ; and in 1812 was appointed to the Puissant, stationary at Spithead.   Whoever is acquainted with the duties of such a situation, is well aware that in time of war it is no sinecure : the attending courts-martial, the constant surveys of men invalided, the attending to the prison-ships in harbour, the examination of candidates for lieutenancies, with various other important matters, render it not only irksome so far as personal exertions are concerned ; but from the number of persons he must necessarily come in contact with, the variety of interests and personal feelings he has in some degree to combat, render it also one of great delicacy : but, by

* See *Naval Chronology*, vol. I. p. 74.

an honest, upright conduct, and consulting only his own honour and the country's interest, Captain Page fortunately succeeded in giving universal satisfaction. In 1819 he was made a rear-admiral, and now resides at the place of his birth, esteemed and respected by all who know him either afloat or on shore. Indeed, we are assured that he is one of the best of men and best of officers in the British navy, of unblemished integrity, high feelings and professional attainments.

HISTORICAL MEMOIRS OF
ADMIRAL JOHN BLIGH, C.B.

To all readers of naval history, to all observers of the rapid strides made by the British navy in obtaining its present elevated situation, the name of Bligh must be familiar, having always maintained a high professional reputation. Admiral Bligh is the son of Captain John Bligh, R.N. and nephew of Admiral Sir Richard Rodney Bligh, G.C.B. whose services we have already recorded. His grandfather, Richard Bligh, was also in the navy, and served as a lieutenant of the Rainbow frigate, with Captain (afterwards Lord) Rodney in 1749. He was born in August 1771, and at a proper age was placed in the royal grammar-school at Guildford, where he remained till 1783, when he became a member of the profession, and went to sea on board the Trimmer brig, being at that time only twelve years old. In the following year he joined the Bulldog sloop, in which he sailed for Jamaica; but on the death of her captain, Marsh, in 1786, he joined the Camilla, Captain Hutt, with whom he returned to England in 1787. He then joined the Pegase of 74 guns; but on her being paid off in February 1788, he removed to the Colossus, and in October joined the Crown of 64 guns, Commodore Cornwallis, with whom he proceeded to the East Indies. In 1791 he was promoted to a lieutenancy on board the Thames, Captain T. Troubridge, and returned to England in December following. In the following year he was appointed to the Lizard, commanded by the present Sir T. Williams; and at the commencement of hostilities in February 1793, he removed to the Courageux, commanded by his particular friend, the Hon. W. Waldegrave. He then proceeded with the fleet under Lord Hood to the Mediterranean; and after the surrender of Toulon accompanied Admiral Linzee to the attack of St. Fiorenzo, whence, being defeated, they returned to Toulon, and it was with much difficulty the Courageux reached the port, as she made seven feet water an hour: the ship was then hove down in the arsenal, and Lieutenant Bligh was employed in the batteries till the final evacuation. Captain Waldegrave having returned to England, been promoted to the rank of rear-admiral, and ordered to hoist his flag on board the Barfleur, Lieutenant Bligh became a follower of his fortune, quitted the Courageux, and proceeded overland to England, when he became first lieutenant of the Barfleur, again proceeded to the Mediterranean, and continued under the orders of Sir John Jervis till after the glorious victory off St. Vincent. He was then promoted to the rank of commander, appointed to the Kingfisher brig, and having sailed on a cruise, captured Le Général privateer, off Oporto, pierced for 18 guns, and having on board 104 men.

Having returned to Lisbon, Captain Bligh was ordered to England in the Flora frigate, with Admiral Waldegrave; and on his arrival obtained his post-commission, bearing date 25th April, 1797. He was then appointed to the Latona frigate, bearing the flag of Admiral Waldegrave, appointed to the chief command at Newfoundland, and continued on that station till 1800, commanding in succession the Romney of 50 guns and Agincourt of 64. In 1801 he was appointed to the Theseus of 74 guns, and in December hoisted the flag of his friend, Admiral Waldegrave, as commander-in-chief in the East Indies; but, as the admiral was shortly after made an admiral of the Blue, and created an Irish peer, it was again struck on the 28th of the month. In February 1802 Captain Bligh sailed under the orders of Admiral G. Campbell to Jamaica.

After the commencement of hostilities Captain Bligh was employed in the blockade of Cape François; and on the 8th September, having found it extremely difficult to prevent small vessels from passing into Cape François with provisions from the little ports on the northern part of the island, in consequence of their finding a safe retreat from his pursuit under the batteries of Fort Dauphin, and conceiving the port to be of importance to the enemy, he deemed it necessary to make some efforts for the reduction of the place and the capture of a ship of war at anchor there. He accordingly proceeded to Manchernel Bay, leaving the Hercule and Cumberland on their station, and having brought up within musket-shot of Fort Labouque at the entrance of the harbour, opened such a well-directed fire, that the guns of the battery could not be pointed with any precision, and the colours were soon afterwards hauled down. With the assistance of the boats, the Theseus was then worked into the harbour, and having fired a few shot at the ship of war, she likewise surrendered, and proved to be La Sagesse of 28 guns. The commandant of the fort conceiving the place to be no longer tenable, and under some apprehension of being exposed to the rage of the Blacks, whom he considered a merciless enemy, claimed British protection, and surrendered the fort and garrison at discretion. Having spiked the guns and destroyed the ammunition, the garrison and inhabitants were embarked, and landed under a flag of truce at Cape François. Being informed by the prisoners that their general (Dumont) and his suite had fallen into the hands of the Blacks, and that they were in the most imminent danger, Captain Bligh, actuated by those motives of humanity which do honour to men in all situations, interested himself to obtain their release; and by his earnest application to the Black chief, his request was complied with, and they accompanied the rest of the prisoners to Cape François*.

On the 18th Nov. the French under Rochambeau surrendered Cape François to the Black general, who attacked it at the head of his army; and by the articles of capitulation the garrison was allowed till the 30th to complete the evacuation, when all the stores and ammunition were to be given up to Dessalines. In the interval, the French general opened a communication with Captain Loring, the senior officer of the British squadron, proposing terms for capitulating to him†; but as they were deemed inadmissible, he broke them off, flattering himself, it is supposed, that the tremendous weather which the blockading squadron was then experiencing would enable him to escape with his ships: but the perseverance and watchfulness of the former precluded him from even attempting it. On the 30th the colours of the Blacks were hoisted on all the forts, which induced Captain Loring, the senior officer of the British squadron, to dispatch Captain Bligh to the Cape, to ascertain the situation of the French, and their reason for remaining in port; with power to act as he should consider most beneficial to the honour and reputation of his country. On entering the harbour he met the French commodore, Barré, in his boat, who pressed him in strong terms to go on board the Surveillante, and enter into some capitulation which should place them under British protection, and prevent the Blacks from destroying them with red-hot shot, which they had threatened, and were preparing to do. Indeed the critical situation of their ships and troops was obvious, aad rendered a capitulation necessary for their preservation. Articles, which had been already drawn up, were then hastily presented to him for his signature‡, which, after some objections

---

* Official letter, see RALFE's *Naval Chronology*, vol. I. p. 18.
† See RALFE's *Naval Chronology*, vol. I. p. 22.   ‡ *Ibid.* p. 23.

on the part of Captain Bligh, and the verbal promise of General Rochambeau that they should be altered on their arrival at Jamaica, were
agreed to. Captain Bligh then hastened to the Black general, Dessalines, to acquaint him of the circumstance. Notwithstanding which, it
was with much difficulty Captain Bligh could prevail upon him to desist
from his intention of firing into the ships, requesting, as the price of his
forbearance, that eight French officers, whom he named, should be given
up to him; but upon Captain Bligh explaining the impossibility of his
acceding to such a request, in violation of the treaty he had just concluded, and threatening him with the vengeance of British hostility in
case he should carry his plan into effect, finding himself thwarted,
the general became enraged, ordered Captain Bligh into confinement,
kept him a close prisoner, and repeatedly threatened to shoot him; but
as this had not the desired effect, he reluctantly desisted from his object, and dismissed Captain Bligh, but wreaked his vengeance on the
French troops who were left in the hospital, the whole of whom were
put to death that night.

This service being completed, Captain Bligh proceeded to Jamaica,
and shortly after was intrusted by Sir John Duckworth with the command of a squadron, to consist of three sail of the line and two frigates,
to make an attack on the Island of Curaçoa; "having," said Sir John,
"received certain information that the garrison of Curaçoa has not been
strengthened since the commencement of the war, and consists of only 160
troops, with a frigate in the port, whose officers and crew are said nearly
all to have fallen victims to the climate." The Vanguard, however, not
having joined, the squadron consisted of only the Theseus and Hercule
74's, Blanche and Pique frigates, and Gipsy schooner. Captain Bligh
was directed to summon the island upon liberal conditions; but in case
of refusal, and he had reason to believe there had been no augmentation
of the enemy's garrison, he was to land a part of the crews of his ships.
Then follows this advice: "But it is my duty to caution you by no
means to hazard more than the object is worth." On the 31st January,
1804, Captain Bligh and his squadron arrived off the island, about six
miles to the eastward of the town and harbour of St. Anne, when Captain
C. B. Ross was dispatched with a flag of truce to the governor, requesting him to surrender the island: this, however, was refused. As Captain Bligh had been informed by Sir John Duckworth, that it was not
his intention that the line-of-battle ships should be risked by attempting to

force the harbour of St. Anne, he bore up with them for a small cove, which had been pointed out as an eligible spot for debarkation, leaving the two frigates to blockade the harbour and cause a diversion of the enemy's force. " In passing Fort Amsterdam, situated on the S.E. side of the entrance to St. Anne, the two 74's were fired at, but without effect, the shot falling short. At 11h. 30m. Fort Piscadero, mounting ten Dutch 12-pounders, and protecting the intended point of disembarkation, opened a fire. This was immediately returned by the Theseus within half-musket-shot, although the ship was unable to remain along side, owing to a strong head wind and lee current. By making short tacks, however, she brought her guns to bear with such effect, that the fort fired only an occasional gun when the ship was in stays. At one p.m. the first division of seamen and marines in the boats stormed and carried the fort without loss, and struck the Dutch colours, which the enemy, on retreating, had left flying. By a rapid movement the British gained the heights, and, with the loss of only four or five killed and wounded, drove the Dutch soldiers from their position. This done, the remainder of the seamen and marines (the whole consisting of about 600 men) were landed, and the Gipsy schooner anchored in the cove. Captain Bligh also went ashore; and, as there was no anchorage for them, the Theseus and Hercule continued to stand off and on, but, owing to the wind and current, found a great difficulty in keeping their stations. During the night several shots were fired at the ships from Fort Amsterdam, but although two or three went over the Theseus, not one shot struck either ship. On the 1st February two 18-pounder carronades and a light field-piece were landed from the Theseus, and, with great difficulty and some danger, were dragged four miles to the advanced post on the height. This post was situated about eight hundred yards to the westward of the town of St. Anne, which it in part overlooked, and was placed under the command of Lieutenant N.J. Willoughby, while the post between that and the point of disembarkation was commanded by Lieutenant Hills." On the completion of those works, a constant cannonade was kept up on the Dutch batteries, including Fort Republique; but without any sensible effect, though the town was partially set on fire. Continual skirmishes also took place with parties of the enemy, some of which consisted of near 500 men; but though they terminated in favour of the British, still it was not without loss, particularly from the guns of Fort Republique. They were also attacked by a more formidable enemy, the dysentery, and seeing there was no possibility of a speedy successful termination of the contest, and as the enemy had received a strong reinforcement, Captain Bligh was induced to abandon the attempt, which he did on the 4th March, after having sustained a loss of 18 killed and 43 wounded, fired away every 18-pound shot in the squadron, and performed every thing which human bravery and foresight could suggest. " Notwithstanding the ill success which had attended this, as Sir John not unaptly termed it, child of his own brain, the addition of the Vanguard's seamen and marines, and a heavy mortar or two, would have enabled Captain Bligh to cut off the water from the Dutch garrison, and probably compelled the French faction that ruled the island to accede to the proposed capitulation. The British officers and men behaved most admirably; and the masterly manner in which, for so long a time, Lieutenants Hills and Willoughby, the latter in particular, maintained their respective posts, elicited the strong praise of Captain Bligh*."

In July following Admiral Dacres having hoisted his flag on board the Theseus, Captain Bligh requested Sir John Duckworth to appoint him to the Surveillante; and he then continued on the Jamaica station till June 1806, when he proceeded to England with 200 sail under his convoy. On the morning of the 9th July, being about four leagues to windward of the Havannah, he fell in with twenty-six sail of Spanish vessels, under convoy of two gun-boats, each carrying a brass 24-pounder, the whole of which were captured, and found to be laden with sugar, soap, and indigo; but being unwilling to detain the vessels under his charge, he ordered the whole to be destroyed; during which operation a Spanish 74-gun ship was about three miles to leeward, and on the Surveillante and Fortunée bearing up in chase of her, she made sail and anchored under the Moro castle. Shortly after his arrival in England the Surveillante was paid off, and Captain Bligh did not again go to sea till March 1807, when he was appointed to the Alfred of 74 guns, and accompanied Admiral Gambier to the attack on Copenhagen, where he superintended the landing of the army and ordnance-stores. On his return from thence he proceeded to the coast of Portugal under the orders of Sir C. Cotton; and in the month of July 1808, Sir Charles having received a dispatch from some of the inhabitants of Figueras, requesting assistance against the French troops, selected the Alfred for

* James.

that purpose; and Captain Bligh, with the marines of the squadron, landed at that place, and was directed to keep it till the arrival of Sir Arthur Wellesley, which, by his ability and perseverance, was most effectually performed. On the arrival of the troops under Sir Arthur, in August, the marines were re-embarked, and the army landed, when they immediately marched towards Lisbon, the Alfred accompanying them down the coast with victuallers and ordnance-store-ships, keeping up a daily communication with Sir Arthur. Captain Bligh also superintended the landing of the different divisions of troops as they arrived, under Generals Anstruther and Acland, the former on the 18th, consisting of about 3500 men, the latter on the 20th, consisting of nearly 6500. He also superintended the landing of the army under Sir J. Moore at Macira, after which he proceeded to Lisbon and rejoined Sir C. Cotton. The Russian admiral having been under the necessity of surrendering the squadron under his command, then lying in the Tagus, the Alfred was one of the ships ordered to escort them to England. In January 1809 Captain Bligh was appointed to the Valiant, considered a better ship, then cruising off l'Orient, under Captain Beresford; and he accordingly sailed for that station, having the temporary command of the Revenge of 74 guns. It was in effecting his junction with Captain Beresford that Captain Bligh fell in with eight sail of French line-of-battle ships*, which he kept ahead of for about two miles, but which made no attempt to attack him; and having joined Captain Beresford, he proceeded with him to Basque roads. The morning after the attack made on the enemy by the fire-ships under Lord Cochrane, Captain Bligh was ordered by Admiral Gambier to proceed with the Valiant, Revenge, Bellona, several frigates and bombs, to anchor within range of the shells from the forts on Isle d'Aix: the instant he had anchored the ships intrusted to his care, he waited on Lord Gambier, and requested permission to proceed to the inner road to the assistance of Lord Cochrane; this being granted, he again weighed, and about three o'clock anchored in the inner road. At that time, and indeed throughout, the resistance both from the forts and ships of the enemy, except at parts, was very trifling: he there joined in the attack of the Varsovie and Acquilon, both of which struck their colours, and he was ordered by Rear-Admiral Stopford to remove the prisoners and set them on fire; which was effectually performed as they lay over on their sides, with the water up to their orlop-decks.

* See *Memoir of Sir J.* BERESFORD.

After these services had been performed, Captain Bligh was still employed on Channel service; and on the 3d February, 1810, captured off Bellisle the French ship Confiance (formerly frigate Cannonière), with a valuable cargo. Although the capture of this vessel afforded no opportunity for a display of courage, there were some circumstances attending it which shew the peculiar good fortune of Captain Bligh. On the 1st February the Defiance, Captain Hotham, and the Valiant were in company together, when Captain Hotham, as senior officer, made the Valiant's signal to follow him, to join the squadron in Quiberon Bay. The Valiant being then astern of the Defiance, could not weather the point to get round into the bay, but the Defiance did. It being light winds, the following day the Valiant could make no progress; and in the course of the night she fell in with the Cannonière, and chased her from daylight until noon, when the wind took the enemy by the head, threw her round upon the Valiant's broadside, and she struck, no other ship being in sight. Her capture was entirely attributed to light baffling winds, with which the Valiant rather gained upon her, as she was three miles from her at daylight and one mile when she struck. Under any other circumstance she would have escaped, as she had outsailed in six hours every ship that had chased her before. She had been ninety-three days from the Isle of France, and had been chased fourteen times during the passage. It had been long known that she was to return to Europe laden with the spoil of the principal captures which the enemy had made in the East Indies during the three preceding years. The British squadron off the Isle of France and cruisers to the westward were on the most vigilant look out for her: she, however, escaped them all, and but for the seemingly untoward circumstance of the Valiant not being able to fetch Quiberon Bay at that particular time, she would have been safe in Bellisle in a few hours after the time she was fallen in with. On her passage out to the East Indies, she ran into the Cape of Good Hope soon after it had been taken by Sir Home Popham; but perceiving the English flag flying, she cut her cable and escaped. She afterwards cruised in the Indian seas, to the terror of the British traders; but wanting repairs, which could not be effected at the Isle of France, the governor of the island, De Caen, lent her for a consideration to the merchants, to convey their goods to France: her cargo cost 800,000 dollars there, and the merchants called her La Confiance. She was previously La Minerve, in the British service, and taken off Cherbourg by running aground in a fog. She had only 18 guns when captured, the remainder having been left at the Isle of France*. For this fortunate capture Captain Bligh received 14,014*l.* He continued in the command of the Valiant till the month of May, when he was obliged to resign her in consequence of ill health. In 1815 he was made a Companion of the military Order of the Bath, and in July 1821 was made a rear-admiral.

Admiral Bligh has been twice married: first, in 1798, to Sarah, daughter of H. S. Leeke, Esq. of Yaxley-Hall, Suffolk; and, secondly, in 1809, to Cecilia, daughter of the late Governor Moultrie.

HISTORICAL MEMOIRS OF

Captain Sir P. BOWES VERE BROKE, Bart*. K.C.B.

FROM a pedigree, now in the possession of the family, it appears that Sir Philip Bowes Vere Broke is descended from Willielmus de Doyto del Brooke, the son of Adam, lord of Leighton, in Cheshire, who lived previously to the reign of King Henry III. From Willielmus de Doyto del Brooke descended Sir Richard Broke, of London, Knight, Chief Baron of the Exchequer in the reign of King Henry VIII. the lineal ancestor of Sir Philip, who is the eldest son of the late Philip Bowes Broke, of Nacton, in the county of Suffolk, Esq. and of Elizabeth, daughter of the Rev. Charles Beaumont, of Witnesham, in the county of Suffolk, M. A. and was born at Nacton on the 9th September, 1776; where, situated on the banks of the Orwell, he gave very early indications of a nautical turn of mind, by his fondness for making ships and sailing them on the river, by the banks of which he would remain for hours together, regardless of all other amusement: indeed so strong did his propensity continue to be by the water-side, that his parents found themselves under the necessity of having him narrowly watched, lest any accident should befall him. Notwithstanding their care, however, he one day effected his escape, and was found upon a plank in the act of pushing off from the shore, to reach some boats which were just then in sight. On being reprimanded, and told of the danger which he might have encountered, his answer, dictated by the high-spirited confidence of inexperienced boyhood, was, " Depend upon it I could have managed it." He commenced his education at Cheam school, in Surrey, under the care of Dr. Gilpin; but the time which he was enabled to devote to classical pursuits was very short. At twelve years of age his father, not being satisfied with the progress which he had made, deliberated on the propriety of removing him to another seminary. Philip requested his father rather to permit him to go to sea; but when Mr. Broke observed to him, that a good and liberal education was equally essential in the naval profession as in any other, he cheerfully assented

* From the *East Anglian Magazine.*

to the justness of his remarks, with the assurance, that if he would yield to his desires, and promise to place him in the navy, he should have no reason to complain of his want of assiduity. His wishes were accordingly complied with; and for this indulgence his father had the satisfaction of experiencing the most grateful return.

From this moment young Broke must be considered as wedded to the sea; and in perusing the Memoir of his life, he will be seen to afford one example out of numbers which exist in the navy, of having passed twenty years of persevering service without a single intervening opportunity presenting itself of obtaining distinction. Indeed it too frequently happens in the navy that an entire life is spent in the unremitting discharge of public duties, without the possibility of achieving any great exploit. To Sir Philip Broke, however, Fortune has been more favourable. When twelve years old, he was placed at the Royal Academy at Portsmouth, where he displayed much diligence and ability in prosecuting his nautical studies till the age of fifteen. As the period of his study was limited, he was anxious that no time, no opportunity of improvement, should be lost: his mind therefore was intensely occupied; his attentions were indefatigable. He allowed himself only four hours' rest from his studies in the four and twenty; and to withhold from his tutor the knowledge of the late hours which he kept, it was his nightly custom to place the blankets of his cot before the door, that no light might be seen from without. Having acquired the theory of his profession, it was very soon his lot to enter on its practical duties. On the 25th June, 1792, he embarked as midshipman on board the Bulldog, under the command of Captain George Hope, under whom he acquired much of the professional skill by which his conduct has been uniformly marked. Mr. Broke continued in the Bulldog, on the Mediterranean station, till the month of August 1793, when he was removed, with Captain Hope and part of the Bulldog's crew, into L'Eclair, a French prize corvette. In that vessel he served some time under Captain Hope, but latterly under Captain George Towry, till the 25th May, 1794. He then joined the Romulus frigate, to the command of which Captain Hope had been just appointed. The nature of the service on which L'Eclair was employed during the time that Mr. Broke was in her was rather active than brilliant: she was occasionally in Toulon whilst the British had possession of that place; and she afterwards joined the fleet, under Lord Hood, at the memorable blockade and siege of Bastia.

In the Romulus Mr. Broke nearly completed the period of his service as midshipman. That ship was principally employed in cruising with the squadrons off Gourjean Bay or Toulon, under Admirals Hotham and Goodall. The Romulus was also the repeating frigate to the rear squadron under Sir Hyde Parker, in Admiral Hotham's action with the French fleet on the 14th March, 1795. After the engagement the Romulus proceeded with the fleet off Minorca, where, on the 8th June in the same year, Mr. Broke was removed to the Britannia, the flag-ship of Admiral Hotham, the commander-in-chief: he was consequently in the indecisive action which took place between the English and French fleets off Frejus on the 14th July. Having passed his examination, Mr. Broke was appointed third lieutenant of the Southampton frigate, commanded by Captain William Shield. The Southampton was some time employed in the little squadron under Commodore Nelson's orders, in harassing the enemy's coasting trade under the western shores of the gulf of Genoa, and in co-operating with the German army, which was then encamped at Savona.

In the month of September 1795, on the return of the Southampton to Leghorn, Captain James Macnamara took the command of her, and proceeded off Genoa to blockade the French frigate La Vestale, which, with the corvette La Brune of 28 guns, two brigs of war of 16 guns each, and several gun-boats, was there, watching for an opportunity to convoy a fleet of vessels, with corn, to Toulon. Observing the Southampton to have detached her consort, the French squadron sailed in the night with their convoy. The Southampton, which appears to have " kept a sharp look-out," boldly attacked La Vestale. She was immediately forsaken by the other ships of the squadron, and after a short but close skirmish she also bore off, and by superior sailing effected her escape, though she was followed by the Southampton till she had nearly got into Villa Franca. The Southampton refitted at Ajaccio, and afterwards went up the Adriatic, for the protection of the trade. On her return she joined the fleet, at that time under the command of Admiral Sir John Jervis, and was some time employed in cruising off Toulon and Marseilles, harassing and destroying the enemy's coasting trade.

Mr. Broke was now on the eve of participating in a most gallant and daring enterprise. In the evening of the 9th of June, 1796, Sir John Jervis discovered a French cruiser working up to Hieres Bay, within the islands, and immediately singling out the Southampton, called her commander on board the Victory, pointed the ship out, and directed him to make a dash at her through the Grand Pass. The Southampton instantly got under weigh, and went in, in view of the entire British fleet, which, with agonizing suspense, witnessed the boldness of an attempt that scarcely any thing but complete success could have justified. The admiral, on this occasion, even refused to give a written order for the enterprise; he only said to Captain Macnamara, " Bring out the enemy's ship if you can; I'll give you no written order; but I direct you to take care of the king's ship under your command." This enterprise was executed in a most masterly manner, and, as Sir John Jervis's letter expresses it, " with admirable skill and alacrity." The details of this affair are highly interesting. On receiving his orders, Captain Macnamara pushed through the Grand Pass, and hauled up under the batteries on the N. E. end of Porquerole, under easy sail, in the hope that he might be mistaken for a neutral or French frigate; a stratagem which succeeded so well, that he arrived within pistol-shot of the enemy undiscovered. Captain Macnamara then cautioned the French captain, through a trumpet, not to make a fruitless resistance; but he immediately snapped his pistol at him, and fired his broadside. At this instant, being very near the heavy battery of Fort Breganson, the Southampton laid the enemy on board, and Lieutenant Lydiard, at the head of the boarders, with an intrepidity which no words can describe, entered and carried her in about ten minutes, although he met with a spirited resistance from the captain (who fell) and a hundred men under arms to receive him. After lashing the two ships together, Captain Macnamara found some difficulty in getting from under the battery, which kept up a very heavy fire. Lieutenant Lydiard, suspecting the cause of the difficulty, passed from stem to stern, sword in hand, searching in darkness for the hawser, which he supposed connected the ship with the shore. He soon had the satisfaction of finding that his conjecture was right; and by dint of repeated blows with his sword, he released the ship from the tie which had been so well contrived on the part of the enemy. About half after one in the morning the Southampton, with her prize, got through the Grand Pass, and joined the fleet. The prize proved to be L'Utile corvette, commanded by Citoyen François Veza, of 24 guns and 130 men, 25 of whom were killed and wounded, and several had escaped on shore in the launch. Captain Macnarama, his officers and crew were highly complimented upon this brilliant achievement; and the gallant Lydiard was most deservedly promoted to the command of the prize.

The Southampton was next employed with Commodore Nelson's squadron in occupying Ferrajo, in evacuating Caprea and Corsica, in the expedition against Piombino, and in the siege of Castiglione. In the month of December, whilst cruising off Cape del Mel, she took the Spanish man-of-war brig Corso. Soon afterwards she went down the Straits with convoy, passing close to the Spanish fleet, and joined the force under Sir John Jervis, off Cape St. Vincent, three days before the celebrated action which was fought off that point on the 14th February, 1797. In this important engagement the Southampton and the other frigates attached to the fleet were employed in towing the enemy's ships to leeward as soon as they had struck. The Southampton remained on the Lisbon and Mediterranean stations till the month of June following, when she returned to England and was paid off.

Thus at the commencement of his professional life Mr. Broke appears to have been engaged for five years in active and unremitting service. He very soon afterwards joined the Amelia frigate as third lieutenant, under the command of the Hon. Charles Herbert, attached to the Channel fleet under Lord Bridport, and generally acting as repeating-frigate. Occasionally, however, she was detached, and was then remarkably active in annoying the coasting trade. In the month of September following the Amelia joined the Ethalion and the Sylph in the anxious duty of watching a French squadron under M. Bompart, proceeding from Brest to Ireland with troops and arms for the rebel forces. Having parted from her consorts, the Amelia joined Commodore Sir John Borlase Warren, who was on a cruise off Achill Head in quest of Bompart's squadron, of the sailing of which he had received certain intelligence. On the 11th October the enemy was discovered, and on the following day an action took place, which terminated in the capture of the Hoche and three frigates. In January 1799, Lieutenant Broke was promoted to the rank of commander, and appointed to the Falcon fire-brig at Sheerness. That vessel, however, was not manned, and she remained at moorings in the Medway. In the Autumn following Captain Broke was appointed to the Shark sloop, in which he joined the North-Sea fleet under Lord Duncan. The Shark was constantly at sea, convoying to the Elbe or to the Baltic, or cruising on the Dutch coast; but she sailed badly, and made no captures of note.

On the 14th February, 1801, Captain Broke had the satisfaction of attaining post-rank, when for a time he retired on half-pay. Not being able to obtain a ship at the commencement, or rather renewal, of the war in 1803, and an immediate invasion being expected on that part of the coast on which he resided, he most laudably employed himself in training the peasantry to arms. To that service he, with much success, devoted a considerable portion of his time; but in the month of April 1805 he was appointed to the Druid of 32 guns. At that time men were so exceedingly scarce that many ships were lying idle for want of hands: Captain Broke therefore volunteered to proceed to sea with a number barely sufficient to work the ship; and his offer being accepted, he sailed upon a cruise for men off the Land's-End and in the British Channel. He soon made up his complement, and the Druid was then attached to the squadron on the Irish station, under the orders of Lord Gardner. On the 2d February, 1806, he captured the Prince Murat, French privateer of 18 guns and 127 men; and on the 1st May following he fell in with Le Pandour, French brig-corvette, of the same force, which, after a run of one hundred and sixty miles, he drove into Admiral Stirling's squadron, where, by the admiral's permission, he took possession of her, and sent her to Plymouth. He also took some smaller vessels; and about the same time he chased the French frigate Topaze into the Raz Passage, but could not come up with her. In the succeeding month (June) Captain Broke was appointed to the Shannon, a very fine frigate of 38 guns; but as he was then at sea, he did not join her till the 14th September. On his taking the command, he immediately completed her crew, and she was then attached to Commodore Owen's squadron off Boulogne, and was employed in the grand rocket expedition. Captain Broke remained on that station, and off Havre, till April 1807; when, in consequence of the Greenland whale-ships having been molested by a French squadron of frigates in the preceding year, he was ordered to proceed, with the Meleager, Captain Broughton, to the Greenland seas, to protect them. Having received information from some of the whalers first spoken with, that the greater part of the ships were fishing upon the coast of Spitzbergen, Captain Broke thought it his duty to proceed thither, accompanied by the Meleager. On the 7th May they fell in with the ice; and, persevering with much difficulty in pushing through it, they, on the 17th June, after speaking several of the scattered whalers, made the southern land of Spitzbergen. Thence

N N 2

they proceeded to Magdalena harbour, where they anchored on the 23d. That port lies in almost the 80th degree of north latitude, which is nearer to the pole than any ships of war had reached before, excepting the discovery-ships under Captain Phipps, afterwards Lord Mulgrave. Having observed that, in the charts to which the whalers generally trusted, there were so many errors as to render it a place dangerous to resort to, Captain Broke, during the time that the frigates remained there to water, made a correct survey of the bay and harbour.

The Shannon and Meleager sailed from Magdalena harbour on the 4th July, and stood to the northward as far as the ice would allow (being then in the lat. of 80 deg. 6 min. north); but not finding any of the whalers, they returned to the westward, coasting the great western ice through the loose drifts. After speaking several vessels, they, on the 23d June, made John Mayen's Island, and thence returned homeward; but from that time they were so constantly enveloped in fogs, that they saw no more of the fishers. On the 23d August, having remained three months within the Arctic circle, and altogether longer on the station than any of the whalers ever staid, they arrived in Leith roads; whence, after hastily completing their provisions, they, on the 27th, sailed on a cruise off Shetland, where they continued till the 20th September. The frigates having separated, the Shannon captured some small Danish vessels. On the 25th she anchored at Yarmouth, and afterwards proceeded to Spithead, where she fitted for foreign service; thence to Plymouth, where she joined the squadron under the command of Sir S. Hood, and sailed with him to Madeira. On the 24th December the squadron ran into Funchal roads, and, anchoring close to the walls of the town, intimidated the governor into an unconditional surrender. The Portuguese had armed a numerous militia for the defence of their works, which by position were strong; and as there was reason to suppose that they had received aid from two French frigates, every disposition had been made for a most vigorous and determined assault. They were wavering in their councils whether they should adhere to the mother country, or follow the fortunes of the Prince of Brazil; but on the appearance of so large a force of those whom they knew to be the friends of their prince, they soon decided.

The island having been taken possession of, the respective ships of the squadron dispersed on various destinations: the Shannon sailed homeward, with the transports under convoy. Her next cruise was, under the orders of Lord Gardner, in the Bay of Biscay; after which she was attached to the Channel fleet, under Lord Gambier, and sailed to join the squadron off l'Orient. Captain Broke was thence detached to the Loire, where, with a small force under his orders, he remained closely blockading two French frigates and harassing the coasting trade for five months. During this irksome service, Captain Broke employed much time in surveying the anchorages and passages in the entrance of the Loire.

On the 10th November, at midnight, having been relieved in charge of the blockade by the Naïad, the Shannon fell in with the Amethyst, Captain M. Seymour, just at the close of her gallant action with the French frigate Thetis. In the morning the Shannon assisted to man the prize and took her in tow, and on the 15th she arrived with her at Plymouth. The Shannon's next station was off the Black Rocks, watching the enemy's force in Brest. Having captured a large privateer, and being relieved by another frigate, she proceeded to Plymouth to land her prisoners. On her return off Ushant, on the 21st February, the look-out frigate intimated by signal that the enemy's fleet had sailed from Brest. Captain Broke having detached vessels to the fleet under Lord Gambier and to Plymouth with this intelligence, reconnoitred the port again; and ascertaining that the enemy's force had all escaped, he sent a cutter, which had joined, to convey the information to the squadrons off l'Orient and Rochefort. The Channel fleet came round Ushant on the 23d, and Lord Gambier detached Sir John Duckworth with eight sail of the line and two frigates, of which the Shannon was one, in quest of the enemy. The Shannon was sent ahead of the fleet to reconnoitre Ferrol; and, on rejoining, she was again detached to Lisbon, to obtain reinforcements from the squadron under Admiral Berkeley, and to apprise him that the enemy was at sea. Two 74's were in consequence detached from the Tagus, and some other ships joined Sir John Duckworth off Cape Finisterre. The Shannon was again sent ahead of the fleet, to procure intelligence and refreshments at Tangiers. On her return, she went with dispatches to Cadiz, the fleet remaining in the offing. Reports having arrived that the enemy's force had put into Rochefort, and was blockaded by Admiral Stopford, Sir John Duckworth proceeded homeward, touching at Madeira for more certain intelligence. The Shannon, occasionally touching at Plymouth for refreshments, was then employed in Channel service till the 17th November,

1810. In December she went out to join the squadron in Basque roads, then under the command of Lord A. Beauclerk, who detached her successively to cruise off Bourdeaux, Bellisle, and the Glennans. On the 20th March, 1811, she returned to Basque roads. The squadron was then under the command of Sir Harry Neale, who, on the 10th April, again detached the Shannon to cruise in the offing and off Bourdeaux till the end of May, when she was ordered home. During these cruises the Shannon chased many vessels, but captured few, as, from her copper being foul, she sailed very badly. At Plymouth she was docked and new-coppered, and ordered round to Portsmouth to complete for foreign service.

On the 30th July Captain Broke sailed from Portsmouth, under sealed orders, with the Hyacinth and a large convoy for Lisbon and the Mediterranean. Having seen the Lisbon ships into the Tagus, and opened his orders, Captain Broke, in pursuance thereof, detached the Hyacinth and a convoy to Gibraltar, and with the Shannon he made sail for Halifax, to place himself under the orders of Admiral Sawyer, where he arrived on the 24th September, and by whom he was employed on various important services: yet at this time, although Captain Broke had been six years almost constantly cruising, he had never once seen an enemy's frigate at sea!

On the 26th June the Shannon sailed from Bermuda for Halifax in company with the Æolus, Lord J. Townsend. On the evening of the 30th, off Vambro, they spoke the Rattler and the Indian, which informed them of war having been declared against Great Britain by the United States, and of the Belvidera's (Captain Byron) gallant action with the American squadron under Commodore Rodgers. Next morning the Shannon and Æolus joined Vice-Admiral Sawyer at Halifax; and it being reported that Commodore Rodgers's squadron was still cruising off Nantucket, or New-York, for the protection of the American trade, Captain Broke was detached with the Africa and three frigates in quest of the new enemy. On the 9th he was joined by the Guerriere, from Bermuda, as yet unacquainted with the war. Captain Broke, agreeably to arrangements with the admiral, attached her to his squadron, and proceeded to Long Island. Having been ordered to blockade the enemy in any port in which they should take shelter, and being in constant expectation of a rencontre, the Africa sailing so badly that she could not keep company in chase, it was highly important to keep the frigates fully manned; Captain Broke therefore determined not to detach men in prizes, unless when there should be occasion to forward information to the admiral: they in consequence burned all the prizes they took. On the 14th July, off Montang lighthouse, they received intelligence that Commodore Rodgers was at sea; and, as he was expected soon at New-York, they pushed immediately towards that port. On the 16th, after a brisk chase, they captured, off Sandy-Hook, the United States brig Nautilus of 16 guns and 106 men, which had sailed from New-York the evening before. Captain Broke now obtained certain information that Commodore Rodgers, with his squadron, had gone off the banks of Newfoundland, with the view of intercepting our valuable homeward-bound convoys from the West Indies. By remaining off the American ports, the British squadron would have effected immense destruction to the trade of the Americans; but as the protection of our own appeared to Captain Broke and his brother officers a more important object, connected, too, with the hope of crushing the American navy, it was immediately decided to proceed off the Grand Banks, crossing the route of the convoys. The Guerriere, however, which had been detached on a chase in the morning, and which had spoken the object of pursuit, was still at a great distance from the squadron, to the southward. Towards evening another large vessel was discovered in the same quarter, which afterwards proved to be the American frigate Constitution. The Guerriere and she had been mutually striving to meet each other. The squadron now made sail towards them, but it was nearly calm all the night. At dawn the next morning, the American frigate and the Guerriere were almost within shot of each other, and at the same distance to leeward of the squadron, which, with a light air, was rapidly closing upon the enemy. The capture of the Constitution appeared certain; but the wind suddenly shifting round, took the squadron aback, and left her to windward. It now fell calm at intervals, during which great exertions were made both by the chasers and the chased, some towing with boats, and others warping ahead with cadges; but the endeavours of the squadron were frequently frustrated by light breezes, which arose and payed the ships off, and rendered it again necessary for them to set and trim their sails. This fatiguing pursuit lasted the whole of the day. The Belvidera got near enough to exchange shots with the enemy; but a light breeze favouring him towards dusk, he increased his distance, and though closely pursued during the night, and the day and night following, he finally effected his escape by superior sailing. The Africa was run out of sight in the chase; but the four frigates, each of which had chased independently, carrying the utmost sail and trying their speed on every point, were all nearly close together when the pursuit was given up. After this mortifying disappointment, the squadron, rejoined by the Africa, shaped their course towards the banks of Newfoundland, destroying many American merchant-ships which they met with on their way. The Nautilus was dispatched to Halifax. On the 20th July they joined the homeward-bound West India convoy, consisting of about sixty sail, under charge of the Thetis; and having informed them of the war, escorted them over the banks of Newfoundland. The Africa was afterwards sent back to Halifax for provisions and to carry prisoners.

The Guerriere having casually separated from the squadron whilst chasing in foggy weather, the other frigates now steered towards Boston, in the hope, from information which they had received, of crossing Rodgers on his return home, and to continue on the usual convoy track. After burning some ships, they lost sight of the Belvidera, whilst chasing in a dark night. The Shannon and Æolus continued the cruise, as before designed, and must have passed very near the American squadron. On the 28th of August the Æolus, having supplied the Shannon with water, was sent to Halifax to complete. The Shannon remained off Long Island (the rendezvous at which she was to receive assistance and supplies) as long as her provisions would allow her; but having been led to the southward in chase, her stores were exhausted before she fell in with them, and she was eventually obliged to return to Halifax, where she arrived on the 20th September, and learned the mortifying news of the capture of the Guerriere. During the latter part of this cruise the Shannon and Æolus recaptured some British vessels, and took or destroyed several Americans. On the 4th September the Shannon had chased the Essex; but the latter, having cautiously hauled up at a great distance, made her escape in the night, leaving a merchant-ship, which had been in company with her, to be destroyed by her pursuers. Commodore Rodgers' squadron and the Constitution had arrived at Boston before the Shannon reached Halifax.

Intelligence having arrived at Halifax of the wreck of the Barbadoes on Sable Island, the Shannon, accompanied by the Bream schooner, was sent thither, on the 3d October, to bring off her crew and the specie which had been saved from her. After waiting some days before the weather would allow them to communicate with the island, they, on the 8th, effected their object; and on the 12th, having captured a privateer on their way, returned to Halifax. On the 18th October reports having arrived that Commodore Rodgers was again at sea, Captain Broke sailed, with the Tenedos, Captain Hyde Parker, the Nymphe, Captain Epworth, and the Curlew brig, Captain Head, with orders to sweep over the banks of Newfoundland, for the protection of the trade homeward-bound from St. John's, and thence to go in search of the American squadron. In the execution of this order the English force was frequently near the enemy, but never got sight of them. They encountered much bad weather; and after a circuitous cruise, from the banks of Newfoundland nearly to Bermuda, and thence back to Sable Island, having captured only a large American privateer-brig and recaptured one British vessel, they returned to Halifax on the 24th November.

On the 7th December the commander-in-chief, Sir J. Warren, sailed in the San Domingo, with the Statira and Junon, for Bermuda, leaving Captain Broke in charge of the naval force stationed on the coasts of Nova Scotia and New England for the winter. This force consisted of the Shannon, Nymphe, Tenedos, Curlew, and Rattler, with another division of sloops and small craft in the Bay of Fundy. Agreeably to orders, a few days after the admiral's departure, Captain Broke sailed with the frigates and the Curlew to escort a homeward-bound convoy half way across the Atlantic. Having parted with them in lat. 45 deg. N. long 45 deg. W. the westerly winds preventing the direct return of the squadron, they went round the Azores, and proceeded off Bermuda; and finding that Commodore Rodgers had returned to port, they went into Halifax to refit on the 23d February.

The severe weather at that season occasioned much delay in the equipment of the squadrons, two of the frigates having to shift their lower masts and to undergo other repairs. The Tenedos rejoined on the day of their arrival in the harbour, with a vessel which she had captured. On the 21st March Captain Broke sailed with his squadron to blockade the enemy's frigates in Boston harbour, the President and Congress, as was reported, being nearly ready for sea. Large reinforcements having arrived from England, Captain Oliver, in the Valiant, was sent, with La Hogue, to take the command of the northern stations; and meeting with Captain Broke's division off Halifax, he took them under his orders. The Shannon and Tenedos having been separated from the squadron in a gale, reconnoitred Boston on the 2d April, which was as soon as the westerly gales and the snowy weather would admit; and having then observed the Congress ready for sea, the President nearly so, and the Constitution under repair, they returned to the rendezvous, as ordered, to make their report. The weather being very foggy, they passed between Nantucket and the shoals at the same time that the Chesapeake got into Boston through the eastern channel. Captain Oliver, having been ordered off New-York, left the Hon. Captain Capel in charge of the squadron off Boston. For the greater chance of intercepting the enemy's vessels, that officer disposed of his ships in two divisions, cruising himself, with others, in the offing, and detaching Captain Broke, with the Shannon and Tenedos, to watch the enemy in the harbour, occasionally communicating with him, to report and receive such observations as they might respectively make. The President and Congress now appeared ready for sea, the Chesapeake was refitting, and the vast trade of the Americans running under licences, and their privateers, kept the squadron in constant employ. As the in-shore frigates, however, could not leave their stations, they captured but few vessels. The grand object was to bring the enemy's frigates to action or to prevent their sailing. The enemy's coasting trade was much distressed by the presence of the British frigates; but, in despite of their vigilance, foggy weather and on-shore winds compelled them to keep an offing during the last week in April; and on the 1st May, favoured by a sudden shift of wind, the President and Congress made their escape. Sailing along shore by Cape Anne and the Isles of Shoals, they passed, unseen, to the northward of the Shannon and Tenedos. Those ships, which lay in the latitude of Boston, at dusk the same evening reached close in shore near Salem, and had the vexation of finding that the enemy was gone.

During the month of May the Shannon, with the Nymphe and Rattler, captured some privateers, and recaptured some British vessels and a French privateer (L'Invincible) of 18 guns, which had been previously taken by the Mutine, Captain de Courcy, and retaken by the American ship Alexander. The Alexander had run the Invincible on shore near Gloucester, and the American militia came down to protect her; but they were soon dispersed by the guns of the frigates, and their boats brought off the prize.

Towards the middle of the month the Chesapeake appeared nearly ready for sea, and engrossed all the attention of the two frigates stationed to watch her. For various reasons, their anxiety was naturally great. The Chesapeake seemed to present the last chance that season of avenging the insulted honour of the British flag ; of confounding the insolent pretensions of an enemy whose triumphs had originated solely in superiority of force; of making the Americans feel, that, upon equal terms, they were unequal to contend, successfully, against the prowess of their parent stock. Serious apprehensions were therefore entertained lest this last remaining frigate of the enemy might escape from her antagonists, as others, favoured by the weather, had lately done. Should the Chesapeake once pass the blockading force, she would inevitably effect much mischief among the British trade where least expected; and she might probably fall in with English ships of war, which, being of inferior force, or weakened by the manning of prizes, would be less capable of supporting the national fame than the Shannon and Tenedos, which had been particularly appointed to watch, and were thoroughly prepared to meet her. Under these considerations Captain Broke regarded it as an important duty to obtain by any honourable means a meeting with the enemy. He had previously sent several verbal invitations to Commodore Rodgers, to meet the Shannon and Tenedos with the President and Congress. The contest would indeed have been very unequal; but Captain Broke trusted that his gallant second, Captain Parker, would vanquish the Congress in time to assist him against the President, should there be occasion for aid. The badness of the weather, however, as already stated, prevented the continuance of a close blockade, and afforded Rodgers the opportunity of escape. It is probable too, that, independent of his having other objects in view, the American commander, when out, might not have deemed it prudent to seek a meeting with the British frigates, without an assurance, on their part, that they would not receive assistance from other ships. This consideration induced Captain Broke to draw up and combine, in a written form, the substance of the different proposals, which, by the masters of licensed vessels, he had already sent in to the captain of the Chesapeake. In this letter, which was expressed in the following terms, Captain Broke endeavoured to answer every objection that could possibly be made to his wishes:

H M. S. SHANNON, *off* BOSTON, *June* 1813.

SIR,—As the Chesapeake appears now ready for sea, I request you will do me the favour to meet the Shannon, ship to ship, to try the fortune of our respective flags. To an officer of your character it requires some apology for proceeding to farther particulars. Be assured, sir, that it is not from any doubt I can entertain of your wishing to close with my proposals, but merely to provide an answer to any objection which might be made, and very reasonably, upon the chance of our receiving unfair support. After the diligent attention we had paid to Commodore Rodgers, the pains I took to detach all force, but the Shannon and Tenedos, to such a distance that they could not possibly join in any action fought in sight of the capes, and the various verbal messages which had been sent into Boston to that effect, we were much disappointed to find the commodore had eluded us by sailing the first chance after the prevailing easterly winds had obliged us to keep an offing from the coast. He perhaps wished for some stronger assurance of a fair meeting; I am therefore induced to address you more particularly, and to assure you that what I write, I pledge my honour to perform to the utmost of my power. The Shannon mounts 24 guns upon a broadside and one light boat-gun, 18-pounders on her main-deck, and 32-pound carronades on her quarter-deck and forecastle; and is manned with a complement of 300 men and boys (a large proportion of the latter), besides 30 seamen, boys, and passengers, who were taken out of recaptured vessels lately. I am thus minute, because a report prevailed in some of the Boston papers, that we had 150 men additional, lent us from La Hogue, which really was never the case. La Hogue is now at Halifax for provisions, and I will send all other ships beyond the power of interfering with us, and meet you, whenever it is most agreeable to you, within the limits of the under-mentioned rendezvous; viz.

From six to ten leagues east of Cape Cod lighthouse; from eight to ten leagues east of Cape Ann height, on Cashe's ledge, in latitude 43 deg. N. at any bearing and distance you please to fix off the south breakers of Nantucket, or the shoal on St. George's bank.

If you will favour me with any plan of signals or telegraph, I will warn you (if sailing under this promise) should any of my friends be too nigh, or any where in sight, until I can detach them out of my way; or I would sail with you, under a flag of truce, to any place you think safest from our cruisers, hauling it down when fair to begin hostilities.

You must, sir, be aware that my proposals are highly advantageous to you, as you cannot proceed to sea singly in the Chesapeake without imminent risk of being crushed by the superior force of the British squadrons which are now abroad, where all your efforts, in case of a rencontre, would, however gallant, be perfectly hopeless. I entreat you, sir, not to imagine that I am urged by mere personal ambition for your acceding to this invitation : we have both noble motives. You will feel it as a compliment if I say, that the result of our meeting may be the most grateful service I can render to my country; and I doubt not that you, equally confident of success, will feel convinced that it is only by repeated triumphs *in even combat* that your little navy can now hope to console your country for the loss of that trade it cannot protect. Favour me with a speedy reply. We are short of provisions and water, and cannot stay long here. I have the honour to be, sir, your obedient, humble servant,

(Signed,)　　　P. B. V. BROKE, *Capt. of H. M. S. Shannon.*

N. B. For the general service of watching your coast, it is requisite for me to keep another ship in company, to support me with her guns and boats when employed near the land, and particularly to aid each other if either ship in chase should get on shore. You must be aware that I cannot, consistently with my duty, wave so great an advantage to this general service by detaching my consort without an assurance on your part of meeting me directly; and that you will neither seek nor admit aid from any other of your armed vessels, if I detach mine expressly for the sake of meeting you. Should any special order restrain you from thus answering a formal challenge, you may yet oblige me by keeping my proposal a secret, and appointing any place you may like to meet us (within 300 miles of Boston), in a given number of days after you sail ; as unless you agree to an interview, I may be busied on other service, and perhaps be at a distance from Boston when you go to sea. Choose your terms, but let us meet.

To the Commander of the U. S. frigate CHESAPEAKE.

(Indorsement on the envelope.)

We have 13 American prisoners on board, which I will give you for as many British sailors, if you will send them out; otherwise, being privateer's-men, they must be detained.

Some rough weather occurring, it was not found practicable to send the letter in till the morning of the 1st June. In the interim, however, the proposed measures had been taken to secure fair play to the enemy. Captain Capel having left Captain Broke in charge of the blockade whilst he went into port for water, the Chesapeake had no line-of-battle ship to fear, and Captain Broke detached all the remaining ships to such a distance as precluded the possibility of their affording him any assistance in the anticipated action. On the 1st June, observing that the Chesapeake lay a long while with her sails loose, and waiting the morning, though she had a fair wind to come out, it was apprehended that she might not sail that day; Captain Broke therefore sent in his challenge to quicken her movements. The Chesapeake, however, stood out of the harbour before the boats reached the shore; and Captain Broke having no assurance that she would not receive aid from other armed craft in Boston, in case of being crippled in action, stood across the bay, till about five leagues from the land, directly opposite to Boston lighthouse. There he lay-to to wait for her, in such a position that the action might be seen from the heights over the town.

The approaching action excited the liveliest interest and the most confident anticipations of victory amongst the people of Boston: a number of pleasure-boats came out with the Chesapeake, to see the Shannon compelled to strike; and a grand dinner was actually preparing on shore for the Chesapeake's officers against their return with the prize. Soon, however, was their joy turned into sadness, their cheering shouts into cries of mourning and lamentation. In fourteen minutes from the time the action commenced the Chesapeake was no longer an enemy; " the American flag was hauled down, and the proud old British Union floated triumphantly over it." The Shannon was lying-to under top-sails, top-gallant-sails, jib, and spanker, with just steerage-way, awaiting the approach of the Chesapeake, and leaving it in her power to commence the action as she pleased, either at a distance or close, either on the larboard or starboard side. She came down in a very gallant style on the Shannon's weather and starboard quarter, till within half-pistol-shot. The Shannon's men having orders to fire as they could get their guns to bear, commenced by firing first their after guns on the main-deck, and then their aftermost carronades on the quarter-deck, just as the Chesapeake's bows were upon their quarter: these two guns were distinctly heard before the Chesapeake 'returned her fire, which then became furious on both sides; but the superiority of the Shannon's was so great, that, at her second broadside, nearly all the men were swept from the upper-deck of the Chesapeake. About this time the ships came in contact, and the Chesapeake having shot rather ahead, was caught by one of the Shannon's anchors, and lay obliquely athwart her starboard bow, exposed to a most tremendous fire from the Shannon's after guns, which, battering her lee quarter and entering her port-holes from thence towards the main-mast, strewed her main-deck with killed and wounded. A small open cask of musket-cartridges, in an open chest abaft the mizen-mast of the Chesapeake, now caught fire and blew up, and when the smoke it occasioned had blown away, Captain Broke saw the favourable moment, and instantly, with a few men, not exceeding twenty, boarded her, about the mizen-rigging, from her starboard bow*. Not a man was left standing on the Chesapeake's quarter-deck when she was boarded; but about twenty made a slight resistance on her gangway, who were instantly driven before the fore-mast, and then being obliged to stand, fought desperately, but were quickly overpowered. A few endeavoured to get down the fore hatch-way, but in their eagerness prevented each other; some jumped over, and one or two of them escaped by getting in again at the main-deck ports. Captain Broke and his first boarding party were almost immediately followed by between 30 and 40 marines, who secured possession of the Chesapeake's quarter-deck, dislodged the men from the main and fore-tops, that were firing down upon the boarders, and kept down all who attempted to come up from the main-deck. Being thus completely captured, Mr. Watt, the first lieutenant, ran aft, and seizing the British colours from a sailor who brought them from the Shannon, bent them, and was in the act of hoisting them over the American, when he was struck in the forehead by a grape-shot, and killed in the very moment of victory. He was shot by one of the Shannon's main-deck guns, the officers of which did not know that the contest was already decided†.

At the commencement of the brief contest with the Chesapeake, Captain Broke had the misfortune to be wounded. He was in the act of charging a party of the enemy who had rallied on their forecastle. He first parried a blow from the butt-end of a firelock, which had been raised to strike him; at the same instant, as it were, another of the Americans made a charge at him with a bayonet; but that also he successfully turned aside. The colours of the Chesapeake were down when Captain Broke received a severe wound with a sabre from one of three men whom he was earnestly calling upon his brave followers to spare. The man was instantly dispatched; and one of the Chesapeake's midshipmen, who, having been in the fore-top, slid down a rope and alighted close to Captain Broke at the moment, would probably have experienced a similar fate but for his humane interference. The capture having been completed, Captain Broke, in a state of exhaustion and in-

---

* Captain Broke was the first man on board the Chesapeake.

† These particulars are extracted from one of the Halifax papers, which related some of the details of the action more fully than Captain Broke's modesty permitted him to do in his official letter.

sensibility from exertion and loss of blood, was taken on board his own ship, which, with her prize, afterwards proceeded to Halifax*.

On the receipt of the dispatches relating to the action, the Lords Commissioners of the Admiralty very promptly and handsomely acknowledged the services which had been rendered to the country by the captain, officers, and ship's company of the Shannon, in a letter addressed by Mr. Secretary Croker to Admiral Sir J. B. Warren, of which the following is a copy :

ADMIRALTY-OFFICE, *July 9, 1813.*

SIR,—I have had the pleasure of receiving and communicating to my Lords Commissioners of the Admiralty a letter from Captain the Hon. B. Capel of his Majesty's ship La Hogue, inclosing a copy of his letter to you, and of that of Captain Broke to him, announcing the capture, in fifteen minutes, of the United States frigate Chesapeake, of 49 guns and 440 men, by his Majesty's ship Shannon. My lords have before had occasion to observe, with great approbation, the zeal, judgment, and activity which have characterized Captain Broke's proceedings since the commencement of the war ; and they now receive with the highest satisfaction a proof of professional skill and gallantry in battle, which has seldom been equalled, and certainly never surpassed; and the decision, celerity, and effect with which the force of his Majesty's ship was directed against the enemy, mark no less the personal bravery of the officers, seamen, and marines, than the high discipline and practice in arms to which the ship's company must have been sedulously and successfully trained.

My lords, to mark their sense of this action, have been pleased to direct a medal to be presented to Captain Broke ; Lieutenants Wallis and Falkiner, who, in consequence of the wound of Captain Broke and the death of the gallant first lieutenant, Watt, succeeded to the command of the Shannon and the prize, to be promoted to the rank of commanders; and Messrs. Etough and Smith, to that of lieutenants ; and my lords will be glad to attend to the recommendation of Captain Broke in favour of the petty officers and men who may have particularly distinguished themselves.

You will convey to Captain Broke, his officers and ship's company, these sentiments of their lordships, with an expression of their satisfaction at hearing that the captain's wound is not likely long to deprive his country of his services.

To Admiral WARREN.   (Signed,)   J. W. CROKER.

On the 25th September following his Royal Highness the Prince Regent was pleased to confer upon Captain Broke the dignity of a baronet

* For the official letter and representation of the action, see RALFE's *Naval Chronology,* vol. III. p. 210.

of the kingdom of Great Britain and Ireland; and on the 1st February, 1814, as an additional and especial mark of royal favour, his royal highness was pleased to allow him and his descendants to bear, " as a memorial of his highly distinguished conduct and gallantry," the following crest of honourable augmentation: " Issuant from a naval crown a dexter arm embowed, encircled by a wreath of laurel, the hand grasping a trident erect; together with the motto, ' *Sævumque tridentem servamus.*' "

Among the tributes of a more substantial nature which have been paid to the skill, intrepidity, and noble disinterestedness of Captain Broke, that of the underwriters of Halifax, in Nova Scotia, stands first in the order of time. As a grateful memorial of the estimation in which they held his services—services which had contributed in an unusual manner to the protection of their trade—they presented him with the following address, accompanied by a piece of plate of the value of one hundred guineas:

SIR,—The Committee of Underwriters of Halifax, on behalf of their constituents and themselves, composed of a number of the principal merchants of the town, beg leave to offer their congratulations on your recovery, not in the ordinary style of addresses, but with heartfelt and unfeigned satisfaction and joy.

We do not attempt to express at large our sense of your magnanimous and disinterested conduct while engaged in the command of a squadron, or singly cruising after the enemy, lest it should appear like flattery, which neither our candour nor our regard for your feelings would allow us to offer; but we feel particular pleasure in observing the manner in which the Lords of the Treasury have marked such conduct, and their having recommended it to the notice of his Royal Highness the Prince Regent in the disposal of American prizes condemned as droits of the crown. As underwriters, we are more especially called upon to express our thankfulness for your exertions in our favour, under the pressure of such difficulties as you had to encounter in recapturing and preserving some of our most valuable risks, and sending them home to us, even while in the face of the enemy; at the same time declining to send in valuable prizes, but preferring to destroy them rather than weaken the force of your ship. To a late brilliant event we will point only in silent admiration, well knowing that our feelings are in perfect unison with those of the nation at large, the public expression of which, from the highest authority, no doubt awaits you and the brave officers and crew of the Shannon.

In farther testimony of our esteem, we beg your acceptance of a piece of plate, value one hundred guineas, which will be presented to you in London by a gentleman who was lately one of our number.

(Signed,)   LAWRENCE HARTSHORNE,

Halifax, Aug. 25, 1813.   *Chairman.*

The Court of Common Council of London also voted Captain Broke their thanks, with the freedom of that city and the present of a sword of one hundred guineas value.

To the freedom of the corporation of Ipswich Captain Broke was entitled by birth; but (September 8), on the motion of R. A. Crickit and J. Round, jun. Esqs. the representatives in Parliament of that borough, the thanks of the court were unanimously voted " for the brilliant victory obtained by him, in his Majesty's ship the Shannon, over the American frigate Chesapeake." The thanks of the corporation were accordingly presented to him, January 27, 1814, in London, by S. Jackaman, Esq. in his official capacity of town-clerk.

About the time that the thanks of the corporation of Ipswich were voted to Captain Broke, a subscription was opened among the gentry and other inhabitants of the county of Suffolk, for the purpose of presenting him with a piece of plate, testifying their sense of his distinguished valour in capturing the Chesapeake, and commemorating that brilliant event. The subscription closed on the 8th January, when it amounted to about 730*l.* The amount would probably have been much larger but for a misconception which unfortunately appeared to prevail. The object was not so much to make a heavy purse, as to express the universal sentiment of the county. With the view therefore of rendering the subscription as general as possible, and that the humblest individual might not be deterred from subscribing by the appearance of great names and large sums, it was resolved, at the first meeting which was holden upon the occasion, that no person should be allowed to subscribe more than two pounds. In the interim the Free and Easy Club, a convivial society composed of the professional gentlemen and more opulent tradesmen of the town of Ipswich, formed the determination of presenting to Sir Philip an approving testimonial of their own. Most, if not all, of the members of the club had set their names down to the general county subscription; but no sooner was the proposal made, than it was agreed to, and the sum of one hundred guineas was subscribed almost instantly, which was immediately applied to the purchase of a silver cup, bearing an appropriate inscription.

On the return of Captain Broke to England, the Shannon, from constant long-continued wear and tear at sea, was unfit for farther service, and it became necessary that she should be paid off. Lord Melville, in consequence, wrote to Captain Broke, proffering him the command of one of the new ships, built to match the large American craft, misnamed frigates: but his wound was not then sufficiently healed to allow of his immediately serving again; in addition to which, his many years' absence from home required that, for a time, he should devote his attention to his own private concerns. He was therefore induced to decline his lordship's polite and flattering offer.

In January 1815 Sir Philip was nominated a K.C.B. He married, in November 1802, Sarah Louisa, daughter of Sir W. Middleton, Bart, and has several children.

HISTORICAL MEMOIRS OF

Captain Sir JAHLEEL BRENTON, Bart. K.C.B.

THE services of this gentleman have been fully stated in the published work of his brother*, where, however, they are necessarily thrown over several volumes; but in judging of the abilities of an officer, and in estimating the degree of praise to which he is entitled, no just conception can be formed, no fair opinion can be delivered, even from leading circumstances, if taken singly, and considered on the bare ground of their own merit, without reference to other parts of his conduct. To estimate it fairly and correctly, the whole should be collected into one view, and each act considered in connection with those which have preceded it; but this is an object which cannot be met with in a general history, and is to be found only in works of a biographical description. In the present instance therefore we have only to collect and place under one head that which has already been published, of course from the best authority, and which will, at once, inform the reader of the important services of Sir Jahleel Brenton. He is the son of the late Rear-Admiral Jahleel Brenton, by Henrietta, daughter of Joseph Cowley, Esq. of Wolverhampton, by Penelope, daughter and heiress of Edward Pelham, Esq. He was born August 22, 1770, received his education at the maritime school at Chelsea, and, after serving for some time in the British navy, passed over into that of Sweden, and was in the battle between the Russians and Swedes in the gulf of Wibourg. He obtained the rank of lieutenant in 1790, and, at the commencement of the war in 1793, commanded the Trepassey of 12 guns, on the Newfoundland station; and subsequently served as a lieutenant of the Barfleur, bearing the flag of Rear-Admiral Waldegrave, with whom he served in the action with the Spanish fleet off Cape St. Vincent in February 1797†. He was afterwards promoted to the rank of commander, and appointed to the Speedy brig of 14 guns and 60 men. On the 9th August, 1799, being in company with the Defender, a privateer of Gibraltar, of the same force, he gave chase to three Spanish armed vessels, which took refuge in a bay five leagues to the eastward of Cape de Gat, where they moored

---

* *Naval History,* by Captain E. P. Brenton.   † Marshall.

in a line within a boat's length of the beach. Captain Brenton having engaged them for three quarters of an hour*, under sail, and not making any impression, ran in, and let go his anchor so close to the centre vessel as nearly to touch her: the Spaniards could stand this no longer, and, taking to their boats, fled, and left all the vessels† to the victors, who brought them out in triumph, with only two men wounded in the Speedy, and one in the Defender. In October Captain Brenton went with his boats into a bay near Cape Trafalgar, where, under a heavy battery, and in defiance of the enemy, who lined the shore with musketry, he boarded and destroyed four Spanish merchantmen, and returned without any one in his boats being hurt‡.

The Speedy's next encounter with the enemy was in the Straits of Gibraltar, which she had entered with a convoy from Lisbon. The gun-boats from Algeziras put out to attack them. The captain of the Speedy allowed the enemy to approach as near as they thought proper: they had thirteen boats, with long 32-pounders, and full of men: reserving his fire so long, the spectators on the rock began to exclaim that he was failing in his duty; but in an instant the royals and studding-sails of the brig were taken in, and, passing through the midst of the gun-boats, so near as to carry away their oars, he poured in from either side such volleys of round and grape, that the enemy fled in confusion, and the Speedy got safe into the bay with all her convoy. Soon after this, he had another brush with the gun-boats under the guns of Europa point, and was nearly sunk, but escaped from them by the same bold manœuvre. The officer of the guard in the south fired a shot at the enemy, for which he was put under arrest by the governor. The Speedy got into Tetuan, where she stopped her shot-holes, and the next day returned to Gibraltar Bay; the captain and crew much out of humour with General O'Hara, the governor. But when Captain Brenton waited on him, his excellency thus addressed him: " I conclude, sir, you think I have treated you very ill in not affording you assistance; but I have made arrangements with the governor of Algeziras to prevent this town being kept in constant alarm and annoyance by the Spanish gun-boats, which, in consequence, are never to be fired at from the rock. There is the

---

* The Gazette letter says *an hour* and three-quarters.

† One vessel of 8 guns, one ditto of 10 guns, and one ditto of 4 guns.

‡ In transmitting this account to the Admiralty, Sir J. Duckworth said, " It is but justice to this officer to observe, that his exertions and gallantry at all opportunities do him the highest honour."

copy of a letter which I have written to the Admiralty, and I most sincerely wish you may obtain your promotion." The letter was so handsomely worded, that Captain Brenton could say nothing about the transaction of the preceding night; and shortly afterwards he was promoted to the rank of post-captain, and to command the Cæsar of 80 guns, the flag-ship of Sir James Saumarez. For the services he performed whilst in that situation, his conduct when in action with the French squadron in Algeziras Bay, refitting the Cæsar at Gibraltar, and the subsequent battle with the combined squadron, we must refer the reader to the Memoir of Sir James Saumarez, contenting ourselves with recording the opinion of that great and distinguished commander, who, in his official letter, said, " I feel it incumbent on me to state to their lordships the great merit of Captain Brenton of the Cæsar, whose cool judgment and intrepid conduct, I will venture to pronounce, were never surpassed." Such an opinion, from such an officer, is the most gratifying proof of transcendent abilities.

Captain Brenton continued to command the Cæsar till after the peace of Amiens, when he was appointed to the Minerve frigate; and after the recommencement of hostilities, was placed under the orders of Sir James Saumarez on the Guernsey station. At daylight on the 2d July, 1803, a detachment of French gun-vessels was seen close under the land, steering for Barfleur, which they reached, notwithstanding every effort made by the Topaze and Minerve to prevent it. The former returned to her station off Havre; and in the evening the Minerve, running close in with Cherbourg, in a thick fog, mistook Fort de la Liberté for Pelée, and a number of vessels being seen to eastward, the pilot assured the captain he might run amongst them without hesitation. The helm was accordingly put up for the purpose, when just as the ship was about to open her fire, she grounded, and the fog at the same time dispersing, discovered her to be in a very perilous situation. She was on the western Cone-Head, about six furlongs from Fort de la Liberté, of 74 guns and 15 mortars, and one mile from the Isle of Pelée, of 100 guns and 25 mortars, from both of which a fire almost immediately opened. This happened about nine o'clock in the evening. Captain Brenton, aware that strong and decided measures were necessary, and that the launch of a frigate was not calculated to carry out a bower-anchor, immediately dispatched his boats, armed, to cut out a vessel from under the batteries of sufficient capacity for the purpose; whilst the launch, with her carronade, should be employed in diverting the fire of two gun-brigs, lying in such a position ahead of the Minerve as to annoy her greatly by a raking fire. The yawl, being the first boat in the water, was sent under the orders of the Hon. Lieutenant W. Walpole, and the other boats were directed to follow as soon as ready; but the gallant officer to whom the enterprise was intrusted found his own boat sufficient. He proceeded under a heavy fire of round, grape, and musketry, and from her position close to the batteries, cut out a lugger of 50 tons, laden with stone for the works, and towed her off to the ship. Before the bower-anchor could be placed in this vessel, it was necessary to clear her of her cargo; and that this might be done without adding to the shoal on which the ship lay, she was veered astern by the ebb tide to the length of a hawser. Unfortunately the moon shone with great brightness: the enemy's fire became very galling; the more so, as no return could be made but from the two forecastle guns, those of the main-deck having been all run close forward, for the purpose of lightening the ship abaft, where she hung. At eleven p.m. the lugger, being cleared, was brought under the larboard cathead to receive the small bower-anchor, and during this operation was so frequently struck from the gun-brigs, as to keep a carpenter constantly employed in stopping the shot-holes. By midnight all was ready; a kedge-anchor had been previously laid out for the purpose of warping the lugger, but the moment the hawser was made taut, it was shot away. Every thing now depended upon the boats, which were sent to take the lugger in tow, and succeeded, under a severe fire, in gaining their object, and the anchor was let go in a proper position. At three a.m. the wind had entirely subsided, and the captain, almost hopeless of being able to save the ship, contemplated the probable necessity of being obliged to abandon her. With this view he caused the wounded men to be brought up and put into the lugger, destroyed his private signals, and prepared fires in the store-rooms, to be lighted in the last extremity. A fine breeze, however, springing up from the land as the tide rose, revived the hope of saving the ship, and the wounded men were returned to the cockpit. The lugger's masts were soon after shot away by the guns of the batteries, over the gangway of the Minerve. At four the capstan was manned, and many of the crew were killed and wounded as they hove at the bars. At five the ship floated, under the most heartfelt cheers of the crew. It was considered as a certainty, that in the course of two or three minutes they would be out of gun-shot of the batteries; and consequently out of danger; but this pleasing prospect soon vanished. The wind again declined into a perfect calm, and the last drain of the flood tide carried the now helpless ship into the harbour, and laid her upon a broken cone. In this situation she remained till the top of high water, when she surrendered, after sustaining the fire of the enemy for ten hours, and having 11 men killed and 16 wounded. Such was the state of her masts, that had there been a moderate breeze they must have gone by the board. She was lightened in the course of the day by the French, and got off. The capture of so fine a frigate, at the commencement of the war, occasioned great triumph, and was announced in the theatre at Brussels by Buonaparte in person, who, addressing the audience, stated the circumstance in the following terms: " La guerre vient de commencer sous les plus heureuses auspices; une superbe frégate de l'ennemi vient de se rendre à deux de nos chaloupes cannonières !" The ship was called the " Cannonière," to support this despicable falsehood.

The moment the Minerve was taken, Captain Brenton was ordered to prepare for a march into the interior. He had no means of procuring money for bills, either for himself or his officers, and was obliged to offer his watch for sale; but the sum tendered was too small to be accepted. At length a stranger appeared, and demanded to see the watch; he did not want to purchase it, he said, but offered to receive it as a pledge for the sum of twenty-five louis. The offer was thankfully accepted, and the stranger went away; but soon after returned, exclaiming, " Sir, my conscience wounds me: I am shocked at the unworthy caution of taking a pledge from a brave officer suffering under the fortune of war. Here, take your watch, and give me a note of hand for the money." This being arranged, the stranger departed a second time, and again returned, observing, that his conscience still troubled him: " and I have been considering," said he, " how I can best relieve it. I am, sir, a merchant of l'Orient; my name is Dubois; I am returning home, and having examined my purse, I find I have just twenty-five louis more than I shall require for my journey. Here," said he, as he destroyed the first note of hand, " add them to the others, and give me a note for the whole." On such an incident it would be superfluous to comment; we mention it as a tribute of gratitude to the generous Dubois, and sincerely hope that such an example in future wars may find many imitators on both sides of the water. The house of Perigaux, the banker at Paris, shewed equal readiness in relieving the wants of the prisoners. They sent a clerk to meet Captain Brenton at St. Denis, with three hundred louis, and an order for four hundred more on his arrival at the place of his destination; promising, at the same time, that any bills drawn by the captain should be immediately honoured. When the prisoners marched through St. Lo, General Delgorgue paid them the kindest attention, extending his hospitality to as many of the officers as his table would hold. The others, with the young gentlemen, were billeted among the inhabitants, who, we believe, *without any exception*, made a point of calling their relatives together and making a feast, as far as their means would go, for the prisoner who had become their inmate; and in no case would any of them, although *bourgeois* or shopkeepers, receive the smallest remuneration. Many other instances of kindness and attention were shewn to the sufferers as they passed on their weary and painful journeys; but they were all from individuals, and performed in stealth, and under the greatest apprehension of being discovered by the official departments, whom the affair at St. Lo had displeased. It is highly desirable that these instances of individual kindness and benevolence should be known and cherished in the recollection of every Englishman; and, in doing this, we must at the same time acknowledge, that the spirit of humanity and charity has not been confined to one side of the Channel. The conduct of the French government was, however, exactly the reverse. When the first detachment of the crew of the Minerve reached the depôt at Epinal, the officers were permitted to take lodgings in the town; the seamen, confined to an old convent, were allowed three sous a day, a pound and a half of bread, and sixteen pounds of straw, in lieu of bedding, once a fortnight to each man. As they were destitute of clothes, blankets, shoes, and hats, and had performed a march of 500 miles, their deplorable state may readily be conceived. The incessant applications of Captain Brenton to the general commanding the district, for some relief to his men, were unavailing.

In the month of September the weather became excessively cold, and the people suffered greatly: the straw in a few days became a dungheap; and to reiterated representations, the only answer was, that the blankets were daily expected; that they were to be sent from Lisle, having been left by the army when on service in that quarter; and that orders had been given for their being *mended* and forwarded to Epinal for the use of the prisoners. When we consider how long a time had elapsed from the period when the army was in Flanders, and the state of that army, particularly the inveterate itch which it had been subject to, much could not be expected from that source of supply. Accordingly when the blankets did arrive, which was not till the end of October, they were found to be of the most wretched description. In the mean time no measures were taken by the government to provide a temporary relief for their prisoners. The officers of the Minerve, with a few of the masters of merchant-vessels, formed a small fund by subscription, with which was purchased a quantity of old tapestry from the walls of the ruined chateaux in the neighbourhood, and distributed it amongst the seamen: this for several weeks was their only covering. Every morning, after the distribution of bread and three sous to each man, privileged suttlers, with the very worst description of ardent spirits and a quantity of offal meat, generally bullock's liver, were allowed to enter the prison, and the three sous were laid out by the prisoner in the purchase of a poisonous dram and a morsel of meat, the bread being his only subsistence for the remainder of the twenty-four hours. At the request of the captain, this sum was at length paid to a person appointed to receive it in a mass, and, with the addition of a weekly subscription from the officers, laid out by a committee of the prisoners in the purchase of meat and vegetables, by which means their fare was considerably improved. Early in November the prisoners were ordered to march to the little fortress of Phalsbourg, in the Vorges mountains, which they reached in the most deplorable state of suffering, from fatigue, sore feet, and cold. Provision was made for the sick in the military hospital; but for the others, none beyond the wretched barrack and the portion of straw. The mayor, M. Parmentier, at his own risk, most kindly ordered nearly the half of them into the hospital, not confining the admission to those who were actually in a state of disease, but wishing to extend the comforts of food and bedding to as many as the building would hold; and to which we gladly allude as another act of private benevolence. In about ten days afterwards they were ordered to counter-march as far as Luneville, and proceed from thence to Givot, in the Ardennes, through Nanci and Verdun; the officers remaining on their parole at the latter place. Shortly after the arrival of the men at their destination, Captain Brenton received a letter, stating that their distress and suffering had become intolerable. He immediately waited upon the general, expressed his wish to visit the prisoners, in order to distribute succours furnished by England, received permission, and set out for Givot under the escort of a *gens-d'arme*. He found the prisoners confined in Charlemont, the greater part of them in rags, having, either from distress or improvidence, sold the clothes they had, without any farther supply from the French government. The old system of the three sous and the privileged suttlers was renewed, under every possible aggravation. Captain Brenton was at the same time informed, that it was intended to remove the prisoners to the barracks at Givot, on the banks of the Meuse. He immediately visited those barracks, and received from the commandant every information and every kindness which, as an individual, it was in his power to bestow: he was allowed to distribute the prisoners into messes as he thought proper, and to assign them rooms for their residence, provided the number corresponded with the official regulation; but it was all that the commandant could grant, for the arrangements of his government went no farther. The prison-allowance remained the same; the supply of clothing and bedding underwent no alteration; the prisoners received their portions of straw from the French government, and found their own sackings to put it in, so as to preserve it and form a bed. Bedsteads were hired, kettles also for cooking their provisions, and a proportion of fire-wood was furnished out of the remittance from England. Blankets and clothes were supplied from the same fund, and four sous a day added to the French allowance to each prisoner; those belonging to his Majesty's ships and packets received six sous, the additional two being considered as an advance upon the pay due to them. With this assistance, and under the superintendence and management of their own officers, they certainly did live, not only with comfort, but with great respectability.

Captain Jurieu, of the French frigate Franchise, a prisoner in England, was allowed to go to France on his parole to procure the exchange of Captain Brenton, under a promise to return should he not effect his purpose. The gallant Frenchman, faithful to his word, and unable to procure the release of the British captain, was preparing to return to England, when he was ordered to Brest, and officially informed by his government that he should be shot if he attempted to go back. He, however, never accepted of service, and wrote three years afterwards to Captain Brenton, stating these facts, and requesting that he would still use his influence to effect the exchange. On the return of Captain Brenton to England in January 1806*, being tried by a court-martial, he was most honourably acquitted, and immediately appointed to the Spartan, a new frigate of the largest class, in which he was sent to the Mediterranean, and where he eminently distinguished himself.

On the 14th May, 1807, the Spartan met with a severe loss off Nice. She had been all day chasing a polacre-ship, and at sunset both were becalmed at the distance of about five miles from each other: the vessel appeared to be an armed merchant-ship; the boats of the Spartan, with the two senior lieutenants, Weir and Williams, and 70 of the best men, pulled along side in two divisions, and attempted to board her on the bow and quarter, with the usual determination and valour of British seamen; but the vessel was defended by a numerous and equally gallant crew, with boarding-nettings and every other means of resistance. The first discharge from their great guns and musketry laid 63 of our brave fellows low, the first and second lieutenants and 26 men being killed or mortally wounded: seven men only remained unhurt! The few remaining hands conducted the boats back to the ship†. Before she had recovered from this misfortune, the Spartan had a narrow escape from capture. Proceeding from Palermo towards Toulon, she fell in with

---

* It is so stated in Captain Brenton's History: the trial, however, took place in February 1807.

† The narrow escape of one of the men was very remarkable. James Bodie, the coxwain of the barge, was missing. The deceased men were all laid out on the deck; the wife of Bodie, a beautiful young woman, flew with a lantern from one to the other in search of her husband, but in vain: all the survivors declared that he had undoubtedly perished; they saw him wounded, and fall between the ship and boat. The poor woman became delirious, got into the barge on the booms, and taking the place lately occupied by Bodie, could with difficulty be moved from it. A few days, with the soothing kindness of the officers and crew, produced a calm but settled grief. At Malta a subscription of eighty guineas was made for her, and she was sent to her parents in Ireland. Some weeks elapsed, when the Spartan spoke a neutral vessel from Nice, and learned that a polacre had arrived there, after a severe action with the boats of a frigate; that she had beaten them off, and that when they had left her, a wounded Englishman was discovered holding by the rudder-chains. He was instantly taken on board, and after being cured of his wounds, sent off to Verdun. Captain Brenton, concluding this could be no other than his coxwain, wrote to his friends at that depôt; and the fact turned out to be as he had supposed. Mrs. Bodie was made acquainted with the miraculous escape of her husband, who remained a prisoner four years. He was at length restored to his family, and afterwards enjoyed a berth on board the Royal Charlotte yacht, Captain Brenton, having his wife with him, both of whom were highly and deservedly respected.

a French 74-gun ship, two frigates, and a brig. Captain Brenton determined to watch their motions during the night, and the enemy gave chase
to him.   At daylight they had got within three miles; but a light breeze
springing up, the Spartan ran along the east side of Cabrera, pursued
by the ship of the line.   The frigates and the corvette went round the
west side, in hopes of cutting her off; the Spartan lying nearly becalmed,
while they were coming up at the rate of seven miles an hour: the headmost frigate being within range, tried single shot, which striking the
object, she gave her whole broadside. The effect of firing in light winds
has been before noticed in this work; we shall now see the consequences
fairly illustrated. Captain Brenton would not allow a shot to be returned.
In a few minutes the French frigate was involved in a dense cloud of her
own smoke, and lay becalmed; while the Spartan, having received very
little damage from their shot, kept the breeze, and left her unskilful pursuers to themselves.   We notice this fact as a warning to young officers,
when similarly situated, to confine their whole attention to trimming their
sails; for not only does the firing destroy a breeze of wind, but even in
fresh gales the motion of the guns and the men are unfavourable to the
velocity of the ship. In 1808, Captain Brenton became under the orders
of Sir Richard Strachan, by whom he was detached to Palermo, for intelligence respecting the French squadron which had escaped from
Toulon.   The Spartan touching at Cagliari, learned that Gantheaume
had been seen steering to the southward.   This information was immediately conveyed to Lord Collingwood, who was fallen in with off Mari-
timo, in quest of the enemy.   His lordship going first to Naples, sailed
thence round the south-west end of Sicily, detaching the Spartan to cruise
between Cape Bonn and Sardinia, where, on the 1st April, she discovered
the French fleet carrying a press of sail to get to the westward.   Captain Brenton, placing his ship about two leagues on the weather-beam
of the French admiral, under an easy sail, watched his motions during
the day: the enemy chased, but without gaining on him. In the evening,
having previously prepared his launch with a temporary deck, he hove-
to, and sent her, under the command of Lieutenant Coffin, with dispatches
to Trepani, then 130 miles distant.   The launch reached Malta on the
third day, and vessels were dispatched in every direction in search of the
British fleet. The enemy, in the mean time, continued in chase of the
Spartan, dividing on opposite tacks, to take advantage of any change of
wind, so frequent in the Mediterranean. Confident in the sailing qualities

of his ship, the captain at night again placed himself on the weather-beam of the French admiral; and at daylight made sail from him on the opposite tack, to increase the chance of falling in with the British fleet. The enemy tacked in chase; the Spartan was becalmed, whilst they were coming up with the breeze, and for a short time her capture appeared almost inevitable; but as she caught the breeze, she again took her position on the admiral's weather-beam. This was the close of the third day, when a frigate was seen to run along the enemy's line, and speak all the ships in succession. Soon after the whole of them bore up, steered with the wind abeam, and the captain of the Spartan concluding that the French admiral had shaped his course to the gut of Gibraltar, and had given up the chase, steered the same way with a strong breeze at N.N.W. The night was excessively dark, and a most anxious look-out was kept for the enemy: at half-past seven they were discovered on the lee-quarter, close hauled, and very near: this was evidently a stratagem of Gantheaume's, to get to windward of his enemy; but the manœuvre failed. All hands were on deck and at their stations; the Spartan wore, and crossed the enemy within gun-shot, before they could take any advantage of their situation: the French squadron also wore in chase, and the next morning was hull down to leeward. The fourth day was passed in the same manner; the Spartan keeping a constant and anxious look-out for the British fleet, while the enemy crowded every sail in pursuit of her. In the evening a shift of wind brought them to windward, and the night being very squally and dark, Captain Brenton lost sight of them, and made the best of his way to Minorca, to ascertain whether Gantheaume had gone there, to get possession of the Spanish ships in the harbour of Mahon. Making Mount Toro, a heavy gale prevented his reconnoitring the port, and he steered for Cadiz, to put Admiral Purvis on his guard. Gantheaume, notwithstanding the vigilance with which he was watched, eluded the pursuit of his enemies, and returned to Toulon, where he was closely blockaded*.

On the 23d April, 1809, Captain Brenton, having under his orders the Amphion and Mercury, attacked the town and harbour of Pesaro, in the Adriatic, where a number of vessels lying in the mole attracted his attention; to effect the capture or destruction of which, the boats were dispatched under the orders of Lieutenant G. Willes, first of the Spartan. Before the boats approached, Captain Brenton sent a flag of

* See *Memoir of Lord* COLLINGWOOD.

truce on shore to the governor, demanding the surrender of all the vessels; adding, that should any resistance be made, his excellency must be answerable for the consequences. Half an hour was allowed to deliberate; at the expiration of which time no answer being returned, and the troops being observed to assemble in the streets and on the quays in considerable numbers, while the inhabitants were employed in dismantling the vessels, the flag of truce, which had been flying on board the Spartan, was hauled down, and a firing commenced from the ships and boats. After this had continued a short time, flags of truce were displayed in several parts of the town: the signal was instantly made to discontinue the action. Lieutenant Willes landed, and was informed that the governor, with all the troops, had made their escape. The marines under Lieutenant Moore were landed to enfilade the streets, and thirteen vessels deeply laden were brought out. Captain Brenton contented himself with blowing up the castle, and withdrawing the ships and prizes to Trieste, without a man being hurt. On the 2d May, the Spartan and Mercury chased two vessels into the port of Cesenatico: a long flat lies before the place, over which the frigates carried for a considerable distance no more than three and a half fathoms water. The place was defended by a castle and a battery of two 24-pounders. By keeping the boats ahead and sounding, the frigates were enabled to come within grape-shot distance of the battery, which was very soon silenced; when the boats, under the command of Lieutenant Willes, landed and took possession of it, turning the guns upon the castle and town, which the enemy then deserted. The magazine was blown up, the battery destroyed and guns spiked, and twelve vessels captured. But, unfortunately, the valour of the captors was not rewarded with the return of wealth which they had a fair right to expect: the prizes having been all sent to Trieste, were found in that harbour by the French when they suddenly appeared and surprised the Austrians a few weeks after. Captain Brenton afterwards proceeded in the Spartan to the gulf of Fiume, where he received information from Colonel Peharnie, commanding a corps of Croatians, that the French were fortifying the Island of Lusin Picolo. He proposed an immediate attack on the place, provided the Croatians would co-operate. This being agreed to, part of the Croatian troops were received on board the Spartan, and the remainder placed in two trabacolis. The forts were attacked, and the enemy fled; the Spartan ran up the harbour, and anchored with springs on her cable abreast of the town, and within half a mile of the castle, at the base of which was a battery of eleven guns. By this battery one of the trabacolis was sunk in going in. Some of the marines and seamen of the Spartan were landed to assist the Croatians, while the frigate opened a fire on the castle, which she continued during a great part of the night. At six in the morning the French commandant, after vainly using every artifice by flags of truce to gain time and remount his guns, was compelled to surrender. Many vessels were found in the harbour; but being claimed by the subjects of the Emperor of Austria, under whose dominion the island now returned, they were not made prizes of.

In the beginning of October Captain Brenton assisted at the reduction of the Islands of Zante and Cephalonia, under the orders of Captain Spranger of the Warrior; and was subsequently detached, with a small body of troops under Major Clarke, to attack the Island of Cerigo, which had long been a harbour for privateers of the worst description; pirates, who respected no flag or nation, and from whom a desperate resistance was expected. Captain Brenton, having landed with the troops and marines, on the 10th October marched towards the castle, followed by one watch of the Spartan's ship's company, dragging three field-pieces. These, owing to the extreme difficulty of the country, did not get into action till ten o'clock the next morning. The troops and seamen occupied a position on the heights on a level with the castle, within four hundred yards of it, and a fire was kept up on both sides with guns and musketry, which continued the greater part of the day. In the evening some Congreve rockets were added, and on the following morning the place capitulated. The zeal, skill, and resources of Captain Brenton during these operations were duly acknowledged by Captain Spranger and Lord Collingwood in their official letters.

In the following year the Spartan and Success were stationed off the Bay of Naples, to counteract the movements of the enemy's ships in that port. On rounding the Island of Ischia on the 1st May, the two British frigates discovered the Neapolitan squadron cruising in the bay. The enemy's force consisted of the Ceres 44, Fama 28, and a cutter, with part of the flotilla: when chased by our ships, they ran into the mole of Naples for protection. On the 2d, Captain Brenton, convinced that they would not leave the port-whilst two British ships were in the bay, directed Captain Ayscough of the Success to proceed ten leagues S. W. of the Island of Capri, whilst the Spartan remained in sight of Naples, in the hope that such a disparity of force might induce the enemy to come out. On the 3d, at daylight, when the Spartan was about five miles from Naples, and standing in with a light breeze from the S. E. the enemy was seen coming out of the mole, reinforced by the Sparvière, a brig of 10 guns (Murat's yacht), and eight gun-boats: four hundred Swiss soldiers were distributed amongst the different vessels. The Neapolitan commodore and the Spartan crossed each other on the opposite tacks; the water was perfectly smooth; the Spartan had every sail set on a wind; the enemy was steering large with the wind abeam. At fifty-six minutes after seven, the Ceres, coming within pistol-shot, fired her broadside into the Spartan's larboard bow, and did her considerable damage: the latter reserved her fire until every gun was covered by her opponent, and returned a most destructive broadside, treble-shotted on the main-deck. The carnage on board the Ceres was very great, particularly amongst the Swiss soldiers, who were drawn up in ranks, and extended from the cathead to the taffarel, in readiness for boarding. The Spartan next returned the fire of the Fama and the brig, as she passed them in succession, and cut the line astern of the brig, by which she separated the cutter and gun-boats from the squadron, and having given them her starboard guns, hove in stays, engaging on both sides as she came round. The enemy's frigate wore, followed by the corvette and brig, and stood in for Baia. The Spartan, in attempting to follow them, was for a moment becalmed, with her head to the frigate's broadside, the corvette and brig on her starboard bow, the cutter and gun-boats under her stern and quarter, and received much injury from their fire. A light breeze at length enabled her to get upon the starboard quarter of the frigate, whilst the corvette lay upon the Spartan's beam, the brig upon her quarter, and the flotilla retaining their advantageous position directly astern. The land-wind now entirely died away, and the sea-breeze soon after coming in, the frigate took advantage of it, to make sail for the batteries of Baia. The corvette, having lost her fore-top-mast, was upon the point of surrendering, when the gun-boats came down in a most gallant manner, and towed her from under the guns of the Spartan: the brig, having her main-top-mast cut away, was obliged to surrender; and the Spartan paraded with her prize in tow before the mole, into which her defeated consorts were running for shelter. About the middle of the action Captain Brenton, whilst standing on the capstan, the only place where he could see his various opponents, was wounded in the hip by a grape-shot, and was carried below. His place was nobly supported by Lieutenant G. W. Willes, who would certainly have captured the frigate and corvette, but for the Spartan's rigging having suffered so much as to render her unmanageable, whilst his enemies were assisted by the breeze and the gun-boats. The loss on board the Spartan was 10 killed and 22 wounded; that of the enemy was stated, by various authorities, to have been immense, amounting to 150 killed and 300 wounded. These round numbers are probably exaggerated; but the slaughter, particularly on board the frigate, from her crowded decks, the close position, and smoothness of the water, must have been very severe.

Murat, the King of Naples, was on the mole, about four miles from the scene of action, exulting in the certainty of success, and on the capture of a fine British frigate. On the retreat of his squadron and the loss of his yacht, his rage was ungovernable, and vented itself in reproaches on the officers. Of these the first captain lost his arm, the second was killed, and the first lieutenant took the ship out of action. The King of Sicily, to testify his sense of the services performed by the Spartan on that day, was pleased to confer the honour of Commander of the Order of St. Ferdinand on Captain Brenton, and that of Companion on Lieutenant Willes and Captain G. Hoste of the royal engineers: the latter was on board the Spartan as a passenger, and directed the fire of the quarter-deck guns. The Spartan was, in consequence of her damages and the very severe wound of the captain, sent to England, where she arrived in the month of July. Captain Brenton being incapable of resuming his situation, retired on half-pay; and on the restrictions from the regency being removed, his Royal Highness the Prince Regent was pleased to create him a baronet. Towards the conclusion of the war he was appointed to the Stirling Castle of 74 guns; in January 1814, to superintend the naval arsenal at Port Mahon; about June following, to command the Dorset yacht; and in the autumn of the same year, to be resident commissioner at the Cape of Good Hope. The establishment of the latter place being reduced, he returned from thence in January 1822, and was afterwards appointed to the Royal Charlotte yacht. In consequence of the severity of the wound he received in the action with the Neapolitan squadron, he had a pension of 300l. a year conferred upon him.

Sir Jahleel Brenton married, first, in 1802, Isabella, daughter of A. Stewart, Esq.; and, secondly, in 1822, Harriet, daughter of the late J. Brenton, Esq. of Halifax.

HISTORICAL MEMOIRS OF

Captain Sir MICHAEL SEYMOUR, Bart. K.C.B.

Captain SEYMOUR was born on the 8th November, 1768, at the glebe-house at Palace, in the county of Limerick; and if the descent from virtuous and honourable parents be gratifying, he is in that respect eminently fortunate. At the time of his birth, the Rev. John Seymour, his father, was rector of Palace; a man of exemplary piety, of a most amiable and benevolent disposition, and endowed with considerable learning*. At the age of twelve years Captain Seymour entered the service, on the 15th November, as a midshipman on board the Merlin sloop, under the auspices of his gallant and kind friend, the Hon. James Luttrell, who then commanded her. He afterwards served with him in the Portland of 50 guns and Mediator of 44, employed in the Channel service till April 1783; and during that time partook of an action which clearly demonstrates that there then existed in the British navy a spirit as daring as any which has since been exhibited. On the 12th December they fell in with a French squadron, consisting of the Eugene of 36 guns, American brig of 14, Menagère, _armée en flute_, 34, Alexandre of 24, and Dauphin Royal of 28; but notwithstanding their formidable appearance, Captain Luttrell determined to attack them: he passed along their line, and, by a skilful manœuvre, cut off the Alexandre and compelled her to strike. Seeing the fate of one of their companions, the rest took to flight; but Captain Luttrell having secured his prize, again went in pursuit, and having come up with them, brought the Menagère to action, and obliged her to surrender. On leaving the Mediator Mr. Seymour was placed on board the Ganges, a guard-ship at Portsmouth, in which he remained till September 1783, when he removed to the Europa of 50 guns, and sailed to the West Indies, where, in April 1784, he removed to the Antelope; but in July was placed on board the Janus of 44 guns, and continued on that station till September 1785, when he returned to England on board the Ariel, in consequence of ill health. In June 1786 he was, however, placed in the Pegase of 74 guns, stationed as a guard-ship at Portsmouth, in which he remained till

* _Naval Chronicle._

June 1787, when he became master's mate of the Magnificent of 74 guns, employed as a guard-ship, and also in attending on the king at Weymouth. In October 1790 he was made one of the lieutenants of the Magnificent, and was employed for twelve months in Channel service. In March 1793 he was appointed to the Marlborough; and in the battle of the 1st June, he was so severely wounded in the left arm as to be obliged to submit to amputation. In February 1795 he was appointed to the Formidable of 98 guns, in June to the Commerce de Marseilles, and in August to the Prince; but in a few days afterwards he was promoted to the rank of commander, and served as acting-captain of the Racehorse and another vessel till August 1796, when he was appointed to the Spitfire of 16 guns, and continued in her for four years employed in the Channel service. But during this period of active service we have no extraordinary tales of wonder to relate, nor praise to bestow. We wish, however, to observe, though no particular opportunity occurred for daring enterprise or gallant heroism, yet every cruise afforded ample testimony, both summer and winter, amidst calms and storms, that the Spitfire was in active duty. Amongst other vessels captured were, the Allegrée, a French vessel laden with ammunition and other warlike stores; six privateers, carrying in the whole 57 guns and 301 men, and a transport armed with 14 guns*. In August 1800 he was promoted to post-rank, and served in the Sphynx of 20 guns and Ville de Paris of 100 as acting-captain. In November 1801 he was appointed acting-captain of the Fisguard, which, however, he retained only four months.

After the renewal of the war in 1803, he served during that and the succeeding three years in four different ships as acting-captain, the Ville de Paris of 100 guns, Colossus, Illustrious, and Warrior of 74 each, for the respective periods of one, four, three, and six months. In July 1806 he was appointed to the Amethyst of 36 guns, in which he was again employed in Channel service and the blockade of the French ports in the Bay. For fourteen weeks he cruised off l'Orient, and during that time violent gales of wind prevailed, which consequently greatly added to the perils of a coast at all times sufficiently dangerous. On the night of the 10th November, 1808, he was, however, sufficiently repaid for all his toil and watchfulness. The night was unusually dark, not a star to be seen, and every circumstance seemed to favour the escape of the enemy from the port: Captain Seymour therefore stood close in

* Marshall.

to the N.W. point of Groa, to render ineffectual the endeavours of the enemy should they make the attempt. About seven the flashes and reports of cannon were distinctly seen and heard from a battery on the French coast, in a direction contiguous to the alarm and signal-posts. The conjecture of the moment supposed it to be in consequence of the near approach of the Amethyst; but it was in reality directed against one of their own frigates, of the sailing of which they were ignorant. About half-past seven a sail was descried just ahead; it was supposed to be a small armed vessel, or something still more contemptible, and the deception of night favoured the supposition. A musket was ordered to be fired; no notice was taken—she grew larger. The Amethyst still continued under an easy press of sail. A gun was now fired, and the crackling noise of the shot was heard as it passed through the cabin-windows. This by the enemy was instantly returned, and the veil of darkness, which had hitherto obscured her, was removed by lights flying in every part of her; every inch of canvas was set, her boat cut from her stern, and a ship of war appeared anxious for escape, though capable of resistance. The Amethyst immediately spread more canvas, but allowed her to gain a little, lest her apprehensions might induce her to run on the shore, which was then so near them. About nine, however, these apprehensions were at an end, and the Amethyst closed fast. Her adversary, now finding all hopes of escape at an end, made her best disposition to receive the Amethyst, and suddenly luffed-to on the starboard tack, to put herself in a raking position. Seeing this manoeuvre, Captain Seymour ordered his helm to be put hard astarboard, and the moment the enemy's guns were discharged, again shifted it to hard aport, cleared the enemy's starboard quarter, and brought up right abreast of her to windward. The action then commenced, which continued with very little intermission until about twenty minutes after twelve. The French ship fell on board the Amethyst a little after ten : she extricated herself from that position; but a little after eleven she intentionally laid the Amethyst on board, and from that time until the moment of her surrender, which was about an hour, the contending ships were locked together, the flute of the Amethyst's best bower-anchor having entered the foremost main-deck port of La Thetis. After a great slaughter, the enemy was boarded and taken possession of, and some prisoners were received from her before the ships were disengaged. The Triumph, Captain Sir T. Hardy, shortly afterwards came up, and subsequently the Shannon, which took the prize in tow. In this long and sharply contested action the rigging and sails of the Amethyst were much cut, her mizen-mast shot away, with her fore and main-masts greatly injured; 19 of her crew were killed and 51 wounded. The loss sustained by the Thetis was, however, much greater: out of a crew of 436 men, she had, exclusive of her captain, 134 men killed and 102 wounded, amongst whom were all her officers except three; in addition to which she was totally dismasted*. When the great disparity of force between the Amethyst and Thetis is considered, the conquest achieved is marked by particular brilliancy. The Amethyst mounted only 42 guns, and had only 260 men on board; the Thetis had 44 guns, her metal was of superior weight, and her crew consisted of 436 men, including soldiers, who had served for years together: added to this, M. Pinsun, her commander, was a man of approved courage, much beloved by his men, and deserving, in every respect, the commendation of an excellent officer. Indeed there are but few instances on record, in which a French ship is known to have had so long, so spirited, and so determined a conflict. But the contest was never for a moment doubtful; all were animated with the glorious spirit that leads to victory, and the guns were served with the same zeal and alacrity in the last hour of the fight as in the first. Such is the simple detail of this distinguished action, which, for gallantry, skill, and bravery, has never been exceeded†. For his distinguished conduct in this action Captain Seymour received the honour of knighthood, and was presented by his Majesty with a gold medal. He also received the freedom of the cities of Limerick and Cork, and from the Patriotic Society at Lloyd's one hundred guineas, for the purchase of a sword.

In the beginning of the following year Captain Seymour was employed, under Rear-Admiral Stopford, in Basque roads; and on the 5th April, whilst cruising off the Cordouan lighthouse, with the Emerald frigate within signal-distance astern, a strange sail was discovered bearing E.S.E. and steering to the westward, with the wind at east; but, on discovery, the Amethyst instantly hauled to the S.S.E. All sail was immediately made in chase; but at seven p.m. the Amethyst lost sight both of the enemy and the Emerald. Soon after dark Captain Seymour altered his course, to meet the probable route of the enemy, not doubting that he would, on losing sight of the Amethyst, resume his course to the

---

* For official letter and plate, see RALFE's *Naval Chronology*, vol. II. p. 79.

† *Naval Chronicle.*

westward. This proved to be the case; and about half-past nine Captain Seymour had the gratification again to discover the enemy's ship on his weather beam. All sail was again set in chase, and at eleven he got within half-gun-shot: a running fight then took place; but owing to the enemy's extraordinary sailing, nothing serious was effected till one o'clock a.m. on the 6th; the Amethyst then succeeded in getting upon the enemy's larboard quarter, and a close action commenced, which continued till about a quarter past three, when the enemy having had her mizen-mast and maintop-mast shot away, and being on fire in the main-top, her fire partly ceased. The Amethyst shortly after ceased firing also, and bore up to place herself under her opponent's stern; but whilst in the act of so doing, her main and mizen-masts fell over her lee quarter, about which time also the remainder of the enemy's mizen-mast also came down; and as the Arethusa, Captain Mends, just at the same moment appeared in sight, the enemy made her signal of submission. She proved to be Le Niemen of 46 guns and 319 men, 47 of whom were killed and 73 wounded: the day after her capture her only remaining mast fell over the side*.

The result of this action was even more creditable to Captain Seymour than the capture of La Thetis: the Niemen not only mounted two more guns, 36-pound carronades, but the crew of the Amethyst was very short, having two lieutenants and 37 men absent in prizes, and had 69 prisoners on board. She had 8 killed and 37 wounded; among the latter was Lieutenant H. Waring of the marines. On his return to port Captain Seymour was created a baronet, and his first lieutenant, William Hill, promoted to the rank of commander.

In the ensuing summer Captain Seymour was employed in the Walcheren expedition; and in the month of October was appointed to command the Niemen, which by his exertions had been added to the British navy. He continued in the command of the Niemen, and employed in the Channel, for two years and seven months, when he was appointed to the Hannibal of 74 guns, and attached, at different periods, to the squadrons blockading the enemy's ports of Rochefort, Cherbourg, and Brest. On the 26th March, 1814, in company with the Hebrus, Captain E. Palmer, and Sparrow brig, Captain F. E. Loch, he fell in with two French frigates, which, on being pursued, separated; one of which was followed by the Hebrus and Sparrow, the other by the Han-

* For plate and official letter, see *Naval Chronology*, vol. II. p. 126.

nibal, and both captured.   The one which surrendered to the Hannibal, after discharging her broadside, proved to be the Sultane of 44 guns and 319 men.   Sir Michael Seymour afterwards proceeded with a convoy to the West Indies; and the war having terminated, he was paid off, after having had a successful and certainly glorious career.   In January 1815 he was made a Knight Commander of the Bath, and afterwards appointed to one of the royal yachts.

Sir Michael married Jane, daughter of Captain James Hanker, R. N. and has several children.

HISTORICAL MEMOIRS OF
CAPTAIN WILLIAM MOUNSEY, C.B.

THIS highly esteemed and most efficient officer entered the naval service, in February 1780, as a midshipman on board the Royal Oak of 74 guns, Captain Sir Digby Dent, and sailed with a squadron of six sail of the line, under Admiral Graves, in pursuit of a French squadron destined for North America. Subsequently Admiral Arbuthnot hoisted his flag on board the Royal Oak, and Sir Digby Dent removed to the Raisonable, taking with him Mr. Mounsey, who accompanied him to England. He then removed with Sir Digby to the Repulse, a new 64-gun ship, and served with him in the Channel fleet under Admiral Darby, with whom they proceeded to the relief of Gibraltar. On their return from that important service Sir Digby removed to the Cumberland, again accompanied by Mr. Mounsey; but Sir Digby having been obliged to resign the command of that ship on account of ill health, was succeeded by Captain William Allen, who sailed in the squadron under Sir Richard Bickerton for the East Indies, where they arrived in time to be in the last action fought between the British and French fleets under Admiral Hughes and Suffrein. In 1783 the Cumberland returned to England with the squadron under Sir Richard King; and shortly after their arrival Mr. Mounsey removed to the Orestes sloop of war, Captain Manley Dixon, with whom he served the remainder of his time as a midshipman. Having passed his examination as a lieutenant, he went as master's mate of the Arethusa frigate, Captain John Stanhope, and from thence into the Duke of 98 guns, bearing the flag of Lord Hood, and afterwards removed with his lordship to the Victory, and sailed with him to the Mediterranean; but immediately on quitting the Channel, he was appointed third lieutenant of the Ardent, Captain Manners Robert Sutton, in which he was confirmed by the Admiralty. On the arrival of the fleet off Toulon he was appointed to the Lowestoffe, Captain Wolseley, in which he served at the reduction of St. Fiorenzo, Calvi, and Bastia. He also commanded the boats of the Lowestoffe in cutting out a vessel from under the guns of the Island of Cabrira. She was laden with powder, intended for the French garrison at Bastia.　After the surrender of the island, Captain Wolseley was appointed to the Imperieuse, and Mr. Mounsey second lieutenant of the same ship, in which he sailed for England, under the orders of Admiral Crosbie, with the French ships taken at Toulon.　Shortly after his arrival he was appointed to the Trident, Captain Theophilus Jones, and subsequently to the Impregnable, Captain J. T. Duckworth, Duke 98, Captain J. Holloway, Defence 74, Captain R. Shivers, and Clyde frigate, Captain C. Cunningham, on various services in the Channel and Mediterranean, till the peace of Amiens, when he was promoted to the rank of commander, and appointed to the Rosario sloop of war, in which he was employed on the Channel and Irish stations under Lord Gardner, and in the West Indies under Sir A. Cochrane, till the end of 1806, when the Rosario was paid off, being unfit for further service.　He was then appointed to the Bonne Citoyenne, and, in June 1809, ordered by the Admiralty to take charge of a convoy for Quebec.　He left Spithead on the 18th June, but on the 2d July lost sight of the convoy whilst reconnoitring a suspicious sail astern; and by traversing between the parallels of 43 and 44 deg. north, edging to westward in proportion to the distance he supposed they would sail with such winds as prevailed, in order to regain a sight of them, he fell in with, on the 5th July, La Furieuse French frigate, which, after a long and well-fought action, he fortunately captured on the following day*.

When first discovered she was in the act of taking possession of an English merchant-ship, but which, on the approach of the Bonne Citoyenne, she relinquished, and made sail to the northward, followed by Captain Mounsey.　The chase continued for eighteen hours, when, at twenty-five minutes past nine a. m. on the 6th, the enemy having brought-to to receive him, he laid the Bonne Citoyenne along side his huge antagonist.　A brisk cannonade was now opened, which continued for six hours and fifty minutes, during which the enemy fired above seventy broadsides; whilst the Bonne Citoyenne, not less sparing, discharged one hundred and twenty-nine, alternately from starboard or larboard side, as circumstances would permit, so as to prevent the guns from getting over-heated, three of which were dismounted and rendered useless early in the action.　The fatal effects of the action were visible in the crippled state of both vessels, particularly that of the enemy; and as the Bonne Citoyenne had fired away nearly all her powder, Captain

* See official letter and plate, RALFE's *Naval Chronology*, vol. II. p. 247.

Mounsey, who worked round his opponent like a cooper round a tub, gallantly determined to carry him by boarding with all hands, for which purpose he took a position across the enemy's bows. This decided the contest, and the enemy, without farther opposition, hauled down their colours. She proved to be La Furieuse, a French frigate of the largest class, pierced for 48 guns, but having on board only 12 42-pound carronades and two long 24-pounders on the main-deck, with six of smaller calibre, 40 soldiers at small arms, her full proportion of officers, and a complement of 200 men, besides the colonel, two lieutenants, and a detachment of the 60th regiment of the line. Of this number she had 35 killed and 36 dangerously wounded; the number of those slightly wounded Captain Mounsey did not state, but they probably amounted to as many more : while the loss of men sustained by the Bonne Citoyenne amounted to only one killed and five wounded, the smallness of which Captain Mounsey attributed to her decks being so low, and keeping so close under the guns of the enemy. A great deal, however, must be attributed to his own skilful manœuvres, in taking up such raking positions that he was enabled to fire at times almost with impunity. On being taken possession of, the prize was found to be in a most dangerous situation, having fourteen shot-holes between wind and water, and five feet water in her hold; her top-masts and all her yards, except the cross-jack and spritsail, shot away, and her lower masts so badly wounded as to render it almost impossible to prevent them from falling. The Bonne Citoyenne was also reduced to a mere wreck, having all her lower masts badly wounded in several places, as well as her fore and main-top-masts shot away ; nearly all the standing and every part of the running rigging, sails, boats, &c. cut to pieces. Notwithstanding all these great and trying difficulties, and that the number of prisoners was equal to his own crew, still, with the aid of the indefatigable exertions of the officers and ship's company, who were constantly on deck for twenty-five days and nights, Captain Mounsey surmounted them all, and succeeded in carrying his prize, that noble trophy and proof of his heroic conduct, into Halifax.

For the conduct manifested by Captain Mounsey on this occasion, he had not only the satisfaction of receiving the thanks of the Amiralty through their secretary, but also the following letter from Lord Mulgrave, dated September 20, 1809 :

Sir,—I did not fail this day to lay before his Majesty the particulars of your conduct in the attack and capture of the Furieuse French frigate. The enterprising gallantry with which you approached and attacked a ship bearing such an appearance of a commanding superiority of force, and the skill, courage, and perseverance manifested by you, and the officers, seamen, and marines under your command, during an action of such long continuance, and so warmly contested, have received his Majesty's fullest approbation; and his Majesty has been graciously pleased to bestow upon you a medal, as an honourable memorial of your very gallant and distinguished conduct on that occasion. It has given me the greatest satisfaction to sign a commission promoting you to the rank of post-captain, and appointing you to the command of the fine frigate which you have so nobly added to the naval force of the country. I have also great pleasure in notifying to you the promotion of Lieutenant Symes to the rank of commander; and I have to request that you will transmit to me the names of the warrant officers of the Bonne Citoyenne, with a view to their promotion in their several ranks, together with the name of the mate or midshipman whom you shall recommend for the rank of lieutenant; and the names of any very meritorious petty officers severally under the boatswain, gunner, and carpenter, who may be deserving of promotion, and qualified to receive it.

I trust that this general promotion through every rank serving in the Bonne Citoyenne may be a satisfactory testimony of my estimation of the action which has been achieved, and may operate as an incentive to others to emulate an example so worthy of imitation and applause.

I have the honour to be, with the highest esteem,

MULGRAVE.

In the Furieuse Captain Mounsey was employed in the Mediterranean under the orders of Sir Edward Pellew, by whom he was stationed with the in-shore squadron to watch the enemy in Toulon; from whence he was removed to blockade the Neapolitan squadron in the Bay of Naples, under the orders of the Hon. Captain Duncan. In February 1813 he was directed by the senior officer on the station to place himself under the orders of Captain Napier of the Thames, and, having taken on board the 10th regiment of foot, to proceed against the Island of Ponza. This order was carried into effect on the 26th, and the island captured in a neat and gallant style by both frigates running direct into the harbour, the entrance of which is only a quarter of a mile wide, defended by batteries, silencing the forts, landing the troops, and carrying the place by assault*.

* See plate and official letter, *Naval Chronology*, vol. III. p. 199.

Shortly after this exploit, the boats of the Furieuse cut out a convoy of eighteen sail of coasting-vessels from the harbour of Murinello, five miles to the eastward of Civita Vecchia, after taking the forts and spiking the guns. Captain Mounsey was subsequently employed, under the orders of Sir Josias Rowley, in the reduction of Porto Spezzio, Genoa, and its dependencies. After the surrender of Savona, he was sent with the Iphigenia, Euryalus, and Bacchante, with a convoy of transports, having two regiments on board, to Bermuda, to join the squadron under Sir A. Cochrane. He was then employed in active operations on the American coast, and, after the surrender of the port and town of Custine and its dependencies to General Sherbrook and Admiral Griffith, he was stationed in the Furieuse, with two sloops of war under his orders, to co-operate with General Gossling in the protection of the port, and remained on that station till the termination of the war, when he returned to England, and was paid off. He was nominated a Companion of the military Order of the Bath, to point him out as one who had by merit and abilities deserved well of his country.

During the whole career of Captain Mounsey, he appears to have maintained the character of a brave, active, and diligent officer; he was ever foremost in volunteering to partake of all services going on, whether on board or detached; and almost every captain and admiral under whom he served, gave him some proof of the high estimation in which they held his manners, conduct, and abilities.

HISTORICAL MEMOIRS OF
CAPTAIN THOMAS SEARLE, C.B.

CAPTAIN SEARLE is a native of Devonshire, was born 29th May, 1777, and commenced his naval career, in October 1789, on board the Mutine cutter. In that vessel, the Sphynx, Active, Artois, and Royal George, he passed the probationary period of his service, and on board the last-named ship he was present at the capture of three ships of the line off l'Orient by Lord Bridport. In August 1796 he was promoted to the rank of lieutenant, in consequence of the great exertions he made in saving the lives of seven men who had been swamped in a boat along side during a heavy gale of wind. To all those who delight in the good and happiness of others, the knowledge of such a circumstance must be highly pleasing; but to be the means of saving the lives of our fellow-creatures, of snatching them from the grave, and preserving them for the benefit of their relations and their country, must be peculiarly gratifying. Mr. Searle experienced this to the full: neither is it less gratifying to find that his exertions were so promptly rewarded; he was not only made a lieutenant, but appointed to command the Courier hired cutter of 12 guns and 40 men. On the 15th April, 1799, he recaptured the Nelly from the French privateer Le Vengeur of 14 guns; and on the 12th May, being off Winterton, he discovered a French privateer of 16 guns in the act of capturing a merchant-sloop: he immediately made all sail, and shortly after brought her to close action, which continued for one hour and forty minutes, when, after every exertion was used, her superiority of sailing was such, together with her having the advantage of the wind, that she effected her escape. Lieutenant Searle continued in chase of her till midnight, when it came on thick and foggy, and he lost sight of her. At daylight on the following morning he discovered a vessel in the N. E. and, supposing it to be his late opponent, he again made sail in chase; at eight o'clock he came up with, and captured, Le Ribotteur of 6 guns. What considerably adds to the merit of the above action is, that, during the whole of its continuance, another French lugger-privateer was lying at some distance to leeward, but made no attempt to take part in the action. In the above affair the Courier had two men killed and five wounded. He then became under the orders of Captain Winthrop, who commanded a squadron of small ships under the chief command of Lord Duncan; and, on the 10th July, assisted at the capture of three vessels, which was thus described by Captain Winthrop: " The boats of our little squadron made another dash into the Watt, at the back of Ameland, last night, and brought out three valuable vessels, laden with sugar, wine, and brandy; they also burnt a large galliot, laden with brass ordnance and stores, which could not be brought off, notwithstanding the perseverance of Captain Mackenzie, to whom I am very much indebted for his coolness and judgment in the management of this affair; and also to Captain Boorder, whose local knowledge has been of great use to me. Lieutenant Searle, who commanded a schuyt converted into a gunboat, and Lieutenant Parole, who commanded the Circe's boats, upon this, as well as upon a former occasion, conducted themselves much to my satisfaction; as did the honest fellows under their command, who were at their oars fifteen or sixteen hours, in a very hot day, opposed to an enemy of superior force; but I am happy to say, not a man was hurt."

On the 11th August Lieutenant Searle was employed in a very spirited and gallant attempt to cut out some vessels from Schiermonikoog, which proved completely successful. The Courier, working faster to windward than her consorts, was ordered to engage the Crash (formerly British) gun-brig, until the Pylades or L'Espiègle could get up, " which she did," said Captain Mackenzie, " in the most gallant manner, considering the enemy is five times the cutter's force." Besides the Crash, several small vessels were captured. They also landed on the island (having previously drove the men from the batteries), spiked four pieces of cannon, and brought off two brass field-pieces. In forwarding the particulars of this affair to Lord Duncan, Captain Sotheron stated, " I have to transmit two letters I have received from Captain Mackenzie. It is impossible for me to express by words the high sense I have of his (Captain Boorder's) and Lieutenant Searle's conduct; I mention their names as being commanders of ships who had the honour of acting on this occasion. The more this attack is inquired into, the more I am convinced it will redound to the honour of his Majesty's arms." Lord Duncan also said, " I shall not trouble their lordships with a comment on the gallantry and the exertions of the officers and men employed on that service, as it speaks for itself; and shall only say, I think Captains

Mackenzie and Boorder deserve the attention of their lordships, as does also Lieutenant Searle of the Courier."

On the 21st November, being in Yarmouth roads, Lieutenant Searle was ordered by Lord Duncan to reconnoitre the ports of Helvoetsluys and Flushing; and having proceeded to sea, at five p.m. on the following day, he observed a suspicious sail bringing-to a bark, upon which he hauled his wind to speak to them; and upon passing the latter, was informed the chase was an enemy. He immediately made all possible sail after her, and fortunately came up with her the following morning; and, after a close action of fifty minutes, obliged her to strike her colours: she proved to be Le Guerrier cutter-privateer of 14 guns and 44 men. His conduct on this occasion again called forth the approbation of Lord Duncan, who strongly recommended him to the notice of the Lords of the Admiralty, and he was promoted to the rank of commander; but we do not find that he was again so far favoured by Fortune as to meet with any other opportunities of distinguishing himself previous to the treaty of Amiens.

After the recommencement of hostilities, Captain Searle was appointed to the Perseus bomb, and also the Helder defence-ship, as well as the Autumn sloop of war. He was also employed, under Lord Keith, in the expedition against the Boulogne flotilla, on which occasion he commanded one of the explosion-vessels. In 1806 he was appointed to the Fury bomb, and also to the Grasshopper brig; in the latter of which he sailed to the Mediterranean, where, in December 1807, whilst cruising off Carthagena, he discovered several vessels at anchor under Cape Palos, which he continued to watch. On the 7th, however, the Spanish ships of war, San Josef of 12 24-pounders and 99 men, Medusa of 10 guns (24-pounders) and 77 men, and Aigle of 8 guns (same calibre) and 50 men, came out to attack the Grasshopper. Notwithstanding their great superiority, Captain Searle immediately brought them to action; but in fifteen minutes the San Josef struck her colours and ran on shore. The Grasshopper was then brought to an anchor, and, owing to the great exertions of her officers and crew, the prize was got off. The other two vessels, the moment their consort surrendered, bore up and made all sail, or no doubt they would have shared her fate.

Captain Searle now received the approbation of his great commander, Lord Collingwood, who, in writing to the Lords of the Admiralty, said, "I have great pleasure in making this circumstance known to their lordships, who will see in it an instance of that zeal and enterprise which mark the general conduct of Captain Searle." On the 4th April, 1808, he had another opportunity of highly distinguishing himself; but his conduct is so fully described by Captain Maxwell of the Alceste, under whose orders he served, that we shall transcribe that part of his letter:

" When at anchor to-day, with the Mercury and Grasshopper brig, St. Sebastian's lighthouse S. E. distant three miles, wind W. S. W. a large convoy of the enemy was discovered coming close along shore from the northward, under the protection of about twenty gun-boats and a numerous train of flying artillery on the beach. At three p. m. I made the signal to weigh and attack the convoy, and stood directly in for the body of them, then off the town of Rota. At four the enemy's shot and shells, from the gun-boats and batteries, going far over us, his Majesty's ships opened their fire, which was kept up with great vivacity until half-past six, when we had taken seven of the convoy, and driven a great many others on shore on the surf; compelled the gun-boats to retreat, which they did very reluctantly, and not until two of them were destroyed; and actually silenced the batteries at Rota; which latter service was performed by the extraordinary gallantry and good conduct of Captain Searle in the Grasshopper, who kept in upon the shoal to the southward of the town so near as to drive the enemy from their guns with grape from his 32-pound carronades, and at the same time kept in check a division of gun-boats that had come out from Cadiz to assist the others engaged by the Alceste and Mercury. It was a general cry in both ships, ' Only look how nobly the brig behaves!' The situation of our little squadron was rather a critical one, tacking every fifteen minutes close on the edge of the shoal, with the wind in, and frequently engaged on both sides."

The boats were then sent in under Lieutenant Allen Stewart, accompanied by Lieutenants Pipon, W. O. Pell, Gordon, and Whyloch, and Hawky of the marines, who boarded in the most gallant manner, and brought out seven tartans from under the protection of the barges and pinnaces of the combined fleet, which had by that time joined the convoy. The captured vessels were all loaded on government account for the arsenal at Cadiz, and had a considerable quantity of valuable ship-timber on board. His conduct on this occasion procured Captain Searle the thanks of the Admiralty, and a more substantial proof of their lordships' approbation by his being promoted to post-rank. It is gratifying to see service and reward so quickly follow each other; but before this news could reach Captain Searle, he had given farther proofs of his merit, and of his claim to that reward which had been bestowed. The following is an extract from his dispatch:

" Yesterday morning (23d April), in company with his Majesty's gun-brig Rapid, I had the good fortune to fall in with two Spanish vessels from South America, under the protection of four gun-boats, when, after a short chase, they anchored under a battery, close in with Faro, among the shoals. I immediately anchored within grape-shot range, and, after a very severe action of two hours and a half, the people on shore deserted their guns, two gun-boats struck, and the other two we drove on shore and destroyed. The cargoes on board the two Spanish vessels, which we also captured, are worth 30,000*l.* each. We had one man killed, myself slightly* and three seamen severely wounded : both vessels suffered much in their sails and rigging. The enemy's loss was very great in the two gun-boats captured ; they had 40 killed and wounded : 14 of the latter I sent on shore to Faro, as I had no means of taking care of our own wounded men and those of the enemy."

Ever alive to distinguished merit, the Committee of the Patriotic Fund seized this opportunity to present Captain Searle with a piece of plate, value one hundred and twenty guineas, as a mark of their admiration of the services he had performed ; and the crew of the Grasshopper, on his leaving that vessel on account of his promotion, presented him with a sword value eighty guineas ; a sure sign of the respect and esteem they entertained for him. Having served in the Frederickstein of 32 guns and Elizabeth of 74, he was appointed to the Druid frigate, in which he acted for several months as senior officer at Cadiz, and subsequently at Tariffa, when that place was besieged by the French troops under Marshal Soult. In 1815 his Majesty, duly considering the important services of Captain Searle, was graciously pleased to appoint him a Companion of the Bath. In 1818 he was appointed to the Hyperion frigate, in which he sailed to South America, where he remained till 1821, and then returned to England, with specie to the amount of half a million sterling.

Captain Searle married the daughter of J. Madoch, Esq. royal dock-yard, Portsmouth, and has several children.

---

* He was shot through the thigh by a musket-ball.

HISTORICAL MEMOIRS OF
CAPTAIN JAMES ANDERSON.

WE have frequently observed, that there is no circumstance tends more forcibly to the encouragement of enterprise and exertion than the conferring honorary rewards. It is almost immaterial in what they consist, so that their distribution is marked with a spirit of impartiality. There are none which are more esteemed than titles or medals; but both army and navy should be put upon the same footing. Whilst the former, down to the common soldier, who served in the battle of Waterloo, are decorated with medals, no such system prevails in the navy, though the individual may have fought in the actions of Rodney, Howe, Duncan, St. Vincent, or Nelson. Such things, however, should not be; whenever gallantry is displayed, whenever diligence is exerted, whenever talents are exercised in the service of the country, and more especially in fighting her battles, then ought rewards and distinctions to follow. Were this system to prevail, then Captain Anderson's breast would not be without that decoration which some have obtained without rendering to the country half the services which she has received from him.

Captain Anderson is descended from the ancient and respectable family of Airderbreck in Scotland; but his grandfather having, from conscientious motives, attached himself to the House of Stewart, unfortunately took an active part in endeavouring to replace that family on the throne; and in defending his principles with his life and fortune, had his horse shot under him, and was so severely wounded in the leg as to be obliged to submit to amputation: he escaped with his life by a hasty removal, but being known, his property was forfeited as a matter of course. The parents of Captain Anderson, being of pious and religious habits, wished to educate their only son for the church; for which purpose he was placed at the grammar-school at Keith, from whence he was sent to the University of Aberdeen, where, before he was fourteen years of age, he gained by competition one of the first burses competed for at King's College. The ecclesiastical profession did not, however, accord with the activity of his mind, and, like his great countryman, Duncan, he chose the navy in preference to the church. Having, through the interference of a friend, procured an introduction to Sir John Lockhart Ross, he served with him for some time on board the Royal George, and then with Admiral Kempenfelt, and was present at the capture of a large convoy laden with warlike stores, and also of the Pegase of 74 guns. He was afterwards on board the Edgar with Commodore (afterwards Lord) Hotham, proceeded with him, under the chief command of Lord Howe, to the relief of Gibraltar, and was, of course, in the action with the French fleet, when he received a contusion on the breast by a splinter from the main-mast. He continued in the Edgar during the remainder of the war, when he was paid off. He then served for three years on board the Barracouta cutter, a vessel cruising in the Channel, and with the boats of that vessel had several contests with smugglers. He shortly after proceeded to the West Indies, where he commanded for several years an armed vessel attached to the commander-in-chief of the forces. Although this was not immediately in the navy, it was still in the king's service, as he was regularly commissioned by General Matthew for the command. He now became intimately acquainted with all the ports and harbours of that hemisphere, and was honoured with the notice of Sir John Laforey, whose ship, the Trusty, he piloted into the proper anchorage at the capture of Tobago in 1793. On the return of Sir John Laforey to the West Indies in 1795, he prevailed on Mr. Anderson, by promises of patronage, to relinquish his situation, and again enter into the regular naval service of his country. He first became a volunteer on board the flag-ship, soon after which he was made a lieutenant, and employed in an express-boat among the islands. Sir John, having shortly after been superseded by Sir Hugh Christian, had no opportunity of fulfilling his promises to Mr. Anderson, but strongly recommended him to his successor, who continued to employ him on the same fatiguing service. In proceeding from St. Lucia with dispatches from Sir H. Christian to Sir J. Laforey at Antigua, he fell in with three French frigates, under Guadaloupe, from which he escaped only by great exertion and address. Sir Hugh was so well pleased with his conduct on this and other occasions during the siege of St. Lucia, that he signified his intention of taking him into the flag-ship on promotion; but was unfortunately prevented from thus rewarding Mr. Anderson, agreeably to his deserts, by the arrival of Admiral Harvey to assume the chief command. Having now been eleven years in the West Indies, during which he had been employed in a variety of difficult and laborious services, and finding, from the excessive fatigue he experienced in a small uncomfortable pilot-boat, his health considerably impaired, he returned to England, without hopes of recovery. Being, however, partially restored, though still much debilitated, he again applied for employment, and, as he was unable to make any vigorous exertion, was appointed to the signal-station at North Yarmouth, in which service he obtained the most flattering testimonials of approbation from Lord Duncan, Sir A. Dickson, and Sir T. Graves.

After the renewal of the war in 1803, Lieutenant Anderson was appointed to the Atlas, in which he served in the North Sea and Channel, and then went to the West Indies, where he exchanged as first lieutenant into the Africaine frigate, and in her returned to England with a large convoy, the charge of which devolved upon him in consequence of the illness of the captain, who was attacked by a most malignant fever, which carried off one-fifth of the crew. The ship being paid off, on the 22d January, 1806, he was promoted to the rank of commander. In the following year he was appointed an agent of transports on the expedition to Copenhagen: he accordingly took charge of a division of transports, having on board the troops under Generals Baird, Grosvenor, and Warde, at Harwich, and conducted them to Copenhagen; after the capture of which he offered his services to Admiral Gambier to fit out any of the captured line-of-battle ships, for which he received the thanks of the admiral*, and by him was directed to superintend the embarkation of the ordnance stores and artillery. To this duty he applied himself with such alacrity and zeal, that, notwithstanding he had only the boats and crews of his own division of transports, consisting of about thirty small brigs, from 160 to 250 tons, he embarked the whole in three days. The next service on which he was employed was embarking a division of troops again at Harwich, and conveying them to Gottenburgh, to serve under the orders of Sir John Moore; and having returned with them to Spithead, was afterwards ordered to Maceira Bay, on the coast of Portugal, where he was directed by Captain Pulteney Malcolm to superintend the landing of the troops and artillery; which he performed in a manner highly satisfactory to that distinguished officer. Having effected this important service, he was ordered to Lisbon to assist in em-

---

* SIR,—I have received your letter of yesterday, and cannot but applaud the offer you have made of your services to assist in fitting the Danish ships, although I cannot accept them, as all your exertions will be required to forward the embarkation of the ordnance stores of the army.

Captain ANDERSON.   （Signed,)   GAMBIER.

barking the French troops which had capitulated by the convention of Cintra. Here, by his experience and arrangements, he effected a saving of 12,000 tons of the transport shipping; and having embarked the first division of prisoners, about 8000 men, conducted them to a French port, agreeably to the articles of capitulation. He then returned to England, but was immediately ordered, with all the transports that could be got ready, to proceed to Vigo Bay, and join Commissioner Bowen, in order to receive the army under Sir John Moore, who was expected to retreat upon that point; but after waiting several days, he was detached with a division of transports to Corunna, where he joined Admiral de Courcy; and on the arrival of the troops at that place, all the sick and wounded, together with the prisoners, artillery, stores, baggage, and some horses, were immediately conveyed on board*.

* With such activity and zeal were all these services performed, that he received the highest commendations from the officers of both army and navy, and called forth the particular approbation of the chiefs of those departments under which he was more immediately employed, as the following documents will satisfactorily prove:

HORSE-GUARDS, *May 9, 1808.*

GENTLEMEN,—I have the commander-in-chief's commands to acquaint you that the conduct of Captain Anderson, agent for transports, has been reported so favourably during the embarkations at Harwich, that his Royal Highness thinks it due to that officer that the same should be made known to you.

(Signed,)   R. BROWNRIGG, *Quarter-Master-General.*

To the Commissioners for the Transport Service.

TRANSPORT-OFFICE, *Feb. 6, 1809.*

SIR,—I am directed by the Board to transmit herewith a copy of a letter from the Right Hon. Lord Castlereagh, signifying his lordship's satisfaction and approbation of the manner in which the service of the re-embarkation of the army at Corunna was conducted by Commissioner Bowen, and the several agents and others employed under his direction; and I am to desire that you will communicate the same to the several agents who were under your charge.

To Captain ANDERSON.   (Signed,)   ALEXANDER M'LEARY.

OFFICE OF ORDNANCE, *March 1, 1809.*

SIR,—The ordnance department having experienced very great attention and accommodation from the active exertions of Captain Anderson, R. N. in his situation of agent for transports at Corunna, and also from the essential service derived from his exertions during the re-embarkation of the heavy ordnance and stores on the expedition to Copenhagen; I have the Board's commands to request you will represent Captain Anderson's attention and good conduct, during his employment on those services, to the Lords Commissioners of the Admiralty, which the Board hope may induce their lordships to consider in a favourable point of view when an opportunity offers.

To the Hon. W. W. POLE,   (Signed,)   R. H. CREW.

Secretary to the Admiralty.

This service being completed, Captain Anderson was appointed to carry the crews of the Russian ships detained at Lisbon (but then lying at the Mother-Bank) to Russia; but before he had embarked more than the baggage, he was directed to return every thing on board the respective ships, and proceed to Harwich, where he was employed, for the third time, in embarking troops for Walcheren; and proceeded with the division, having on board that portion of the army under General Grosvenor, to Campvere. After a good deal of hard service in the Scheldt, embarking and disembarking troops, and passing the transports through the Slough passage, he returned to England, and was immediately appointed to command the Rinaldo of 10 guns. During his first cruise in that vessel he was fortunate enough to fall in with and capture the Maraudeur, French privateer of 14 guns and 80 men, after a sharp contest, in which her captain and four men were wounded*. As the Rinaldo was one-fourth short of her complement, and every way inferior to the privateer, he received the thanks of the Board of Admiralty. He was afterwards stationed between Dungeness and the Goodwin sands, where he afforded the most complete protection to the trade by his vigilance in looking after the enemy's cruisers. On the 17th December, 1810, being on his return from Portsmouth, whither he had conducted a convoy of trading vessels, and being near the Owers light, he discovered four privateers in the offing, lying with their sails lowered, without the track of the trade, and as he knew he had no chance of getting near them by a direct chase, he determined to endeavour to decoy them under his guns; for which purpose he altered his course and steered in shore, trimming his sails bye, to enable the enemy to come up with him about dark, at the same time keeping the brig in such a position as to prevent them from making her

---

* On this occasion Captain Anderson had a very narrow escape. While leaning over the gangway, the privateer being close along side, and his men rushing on board of her, he felt something hot close to his ear, and supposing it came from the musket of the corporal of marines, who was standing close to him, said, " Corporal, stand farther off, or you'll be shooting me presently!"—" It was not me, sir," was the reply; " but that big fellow of a Frenchman: however, I'll soon shoot him."—" By no means," said Captain Anderson; " the boarders have now got possession."

This Frenchman was a remarkably stout man, a member of the Legion of Honour, and sailing-master of the privateer. On the following morning, observing the indifferent crew the Rinaldo had, he said to Captain Anderson, " Capitaine, your crew are only boys."—" True," was the reply; " but you find English *boys* can beat French *men.*"— " Eh bien! la fortune de guerre; if we had known you had so bad a crew, we would have taken you."—" Remerci, monsieur," said Captain A. " I am quite satisfied as it is."

out to be armed. This had the desired effect; the enemy made all sail in chase, and about five o'clock, the Owers W.N.W. half a mile, the two largest of the enemy arrived up under the Rinaldo's stern, hailing her, in very abusive and peremptory terms, to strike, and at the same moment poured into her a volley of musketry. This, however, was taken no notice of, and the moment they reached her quarter, the Rinaldo tacked, giving each of them a broadside; then wore round on her heel, and gave the largest a second broadside within half-pistol-shot. The enemy now discovered their mistake, and endeavoured to sheer off by bearing up, at which moment all his masts went by the board, and being in a sinking state, he called for quarter. The second privateer was then observed running for the Rinaldo's bow, keeping up a constant fire: the Rinaldo consequently abandoned the first to her fate, to attack the second, with which a closer action commenced; after which she ran within the light-vessel, lowered her sails, and called for quarter. Unfortunately, however, the Rinaldo, in wearing round to take possession of her, was carried by the tide, which was then at strong ebb, with little wind, on board the Owers light-vessel, by which accident the boats were prevented from being sent away, and before she could be extricated from her situation, the other two privateers arrived within gun-shot. The one which had struck then rehoisted her colours, and by the assistance of her companions was enabled to make sail and effect her escape: the first, however, named La Vieuse Josephine, of 16 guns and 80 men, sunk with all her crew, except the captain and two men.

Captain Anderson was afterwards stationed off Dover, and, during the most tempestuous season of the year, continued to keep his station, when scarcely any other cruiser remained on the coast; and was fortunately enabled, by his vigilance and perseverance, to keep it so clear of privateers, which generally abound at that period, that not a single merchantman fell into the hands of the enemy. Such conduct excited the notice of Admiral Campbell, the commander-in-chief, who particularly mentioned him to the Lords of the Admiralty. From an authenticated copy of the Rinaldo's log, signed by Sir T. Foley, it appears that, between the 17th December, 1810, and 31st March, 1811, she chased fifty privateers into their own ports, or under the protection of their batteries; that during the same period she blockaded forty others; and in an action with four, she sunk one of them. Although it may at first sight appear strange that so many privateers should have been fallen in with, and so few captured or destroyed, the surprise will cease when it is considered that these vessels seldom or never venture without the protection of their batteries in the daytime, and only run across the Channel in the night, when they generally lie, with their sails down, near the track of the trade, and always return in the morning; that they lie nearly as low on the water as a row-boat; that they are remarkably fast sailers; that they keep all hands constantly on deck whilst in this situation, looking sharply out, and ready to make sail off the moment they discover a cruiser; and that the distance the cruisers, between Dungeness and the South Foreland, have to chase before they find themselves under the enemy's numerous batteries, is very short (these batteries being always on the look-out to protect them)—when these circumstances are fairly considered, the wonder is, that any of them are ever got hold of on that part of the coast; and indeed it is only when by any lucky chance they are caught in some particular situation, or decoyed by stratagem under the cruisers' guns, that any of them can ever be got hold of. *The protection of the trade* therefore up and down the Channel is the principal object of the cruisers; and Captain Anderson had the great satisfaction of knowing, *that not a single merchantman* was captured on that most difficult and dangerous part of the coast during the time he was on the station; but their privateers were either prevented from getting out of the protection of their batteries, or invariably driven back without making any capture; and even vessels captured to the westward have been recaptured by him, in endeavouring in the night-time to get into Boulogne or Calais.

It is not supposed that all these privateers were different vessels, but many of them, no doubt, the same vessels chased at different times; but Captain Anderson's character for vigilance and zeal is not in the least diminished by this circumstance. About this time it was thought proper to alter the mode of cruising, and instead of each cruiser having a particular station allotted to her, and being confined to a small space of the coast, they were placed in small divisions, with extended cruising ground, and under particular officers. Admiral Campbell, who had the appointing of officers to those commands, being convinced of the zeal and enterprise of Captain Anderson (although there were many senior officers on the station), appointed him to the important command off Calais and Boulogne, where the greatest activity prevailed in fitting out flotillas. He had also orders from Admiral Foley to keep a vigilant look-out for the squadrons of the enemy from the Texel and Scheldt, which were expected to leave those places at the equinoctial spring tides, and endeavour to reach Brest; in which case he was to communicate the intelligence to the commanders at Deal, Portsmouth, off Cherbourg, and Ushant. He consequently placed the brigs under his orders in such a position across the Channel, as to render it impossible for any ship to pass without being discovered. No enemy, however, appeared, and, as the tides took off, he resumed his station. He then received orders to make a weekly report of the apparent number of troops on the heights about Boulogne, and of any observations he might be able to make respecting their increase or diminution; for all which services he met the entire approbation of his commander-in-chief. On the 15th May a sloop and several boats were observed coming out of Calais, and steering for Boulogne. The boats returned to Calais on his giving chase, but the sloop anchored within half a cable's length of the beach; upon which he immediately sent his boats to board her, standing in with the brig to cover them from the fire of the batteries, which was attended with the desired success, and the sloop was brought out without the loss of a man. On the 18th June, when cruising off Boulogne, nine brigs, four long 24-pounders each, and two luggers, came out of the harbour, and stretched away towards Cape Grinez. Captain Anderson, with the Redpole and Apelles in company, immediately proceeded in chase, upon which they sought shelter under the protection of the batteries; notwithstanding which Captain Anderson brought them to action, and succeeded in driving two of them on shore, whilst the others made their escape to the westward of Boulogne, where they were blockaded by Captain Anderson till the 3d July, when it having come on to blow strong from the N. E. at half-past seven p. m. they weighed and began to run for the harbour: Captain Anderson immediately stood close in, brought the French commodore to action, and drove him ashore to the westward of the pier-head, where it was ascertained afterwards that he received considerable damage. At this moment the Rinaldo had only three fathoms water, and was within half a mile of Fort Imperial, which, with the whole of the batteries round the bay, commenced a brisk fire of shot and shells upon her and her two consorts, the Skylark and Apelles, but fortunately did them no injury. During the remainder of that, and in the following month, Captain Anderson frequently stood in and endeavoured to bring the enemy to action, but did not succeed till the 3d September, when a part of their flotilla, consisting of four praams of 12 guns each, one bearing an admiral's flag at the main, four brigs of four guns, and seven gun-boats of one long gun each, was observed getting under weigh about eleven o'clock a. m. in the west end of the bay, upon the flood tide, to shift their berth, as was supposed, under the eastern land, the wind being E. N. E. a strong breeze. Captain Anderson, although he had only the Redpole in company, hoping that a chance might offer of cutting off some of them, should they venture a little way off the shore, hovered about them to windward. Observing one of the ships and a brig somewhat astern of the others, he immediately made all possible sail, in hopes of cutting one or other of them off; but they succeeded in getting within the Basse bank, and joined the others, which were lying-to there for them. He, however, pursued them within the bank, shortened sail, and at one p. m. commenced action, and drove the whole close under the batteries. The enemy, however, tacked and stood off again in two lines towards the brigs, which, having wore round, were lying-to to receive them. The enemy began to fire very briskly as soon as they got their heads off shore, as well as when in stays; but were so warmly received by the brigs, which, by stretching a little ahead, were enabled to rake them as they stood off, that they soon wore round (firing their broadsides as they wore), and stood in again; the brigs also wearing, and raking them as they stood in. In this manner they stood off and were driven in to the shore *three times successively,* the gun-luggers lying all the time to windward, firing on the brigs as occasion offered, and ready to take any advantage that might occur in the event of the brigs being disabled, or to tow in their own vessels should they want that assistance. Finding they could make no impression on the two brigs, the enemy bore round up and stood in to their former anchorage. Soon after the commencement of the action, one of the gun-brigs and two of the lugger gun-boats ran directly into the harbour, in consequence of the damage sustained. The ship carrying the admiral's flag having approached nearer the brigs, in consequence of her being the leading ship, and being particularly attacked by them, received so much damage in the hull, that she was carried into the harbour the next morning to be repaired. Several others also received considerable damage. It afterwards appeared that it was Marshal Ney's flag which was on board the praam, and that he was on board of her himself, and had had selected a number of able cannoniers from that part of the flotilla remaining at anchor, for the purpose of capturing the two little brigs.

When the great disparity of force which existed on this occason is considered, nearly seven to one, besides forty-four other vessels at anchor close to them, those qualities which distinguish the seaman must have been displayed by Captain Anderson, and his gallant associate, Captain Colin Macdonald. Captain Anderson continued to blockade the enemy until their flotilla amounted to sixty-three vessels of all descriptions, when he was reinforced by the Castilian of 18 guns, Captain D. Braimer, and the Viper cutter, Lieutenant E. A. d'Arcy. On the 17th September Buonaparte arrived at Boulogne, to accelerate the equipment of the flotilla and review the whole. On the 18th the Naïad, Captain Carteret, arrived off Boulogne, and on the 20th an attack was made upon her by the flotilla as she lay at anchor; but as it was nearly calm, Captain Anderson could afford her no assistance, having been carried, with his brigs, to leeward by the tide. On the following day, at seven a.m. moderate breezes and fine weather, wind S.W. seven large praams, carrying twelve long 24-pounders each, five gun-brigs of four and six guns, several luggers of one long gun each, and a sloop fitted as a bomb-vessel, the same force which attacked the Naïad on the 20th, got under weigh near Point la Crèche, on the weather tide, and stood to the westward on the larboard tack, formed in two lines. The weathermost line consisted of three praams, the leading one carrying a rear-admiral's flag, and the second a commodore's broad pendant; the lee line consisted of four praams; the brigs and luggers taking stations as most convenient in the rear of the two lines, with openings between them and the bomb, close to the rear-admiral. The squadron under the immediate orders of Captain Anderson having worked to windward during the night with great diligence and perseverance, and having stood within the Basse bank, in the westernmost part of the bay, near Fort l'Heurt, tacked and hove-to with their heads to the W.N.W. to wait the enemy's coming without the range of their batteries. While in this situation, Boulogne bearing S.E. by E. five or six miles, the Naïad got under weigh and joined them, and the whole continued to lie-to till half-past nine, when the outermost or leading praam of the enemy's weather line having come within long gun-shot, hove in stays, as did all the others at nearly the same instant, firing their broadsides as they came round. The moment the praam's helm was put down, the British squadron, by signal from the Naïad, instantly wore round; and the brigs, making all sail in chase, soon passed the Naïad, which seemed steering for the admiral's praam, now the sternmost praam of their weather line. The Rinaldo and Redpole directed their course for the large praam which led the enemy's lee line, but now the sternmost of that line, with the intention of laying her on board, the Rinaldo on her weather bow, and the Redpole on her lee quarter, agreeably to a plan previously arranged by Captain Anderson with Captain Macdonald. Having passed the Naïad about three-quarters of a mile or rather more, and when nearly up with the praam, the Naïad made the signal for them to take more open order, and so leave the above praam to her. Upon this they bore round up, shortening sail at the same time, and the Rinaldo running under the praam's stern, poured two well-directed broadsides into her, and then hauling up under her lee within half-pistol-shot, at fifty-eight minutes after nine commenced a close action with her, supported by the Redpole. By the first two broadsides the Rinaldo severely wounded the praam's masts, brought down her mizen-top-sail and mizen, much cut her other sails, wounded her stern-post and rudder, and hulling her each time, killed and wounded many of her crew, and drove the rest below from their quarters, except a few in the tops.

While the praam was reduced to this state, the Naïad, having made sail, came up on her weather quarter; and to get out of the way of her shot, some of which were flying over and between the masts, the two brigs made sail to attack the next praam ahead. When the Naïad got on the praam's starboard bow, she put her helm to starboard, and wore right round, carrying the praam, already disabled, round with her, and taking her in tow, stood off to sea with all sail set. The Rinaldo and Redpole, however, continued the contest with the greatest perseverance and bravery, exposed to the whole fire of the enemy, as well as of the bomb-vessel, the shells from which continued to fall about them. The Redpole was a little to leeward of the Rinaldo, and so situated, that she could seldom fire upon the enemy without the danger of firing into her; and having reached near the shore, exposed to the raking fire of the vessels at anchor, she was very properly wore round, for the purpose, by making a short stretch off, of being enabled to close with the enemy, and more effectually support the Rinaldo in the unequal contest she had to maintain. The Castilian, which was still farther to leeward, and could rarely fire during the action without firing over or into the other two brigs, followed the example of the Redpole, with the same intentions. The Rinaldo was by this time close into the enemy's anchorage, the vessels in which began to fire upon her, as well as the whole of the vessels under weigh; and the entire of the batteries all round the heights, with the Forts l'Heurt and la Crèche, built at low-water mark, opened a tremendous cannonade upon her, she being the only object within their reach. Being in three fathoms water, she wore round amidst all this fire, continuing the action as long as her guns would reach, and stood out to join the Naïad, which, with the disabled praam in tow, was standing off under all sail, and had gained a considerable distance in the offing. During the action the Rinaldo fired forty-two broadsides, her guns double-shotted each time*.

Such are the particulars of the capture of the famous Ville de Lyons.

* Captain Anderson afterwards proceeded on board the Naïad, not very well pleased with the result of the day's adventure, and after some preliminary observations, the following conversation took place between him and Captain Carteret:

Captain A. I am sorry to say, commodore, that you have not treated us (the brigs) altogether fairly to-day: you know that I have been watching all the summer for the opportunity which this day presented, and you have by your signal prevented me from reaping the advantage of it. You appeared to direct your attention to the enemy's weather line, and I therefore expected you would leave the lee line to the brigs: if you had done so, I venture to say, that we should have given a good account of it.

Captain C. Why I saw that *only one* could be taken, and I thought it best to secure her with this ship, as your going along side of her might have been attended with the loss of many lives: that was my reason for making the signal.

Captain A. I am sorry you thought so; for if officers going into action were to stop short and enter into calculations of the loss they might sustain, none of those brilliant exploits which have distinguished so many gallant officers could have been achieved. As to the idea that only one could have been captured, I will venture to say, that had the Naïad made sail when the brigs did, that more might have been captured or destroyed.

Captain C. The reason why I did not make sail sooner was, that I thought it would be attended with considerable confusion to go into action with a crowd of sail, especially as we were coming up with them.

Captain A. You saw that the brigs were under a crowd of sail, every thing they could pack, except steering sails: yet no confusion took place in either of them, although they did not shorten sail till your unexpected signal, when they were obliged to go to leeward. However, what is past cannot be recalled: but I hope you will in your letter give the brigs the credit they deserve; for you must be aware, that if the Rinaldo and Redpole had not disabled the praam, you could not have got up with her; besides, the capture of a 12-gun praam by a frigate of 48 guns cannot reflect any very great credit upon her, though it might upon a brig of 10 guns.

Captain C. The brigs behaved exceedingly well, and I am much pleased with their conduct.

praam, and although they differ materially from those contained in the official account, we can answer for their correctness. We have been at considerable pains to ascertain the truth, particularly as the return of the Naïad's killed and wounded may appear to afford some contradiction; but on examining her surgeon's journal, we find that most of the wounds were caused by an explosion of some cartridges on board the Naïad; and none are said to have been killed on that day, or hurt by a cannon-shot, though some were wounded. The Naïad having proceeded with the praam to the Downs, and Captain Anderson having put his little squadron in a condition to renew the action, again stood into the bay, to shew the enemy he was ready to meet them, although he was no longer assisted by the frigate. During the night, however, the enemy ran, some into Boulogne, some into Vimereaux, and some into Abbeville, where they were closely blockaded by the Rinaldo and Redpole till the 3d October, when they were dismantled and laid up. Thus may it be said, that by his judgment in properly applying a very small force for the attainment of an important object, was he enabled to defeat a very superior enemy, and prevent them from carrying those plans into execution which they had laid for the annoyance of his country. The flotilla being thus laid up, and part of their crews turned over to privateers, Captain Anderson's attention was of course directed to them, eleven of which were lying at Boulogne: one of them he drove on shore and destroyed near Etaples, notwithstanding a heavy fire took place from the batteries, which did considerable damage to the Rinaldo's sails and rigging, though without hurting a man. Having continued on this station till the end of October, and the time of his cruise being expired, he returned to the Downs, from whence he was ordered to Sheerness to refit.

In January 1812 he resumed his station off Calais, and on the 1st February he sent in his boats, under Lieutenant Miller, to destroy a gun-brig which was aground; and which was effectually performed under the fire of the Rinaldo, although the alarm had been given on shore, and several field-pieces had been brought down for her protection. She proved to be No. 276 of the flotilla.

On Captain Anderson's return to the Downs, shortly afterwards he had the gratification to find, that his active and meritorious services were duly appreciated and rewarded by his promotion to post-rank. In thus closing his services as a commander we must offer a few observations. When he took the command of the Rinaldo she had not an officer belonging to her, very few men, and those of an inferior description; but when he resigned the command of her, in consequence of his promotion, she was one of the best manned sloops in the service, two able seamen above her complement, all the crew raised by himself, and every man a volunteer. Another very peculiar circumstance attended him: notwithstanding the many severe contests he had been in, he had not a single man killed or wounded, except a pilot slightly on the 21st. What a laborious and important service he had been employed on for two years and a half will be best understood, and his exertions best appreciated, by those most conversant with the nature of such a service, and the difficulty of performing it with so inferior a force. The efficiency of his abilities may be also known from the circumstance, that not a single privateer was enabled to cross the Channel from Calais, or made a single capture, during the time he was stationed off that port; nor did a single vessel of the flotilla ever get beyond the reach of their own batteries. The trade of his country consequently obtained the most complete protection, so far as in him lay, and the mercantile interest was most effectually promoted.

Notwithstanding several applications, Captain Anderson did not receive any other appointment till August 1814; he was then sent for to the Admiralty, and asked if he would accept the Zealous of 74 guns, which was, in the first place, to go to Halifax, where she might remain the winter. The command was accepted, on the understanding that if she was put out of commission he should immediately have another ship. Two days afterwards he was told that it was determined to send the ship to Quebec; that she was to carry two hundred seamen for the lakes, and to be unincumbered with convoy, as it was important that she should make the best of her way; that the ship was fully manned and ready for sea; and that as the reinforcements were much wanted, he must immediately join her. With his usual zeal he instantly started for Portsmouth, where he arrived on the 15th; but instead of finding the Zealous ready for sea, her fore-mast and main-yard were in the dock-yard, all her sails and rigging on shore, and two gangs of shipwrights and caulkers on board fitting her out; added to which, her crew was in a most inefficient state, scarcely a man being able to perform a seaman's duty. This inefficiency was occasioned by the greater part of the crew having been discharged as long-service men, and their places supplied by men totally unacquainted with square-rigged vessels. The master, purser, boatswain, and carpenter were ordered to be discharged; and the first and third lieutenants were invalided on the morning Captain Anderson took the command, having been surveyed by application from his predecessor: he consequently wrote to the Admiralty for two others, but received a letter from Mr. Croker, expressing *their lordships' surprise that he should have made such an application, when the ship was directed for a particular service; and that they had ordered the two lieutenants to be resurveyed.* But surely this was the strongest possible reason why he should have efficient officers; and we believe that the resurvey was the first of the kind that ever took place under such circumstances: it, however, sanctioned the previous one. With a fatuity or negligence wholly unaccountable, the fore-mast was replaced by one of tick, and so heavy that the officers of the sheerhulk declared, that in hoisting it in it brought the hulk a streak and a half lower in the water than the Caledonia's main-mast had done. Notwithstanding these circumstances, and the most vexatious delays and interruptions arising from contradictory orders which he received, such as taking on board one day a variety of articles, and sending them on shore the next to make room for others, and in the end the whole being discharged to make room for a number of artificers from the dock-yards, with their tools and baggage, he reported the ship ready for sea on the 28th: but after this he was detained a week at Spithead, five days of which the wind was fair, waiting for more artificers; and to make room for them he was obliged to send the lower-deck guns on shore, and to return to the guard-ship fifty of the supernumeraries for the lakes. At last upwards of two hundred and forty artificers, with an enormous quantity of baggage, were embarked, and the Zealous sailed on the 5th September, when she beat down Channel with a westerly wind, loaded like a collier.

During the passage continual gales of wind from N. W. and S. W. were experienced, but by dint of perseverance Captain Anderson subdued every obstacle; and on the 14th Oct. made St. Paul's Island, at the entrance of the gulf of St. Lawrence, having then tolerably fair weather; but which afterwards became so thick and hazy, with a strong gale, that the next land seen was on the Island of Anticosti, near Jupiter river, passing all the islands at the entrance of the gulf without seeing one of them*.

* In addition to the other difficulties and perplexities he had to contend with on the passage, the artificers made an attempt to mutiny and disobey the standing orders of

On the 21st the ship anchored at the Brandy Potts, and Captain Ander-son prepared to carry his orders into execution, which were, after placing the ship in a secure situation, to communicate with Sir J. Yeo, and place at his disposal all the officers and men of the Zealous, leaving only a sufficient number to take care of the ship, and to send all her guns, masts, yards, sails, rigging, stores, &c. to the lakes ; but the pilot having started many difficulties about carrying the ship through the Traverse, as she drew twenty-three feet nine inches of water, Captain Anderson, on the following morning, made the signal to the signal-post on Hare Island, that he had on board artificers and seamen for the lakes, and requested transports might be sent down to receive them. On the evening of that day the Junon arrived at the Brandy Potts, and Captain Anderson then learned from Captain Upton the impossibility of wintering the ship in any place at or near Quebec, and recommended him to leave the St. Lawrence as soon as he had forwarded the supplies for the lakes. He was also waited on by Mr. Lumley, the harbour-master of Quebec, who likewise assured him of the utter impracticability of wintering the ship at Quebec. Mortified and disappointed at being thus prevented from carrying the whole of his orders into execution, he proceeded as high as the Kamarouski Islands, and having forwarded every thing to the lakes that could be spared out of the ship's stores, he considered it now as his only duty to take every measure for the safety of the ship; and conceiving it would be unjustifiable in him to run the double risk of passing the Traverse by going up and coming down again, he returned, with a most heavy heart and anxious mind, to the Brandy Potts, to wait the arrival of stores and provisions from Quebec, and then returned to England. On his arrival at Spithead he sent the following letter to the Admiralty, explanatory of his conduct and motives:

H. M. S. ZEALOUS, SPITHEAD, *Dec.* 15, 1814.

SIR,—Their lordships would be informed by my letter of the 30th October (No. 5) of the impracticability of the Zealous wintering at Quebec, and that I wished for the benefit of Captain Hancock's advice for my future proceedings. He arrived at the Brandy Potts on the 9th November, and I had not been many minutes on board the Liffey when I received a letter from Sir George Prevost, requesting that I would take transports with the 27th regiment under convoy

the ship, at the instigation of their preachers, who were the most troublesome persons on board : by a happy application of firmness and lenity, Captain Anderson was, however, able to suppress it in the bud, without having recourse to severe measures.

to Halifax, whither he understood, as he said, the Zealous was to sail on the 15th. Although I had never expressed any design of going to Halifax at that late season of the year without a pilot, who could not be procured, I did not hesitate, having the sanction of Captain Hancock's approbation, to undertake seeing them in there, provided they arrived at the Brandy Potts so as to enable me to sail at the appointed day; which they could not fail to do with only common diligence, as they were embarked at Montreal on the 6th, and were to be at Quebec on the 9th. At the same time I acquainted Sir George, through the quarter-master-general's department at Quebec, that the ship would be ready by the 12th, and might have been so much sooner, had it not been for the unaccountable delay in getting supplies from Quebec; but that notwithstanding the lateness of the season, I would wait till the 15th. In the mean time I forwarded from this ship, by different vessels, the ordnance stores mentioned in the inclosed list to Sir James Yeo, and completed my water. Seeing no appearance of the transports with the 27th regiment, although the wind had been fair from the day of their embarkation, I sent a telegraphic dispatch on the 13th, stating that the ship was ready for sea, and waited only for the transports to sail. On the evening of the 14th a very strong N. W. wind set in, which, continuing during the night with great violence, gave me great apprehension for the safety of the ship, the winter having already set in with greater severity and much sooner than had been known for twenty years before. The pilot expressing his uneasiness if the ship continued longer, the N. W. winds having now, as he supposed, set in, and it becoming more moderate on the morning of the 15th, I sailed at noon, with the wind at N. N. W. and got clear of the gulf of St. Lawrence on the 21st, after experiencing a very heavy gale from the N. E. with very thick hazy weather, rain, sleet, and snow.

Left thus to the exercise of my own discretion, I conceived it my duty, as there was a commander-in-chief on the station, to repair to Bermuda and join Sir Alexander Cochrane; but having made little progress, in consequence of experiencing hard gales of wind, in which I split two main-top-sails (one not repairable), and on the morning of the 28th the wind coming to S. S. W. and increasing to a perfect storm, and directly against my proceeding to Bermuda, having only a fore-top-sail bent for a main one, the other sails much worn; no spare top-mast on board in case of accident; an old fore-top-mast, sprung in two places, for a main one; no rope to reeve for lifts, braces, &c. and those now in use several times spliced and unfit to be trusted, from the almost constant gales the ship had been in from her leaving England; and the carpenter reporting that the ship was very weak and complained much forward, making at the rate of from eight to twelve feet water in the twenty-four hours; I called the officers together to consult on the propriety of contending longer against contrary gales of wind in the state the ship was in, and their unanimous opinion was, that it would be unsafe to contend farther, and that it would be most proper to bear up for a port in England, while there was yet a prospect of doing it with any probability of success : I accordingly bore up under a reefed fore-sail in a heavy gale of wind, with a high sea, which continued, with more or less violence, ever since, and having brought the ship nearly eight hundred leagues in a constant gale of wind, I have the honour of acquainting you, for their lordships' information, with her arrival in this port almost a complete wreck.

   J. W. Croker, *Esq.*   (Signed,)   James Anderson.

But these reasons not being considered satisfactory, a court-martial was held upon him in the month of January 1815, a month after his arrival, and he was tried for neglect of duty in not communicating with Sir J. Yeo; for disobedience of orders in not wintering the Zealous at Quebec; and for not remaining at the Brandy Potts till the arrival of the transports with the 27th regiment on board. Captain Anderson, however, most fully and satifactorily proved, that he did communicate with Sir James Yeo the very first opportunity he had of so doing; that there was no place at or near Quebec where so large a ship as the Zealous could be laid up with safety during the winter; and that, from the tempestuous state of the weather, and the advanced season of the year, the ship could not remain in the river longer than she did, waiting for the transports, without the most imminent danger to both ship and crew. The court therefore, after maturely and deliberately considering the case, unanimously came to the following sentence : " *That it was not practicable for the said Captain Anderson to have proceeded at that advanced season of the year from the Brandy Potts, in the river St. Lawrence, to Quebec, in his Majesty's said ship Zealous, without an unjustifiable risk of the safety of the ship; that he communicated with Commodore Sir James Yeo, both by telegraph and letter, as soon as he had an opportunity of so doing; and that, from the information he obtained from the most competent sources, and the repeated urgent representations of the pilot, he was fully justified in returning down the river St. Lawrence at the time he did so, without longer waiting for the transports with the first battalion of the 27th regiment; and doth adjudge the said Captain Anderson to be acquitted, and he is hereby acquitted accordingly.*"

On returning his sword, the president complimented him in very flattering terms, as did all the officers composing the court. The Zealous having been paid off, Captain Anderson waited on Lord Melville, when a conversation is said to have taken place on the subject, of which the following is the substance: His lordship having expressed his disappointment, and that of the Admiralty, at Captain Anderson's not wintering at Quebec according to his orders, the latter said, "that he was also much disappointed, as well as mortified, to find that he was sent on a service which it was impossible to perform;" and then added, "had your lordship sent me on any duty that was practicable, you would not have been disappointed, nor should I have been subjected to the mortification I have experienced: but I suppose your lordship is now convinced there is no place about Quebec where the ship could have wintered in safety."—"Oh!" said his lordship, "*if you had lost the ship there would not have been a word said about it!*"—Naturally surprised at such an assertion, Captain Anderson replied, with some degree of warmth, "My lord, I could not expect such an avowal, much less that it would have been acted upon: I have been all my life in his Majesty's service, and this is the first time I ever heard it insinuated that it was the duty of a captain of a man-of-war to lose his ship, except to prevent her falling into the possession of the enemy. Had I obstinately persevered, after all the information and warnings I received, as to the danger, from those best acquainted with the place, I should not have had so complete a justification to offer for my conduct, as I was fortunately enabled to produce to the court-martial by which you were pleased to try me." His lordship continuing to make several inquiries whether the ship might not have been laid up at several places, Captain Anderson endeavoured to point out the reasons why it was impossible; but on his lordship appearing dissatisfied, Captain Anderson continued: "My lord, I have proved to the satisfaction of a court-martial, some of the members of which were well acquainted with the St. Lawrence, that it was altogether impracticable for a ship of so large a size to lie in safety during the winter; and I beg to thank your lordship for having brought the subject to a trial, as the unanimous acquittal of the court puts it out of the power of *any one* to make any unfavourable observations or insinuations on my conduct." To which his lordship immediately added, "All I have to say is, *that if Canada fall, it will be entirely owing to your not wintering the Zealous at Quebec!*" At hearing this heavy and serious accusation, Captain Anderson was of course greatly surprised and astonished; but, after a few moments of reflection, he replied, "I am very sorry to differ so much in opinion from your lordship; but this assertion goes the length of saying, that if Canada fall, it will be *in consequence of my not having performed an impossibility*. Should it, however, fall, I rather think, *it will be in consequence of proper supplies, in proper ships, not having been sent there at a proper season of the year*." Here the conversation ended.

To some persons enough may appear to have been said on this subject, but we cannot dismiss it without offering two or three observations. From authentic documents, it appears, that commissioners from the United States and Great Britain met at Ghent 6th August, 1814; and though it was well known that Canada was in great want of warlike stores and supplies, none were attempted to be sent till the negociations had failed: great exertions were then made to repair this neglect, and some transports were ordered to sail thither on the 1st September from Spithead, and others again from Cork towards the end of that month, the time which, in common prudence, they ought to have been at Quebec; while the particular reinforcements required by Sir James Yeo on the lakes were delayed to a still longer period. They indeed appear not to have been thought of till the very last moment, when it was hastily resolved to send the Zealous, an old rotten ship, which had long previously been doubled, though in some degree strengthened with additional knees, while her decks were kept from falling in by long clamps of wood placed diagonally from her keel to her quarter-deck; which, in fact, had six years before been surveyed, and, after a slight repair, reported fit only for Channel service for two years! Such was the condition of the ship that was now fixed on by the Admiralty-Board to perform one of the most dangerous and difficult services a ship could be sent on at that season of the year. It was indeed considered by the shipwrights at Portsmouth dock-yard, when she was taken into dock, quite a miracle that she had survived the gales of wind, snow-storms, and other dangers which she had experienced; and her being at last safely in port was attributed solely to the experience and professional abilities of Captain Anderson. To prove still farther the dangers and difficulties experienced on this unfortunate occasion, we may observe, that the weather was so thick, both on entering and leaving the St. Lawrence, as prevented any one on board from seeing any one of the islands lying in its entrance between St. Paul's and Anticosti; and that shortly after her arrival at Spithead (which she reached under reefed courses—a circumstance, we believe, which seldom happens), she was surveyed, and being found completely rotten, was broke up. It ought also to be observed, that Captain Anderson carried the ship from the Western Islands to the Kamarouski Islands, in the river St. Lawrence, with a fore-top-mast sprung in two places and reefed for a main-top-mast, and being unable to get a supply of top-masts from Quebec, he was obliged to proceed to sea again, and brought the ship to Spithead in the same manner.

From the very ungracious reception which Captain Anderson met with at the Admiralty, we think we are warranted in saying, that the Board never expected the Zealous would again reach England; and judging from the expression of Lord Melville, that if Captain Anderson " had lost his ship, there would not have been a word said about it," we cannot believe that he wished she ever should return. The reason for this appears obvious: for had the war continued during the ensuing spring, and any disaster had befallen Canada, or any disasters had occurred on the lakes, in consequence of the shameful neglect in sending out reinforcements at the proper season; had the ship been lost, which appears to have been so fully expected; had the disaster been what it would, it would, no doubt, have been attributed to her loss; and she could easily, by a flourish of rhetoric, have been described as full of stores and every thing requisite for the object in view, although, in fact, she had not sufficient for her own use for three months: hence a wide field would have been left open for exclaiming against the winds, the weather, tempestuous seas, and a war of the elements; and hence a justification of the conduct of those who had so shamefully neglected their duty.

We shall not assert that the sending out such an old, worn-out, rotten ship as the Zealous, with such a cargo, at such a season, to such a place, without obtaining better information as to its capacity to afford her proper shelter during the winter, was a wanton, cruel, or designed exposure of the ship and the lives of 800 men, to answer a political or private purpose, but shall leave it to others to say, whether a more rash, inconsiderate, inconsistent, deplorably ignorant and desperate undertaking could possibly have entered the imagination of man. So irresolute, undetermined, and confused were the ideas of those who ordered her on the service, that during the time she was fitting out scarcely a day passed without some alteration in her orders; first in her destination, next as to the description of persons to be sent out, and then again as to what articles should be sent out. We must also mention another circumstance, which forms a most remarkable feature in this remarkable case, and which perhaps will scarcely be believed—that during the time the Zealous was fitting out, two troop-ships, fully adequate to the intended service, were then lying at Spithead ready for sea, and it is believed were there on her return.

The court-martial, however, gave Captain Anderson an opportunity to vindicate his character, which he did in so ample and satisfactory a manner, as greatly added to his high professional character, and thus, as he told Lord Melville, put it out of the power of any one to make remarks upon his conduct which should be detrimental to his fair fame and reputation. The sentence of the court was of course highly satisfactory to his feelings, and as naturally galling to those by whom it was ordered. Respecting the first charge, the court plainly stated that it was not practicable for him to execute his orders. What then must be thought of those who could thus unnecessarily expose the lives of 800 men? On the second charge his accusers were convicted of wilful misstatement, in charging him with not having communicated with Sir J. Yeo, as he proved that he had done so, and that he had sent them copies of his correspondence. From the sentence on the third charge, it appears that the court confirmed his judgment in preferring the opinion and experience of those on the spot, to that of their lordships at a distance, who were totally ignorant of the local inconveniences; as every one will allow, that to be in danger, and to view it at a distance, are two distinct things. But it would seem that they overlooked all minor considerations for the purpose of gratifying a spirit of revenge, raised by the disappointment they experienced in the ship not having been lost, as Captain Anderson clearly proved that he waited for the 27th regiment as long as he promised to do, or was even requested to do, and perhaps longer than was altogether prudent at that late season of the year, all the pilots declaring that so large a ship had never been in the St. Lawrence so late in the season.

From memorials and documents presented by Captain Anderson to the Admiralty, we there find it stated, that he has been in one general action with the enemy's fleets; has been upwards of forty-five times in action with the enemy, either with their batteries or their ships of war or privateers; and that his conduct has been invariably honoured with the approbation of some of the most distinguished officers in the navy and of the Admiralty-Board. Indeed, from all that we have been able to ascertain, he is considered by all those who have been on service with him as a most skilful officer, and equal to any situation in the service. When he commanded a sloop of war in the Downs, she was held up as an example of neatness, good order, and discipline, and that too without any severity of conduct being indulged in. Indeed his character became so well known for his attention to the comforts and accommodation of his crew, that whenever any impressed men were sent on board, they never failed to enter before they had been there twenty - four hours. It is but justice to the crew to observe, that, animated by the example which was invariably set them by their captain, they never failed in the performance of their duty, whether at sea, in port, or against the enemy. In his early youth Captain Anderson had the good fortune to receive a superior education, so that when he left school he was considered an excellent classical scholar: the profession, however, which he made choice of is not very favourable to study; and it is therefore not very extraordinary that he should have neglected classical pursuits. Study, however, was not entirely omitted, as he steadily pursued those branches which might be beneficial to him in his profession; and we understand he is well versed in mathematics, and knows sufficient of astronomy to be able to calculate the eclipses of the sun and moon. He has also written several pieces, principally relating to the navy, which were published in the periodical publications of the day; and during the period that Lord Mulgrave presided at the Admiralty, he presented his lordship with a plan for the preservation of the health of seamen in the West Indies; and when Mr. Yorke was at the head of the Admiralty, he proposed a plan for the checking of smuggling in the narrow seas, for both of which he received the thanks of Mr. Yorke and the Board. The only production, however, in print which bears his name is, " Observations on the Peculiarities of the Tides between Fairleigh and the North Foreland," inserted in the Transactions of the Royal Society for the year 1819*.

* From a vast variety of documents, now in the Record-Office, and which were written by some of the most respectable and distinguished officers in the navy and army, all proving, in the most satisfactory manner, the zeal and abilities manifested by Captain Anderson on various occasions, we select the following as a specimen :

DEAL, *Jan.* 16, 1812.

SIR,— I have perused with much pleasure the contents of the several letters you gave me yesterday, and I congratulate you on having obtained the approbation of such dis-

Captain Anderson was born in April 1765, and married, in September 1790, Jane Ann Thornhill, daughter of the Rev. Thomas Harris, A.M. rector of St. Lucy's parish in the Island of Barbadoes; a lady descended, both by father's and mother's side, from the most distinguished of the old Scotch and English families who there sought an asylum from the political or religious persecutions of the times at home. They have had a large family, but none now survive.

tinguished officers for your conduct on so many important services; I am happy to add mine in testimony of your merits since you have been under my command.

(Signed,)   THOMAS FOLEY.

HISTORICAL MEMOIRS OF
CAPTAIN WILSON RATHBORNE, C. B.

THIS gentleman has the character of being one of the most skilful, worthy, and modest men in the British navy: but though the latter quality is highly praiseworthy, it may be carried too far; and we fear that to this circumstance is to be attributed the slowness which took place in his promotion. Such a man is sure to have the love, the friendship, and good wishes of all mankind, though at the same time he finds himself opposed and thwarted in his views, and others, from their more boisterous and confident conduct, preferred before him. We may, however, affirm, that real personal courage and true fortitude of mind are more likely to be found in the modest humble man, than in the proud and presumptuous: " pride may make a man violent, but humility will make him firm."

Captain Rathborne is a native of Ireland, being born in Galway, July 16, 1748, but descended from a Lancashire family; his father was the Rev. Richard Rathborne, a clergyman of the established church, and his mother was a daughter of Commodore Wilson, who served his country with great credit during the reign of Queen Anne. He first entered the naval service, in 1763, as a midshipman on board the Niger, commanded by his friend and patron, Sir Thomas Adams, Bart. with whom he continued in different ships and on different stations till the hour of his death, which took place, in 1770, on board the Romney of 50 guns, on the North American station. In that ship Mr. Rathborne returned to England and continued in her till the following year, when he was removed to the Royal William, at the particular request of the late Lord Hood, who commanded her. He afterwards joined the Hunter sloop, commanded by Captain Thomas Mackenzie, with whom he again proceeded to North America. During the siege of Quebec by the Americans, Mr. Rathborne was attached as first lieutenant to the naval battalion formed from different ships, and landed to co-operate in its defence; and when the enemy attempted to carry the town by storm, he was detached to cut off their retreat: the attempt of the enemy proving abortive, they were intercepted on their return, and the whole made prisoners. Sir Guy Carleton, in his dispatches announcing the event, acknowledged the important services of the naval battalion; but it was not attended with any promotion to Mr. Rathborne. In the ensuing spring he was in the left wing of the army which marched out under Lord Dorchester to raise the siege, which was fortunately attended with the most complete success. For four years subsequently Mr. Rathborne acted as master of the Hunter sloop, was still employed on the North American station, and during that period saw and partook of a great variety of service. In 1780 he returned to England, and being introduced by Captain Thomas Mackenzie to Lord Sandwich, he was presented with a lieutenant's commission; and still at the recommendation of Captain Mackenzie, he went with Captain Sir Edmund Affleck in the Bedford, and shared in two general actions on the coast of America— those between Admirals Arbuthnot and M. de Ternay, and Admiral Graves and the Count de Grasse. He afterwards proceeded to the West Indies, where he participated in the honours acquired by Sir Samuel Hood at St. Kitt's, and by Sir George Rodney on the 9th and 12th April, on which occasions the Bedford was particularly distinguished. After the latter action he became first lieutenant of the Bedford, and continued in that situation during the remainder of the war, which unfortunately terminated without any farther notice or attention being paid to the merits and services of Lieutenant Rathborne. During the Dutch armament of 1787, Sir Edmund Affleck was nominated for the chief command on the Jamaica station, and Lieutenant Rathborne was appointed to his flag-ship, the Atlas of 98 guns; but in consequence of the existing dispute being amicably arranged, Sir Edmund's appointment did not take place, and he recommended Lieutenant Rathborne to Captain H. C. Christian, who received him on board his ship. In the same year, however, Sir Edmund was appointed to the chief command at Portsmouth, and being anxious for Lieutenant Rathborne's welfare, again applied for him; but he unfortunately died the day he was to have hoisted his flag : Lieutenant Rathborne therefore remained with Captain Christian in the Colossus.

In 1792, Mr. Rathborne was appointed first lieutenant of the Captain of 74 guns, and sailed to the Mediterranean. "After the occupation of Toulon, the Captain was sent by Lord Hood to dismantle the forts and batteries on the Hieres Islands and opposite shore; the latter and most difficult part of which duty was performed by Lieutenant Rathborne, in the presence of a vastly superior republican force. He afterwards distinguished himself by his exertions in weighing the Imperieuse, a large frigate that had been scuttled by the French in Port Especia; and on her being commissioned by Captain Charles Cunningham, he was appointed to act as commander in the Speedy of 14 guns, from which vessel he returned to the Captain, in consequence of his being superseded a few days after by one of the admiral's own lieutenants, the present Sir George Cockburn. During the ensuing siege of St. Fiorenzo, Lieutenant Rathborne served on shore, under the orders of Captain Samuel Hood*." He was also present in Admiral Hotham's action, and whilst closely engaging the Ca Ira, he was severely wounded in the right arm and head, through which he lost the sight of his right eye. For his conduct on this occasion he was promoted to the rank of commander, but obtained no farther employment till 1797, when he was appointed to the Good Design, an armed ship, and was constantly employed with convoys till 1800, when he was removed to the Racoon of 18 guns, and employed off Boulogne for fourteen months; during which time no British vessel was carried into that port, and only one into Calais. He continued in the command of the Racoon, serving in the Channel, Mediterranean, and the West Indies, till October 1802, when he received a commission as post-captain, which ought in fairness and justice to have been bestowed upon him years before. He was then appointed, whilst on the Jamaica station, to the Santa Margaretta; and in 1803 returned to England with a convoy, under the orders of Captain Bayntun. During the voyage he was in a gale of wind, and was separated, with a great part of the convoy, from the commanding officer for several days; but the whole arrived in perfect safety, and Captain Rathborne had the satisfaction to receive the thanks of the merchants of London connected with the convoy through the secretary of the Admiralty. The Santa Margaretta having been refitted, he was employed in Channel service, cruising along the French coast, and harassing the enemy's trade. "Whilst thus employed, she fell in with the squadron under Sir R. Strachan, whose success in capturing four French line-of-battle ships in November 1805, may be in a great measure attributed to the persevering exertions and gallant conduct of Captain Rathborne, who, availing himself of his frigate's superior sailing, closed with and harassed the enemy for three hours and a half before Captain Baker of the Phœnix got up to his assistance, and for six hours and a half before the commodore and his

* Marshall.

squadron arrived.   On that occasion his ship, although she had only one
man killed and one wounded, suffered much in her hull, masts, sails, and
rigging : her conduct indeed was conspicuous throughout ; and the officers of the French admiral's ship afterwards asserted, that she killed and
wounded several of their men, among them the nephew of Murat King
of Naples, shot away much of their rigging, and greatly impeded their
progress.   Sir Richard Strachan was so much pleased with the conduct
of Captain Rathborne, that he had a drawing made of the action, representing the Santa Margaretta harassing the enemy's rear, and presented
it to him as a mark of his admiration; and from which the plate was
copied which we have inserted in the *Naval Chronology**.   Captain
Rathborne was also presented with a sword by the Committee of the
Patriotic Fund.

" Captain Rathborne was soon after appointed to the Foudroyant of
80 guns; a circumstance that gave him considerable pain, as, independent
of his disinclination to remove from a cruising frigate to a blockading
ship, he was unwilling to part from his officers and crew, whose conduct
on every occasion had given him the greatest satisfaction, and in whom
he had every confidence.   Captain Loring, the officer who had been appointed to succeed him in the Santa Margaretta, observed his distress,
and generously forbore to use the commission he had received from the
Admiralty, until the pleasure of their lordships could be ascertained; a
forbearance worthy of record.   The result proved highly gratifying to
both parties; Captain Rathborne being continued in the command of
the Santa Margaretta, and his worthy brother officer soon after compensated for the spontaneous sacrifice he had made by an appointment to a
frigate of superior class."   In 1806 he was detached from the Bay with
ten sail of West Indiamen: on the passage he fell in with two French
squadrons, from which he had the good fortune to escape; and on his
safe arrival at Barbadoes, the masters of the ships under his convoy
presented him with their thanks for the great skill, care, and attention he
had manifested throughout the voyage.

Captain Rathborne continued in command of the Santa Margaretta
till December 1807, when, being completely decayed and worn out, she
was put out of commission.   In 1808 he was appointed to command the
Essex sea-fencibles; in 1810, to regulate the impress service at Shields,
Sunderland, and Newcastle; and in 1822, to superintend the ships in

* Vol, I. p. 141.

ordinary at Chatham. Whilst engaged in the impress service, he made several applications to be employed afloat, but they all failed. This disappointment, however, did not cause him to relax his exertions in the service committed to his charge; and he had the satisfaction to know, that he raised double the number of men, at those places, that had previously been done in the same period of time. In 1815 he was nominated a Companion of the Bath. From the number of distinguished officers under whom Captain Rathborne has been employed, and amongst whom may be enumerated Lords Keith and St. Vincent, Sir W. Cornwallis, Sir C. Cotton, Sir T. Duckworth, Sir T. Graves, Sir R. Strachan, Sir P. Durham, Sir I. Pellew, Sir H. Hotham, Sir R. King, Sir H. Bayntun, and Sir J. Wood, from all of whom he received the highest testimonials of professional merit, his character must be considered as standing high in the service.

Captain Rathborne married, in 1805, the youngest daughter of John French, Esq. late of Loughrea, in the county of Galway, by whom he has three sons, one of whom is a midshipman in the navy. His sister was the mother of John Wilson Croker, Esq. secretary to the Admiralty.

HISTORICAL MEMOIRS OF

CAPTAIN SIR CHRISTOPHER COLE, K.C.B.

PATRIOTISM, in the unsophisticated sense of the word, comprises nearly all that is elevated in the human mind. The real patriot, superior to all party, acts, feels, and lives for his country; he deplores her poverty, but rejoices in her wealth; sympathizes in her losses, but exults in her success; mourns over her defeats, but triumphs in her victories; shudders at the idea of her disgrace, but experiences a glowing pride in all that adds to her honour or increases her splendour. To all therefore in whom the spark of patriotism glows, the conduct of Sir Christopher Cole will be read with interest*. His services have been directed to the preservation of his country's interest and honour, and he fortunately " succeeded in realizing the most romantic daring of the age of chivalry†."

Sir Christopher entered the naval service in 1780, before he had completed the tenth year of his age, on board the Royal Oak of 74 guns, commanded by Sir Digby Dent, in which he immediately sailed to America. In the following year he joined the Russell, Commodore F. S. Drake, removed with him into the Princessa, and with that gallant officer shared in five general actions—under Sir Samuel Hood, off Martinique; Admiral Graves, off the Chesapeake; Sir Samuel Hood, at St. Kitt's; and Sir G. Rodney, on the 9th and 12th April. After the last decisive action the fleet rendezvoused at Port Royal, when four brothers out of five, then engaged in the naval and military services of their country, met together. One of the four was the late Captain Francis Cole of the Revolutionaire, who died at the early age of thirty-eight, after having distinguished himself by his gallantry and high professional merit.

During the ensuing ten years, the subject of this Memoir was constantly employed as a midshipman in various parts of the world: with his brother, in the Trepassey, on the Halifax station; in the Atalante,

---

* *Naval Chronicle.*
† Mr. Percival's speech in the House of Commons, when speaking of the capture of Banda.

Captain T. Foley, on the same station; in the Winchelsea, Captain Edward Pellew, on the Newfoundland station; and the Crown, Commodore Cornwallis, in the East Indies. Under such officers he could not fail of acquiring a considerable degree of professional knowledge; and though the time was unfavourable to promotion, yet the excellent foundation which he had laid, and the store of useful information he had collected, in the hour of need brought him into notice, and his advancement in the profession as quickly followed. In 1793 he obtained a lieutenant's commission, and in the following year, in consequence of the character he had obtained under his former commanders, he was appointed by Lord Chatham first lieutenant of the Cerberus, a new frigate, commanded by Captain Drew; although his rank as a lieutenant was only of two months' standing, and two junior lieutenants, the late Captains Stackpoole and Younghusband, were at the same time appointed to her, to secure the situation of first lieutenant to Mr. Cole. We mention this circumstance as a proof, that a sense of his ability and good conduct during the severe trial of a long servitude in a subordinate situation was not lost. In the following year he was appointed to the Sans Pareil, the flag-ship of Lord Hugh Seymour, with whom, in 1799, he proceeded to the West Indies in the Tamar frigate; and after the capture of Surinam, he was promoted to the rank of commander into a corvette taken on that occasion and named after the colony. The active exertions of Captain Cole whilst in command of the Surinam recommended him to Sir John Duckworth, who succeeded Lord Seymour in the chief command, and who, in 1801, appointed him to command his flag-ship the Leviathan. His post-commission was not, however, confirmed till April 1802, in which year he removed to the Southampton frigate, and returned to England. In 1804 he was appointed to the important situation of flag-captain under his old friend Sir Edward Pellew, and sailed with him in the Culloden to the East Indies, where, under the eye of that celebrated commander, he distinguished himself by such a display of zeal, activity, diligence, and seamanship, as to secure his lasting esteem and friendship. In 1807 he was appointed to the Doris, a new frigate launched at Bombay, and served with great credit in every part of the Indian seas, from the Persian Gulf to the Pacific Ocean. He conveyed Colonel Malcolm, ambassador to the Persian court, to Abashir, and having remained there for some time to protect the trade, afterwards received a present of 500*l.* from the governor-general in council. He was afterwards employed in the China seas; and intelligence of the favourable change of affairs in Spain and Portugal being received on that station, he was employed by Admiral Drury, accompanied with the Psyche, on a mission to the governor of the Philippine Islands; and having succeeded in conciliating the constituted authorities, and establishing a friendly communication with those colonies, he received information that two French frigates were on the coast of China, in quest of which he immediately sailed. His exertions, however, were ineffectual, and the crews of both ships suffered greatly from the scurvy and dysentery. So great indeed was the mortality and sickness that prevailed, that when the Doris anchored in Malacca roads, Captain Cole had only one lieutenant, the gunner, and fifty-six men who were capable of assisting him in doing the duties of the ship.

In 1810 Captain Cole was appointed by Admiral Drury to the Caroline frigate, and immediately afterwards was ordered to proceed, with the Piedmontaise frigate, Baracouta brig, and Mandarin transport, having on board 100 men of the Madras European regiment, with a considerable sum in specie, besides large supplies of provisions, to Amboyna, for the protection of that colony. He quitted Madras in the month of May, to effect the passage against a south-east monsoon. On his arrival at Pulo Penang, he determined to attempt the reduction of some of the settlements of the enemy he had to pass on his route to the Banda seas; for which purpose he solicited and obtained from the Company's government at that place a supply of two field-pieces, several scaling-ladders, and twenty artillery-men, with a subaltern officer. After a most difficult passage through innumerable coral reefs, a great part of which had never been traversed by a large ship, the squadron arrived in the sea of Banda the beginning of August. " During the whole of this long passage, the ships' companies had been daily exercised in the use of the pike, sword, and small arms, and in mounting the scaling-ladders, placed against the masts, preparatory to any attempt at escalade. The expertness with which they handled their weapons, and the emulation displayed by them when imitating the storming of a fortress, added to their excellent health (not a man having died since they left Madras) and high spirits, convinced Captain Cole, that, however deficient in numbers, no men could have been found better calculated to ensure success to any hazardous enterprise." When the great strength of the place against which he was about to proceed, which mounted 140 pieces of cannon, and was garrisoned by

700 regular troops and 800 militia, the difficulties of the undertaking, and the vast disparity of the attacking force to that of the enemy, are all duly considered, the capture of Banda will appear, as it really was, an achievement- which, for boldness of conception and courage in the execution, has rarely been equalled, and perhaps never excelled, in the annals of British enterprise. " The Caroline, Piedmontaise, and Baracouta arrived off Banda on the 8th August, and hove to at a considerable distance from the land, to avoid being seen (a hope which was frustrated by some fishing-boats). At ten at night, being about four miles from the harbour, the boats were hoisted out and assembled along side the Caroline, containing 390 men. At twelve they shoved off, under the command of Captain Cole, the weather being then tolerably fine: it soon, however, became dark and squally, attended by a boisterous sea, which occasioned a separation of the boats; and on arriving at the appointed rendezvous, Captain Cole found the original force diminished to 180 men. After remaining until three o'clock, in hopes of being joined by the missing boats, it became necessary to push on for Banda Neira, still three miles off, or to return to our ships, mortified and disappointed. Captain Cole fortunately determined to go on; and, on approaching the shore, we found, by several alarm-guns being fired, that the enemy were expecting us. The badness of the weather, which had before acted against us, now became our protection; for the boats grounded undiscovered, in a heavy squall of wind and rain, within one hundred yards of a battery of ten 24-pounders, which was stormed in the rear; the sentinel was killed by a pike, and sixty men were disarmed without firing a shot. After leaving a guard in the battery, the storming party, headed by Captain Kenah, and the reserve by Captain Cole, proceeded to Fort Belgica, by a narrow path on the skirts of the town. The bugle was then sounding the alarm of our landing : the enemy in Belgica reserved their fire until we got close to the walls. The scaling-ladders were then placed between the guns, and mounted with a rapidity exceeding all belief, notwithstanding a heavy sharp fire from the citadel and the surrounding bushes. After gaining possession of the lower works, the ladders were hauled up and placed against the inner wall. The interval occasioned by this seemed to give the enemy fresh courage; but when they saw the ladders firmly fixed, they seemed quite panic-struck, and fled in all directions, leaving the colonel-commandant and ten men killed, and two captains and thirty men prisoners. The guns near which

the ladders were placed fortunately burnt priming, owing to the heavy rains; and thus we found ourselves in possession of this strong citadel, without the loss of a single man, just in time for the sun to rise on the British flag, and to shew us our commanding situation, having Fort Nassau and the town immediately under our guns. A flag of truce was immediately dispatched by Captain Cole to the governor, offering protection to private property, on the surrender of the island, which was refused. However, a shot from Belgica, and a threat of storming the town and forts, produced an immediate and unconditional surrender; and 700 disciplined troops and 300 militia grounded their arms to us. Captain Cole's feelings at this moment must have been in unison with his followers—proudly grateful. The enemy had notice of the squadron's approach at six o'clock in the afternoon, and dispatched a great part of their force to the place where Admiral Ranier formerly landed; an event which Captain Cole had foreseen*."

Such gallantry and perseverance naturally excited the highest admiration in all who knew how to appreciate heroic conduct; and Captain Cole received the most unbounded praise from the Admiralty, the commander-in-chief, and governor-general in council of India; whilst the enthusiasm and attachment created in the minds of Captain Cole's companions and followers had scarcely any bounds. Captains Foote and Kenah took the lead in bearing testimony to his merits, by sending him the following letter:

Dear Cole,—Kenah and myself request your acceptance of a piece of plate (to be made in England), in commemoration of the gallant manner you led on to and directed the attack and capture of the forts at Banda: it may possibly have been equalled, but can never be surpassed. We therefore hope you will receive it as a testimony of our high esteem and friendship, and admiration of your spirited and noble conduct on the 9th of August. Most sincerely do we both wish that you may live long to enjoy the fruits of your labour, and to follow up your present success. Believe us, dear Cole, your sincere and affectionate friends,

(Signed,)   Charles Foote,
              Richard Kenah.

The officers of the Caroline, Piedmontaise, and Baracouta also presented him with an address of congratulation, and a sword value one

---

* Lieutenant Lyons of the Baracouta's account.—For Captain Cole's official letter, with a representation of the landing of the troops, see Ralfe's *Naval Chronology*, vol. III. p. 64.

hundred guineas, in testimony of their approbation of the gallant and judicious manner in which he conducted the attack.

From the officers of the Hon. Company's troops serving under his orders he received the following address:

Sir,—In addressing you upon the capture of Banda Neira and its dependencies, which secures to the British flag a conquest of great value, the officers of the Hon. Company's troops engaged in that enterprise have to congratulate you and themselves upon the successful issue, under every disadvantage of wind and weather, upon a hostile shore lined with numerous batteries, the enemy aware of and prepared for an attack, so wisely planned and so ably carried into execution under your personal direction. The confidence you inspired all with on the approach to assault Belgica, we are convinced contributed, in a great measure, to the success of the escalade. Your bravery and gallant conduct were so conspicuous on that occasion, that it must secure to you the esteem and admiration of all who are acquainted, as we are, with the circumstances attending the reduction of that strong and important citadel.

As a memorial of the high sense we entertain of the services performed by you on this occasion, and as a mark of our personal esteem and respect, we request you will do us the honour to accept of a sword of the value of one hundred guineas. We further beg leave to assure you, that our warmest wishes for your future success and happiness will always attend you, in whatever situation it may please Providence to fix your lot.   *(Signed by the several Officers.)*

The Dutch colours and two brass guns were presented by Captain Cole to Admiral Drury, the commander-in-chief on the station, from whom he received the following letter:

Sir,—I have great satisfaction in the highly flattering communication you have made to me of the sentiments of yourself and of your brave companions, who so nobly and so successfully carried the supposed impregnable fortress of Banda Neira, the colours of which and two guns taken under your auspices by a handful of men composed of seamen and marines, and the intrepid officers and soldiers of the Madras European regiment, confer on me an honour and happiness far beyond my deserts, but most gratefully and thankfully received as coming from a body of men so highly and particularly distinguished. I beg you to make my acknowledgments to the Banda heroes, whose heartfelt encomiums on their gallant leader do equal honour and justice to themselves, and place on your brow a never-fading laurel.

(Signed,)   W. O'Brien Drury.

From the governor-general in council, through their secretary, he received a highly flattering and complimetary address, from which the following is an extract:

"The details of this brilliant achievement, and of your arrangements for the administration and security of the islands, have been communicated to his lordship in council, who observes, with just admiration, the judgment, ability, and foresight manifested by you in the plan of attack, and the zeal, intrepidity, and precision with which it was carried into effect by the gallant officers and men of the naval and military services under your direction. His lordship and council consider the rapid conquest of a place so strongly fortified by nature and by art, in the face of a superior force, without the loss of a man, as forming a singular event in the annals of British enterprise, reflecting a peculiar degree of credit on your professional skill, and affording an extraordinary instance of discipline, courage, and activity on the part of the men under your command."

In the beginning of the following year, Admiral Drury projected an expedition against the Island of Java; the arrangements for which, in consequence of the illness of the admiral, which caused his death, were superintended by Captain Cole, till the arrival of Commodore Broughton, at which time the whole were nearly ready to sail. On arriving off the island, Captain Cole was intrusted with the direction of landing the troops. "The sloops of war and the Hon. Company's cruisers anchored near the beach in readiness to scour it, and the troop-ships without them, covered by the Caroline, Modeste, and Bucephalus. The rapid approach of the fleet had prevented the enemy from ascertaining the intended place of landing in time to send a force thither to guard it: this being noticed by Captain Cole, he made the signal from the Caroline for the advance of the army to land immediately, then hoisted out his boats, tripped his anchor, and dropped the Caroline nearer to the shore. No time was occupied in arranging the order of the boats, they being ordered to shove off when manned and filled with troops. His example being followed by Captains Elliot and Pelly, and the boats of the men-of-war being sent to assist in conveying the troops, about 8000, with their guns, ammunition, and provisions, were landed in safety by half-past six o'clock. Soon after dark, the British advanced guard had a skirmish with the enemy's patroles, who, but for Captain Cole's alacrity and promptitude in making the above signal, without waiting to complete the arrangement of boats, as usual in such cases, would have taken post in a wood at the back of the beach, and might have occasioned great loss to the invading army. We should here observe, that

Captain Cole had previously volunteered to command the naval battalion appointed to serve on shore; but the presence of Captain Sayer, who was his senior in rank, and equally desirous of the honour, prevented Commodore Broughton from placing him in that honourable post. He subsequently obtained permission from Admiral Stopford to proceed to head-quarters and make an offer of 400 additional seamen, to be commanded by himself, to assist in storming Meester Cornelis, or any of the enemy's positions; but his co-operation was necessarily declined, as such an increase of force was not wanted*." His spirited offer and zealous co-operation throughout the whole of the expedition were highly exemplary, and did not pass without notice. Admiral Stopford intrusted to him the dispatches for the Admiralty, and in noticing Captain Cole's conduct, said, " I send this dispatch by the Caroline; and I am happy to have so good an opportunity as is offered by Captain Cole, who has had a large share in every thing relating to this expedition, and, from his knowledge of all the parts of the operations, can communicate to their lordships the fullest account of them."

In January 1812 the Caroline was paid off, and on that occasion Captain Cole had the gratification of receiving the following address from the crew of that ship, which, if it was not drawn up with all the elegance of diction, conveyed their admiration of his conduct, both as it respected his solicitude for their welfare and his bravery as an officer:

" We, the crew of his Majesty's ship Caroline, wish to give you our most gracious thanks for the care and favour you have shewn to this ship's company, by making you a present of a sword, amounting to one hundred guineas, for your noble and brave conduct when you led us to the storm of Banda, and likewise the zealous bravery in landing our troops at Batavia ; and by accepting of this present you will gratify the wishes of your most obedient ship's company,

(Signed,)   " THE CAROLINES."

The sword was afterwards presented to Captain Cole by the person employed on the occasion, accompanied by the following address:

" SIR,—I am requested by James Macdowal and others, on the part of the crew of his Majesty's frigate Caroline, to present you with this sword, as a testimony of the high esteem and respect they entertain for you as their late commander, in return for the marked attention you at all times paid to them ; for the gallant manner in which you took them into action, and for the honourable manner in which you brought them out of it; for the unceasing zeal you inva-

* Marshall.

riably have manifested for your country's cause, and for the comforts they
have enjoyed whilst they served under your command. They humbly trust you
will accept the same as a pledge of gratitude and a token of veneration for you,
which no time can efface from their memory."

In the month of May Captain Cole received the honour of knighthood, and in the same year was presented with the degree of LL.D.
from the university of Oxford, and also a piece of plate, value three
hundred guineas, from the East India Company. In 1813 he was appointed to the Rippon of 74 guns; and in the month of October, in
company with the Scylla and Royalist, captured the Weser frigate; and
in February 1814 was present at the capture of the San Juan, Spanish
treasure-ship, with a valuable cargo, besides 600,000 dollars in specie on
board. This was the last important act of Captain Cole's professional
career; peace shortly after took place, and he then returned into private
life, having been thirty-four years almost constantly at sea, eighteen of
which he had passed in the East and West Indies; and we may confidently assert, that but few officers have obtained in a greater degree the
confidence and regard of those whom they have commanded.

In 1815 Captain Cole was nominated a K.C.B.; and in the same
year married Lady Mary Talbot, daughter of the late Earl of Ilchester,
and widow of T. M. Talbot, Esq. of Margam Park and Penrice Castle,
Glamorganshire. In 1817 he was elected M.P. for the county of Gla-
morgan, and in 1820 re-elected for the same place.

HISTORICAL MEMOIRS OF
ADMIRAL LORD JAMES O'BRYEN.

HAD not experience proved that every profession has an effect on the mind, manners, and customs of their respective members, it would be worth while to inquire into a circumstance so apparently remarkable: it is, however, self-evident; and perhaps none are more distinguished for those qualities which call forth our admiration, than naval men. We have now had a tolerably extensive opportunity of judging of the conduct, tempers, and dispositions of many of its members, and think we may, without arrogance, assert that, as a body, they yield to no other class or profession in every thing that reflects honour on human nature. In public their actions have borne the most noble testimony of their worth and importance; whilst in private they appear honourable, social, pleasant, generous, and open-hearted, qualities which add lustre to crowns and coronets, stars and ribbons. To embellishments of this description, which are fully participated in by Lord O'Bryen, he adds a most illustrious descent, tracing it in a clear line to the kings of Thomond and Munster. He is the brother of the Marquis of Thomond, and first entered the naval service in 1783, on board the Hebe frigate, commanded by Captain (now Sir) E. Thornborough, who was afterwards joined by Prince William (now Duke of Clarence), as third lieutenant. From this period a close intimacy was formed between young O'Bryen and the prince. On the appointment of his royal highness to command the Pegasus, the former was removed to her as one of the midshipmen, and he continued with the prince during the whole time that his royal highness remained an active member of the profession, not only whilst he commanded the Pegasus, but also the Andromeda and Valiant, from which last ship he was promoted to a lieutenancy, being one of the six which his royal highness had the nomination of at the termination of the Spanish armament. When the war commenced in 1793, Lieutenant O'Bryen was nominated one of the lieutenants of the London, Captain R. G. Keats, the intended flag-ship of his Royal Highness the Duke of Clarence, and she joined the Channel fleet under Lord Howe. His royal highness, however, did not join her; and on its being made known that he did not intend to do so, Lieutenant O'Bryen removed into the Artois, with his relative, Lord Lecale, and afterwards into the Brunswick, in which he was present at the glorious retreat made by Admiral Cornwallis, and remained till she became the flag-ship of Admiral Harvey, when he was appointed first lieutenant of the Indefatigable, Captain Sir Edward Pellew (now Viscount Exmouth), with whom he continued for six months, when he was promoted to the rank of commander into the Childers sloop, and, at the request of Sir Edward, attached to his squadron of frigates. On the 14th February, 1798, he was promoted to post-rank, and appointed to the Thisbe, which ship was shortly after paid off. In 1800 he was appointed to the Emerald frigate, and sailed with a convoy to the West Indies, where he remained till 1804. At the commencement of hostilities, he was at the capture of St. Lucia, on which occasion he led in to cover the landing of the troops, in doing which the Emerald ran aground. Nevertheless, he succeeded in his important object; and on that being completed, the ship was got off, and, with the utmost zeal and promptitude, proceeded in chase of a fine schooner, which was endeavouring to make her escape out of the harbour, but which he captured, after a run of seventy miles to leeward; and for the conduct he displayed throughout received the thanks of Sir Samuel Hood. He was afterwards at the capture of Surinam; and the following extract from Sir Samuel Hood's official letter will prove the active part he took on that occasion:

" Brigadier-General Hughes was ordered on board the Pandour, to endeavour to gain possession of Braams Point; and instructions were sent to Captain O'Bryen, then lying off the bar, to carry this service, in concert with the brigadier, into execution. He, with his usual intrepidity, lost not a moment, but as the tide flowed pushed in over the bar, and anchored close to the battery of seven 18-pounders, followed by Captains Nash and Ferris, in the Pandour and Drake. The fort commenced a brisk fire on the Emerald, but was silenced by a few broadsides after the ships had anchored, without any loss on our side. In it were captured forty-three officers and men, three of whom were wounded*. Not being able to approach nearer in the Centaur, the general and myself removed next morning into the Emerald, and having summoned the colony, received an answer containing a refusal of the terms. The moment, therefore, the tide

* On this occasion Captain O'Bryen was the first who landed, striking the Dutch colours, and substituting in their place those of England; but in the execution of this duty was slightly wounded.

served, every effort was made to get up the river, which, from the shallowness of the water, was very difficult, the Emerald having passed through the mud in three feet less than she drew.

" The indefatigable zeal of Captains O'Bryen and Nash in arranging and forming the supplies, and Captains Maxwell, Ferris, Waring, and Richardson in giving aid to the army, as well as Captain Kemp, agent for transports, claims my warmest applause*."

After the reduction of Surinam, Captain O'Bryen proceeded to Antigua with prisoners, and remained cruising for the protection of that and the adjacent islands. At that moment the notorious Victor Hughes commanded at Guadaloupe, who, at a former period, declining no arts however inhuman, and no measures however dangerous, for extending the arms and influence of republicanism, by fitting out small expeditions, and aided by means of numerous emissaries and a laxity of vigilance on the part of his opponents, was too often successful, now attempted a repetition of his former conduct, and ordered one of his marauding armaments to make a descent on the Island of Antigua. Of this intention of the enemy Captain O'Bryen fortunately obtained information, and fell in with it shortly after it left Basse-Terre; but being to leeward and in a calm, he could not, during daylight, get sufficiently near to prevent their getting into one of their small harbours: here, however, he attacked them with his boats, though protected by a battery, drove the greater part on shore, and brought out an armed schooner; and by orders found on board, it appeared that a general officer and a number of troops had been embarked; that a landing was to have been effected on the Island of Antigua, the arsenal to be burnt, the island plundered, and the governor conveyed to Basse-Terre, for whose release, no doubt, a considerable ransom was expected. Had the enemy been successful, it is evident that much slaughter, if not total destruction, to the inhabitants of Antigua would have been the result; but from this calamity they were rescued by the zeal and activity of Captain O'Bryen, and it was consequently duly appreciated by the legislature and the whole colony. Upon the receipt of the intelligence, Lord Lavington immediately dispatched a message to the assembly, in which he said, " I am persuaded that you will concur with me in opinion that we cannot pause a moment on the extent of our obligations to Captain O'Bryen, without deciding on the public acknowledgments

---

* For official letter, see RALFE's *Naval Chronology*, vol. I. p. 72.

which are due to the vigilance and activity of that excellent officer, and the gallantry of those brave men employed in this service."

The privy council immediately came to the following resolutions:

"His Excellency the Captain-General having informed the Board that he had received a letter from Captain O'Bryen of his Majesty's ship Emerald, giving him an account of his having intercepted, to the north-ward of Guadaloupe, a number of French sloops and schooners, having on board a body of troops, apparently with an intent of coming over to this or some of the neighbouring islands; and his excellency having laid Captain O'Bryen's letter on the subject before the Board, and desired its advice, it was of opinion, that his lordship should be requested to communicate to Captain O'Bryen the high sense which this Board enter-tains of the vigilance, zeal, and good conduct of Captain O'Bryen on this occasion; and to desire Captain O'Bryen to accept the unanimous thanks of the Board for the essential service he has performed to this and his Majesty's other islands in these seas, by defeating the armament that had sailed with a view to make a descent on some of the islands, and for his spirited exertions in cutting out three of the vessels that had formed the expedition, from under the enemy's guns in the bay of the Hayes.

" That it is the opinion of this Board, that his lordship should further be requested to send a vessel, at the public expense, to the commanders-in-chief of his Majesty's land and sea forces, to inform them of the pre-sent danger that threatens this island, and English Harbour in particular, and to solicit such a force for the protection of the same as the circum-stances of the case require; and, in the mean time, to use his exertions with Captain O'Bryen to get him not to leave the neighbourhood of Gua-daloupe and these islands until an answer shall arrive from the com-mander-in-chief, that thus he may have an opportunity of completing the work which he has commenced with so much honour to himself and those under his command, and with so much advantage to these colonies."

The House of Assembly came to similar resolutions; and, as a further proof of the high estimation in which they held the services performed by Captain O'Bryen, voted a sum of two hundred guineas, for the pur-chase of a sword to be presented to him. In the month of October 1804 he sailed for England, with a convoy under his protection: but before he did so, in consequence of his attention to the mercantile inter-ests, the merchants of Antigua came to the following unanimous resolution: "That the thanks of this meeting be given to Captain O'Bryen, commanding his Majesty's ship Emerald, for his judicious, disinterested, and effectual attention to the application made by his Excellency Lord Lavington, on the sailing of the homeward-bound fleet in July last, by affording convoy in the ship under his command to the vessels at this island, to the number of fourteen, to the Island of Tortola; by which means alone the said ships (which otherwise must have remained in port) were enabled to arrive safe at the general rendezvous and proceed home with the fleet, his Majesty's revenue was secured, and the trade and credit of the colony protected and promoted."

In about ten days after leaving the West Indies, in the month of October, he experienced a severe gale of wind, which carried away the Emerald's rudder, and otherwise caused her considerable damage. Not judging it prudent at that season of the year, especially with a crew in so weakly and sickly a state as the Emerald's then was, to enter the Channel in so crippled a state, he made every arrangement he could for the safety of the convoy; he stood to the northward and westward, and having reached Madeira, he had there a rudder made, which brought the ship to England, which he reached in February 1805. On arriving at Spithead, every ship that could be sent to sea was preparing to join the Channel fleet under Sir A. Gardner, in consequence of information being received that the Brest fleet was about to sail. The Diadem was then lying at anchor, and in consequence of her captain, Sir H. Popham, being in London attending an investigation in the House of Commons, Captain O'Bryen immediately offered his services to carry her to sea, which were accepted, and, by telegraph, he was ordered to proceed in her off Ushant. Having cruised under the orders of Admiral Gardner for about a month, and the enemy shewing no intention to put to sea, he returned to Spithead, and the Emerald having been paid off, he retired on half-pay. In November 1809 his Majesty was graciously pleased to grant, as an especial favour, to Captain O'Bryen, his brothers and sisters, the same precedency as if their father, who died in 1801, had survived his brother, the late marquis, who died in 1808 without male issue.

In 1813 he was appointed to command the Warspite, attached to the Channel fleet; and in June 1814 embarked troops in the river Charente for service in America, to which coast he proceeded, accompanied by the

Asia and a convoy. He sailed up the river St. Lawrence, and anchored opposite the city of Quebec, being the first instance, we believe, of a line-of-battle ship of that class going so high up. It is not, however, generally considered safe for them to proceed beyond the Brandy Potts. On his return to England the Warspite was paid off; and in May 1825 he was promoted to the rank of rear-admiral.

His lordship has been twice married, and is heir presumptive to the marquisate of Thomond, now enjoyed by his brother.

HISTORICAL MEMOIRS OF
ADMIRAL ANDREW SMITH.

OWING, we believe, purely to a want of interest, it has been the lot of this gentleman to pass the greater part of his life, at least of the time which has elapsed since the date of his post-commission, without any active employment. This is the more extraordinary, seeing how actively he was employed all the preceding part of it, with what great and distinguished characters he acted, in what scenes he was an actor, and in what glories he shared. He is a native of Scotland, descended from a respectable family, and was born in Edinburgh on the 20th March, 1763. Having completed an education suitable for his intended mode of life, Mr. Smith first went to sea in 1779, on board the Princess of Wales hired armed ship, employed in the Channel and North Sea. He was afterwards placed on board the Santa Margaretta, and from thence removed to the Victory, bearing the flag of Admiral Geary, with whom he assisted at the capture of a valuable convoy of French merchant-vessels from St. Domingo in July 1780. In the following year he was placed on board the Fortitude, Captain (the late Sir Richard) Bickerton, with whom he proceeded, under the chief command of Admiral Darby, to the relief of Gibraltar.

Sir Hyde Parker having hoisted his flag on board the Fortitude, Mr. Smith proceeded with him to the North Sea, and was of course present at the hard-fought and bloody battle off the Dogger bank, when the Fortitude had 20 men killed and 67 wounded. Sir Hyde having struck his flag, the Fortitude, having been repaired, was attached to the Channel fleet, under the command of Admiral Barrington, and assisted in the capture of Le Pégase and a convoy of transports and merchantmen. She was afterwards put under the command of Lord Howe, proceeded with him to the relief of Gibraltar, and in the action with the combined fleet had two men killed and nine wounded. During the ensuing peace Mr. Smith proceeded to the coast of Guinea, and thence to the West Indies, on board the Rattler sloop: on the latter station he was removed by Sir Richard Hughes into his flag-ship, the Adamant of 50 guns, and continued with him till his arrival in England in 1786. In 1789 he proceeded with Sir Richard to the coast of America, and was promoted by him to the rank of lieutenant in the Rattler on the 10th August, 1790, in which he continued for two years.

Immediately after the commencement of hostilities in 1793, Lieutenant Smith was appointed to the Incendiary fire-ship, in which he served till August 1794, when he was appointed first lieutenant of the Defence of 74 guns, Captain Gambier, and afterwards removed to the Prince George of 98 guns, in which he served in the action off l'Orient; and for his conduct on that occasion was promoted to the rank of commander. He shortly after had the command of the Calypso sloop of war, in which he was actively employed in the Channel for several months; but that was the only vessel he commanded previous to his promotion to post-rank, which took place in January 1797.

It is, however, a remarkable circumstance, that notwithstanding he had been so long and actively employed as a junior officer, notwithstanding he had during the whole time that he was a lieutenant always held the situation of first lieutenant, mostly in line-of-battle ships, repeatedly distinguished himself, and had received the thanks of his superior officers, he could not succeed in obtaining a post-ship till November 1813, when Admiral Sir W. Johnstone Hope selected him for his flag-captain of the Latona, when he was commander-in-chief at Leith. The interim was not, however, passed in idleness or inactivity, as in 1805 he was appointed to command the sea-fencibles at Lynn, from whence he was removed to Berwick on the same service in September 1807, where he remained till 1810. He was then appointed to command the impress service at Greenock, the most unpleasant duty in the profession; but such was here his activity and zeal, that he raised double the number of men ever sent to sea by any of his predecessors in the same space of time. His life and conduct had therefore been useful and praiseworthy, and fully entitled him to promotion to a flag, which took place in July 1821.

Admiral Smith married in 1795 Maria, only child of W. Hulke, Esq. by whom he has two sons and two daughters.

HISTORICAL MEMOIRS OF

ADMIRAL CHARLES EKINS, C. B.

CURIOSITY naturally prompts us to search for and inquire into the ancestry of all those who, by their own acts, leave behind them examples to be followed. Mr. Gibbon indeed, who stood in need of no rank or titles to render his name illustrious, has declared, that if he could draw his pedigree from a general, a statesman, or a celebrated author, he would study their lives with the diligence of filial love. In this respect Admiral Ekins is peculiarly fortunate. His family was originally from Northamptonshire, and is very ancient. His grandfather possessed the living of Barton-Seagrave, in that county, which he afterwards exchanged for the rectory of Quainton, in Buckinghamshire, which now belongs to the family. Both his father and uncle were educated at Eton, from whence they went to Cambridge, where they became tutors to most distinguished individuals—his father to the late Earl of Carlisle, and his uncle to the Duke of Rutland. His father was afterwards presented, by Lord Carlisle, when Lord-Lieutenant of Ireland, to the bishopric of Dromore, which he exchanged with the late Dr. Percy, and died Dean of Carlisle. His uncle (who married the sister of the admiral's mother), through the Rutland interest, became Dean of Salisbury. The admiral's mother was the daughter of Philip Baker, Esq. of the War-Office, and combined in herself both beauty and goodness. By this marriage the admiral became connected with the family of the Harmans, whose names stand so celebrated in naval history. Lieutenant Philip Harman Baker, the last male branch of the family, and a cousin of the admiral's, was lost in the Defence; and on his death his sister presented the admiral with the medal* bestowed by King Charles II. on Captain Thomas Harman, for a desperate engagement he had with, and capture of, an enemy's ship off Cadiz, a representation of which now decorates the walls of Greenwich Hospital; and also an original letter† which Captain Harman wrote to his father respecting it.

* It formerly had a chain attached to it, which was sold by an old lady for 200*l.*
† The following is a copy: *March* 21st, 1694.
HONERED SUR,—I should be hartily glad to haue euery two or three month a letter from you: seuerall, fouer or fiue, letters I haue rote to you, but neuer receued an answer,

For some time the admiral and his elder brother were placed under the care of Dr. Moises at the public school at Newcastle*, at which time their father held the living of Morpeth. They both afterwards went to Winchester, from whence the eldest was removed to New College, Oxford, and educated for the church; but Charles, having an impediment in his speech, was sent to Edinburgh, and placed under the care of Mr. Braidwood, who was the first person who undertook to teach the dumb to speak in this kingdom. From that gentleman's advice he received considerable benefit, and he afterwards went to sea as a midshipman with the Hon. Keith Stewart, on board the Berwick of 74 guns. In that station he appears to have led an active and important life, having been present in the hard-fought action off the Dogger-bank in 1781, in which the Berwick suffered severely; and afterwards with the same captain, in the Cambridge of 80 guns, in the action with the combined fleet after the relief of Gibraltar by Lord Howe, on which occasion he was wounded whilst acting as aide-de-camp to Captain Stewart. In the ensuing peace he served on board the Marquis de Seignally sloop with Captain Hunter, then with the Hon. Seymour Finch on board the Pearl frigate, and then with the same officer in the Lion of 64 guns. In that ship he was promoted to a lieutenancy, and afterwards removed to the Flirt brig, in which he sailed to the West Indies. He then became lieutenant of the Alarm, and afterwards of the Boyne of 98 guns, from which he was burnt out at Spithead. He was shortly after promoted to the rank of commander, and appointed to the Ferret sloop, in which he captured the Eléonore French privateer. He then proceeded to the Cape of Good Hope under Admiral Elphinstone, from whence he was sent on a wild-goose sort of chase to the Indian seas, in search of a ship actually broken up at the Cape.

Feberary 19th I had the good fortune to haue the uectory ouer a Hollands man-of-war. I began the fite about 12 o'clock; about two I had the uectory: he had abord about 270 men; and I had the fortune to haue kelled 127 and wound 97, whare of 59 is dead. It was sertanly one of the gretes uectories that euer was gaued at see. I lost 9 men and 28 wounded: the last small gun that was fiered shot me in the hand, and I haue lost one of my eyes, and at the righting this letter haue lay wounded 17 days. I hope in God to be well in 10 days more. The king hath send me an order to cum home; therefore I suppose to see England in 2 mo. and hope to see you in good health.

Sur, your obediant and affec. sone,

THO. HARMAN.

* Where the present Lords Eldon and Stowell were educated.

In December 1796 Captain Ekins obtained post-rank, and returned to England in the Havick of 18 guns. He was then appointed to the Amphitrite, and sailed with a convoy, under the orders of Captain Bagot of the Trent, to the West Indies; on which station he captured a great number of the enemy's vessels, among which were seven privateers, carrying 62 guns and 466 men. He also assisted at the taking of the Dutch colony of Surinam by the naval and military forces under Lord H. Seymour and General Trigge, on which occasion the Amphitrite bore the admiral's flag. He afterwards, in company with the Unité, commanded by the present Sir J. Beresford, assisted at the surprise and capture of the Devil's Islands on the coast of Cayenne*. In March 1801 the Amphitrite accompanied Sir J. Duckworth on an expedition against the Virgin and other islands, of which it had been determined to take possession in consequence of the hostile measures adopted against Great Britain by Denmark, Sweden, and Russia; but unfortunately Captain Ekins, being sick, was obliged to remain at Barbadoes. However, a reinforcement arriving from England, escorted by the Coromandel and Proselyte, he took a passage on board the latter, and joined the commander-in-chief in time to be intrusted with the superintendence of the debarkation on the Island of St. Martin, and to assist in the subsequent operations†. His exertions on this occasion having brought on another attack of yellow fever, by which he had been previously much reduced, Rear-Admiral Duckworth was induced to send him home with his dispatches; and he accordingly returned to England in the Fanny cutter-brig, commanded by Lieutenant Frizell. In April 1804 he commanded the Beaulieu, and proceeded to the West Indies, from whence he returned in March 1806, then joined the Defence, and in the following year sailed with Admiral Gambier on the expedition against Copenhagen but he was prevented from being present at the surrender of that capital and the Danish navy, in consequence of having been detached with the Comus of 32 guns to cruise in the Sleeve, when the Danish frigate Frederickswarn was captured under his orders; the particulars of which are contained in the following extract of a letter, dated Defence, August 16, 1807:

" Finding that ship (the Comus of 24 guns, Captain Heywood,) in light winds had much the advantage of the Defence in sailing, and seeing the enemy soon after leaving the Sound, I directed Captain Heywood to give chase. At one

* See *Memoir of Sir J.* BERESFORD. † Marshall.

o'clock on Saturday morning he brought him to close action, the Defence being too far astern to render any assistance; and in about fifty minutes, having killed 14 and wounded 20, at length by boarding compelled him to surrender. The Comus, I am happy to say, had but one man (the pilot) wounded, and is very little damaged. The Danish frigate mounts 26 12-pounders on her main-deck, and 10 on her quarter-deck and forecastle, with 230 men. In her masts and rigging she has received considerable injury, the fire of the Comus having been so much better directed than that of the Dane."

The weather off that part of the coast of Norway where Captain Ekins was directed to cruise was extremely boisterous; to prove which it is only necessary for us to insert an extract of another letter, dated October the 12th, at the anchorage under the Scaw*:

" Since I had the honour of addressing you by the Clio, we have experienced such very heavy gales from the northward and westward, that I thought proper on Friday morning, the 9th instant, to bear up for this anchorage, and, with H. M. ship Comus (the Pelican having separated in thick weather the Monday preceding), arrived here at three p. m. on the same day. Excepting for a few hours yesterday, it has continued blowing with almost unabated fury; and I am strongly of opinion, that the weather at this advanced period of the season will prove an insuperable bar to all hostile operations on the coast of Norway. Under this impression, should I in the mean time receive no farther directions from you, I shall consider it my indispensable duty to consult the preservation of the ships, with their crews, by returning with them to England.

" A rapid succession of storms or calms, always accompanied with rain, by preventing us from drying the sails, has rendered those upon the yards scarcely to be depended upon; and but one spare top-sail remains on board this ship."

Captain Ekins, however, for some time hesitated; but the hard gales from the N. W. and W. N. W. having continued, drove him towards the Scaw, and he was again obliged to take shelter under it. The wind, however, having moderated, and drawn round to the eastward, he determined upon an immediate return to England, where he arrived on the 27th October, and subsequently found his conduct in so doing approved of by the Admiralty.

Captain Ekins afterwards joined the squadron under Sir C. Cotton off the Tagus, and by him was directed to proceed off St. Ubes, and there endeavour to smuggle on shore and circulate some manifestos among the

* A Danish 74-gun ship was reported to be on her return to Copenhagen at this time, and the Defence and Comus, after the capture of the frigate, were desired to look out for her: she, however, eluded their vigilance, and shut herself up in Christiansand.

Portuguese, as well as to open a communication with the Russian admiral in the Tagus, Lisbon being at that time in possession of the French. Whilst on this service he received information that a squadron of French ships had just been discovered, supposed to be steering for the West Indies: he lost no time in proceeding thither, to put the British admiral on that station on his guard; first dispatching the following letter to Sir C. Cotton, dated January 23, 1808, 11 a. m.:

" Sir,—Captain Jones of H. M. S. Talbot having just informed me that six sail of large ships passed close to him at four o'clock this morning, that he is convinced four of them were line-of-battle ships, and that two of them bore top and stern lights, were steering W. S. W. under a press of sail, and from their movements deeming them a squadron of the enemy; I have therefore thought it my indispensable duty to follow them immediately, sending the Spaniards and Portuguese prisoners on board the Talbot, to rejoin you without loss of time. I trust this circumstantial information of Captain Jones will warrant this proceeding on my part, though I consider the Defence little equal to a foreign voyage. The hard N. E. gales* have prevented my executing your order: in leaving it unexecuted to pursue the enemy, and to reinforce the commander-in-chief in the West Indies, I hope and trust I am only doing right."

On arriving at Barbadoes Captain Ekins made known his arrival to and soon joined Sir A. Cochrane; on the morning after which they were joined by Sir J. Duckworth, who had, in like manner, left his station in quest of the enemy; who, however, did not proceed to the West Indies, but escaped into the Mediterranean.   At the end of about three months Captain Ekins was ordered to England with a convoy of about 200 sail, having under his orders the Cerberus and Melville, with which he arrived perfectly safe; but shortly after coming to an anchor in the Downs, he received a letter from the Admiralty, severely reprimanding him for leaving the Lisbon station without orders; and upon his reaching the Medway, the crew of the Defence, being then in the highest state of discipline and health, were drafted away into five different ships of war fitting out there, without, it would seem, any necessity for so doing, at least any arising from the defects of the Defence, as she only remained one month in dock.   We are almost afraid to offer any observations on such conduct; it appears to us mean and pitiful, and that it would have

---

* In these gales the Defence sprung her bowsprit, and carried away her cross-jackyard. As soon as the weather permitted, a boat was lowered from her quarter for Captain Jones, who had made the signal for seeing an enemy from the first of the morning.

been better to have deprived Captain Ekins of the command altogether, rather than that the service should suffer by a wish to mortify him for doing that which at the worst could be considered only as an over-zeal for the benefit of his country. It has always been a great complaint amongst seamen, that they are drafted about to different ships, and with officers of whom they know nothing : in the present instance they had been long together, and nearly two years under the command of Captain Ekins, and were well satisfied with all their officers. We may perhaps be incompetent to judge correctly of the effect such treatment is likely to cause, but we are sure that to a feeling mind the reprimand must have been acutely felt; for to deprive an officer under such circumstances of his ship's company must have been the completion of his distress and mortification.

Captain Ekins was afterwards ordered to proceed to the Baltic ; and, upon his arrival at Nargen, the rendezvous of the fleet under Sir J. Saumarez, he was almost immediately (2d August) detached across the gulf to Makelota Bay, situate to the westward of the lighthouse on Porkala Island, to cut off the supplies sent by the Russians to their army in Sweden. To shew, however, the difficulty of the service he was then employed on, we must observe, that the pilots (from Yarmouth) were entirely ignorant of the coast, and not one of the officers in the ship had even been there before. The Cheerful cutter, Lieutenant Carpenter, was therefore sent ahead to guide her to the anchorage amidst rocks breaking above water in every direction, whilst the rugged coast of Finland was in the rear ; lurking unseen dangers were likewise numerous, requiring the most vigilant attention and look-out, and to avoid which the Cheerful kept reporting soundings as she advanced. In this manner they got into what they considered tolerable ground for the night, in seventeen fathoms. On the following morning they were joined by the Bellerophon, Captain S. Warren, who was placed under the orders of Captain Ekins, when the pilots of both ships were employed to take the best survey of the place that circumstances would permit, and from the information transmitted to the commander-in-chief of the whole of the proceedings, the following is extracted :

" A light breeze offering on the 5th, the ships were moved about three miles to the N. E. by N. with regular soundings all the way, and the anchors let go in thirteen fathoms. But notwithstanding we had deep water all around us within half a cable's length, we found but seven fathoms and a half along side, and at ten p. m. the wind coming from the land, the ship tailed upon a sunken rock, but not violently. The anchor was weighed, and the ship cast, but again settled upon the rock, where she hung about an hour, when, by removing some of the guns and making sail, she went off, without receiving any injury, and was again anchored in deep water. The wind was very light, and the water perfectly smooth; the rock also seems to have been smooth and round, on which the ship appeared to rest almost insensibly. Upon reaching this second place of anchorage, the master and pilots were well satisfied with their good fortune, and thinking the ship in a safe berth, were congratulating each other on their success over a glass of grog, when the striking of the ship dashed the cup of joy from their lips, and roused the captain from his slumbers.

" On the 13th August twenty-four gun-boats came down from Por-kala Point along shore, sailing and rowing. The ships and cutter immediately weighed with a light southerly wind, but were not able to get within reach of them, stealing behind every island and rock in their progress. They were much too numerous and powerful for the boats, rowing about twenty oars, and each having a little row-boat attending it. Six or seven ships of war were, at the time, lying in Swibourg, intending also to come that way."

On the 23d August Captain Ekins writes thus :

" The two ships under my orders are now anchored in such situations, that it will be difficult for the gun-boats of the enemy to pass us without considerable molestation; and the better to favour it, or molest them, I have thought it expedient to cause a battery to be erected on the northern extremity of the Island of Trasken, and which completely commands the passage. The enemy's battery on Porkala Point has been destroyed without opposition, and five guns are now mounted upon Fort Sauma-rez; a twelve-pound shot is sent with ease to the enemy's hill on the Point; upon which, however, could they erect a mortar battery, I fear they would dislodge our little garrison, and oblige the ships to move to a greater distance. If you will have the goodness to send the Fury to us, we shall then be able to keep our position, and to bid defiance to almost any force the enemy may send against us, and thus effectually cut off all supplies by this route to the Russian army. The fort is to be garrisoned by 100 men, and the command given to Captain Anthony Stransham, royal marines, of this ship, with the authority of captain-commandant. Eleven Swedish and Porkala pilots await your disposal. I secured as many as I could, to prevent their assisting the Russians, many of them having conducted the last division of gun-boats to Hango."

The commander-in-chief was highly satisfied with all these measures, and reinforced Captain Ekins with a gun-boat. We should have observed that the lighthouse had been taken possession of at an early period, and a midshipman and party kept constantly residing in it to take care of the light, which had been abandoned on the arrival of the British fleet. The ships kept their stations till the 21st September, when, as the season was closing, Captain Ekins received orders to return to Nargen; upon which the garrison was withdrawn, and he rejoined the commander-in-chief, the captain of the fleet, G. Johnstone Hope, observing that he had completely check-mated the Russian gun-boats.

Captain Ekins shortly after returned to England, and having been long afflicted with a serious complaint, applied for an *acting-captain*, in order that he might procure the best advice: it was, however, refused; and he was in consequence under the necessity of requesting to be superseded. In three months he obtained a perfect cure; but the circumstance had unfortunately thrown him out of employment, and he did not again receive any till 1815, when he was appointed to the Superb of 78 guns, and afterwards proceeded with Lord Exmouth to the Mediterranean.

In the plan of attack on Algiers, the Superb was situated as the second astern of the commander-in-chief, and in following the wake of the Queen Charlotte, having so nearly gained her allotted station as to have clewed up the main-top-sail, running under the fore and mizen-top-sail only, the signal 3. 6. 5. (Sir Home Popham's code) was made to the Superb, and reported to the captain to be " to anchor instantly." Captain Ekins, however, not thinking the ship (agreeably to the circular order of attack before given out) near enough to the commander-in-chief, was, for a short time, apprehensive of some mistake; but finding, on comparing the signal with the signal-book, that it had been correctly reported, and as quarter-masters were ready in the main-chains on both sides with sharp axes, Captain Ekins, who upon this occasion conducted the duty himself, ordered them to cut away, and by two frigate's anchors, the remaining top-sails being at the same time taken in, the ship was brought up by the stern, the cables being secured to the new after-bits. During the short hesitation which occurred respecting this signal, the

Superb was still slowly advancing, and at length placed, though not quite so close to the Queen Charlotte as at first directed, still in an excellent position, having her starboard broadside immediately opposed to a battery of a double tier of guns, at the same time that her after-guns on the same side enfiladed all the enemy's batteries from the angular part, or large arch, to the lighthouse, and which proved an essential advantage, when the battery abreast of her was silenced, by supporting the attack of the ships astern of her*. For greater security and to preserve her station, a bower and a frigate's anchor, with a chain-cable, were let go from the bows: the ship was then fast both ahead and astern; but Lieutenant Caswell, who commanded the foremost guns of the lower deck, having reported that the ship's head was so much inclined to the shore, that he could with difficulty bring his guns to bear, the fore-topmast stay-sail was immediately run up, and the cable ordered to be paid out. The sail was knocked into a thousand ribbons in an instant, and the ship's head did not appear to swerve; it was then found that she was bound by the chain-cable of the frigate's anchor, the range not being sufficient for the depth of water, which proved to be deeper than what is laid down in Captain Ward's chart. Upon more of the chain being given to the ship, her head paid off, and in a little time the officers and men had nothing to attend to but the guns, the ship's battery being parallel to that of the enemy. In this manner she continued to keep up an incessant fire from a quarter before three p. m. till a quarter before nine,

---

* We must here explain more particularly the object of the admiral's signal to the Superb, 3. 6. 5. which was imperative upon her to anchor instantly. In taking his masterly position off the mole-head, Lord Exmouth had rounded a little point of the beach which projected from it; and as the Superb was following in his track, his lordship was fearful Captain Ekins might not be aware of, and run upon it. This new position of the Superb could not affect those to be taken by the remainder of the squadron but in the most trifling degree, as her anchor was let go only about half a cable's length short of the situation which was originally intended for her. This circumstance afforded an opportunity to that excellent officer, Captain W. F. Wise, of the Granicus frigate, to distinguish himself in a brilliant and particular manner: having waited till his seniors had taken their stations, and seeing the opening which this signal had caused, he immediately made sail, in the coolest and most skilful manner, on the starboard side of the Minden, and the larboard or off side of the Superb, silently cheering as he passed, clewed, and brought his ship up by the stern immediately in the grain of the Superb, and was instantly in the hottest fire. Warps, as directed by the commander-in-chief, were then exchanged between the Superb and Granicus, for mutual security, and both ships preserved their positions in the steadiest manner, keeping up a tremendous cannonade.

when the commander-in-chief sent Captain F. Mitchel round to each ship of the squadron to order it off, and come to an anchor in the bay.

The battery abreast of the Superb had ceased firing for some time, and her crew were taking some rest by their guns; powder was also being removed from the fore to the after magazine, and shot brought up to replace those which had been expended. Not suspecting that they would be again molested, Captain Ekins ordered " to pipe up anchor," and sent all the men from the quarter-deck guns to man the capstan, to weigh the bower anchor, which had been brought-to for that purpose, and the bars were shipped and ready. This was scarcely completed, when a large shot entered, and carried with it all the planking between two of the carronades on the starboard side, which took the captain, first lieutenant (Horn), and another officer, by the heels, and laid them prostrate on the deck. Upon being lifted up, Lieutenant Horn advised the captain to cut, as in all probability the ship would suffer much in staying to weigh, without any particular advantage. The chain-cable was slipped, the bower cut, and the gig and launch, the only boats left, were ordered to tow the ship's head off the battery; and as soon as that object was accomplished, with the assistance of such sails as could be set, the stern cables were to be cut, and every exertion used to get off*. Lieutenant Horn, though badly wounded, continued on deck for some time, to execute these orders; and the captain was led to the cock-pit for an examination of his wounds, as the musket-balls were flying in all directions, and, as it was then dark, to have brought lights upon deck would have proved destruction to every man seen from the shore†. Lieutenants Soady and M'Dougal were then left to extricate the ship from her difficulties, being promptly assisted by Captain R. Riddell, of the Britomart, who came on board the Superb before she left her position, to render any service in his power, and who, after Captain Ekins had left the deck, caused a tow-rope to be made fast from his little brig to the bows of the Superb. The rope was, however, soon shot away, and she was left to scramble out as she could, which at

---

* Captain Paterson, of the Minden, very handsomely volunteered to remain at anchor, and kept up an incessant fire, to cover the Superb as she retired.

† A marine, who, during a short cessation of the firing, had left the quarter-deck, to take a better view of the battle from the poop, received a brace of balls (joined so as to be put into the barrel together) in the centre of his forehead, as he leaned over one of the carronades.

last she successfully accomplished, and about two a. m. anchored in the bay.

During this desperate conflict, there were some peculiar circumstances that took place, which, though they do not come exactly within the plan of the work, we cannot refrain from noticing. In the heat of the battle, the colours flying at the peak were shot away, which being perceived by Mr. Thorpe, the signal-midshipman, quartered on the poop, he, without saying a word, immediately seized the largest blue ensign he could find, was taking it deliberately up the mizen-rigging, and when about half way, was discovered by the captain, who desired him to fix it there, and come down with all speed. He fixed it effectually; but sorry are we to add, that notwithstanding this proof of his coolness and intrepidity was faithfully reported by his captain to the Admiralty, and that he had passed his examination full two years, his conduct and merit were disregarded.

When the ship had been some time engaged, a singularly shaped shot made its way through a closely stowed double row of hammocks and bags on the starboard gangway, and lodged itself in the booms. The boatswain observing it, was going to remove it, for the purpose, as he said, of " giving it them back again by one of the main-deck guns;" but the captain desired him to let it remain. It was similar to one of the American dismantling shots, put in double, and weighing 38 pounds; its length *three feet ten inches**.

That the ship should not have suffered a greater loss of lives than ten killed, is best accounted for by her being anchored so close, and the enemy firing high; also to Captain Ekins not quartering any men in the tops: nor did he permit a man to go aloft from the time she took her position. The only sails that were left loose were the three top-sails, fore-sail, and jib; the former closely clewed and brailed up, according to the directions given by the commander-in-chief: the top-sail-yards were on the cap. To have attempted to replace losses, or repair damages, in the midst of such a conflict, was quite out of the question; but on the following morning, at daylight, all hands were turned up for the purpose. The main-mast was so badly wounded (nine shot having struck it), and the shrouds and rigging so much cut, that no sail could be set upon it on coming out. The sails on the mizen-mast, the remains of

---

* It is now in Admiral Ekins's possession.

the fore-sail, the fore-top-sail, just lifted from the cap, and the sprit-sail, were the only serviceable sails, with the driver, that were left. In four days all the masts were fished, top-masts, &c. shifted, and the ship ready for sea. To shew the care and attention of the gallant chief to those under his command, and who were then bleeding from their wounds, in a letter to Captain Ekins he says, " The Mutine, having joined from Oran with slaves, has three bullocks on board, and I have directed Captain Mould to join you with one for your poor fellows." After some inquiries about wounded officers, he says, " I shall never forget what I owe you and the Superb for your effectual support." Upon another occasion he writes thus: " I could have written with pleasure the name of every captain under my command; I can never do enough to satisfy my feelings, any more than I can ever forget the noble and gallant support you afforded me in that arduous contest: not a man moved till the flag was safe, and we had accomplished the full object of our orders." Such sentiments do as much honour to the writer as to those to whom they were addressed. The flag was, at one period of the battle, in the most imminent danger: the large Algerine frigate which had been boarded and set on fire by the barges manned with volunteers from the Queen Charlotte, had burnt her fastenings, and was drifting out of the mole in one entire stupendous blaze, her main-mast and main-yard forming, for some time, a brilliant crucifix. The Queen Charlotte had already begun to move from her first position, when this mass of flame was drifting rapidly towards her: the whole squadron were in the most painful state of anxiety and suspense for the safety of their chief and his brave companions. So close had the enemy's ship approached to the stern of the Queen Charlotte, and so excessive was the heat felt on board of her, that none but the chief himself and his gallant captain* could remain on the poop ; and lest the flag of the British ensign, so proudly waving over the stern, should be caught in flame, it was hauled into the ship. At this moment the peril was at the highest, and the feelings of the whole fleet consequently excited to the highest pitch: Lord Exmouth himself had scarcely any hopes left ; for turning to his captain, he said, in a low tone, " Brisbane, I fear all is over with the poor Charlotte : but," added he, with the greatest coolness, " we will all go together†." Another fate

---

* The late Sir James Brisbane.

† The Leander, Severn, and Glasgow were also in great danger from the ship on fire.

was, however, reserved for them : at that moment the burning ship was brought up in her course by some of the rigging, from the bowsprit getting entangled with the mast-heads of a little brig, which had been sunk early in the battle, and which were above water*. The warping, towing, and firing were still, however, kept up by the Queen Charlotte, as she could bring her larboard broadside to bear : the progress of the burning ship was, however, not only checked, but she received a different direction, and drifted on her own beach. Thus did Lord Exmouth, by great good fortune, labour, and exertion, triumph over every difficulty, and bring to a glorious termination a contest of unexampled duration, planned, commenced, and conducted by himself. In the Memoir of his lordship, we have endeavoured to do justice to his lordship's character ; but we cannot help here observing, that his skill and intrepidity were illustrated and brought to the noblest proof by his example on this occasion.

On reaching soundings in the Channel, the Queen Charlotte, intending to proceed to Portsmouth, on the evening of the 4th October made the following general telegraphic signal : " Squadron destined for Plymouth : the admiral intends parting : can never forget his obligations for the noble support he has received from his honourable and gallant friends." The well-known *dread of Algiers* was flying at his mast-head when the squadron, with colours up, closed with the admiral, cheered, and saluted him with 17 guns, which he immediately returned with the same number, and then separated†.

---

* When the fleet had arrived at Gibraltar from England, the admiral assembled the captains on board the flag-ship, to explain to them his intentions. With one of Captain Ward's charts before him, he pointed out to them the great object in view, the burning or destroying the enemy's marine ; the mode of proceeding with either a land or sea breeze ; the position he intended to take up, and the course to be followed by the other ships. On this occasion Captain Ekins, in offering the assurance of his best support, struck with the great coolness of the admiral when describing his intention of burning the enemy's ships, said, " Take care, my lord, that you do not involve yourself in flames of your own creating."

† The following anecdote will perhaps shew still stronger than we have hitherto done, the dreadful nature of the contest in which they had been engaged. When the fleet was lying at Gibraltar, an officer from one of the regiments in garrison having obtained leave of absence, volunteered his services in the Superb's gun-boat, fitting out there. He was a young man of good character and approved courage, having distinguished himself in several battles in the Peninsula. He, however, could not long stand the dreadful pelting of grape and musketry to which he was exposed in the gun-boat before Algiers, and

We must now notice the honours conferred upon Captain Ekins for his conduct in the battle, and also the part he took in the presentation of a piece of plate to Lord Exmouth, as well as his exertions to obtain for those on board the Superb that promotion which they deserved. By his own sovereign he was nominated a Commander of the Bath; and by the King of the Netherlands a K. W. N. which entitles him to the rank of a chevalier in that kingdom; and by the twenty-five young gentlemen of his quarter-deck he was presented with a very handsome gold snuff-box, with the following note:

" The under-mentioned gentlemen, impressed with the highest sense of grati-tude and respect, humbly beg Captain Ekins will be pleased to accept this small token of their esteem, which can never be erased from the memory of those who had the honour to serve under his command on the glorious 27th August."

To this address, so gratifying to his feelings, Captain Ekins returned the following answer:

" GENTLEMEN,—I fear I cannot convey to you in adequate language the proud and grateful feelings you have excited, by presenting me with so liberal, so appropriate, and so elegant a testimony of your esteem and regard ; and if my conduct on the 27th August met with your admiration, I can but with justice ascribe it to a firm reliance on the Almighty will, and a perfect confidence in those I had the honour to command, of whom the junior officers of the Superb, as they bore a large and very conspicuous part in all the dangers and fatigues of the day, will ever claim my sincere and grateful acknowledgments. Allow me to repeat my best thanks to you all for this unexpected and highly gratifying token of your approbation.*"

actually left the deck in consequence. He was, however, subsequently manly enough to acknowledge the circumstance at the head of his own mess-table, in presence of some of the officers of the Superb, and declared that all he had hitherto seen was mere farce and child's play, compared to what he then saw. Lieutenant Johnson, a very brave officer, commanded the gun-boat, and had a very narrow escape. Lieutenant Pitfield commanded the rocket-boat, and was equally distinguished by his activity and bravery.

* On the outside of the box is engraved the Turkish arms, with the word " Algiers," encircled with laurel. Within is the following inscription:

" This box was presented to Captain Charles Ekins by the junior officers of H. M. S. Superb, as a mark of their esteem, and admiration of his conduct on the glorious 27th August, 1816, on behalf of the following officers:

Messrs. Barclay,	March,	Mills,	Whateley,	Parlby,
Barrs,	Sweeting,	Dobbs,	M'Lean,	Williams,
Thorpe,	Church,	Stephens,	St. John,	Burt,
Wolesley,	Ferris,	Belcher,	Webbe,	Barnett,
Prust,	Fairbairn,	Welch,	Wilkinson,	Watts."

To these young gentlemen, and indeed to all who had ever sailed with him, Captain Ekins had behaved with the kindness and attention which are dictated by the purest motives of friendship and an anxious desire to promote their welfare: their recent conduct before Algiers he had every reason to be satisfied with; and he now endeavoured to obtain for two of them, who he thought had particular claim to his attention, that promotion which he conceived they deserved, and he consequently wrote the following letter to Lord Exmouth:

My Lord,—Agreeably to your lordship's directions, signified in your letters of the 6th and 7th inst. I have the honour to state to you, that Lieutenant Philip Thickness Horn, first lieutenant of the Superb at the attack of Algiers, is highly and justly entitled to the rank of commander.

That Mr. Peter Fairbairn is the surgeon's assistant, who, by his services and his conduct, merits the situation of surgeon; and that Mr. Charles March and Mr. William Sweeting, *Admiralty* midshipmen, are those I nominate for the rank of lieutenants, conformably to the arrangements of my Lords Commissioners of the Admiralty.

In fixing upon a midshipman of the ship for the preference of recommendation, I found it not so easy a task, and of two gallant young men of equal claims and merit, I was under the painful necessity of desiring them to draw lots; although one of them (Mr. Edward Hall Thorpe), with a modesty and generosity much to his honour, would willingly have resigned his pretensions entirely in favour of the other (Mr. Francis Barrs), who proved to be the fortunate candidate.

In this arrangement of their lordships, I cannot but with feelings of mortification and disappointment observe, that, independently of the increased numbers of deserving midshipmen in ships of the line, the privilege of patronage of a post-captain of nearly twenty years, and the *senior* under your lordship's orders, is considered only as on a par with that of a *commander* of *yesterday*; and I have still to learn, except in the most honourable post your lordship was pleased to assign me on the day of battle, in what the benefits or advantages of seniority consist. I have the honour to be, &c. &c.　　　CHARLES EKINS.

To the Right Hon. Lord VISCOUNT EXMOUTH, *&c. &c.*

But notwithstanding Captain Ekins was the senior captain of the fleet, he was put on a level with the youngest commander in it, and not allowed by the Admiralty to recommend more than one midshipman for promotion; although their lordships thought proper to promote two other out of the Superb, who had no particular claims, and who had joined the

Superb only a few days before she left Plymouth Sound. Upon such
conduct we shall make no comment, but proceed to observe, that Captain
Ekins being called upon to be the medium of conveying to Lord Exmouth the expression of high and ardent feelings for the noble and intrepid conduct he had displayed before Algiers, he sent to his lordship
the following letter, dated 27th August, 1818:

My Lord,—Deputed by the rear-admiral, the captains and commanders, who
had the honour to serve under your lordship's command at the memorable attack
on Algiers on the 27th August, 1816, it is with feelings of peculiar pride and
gratification I have to offer to your lordship's acceptance the accompanying tribute of their admiration and respect; and by presenting your lordship with this
token of their esteem, endeavour to express the high sense they entertain of the
judgment which planned, the experience and ability which guided, and the daring
intrepidity which so nobly executed, one of the boldest achievements recorded in
the pages of our naval history; an event which, by having for its sole object
the extinction of Christian slavery, sheds a never-fading lustre over the arms and
character of the British nation.

In conveying to your lordship this testimony of our united sentiments upon
that occasion, accept, my lord, the assurance of respect and esteem with which I
have the honour to remain your lordship's most obedient, humble servant,

CHARLES EKINS.

And to which he received the following reply:

ADMIRALTY-HOUSE, PLYMOUTH, 27th August, 1818.

Dear Sir,—I accept with the most lively satisfaction the elegant piece of plate
which Rear-Admiral Sir David Milne and the captains and commanders of his
Majesty's squadron who so nobly seconded the attack upon Algiers on the 27th
August, 1816, have conferred on me, to mark (as your kindness has led you to
say) their admiration of my services on that occasion; and I request you will convey to them my warmest thanks for this very flattering testimony of their esteem,
which will perpetuate in my family the pleasing recollection of a service from which
resulted honour to the British name, the emancipation of thousands of suffering
victims, and the total abolition of Christian slavery.

The highest gratification an officer can receive in the discharge of his public
duty arises from the respect of those he has had the honour to command, especially when sanctioned by distinguished services and experience; and such sentiments are rendered doubly acceptable when conveyed by an officer who himself
fought and bled in this cause so interesting to humanity.

I request that you will do me the favour to receive my best acknowledgments
for the very flattering manner in which you have communicated to me the wishes

of your brave associates. I have the honour to be, with much esteem, dear sir, your most obedient, humble servant,   EXMOUTH.

In August 1819 Captain Ekins was advanced to the rank of rear-admiral.

In addition to the benefits derived to the country from the services of Admiral Ekins, she is also indebted to other members of his family; for he lost two brothers serving in the army whilst fighting in her defence: the youngest, John, was badly wounded and taken prisoner at Point-à-Petre, and died through bad food and worse treatment, under Victor Hughes. The other was at the capture of St. Vincent by General Abercrombie, and there died. His elder brother is now rector of Morpeth.

Since the conclusion of hostilities, Admiral Ekins has not been idle, but has been assiduously employed in preparing the minds of naval students, and fitting them to combat with success the enemies of their country, should circumstances arise again to call them forth in her defence, by publishing Critical Remarks on Naval Actions, from 1744 to 1814, illustrated with numerous plans; and respecting which we can only observe, that all those officers whom we have heard speak of the work, hold it in very high estimation.

HISTORICAL MEMOIRS OF
ADMIRAL SIR GEORGE EYRE, K. C. B.

IN contemplating the records of those illustrious for talent and virtues, which entitle the possessors to the applause and admiration of after-ages, people in general are apt to complain of the paucity of their number: we confess, however, that we are not of that class; but, on the contrary, are amongst those who believe that all ages have produced individuals who are equal to the situations that emergencies required them to fill; and that, in fact, it is necessity which requires and produces them. That the wars arising from the French revolution created, or rather brought forward, some of the most eminent men that England ever produced, both in a civil and military capacity, cannot be denied; and amongst those must be classed the subject of this Memoir. The family of Eyre has been long established in Nottinghamshire, where it has considerable property, and several of the members have represented it in Parliament. They were also particularly distinguished in military capacities during the civil war, in their support of the house of Stuart, and their endeavours to maintain Charles I. on his throne. Sir George's father was for many years M. P. for Boroughbridge, in Yorkshire, and his eldest brother also represented the county of Nottingham in several successive Parliaments. Sir George was educated at Harrow school; and after passing a few months at an academy at Chelsea, went to sea in 1782, on board the Resistance of 44 guns, commanded by Captain James King, the companion of Captain Cook during his last voyage of discovery, and the writer of the last volume containing the account of it. On his joining the Resistance, a son of Captain Cook's was one of the lieutenants, and they shortly after proceeded with a convoy to Jamaica, where they continued to cruise during the remainder of the war, and captured, after a short action, the Coquette French frigate, commanded by the Marquis de Grasse (a nephew of the count's), and which, we believe, was the last prize made in that war. Shortly after its termination, Sir George returned to England with Captain King, on board the Diamond frigate; but shortly after went out in the Resistance, to join Sir Charles Douglas, at Halifax. As the flag-ship, however, remained principally in harbour, he was sent to cruise in smaller ones, particularly the Mercury, Captain Stanhope, and Atalante, Captain Sir Thomas Foley. Towards the end of 1786, he returned to England in the Resistance, Captain Bentinck, and the following year was appointed to the Adventure, Captain F. Parrey, and appointed commodore on the coast of Guinea. From thence, however, the commodore was obliged to return before the expiration of his command, on account of ill health, and Sir George then proceeded to Newfoundland with Captain Trigge, in the Nautilus. In the Spanish armament he joined the Queen Charlotte, bearing the flag of Lord Howe; and at the close of it (November 1790) he was promoted to the rank of lieutenant. He was then appointed to the Scipio, Captain (now Sir Edward) Thornbrough; and that ship being paid off, he received an appointment to the Aquilon, Captain (now Sir Robert) Stopford, in which he sailed to the Mediterranean. At the commencement of the war in 1793, he was appointed to the St. George, bearing the flag of his relation, Rear-Admiral Gell, and was fortunate enough to be in her at the capture of the St. Jago Spanish register-ship, which had become a prize to the French privateer General Dumouriez. Having joined the fleet under Lord Hood at Gibraltar, the St. George proceeded with him off Toulon, and there Lieutenant Eyre joined in all the active operations which took place. When the marines and detachments of seamen from each line-of-battle ship were ordered to land, he volunteered his services on shore, and in consequence had the command of the party sent from the St. George, and proceeded with them for the defence of Fort la Malgue. On the following day he was ordered to the advanced battery on the heights of Pharon, where he continued till he had, by his good conduct, attracted the notice of Lord Hood, who ordered him to join his flag-ship, the Victory. Shortly after the evacuation of Toulon, he was advanced to the rank of commander, and appointed to the Speedy of 14 guns, in which he assisted at the siege and capture of Bastia. He was then ordered to join the Diadem off Nice; but unfortunately, in his passage thither, he fell in with, on the 9th June, 1794, the French fleet, consisting of seven sail of the line and several frigates, which had sailed from Toulon a few days before, and was standing to the eastward along their own coast. The utmost exertions were now made by the Speedy to escape from the enemy, and she continued standing from them for several hours; but the strength of the breeze and a considerable sea gave the enemy's large ships such a decided advantage, that they eventually came up with, and of course captured her. One of the greatest improve-ments of which modern times can boast, with just pretensions to applause, is the mildness and humanity manifested in war. Notwithstanding the bright example which former ages afforded of heroism, magnanimity, and contempt of death, their mode of warfare was conducted upon a prin-ciple of cruelty and revenge, which happily, in later ages, can find no parallel, except in some instances with the republicans of France, who threw aside "that polish which is almost universally diffused over modern manners; that civilization, that mildness and grace which repress the bursts of furious passions, and soften the ferocity of rudeness and bar-barity." The moment Captain Eyre reached the commander-in-chief's ship, Admiral Martin, who had as a coadjutor Sallicetté, one of the de-puties of the French Convention, immediately addressed him, and asked if he had heard of the recent decree of the Convention, declaring that no quarter should be given to either the English or Hanoverians. And upon his answering in the negative, the French admiral added, "Then I must tell you it is now *un guerre à mort;* and if I had been the first to come along side of you, I should have instantly sent you to the bottom." These words were scarcely concluded when the English fleet hove in sight; Captain Eyre was immediately hurried back to the ship he had first gone into, and the enemy made the best of their way into Gourjean roads, when Captain Eyre was landed, and marched with his crew to Antibes. The Sardinian frigate had been captured by the same squa-dron the day previous to the capture of the Speedy; and her officers and men having been placed on board the French admiral's ship, the Sans Culotte, had been very severely treated, her captain, Ross, not having been allowed to wash or shave himself while on board; and in that state he and Captain Eyre met on shore. On their arrival at An-tibes, Captain Eyre and the Speedy's crew were all confined together in a dungeon, with merely straw to lie upon, there to wait the determina-tion of the French government as to the manner in which they were to be treated, neither the admiral nor local authorities choosing, in cold blood, to put the decree of the Convention into execution. Fortunately for Captain Eyre and his associates, fortunately for humanity, the victory of Lord Howe saved them from an untimely death, and the blood-thirsty wretches who could cruelly pass such a decree were, by a chas-tening hand, brought to a sense of reason; and as so many of their own seamen had been carried captives to England, it was no longer thought advisable to begin "*un guerre à mort.*" Captain Eyre therefore escaped; but he remained for three weeks in his wretched abode, waiting the determination of those regenerators of mankind.   On its arrival, his officers and crew were marched on foot to Aix, in Provence, and there again confined in the common prison; the only difference made between them and the malefactors being, that the former were allowed permission to hire beds, and to have, on paying for it, something better than the prison-allowance.   There they remained for about a month after the fall of Robespierre, when Captain Eyre and his officers were allowed their parole, and conducted to Romans, in Dauphiny; the remainder of the Speedy's crew being sent to other towns, and employed in various works. Captain Eyre remained at Romans till May 1795, when a French officer being sent from England to be exchanged, he was released, and returned home.   A court-martial was, as a matter of course, shortly after held, to inquire into the Speedy's loss, and an honourable acquittal having been pronounced, he was appointed to the Albacore; and on the 6th February, 1796, was made post-captain into the Prompte, in which he accompanied Sir H. Christian to the West Indies, where he was appointed by Sir Hyde Parker to the Regulus of 44 guns, in which he was constantly and actively employed in cruising against the enemy; and by his activity, diligence, and zeal in that service, he not only acquired considerable celebrity, but the number of his prizes were important in a pecuniary point of view.

On the 11th July, 1798, when cruising off Porto Rico, Captain Eyre observed five vessels at anchor in Aguada Bay; but notwithstanding they were under the protection of the batteries, he determined to attempt their capture or destruction; for which purpose the boats were sent in under Lieutenants Good and Holman, accompanied by a prize-schooner, the Regulus standing in as close as possible to protect them.   The wind, however, failed, and neither the Regulus nor schooner could get near enough to render any effectual assistance; notwithstanding which Lieutenant Good pushed on to the attack, and, by the spirited exertions of all employed, obtained possession of the five vessels; but owing to there not being a breath of wind, they were obliged to abandon two of them: the rest were brought out, with the loss of only one man wounded, although a sharp and incessant fire was kept up by the enemy.

In September 1799 he returned to England, having on board Admiral R. R. Bligh; after which he remained unemployed, except for a few months that he commanded *pro tempore* the San Josef, then attached to the Channel fleet, till 1805, when he was appointed to the Ardent; but before she was ordered on any service, he was removed to the Magnificent, a fine new 74, just launched. He was then attached to the Channel fleet under Lord St. Vincent, and was employed, under the orders of Sir Eliab Harvey, in the Bay of Biscay, till June 1807, when he was ordered to the Mediterranean, and joined Lord Collingwood off Cadiz, where he continued till the Spanish revolution broke out; and on the surrendering of the French squadron in that harbour, he was ordered off Toulon, from whence he was detached to the assistance of the Spaniards at Rosas, where he took off Lord Cochrane from the Fort of Trinidad, which he had so gallantly defended. In April 1809 he was appointed by Lord Collingwood to command the squadron in the Adriatic, which was increased to three sail of the line and seven or eight frigates. In the following October he was ordered to join the squadron under Captain Spranger, taking with him the Magnificent, Belle Poule, and Kingfisher, and assist in the reduction of Zante, Cephalonia, Cerigo, and their dependencies; which, owing to the excellent arrangements, was happily accomplished, after a short resistance*: but short as it was, the conduct of Captain Eyre was such as to draw forth the thanks of the commanding officer, Captain Spranger.

The Island of Santa Maura, having been left in possession of the enemy, became very troublesome, from the shelter it afforded to the small armed vessels which infested that part of the Ionian sea, as well as from a body of troops which had collected there, and which seemed prepared to take the first favourable opportunity to wrest from their opponents those possessions of which they had recently dispossessed them: Captain Eyre therefore saw the necessity of making some attempt not only to defeat the projects of the enemy, but also to add Santa Maura to the conquests achieved by the arms of England. That he should know his own abilities was natural; he felt his own powers; and he was also convinced of what could be performed by the forces under his command. In conjunction therefore with General Oswald, he obtained the most correct information respecting the strength of Santa Maura, as well as of its means of defence; and being of opinion that their forces were fully adequate to its reduction, and that the circumstances under which they were placed would justify the attempt, they accordingly made the necessary

* See official letters in RALFE's *Naval Chronology*, vol. II. p. 238.

preparations, and in March 1810 they sailed from Zante; General Oswald, his staff, and a great part of the 35th regiment, being on board the Magnificent, and the remainder of the troops distributed in the other ships of war and transports. A landing having been effected on the 22d, it was observed that the enemy possessed three strong redoubts on a narrow neck of land, which formed the only approach to the fortress, or, as it might be called, the citadel, and they consequently became the principal objects of attack. This was carried into effect the same day, and as the large ships could not co-operate, Captain Eyre landed with the troops, and accompanied the general, in order to facilitate such supplies and co-operations from the ships as the circumstances of the moment might render necessary*. The troops, marines, and a detachment of seamen immediately began their march; and the Leonidas frigate, Captain A. J. Griffiths, was stationed as near the neck of land as the water would admit, in order to cover their advance, and render her co-operation as prompt and available as possible. The troops, with the general at their head, immediately advanced under a heavy fire of grape and musketry to the assault, drove the enemy from their entrenchments at the point of the bayonet, and followed them so close, that they had not time to rally at the second redoubt, but fled through it without stopping, and were pursued close to the walls of the citadel. The acquirement of these posts, which from that moment were kept possession of, was of the utmost importance to the operations of the victors: but in their capture Captain Eyre received a severe wound in the head by a musket-ball, which knocked him senseless to the ground, and he otherwise narrowly escaped death, having at the same time three other balls perforate his clothes. From the severity of his wound, Captain Eyre was obliged to delegate the further naval arrangements to Captain Brisbane till the 25th, when, though still suffering from its effects, he again resumed his active exertions, which terminated in the surrender of the enemy by capitulation on the 16th April†. The conduct of Captain Eyre on this occasion could not fail of exciting the admiration of his superiors; and he accordingly received the thanks of Admirals G. Martin‡,

---

* See official letter, RALFE's *Naval Chronology*, vol. III. p. 32.

† See *Memoir of Admiral* MOUBRAY.

‡ THE CANOPUS, *at* PALERMO, *April* 30, 1810.

SIR,—The Imogen arrived here yesterday, and by her I received your letter of the 18th instant, giving an account of the success of your attack upon the fortress of Santa

Sir C. Cotton*, and the Lords of the Admiralty. As Cephalonia, Zante, and the other islands were by this conquest rendered perfectly secure, the undivided attention of Captain Eyre and General Oswald was then devoted to the blockade of Corfu, in doing which he captured, on the 6th February, 1811, twenty-two vessels out of a convoy of twenty-five, laden with corn and ordnance stores, with 500 troops on board, which sailed from Otranto for Corfu; and also to the annoyance of the enemy in the upper part of the Adriatic, where Captain Eyre had stationed several frigates under that excellent officer Captain (now Sir William) Hoste, where he had that action which has rendered his name illustrious, and which for the amount of the force engaged was one of the most brilliant that occurred during the war. For a period of two years Captain Eyre continued to exercise the command on this station, a period of active and persevering service, never remaining in port beyond eight or ten days, and then only for the purpose of refitting, whilst his cruises were extended to six months. He then received a communication from Sir Charles Cotton†, the commander-in-chief, and was re-

Maura, upon which I beg to offer you my sincere congratulations, and to assure you how highly I appreciate your services on this occasion, and those of every officer, seaman, and marine under your command. I have, &c.   (Signed,)   G. Martin.

* San Josef, *off* Toulon, *June* 3, 1810.

Sir,—I am to acknowledge the receipt of your letter of the 18th April, together with the inclosures severally referred to, detailing your proceedings in an attack of the Island of Santa Maura, and final reduction of the citadel and island; and in making this communication, I cannot desist from expressing the very high sense I entertain of the skill, bravery, and perseverance displayed by yourself, and the captains, commanders, officers, seamen, and marines employed on the occasion, whose efforts have been crowned with the success they merited.

While I offer you my warmest congratulations upon the exploit in question, I cannot but lament the wound you have received; but trust it may not be to an extent to incapacitate you from affording still greater service towards the important operations in contemplation, and to promote which the rigorous blockade of Corfu must be a primary consideration.   (Signed,)   C. Cotton.

† The following is a copy :   San Josef, Mahon, *Feb.* 2, 1811.

Sir,—I cannot but in justice to your unremitted exertions on the station where you have been so long the senior officer, express my perfect satisfaction in every part of your conduct, at least as long as I have held the command in the Mediterranean. The relieving you now was chiefly the result of circumstances—the probability of your being ordered home, and the natural wish of placing a near relation in the most important command I could give him, in lieu of the situation of which he is deprived by a new order of the Admiralty-Board.   (Signed,)   C. Cotton.

lieved by Captain (now Admiral Sir Charles) Rowley, and joined the fleet off Toulon. During the whole period that Captain Eyre had been in the Adriatic, he was upon the best possible terms with all the officers under his command, who admired him for his abilities as an officer, and his character as a man and a gentleman; and as a mark of their respect and esteem, came to the resolution of presenting him with a piece of plate, which was announced to him by the following letter from Captain Brisbane:

Belle Poule, Malta, June 1, 1811.

My dear Commodore,—It is with the sincerest pleasure that I hasten to execute the wishes of my brother officers, of informing you, in the name of all of us who lately served under you in the blockade of Corfu, that we have sent directions to England to have a small piece of plate prepared, which we request your acceptance of, not for its value, but as a testimonial of our high esteem and affectionate regard, and a memorial of the happiness we experienced while serving under your orders. Ever, my dear commodore, yours, with great regard, most faithfully and sincerely,

James Brisbane.

Sir Edward Pellew having shortly after assumed the command of the Mediterranean fleet, and the Spaniards still continuing to defend their country against its invaders, Captain Eyre was ordered to render them the utmost assistance in his power on the coast of Valencia, where he had several opportunities of rendering them great service, particularly in enabling part of the garrison of Oropesa to escape on board the Magnificent, who would otherwise have been obliged to surrender to the enemy; for which he received the thanks of the Spanish general, Blake, and respecting which he addressed the following letter to Sir E. Pellew, dated October 14, 1811:

Sir,—Upon my arrival at this place on the 8th instant, I lost no time in assuring General Blake of my readiness to undertake any service in which I could be useful in forwarding his plans for the defence of this province; and the next day I received from his excellency a letter, containing a request that I would endeavour to relieve the castle of Oropesa, which was closely invested by the enemy, and much distressed for provisions. I in consequence immediately proceeded thither, with three gun-boats, which the general had put under my command, and arrived there on the evening of the 11th, when I learned that the castle had surrendered the preceding day, and that 2000 of the enemy's troops were in the town. A tower, however, about a mile from Oropesa, and only a short distance from the sea, had the Spanish flag still flying, and the enemy were discovered constructing a strong battery against it within musket-shot. Having found means to communicate with the tower, I received a letter from the commandant, informing me, that although he had refused to capitulate when summoned the day before, it would be impossible for him to hold out many hours against such a force as the enemy had brought against him : an arrangement was in consequence immediately made to withdraw the garrison. At daybreak the following morning the enemy opened their fire, which was returned with spirit from the tower; but it was not till near nine o'clock, when the breeze sprung up, that I could proceed in with the Magnificent. I then anchored as close to the shore as the situation would admit, and sent our launch and pinnace, together with the gun-boats, to bring off the garrison, which consisted of two officers and eighty-five soldiers, all of whom I have the satisfaction to inform you were, by the exertions and steady conduct of the officers and boats' crews, embarked by ten o'clock.

" The fire from the Magnificent kept the enemy in check ; but the moment the enemy perceived that the tower was abandoned, they drew down to the waterside, under shelter of a little point of land, and amongst the rocks, in great numbers, keeping up against the boats an incessant and heavy fire of musketry, by which three of our men were wounded."

The conduct of Captain Eyre was indeed throughout marked by great skill and judgment; it enabled the Spaniards to renew their exertions with much vigour, which were attended with considerable success, and drew from Sir Edward Pellew the following observation : " I have to express my complete approbation of Captain Eyre's measures, and have much satisfaction in employing the services of that excellent officer in aid of the Valencia patriots." Captain Eyre continued to assist the Spaniards at every point along the coast, and annoy the enemy by every means in his power; but the enemy becoming superior to General Blake, and he being obliged to give up the city of Valencia, Captain Eyre was ordered to proceed to England : but before he did so, he received the most flattering testimonial of his admiral's approbation, who, in an official letter, bore the most ample testimony to his merits. " In conveying to you these orders," said Sir Edward Pellew—those of the Lords of the Admiralty—" to proceed to England, I am desirous to express to you my sincere regret on losing your valuable services on this station, and the sense I entertain of your meritorious conduct while under my command." And in a private letter, dated 1st November, 1811, he said,

" My dear Sir,—I am greatly pleased by your prompt and wise decision of continuing on the coast of Valencia as long as you can do service ; it is like yourself; and I should be lost to feeling if I did not appreciate, as I ought, your great exertions at Oropesa and on the coast, ever since you have been there; and I entreat you to accept my best thanks, and that you will offer them to Lieutenant Hiat, and all those under him. I shall not fail to inform their lordships of their meritorious conduct.

" I am pretty confident one, if not two, ships will arrive before this month ends, and you shall be off on the arrival of the first, much as I shall regret your absence. I shall leave it to your choice to go direct to Gibraltar, instead of Mahon, whenever you are relieved, and send you orders accordingly."

On the arrival of Captain Eyre in England the beginning of 1812, having been five years on a foreign station, and being in a very indifferent state of health, he solicited and obtained leave to go on shore, where he continued unemployed during the remainder of the war; but as a mark of his Majesty's approbation of the conduct displayed by Captain Eyre, during the time he commanded a detached squadron in the Adriatic and on the coast of Spain, he was pleased to confer upon him the honour of knighthood. In June 1814 he was appointed a colonel of marines; and, as another mark of his sovereign's approbation, he was, on the extension of the Order of the Bath, in the first list of those who were appointed Knights-Commanders. In 1819 he was promoted to the rank of rear-admiral, and very soon after received an offer from Lord Melville to command on the Cape and St. Helena stations*, but which he was prevented from accepting by circumstances of a private nature. In 1823 he was appointed to the chief command in South America; and although it was no field for enterprise or glory, it was nevertheless a station of peculiar interest, from the recent changes which had taken place in that part of the world, the Spanish colonies having proclaimed their own independence, and, unaided by foreign states, put it on a firm and substantial foundation. This conflict with the mother country was attended with many circumstances of a peculiar and intricate nature, which made

* ADMIRALTY, *Nov.* 4, 1819.

SIR,—As the period is arrived when a successor ought to be appointed to Admiral Plampin on the Cape and St. Helena stations, I am desirous of knowing whether it would be agreeable to you to accept that command. It may be proper that I should mention, in regard to any extra expenses that might be incurred there, that, in addition to the ordinary pay of a rear-admiral and the allowances as commander-in-chief, a further sum of 2l. 5s. *per diem* has been granted, and a house is also provided at St. Helena. I have the honour to be, &c.   (Signed,)   MELVILLE.

it difficult for the British commander to protect the maritime rights of his country and the lawful commercial pursuits of her merchants, and at the same time preserve a good understanding with the various authorities: in all these objects, however, Captain Eyre fortunately succeeded; and after remaining on the station for three years, was relieved by the gallant and intrepid Admiral Sir R. Otway.

Sir George arrived at Spithead on the 10th December, 1826, and on the 12th received a communication from Lord Melville, informing him that his lordship had given directions that the orders, in the usual form, for striking his flag, should not be issued previously to Sir George's arrival in London, and requested him to proceed to the Admiralty the next day: he had then the gratification to receive from his lordship the tender to command the squadron then fitting out for Lisbon, and just upon the point of sailing. But, however flattering and gratifying such a circumstance must be to the feelings of any officer so situated, strongly proving, as it did, the approbation with which the Admiralty viewed the whole of Sir George's conduct, his health would not, unfortunately, permit him to accept it: his three years' residence in a hot climate, and the sudden change to a European winter, brought on an attack of gout; and his lordship having intimated that Sir T. Hardy was on the spot with his squadron, and that the service would not be impeded if he considered his health too much impaired to undertake the command, Sir George respectfully declined the offer.

Sir George was married in 1800 to Georgiana, a daughter of Sir George Cooke, Bart. of Wheatley, near Doncaster, and has a family of eight children.

HISTORICAL MEMOIRS OF
ADMIRAL SIR THOMAS TROUBRIDGE, BART.

WERE it possible to transmit to their heirs those virtues which most men possess in some degree, a noble and amiable ancestry would be the greatest and most desirable inheritance a man could enjoy, as he would then combine in himself all those qualities which would render him illustrious and admirable. As, however, this cannot be, and we must depend upon our own exertions for celebrity, ancestry becomes, in the eyes of most people, of a secondary consideration: but however it may be contemned by the severe moralist, and sneered at by those who do not possess it, or who have it not in their power to point to one who left his name behind associated with either honour, glory, or merit, we confess we are amongst its admirers, and think an illustrious pedigree entails upon its possessors an anxiety to keep up the responsibility of their class, and render themselves worthy the name they bear by their own conduct and exertions. But much as we admire men who are so situated, our admiration must be divided between those who are so situated and those who, without those advantages and inducements, but stimulated by their own innate desire of distinction and celebrity, by honourable and intrepid conduct free themselves from those shackles which, at their birth, they seem doomed to bear, and by persevering in the road to honour, obtain for themselves, and transmit, for the benefit of their descendants, those titles which are sought by men of the greatest wealth. In the British navy there are many instances of men, who, from the humblest stations of life, have, by their merit, obtained the most splendid remunerations; and amongst them must be placed the name of Troubridge, who, for the rank which he enjoyed, and the title he obtained, was indebted solely to his own bravery, exertion, and intrinsic worth.

In a Memoir of the professional services of Sir Thomas Troubridge inserted in the *Naval Chronicle*, it is there said, " It becomes our duty to make an humble offering at the shrine of departed merit; to collect, as it were into a focus, some of those brilliant actions which singly irradiated the earlier pages of our work ; to deliver down to posterity a brief memoir of the public services of one who will long be remembered as a pattern of professional excellence, of undaunted valour, and of patriotic worth. We obtrude not these sentiments merely as our own, but as comprising the opinion of one whose judgment will not be slightly called in question—the illustrious Nelson." His entrance into the service is thus described in the same work:

" Sir Thomas was the son of a Mr. Troubridge, a baker in the city of Westminster. Sir Charles Saunders, the companion of Anson, the naval conqueror of Quebec, an admiral and first commissioner of the Admiralty, residing in Spring Gardens, was frequently afflicted with the gout, of which he afterwards died: to ease the agonizing tortures of this dreadful chronic, it was customary for him, in his worst paroxysms, to have his legs rubbed by the hands of his housekeeper, an acquaintance or relative of Mr. Troubridge. The daughter of the latter, a little girl, occasionally visited her: the old lady having been taken ill during one of the admiral's worst fits, sent the child to attend him: the soft hand of youth, and the pleasing manners of infantine simplicity, were more agreeable than the frigid exertions of age; he sent for Mr. Troubridge, and requested he would allow a continuance of the child's attention, that afforded him such relief. He inquired whether he had any sons who wished to enter the naval service, acquainting him of the influence he possessed. Mr. Troubridge informed him that he had a son, then a cabin-boy in a West-Indiaman, who, he believed, was a promising lad, and to whom he had given the best education in his power. On his return home he was placed as a midshipman in the Seahorse, which sailed for the East Indies in 1773; but as Sir Charles died in 1775, his prospects became obscured: fortune and merit, however, did that for him which interest does for thousands. He was, however, in the right road, the wedge had obtained an entrance, and he was determined to drive it home. The Sartine, dispatched from France with supplies for Hyder Alli, was chased and captured by the Seahorse, much her inferior in force. The result of the battle was facilitated by the gallantry of Mr. Troubridge, who, seizing a favourable opportunity, boarded from the forecastle, routed the enemy, and hauled the colours down with his own hands. At that time capturing a frigate was not so common an achievement as it has been since, particularly by a vessel of inferior force, and it established a reputation for Captain Farmer, who, while dining with Sir Edward Hughes, the commander-in-chief, was overwhelmed with felicitation, but who, with a true greatness of mind, declared it was entirely owing to the gallantry of a young midshipman named Troubridge. Sir Edward, surprised, required an explanation: the noble captain explained the circumstances: the worthy and excellent admiral declared he would be the father of his future fortunes, and received him into his flag-ship. On this station he participated in all the active service then going on, and received very rapid promotion, having passed through the ranks of lieutenant and commander, and obtained post-rank on the 1st January, 1783. He was then appointed to the Active frigate, and joined in the attack on Cuddalore. The termination of hostilities, however, put a period to his exertions for a time, and in the following year he returned to England as flag-captain to Sir Edward Hughes. In 1790 he was appointed to the Thames frigate, and again sailed to the East Indies, serving under the command of Commodore Cornwallis; but returned to England previous to the French revolutionary war, at the commencement of which he was appointed to the Castor of 32 guns, and in May 1794 was ordered to proceed to Newfoundland with a convoy of fourteen vessels; but when running through the Bay was intercepted by part of the French fleet, and was of course captured. The Castor was, however, shortly after retaken by the Carysfort, Captain Laforey; but Captain Troubridge had been removed to the Sans Pareil, Admiral Nieuilly, and in that ship was in the action of the 1st June, on which day a curious scene occurred on board. After Lord Howe had taken his position, and had drawn his line parallel to that of the enemy, he brought-to, and made the signal to go to breakfast. Troubridge knew the purport of the signal, and telling it to the French admiral, they took advantage of the time allowed them for the same repast. Troubridge, whose appetite never forsook him on those occasions, was helping himself to a large slice from a brown loaf, when the French captain observed to him, by an interpreter (for Troubridge would never learn their language), that the English admiral shewed no disposition to fight, and he was certain did not intend it. ' What!' said the English hero, dropping his loaf, and laying his hand almost too emphatically on the Frenchman's shoulder, while he looked him furiously in the face, ' not fight! Stop till they have had their breakfasts: I know John Bull damned well, and when his belly is full, you will get it.' In a few minutes after this the British fleet bore up to engage. Troubridge was sent into the boatswain's store-room, where, for a length of time, he leaned against the fore-mast, and amused himself in pouring forth every invective against the French and the man appointed to guard him. Suddenly he felt the vibration of the mast, and heard it fall over the side ; when, grasping the astonished Frenchman with both his hands, he began to jump and caper with all the gestures of a maniac. The Sans Pareil soon after surrendered, and Troubridge assisted in setting her to rights and taking her into port*."

Captain Troubridge having been tried and acquitted for the loss of the Castor, was appointed to the Culloden, and employed in Channel service. On the 3d December, at ten p. m. as the Culloden lay at Spithead, the greater part of her crew, bursting into open rebellion, unshipped the ladders, and barricaded themselves below. The officers having got the marines under arms, sent to acquaint the admiral of the Channel fleet, and the captain of the ship, who was then on shore. On the next morning, at seven a. m. the petty officers, who had been confined below by the mutineers, were allowed to come on deck ; and several of the well-disposed among the people took that opportunity of effecting their escape. On calling a muster at a few minutes before noon, the well-disposed were found to consist, besides the commissioned and warrant officers, of the whole of the petty officers, all the marines but six, and 86 of the seamen, leaving about 250 for the number of the mutineers. In the course of the afternoon, Admirals Bridport, Cornwallis, and Colpoys came on board, and endeavoured, but in vain, to persuade the men to return to their duty. Matters continued in this alarming state during the whole of the 8th, 9th, and 10th, except that on the latter day the mutineers permitted the necessary water and provisions to be got up from below. On the 11th, Captain Thomas Pakenham went on board, and succeeded at last in persuading the men to return to their duty. The ship's company was then mustered, and the ringleaders, ten in number, seized and sent on board different ships, there to await their trial. It was discovered that the mutineers had broken into the magazine, raised a barricade of hammocks across the deck between the bits, and loaded with grape and canister shot the two second guns from forward, and pointed them towards the hatchway, and had collected upwards of fifty muskets and tomahawks. On the 15th December a court-martial sat on the ten mutineers, two of whom were acquitted, and eight sentenced to be hanged. On the 13th January five of them were hanged on board the Culloden at Spithead, and the remaining three received the king's pardon.

* Brenton.

In May 1795 Captain Troubridge was ordered to the Mediterranean, and where he was present at the indecisive action of the 13th July. A course of important and active operations were, however, about to take place, and in all of which it will be seen that he bore an ample and important part. In 1796 he was employed by Sir John Jervis, with a small squadron under his command, to watch the enemy in the port of Toulon, where he strongly evinced his zeal and perseverance; but, with Sir John Jervis, he was obliged to retreat from the Mediterranean, in consequence of the junction between the Spaniards and the French, and the great superiority of their force: but he succeeded in capturing the Nuestra Senora del Carmen, with 30,000*l.* on board, which he carried safely into Lisbon. The battle of St. Vincent shortly followed: on that day he led the British fleet, " which he did," said Sir John Jervis in a private letter to Lord Spencer, " in a masterly style. That gallant officer opened his fire on the Spanish ships to windward, which effectually separated the sternmost and leewardmost from the main body, then tacked, and thus prevented their rejunction. As soon as he had succeeded in passing through the enemy's fleet, he gave his starboard broadside to the nearest of their ships as he threw in stays: his example was followed by the van of our fleet, and thus the action became nearly general, by the British ships coming in the same tack with those of Spain*."
In this action the Culloden had 10 men killed and 47 wounded. The thanks of Parliament were voted to the victors; and Captain Troubridge also received a gold medal, to commemorate the victory. He afterwards assisted at the bombardment of Cadiz, and, by his activity, the launch of the Ville de Paris was raised, after she had been sunk by a raking shot from one of the enemy's gun-boats. The attack at Teneriffe succeeded this futile attempt to destroy the Spanish fleet; but as we have, in the Memoirs of Lord Nelson and Sir S. Hood, stated the particulars of that unfortunate affair, it will be unnecessary to say more on the subject, than to insert the following letter from Captain Troubridge, detailing the proceedings of the party under his immediate command:

" From the darkness of the night, I did not immediately hit the mole, the spot appointed to land at, but pushed on shore under the enemy's battery, close to the southward of the citadel. Captain Waller landed at the same time, and

* Brenton.

two or three other boats. The surf was so high, many put back : the boats were full of water in an instant, and stove against the rocks, and most of the ammunition in the men's pouches was wet. As soon as I had collected a few men, I immediately advanced, with Captain Waller, to the square, the place of rendezvous, in hopes of meeting you and the rest of the people, and I waited about an hour ; during which time I sent a serjeant, with two gentlemen of the town, to summons the citadel. I fear the serjeant was shot on his way, as I heard nothing of him afterwards. The ladders being all lost in the surf, or not to be found, no immediate attempt could be made on the citadel ; I therefore marched to join Captains Hood and Miller, who, I had intelligence, had made good their landing with a body of men to the S. W. of the place I did. I then endeavoured to procure some account of you and the rest of the officers, but without success. By daybreak we had collected about 80 marines, 80 pikemen, and 180 small-armed seamen : these I found were all who remained alive of those who had made good their landing ; and with this force, having procured some ammunition from the Spanish prisoners we had made, we were marching to try what could be done with the citadel without ladders, when we found the whole of the streets commanded by field-pieces, and upwards of 8000 Spaniards and 100 French under arms, approaching by every avenue. As the boats were all stove, and I saw no possibility of getting more men on shore, the ammunition wet, and no provision, I sent Captain Hood with a flag of truce to the governor, to declare I was prepared to burn the town, which I should immediately put in force if he approached one inch farther ; and at the same time I desired Captain Hood to say it would be done with great regret, as I had no wish to injure the inhabitants, and that, if he would come to my terms, I was willing to treat, which he agreed to*."

Captain Troubridge thus concluded his letter :

" From the small body of men, and the greater part being pike and small-armed seamen, who can only be called irregulars, with very little ammunition in the pouches but what had got wet in the surf at landing, I could not expect to succeed in any attempt upon the enemy, whose superior strength I have before mentioned. The Spanish officers assured me they expected us, and were perfectly prepared, with all the batteries, and the number of men already mentioned, under arms. This, with the great disadvantages of a rocky coast, high surf, and in the face of 40 pieces of cannon, will shew, though we were not successful, what an Englishman is equal to ; and I have the pleasure to acquaint you, that we marched through the town on our return with the British colours flying at our head."

* See *Memoir of Sir* S. Hood.

Such conduct requires no comment; but we must add, that Nelson, in sending the above account to Earl St. Vincent, observes, " I cannot but express my admiration of the firmness with which Captain Troubridge and his brave associates supported the honour of the British flag."

Captain Troubridge afterwards rejoined Lord St. Vincent off Cadiz; and in May 1798 ten sail of the line and a 50-gun ship were placed under his command, with orders to proceed into the Mediterranean, and join Rear-Admiral Nelson, who had been previously dispatched thither to watch the enemy's fleet in Toulon. He proceeded with him to Egypt, shared in all his anxiety of the chase, and was, by an unfortunate circumstance, prevented from sharing in the glory of the subsequent conquest off the Nile. He had been detained by towing a prize which he had taken off Coron, but obtained leave, when two leagues to the eastward of the admiral, to cast her off. Like the rest of the squadron, he had kept constantly sounding as he advanced, but he was so much astern of them, owing to the above-mentioned cause, that when our van ships were nearing the French, the lower-deck ports of the Culloden were just out of the water. The day was now closing in, which added considerably to his difficulties, when suddenly, after having sounded, and found eleven fathoms water, before the lead could again be hove, the Culloden was fast aground on the tail of the shoal running from the small Island of Bequieres, on which were two batteries of the enemy. Notwithstanding his own incessant exertions, with those of Captain Thompson in the Leander and Captain Hardy of the Mutine brig, both of whom immediately came to his assistance, the Culloden could not be got off so as to enter the action. The sufferings and agitation of Captain Troubridge, whose presence in the battle would have been severely felt by the enemy, corresponded with his determined character and zealous disposition. The Culloden did not get afloat until the next morning: it was, however, some satisfaction to the mortified feelings of her commander, that his ship served as a beacon to the Alexander and Swiftsure, which, from having been detached, were late before they could get into action*.
" Every exertion in my power," said Captain Troubridge, " was used to save his Majesty's ship; but it was long doubtful whether I should be able to keep her afloat, after I had got her off: the rudder was gone, and she was making seven feet water in an hour. However, by great

* Clarke and M'Arthur.

labour, on the third day we got a new rudder made and hung, and, with thrummed sails, reduced the leak considerably. The false keel is gone, and probably part of the main, as she struck very hard for nine hours, with a heavy swell: all the gripe I can see is off. I shall use every exertion to patch the poor Culloden up again; and I flatter myself I can still fight a good battle in her, if opportunity offers. I am now fagging hard at the leak, and in the first harbour we make I must and will patch the old ship up, and make her last as long as your lordship has the command. Two pumps going I shall not mind; we are fully equal to that. I endeavour, and I believe succeed in making my men believe, that the leak is nothing, for they dance every evening as usual." With the rest of the officers under the command of Admiral Nelson, Captain Troubridge received the thanks of Parliament and the gold medal: notwithstanding which, the first lieutenant of that ship was passed over in the general promotion which took place, under the plea that the ship had not been engaged; which induced Lord Nelson to write to Earl St. Vincent on the subject, and in which, after alluding to the circumstance, he said, " For Heaven's sake, for my sake, if it be so, get it altered. Our dear friend Troubridge has endured enough; his sufferings were in every respect more than any of us: he deserves every reward which a grateful country can bestow *on the most meritorious sea-officer of his standing in the service*. I have felt his worth every hour of my command, and I now place Troubridge in your hands." This request was forwarded to the First Lord of the Admiralty, Lord Spencer, who returned the following answer:

" The exception of the first lieutenant of the Culloden was necessary, on account of that ship not having got into action, from the circumstance of being aground. I am, however, so fully convinced of the merit, both of Captain Troubridge and his officers, on all occasions, that I beg you will be so good as to give the first vacancy of commander that arises to the first lieutenant of the Culloden."

These sentiments were fully acceded to by Earl St. Vincent, who, in his reply, said,

" Your lordship's distinction, touching the first lieutenant of the Culloden, is very just; for it certainly would establish a precedent liable to great abuse. Having admitted thus much, I beg leave to remind you of the very eminent services of the Culloden. After she took the ground, the promptitude of making the signal to avoid the danger prevented the Alexander and Swiftsure from being inevitably wrecked, thereby contributing largely to the ultimate glorious success. The Culloden made 120 tons of water an hour : yet by the astonishing resources of her captain, and the happy manner he possesses of making his officers and men think and act like himself, the ship was preserved, and her damages have been since repaired. Nor was Captain Troubridge's attention entirely taken up with his own ship when in such critical circumstances off the Nile; for after the action, he obtained sheep and other refreshments for the wounded men of the fleet; conducted the exchange of prisoners, and assisted in jury-masting our own dismasted ships and the prizes : I shall therefore obey your lordship's commands with inexpressible satisfaction."

Captain Troubridge followed Lord Nelson to Naples, where he arrived in the month of September, and was soon in all the active scenes of that important period : but he soon found occasion to execrate those who called themselves the allies of England ; and, great as his detestation of the enemy was, he was still louder in his complaints of the faithless conduct of those who professed to act with him. He appears, however, to have soon obtained a knowledge of their character; but, unlike the admiral he served under, he was not to be cajoled out of his senses by the slippery tongue of a female. On the 6th November, 1798, in writing from Naples to Lord Nelson, he said, " I told the marquis and *squad* of the taking of Goza: he replied, ' *I could have done that any day; but it was of no moment—Malta was the thing.*' I bowed, and we parted. He has ordered the ships to be got ready with all possible dispatch : some are doing it, and some are thinking about it. I think they are cheating us about the wine: but that is nothing new here; for, between ourselves, for a carline I could buy all the generals in the place, from Pignatelli downwards. I long much to see you. God send I may never behold this degenerated place again! Every man here is our bitter enemy." He was subsequently stationed off Leghorn, and after the French army had entered the Neapolitan states, he addressed Lord Nelson as follows:

" *Dated Dec.* 1. As soon as your lordship was gone, I went on shore, and found a general hurry and movement. I advised the old general to seize immediately all the French in the mole, or let me do it; but he said his orders were very particular not to make war with the French. I asked him, whether taking Rome was to be considered as a hostile transaction of the King of Naples : if it were, why not act as his king had done? At last he agreed, but took two days, and then wanted the whole of the Genoese vessels in ballast to be let go. I represented the matter to Mr. Wyndham as being quite contrary to our agreement, and we settled how I should act. I believe the only thing which at last brought the general to take any steps was, my telling him the mole would be destroyed by fire, and probably the town; and in the bustle, the French, Genoese, &c. might take the town from him. This staggered him; and he agreed, as I have told you, to a half measure."

" *Dec. 5.* I inclose General Naselli's proclamation. Mr. Wyndham has been with the general, to press him to put his proclamation in force, which ordered all the crews of the French ships and the vagabonds to depart in two days: four have now elapsed, and no orders are given, nor any attempt made to force the substance of the proclamation to be executed: *the true Neapolitan shuffle takes place on all occasions.*"

At the end of the year, Lord Nelson appears to have heard of Sir Sidney Smith's appointment to the separate command off Egypt, and to have been much hurt in consequence; and in a letter to Lord St. Vincent he said, " As soon as I can get hold of Troubridge, I shall send him to Egypt, to endeavour to destroy the ships in Alexandria: *if it can be done, Troubridge will do it.*" He accordingly proceeded thither, but every endeavour to destroy the transports at Alexandria proved ineffectual. The French had, after the departure of Lord Nelson, very strongly fortified all the points of the harbour, and the transports could not be destroyed by shells, as all the mortars burst, and six fire-ships were lost in a gale of wind.* On the 5th of March, 1799, he gave up the blockade to Sir Sidney Smith. In writing afterwards to Lord Nelson, he gave an account of the manner in which he had discovered and taken a person who had been sent by Buonaparte to mislead the Turks.

"On the 14th February I detained the caravella, that had at last been permitted by the French to leave Alexandria; and having received information from a spy on board her, sent for the captain, and shewed him a firman from the grand seignor, taking care not to let him read it. I told him it was a hattesheriff for the head of a traitor: on this he appeared alarmed, and acknowledged he had a Mons. Beauchamp on board, habited like a Turk, and a French pilot. I immediately sent and seized the ambassador, as they called him, and his Greek servant, and by sharpening an axe, and playing him off with the hattesheriff, I so alarmed the Greek domestic, that he shewed us where they had concealed their instructions from Buonaparte on board the caravella. It appeared to me that the grand seignor would do this fellow more justice than I could: I therefore sent him in the Swiftsure to Rhodes, *recommending him strongly for decapitation.*"

* Harrison.

At this period every exertion was making by Lord Nelson, in concert with their Sicilian Majesties, to effect the recovery of Naples from the dominion of the French. Cardinal Ruffo, who united in himself the three important characters of statesman, prelate, and general, had raised a large army of loyalists in the provinces, and a strong spirit of insubordination against the French prevailed in Naples itself. It was therefore resolved that an English squadron should be sent into the bay, to prevent the enemy receiving any supplies of corn or other articles by sea; and also to obtain possession, if possible, of the Islands of Procida, Ischia, and Capri; and it was at the same time determined that this squadron should be under the orders of Captain Troubridge. He in consequence sailed on the 31st of March, for the purpose of carrying these orders into effect. But, "it is a singular fact, that even at this very period, when Lord Nelson was thus engaged in securing Sicily from the French, as well as labouring to obtain the restoration of Naples, attempts were making by the governor of Messina, then actually protected by British troops, to prevent the condemnation of a French prize which had been taken near the entrance of that port, as if it were still in a state of neutrality." On his arrival in the bay, Captain Troubridge immediately commenced the most active operations. Procida, Ischia, and Capri were soon taken possession of; but the inhabitants were in the most wretched and deplorable condition, bordering indeed on a state of starvation. It was in vain that he solicited from the Sicilian government provision for their support, for so wretchedly were its affairs administered, that none could be procured; and had it not been for the humanity of Captain Troubridge, many of them must have perished from actual want. But while he distributed food with one hand to the loyal part of the inhabitants, he was no less active in discovering and putting into confinement those who had betrayed the interests of their sovereign. All the principal traitors that were taken on the islands were distributed among the ships of the squadron, to await the punishment due to their crimes. He solicited a Neapolitan judge to try the offenders; but it seemed to be the wish of the imbecile ministry to cast all the odium of every execution upon the English, and some time elapsed before he could obtain the object of his desires. Captain Brenton says, "Had there been one spark of virtue or courage in Ferdinand and his base associates at this period, Naples might have been again happy; but her day was past. Of the Italians who figured in this eventful scene, we only know of two who deserved the name of men, Ruffo and Caracciolli. Thirsting for the blood and property of each other, there was no act degrading to men which the degenerate Neapolitans scrupled to commit; cowardice and treachery were the prominent features of their character. Whatever courage or talent might be found among them was (with the exception of Ruffo) always exerted against the king. The following anecdote was given to the author by a friend, on whose veracity he can rely: Troubridge was asked by a lieutenant-colonel, *a stanch royalist,* for two English sloops of war, with which he was to take some little fort. The request was granted: but the warrior returned and begged for two frigates; these were given him in lieu of the sloops, when another request was preferred for two ships of the line. His last application was made in the cabin of the Culloden: suddenly the doors burst open, and out flew the lieutenant-colonel, with Troubridge at his heels, kicking him along, while the commodore, foaming with rage, exclaimed, 'The cowardly rascal! first sloops, then frigates, then ships of the line, and then, damn him, he is afraid to fight after all!' No man so justly appreciated the character of these people as Troubridge: he hated the French, but he despised the Neapolitans."

The conduct of Captain Troubridge during the ensuing month of July, throughout the sieges of St. Elmo, Capua, and Gaieta, afforded continual examples of the vigilance, enterprise, and inexhaustible resources of that great officer. He had landed, agreeably to Lord Nelson's orders, with the English and Portuguese marines of the fleet, on the 27th June, and after embarking the garrisons of the castles of Uovo and Nuovo, composed of French and rebels, had left a garrison in each under Captain Hood; and on the 29th of the same month, had taken possession of Fort St. Elmo, which he summoned to surrender. This fort, garrisoned with 800 troops, was commanded by a French republican, Mejan, the commandant of the French Neapolitan army, whose rude manners and insolent behaviour were peculiarly obnoxious to the king. "*Je m'amuse, monsieur,*" said this republican in a letter which he sent to Captain Foote, "*de l'existence politique que vous voulez bien donner au fantôme de monarque que vous appellez Majesté Sicilienne. Il ne tardera pas lui-même à subir le traitement dû à un monstre, qui n'a existé que pour le malheur du genre-humain, tout comme le sont les tyrans de son espèce. Du reste, nous sommes persuadés que les gouvernemens de Londres ou de Palerme, si vous le voulez, ne se comprometront pas jusqu'à maltraiter Citoyen Ribaud, consul de France à Messine. Il suffit qu'il soit revêtu du caractère d'un citoyen Français pour que tous les tyrans insulaires le respectent.*" Captain Troubridge having resorted to Antigniano, near St. Elmo, in eight days brought this proud republican to his senses, and to a consciousness of his inferiority. Notwithstanding bad powder and damp cartridges, Captain Troubridge opened a battery on him of three 36-pounders and four mortars, on the 3d July, within 700 yards of Fort St. Elmo: about twelve Jacobins were in the castle, with their chief, named Mattera, and in the adjacent convent of Martini were eight Italian republicans.

" It is difficult," wrote Captain Troubridge to Lord Nelson, " to make approaches, the castle stands in so commanding a situation. Your lordship may rely on every exertion being made. Several of the shells fell well, and I hope broke some of their shins."

" *July 3.* We are preparing fascines, &c. for a battery not more than 200 yards from the wall; but every article is so difficult to get, that our progress is not so quick as I could wish. The mortar-beds are quite old, and a variety of causes have stopped us this morning: by the time your answer comes we shall begin. I shall observe strictly what your lordship hints, and will knock up Micheroux altogether. Ball was instructed this morning, if they offered terms, to say they must be prisoners of war. Micheroux has been a cipher with us, and cannot have the smallest influence; we have suspected him, as Ball will inform you: I think he is off. When all is over, I shall have a settling with these youths. I had, prior to your lordship's letter, sent eighty picked men, with two of the best captains and lieutenants I could select, to restore order in Naples. In short, my lord, the cardinal's secretary is making a fortune by giving protections to Jacobins; and the greatest discontent prevails at the conduct of the villanous lawyers who are trying the culprits at the granary; they all escape: the lawyers are bribed."

"*July 4.* You must not fret at our not getting on so fast as you expect. The musketry last night frightened away the whole of our workmen, even those who were out of the direction of the fire, and they were not to be found until late this morning. Our next battery will be so very close, that we are obliged to make regular approaches. I am really making the best I can out of the degenerate race I have to deal with; the whole means of guns, ammunition, pioneers, &c. with all materials, rest with them. With fair promises from them to the men, and threats of instant death if I find any one erring, a little spur has been given. Four of our mortars are nearly done up; their touch-holes are as big as a half-crown."

On the 5th July Captain Troubridge opened another battery of two

36-pounders, 200 yards from St. Elmo. The Russians under Captain Baillie also opened a battery of four 36-pounders and four mortars against the opposite angle, in order to assist in storming it in different places as soon as two practical breaches were made: Captain Troubridge at the same time was making every preparation for opening a fourth battery, and also a fifth within 100 yards of the wall of the garrison. When writing to Lord Nelson, he said,

"I am really sorry to see you so low-spirited: all will go well; but the devilish fort is so high and commanding, that our batteries are obliged to be mountains. When we get their works beat off, I hope we shall soon be able to mine the fort. I am a strong advocate, if we can accomplish that, to send them, hostages and all, to Old Nick, and surprise him with a group of nobility and republicans."

The insolence of Mejan gradually abated in proportion as this resolute enemy approached; and in making a request to him respecting the sick and wounded Frenchmen, the commandant, instead of speaking of " insular tyrants" and " royal monsters," as had been his custom, prefaced his request with, " *Je sais, monsieur, qu'au milieu des qualités que vous distinguent, la bienfaisance et la humanité n'occupent pas la plus petite place. Cette reputation que vous honore ne me laisse aucun doute.*" Troubridge, suspecting treachery, declined interfering, and continued his approaches. In a letter to Lord Nelson, he said,

" I have intercepted a letter from Micheroux, wherein he tells his brother, *too many cooks spoil the broth.* I think he wanted the rich part, and for us to eat the soup-meagre: he has been some time carrying on this farce. Since finishing my letter, the governor has, through Micheroux, sent an offer to surrender for 150,000 ducats: I treated the offer as it deserved. Be assured, my lord, we are getting on. I constantly hold out rewards and promotion for those who behave well and exert themselves, and a halter for traitors. Our new work is going on fast. I have a good redoubt in the middle of the work, and a famous trench."

" *July* 7. I am going to order that all persons living near our out-posts must remove. We are so surrounded with villains, that it becomes necessary to do so. I have had a Frenchman taken up at Naples, who says Micheroux gave him permission to be at large in that city: he was in one of the castles, either Uovo or Nuovo."

" *July* 9 Your lordship will see I have made Mr. Mejan write like a gentleman. I sent word by his officer, that none of his letters with the insolent printed words at the top, *Liberté, Egalité, Guerre aux tyrans,* &c. would be received. If he wrote to me like a soldier and a gentleman, I would answer him in the same style; the others would have no answers whatever. I was yesterday busily employed in sifting to the bottom a diabolical good understanding between our Neapolitan officers stationed at the advanced posts and the enemy. I inclose your lordship the depositions of the two men who were employed to carry it on. The general told me the council of state would condemn them directly; I therefore sent them to the cardinal last night: he declined having any thing to do with it: such damned cowards and villains I never saw. Your lordship must therefore endeavour to fret as little as possible—we shall succeed."

" *July* 12. The new battery brought the vagabonds to their senses after much trouble and palavre. I send your lordship the capitulation regularly signed; and the moment I have got the fort arranged, I shall pay you my respects, and bring the colours and keys."

Thus did the French garrison of St. Elmo surrender themselves prisoners of war; and respecting which, Lord Nelson said, " The very great strength of St. Elmo, and its formidable position, will mark with what fortitude, perseverance, and ability, the combined forces must have acted. I have now to state to your lordship, that although the ability and resources of my brave friend Troubridge are well known to all the world, yet he had difficulties to struggle with, in every way, which the state of the capital will easily bring to your idea, that have raised his character even higher than it was before; and it is my earnest request, that your lordship will mention him in that way to the Board of Admiralty, that his Majesty may be graciously pleased to bestow some mark of royal favour on him."

In a letter to Earl Spencer, he added, " It would be supposing you, my dear lord, were ignorant of his merits, were I to say more than that he is a first-rate general." In a letter to the Duke of Clarence, he again alluded to the merits of Captain Troubridge, by saying, "I find, sir, that General Koehler does not approve of such irregular proceedings as naval officers attacking and defending fortifications. We have but one idea—to get close along side. None but a sailor would have placed a battery only 180 yards from the castle of St. Elmo. A soldier must have gone according to art and the ~~ way; my brave Troubridge went straight, for we had no time to spare."

The sieges of Capua and Gaieta followed, and were crowned with equal success; but in which Captain Troubridge experienced a repetition of all his troubles and difficulties, as will be seen from the following account in one of his letters to Lord Nelson:

" I hope to acquire a little patience; but the Neapolitan government is so deranged, that it is impossible for things to go on as we could wish: of a bad bargain, we must make the best. The poor devils of workmen have had no provisions to-day; I offered my own cash, but I could not procure bread, so we must stand fast to-night. The damned cardinal writes a flaming letter, saying 40,000 ducats a week have been ordered; when the whole are calling for payment, and on being told it only exists on paper, are quite disheartened. I lent an officer to-day 60 ducats to buy him a dinner. Several deserters came in to-day: they all agree that the enemy have not the smallest intelligence of us. I hope to astonish their weak minds to-morrow.—*Eight p. m.* The *etat-major*, with all its forms, ruins us, and instead of having the batteries ready to play on the enemy, we have not a single thing or workman arrived. At St. Elmo I had the vagabonds within hail. I do not mean this as a complaint, as I have hopes that workmen, &c. will arrive to begin at the dawn of day. Your lordship must make a little allowance for the people and staff; the latter, you know, have too much method for us: however, we shall do."

On the 25th the trenches were opened, with one battery within 500 yards of the glacis. In his official letter, he says.

" Our battery was finished yesterday by four o'clock p.m. but I did not think it adviseable to open it until this morning at half-past three o'clock. After three rounds from the guns and mortars, I sent Hallowell to propose the terms your lordship directed. They answered they would not surrender, and hardly believed that St. Elmo was taken: nothing but the sight of Mejan's signature could make them believe it. Our batteries are again opening, but the powder is so bad that the shells hardly break; many fall short, though not above 300 toises. I really suspect some treachery. If your lordship could spare us 40 casks of our powder, it would be very useful for the mortars. If you comply, it will be necessary that some person belonging to us should accompany it, or they will steal one half and change the other. I have moved the camps, to enable us to erect two more batteries in a very commanding situation, within 200 yards of the works."

" *July* 28. As there is no dependence to be placed on the metal of the Neapolitan mortars, I submit to your lordship if we had not better get our 10-inch sea mortars fitted in land-beds. Pray lend us all the spades and iron shovels from the ships; the tools these country people have work too slow for us.—*Nine p. m.* We gain ground daily; if we can complete the trench to-night for two batteries of four guns each, I think, with the mortars, to bring the governor to his senses. The difficulty is to get the workmen to stand a little fire."

" *July* 27. The French sent out this morning, in the usual way, demanding protection for their patriots: I answered—inadmissible; and offered the terms of St. Elmo, and to include Gaieta in the capitulation. They desire until to-morrow to hold a council. They offered Gaieta if I would omit the patriots, and promise that they should not be molested, and their property be secured, which I positively refused."

" *July* 28. I have the honour to inclose your lordship a copy of the capitulation, signed by all but the Turk: I shall get his signature to another in the course of the day. I had gone too far before your letter reached me at midnight, to insist on Gaieta. The governor offers, if his Majesty will allow that garrison to take their arms, he will give orders for its immediate evacuation."

" *July* 29. I have sent in the greater part of the marines belonging to the ships gone to Mahon, as well as those which are to follow. The French general, when he found that we gave in for the arms, refused to issue any orders until you permitted the garrison of Gaieta to go without being prisoners. As I was not authorized to do that, I told him he was not a man of honour, and I should leave them and him to their fate. Gaieta may be reduced by the Russians and king's troops, without our assistance. I shall remain here to-day, to stop all the villanies going on. Their baggage is enormous—some antiques may be in it. I pray that may be a business of Count Thurn, if found necessary. *Every man, you see, gentle and simple, are such notorious villains, that it is necessary to be with them.* I am endeavouring to get a return of prisoners, powder, guns, &c. but as it is the interest of the thieves here to prevent it, they are trying to do it, and I am trying against them. His Majesty shall have as good an account as I can get. There are immense quantities of powder and fine ordnance. Colonel Gams has just sent me word that he is obliged to form a hundred stratagems to get clear of the Calabrians: these vagabonds have killed sixteen of their officers within this month."

On the 29th and 30th of September Captain Troubridge, with 200 seamen and marines, took possession of Civita Vecchia, Cornatto, and Tolfa, under articles of capitulation, from which places he embarked about 5000 Frenchmen. By another convention with the French general, Garnier, the Roman states were cleared of the enemy.

Respecting these and other important events, he gives the following particulars* :

" *Sept.* 12. The news from Rome is very unfavourable. Bouchard has with him about 2000 regulars and 7000 vagabonds. The Romans, it is said, have all armed to resist him, declaring that the Neapolitans are such thieves, no reliance

---

* Clarke and M'Arthur.

can be placed on their word : the Romans are therefore determined not to be under their yoke. I wish, my lord, there was not so much truth in what they assert. Although Naples is certainly quiet at present, yet much discontent prevails at the absence of the court and nobles. It really appears to me that means are taken to create discontent. The officers only receive their three carlines a day, the same as the soldiers. The distress I daily meet with hurts me much. Many I relieve, and thousands I abandon to their fate. The letters from Palermo mention the feasting, and the immense sums of money that are spent there. It has caused the Neapolitans to murmur ; and they very justly say, ' If the money were spent in the capital, it would relieve many thousands.' The report to-day is, that the Pignatellis are only to be banished : Prince Tarella the same. Riario is also destined for Maretimo, with a few others. They must finish soon, or every family here will be interested in making a disturbance. They should make some examples, and pass an act of oblivion, and let all be forgotten. At present there are upwards of forty thousand families who have relations confined. If some act of oblivion be not passed, there will be no end of persecution; for the people of this country have no idea of any thing but revenge, and to gain a point would swear ten thousand false oaths. Constant efforts are made to get a man taken up, in order to rob him. I have seen many instances, which induces me to make this representation to your lordship. I shall be ruined, if I stay here much longer. I fear the property that is confiscated does not reach the king's treasury—all thieves ! If the king knew as much as I do, he would certainly come to Naples. The property of the Jacobins is selling for nothing, and his own people, whom he employs, are buying it up, and the vagabonds pocket the whole. I should not be surprised to hear that they brought a bill of expenses against him for the sale. His Majesty's custom-house is carried on in the same iniquitous manner. If the king does not come and settle his kingdom of Naples, all must go wrong : they are now greater villains, if possible, than before the revolution."

Having sent Captain Louis to Civita Vecchia, with proposals for a capitulation, he followed on the 18th ; and, on his arrival, found that his proposals had been forwarded to the French general at Rome. But as it appeared to him that the general wished to get off from the Roman states, and as Civita Vecchia had no powers to treat separately, he took upon himself, without a moment's loss of time, to offer the Gaieta terms for all the Roman states, except Ancona. These terms, however, were not accepted with that readiness which he expected, which he found was attributable to the French ambassador; and he wrote the following to Lord Nelson :

" The council the French general talks of is the damned ambassador and commissaire, who assume a power over Garnier. The stuff the French proposed made me sick: the ambassador was the cause of it: the thief is afraid to go to France; he would stay where he is not wanted. He called the Roman territory the property of the French republic by right of conquest: I settled that by saying, *It is mine by reconquest;* and he was silenced."

Terms were at length settled; and in forwarding them to his admiral, on the 27th, he said,

" If the copy of the very voluminous capitulation is not so correct as I could have wished, your lordship will, I hope, pardon it. I am really tired and worn down; very little sleep since I have been here, and am unable to give your lordship all my strong and weighty reasons for offering the French general such good terms. I have sent Louis up to Bouchard, to secure the tranquillity of Rome. The public property is immense, by the French accounts. The Austrians offered any terms, but I out-manœuvred them, and brought General Garnier on board the Culloden, and settled all, as your lordship will see. I pray you suspend your opinion, if you think I have acted wrong, until I have the honour of seeing you. I am sure I can then give such substantial reasons for all I have done, as wholly to clear every thing. The policy of the Germans to get hold of the state, your lordship is well acquainted with, particularly as the Pope is dead. I wrote to the cardinal, but did not tell him the papal chair was to let."

For his important services in the Mediterranean, Captain Troubridge was presented with the Sicilian Order of St. Ferdinand and Merit; and in the same year (1799) had the farther honour of being created by his own sovereign a Baronet of Great Britain.

This active and indefatigable officer was now ordered off Malta, and to exert his great abilities in the reduction of that important place, as well as to watch the French ships in the harbour. But here it seems the imbecility of some of the Neapolitans, the intrigues of others, and their villany, were as apparent, and perplexed him as much, as when he was exerting himself on the Italian coast. " The difficulties," say Clarke and M'Arthur, " which Sir Thomas Troubridge had experienced, through want of a supply of corn from Palermo, during the preceding summer, were, at the beginning of 1800, greatly increased throughout his services at Malta. His mind was also much agitated by the continuance of Lord Nelson at Palermo. Troubridge's affection for him was unbounded; and being fearful lest the remnant of the Nile squadron, which had taken refuge at Malta, might, in an attempt to escape, be captured without the presence of the admiral, the dejected commodore thus expressed the warmth and disinterestedness of his friendship, in a letter dated Malta, Jan. 1:

" We are dying off fast for want. I learn, by letters from Messina, that Sir W. Hamilton says Prince Luzzo refused corn some time ago, and Sir W. does not think it worth while making another application. If that be the case, I wish he commanded at this distressing scene, and not I. Puglia had an immense harvest; near thirty sail left Messina before I did, to load corn : will they let us have any ? If not, a short time will decide the business. The German interest prevails. I wish I were at your lordship's elbow for an hour: all will be thrown on you, depend on it. I will parry the blow as much as it is in my power. I foresee much mischief brewing. God bless your lordship ! I am miserable. I cannot assist your operations more. Many happy returns of this day to you! I never spent so miserable a one. I am not very tender-hearted, but really the distress here would move even a Neapolitan."

" *Jan.* 5. I have this day saved 30,000 people from dying ; but with this day my ability ceases. As the government are bent on starving us, I see no alternative but to leave these poor unhappy people to perish, without our being witnesses to their distress. I curse the day I ever served the Neapolitan government. I, who know your lordship so well, can pity the distress you must suffer: what must be our situation on the spot ? I never expected to be treated in this manner. *** certainly influences the king's council : he complains he cannot get his orders put in force. How can he expect it, when he never punishes any of the traitors ? On the contrary, is he not daily promoting them ? We have characters, my lord, to lose; these people have none. Do not suffer their infamous conduct to fall on us. Our country is just, but severe. I foresee we shall forfeit the little that can be gained. Such is the fever of my brain at this moment, that I assure you, on my honour, if the Palermo traitors were here, I would shoot them first, and then myself. Gergenti, they inform me, is full of corn ; the money is ready to pay for it; we do not ask it as a gift. Oh ! could you see the horrid distress I daily experience, something would be done."

" *Jan.* 7. Your lordship will perceive that some engine is at work against us at Naples, and I believe that, in my former letter, I hit on the proper person. If you complain, he will be immediately promoted, agreeably to the Neapolitan custom. My friend Yauch is in high favour, and at present intriguing deeply. All I wrote to you is known at the queen's : I suspect my letters are opened before they reach you. For my own part, I look upon the Neapolitans as the worst of intriguing enemies ; every hour shews me their infamy and duplicity. It may be necessary to caution General Acton of what is going on : as that can be done in English, you may be sure of what is said. I pray your lordship be cautious : your honest open manner of acting will be made a handle of. It is necessary to be very vigilant over the deceitful set you have to deal with : every nerve of mine shall be exerted to forward your views and the service. I cannot assist you so fast as I could wish, so little depends on me : that little you shall find well done."

" *Jan.* 8. From the Russians not arriving, by the contrivance of these mon- sters, is to be attributed our inactivity, which creates discontent. In short, my lord, when I see you, and tell of their infamous tricks, you will be as much sur- prised as I am. The whole will fall on you, which hurts me much. If you would contrive to come here, and get the credit of the reduction of this very important place, it would much gratify all your friends, and none more than your ever faithful and obliged, " T. Troubridge."

Sir Thomas continued in the Mediterranean till July 1800, when he returned to England, and was appointed captain of the Channel fleet under Earl St. Vincent. A few months afterwards he was appointed one of the Lords Commissioners of the Admiralty; a post which he con- tinued to occupy, with credit to himself and advantage to the country, till May 1804; but on the 23d April preceding he was promoted to the rank of rear-admiral. In April 1805 he hoisted his flag in the Blenheim, having been appointed to the chief command in the Indian seas, to the eastward of Point du Gallo, in the Island of Ceylon, and sailed for that station with ten sail of Indiamen under his convoy, having a body of troops on board for Madras. In the month of August he fell in with Admiral Linois, in the Marengo, to the eastward of Madagascar, having with him the Belle Poule and Atalante frigates of 44 guns, and Bruns- wick, his prize. The Marengo brought the Blenheim to action, most probably under the conviction of that ship being an Indiaman; but feel- ing the effect of her lower-deck guns, Linois very quickly took himself out of gun-shot, and hauled his wind. The Blenheim sailed too ill to attempt the pursuit, and the British rear-admiral continued his course to Madras, where he arrived without any farther accident, and took the command in the Eastern seas*, which he retained till the beginning of 1807, when Sir E. Pellew, who likewise commanded in the Indian seas, by an order from home, assumed the chief command of the whole; at which time Sir Thomas was directed to proceed to the Cape of Good Hope, as commander-in-chief on that station. His flag was still on board the Blenheim of 74 guns, formerly a second-rate, but cut down, and a worn-out ship. Early in 1806 she had got on shore in the Straits of Malacca, where she had received so much damage as to render her un-

* Brenton.

fit to cross the Bay of Bengal; but having repaired her at Pulo-Penang, and rigged jury-masts, Sir Thomas, whose pride was to overcome difficulties, proceeded in her to Madras, where he arrived in safety. Here the defects of his ship became daily more apparent; her back was broken in a most extraordinary manner, and her beams and riders shewed that she was falling to pieces, while the labour of the crew at the pumps barely sufficed to keep the water from gaining on her as she lay at anchor. Captain Bissell commanded the ship, and, as was his duty, represented her state to the rear-admiral. Sir Thomas, however, persisted in his purpose of sailing in her to the Cape; and such was the confidence reposed in his talents, that many passengers from Madras embarked with him. He sailed on the 12th January; the Java of 36 guns, an old Dutch prize frigate, commanded by Captain George Pigot, and the Harrier brig, of 18 guns, Captain Finlay, being in company. On the 1st of February, when in lat. 22° 44′ S. and long. 66° 11′ E. not far from the S. E. end of Madagascar, they were caught in a tremendous gale of wind, and forced to lay-to. In the evening the Java, which was to windward, bore up to close with the Blenheim, both ships having the signal of distress flying. The Blenheim was observed by the officers of the Harrier to have settled much lower in the water, and it was the general opinion that Captain Pigot, even in his own distress, had, while generously attempting to save some, at least, of the unfortunate people on board the Blenheim, ran foul of her, and accelerated their destruction. As night came on, the Harrier bore away for the Cape, where she arrived on the 28th of the same month. Such are the last and only accounts we have ever had of the Blenheim and Java. As soon as Captain Finlay's letter reached Sir E. Pellew, in India, he conceived a faint hope that the two ships might have put into some port to repair: he therefore ordered Captain Troubridge, only son of the rear-admiral, and then commanding the Greyhound of 32 guns, to go in search of his father. He was first directed to proceed to the Island of Roderique, then to the Isle of France, and to send in a flag of truce to the governor for that information which, even in time of war, would not be refused by a generous enemy; after which he was to go to St. Mary's, on the S. E. point of Madagascar, and failing there, was to return to Madras. The gallant and unhappy young officer commenced his melancholy search, pursuing the course marked out by the admiral. On his arrival at the Isle of

France, General de Caen sent him every information which it had been in his power to collect from the different signal-stations, together with a description of certain pieces of wreck which had been cast on shore; but there was nothing which could give the smallest clue to the fate of the Blenheim and Java, beyond the letter of Captain Finlay. Thus perished Sir Thomas Troubridge, one of our most gallant and effective admirals, the friend of St. Vincent, the companion of Nelson. His maxim, never to make a difficulty, copied from his great patron, Earl St. Vincent, he perhaps carried to an extreme: it was the compass by which he had steered, by which he had risen from the lowest to the highest ranks in the service. He was supposed to command more resources in his ship than any other officer of his time. The Culloden was always prepared for service; a proof of which was afforded previously to the battle of the 14th February, when, being disabled in such a manner as would have induced many officers to have gone into port, he refitted her at sea, and had a very distinguished share in that glorious victory*.

In addition to those letters which are here inserted of Lord Nelson's, expressing the high opinion which he entertained of him, we must give the following: June 15, 1798, he says, " Troubridge possesses my full confidence, and has been my honoured acquaintance of twenty-five years' standing." After the battle of the Nile, he said, " Although I keep on, yet I feel that I must soon leave my situation up the Mediterranean to Trou- bridge, *than whom we both know no person is more equal to the task.* I should have sunk under the fatigue of refitting the squadron but for him, Ball, Hood, and Hallowell: not but that all have done well; but these are my supporters."—Again. " Dear Troubridge, whom we went to visit yesterday, is better than I expected: the active business and the scold- ing he is obliged to be continually at do him good. I am not surprised that you wish him near you, but I trust you will not take him from me. I well know he is my superior, and so I often want his advice and as- sistance."

After what has been already said on this subject, it may appear unne- cessary for us to make any comment, but we cannot allow it to pass without offering a few observations; and we more particularly wish to do so, in consequence of having heard it said, that Sir Thomas was much to

---

* Brenton.

blame for leaving Madras with so crippled and disabled a ship; that it was a presumptuous contempt of danger, and a too great confidence in his own powers; that it was trifling not only with his own life, but with the lives of hundreds of others.   In the absence of all authentic information on the subject, we can only hazard a few general remarks.

"It can raise no wonder that temerity is generally censured; for it is one of the vices with which few can be charged, and which therefore great numbers are ready to condemn: it is the vice of noble and generous minds, the exuberance of magnanimity, and the ebullition of genius; and is therefore not regarded with much tenderness, because it never flatters us by that appearance of softness and imbecility which is commonly necessary to conciliate compassion.   But if the same attention had been applied to the search of arguments against the folly of presupposing impossibilities, and anticipating frustration, I know not whether many would not have been roused to usefulness, who, having been taught to confound prudence with timidity, never ventured to excel, lest they should unfortunately fail."

Sir Thomas, we may say, was born in obscurity, and at first experienced all the natural disadvantages attending it: chance brought him into the path of honours; he distinguished himself by brilliant conduct, and to his own merit was he exclusively indebted for his renown.   His skill and bravery were undoubted; his seamanship was held in the highest estimation; and a long, arduous, and indefatigable application to his professional duties, enabled him to acquire a degree of professional celebrity which rendered no disaster unknown, and no situation unusual to him.   He was jealous of fame, careless of safety, enamoured of glory, and " ambitious to shew that courage can triumph over fortune, and magnanimity over force; that nothing is invincible to the brave, or impregnable to the daring."   Was he then to be deterred from crossing the Indian Ocean in company with two other vessels, because his own was defective?   People are generally disposed to censure the justice or policy of an unsuccessful action, but often without inquiring into particulars, or making allowances for circumstances and situations.

"It may be laid down as an axiom, that it is more easy to take away superfluities than to supply defects: and therefore he that is culpable, because he has passed the middle point of virtue, is always accounted a fairer object of hope, than he who fails by falling short.   The one has all that perfection requires, and more, but the excess may be easily re-trenched : the other wants the qualities requisite to excellence, and who can tell how he shall obtain them ?"   But neither merit nor abilities can command success; and if Sir Thomas erred, he erred on the side of glory, genius, perseverance, and fortitude.   In every station he had hitherto distinguished himself by superior valour, rigid discipline, and successful conduct; and we believe him to have been in no respect inferior to the greatest. and most admired commander that the British navy ever produced.

HISTORICAL MEMOIRS OF

CAPTAIN THE HON. FREDERICK PAUL IRBY.

IT has been intimated to us, that the observations which we have in ge-neral prefixed to the Memoirs of officers would have been better omitted; that they appear to indicate a degree of vanity on our part, or a desire of book-making. Whatever appearances they may, however, have, we can-not plead guilty to either of the above conclusions: our only object in in-troducing them has been to vary the subject as much as possible; to divert that sameness which must appear in a work of this description, and to make it as entertaining as the subject and our own abilities would admit. We are, however, now nearly in the situation of the man who has indulged himself in certain habits for a long series of years, and who, though he may wish to adopt a new method, finds his energies gone; is unable to muster sufficient resolution to make an alteration in his mode of living; that neither his faculties nor his bodily strength will allow him to adopt a new mode; and that, in fact, he is too old to change. Were we ever so inclined to alter the plan of this work, it is now too near its conclusion to enable us to do so: but we will fairly own, that we have no such inclination; satisfied with our own intentions, and the good opi-nion of those officers under whose auspices we undertook the task, we shall unhesitatingly pursue them to the end. And though we are by no means indifferent to, or regardless of, the sentiments and opinions of those gentlemen to whom we have above alluded, we must observe, that were the work to be redone, we see but little necessity for any alteration.

The gentleman who is the subject of the present Memoir is the second son of Frederick Lord Boston and Christian his wife, only daughter of Paul Methuen, Esq. and was born April 18, 1779. Having been for some time at Eton school, he entered into the naval service of his country in the year 1791, on board the Catharine yacht, commanded by Sir George Young; and in the following year he proceeded to Halifax on board the Winchelsea frigate, Captain R. Fisher, and continued on that station till the French revolutionary war, when the Winchelsea pro-ceeded to Barbadoes, having on board the 21st regiment of foot. In coming to an anchor in Carlisle Bay, she unfortunately carried away her

mizen-mast by falling on board the Orion of 74 guns: at that moment
Mr. Irby, with about fifteen other midshipmen and boys, was in the
top, about to hand the mizen-top-sail; they all fell with the mast, but
most providentially not one received any injury, except a few bruizes.

In 1793 Mr. Irby was removed to the Hannibal of 74 guns, Captain
Sir J. Colpoys, at Martinique, who afterwards went down to Jamaica,
took a convoy of merchantmen under his charge, and sailed for England.
On entering the Channel she had a most miraculous escape from being
wrecked on the Scilly rocks: an American vessel had reported, that the
French fleet was in the Channel, and the Hannibal was working between
the islands and the main, when at night she got completely within the
rocks, and the lights were not seen till she was quite clear of them.
On the passage home Mr. Irby met with a very serious and alarming
accident: while sitting under a large arm and colour-chest on the poop,
between two other young gentlemen, during a gale of wind, the chest
gave way, and forced his legs under the hen-coop, and jammed him in
by the small of his back. With much difficulty he was extricated from
his critical situation; but he was seriously injured, for a long time was
quite disabled, and indeed never totally recovered from its effects. In
1794 the Hannibal was paid off, when he removed to the Montagu, and
in that ship was in Lord Howe's action of the 1st June, when her captain, James Montagu, gloriously fell. In the Montagu Mr. Irby again
proceeded to the West Indies, in company with the Ganges of 74 guns,
and on the passage they captured the Jacobin French national ship of
24 guns, which, just before the break of day, ran down to the Ganges,
began firing, and actually killed two men on board that ship before she
discovered her mistake and struck her colours. Towards the end of
1795 the Montagu again returned to England, bearing the flag of Admiral C. Thompson, with a convoy; and on her being paid off, Mr. Irby
went on board the London of 98 guns, bearing the flag of Sir John Colpoys, attached to the Channel fleet. In 1797 Mr. Irby was a lieutenant
of the Circe of 28 guns, Captain Halket, which was repeating-frigate to
Admiral Duncan in the memorable battle of the 11th October. On
Captain Halket being appointed to the Apollo frigate, he was accompanied into her by Lieutenant Irby, who was on board when she was unfortunately wrecked on the Dutch coast*. In the following year (1799)
Lieutenant Irby was appointed to the Glenmore frigate, Captain G.

* See *Memoir of Admiral* HALKET.

Duff, on the Irish station; and in 1800 was promoted to the rank of commander in the Volcano bomb, attached to Admiral Dickson's squadron, sent into the Baltic to enforce Lord Whitworth's embassy to the Danish court. In 1801 Captain Irby took the command of the Jalouse brig of 18 guns, and cruised in the North Sea with much success. In 1802 he was promoted to post-rank; and in 1805 he was appointed to the sea-fencibles in the Harwich district, under the command of Sir C. Hamilton, Bart. In 1807 Captain Irby was appointed to the Amelia of 38 guns, at Deptford, from whence he proceeded to North Yarmouth with specie, to be transmitted to Sweden in the Stately and Nassau. In consequence of the Amelia being at this time only half-manned, she remained at Yarmouth for some time with the flag of Vice-Admiral Russell; but in 1808 she proceeded to Quebec with a convoy. During their passage, one of the convoy, having on board the Bishop of Quebec and family, sprung a leak, and having twice made the signal of distress, and the carpenter of the Amelia having reported her in a dangerous state, Captain Irby, during a heavy gale of wind, removed the bishop and family to the Amelia, having previously on board, as passengers, Major-General Gordon Drummond, his family and suite; but in the performance of this object one of the Amelia's crew was unfortunately drowned. In the following September the Amelia returned to England, and then, in company with the Loire, Captain Schomberg, convoyed General Baird's army, in 152 transports, to Corunna; Generals Warde and Manningham, with their suites, being on board the Amelia. From Corunna Captain Irby proceeded with transports to Lisbon, and brought General Sir Harry Burrard to England. He was then attached to the Channel fleet, and whilst blockading l'Orient, under the orders of Sir J. Beresford, he fell in with the wreck of a French merchant-brig, which had upset the previous day, all her crew having perished, except a man and a boy, whom Captain Irby, with great humanity, ordered to be landed on the French coast. On the 21st February, 1809, the Amelia was on her station off the S. E. end of Groa, with yards at the mast-head and sails stopped by rope-yarns, ready to slip or weigh, the enemy's squadron being expected out; and at daylight on the following morning a French squadron from Brest, consisting of eight sail of the line and a frigate, was observed outside the Amelia, while a frigate and a brig were off the mouth of l'Orient, making signals to the ships in port; at which time none of the British squadron was in sight from the Amelia, though it appears they were from the enemy's ships. Captain Irby immediately weighed, and was followed for some time by two ships of the line; but standing close in shore, and running down to Quiberon, to apprise the vessels lying there of the enemy's being at sea, they left off chasing. In the evening he again stood out, and fell in with the squadron under Sir John Beresford, who had been led from the enemy by the Amelia's signals, and the mistake was not discovered till daylight, when the ships stood in shore again; where three of the enemy's frigates from l'Orient were standing to the southward, followed by the Dotterel brig. The Amelia joined in the pursuit by signal, and parted from Sir J. Beresford: during the night, when passing between Isle Dieu and the main, Captain Irby arrived so close as to hear the enemy hail each other. On the morning of the 24th, a squadron was seen to windward, and the enemy's frigates stood in for the Sable d'Olonne; but in crossing on opposite tacks, the Amelia exchanged broadsides with the sternmost ship, the Italienne, by which (from the report of prisoners afterwards made) she had three men killed and several wounded. He then joined in the attack made on the enemy by Rear-Admiral Stopford*, and afterwards continued under the command of Lord Gambier in blockading the enemy in Basque roads; and on the 1st April was sent in to prevent a battery being erected on the Boyart shoal, which he fully accomplished. On the 5th he was sent, with the Alcmene frigate, to watch two French frigates ready for sea, and two others fitting in the Loire. On the 30th, the two frigates stood to reconnoitre the enemy, previous to rejoining Lord Gambier, when the Alcmene struck on the Three Stones at the north end of la Blanche shoal, and, notwithstanding every exertion was made to get her off, she was wrecked. For six days Captain Irby used every effort which skill and genius could suggest for her preservation, but in vain, though he succeeded in saving the whole of her crew and stores, and she was then totally destroyed. He was afterwards employed on the north coast of Spain in preventing supplies being sent to the French army, in which important and desirable service he was particularly fortunate; having, in

---

* Shortly afterwards Captain Irby received the following letter from the rear-admiral :

SIR,—I have great pleasure in communicating to you, by the desire of the commander-in-chief, the high approbation which the Lords Commissioners of the Admiralty are pleased to entertain of your gallantry, as well as that of the officers and men under your command, for their conduct in presence of the French squadron which lately sailed from Brest, and in the attack made on the three frigates belonging to the said squadron.

company with the Statira, captured off St. Andero, La Mouche French corvette, and several other vessels; and at other periods and situations, several others laden with ammunition and clothing, besides rendering great assistance to the Spanish cause by saving many of the patriots from falling into the enemy's hands: amongst that number were General Count Calderon de la Barca and his suite, who afterwards went on board the Amelia, with the Bishop of Saragossa, the great ally of the Prince of Peace, and captured by General Porlier. Captain Irby was also particularly active in destroying batteries erected by the enemy along the coast, and the capture of small vessels in shore, in which services the Amelia had at times some of her men killed and wounded. On this station Captain Irby continued till May 1810, when he joined the squadron off Brest, from whence he was ordered to cruise off Teneriffe, to intercept some English store-ships trading under Spanish colours, and fortunately detained two, the ship Galacia and schooner Palafox: names, however, which were merely assumed; the former being the Queen Charlotte of London, the latter the Mohawk of Jamaica, both of which were condemned in England.

On his passage home Captain Irby captured the Charles French ship-privateer of 20 guns, a vessel well calculated to do considerable injury to the merchant service, owing to her force and the great superiority of her sailing: she had escaped from several vessels which had chased her, and no doubt would have from the Amelia, had she not carried away her main-top-gallant-mast in the chase.

In January 1811 Captain Irby was appointed to the Crescent of 38 guns, a large new frigate; but being much attached to the officers and crew of the Amelia, he obtained permission to retain the command of her; and shortly after, having Generals Houston and Nightingale on board, he convoyed some transports to Lisbon, with reinforcements for the British army. On his return from thence, he was employed off Cherbourg, and assisted in destroying the Amazone French frigate of 44 guns off Cape Barfleur, in which he had one man killed and one wounded. He then convoyed a fleet of merchantmen to Quebec. He there received on board General Sir James Craig, the governor, whom he conveyed to England; and on his arrival it was found necessary for the Amelia to go into dock, in consequence of her having been on shore three times in the St. Lawrence, and nearly wrecked. As soon as she had undergone the necessary repairs, Captain Irby received orders to proceed to the coast of Africa, having some smaller vessels under his command, for the express purpose of suppressing the slave trade, and enforcing the treaty entered into with the Portuguese for confining their traffic in human beings to such places as were in the possession of Portugal; a command which, we must observe, was conferred upon him at the solicitation of the African Institution, dictated by the high opinion which they had formed of him for capturing the Galacia and Palafox. He sailed from Spithead on the 15th October, 1811, and after touching at Madeira and Goree, reached Sierra Leone on the 22d November. After fitting out a tender, he sailed down the coast, to execute to the utmost extent the orders with which he had been intrusted; and in consequence several Portuguese vessels were detained, and condemned in the Vice-Admiralty Court at Sierra Leone. In fulfilling these orders, he had at different times so much communication with the shore, that his crew were generally assailed, more or less, with the fever incidental to the climate, but particularly so on one occasion, when acting in concert with some officers and men belonging to the African Company, who were detached from Cape Coast Castle in the Amelia, in consequence of the natives of Whinnebah having murdered Mr. Meredith, the governor of the British fort, although they were at the time living under his protection from the attacks of the Ashantees; and having confined Mr. James, the succeeding governor, and his officers, with a few men and slaves, in the fort, it was considered, by a committee of the African Company and the officers of the Amelia, necessary to destroy the town and fort, as a punishment to the natives; which was completely effected under the direction of Captain Irby, who received a letter of thanks from the governor in chief and the members in council at Cape Coast Castle, for the services he had rendered to them and to the European residents in general. But in about a fortnight the whole of the officers and men who had been at Whinnebah were attacked with the fever, and 90 of the Amelia's crew were incapable of duty, although, through the attention of the surgeon, Mr. Stephen Williamson, during the whole period of fifteen months she did not lose above ten men. Being, however, short of medicines, and anxious to refresh his crew, Captain Irby found it necessary to proceed to St. Helena: but so positive did he consider his orders to be, that though they were still in a very enfeebled state, he quickly returned to the coast, to fulfill that part of his instructions which yet remained unexecuted. Here he remained till the latter end of 1812, when, considering

that he had completed the object of his appointment, he prepared to return home, and received a considerable quantity of gold-dust on board
from the different forts, for the purpose of conveying it to England: he
then ran down the coast; but having intercepted another slave-vessel, he
was obliged to return to Sierra Leone, and await the trial. Being again
ready to sail, but waiting for some official dispatches, on the 29th January, 1813, a small vessel arrived in the river with Lieutenant Pascoe and
the chief part of the officers and crew of the Daring gun-brig, which
had been chased on shore by the Rubis French frigate, and destroyed,
to prevent her falling into the enemy's possession; and Captain Irby
having received information that the Tweed sloop of war and a convoy
of transports, having money and stores for the different settlements, were
coming down the coast, was on the point of sailing for their protection,
when another small vessel arrived with the master and boat's crew of the
Daring, and the crews of some vessels which had been captured and destroyed by the enemy, who, in addition to the Rubis of 48 guns and 375
men, had L'Arethuse of 48 guns and 380 men, and a Portuguese ship of
20 guns, which they had captured. At the moment of the arrival of the
last part of the Daring's crew, the first lieutenant of the Amelia, in consequence of their sickly state, took them on board; but Captain Irby afterwards sent them on shore, after having given their paroles not to serve
till exchanged. The Amelia left Sierra Leone on the 4th February, and
arriving off the Isle de Loss on the 6th, observed one of the French
frigates at anchor, with the Portuguese ship, and the other frigate also
at anchor at a considerable distance to the northward. On this frigate,
L'Arethuse, getting under weigh, the Amelia stood towards Le Rubis,
which appeared likewise to be preparing to weigh, and to have her top-
sails hoisted. The Amelia not being in an efficient state to meet both ships,
stood out to sea at sunset for the night, and it fell quite calm. On the
morning of the 7th L'Arethuse was still in sight, and it was naturally supposed that Le Rubis was in sight astern of her.

" At five p. m. finding the wind begin to fall, and conceiving that he
had drawn the Arethuse to a sufficient distance from her consort, Captain Irby shortened sail, wore round, and running under his three top-
sails, with the wind on his starboard quarter, steered to pass, and then
to cross the stern of the Arethuse, who was standing under the same
sail, close hauled on the larboard tack. To avoid being thus raked,
Captain Bouvet, at 7h. 20m. p. m. tacked to the S. W. and hoisted his

colours, as the Amelia previously had hers. It was now a fine moon-light night, with the wind very moderate, and the sea nearly as smooth as a mill-pond. At 7 h. 45 m. just as the Amelia had arrived within pistol-shot upon her starboard or weather bow, the Arethuse opened her fire, which was immediately returned. After about three broadsides had been exchanged, the main-top-sail of the Amelia, in consequence of the braces having been shot away, fell aback. Owing to this accident, instead of crossing her opponent, as she intended, the Amelia fell on board of her; the jib-boom of the Arethuse carrying away the Amelia's jib and stay, and the French ship's bumpkin, or anchor-flook, part of the British ship's larboard forecastle-barricade. The Arethuse now opened a heavy fire of musketry from her tops and mast-heads, and threw seve-ral hand-granades upon the Amelia's decks, hoping, in the confusion caused by such combustibles, to succeed in an attempt to board, for which purpose several of the Arethuse's men had stationed themselves in her fore-rigging. Finding that, owing in a great degree to the steady and well-directed fire kept up by the Amelia's marines, her object could not be accomplished, the Arethuse threw all aback, and dropped clear. Setting her main-top-gallant and middle-stay-sails (her jib for the time being disabled), the Amelia endeavoured again to get her head towards the bow of the Arethuse. The Amelia at length did so; but in attempt-ing a second time to cross the bows of her antagonist, a second time fell on board of her, and the two ships swung close along side, the muzzles of their guns almost touching. This was at about 9 h. 15 m. p. m. and a scene of great mutual slaughter ensued. The two crews snatched the spunges out of each other's hands, through the port-holes, and cut at each other with the broad-sword. The Amelia's men now attempted to lash the two frigates together, but were unable, on account of the heavy fire of musketry kept up from the Arethuse's decks and tops ; a fire that soon cleared the Amelia's quarter-deck of both officers and men. Among those who fell on the occasion were the first and second lieute-nants (John James Bates and John Pope), and a lieutenant of marines (G. Grainger). Captain Irby was also severely wounded, and obliged to leave the deck to the command of the third lieutenant, George Wells, who was shortly after killed at his post, and Mr. Anthony de Mayne took the command. The mutual concussion of the guns at length forced the two frigates apart, and in the almost calm state of the weather, they gradually receded from each other, with, however, their broadsides still mutually bearing, until 11 h. 20 m. p. m.*" when the action entirely ceased, by the enemy bearing up, and the Amelia still keeping her head to seaward.

The wind had also come round again from the land, which was of course expected to bring Le Rubis into the scene of action; and as the Amelia had had her three lieutenants, besides Lieutenant Pascoe of the Daring, killed, the captain severely wounded, and all the other officers wounded, making a total of 46 killed and 91 wounded, she was prevented from following the enemy. Joined to the great loss of men which she sustained in the action, must be added the damage done to the ship, and owing to her having been so long on the coast, she was almost destitute of spare sails and stores. Captain Irby, in his official letter†, stated that the enemy carried heavy 24-pounders on her main-deck; and which he did from the circumstance of only three 18-pounders being found on board the Amelia, whilst there were sixteen shot, weighing twenty-seven pounds, besides many others of that weight, in her sides: but from the report of Lieutenant Chads, it appears that the enemy had only 18-pounders on his main-deck.

Respecting the enemy's consort, Le Rubis, it appears, from the report of Governor Maxwell, that she ran on the Arethusa rock on the 7th, the day of the action, and was burnt on the day following, and her crew distributed in the Portuguese ship and L'Arethuse. With regard to the merit displayed by Captain Irby throughout the whole of his arduous command, more especially in his severe contest with the enemy, very little need be said, farther than to insert what has already been advanced by others. In order to shew, in some degree, the baneful effects of the African climate, we shall insert the following extract of a letter from Sir George Collier, printed by order of the House of Commons:

" I will beg leave to conclude this part of my report with the following re-mark: that the vessels employed in the slave-trade are navigated by natives of Africa, or of similar climate, and they are thereby enabled to endure that which no ship manned by Europeans ever can; for I venture confidently to predict, that every British cruiser, exposed to the deluging rains of Africa, during the sickly season, for only a few days, will generate fever of so malignant a nature, that half the crew may be the sacrifice, and herself thereby incapacitated for service. And by no other means can the smaller vessels of war be rendered effective in the sickly season, than by being manned, as the colonial schooner was, by native

* James.—† See RALFE's *Naval Chronology*, vol. III, p. 215.

seamen, who, accustomed to the climate, can resist the disease, which will ever be found the certain destruction of Europeans."

Upon this subject we shall only observe, that the Amelia was fifteen months on the coast, was much exposed in the rainy season, and the weak state of her crew, as well as of the Thais and Kangaroo, proves the truth of Sir George's assertion. The following extract of a letter from Captain Lloyd of the Kangaroo, will put this in a clearer light.

After explaining the reasons for going into the river, he says,

" I now come to a most painful narration. Upon quitting the Gambia, the crew were attacked by a most violent fever and dysentery, which induced me to proceed immediately for Sierra Leone, as our medicines were beginning to fail, and it was impossible to foresee where the sickness would end. Upon my arrival, only a lieutenant and about fifteen men were capable of doing duty. I endeavoured to procure them room in the Colonial Hospital; but, I am sorry to say, it was full: I therefore was necessitated to hire rooms for the worst cases; and I feel pleasure in reporting, that only nine died since the Kangaroo's arrival in St. George's Bay. Of the debility of the crew, mostly convalescent, and generally afflicted with the tertian ague, you will be better able to judge, if you will be pleased to order them to be surveyed."

Extract of a letter from the Hon. Robert Thorpe, judge of the Vice-Admiralty Court, Sierra Leone, dated July 13, 1813:

" When I consider the infirm state of the Amelia's crew, which you preserved, in an enfeebled state, by going to St. Helena, I congratulate you on your escape, and wonder at what you have done."

Lieutenant Chads' report of falling in with L'Arethuse at sea, dated Mercury cartel, 20 March, 1813:

" On the 18th instant, in lat. 33° 36' N. long. 40° 1' W. we were boarded by the Arethuse French frigate, Commodore Bouvet, with a captain under him. I was taken on board the frigate, when it was easily to be perceived that she had been in action, and had suffered most severely, having all her lower-masts, fore and main-yards, gaff, spanker-boom, and mizen-top-mast fished, and upwards of thirty round shot in her hull, on the starboard side, below the quarter-deck. In her cabin was the drawing of an action, said to have taken place on the 7th February, off the coast of Africa, between her and an English frigate; and on the sides of this view was her list of 31 killed and 74 wounded*. I was told they were engaged two hours and a half, when the English frigate, which they thought had suffered severely, but without the loss of her masts, made off. But upon

---

* The *Moniteur* stated that she had 20 killed, and 88 *severely* wounded, including all the officers, except the captain. The slightly wounded not mentioned.

my appearing to doubt this, they allowed she had good reason, *as there was something else in sight besides themselves.* They pursued the English frigate, but lost her after twenty-four hours' chase; from which I concluded they must have a squadron. The Arethuse is a large frigate, and appeared very full of men, mounting 28 18-pounders on the main-deck, 16 36-pounder carronades, and two long guns on the upper-deck. From her very crippled state, and chasing us three days to the N. E. which I do not think she would have done if our courses had not lain together, I am inclined to suppose she must have been bound into port."

The following extract of a letter, dated Portsmouth, Dec. 21, 1813, from Captain Scobell of the Thais, who, from his serving under Captain Irby, was well acquainted with the enfeebled state of his crew, and the difficulties he laboured under, is too important to be omitted:

"Most truly may we say that the events since we parted have been great and critical, and that it is to your exertions the Thais feels indebted for her preservation. I have felt, and still feel, the extreme perplexity of your situation, from the time the enemy reached de Loss: yet, under every result, I must continue to admire the bold decision of your proceedings, and the gallantry with which they were put into execution. Unfortunate, and indeed contrary to its merits, was the termination of your contest; but who can outstretch the power of humanity, or resist the shafts of fate? In truth, however, so extensively did destruction fall on you, that the most unreasonable must exclaim, how gallantly your men fell, and how impossible to have continued the action! To conclude the adventure of the Arethuse, I must congratulate you on the entire self-approbation of your mind on its every suggestion and execution.

"You rightly calculate that my last months in Africa were most tedious and fatal, justly to be dated so from the time of our parting; for shortly afterwards we were assailed with sickness more calamitous than what I even met you in, and which rendered both our ships inefficient: scarce a man escaped disease; nor can an exception be made to enervation and lassitude, a helplessness which does not easily wear off, nor seems yet to give way to our native climate."

Mr. James* adds, "With respect to Captain Irby, his critical situation, without reference to the state of his crew, must not be overlooked. The Amelia commenced, gallantly commenced, the action under the impression that another French frigate, also equal in force to herself, was, although out of sight, at no great distance off. If then there was a probability of the approach of the Rubis when the action began, how must that probability have been heightened after the action had lasted three

* Vol. VI. p. 273. Second edit.

hours and a half, both ships remaining nearly stationary the whole time, and the wind, when it afterwards sprung up, drawing from the eastward, the direction in which the Rubis had been last seen. In addition to all this, the Amelia had on board a considerable quantity of gold-dust, belonging to the merchants in England. Upon the whole, therefore, both frigates behaved most bravely; and although he had no trophy to show, each captain did more to support the character of his nation than many an officer who has been decorated with the chaplet of victory." We shall only add to those observations, that it was in all probability owing to the conduct of Captain Irby, to his going in quest of the enemy, drawing the Arethuse from her consort, and engaging her under such disadvantageous circumstances, that the Rubis was entirely lost to France ; for if the former had been near, she might have rendered such assistance to the latter as would have prevented the necessity of destroying her.

Shortly after his arrival in England, the Amelia was paid off; and the health of Captain Irby having suffered severely in the African climate, prevented him from resuming his professional employment on board another ship, and peace having taken place, terminated, for a time, his public duties.

HISTORICAL MEMOIRS OF

ADMIRAL SIR DAVID MILNE, K. C. B.

FROM a mere brief consideration of the conduct and character of this distinguished officer, it will be seen that he possesses a vast collection of professional talent, and that it has been exerted in rendering the most valuable services to the country; and those qualities have been increased by the possession of those endowments which, though attained by few, are almost indispensable in the character of an officer holding superior rank and authority—affability, kindness, frankness, and gentlemanly, honourable demeanour; conduct which forms such a contrast to those supercilious airs which some persons assume, and which tend only to excite contempt.

Sir David was born at Edinburgh in May 1763, and is the son of David Milne, Esq. merchant of that city. He entered the naval service in 1779, as a midshipman on board the Canada, Captain Hugh Dalrymple, at whose death Sir George Collier succeeded to the command. In 1780 he proceeded with the fleet under Admiral Darby to the relief of Gibraltar, where he was repeatedly engaged with the Spanish gunboats and batteries. On returning to England, the Canada chased from the fleet, and on that occasion captured the Santa Leocadia Spanish frigate of 44 guns, after a brave defence on the part of the enemy. Captain W. Cornwallis afterwards assumed the command of the Canada, with whom Mr. Milne proceeded to America, under the orders of Admiral Digby, and from thence to the West Indies, where he had an opportunity of learning caution from the enemy, and a bold and daring confidence from his captain, who was justly considered one of the best seamen and the most determined officer in the British navy. In the fine display of courage and seamanship exhibited by Sir Samuel Hood at St. Kitt's, the Canada bore a conspicuous part, and excited the admiration of the admiral. The battles of the 9th and 12th April followed; the Canada was again foremost in the fight, and on the last glorious day she closely engaged the Ville de Paris, which she may be said to have subdued, though the enemy struck to the Barfleur. On all these occasions the conduct of Mr. Milne was, as it always has been, cool and collected; and

one of the master's-mates having been wounded on the 12th, he was promoted by the captain to fill that situation.   In the following August the
Canada was ordered to England, with the Ramillies, Centaur, and Pallas
frigate, and also the French prizes, Ville de Paris, Glorieux, Hector,
Ardent, Caton, and Jason, with a very numerous convoy, under the
orders of Rear-Admiral Graves; out of which the Canada and Jason
were the only ships of war which reached England: the Ardent put
back to Jamaica, and the Caton bore away for Halifax; but the rest unfortunately perished in a severe hurricane which took place in September*.
The Canada having been paid off shortly after her arrival, Mr. Milne
joined the Elizabeth as master's-mate, commanded by Captain Kingsmill,
under orders for the East Indies; but the Elizabeth having sprung her
masts in the Bay of Biscay, returned to Spithead, and peace having
taken place, her destination was altered, and she was paid off.

Mr. Milne was now without any prospect of early employment in the
navy; but being determined to follow the profession he had adopted, he
entered into the merchant-service, was almost constantly at sea, and returning from the East Indies on board one of the Company's ships in
the early part of 1793, finding that war was declared against France,
and that an expedition was about to sail under Sir J. Jervis against her
islands in the West Indies, he eagerly returned to his regular professional
employment, was received on board the Boyne, Sir John's flag-ship,
and by him was offered a lieutenancy on board a store-ship.   This
one circumstance will tend to prove his high character and great claims
to notice: finding that the store-ship was not likely to remain with the
expedition, and that he would thus be most likely deprived of any opportunity to manifest either his courage or abilities, he requested Sir John
Jervis to allow him to decline it, preferring to remain as a master's-mate
on board the Boyne, and take the chance of any opportunity to distinguish himself, and thus bring his name into notice, than receive certain
promotion with inglorious privacy; and the event proved that he made a
judicious choice.   He in the first place secured the good opinion of Sir
John Jervis, who, on their arrival at Barbadoes, appointed him lieutenant
of the Blanche frigate, commanded by Captain Christopher Parker, who
was ordered to cruise off Martinique.   After the army was landed, they
were employed sometimes on shore and sometimes in cruising, services
which were repeated during the operations against St. Lucia.   Here

* See *Memoirs of Lord* GRAVES *and Sir* W. CORNWALLIS.

Captain Parker, having been promoted to a flag, was succeeded in the command of the Blanche by Captain Robert Faulknor. On the expedition proceeding against Guadaloupe, it was considered of great consequence to obtain possession of the small islands called the Saints. To have attacked them, however, in the daytime would most probably have been attended with loss of much time and many men, as the tops of the hills which commanded the anchorage were strongly fortified, as also the different islets: it was therefore determined to endeavour to surprise them in the night; and the boats of the Blanche and Quebec were employed on the service. Captain Faulknor, accompanied in his barge by Lieutenant Milne, proceeded against one of the islands; succeeded in getting into the rear of one of the batteries of two 32-pounders, before they were perceived by the enemy; got possession of it, after a discharge of musketry; pursued the enemy, who retreated to the fort at the top of the hill, which they entered with them, and thereby prevented the discharge of a single gun, although matches were lying on them ready for the purpose, and which would have swept the whole approach to them. The other islands were carried by the boats of the Quebec frigate; and thus was that fine anchorage got possession of, which proved of the greatest advantage to the fleet, and greatly facilitated the object of the expedition against Guadaloupe, throughout the operations against which Lieutenant Milne was most actively employed in various situations. After its reduction, the Blanche was ordered to convey his Royal Highness the late Duke of Kent to Halifax; and having performed that service, and cruised for some time on the coast of America, returned to the West Indies in the autumn of that year (1794), and found Guadaloupe, with the exception of Fort Matilda, again in the possession of the enemy. A strict watch was now kept up by Captain Faulknor, who continued cruising round the island, and annoying the enemy in every assailable point, sending in the boats, destroying public property, and cutting out vessels from under the batteries. In all these services Lieutenant Milne took the lead by commanding the boats, and had repeated opportunities to signalize his abilities, particularly on one occasion, when, understanding the enemy were endeavouring to throw supplies of powder and ammunition into the north side of the island for the siege of Fort Matilda, and that the vessels were then lying in Mahout Bay, one with French colours flying, and knowing it was of the utmost importance to capture or destroy her, the Blanche stood into the bay. The batteries opened an animated fire, almost every shot striking her; and on one going through the centre of the main-mast, Lieutenant Milne, after several solicitations, obtained permission to make the attack with the boats: he immediately put off; the guns of the batteries were then pointed against them, and they were nearly covered with water. The vessel, however, was boarded and brought out, notwithstanding the continuance of the fire; and on Lieutenant Milne presenting Captain Faulknor with the Frenchman's sword, he returned it to him, with the most flattering compliments. In a few days afterwards Lieutenant Milne again displayed his courage by cutting out with the boats, from under the batteries of Deseada, a large armed schooner, although she was moored to the rocks with hawsers, and the battery, besides musketry, was within fifty yards of her, from which a continued fire was kept up, by which some men were killed and wounded in the boats. On board the enemy's vessel, which was commanded by the first lieutenant of the Pique frigate, then lying in the harbour of Point-à-Petre, were several killed and wounded, but most of the others escaped on shore. Being in daily expectation of the arrival of vessels with troops on board from France, and finding that there was little probability of their entering the harbour whilst the Blanche continued on the station, on the morning of the 4th January, 1795, the Pique herself was ordered out to endeavour to force her away. Immediately upon seeing her under sail, Captain Faulknor bore up for her; but she kept so close to the batteries, that it was deemed imprudent to attack her. In the evening, however, about eleven o'clock, with a full moon and quite clear, she was observed, with a large schooner in company, steering so as to indicate a determination to bring the Blanche to action. Captain Faulknor immediately shortened sail, and shortly after twelve the action commenced. In the Memoir of Captain Faulknor* we have stated the particulars of that desperate conflict, and have only farther to observe, that on the Blanche's main and mizen-masts being shot away, Captain Faulknor went aft on the quarter-deck, and Lieutenant Milne forward, to avoid the wreck of the mast; and shortly afterwards the gallant captain received his mortal wound (not whilst lashing the enemy's bowsprit to his own capstan, as it has been erroneously asserted): he instantly called out, "Lieutenant Milne!" who immediately replied to his call; but ere he could reach his brave friend and commander, he had ceased to exist. At this time four of the Blanche's main-deck guns were raking the enemy with the most destructive effect through the bows; but from her main

* Vol III. p. 315.

and mizen-masts being gone, her head-sails filled, and she paid off before the wind, the enemy dropping astern; but as his bowsprit was still fast, he was kept in tow, about thirty yards astern, with all his masts shot away. In this position, however, the enemy had for a time an advantage over his opponent, by pointing his quarter-deck guns forward and raking the Blanche, which, not being fitted with stern-ports, had no means of bringing a gun to bear. In this extremity it was determined to blow out the stern-frame: the buckets were immediately filled with water, to be in readiness to quench the fire; the two after main-deck guns were then pointed against the frame, discharged, and the enemy then saw the instruments of their destruction: his main-deck was swept fore and aft, and in this way the contest continued till a quarter-past five o'clock, when the enemy called out that he had surrendered. Both ships were at this time perfect wrecks, and the victors had not a boat left to enable them to take possession; but Lieutenant Milne, calling to a part of the ship's company to follow him, began to descend into the water by the jolly-boat, which was hanging by one end over the stern; but in going down, owing to the tackle having been shot away, she fell over him, and he narrowly escaped death: by great exertions and activity he got clear, swam to the prize, got up to her forecastle by the wreck of her fore-mast, received the French captain's sword on the gangway, and being followed by ten men, took possession of the French frigate La Pique, after as gallant, as persevering and brilliant an action, as can be pointed to in the naval history of the world.

She was immediately carried to the Saints, where the heroic Faulknor was buried with all due honours. Lieutenant Milne was then dispatched by the first lieutenant, Watkins, to Admiral Caldwell at Martinique, with an account of the action; but though every praise was bestowed upon him for his intrepid conduct, he received no reward or promotion, but, on the contrary, had even a junior lieutenant placed over him in the Blanche, on the promotion of Lieutenant Watkins to the rank of commander. He, however, acted as first lieutenant of the Blanche under Captain C. Sawyer during the unfortunate attack on St. Lucia by the forces under General Stewart and Captain Sawyer, and was always employed with the boats, until the troops were obliged to re-embark and return to Martinique. If, however, he felt himself slighted, or experienced any disappointment or neglect, after the capture of the Pique, he was, shortly after his arrival at Martinique, compensated by finding his services had been fully acknowledged in the highest quarter, the Lords of the Admiralty having promoted him to the rank of commander, on being made acquainted with the particulars of his conduct, and appointed him to command the Inspector sloop: but as this vessel was at Tortola, he was ordered by the admiral to act in the Quebec frigate; and on the appointment of Captain James Carpenter to the Quebec, he was removed to the Alarm frigate, in which, having seen a convoy to the northward of the islands, he fell in with a French ship of 20 guns, called La Liberté, which had the temerity to engage the Alarm; but after a short action, she sunk, with several of her crew, though 100 of them were saved through the humanity of the victors: she had on board clothing and ammunition for the French army at Guadaloupe. Captain Milne shortly after joined his own ship, the Inspector, at Tortola, where he remained cruising for the protection of the trade; and so manifest were his exertions and judicious conduct, that the governor and council presented him with a vote of thanks. Having proceeded to Martinique, the Inspector was ordered to England with a convoy; but as much active operations were still going on in this part of the world, and Sir John Laforey, not wishing to part with an officer who had given such eminent proofs of his professional abilities, offered him the first post vacancy that should occur if he would remain on that station, and in the interim take charge of the transport service; an offer which was no sooner made than accepted. He entered upon the duties of this new office with all that zeal and activity which had characterized the whole of his proceedings; and having collected a great number of transports from all parts of the West Indies, which were lying there at a great expense, though perfectly useless, he sent them to England, and thus saved an immense sum to the nation. He was also employed at Martinique, which was daily threatened with an attack from Guadaloupe and St. Lucia; several landings were indeed effected, but the enemy was always repulsed with loss.

Towards the end of 1795, Captain Milne received the promised promotion to post-rank, so that ample amends were now made for former neglect: he was appointed to the Matilda; but so necessary did the commander-in-chief find it to have an officer of his experience and active disposition at hand, that he even then would not allow him to go to sea, but ordered the Matilda to cruise under her first lieutenant. At the close of the year, however, the Pique became vacant by the death of her commander, and she was ordered to Barbadoes to get manned. Naturally ambitious to command that ship, which had, mainly by his valour and intrepidity, been added to the British navy, he solicited Admiral Laforey for the appointment: such a request from such an officer could scarcely be declined, and, however loathe the admiral was to part with him, he immediately acceded to his request; and he accordingly joined the Pique in January 1796, at Barbadoes. An important and arduous duty was now to be performed: several vessels belonging to the unfornate expedition under Sir Hugh Christian, which had been dispersed in the Channel, had arrived at Barbadoes without convoy, or vessel of any description to protect them. Captain Milne immediately saw the danger to which the remainder were exposed, and he represented to General Knox, the commanding officer at Barbadoes, that if a ship of war was not directly ordered to windward of the island, for the protection of the scattered transports and victuallers, the object of the expedition would be totally defeated. There was, however, no other ship at hand but the Pique, and she was incapable of proceeding to sea for want of hands; but her zealous commander offered to sail the next day, if the general would order some soldiers on board to work the guns: this was agreed to. Parts of the 54th and 57th regiments were embarked, and he proceeded to the northward, where his judicious conduct was soon proved, by the capture of the Lacedemonian French brig of 18 guns, and chasing a French ship of 20 guns, a brig, and a scooner off the station, by which means he completely protected the scattered convoy, which arrived safe at Barbadoes.

He afterwards accompanied the expedition to the attack of the Dutch colonies of Demarara, Essequibo, and Berbice, which capitulated on the Pique anchoring close to the batteries of Demarara. In the month of July, a valuable convoy was assembled outside the bar, waiting for a ship of war to take charge of them as far as St. Christopher's, there to join the general convoy for England, and which ship of war the commander-in-chief had signified to the merchants should be sent. No ship of war, however, arrived, and Captain Milne became daily importuned with applications and petitions from the governor and merchants of Demarara, not to suffer so valuable a convoy to go to destruction, as they could not re-enter the river without unloading (they were obliged to take in the last part of their cargo outside the bar, owing to the shallowness of the water); and to sail without protection was exposing them to almost certain capture by the numerous privateers known to be cruising amongst the islands. He was therefore reduced to the necessity of either sacrificing part of this important branch of Britain's greatness, or leave his station without orders: the latter, however, appeared to him the lesser evil; and therefore, having waited till the last hour for the arrival of the expected vessel, he quitted his station, and sailed with the convoy for St. Christopher's, where they arrived on the 28th of July; but, to his great surprise and disappointment, found that the general convoy had sailed for England several days before, contrary, we believe, to what ever previously happened, the 1st of August being the day usually appointed for that purpose. On passing Martinique, he dispatched a tender to the commander-in-chief to inform him of his proceedings, and requesting instructions; but after waiting at St. Christopher's till the 11th, when the hurricane months having commenced, the anchorage becoming quite unsafe, and having received notice that the commander-in-chief had received the dispatches, though he had not sent any orders, Captain Milne was again under the necessity of exercising his discretion, and he again determined to protect the commerce of his country at all risks: he therefore returned to England with the merchantmen under his convoy; a step which met the approbation of the Lords of the Admiralty.

In the mutiny which unfortunately broke out amongst the ships at Spithead in 1797, the Pique was carried, with the rest of the fleet, to St. Helen's: her crew indeed appears to have been very refractory; for after the disaffection had mostly subsided, and the fleet was proceeding down the Channel, with Lord Bridport, to resume the blockade of Brest, when they were dispersed in a fog, they again broke out into acts of violent insubordination, put the boatswain, mate, and another man in irons, assembled on the forecastle, and were proceeding aft in the gangway to take possession of the quarter-deck. Seeing the necessity of immediate personal exertion, Captain Milne called to his officers to arm themselves, and he rushed forward to the gangway to seize the first man, who was the captain of the fore-top, and who instantly leaped down into the waist. Captain Milne immediately followed him, and pursued him to the fore-part of the ship between-decks, where he seized him, and dragged him up to the hatchway to the quarter-deck; having there secured him, he advanced into a body of men collected on the forecastle, seized the first man who offered resistance, and stapled him and the other prisoner to the quarter-deck, when the remainder of the refractory part of the crew ran below.

On the following day, he fell in with the Atlas, Captain Squires, whom Captain Milne informed both personally and by letter of what had happened, and requested that he would take the two prisoners out of the ship, as he meant to try them by a court-martial. This, however, Captain Squires refused, as he greatly mistrusted his own men, and strongly advised Captain Milne to forgive them. This, however, he for some time declined; but Captain Squires having repeated his advice, and the men having written a supplicating letter, expressing their sorrow for what had happened, he at last consented, and the men returned to their duty. Such conduct we know is censured by the strict disciplinarian, and we hardly know whether to defend or condemn it: as a general principle, it must no doubt be censured; but, like most other acts, it must at times stand on its own merits, and seek for a justification in expediency, as well as humanity. We shall therefore only say, that, in this instance, Captain Milne closely followed the conduct of his noble countryman, Lord Duncan, on the same melancholy occasion: like him, he was surrounded with dissatisfaction; like him, he personally seized the ring-leaders and put them in confinement; like him, he pardoned the culprits; and like him, he had never reason to regret the lenity of his conduct; the men having ever afterwards remained in a high state of discipline, though several ships of the Channel fleet continued in a refractory state all the summer.

During his continuance with this fleet, which was till the beginning of 1798, the Pique was always the chasing frigate; but in the summer of that year he was placed under the orders of Sir R. Keats, cruising off the French coast; and on the morning of the 27th of July, being in company with the Jason, Captain Stirling, and Mermaid, Captain Newman, a strange sail was discovered, which was soon made out to be an enemy; and although the Pique was at the moment the leewardmost ship, she was soon first in the chase, which continued the whole day: in the afternoon, the Mermaid was out of sight, and the Jason far astern. The enemy ran into the Pertuit Breton passage; but although the night was very dark, and the two French pilots of the Pique had given up charge of the ship, Captain Milne determined to follow the chase wherever she went, and never lost sight of her for one moment. At eleven

p. m. he succeeded in getting within gun-shot, when a running fight continued through the passage till near two o'clock a. m. when he got close along side. By the flashes of the guns, the Jason had been enabled to keep sight, and about this time arrived close up; Captain Milne hailing her not to pass between him and his opponent, as they were aground; but not hearing this friendly warning, she pushed on, the Pique ceasing her fire as she passed, took the ground, and swung round with her stern to the enemy, without either the Pique or Jason being able to bring a gun to bear. As the Pique held by the stern, Captain Milne ordered all the men to the forecastle and bowsprit, with shot in their hands, by which means she forged a little ahead, and he again opened his fire on the French frigate, upon which she almost immediately surrendered, when he sent a boat and took possession of her. She proved to be La Seine, from the Mauritius, with parts of two regiments on board, in all about 600 men, 150 of whom were killed, and a proportionate number wounded. She mounted 18 and 9-pounders; the Pique only 12 and 6-pounders. The Jason was soon got afloat, but although every exertion was made by shoring the Pique up with spare top-masts and lower-yards, and cutting away all her masts, yet, as the tide fell, the shores broke, and she lay over a complete wreck, the water rising inside of her as fast as the outside, on the rising of the tide. The prize also lay over, her fore-part being dry at low water. In this state they lay three days, during which they privately landed the wounded prisoners, and used every exertion to get the ships off.

The Mermaid arrived shortly after the accident, and on the following day the Phaeton, Anson, and St. Fiorenzo also arrived, under Sir Harry Neale, who anchored the Fiorenzo close to the Pique, and by whose assistance the Seine was got off, with the loss only of her rudder; but the Pique was unfortunately obliged to be destroyed, by which means her captain lost every thing he had on board. Captain Milne and his crew now removed into the prize, and returned to Spithead, where he was tried by a court-martial for the loss of the Pique; and being honourably acquitted, was appointed by Lord Spencer to command the Seine, in which he was employed in blockading the port of Havre.

In October 1799 he was ordered to proceed with the annual store-ship to the coast of Africa, to remain there a certain time for the protection of the trade, and then proceed with a convoy to Jamaica. On his arrival off the African coast in December 1799, he was informed that three French frigates had been there, and done considerable injury to the trade. He immediately proceeded to Acra in quest of them, and found that they had been there, and had sailed a short time before; he then sailed for Prince's Island, but on his arrival had the mortification to find that the enemy had still the start of him. Being now convinced that they had left the coast, he returned to Cape Coast, for the protection of the trade, and gave the necessary instructions for such ships as intended to take advantage of his convoy for the West Indies, to rendezvous at Prince's Island.

One remarkable circumstance connected with his continuance on this station, which was from the beginning of December to the end of April, we must not omit to mention. During the whole of that time he lost only one man by sickness, and he was consumptive when the ship left England; a loss, the smallness of which must, we believe, be attributed to the particular regulations laid down by Captain Milne respecting wooding and watering. At the end of April he sailed for the West Indies, and on his arrival at Jamaica became under the orders of Sir Hyde Parker, who was shortly after relieved by Lord Hugh Seymour, by whom he was directed to cruise for a French frigate bound to France from Curaçoa.

On the 20th of August, a large ship was discovered under St. Domingo, on the larboard tack, standing to the northward, through the Mona passage, which was soon discovered to be the one he was so anxiously looking for, and he immediately made all sail in chase. The wind having come from the north, obliged her to tack, as she could not weather Cape Raphael, on the St. Domingo shore; she then stood S.S.E. and made all sail, but about twelve at night Captain Milne was enabled to get within gun-shot, when a running action commenced; the enemy baffling for a long time every attempt of Captain Milne to get along side, and both ships suffered so severely in their sails and rigging as to separate, to repair their damages. At daylight the action was renewed, and Captain Milne again endeavoured to bring his enemy to close action, by repeated efforts to get down on his weather quarter, which he avoided by going with the wind on his beam and luffing up, by which means he succeeded in raking the Seine, and cutting her rigging in pieces. To avoid this, Captain Milne kept close on his lee quarter, and although much damaged by his stern guns, closed with him, and luffed close to his weather quarter, when a severe and bloody contest ensued, in which the enemy was totally dismasted. After about an hour and a half's hard fighting, the enemy called out from their bowsprit that they had surrendered.

Thus closed a battle which we may safely say, from the force of the enemy, the ability with which he fought his ship, the long continuance and severity of it, was not surpassed by any frigate action during the war. She proved to be the Vengeance, mounting 28 18-pounders on her main-deck, 16 12-pounders and 8 42-pounder carronades on her quarter-deck and forecastle, and brass swivels on the gunwale, with shifting guns on the main and quarter decks*.

In his official letter, Captain Milne bore the most honourable testimony to the distinguished merits of his officers and ship's company.

" To my first lieutenant, Mr. Cheetham, I am greatly indebted, for his cool and steady behaviour, and for the amazing fire kept up from the main-deck, which nothing could surpass. My second lieutenant, Mr. George Milne, fell, fighting nobly, about the middle of the action. In him his Majesty has lost a valuable and as zealous an officer as any in the service. To my third lieutenant (Mr. Edevin, whom I mentioned in a former letter, when gunner of the Pique,) I am equally indebted for his services ; as likewise to Mr. Barclay, the master, and Mr. Macdonald, lieutenant of marines, who was taken down wounded, and came up again, when dressed, but was obliged, from a second wound, to be taken below : but I am happy to state, the life of this valuable officer will be saved, to render farther services to his Majesty. The heroism of the petty officers, seamen, and marines was such as does them the highest credit."

In this contest the Seine had 13 killed and 29 wounded. The enemy's loss does not appear to have been ascertained: she had a complement of 453 men at the commencement of the action; some general and artillery officers and men were likewise on board, and served at the guns; and a captain of a line-of-battle ship was also on board, who was mortally

---

* The Vengeance was the same frigate which had, six months before, been engaged by Commodore Truxton, in the American frigate Constellation, who bore down on the Vengeance under English colours. But after sustaining an action for a considerable time, the commodore set off before the wind, leaving the Vengeance a mere wreck: notwithstanding which, on his arrival at Jamaica, he declared he had sunk the Vengeance, and was accordingly entertained by the British officers and merchants with a dinner.

wounded. The prize was carried into Jamaica, where she was purchased into the British service. The first lieutenant of the Seine was promoted to the rank of commander, but Captain Milne received neither honour nor reward; and here is another instance of the shameful neglect which is sometimes experienced by those who deserve well of their country. Nothing can be more gratifying to the liberal and the just, than to see the merits of the brave recorded with the grateful acknowledgments due to their intrepidity; acknowledgments which excite emulation, and lead to eminence in the career of honour: and, on the contrary, nothing can be more grating to the feelings, nothing more mortifying to the patriot and the lover of justice, than to see them neglected; to see the faithful and zealous servants of the country go unrewarded; men who should be the adopted sons and brothers of the great and powerful, of every friend to his king and country, and of every one who possesses the least spark of honour and justice. That this, however, is unfortunately not always the case, it has been the painful part of our labours to record; and the treatment experienced by Captain Milne on this occasion is another proof of the melancholy truth.

The Seine having been refitted, Captain Milne was ordered off the Havannah, and in the following year was employed in blockading the Mississippi, where he captured and destroyed many of the enemy's vessels. At the end of the year he returned to Jamaica, and in January 1802, in consequence of the peace of Amiens, he was ordered to return to England, where he was paid off in the month of April. At that time Lord St. Vincent filled the situation of First Lord of the Admiralty, and offered to retain Captain Milne in commission by appointing him to a large frigate; an offer he was compelled to decline, on account of his health having suffered much from hot climates, and of course he wished to retire for a short time to his native country. On the first appearance of the renewal of hostilities, he hastened to London, offered his services, and solicited the command of his old ship, the Seine. She had been ordered to be fitted up as a block-ship, to lay in the mouth of the Thames; but in consequence of his application, she was ordered by Lord St. Vincent to be fitted as a cruiser.

In the month of April, exactly one year from the time of her being paid off, Captain Milne resumed the command of his favourite ship at Chatham. Men were at that time scarce; but as they were allowed to volunteer from ships coming home to particular vessels, the Seine very shortly had her full complement, when she sailed to Sheerness, where the men were to receive their wages. At this time Lord Keith, commanding at the Nore, received intelligence that seven sail of the line had been seen to the north of Ireland, standing, as it was supposed, for the North Sea. Without a moment's notice, and before the crew had been paid their wages, although a great many of them had just arrived in the Romney from the East Indies, she was ordered to sea to watch their motions. Captain Milne immediately proceeded off the Texel, and was then directed by Admiral Thornbrough to blockade the Elbe, having received two pilots for the North Sea from the flag-ship at Sheerness; but on the 21st July, whilst standing towards the land, with fine clear weather and smooth water, proceeding to his station, the ship was run on a sand-bank and totally lost. Respecting this unfortunate event, Captain Milne wrote the following particulars to the commander-in-chief:

July 23, 1803.

SIR,—I am exceedingly sorry to inform you that his Majesty's ship (Seine) has been unfortunately wrecked, by running on a sand-bank off Schelling Island, on the morning of the 21st instant.

This melancholy event was caused either by the total ignorance or wilfulness of both pilots. At eight a. m. we were standing on the larboard tack, E. by S. close hauled in towards the land, beating up to the station I was ordered by you, off the river Elbe. Both pilots came on deck, and the master informed me, as I came up, at half-past eight, that there was fourteen fathoms water, and that the pilots said we should deepen directly more, as we were only crossing a sand-bank; a man was in the chains, and the lighthouse on Schelling Island was at this time seen nearly right ahead, or rather on the lee bow. I repeatedly told the pilots not to stand any nearer than was necessary, and pointed out a buoy to them on the lee bow, which they seemed to know of, and constantly said there was no danger, and plenty of water.

At forty minutes past eight the ship struck, when the helm was immediately put a-lee: the pilots said she did not strike; that it was impossible she missed stays, owing to having taken the ground: we then let her come round on her heel, and filled on the other tack, the ship still striking; she went ahead a considerable way, then stuck fast. The master in the boat reporting shoaler water on her lee quarter, the best bower-anchor was let go, and she brought it ahead about fifteen fathoms, it being high water, and no possibility of getting her off that tide. I called a consultation of the officers, when it was agreed to strike the lower yards, to shore the ship up, and get the spare top-mast over the side for the same purpose, which was done immediately, and top-gallant-masts got on deck. Observing a brig and galliot under neutral colours coming down, we fired a gun, and brought them to an anchor about two cables' length, in twelve fathoms ahead of us, to warp off, if possible, the next high water. The stream-cable and hawsers were directly got out to them, and hove taut. We then began to start the water, and got six of the main-deck guns and carronades overboard, on the side she would swing from. In the mean time, we endeavoured to get a bower-anchor carried out, by means of making a raft of the launch ; but, from the increasing wind and heavy swell breaking over the sand, found it impossible.

At six p. m. the tide of flood made, and we hove a considerable way towards the two vessels : at this time the wind from N. N. W. had increased so much as to occasion a very heavy sea, and the ship to strike very hard and roll deep : at ten the rudder was unshipped, and the stern-post working very much ; at half-past eleven the carpenter reported the water to be above the cock-pit deck. A few minutes before this the pumps had sucked.

His Majesty's ship being reported in this state, I called the officers again on deck, and asked if it was possible for any thing more to be done to save the ship. It being the opinion she was now irrecoverably lost, and sinking fast in the sand, it became my duty to save the crew as fast as possible, by sending them on board the two neutral vessels, which I am happy to say was effected, without the loss of a man, by three o'clock, although a very heavy breaking sea ran between us and the vessels; and when I left the ship the water was above the cables.

Three armed national vessels, with row boats full of men, having attempted to get near us, made it appear to myself and officers that they meant to get possession of such rigging and stores as might be left; I therefore thought it proper, to prevent any thing from falling into the hands of the enemy, to order the ship to be set on fire, which at four a. m. was accordingly done. At this time the water was upon the main-deck. We kept near her until she was consumed to the water-edge.

Thus has perished his Majesty's ship Seine, by what I conceive to be the total ignorance or wilfulness of both pilots.

My feelings, sir, I cannot express, on the present unfortunate occasion; but I feel confident, when the Lords Commissioners of the Admiralty shall be pleased to order an investigation, it will appear that no blame will be attached to myself, officers, or crew.   (Signed,)   DAVID MILNE.

On the 4th August Captain Milne, his officers and crew, were tried by a court-martial, and the whole of them honourably acquitted, with the exception of the two pilots, who were sentenced to be mulcted of all their pay, to receive two years' solitary confinement in the Marshalsea, and rendered for ever incapable of serving his Majesty.

There is hardly any circumstance in the life of a naval officer which causes him so much pain and vexation as the loss of his ship, even though he be perfectly free from blame. Although, in the present instance, fortunately all the crew were saved, it proved a great misfortune to Captain Milne, as he not only lost every thing he had on board, but was thrown out of employment in the regular line of his profession. On his waiting upon Lord St. Vincent, then First Lord of the Admiralty, his lordship expressed much regret at the circumstance, as he had not, at the moment, the command of another ship to offer him; but promised Captain Milne shortly to give him an appointment which would be gratifying to his feelings, till he could give him a command afloat. His lordship, however, shortly after left the Admiralty, and Captain Milne's merits were, for a period, overlooked. It was, however, but for a time, when they again shone forth with all their former zeal, and subsequently with additional and striking splendour. The active and enterprising mind of Captain Milne would not, however, allow him to remain dormant, and he availed himself of that opportunity to renew his acquaintance with the rocks and shoals of his native shore, in viewing and contemplating the best means of defence in the event of an invasion of the British dominions. The scientific and nautical knowledge thus acquired was soon called forth for the public benefit; for, from the great preparations of the enemy, particularly in the year 1804, serious apprehensions were excited in the minds of the people, and the government were induced to make every preparation for defending every part of the coast. Sea-fencibles were enrolled; and the Frith of Forth, being an important point, was ordered to be particularly attended to. With every spot around that part Captain Milne was well acquainted, and also with the manners and habits of the fishermen; a particularly bold and intrepid class of men, whose confidence and esteem he fully possessed, and who nobly and generously offered themselves and their boats for the defence of their country, agreeably to any plan which Captain Milne might propose. The best means of employing their powerful energies readily suggested themselves to his mind, and he pointed out to Sir James Sinclair Erskine (now Lord Rosslyn), then commanding a brigade in the district, that the fishing-boats might, at a very trifling expense, be fitted as gun-boats, and carry a 12-pounder carronade; in which case they might be rendered very useful in transporting troops, if required, and without hurting the boats for fishing. This proposition was mentioned by the late Duke of

Buccleuch to Captain Clements, then commanding the sea-fencibles, and to Colonel Smith, commanding officer of artillery at Leith, both of whom declared, that the boats in question could not bear a gun of that description. But Captain Milne, knowing from experience that such boats, thirty feet in length and ten in breadth, could carry, not only a 12-pounder, but an 18-pounder, if required, repeated his opinion in presence of these gentlemen, but to no effect. Shortly after, however, he was asked by the Duke of Buccleuch to superintend the fitting out of two of the boats at his grace's expense. This he readily complied with, and two were accordingly completed, having single slides, for about six pounds sterling. They were then tried with twenty-six rounds of round shot and four rounds of shrapnel-shells, with a full charge of powder, at an elevation of three degrees, firing nearly four times in a minute. They were afterwards examined, but not a bolt or nail had started, nor had the boats received the slightest injury. On these particulars being reported to the First Lord of the Admiralty, the late Lord Melville, Captain Clements was superseded, and Captain Milne appointed to the situation; an appointment which was communicated to him by the Duke of Buccleuch, who was ever foremost in improving the defensive means of the country, and had taken the most lively interest in the success of Captain Milne's plan. Although this was a situation which never would have been sought after by Captain Milne, as he felt anxious for more active employment, he still considered it to be his duty to accept of it; and indeed this appointment must have been attended with a certain degree of gratification, proving, as it did, his superiority in the art of gunnery. He then fitted many of the boats in the same simple and useful manner: but such are the trammels of office, that, after the lapse of a certain period, a person was commissioned by the Navy-Board to superintend the fitting of the boats, which he commenced doing without consulting the owners of them, who had hitherto granted the use of their boats free of expense. All, however, which we shall say upon the plan which he adopted is, that, after going to a great expense in fitting them with cumbrous work, it did not answer the purpose, and became totally useless, besides rendering the owners of the boats discontented. In justice to that meritorious class of persons on the Frith of Forth, as well as to the character of Admiral Milne, we must observe, that, during the time he held that command, they all volunteered their services, at an hour's notice, to embark in his Majesty's ships, for the purpose of proceeding to

Copenhagen, to assist in navigating to England the ships captured by Admiral Gambier. Also, upon another occasion, when it was reported that a French frigate was in the Greenland seas, and the flag-ship of 50 guns, then lying in Leith roads, was incapable of proceeding to sea for want of men: this being communicated to them by Captain Milne, a sufficient number immediately went on board that ship, and were absent ten weeks, though unfortunately they did not fall in with the enemy.

During his continuance on this station, Captain Milne was directed by Lord Melville to report on the best and most desirable spot for a squadron to rendezvous on the east coast of Scotland; and having surveyed every part thereof, he was decidedly of opinion that Aberlady Bay, in the mouth of the Frith of Forth, was the most eligible, having a good anchorage, and from whence ships could proceed to sea with any wind; in consequence of which the flag-ship and ships on the station were ordered to anchor in that bay. The fear of invasion having subsided, and the enemy having withdrawn their troops from the coast in 1809, Captain Milne applied to the First Lord of the Admiralty (Mulgrave) for the command of a ship, but without success. In the following year he renewed his application for active employment, but with the same result. However, on the appointment of Mr. Yorke to the situation of First Lord of the Admiralty, Captain Milne was nominated to the Impetueux of 74 guns, which he joined in the Baltic. He afterwards served under Admiral Young off Flushing; in the winter of 1811 was off Cherbourg; and in the spring of 1812, he was ordered to join the Lisbon squadron under Admiral Berkeley. Dispatches being received from Captain Loring of the Niobe, stating that he had been chased by two French frigates near the Western Islands, Captain Milne solicited and obtained leave to go in quest of them. Being convinced that they were bound to France, he immediately directed his course to Cape Finisterre, and was to the northward of that cape on the 16th May, but they escaped, owing to continued thick and hazy weather, though they did not reach their own ports, being intercepted and destroyed by Sir Henry Hotham on the 22d, endeavouring to get into l'Orient. Not falling in with these ships, as he expected, off Cape Finisterre, Captain Milne proceeded to St. Michael's, and from thence to Madeira, where, having heard that when last seen off the coast of Africa they were short of water, he sailed for Mogadore, thinking they might have run there for a supply; but gaining no farther intelligence of them at that place, he returned to Lisbon, where he found he was superseded in the Impetueux, Admiral Martin having been ordered to hoist his flag in that ship. Having returned to Spithead as a passenger in the Niobe, he was immediately appointed to the Dublin, and afterwards to the Venerable, with an acting order for the Royal Charlotte yacht, until the Venerable's arrival from the coast of Spain. In January 1813, he assumed the command of the Venerable, and was employed as senior officer off Cherbourg, which he effectually and totally blockaded until June, when that ship having suffered much by tempestuous weather was ordered into dock. Captain Milne took this opportunity of having her ballast restowed, by which means she became, from being almost the worst sailing ship in the navy, so improved as to be one of the very fastest*. During the remainder of the year Captain Milne was employed in cruising between the Azores and Newfoundland, and in protecting a convoy to Lisbon. At the close of the year he was removed from the Venerable to the Bulwark, and shortly afterwards proceeded to the North American station. In the summer and autumn of 1814 he had the command of a squadron in Boston Bay, blockading the different harbours and rivers along that part of the American coast, where he destroyed so many of the enemy's vessels that their trade was totally ruined. Indeed, so sharp a look-out was kept, that not a boat could go along shore, and supplies of every kind were effectually prevented from getting into Boston. In the month of June he was promoted to the rank of rear-admiral; but before intelligence of that circumstance reached him, he served at the capture of Castine, in the Penobscot, under the orders of Admiral Griffith. In the month of October he returned to Halifax; but as there was no ship of the line off Boston, to watch the ships there fitting for sea, he offered his services to Sir A. Cochrane for that duty, to which he was accordingly appointed, and where he remained till the end of the month, and captured a large schooner privateer of 300 tons, armed with long 12-pounders. Having been superseded in the command of the Bulwark, in consequence of his promotion, he returned to England in the Loire frigate, and on his arrival at Plymouth received the melancholy intelligence of the death of his amiable wife, who had gone to the south of France for the benefit of her health; and by which melancholy event his two infant children were left at Bourdeaux without any natural protector. With feelings of real parental affection, he immediately proceeded to that city; and on

* See *Memoir of Admiral Sir P. Durham.*

his return from thence had the mortification to find, that, on the extension of the Order of the Bath, his name, contrary to general expectation, had been omitted; and owing to his recent loss, and consequent distress of mind, he was prevented from making that remonstrance on the occasion which he otherwise would have done. The selection, however, that was made on that occasion was certainly a matter of general surprise: some were appointed without one particle of claim, and others omitted, though possessed of every qualification. Some, indeed, whose merits were great, and had received the deserved honours, regretted the circumstance, when they found who were their associates. So that disappointment was experienced by some whose services were rewarded, and by others who were neglected; which reminds us of an allegorical description given of the Temple of Fame, which is said to be seated on the summit of a high mountain, at the foot of which are the bowers of peace, with a long valley leading to it, and on the verge of a boundless plain. The disciples of Virtue are said to press forward in the valley, though sometimes wounded by thorns and bruised by stones; while the votaries of Vice wander on the plain, which was adorned with flowers, though their beauty was transient and their fragrance hurtful. "But all the disciples of Virtue do not ascend the mountain, and the last stage is the ascent of the precipice: to climb is the voluntary labour of the vigorous and the bold; to desist is the irreproachable repose of the timid and the weary. To those, however, who have surmounted the difficulties of the way, the gates of the temple have not, unfortunately, always been opened; nor against those by whom it has never been trodden have they always been shut. The declivity of the mountain, on the other side, is gradual and easy; and, by the appointment of Fate, the entrance of the Temple of Honour has been always kept by Opinion. Opinion indeed ought to have acted under the influence of Truth, but was soon perverted by Prejudice and Custom; she admitted many who ascended the mountain without labour from the plain, and rejected some who had toiled up the precipice in the path of Virtue. These, however, were not clamorous for admittance, but either repined in silence, or exulting with honest pride in the consciousness of their own dignity, turned from Opinion with contempt and disdain, and smiled upon the world which they had left beneath them, the witness of that labour of which they had been refused the reward." Discontent, however, soon reigned in the Temple; and the disciples of Virtue, justly jealous of an eminence which they had obtained by the utmost efforts of human power, made attempts to expel those who had been admitted by Opinion without a claim, and were thus allowed to pollute the temple and disgrace the assembly. Whereupon the goddess flew to Jupiter, and implored him to protect the temple, and not allow it to be possessed by the undeserving. Jupiter, however, replied, that he could not reverse the order of Fate; that admission to the temple must still depend upon Opinion; but he would depute Reason to examine her conduct, and endeavour to put her under the influence of Truth. It was then soon discovered that Opinion, in her selections, had adopted neither rule nor principle, nor shewed the smallest discriminating knowledge, but had been actuated by favour and caprice. Such, we fear, may be said of the new Order of the Bath: if merit had been considered, if truth had been consulted, and justice duly administered, Admiral Milne would not have been denied admittance, but the doors would have been thrown open to receive him. However, as some little recompence for his disappointment, he was shortly after appointed to the chief command at Halifax, and hoisted his flag in the Leander of 50 guns; but previous to his sailing, an expedition was ordered to be fitted out against Algiers, and in that important armament he was placed as second in command.

The fleet, under Lord Exmouth, left Plymouth on the 28th July, and after a pleasant voyage reached Gibraltar on the 9th August. During the passage Admiral Milne and his brave friend and follower, Captain Chetham, were indefatigable in seconding the efforts of the commander-in-chief, by exercising the men, particularly at the great guns, which were fitted with sights upon a new and improved plan of Admiral Milne's. Nothing indeed was too minute or too extensive for his mind and attention; and no ship could be better prepared for the sanguinary conflict which was expected to take place. This was fully proved in the subsequent battle, the Leander having done considerable execution, from the precision of her fire and the steadiness of the men. On the 13th August Admiral Milne shifted his flag to the Impregnable of 98 guns, Captain Brace, and on the morning of the 27th the fleet arrived off Algiers. The time allowed by Lord Exmouth for the determination of the Dey having expired without any satisfactory reply, the signal was made for attack, and for the ships to take their stations. On taking her position, the Impregnable could not get sufficiently beyond the enemy's formidable batteries so as to shut them in, in consequence of the wind failing and the enemy opening his fire, so that she was obliged to take up the position she did, and which was one of extreme danger, opposite the Demi-Lune and the lighthouse tower, where she was exposed to a most destructive fire. A vigorous and animated fire was, however, kept up on her side, and all the enemy's guns exposed to her were soon dismantled, except the lower tier of the lighthouse battery, which was kept supplied from the opposite side of the tower, which very greatly annoyed the ship, and strewed her decks with killed and wounded. Previous to sailing from England, an explosion-vessel was fitted out, for the purpose of being placed in the angle between the lighthouse and the other batteries of Algiers, to protect as much as possible the ships from the fire of the enemy's strong batteries. Captain Powel, a volunteer on board the Impregnable, was then sent by Admiral Milne with a message to Lord Exmouth, requesting this vessel might be placed where she was originally intended for, and which he thought might then be done with effect. This was complied with, and she was run aground in the angle near the lighthouse, where she exploded with a tremendous shock, but with little effect, owing to the thickness of the walls and the batteries being bomb-proof*. Though the enemy were for a time struck with consternation, the cannonade from the lighthouse was soon renewed; but twelve of the Impregnable's lower-deck guns were kept constantly pointed into their embrasures, and were fired the instant the enemy was observed to put the matches to their guns, so that they were repeatedly dismounted. Thus was the fire maintained by the Impregnable till orders were given by Lord Exmouth for withdrawing the ships. The great loss of men sustained by the Impregnable, 50 killed and 154 wounded, plainly shews the important part she took in the glories of the day; while the quantity of powder and shot she expended, proves the severity of her fire†. With the news of this important and brilliant victory, a victory glorious and honourable in every point of view, Admiral Milne was dispatched to England in his own ship, the Leander‡; and the commander-in-chief, in

* In the official letter of Lord Exmouth's, it is stated that the rear-admiral applied for a frigate: but this is a mistake, owing no doubt to the hurry of the moment.

† Fifteen tons and sixty pounds of powder, one hundred tons of shot, besides grape, canister, shrapnel-shells, and other combustible matter.

‡ Upon the arrival of the Leander at Gibraltar, it was found that she was so much damaged, that she could not carry sail; and the admiral, though most reluctantly, shifted his flag to the Glasgow, to the great regret of all the Leander's crew, particularly the wounded, who had fully experienced his bounty and liberality, by the whole of his stock having been given to them for their support and comfort.

his official letter*, bore the most honourable testimony to his merits. " I have confided," said he, " this dispatch to Rear-Admiral Milne, my second in command, from whom I have received, during the whole service intrusted to me, the most cordial and honourable support. He is perfectly informed of every transaction of the fleet from the earliest period of my command, and is fully competent to give their lordships satisfaction on any points which I may have overlooked or have not time to state. I trust I have obtained from him his esteem and regard; and I regret I had not sooner been known to him." The wishes here expressed by his lordship, we believe, were fully gratified; for no one could hold the talents and conduct of Lord Exmouth in higher estimation than Admiral Milne, and he accordingly took an active and prominent part in setting on foot amongst the officers of the fleet a subscription for a piece of plate, which was afterwards presented to his lordship by Captain Ekins.

We have now to notice the honours conferred upon Admiral Milne for his conduct in this brilliant action. By his Majesty he was created a Knight-Commander of the Bath, with additional armorial bearings†; by both Houses of Parliament he was presented with their thanks; by the King of the Netherlands he was nominated a Knight-Commander of the Royal Military Order of William; by the King of the Two Sicilies he was presented with the insignia of the Order of St. Januarius; by

---

* See RALFE's *Naval Chronology*, vol. III.

† After reciting his early services, the *Gazette* says, " And his Royal Highness (the Prince Regent) being desirous in an especial manner to evince the sense he entertains of the distinguished merits of the said rear-admiral in the above brilliant actions, and more particularly his meritorious conduct as second in command at the attack upon the town and shipping of Algiers on the 27th day of August last, upon which occasion he commanded his Majesty's ship Impregnable, and by his signal intrepidity and skill eminently contributed to the glorious and successful result of that memorable day, hath been pleased, in the name and on the behalf of his Majesty, to grant unto the said Sir David Milne his Majesty's royal licence and permission that he and his descendants may, as a lasting memorial of his Majesty's royal approbation, bear the armorial distinctions following: ' *A cross moline, quarterly pierced between three mullets, on a chief of honourable augmentation wavy; a fortified lighthouse, thereon a red flag flying, flanked by a battery of three tiers of guns, with a like flag on the dexter, and another battery on the sinister.*' The whole being intended to represent that part of the works defending the town and port of Algiers to which his Majesty's ship Impregnable, bearing the flag of the said Rear-Admiral Milne, was opposed on the said ever-memorable attack; and for crest, ' *out of a naval crown a cubit arm, holding the flag of a rear-admiral of the Blue, inscribed with the word*—IMPREGNABLE.' "

the city of London he was presented with their freedom and a handsome sword; and last, though not least, he received from Lord Exmouth a gold snuff-box, with an appropriate device, expressive of the effects resulting from the glorious battle in which they had fought; a battle in which Sir David Milne received a severe contusion, in consequence of a large round shot passing between his thighs, which caused considerable lameness for several months, though he would not allow it to be noticed in the casualties of the ship.

In 1817 Admiral Milne proceeded to Halifax to assume the command of the British squadron in America; and on his arrival had a very delicate duty to put in force respecting the fisheries, the Americans having monopolized the whole, and, contrary to treaties, had come to fish in every harbour and creek in Nova Scotia, to the great injury of his Majesty's subjects; and to check which he was obliged to order several of their vessels to be seized, which were condemned in the Vice-Admiralty Court, but subsequently released by order of the British government, who entered into a new treaty with the United States, by which privileges were allowed to the citizens of the latter which had never been conceded by any former treaty. From this station Sir David returned in 1819; but previous to his so doing, he received an address from the merchants of Bermuda, which, as it is drawn up by men who had ample opportunities of judging of his character, we may here insert as a satisfactory proof of the high estimation in which he was held, and of his public and private worth: " Influenced by feelings of personal respect, and actuated by a sense of public duty, we, the merchants and inhabitants of St. George's, are desirous of testifying our estimation of your public, as well as private, character, ere you bid us farewell. Besides the constant and unremitting attention to your own duties as naval commander-in-chief on this station, we have experienced the lively interest you have manifested on all occasions in forwarding our views, by the application of your personal exertions, as well as in pointing out the manner, which your professional and scientific abilities have suggested to you, of advancing our commercial relations. Contemplating, with the rest of our countrymen, the auspicious prospect which the colony presents to us, we cannot but feel grateful for the friendly offices of men who are both able and willing to assist us, and who proffer their kindest exertions in thus advancing our interest; for by this means we are satisfied, that our anticipations of her future wealth and importance are the more likely to be realized. We have, sir, in public and in private, seen you advocating the cause of the colony; and we have found you ever accessible and ever ready to assist us in any thing of importance for the welfare of the people. When a union of talent and perseverance, of uprightness and courage, is manifested, we feel confident that our trust is in good hands: these make the cause of truth not only respectable but irresistible. We cannot conclude, sir, without recurring to your already acknowledged services to your country; but, sir, as history and fame, whose works are imperishable, have recorded those deeds, their recapitulation would be but a mockery by the public chroniclers of a day. When you return to your native land, the rectitude and consistency of your character will ensure you every heartfelt, every generous wish; and although we may seriously deplore your separation from us, your kindness, your affability, and your usefulness to the community, will never be obliterated from our recollections."

Sir David Milne has been twice married: first, in 1804, to Grace, daughter of Sir Alexander Purvis, Bart. by whom he had two sons: the eldest has been educated for the Scottish bar, and has displayed a high degree of scientific talent; the youngest is a lieutenant in the navy, and promises to be an honour to his profession. Sir David married, secondly, Miss Stephen, daughter of George Stephen, Esq. of Grenada. The admiral is now settled at Milne-Graden, in Berwickshire, where his warm hospitality and general benevolence endear him to all around his neighbourhood; while the occupation afforded in the execution of the important duties of a deputy-lieutenant and a magistrate prevents him from experiencing that tedium so frequently observed in naval officers when removed from their own element.

In the course of this Memoir we have stated the care and attention paid by Sir David Milne to the crews of those ships which he commanded, and that by his judicious management, whether in the West Indies or on the coast of Africa, he kept them free from sickness. As this is a subject of the greatest importance, we must more particularly allude to it, in hopes that others may adopt the plan he pursued, and find the same beneficial results. On leaving England for any tropical climate, he always supplied himself with a certain quantity of quick lime, and on arriving on his station, he invariably had the interior of his ship lime-washed, taking care that all the boxes should be removed, and not a single part should escape this operation. It is generally supposed that it is the heat of a climate that engenders fever: Sir David, however, found from experience that this was not the case, and that it is from dampness the most malignant fevers take their rise. To guard against the fatal consequences arising from this cause, he supplied himself with some portable or swing-stoves, and after every shower of rain invariably had them lit, *to dry the decks as quick as possible.* So particular indeed was he on this subject, that he never allowed the decks to be *washed,* except from absolute necessity; but having procured a quantity of common sand, had it baked, so that it was perfectly dry, and every morning had the decks dry-rubbed with this sand and small square stones for the purpose, and which was found to answer completely every object contemplated. Another circumstance must be noticed: it is usual in hot climates to send parties on shore for wood and water *before the sun rises;* but this Sir David never did, feeling convinced that the exhalations arising from the earth at that time of the morning would prove more detrimental to the health of the men than any effects of the sun. He therefore would never allow a man to go on shore till after the sun had risen, and not then unless he had had a *hot breakfast.* Neither would he allow his men to drink *cold* grog, but, with the aid of lemons or lime-juice, had the spirit made into punch, and drank warm. By this continued kindness and attention to the health and comfort of the men, he not only kept them in constant readiness for any service, their valuable lives were not only saved for the defence of their country, but he so firmly secured their admiration and regard, that no commander ever more effectually obtained the hearts and inclinations of those placed under him, than Sir David Milne. We have only farther to add, that Sir David is a most scientific, humane, upright, and honourable man.

HISTORICAL MEMOIRS OF
ADMIRAL SIR JOHN GORE, K.C.B.

THE nearer we approach to the termination of this work, the more anxious are we that the whole should be considered worthy the object we had in view at its commencement—to make known the services of a body of men who, during a reign of unexempled duration and importance, rendered the name of Britain illustrious in every corner of the world; to trace their career from the first dawnings to the close; and to shew, in adequate terms, their claims to public gratitude. But the object, however important, is not new; it has, with ability and perseverance, been before attempted; and we have, therefore, in that part of the subject no claim to originality. We have felt the weight of this objection from the beginning, and also the magnitude of the work; but, during its progress, we have paid unremitted attention to every circumstance connected with it, have been most anxious to obtain every possible information respecting it, and think we may say, that the lives of some of those individuals were never before published; and that many important circumstances, details, and particulars respecting the services of others, were equally unknown. Some indeed there are whose names are not mentioned in the work, or at least who have not a distinct article respecting them; not, however, because we thought them too unimportant, but because we could not succeed in obtaining sufficient information to enable us, in our estimation, to do justice to the character they hold in the profession. But if we have not been able to accomplish every object with which we started, we must find our consolation in our motives, and the knowledge that we have succeeded in part; and that we have so far succeeded, we may adduce the present Memoir as a proof.

Sir John is a native of Ireland, being born at Kilkenny, on the 9th of February, 1772, and is the second son of the late Colonel John Gore, who served many years in the 33d regiment of foot, from the command of which he retired in 1776, upon being appointed lieutenant-governor of the Tower of London, where he died in 1794, and there lies buried in the chapel, with his wife and a daughter. He left three sons and two daughters: Ralph, the eldest, a captain in the 33d regiment; Arthur, a lieutenant in the 73d regiment, who afterwards attained the rank of major-general, and was killed under the walls of Bergen-op-Zoom; and John, the subject of this Memoir.

He entered the naval service in 1780, on board the Monarca of 74 guns, commanded by Captain John Gell; but that ship having put to sea, and proceeded to the East Indies without him, he was received on board the Canada, Captain the Hon. W. Cornwallis, with whom he sailed to North America. The first service on which they were employed was the fruitless attempt made to relieve Lord Cornwallis at York-Town; after which, they accompanied Sir Samuel Hood to the West Indies, and the conduct of the Canada in the manœuvres at St. Kitt's, as well as in the actions of the 9th and 12th of April, we have before detailed, and shall here only observe, that on those occasions she drew forth the admiration of both friends and foes. Mr. Gore returned to England in the Canada, and of course witnessed that tremendous hurricane in which so many ships, with all their crews, perished.

The Canada having been put out of commission, he removed with his captain to the Dragon; and in March 1783 he was placed in the Iphigenia frigate, Captain James Cornwallis, a relation and *élève* of his late captain, with whom he again proceeded to the West Indies; and from whence he returned in 1786. At this time, however, his health was considerably impaired, and he was entered on board the Royal Charlotte yacht, with his first captain and patron, the Hon. W. Cornwallis, with whom he afterwards removed to the Robust of 74 guns, during the armament of 1787; and having passed his examination for a lieutenancy, and the Robust being put out of commission, he entered on board the Hebe frigate, Captain Thornbrough, stationed in the Channel, and continued cruising till October 1788, when his old friend Cornwallis having been appointed commander-in-chief in the East Indies, with the rank of commodore, having his pendant in the Crown of 64 guns, Captain James Cornwallis, Mr. Gore removed to that ship, in which he continued till the 29th November, 1789, when he was promoted to a lieutenancy, and appointed to the Perseverance frigate, Captain James Smyth. In the autumn of 1791 he returned to England in the Crown, in consequence of his health having suffered severely from the effects of the climate, and which, on his arrival in England, prevented him from accepting any other appointment till December 1792. He was then appointed to the Lowestoffe frigate, Captain Wollesley, and afterwards accompanied the fleet under Lord Hood to the Mediterranean, where he was removed to the Britannia, bearing the flag of Admiral Hotham.

During the operations at Toulon, Lieutenant Gore was landed with a detachment of seamen, employed on a variety of services, and was in various actions both ashore and in the floating batteries; and the favourable reports made of him on all these occasions to the commander-in-chief induced Lord Hood to remove him to his ship, the Victory; and as a farther proof of his lordship's confidence, and the high opinion he had formed of his zeal and abilities, he the next day sent Lieutenant Gore with a detachment of seamen from the different ships, to serve as artillerymen in, and defend the important post called Fort Mulgrave. Three times did the enemy attempt to take the fort by storm, and three times were they defeated with loss by the party under Lieutenant Gore. The enemy then brought up a detachment of heavy guns and mortars, and commenced a regular bombardment, during which Lieutenant Gore received a severe wound in the head, so that he was under the necessity of being removed.

On the morning previous to the evacuation of Toulon, he was ordered by Lord Hood to go into the arsenal, and see if any thing could be there effected with fire-ships; and upon making his report, several boats were placed under his orders, and he was directed to tow the Vulcan to a certain position in the arsenal, and then place himself under the immediate orders of Sir Sidney Smith. Having effected the first object, he was subsequently receiving some of the combustible materials out of the Vulcan for the purpose of firing some of the ships in the southern basin, when the Vulcan was prematurely and suddenly fired, and he was blown out of his boat (Lord Hood's barge), and so severely burnt, as to make him totally incapable of rendering any farther service at that most important and critical moment.

The Island of Corsica was the next scene of his exertions, where he was landed with a detachment of seamen to assist in driving the enemy out of St. Fiorenzo. The enemy having been driven from their strong points, took refuge in the Convention redoubt, when it became necessary to form batteries on the two hills which commanded it, but which were nearly inaccessible. Captain Edward Cooke, however, immediately undertook to erect one of them, and Lieutenant Gore as readily offered to complete the other: each had 300 seamen under his orders, with all the aid the squadron could afford; and in forty-eight hours, " by the most surprising exertions of science and labour on the part of the officers and men, several 18-pounders, two 10-inch mortars, and other pieces were placed on an eminence of very difficult ascent, 700 feet above the level of the sea. This rocky elevation, owing to its perpendicularity near its summit, was deemed inaccessible; but the seamen, by means of blocks and ropes, contrived to haul up the guns, each of which weighed upwards of forty-two hundred weight. The path along which these dauntless fellows crept would in most places admit but one person at a time: on the right was a descent of many hundred feet, and one false step would have led to eternity; on the left were stupendous overhanging rocks, which occasionally served as fixed points for the tackle employed in raising the guns. From these 18-pounders, so admirably posted, a cannonade was unremittingly kept up for thirty-six hours; but the first shot which the enemy fired dismounted one of the guns in Lieutenant Gore's battery, which, however, was replaced during the cannonade. At the end of that time, all the enemy's guns were silenced, and their works so much damaged, that an assault was determined on, under the command of Colonel (the late Sir John) Moore, assisted by Lieutenant Gore and the detachment of seamen under his orders; a service which was carried into execution with the wonted vigour of Englishmen, and crowned with that success which skill and courage deserve."

Early on the following morning the enemy abandoned the tower and fort of Fornelli, which Lieutenant Gore was ordered to take possession of; and shortly after he discovered that the enemy were about setting fire to two frigates lying in the bay. This intelligence he immediately forwarded to Lord Hood, and having succeeded in drawing a spike out of an 18-pounder, commenced firing at the nearest, which he sunk at her anchor (she was subsequently weighed and added to the British navy under the name of the St. Fiorenzo); but the destruction of the other one was effected by the enemy. The enemy having evacuated St. Fiorenzo, Lieutenant Gore, with his detachment, returned to the Victory; but on the 2d April was again landed, under the orders of Captain Nelson, to co-operate in the siege of Bastia. With that distinguished officer Lieutenant Gore shared in all the fatigues, the anxious duties, dangers, and hard services of that period, during which he received two severe contusions. His conduct indeed throughout the whole of these important operations could not fail of exciting commendation; and accordingly we find that, on the surrender of Bastia, he was promoted by Lord Hood to the rank of commander on board La Flèche, a French ship-corvette lying in the port. As soon as she could be fitted for sea, he was ordered to Malta, to negociate with the Grand-Master, Rhoan, for a supply of seamen, naval and military stores, &c. Upon his rejoining the fleet, he found it under the command of Admiral Hotham, who, the following day, 12th November, 1794, promoted him to post-rank in the Windsor Castle, bearing the flag of Rear-Admiral Linzee. On the 14th March following, he was in the partial engagement with the French fleet, when the Censeur and La Ca Ira were captured. Captain Gore was afterwards appointed to the Censeur, and ordered to accompany the Fortitude 74 and Bedford 74, with a valuable convoy from the Levant, to England. As the Censeur had lost her main-mast in the action of the 14th March, she was fitted with a 32-gun-frigate's main-mast on the stump of her old main-mast on the lower deck, by which all the frigate's sails had their full effect above deck, and she had all her proper masts and sails in the fore and mizen, which were of the largest dimensions, being a ship of 1800 tons. She had a full complement of officers as a 74, and her crew was composed of a draft of five seamen from every ship in the fleet, 20 men lent from the Argo and 20 from the Juno; in all she mustered at quarters 260 seamen, but no marines. Besides which, she had on board, at the time of sailing from Corsica, seven invalided lieutenants, three surgeons, five boatswains, three carpenters, two gunners, several excellent midshipmen and petty officers from the Blenheim, and all the sick and invalids of the fleet; but she had only a small quantity of powder and shot. To promote and effect the utmost order and regularity in so motley a crew, the ship's guns were divided into batteries of three guns each, at which were stationed a lieutenant, with a certain number of men, who were taught to work them, which they did so effectually, that, on his arrival at Gibraltar, Captain Gore was induced to complete the powder and shot to its full quantity. On the 25th September the whole squadron and convoy left Gibraltar, and on the 7th October arrived off Cape St. Vincent, where they fell in with a French squadron under M. Richery, when the Censeur and many ships of the convoy were captured. The Censeur was a remarkably fast-sailing ship, and the day before her capture was ordered to chase a large French frigate, which had been hanging on the rear of the convoy for two days, and gained so fast upon the enemy, that had she been permitted to continue the chase, the enemy must have been captured before midnight. On the following morning at daylight, while the Censeur was still far to leeward, the enemy's squadron of six sail of the line and three frigates was seen to windward: Captain Gore consequently used every exertion to gain his station in the line and prepare for action, agreeably to signals, which he effected astern of the Fortitude about ten a. m. Signals were then made for the convoy to disperse, and for the ships of war to bear up and steer S. E. preserving the order of battle. In performing this evolution, however, the Censeur rolled so deep, that her fore-top-mast went by the cap, which necessarily retarded her progress. The Fortitude and Bedford kept on their course with all sail set; but Captain Halket of the Lutine offered to take the Censeur in tow; an offer which Captain Gore declined, in consequence of the enemy's shot at that time passing over them, and Captain Halket was ordered to make sail and save his ship. The Censeur was then put before the wind, but was overtaken by the Barras (now Donegal in the British navy), which was received with so steady and well-directed a fire, that, after an action of half-an-hour's duration, the enemy sheared off, with the loss of all her studding-sails, fore-top-sail-yard, and nearly 150 men killed or wounded. One of the enemy's frigates was also effectually crippled; for on attempting to pass outside the Barras, she received three broadsides from the Censeur, and was obliged to drop astern. Such firmness on the part of the Censeur not only prevented those two ships from pursuing the flying convoy, but the enemy's whole squadron was for a time prevented making any attempt on them. Admiral Richery, seeing how roughly his companions were handled, formed his other five ships into a line-of-battle abreast, and about three o'clock closed with the Censeur, by placing two of his line-of-battle ships on each quarter, while the fifth, or centre ship, brought-to across her stern. In this position Captain Gore received the enemy's fire, and returned it with that coolness, vigour, and effect, which had marked his conduct when opposed only to the Barras: escape, however, was out of the question, and having had his mizen-top-mast and main-top-gallant-mast shot away, and sails cut to pieces, a farther sacrifice of life was unnecessary; he therefore put his helm a-starboard at the moment the ensign was hauled down, hoping to run athwart the hause of the Formidable of 84 guns (captured by Sir R. Strachan in November 1805), which had fired red-hot shot, several of which had taken effect, and when Captain Gore left the ship she was on fire in five places. On the surrender of the Censeur the enemy's squadron was brought-to, and all farther pursuit of the valuable convoy abandoned, so that only about fifteen were captured by the enemy's frigates; a circumstance which must be entirely attributed to the bravery and perseverance of Captain Gore, whose conduct throughout was marked with all those traits which distinguished the character of his great friend and patron, Cornwallis; and though he lost his ship, his defence was much more honourable, and the wreath of laurel which he thereby gained was much more valuable, than has often resulted from a more successful termination. His conduct indeed excited the admiration of Admiral Richery, who not only allowed him to exchange with the captain of the Modeste, then a prisoner at Gibraltar, but gave him the Golden Lion, a large transport which had been captured, for the purpose of proceeding to England with his officers and invalids, on condition that a similar number of French prisoners should be allowed to proceed in her to France, for which purpose a lieutenant de vaisseau was placed in her; and to mark still farther the high opinion he entertained of Captain Gore's defence, at his request, he agreed that the remainder of the Censeur's crew should be sent to Gibraltar, on the same conditions, to join Admiral Man's squadron, on board another transport, under the command of Lieutenant Clephane, second of the Censeur: but on the passage, the seamen took the command from the lieutenant and brought her to England, ran her ashore near Hartland Point, and escaped inland. The Golden Lion arrived at Spithead, after a severe passage, with hardly a sail left to the yards; and it is scarcely necessary to add, that the conditions entered into by Captain Gore were faithfully executed by the British government. As a matter of course, Captain Gore underwent the ordeal of a court-martial, by which he was most honourably acquitted; and received from the president, Sir Roger Curtis, the most flattering acknowledgments of the zeal and ability he had displayed.

In the following year (1796) Captain Gore successively commanded the Robust of 74 and Alcmene of 36 guns, in the absence of their captains; and in the month of September he was appointed to the Triton of 32 guns, an experimental frigate, just launched, and was attached to the Channel fleet till 1798, when the French fleet having escaped from Brest, he was ordered to the Mediterranean with dispatches; and on his arrival, was directed by Lord Keith to reconnoitre, with two other frigates, all the ports between Toulon and Cadiz, and in case of discovering the enemy, to watch and report to him their movements. On ascertaining that they had joined the Spanish fleet in Cadiz, and that their united force amounted to thirty-eight sail of the line and eighteen frigates, he stationed himself off that port, and on the enemy again putting to sea, some of their frigates were ordered to drive him away; but the moment they gave up the chase, he immediately hauled his wind, and kept sight of them till he saw them all bear up round Cape St. Vincent and make all sail northward; when he pushed past them under all sail, making the best of his way for England, to inform the ministers of the enemy's movement, and arrived at Plymouth five days before the enemy reached Brest. In a few days afterwards he was intrusted with the command of a squadron of frigates, to watch the movements of the enemy's squadron in Brest; and while on this service a Spanish squadron of five sail of the line and two frigates from Ferrol attempted to enter the harbour through the Passage du Raz; but finding themselves so closely watched by the squadron under Captain Gore, they gave up the attempt, and returned to Ferrol. Sir John Warren, having been ordered in pursuit of the enemy, was accompanied by the squadron under Captain Gore, and on their arrival off Ferrol, finding the enemy's ships were partly dismantled, Sir John Warren rejoined the fleet under Lord Bridport off Ushant, leaving Captain Gore, with the Ethalion, to watch the port of Ferrol, which proved of the most fortunate description. On the morning of the 17th October two Spanish frigates were observed, pursued by two English ones, though at a great distance astern. Captain Gore and his companion, Captain Young, immediately bore up in chase, upon which the enemy separated, one of which was pursued by the Ethalion, and the other by the Triton. About nine o'clock the Ethalion, assisted by the Naïad and Alcmene, captured the Thetis; but the chase of her consort continued till eleven p. m. when, just as Captain Gore was bringing her to close action, the Triton struck on a sunken rock off Cape Finisterre; but by skilful management his ship was soon afloat again and in pursuit of the enemy. Although by this accident she was much shaken, going at the time seven knots an hour, and became very leaky; still, owing to her remarkable qualities of sailing, she again got along side of the enemy by seven a. m. just as she was reaching the Bayonne Islands, and poured into her one broadside, when she struck; at which moment the Naïad and Alcmene joined, and the enemy was taken possession of. This took place within sight of the enemy's squadron in Vigo, five of which put to sea for the purpose of rescuing their friend; upon which the prize was im-

mediately taken in tow by Captain Gore, the Naïad and Alcmene
forming a line ahead and astern, in which position they prepared to receive them; but the enemy no sooner observed their resolute appearance
than they bore up and returned into port, leaving the British squadron
to carry off their prizes, and with which they arrived in safety at Plymouth. The cargoes of these vessels proved of the most valuable description, and each captain shared above 40,000 pounds prize-money.
The Triton having been docked and repaired, Captain Gore again proceeded off Brest, attached to the Channel fleet.

On the 8th of February, 1801, a serious accident occurred on board
the Triton: being in chase of a French cutter off the Penmarks, one of
the main-deck guns burst, by which a lieutenant and two men were
killed, and twenty-two others wounded, amongst whom was Captain
Gore, who received a violent contusion on the back; besides which, the
ship was so much damaged, that Captain Gore was compelled to return
to port for the purpose of having her docked.

From the above account of the services of Captain Gore, it will be
seen that he had led a most active and diligent life; that he had been
almost constantly employed; and during the time he had commanded
the Triton, captured thirteen privateers and three men-of-war brigs, and
suffered a good deal of fatigue in the service. He applied to Lord St.
Vincent for a short leave of absence, for the benefit of his health; but
this favour was denied him, and feeling himself incapable of immediately going to sea, he was actually superseded in command of the Triton. However, upon reporting himself ready for service, he was, on the
1st of May, appointed to the Medusa, a new ship just launched at Woolwich. The moment the Medusa was fitted for sea, Captain Gore was
ordered off Boulogne, to watch the enemy's flotilla in that port. Shortly
afterwards, Lord Nelson was ordered to assume the command, and he
hoisted his flag on board the Medusa, when Captain Gore was directed
to arrange and place the bombs in positions to bombard the flotilla,
which took place under cover of the ships of the squadron.

On the 16th of August a more serious attack took place: the enemy
having brought thirty-six of their largest vessels outside the port, Lord
Nelson decided on making an attempt to destroy them by means of the
boats of the squadron and some flat-bottomed boats with howitzers, the
arrangements of which were confided to Captain Gore. At the appointed time they proceeded to the attack, the Medusa's boats leading

the centre division, and having reached the prescribed point of operations, captured the enemy's advanced look-out vessel, and soon boarded six others off the pier-head; but the enemy had so securely fastened them, that all attempts to bring them away proved fruitless, and they were obliged to be abandoned. In this unsuccessful attempt the boats suffered so severely in killed and wounded, as obliged his lordship to return to Deal to land the latter. He then removed his flag to the Amazon; and on the Medusa's crew being recompleted, Captain Gore was ordered to take the command of a squadron off Dungeness, to protect that part of the coast, and occasionally to menace the Boulogne flotilla; in which service he continued till the termination of hostilities by the treaty of Amiens. He was then ordered to cruise in the Channel, between the Start and the Isle of Wight; and on the 12th of February, 1802, was sent from Spithead to the Mediterranean with dispatches, and joined Sir Richard Bickerton at Malta on the 26th. He was then directed to visit and examine the ports in the Mediterranean; and, subsequently, with a squadron to escort the King of the Two Sicilies from Palermo to Naples.

In 1803 Captain Gore was ordered to convoy the British ambassador, the Right Hon. W. Drummond, from Naples to Constantinople; but, unfortunately, in their passage thither, through the ignorance of the pilot, the Medusa was run ashore in the Thracian Bosphorus, which accident rendered it necessary to remove all her guns and every thing out of her, in order to get her afloat; and so great was the zeal and alacrity shewn on the occasion, that in five days Captain Gore proceeded on his mission. Soon after his arrival at Bynkedery he learned the great probability of the renewal of the war between England and France; and knowing that in such an event the admiral would require the services of all the frigates attached to his squadron, he took upon himself the responsibility of leaving the Dardanelles without orders, and rejoined Sir Richard Bickerton off Toulon in July. He was immediately ordered to take the command of the advanced squadron, and closely watch the movements of the enemy in that port; but on the arrival of Lord Nelson to assume the command of the fleet, on the 9th of July, Captain Gore was ordered to proceed with three frigates and four sloops, to act, as his lordship said, as " his advanced guard off the Straits of Gibraltar."

On beating through the Straits, the Medusa struck on a rock about five p. m. and became so leaky, that Captain Gore was obliged to bear up and carry all sail, so as to reach the mole before dark; and although the ship had four months' provisions on board, she was cleared, hove down, keel taken out, repaired, restowed, and sailed again on the eighth day, to execute his orders, in which he captured or destroyed, at various times, five French privateers; and received from Lord Nelson the most flattering testimonials of his approbation.

That zeal for the service which Captain Gore had invariably displayed never more particularly manifested itself than during the period he remained on this station; and the following circumstance will prove, that he not only had courage to defend the rights of his country in open warfare, but that he had spirit and ability sufficient to maintain her dignity when attempted to be assailed by insidious friendship.

While lying in Gibraltar Bay, whither he had returned the preceding evening to refit, after a three months' cruise, he perceived a cutter coming from the westward, engaged with two large feluccas. At this moment nearly all the officers and most of the Medusa's crew were ashore, obtaining supplies from the dock-yard and victualing-offices; they were immediately called on board, the cables slipped, and being favoured by a fortunate start of wind, he fetched Cabrita point, near to the enemy, one of which was about to board the cutter, the British Fair, charged with dispatches of the utmost importance to Lord Nelson; but perceiving the Medusa approach, the enemy separated on opposite attacks, upon which Captain Gore ran along side one of them, ordered his first lieutenant (now Captain), Henry Hart, to board her, and then continued in pursuit of the other, which he engaged under sail, and though she succeeded in reaching the shore, she was in a shattered and sinking state, and never again floated.

The rapidity with which the whole of this affair was effected, and the great good fortune attending it, rendered it altogether one of those surprising events which partake of the nature of romance. Added to the interest of the scene, the day itself was remarkably beautiful, and drew forth almost every individual in the garrison, who had the gratification to witness his skilful manœuvres, and who afterwards cheered him on his return.

The capture and destruction of these two vessels brought on a long correspondence between General Sir T. Trigge, lieutenant-governor of Gibraltar, the Marquis Solano, captain-general of Andalusia, and General Castanos, governor of Algeziras, which was reported by Sir T.

Trigge to Captain Gore, and which he cut short by the following reply:

Sir,—I have the honour to acknowledge the receipt of your excellency's letter, and the inclosures from the high Spanish authorities; and in reply, I have to request you will be pleased to inform those officers, that so long as they countenance the French privateers lying in Tariffa and other ports, sallying from thence to seize upon the unprotected trade of his Majesty's subjects, thereby transgressing the laws of neutrality, I shall be equally heedless of them; and after the instance they so strongly dwell upon, *I shall feel it my duty to pursue the French privateers into the Spanish ports, and destroy them where I can;* and I shall instruct the captains of his Majesty placed under my command to do so likewise.

(Signed,)   John Gore.

This, as the sequel proved, was not an empty threat; for a very short time afterwards, as the Medusa was watching the movements of a French 74 and a ship-corvette, lying in Cadiz harbour, a French schooner privateer was observed coming from the eastward, within the Pedro shoals, when Captain Gore used his utmost exertions to prevent her from entering the harbour, which he nearly effected close to the lighthouse; so close indeed were they, that the Medusa's shot went into the town. On the following morning the Marquis Solano sent off his aide-de-camp to the Medusa, to acknowledge the honour of the salute; but requested that the next time that Captain Gore might favour him with a similar honour, he would give directions that his guns should not be shotted, producing two of the Medusa's 18-pound shot which had been picked up. Captain Gore, at the same time, received a note from the marquis, requesting his company to dinner, and that of his officers to a bull-fight in the evening, which was accepted by Captain Gore; and the Medusa stood into the harbour. Captain Gore had lived on terms of intimacy with the marquis during his detention at Cadiz, after the capture of the Censeur.

Towards the end of September, Captain Gore received instructions from the Admiralty to intercept some Spanish treasure-ships coming from South America. At that time the Amphion, Captain Sutton, was in company; and on the 30th he was joined by the Indefatigable, Captain Graham Moore, and the Lively, Captain Hammond, when Captain G. Moore, being the senior officer, took the command.

On the 5th they fell in with four Spanish frigates, when an action ensued, which terminated in the capture of three of the Spaniards, and the destruction of the fourth*. The Indefatigable, Amphion, and Lively conducted the prizes to England, and Captain Gore remained on the station; but was soon after ordered to England by Sir Richard Strachan, in charge of the Spanish frigate Matilda, which Sir Richard had detained, and was laden with quicksilver, and bound from Cadiz to Vera Cruz.

Shortly after his arrival, Captain Gore received the honour of knighthood, and his Majesty was farther pleased to express his approbation of his long and meritorious services. The Medusa was now undergoing repairs, and during that period Captain Gore visited Bath for the benefit of his health. Here he heard of the appointment of the Marquis Cornwallis as governor-general of the East Indies: he was the godfather of Captain Gore, had ever been his steady friend through life, and the latter naturally wished to convey him to his destination. He accordingly wrote to him the following letter, dated York-House, Bath, December 15, 1804:

My Lord,—I have just read in the *Courier*, that you are appointed governor-general of India; I do not mean to intrude any question, but if it is so, and your lordship thinks you can be more comfortable with me than with an entire stranger, I can only state, that my frigate, the Medusa, is now in dock at Portsmouth, undergoing a thorough repair, and I am told will be out of dock in February, and that I shall be truly rejoiced to do any thing in my power to render the voyage agreeable to your lordship. I have now only to beg, that, instead of taking the trouble to reply to this, you will signify your wishes to Lord Milville, upon whom, as well as yourself, I will wait the moment I return from Devonshire.

(Signed,)　　　　JOHN GORE.

To this friendly letter Captain Gore had the gratification to receive the following reply, dated London, December 19:

My DEAR GORE,—What you have read in the *Courier* is perfectly true. I am told that I can be useful by going to India; and if I can render my country any service, it is a matter of indifference to me whether I die on the banks of the Thames or the Ganges: I therefore accept your offer with all the kindness it is made. I have seen Lord Melville, who desires to see you as soon as you come to London, and will then make up all necessary arrangements. Believe me your attached friend,　　　　(Signed,)　　　　CORNWALLIS.

* See *Memoir of Sir* GRAHAM MOORE, vol. III. p. 209; and official letter, RALFE's *Naval Chronology*, vol. II. p 56.

On the 15th of April following, he sailed from Portsmouth with the Marquis Cornwallis, and landed him at Calcutta in the month of July. Here Captain Gore continued for four months, when he returned to England with the treaty of peace entered into with the native powers, and also the melancholy intelligence of his lordship's death. His voyage home was performed with the most astonishing celerity; the Medusa having run from the Ganges to the Lizard in eighty days, two of which were spent at anchor in St. Helena roads: she was consequently but seventy-eight days under sail, in which she traversed the immense space of 13,831 miles! The Medusa was only eighty-two days on her passage to India.

On the 28th of February, 1806, he was appointed to the Revenge of 74 guns, in which he joined the Channel fleet; and was successively employed in blockading the ports of Brest, l'Orient, and Rochefort.

In the month of October he was under the command of Sir Samuel Hood, and assisted at the capture of four frigates which had escaped from Rochefort.

Early in 1807, he was ordered to join the fleet under Lord Collingwood, off Cadiz; and in January 1808, was directed to take the command of the advanced squadron, and closely watch the movements of the enemy in that port. In the month of June, he had the pleasure to receive two Spanish officers on board the Revenge, who had been sent by the inhabitants with offers of amity, and to solicit assistance against the invaders of their country. In conjunction with Colonel Sir George Smith, Captain Gore was then deputed by Lord Collingwood to land, and enter into a negociation with the constituted authorities, which, with his usual zeal and ability, he brought to a satisfactory termination. He was afterwards ordered to convey two Spanish commissioners, appointed by the Supreme Council at Seville, to England. On his arrival, the Revenge was taken into dock; and as the health of Captain Gore was in a precarious state, from his long course of anxious services and changes of climate, he found himself under the necessity of soliciting a little relaxation from professional duties; and on the 6th of August he retired on half-pay.

In September 1810 he again solicited employment, and on the 12th of that month he was appointed to the Tonnant of 80 guns. The Macedonian frigate was then placed under his orders, and he was directed to receive on board those ships the 50th regiment, and land them as expeditiously as possible at Lisbon; which having effected, he again anchored in Cawsand Bay on the 3d of October.   He was then directed to take the Poictiers and Mars under his orders, and proceed with them to Lisbon, where, and in cruising with a squadron under the orders of Sir Thomas Williams in the Atlantic, he continued till April 1811, when he returned to Spithead; and was then ordered to join the Channel fleet, having the command of the in-shore squadron off Brest.

In March 1812 he was ordered to join the squadron in Basque roads, to blockade a superior force of the enemy; and whilst employed on this service he met with a severe accident by the falling of some tackle from the main-top, which caused a severe contusion on his head and gave a general shock to his whole frame.   He was then ordered into port; and as the Tonnant required considerable repairs, she was put out of commission, when Captain Gore obtained respite from professional toils, and thus had an opportunity of re-establishing his health.

On the 27th of November following he was appointed to the Revenge of 74 guns, and ordered to join the fleet under Sir Edward Pellew in the Mediterranean.   Immediately on his arrival off Toulon, he was appointed to command the in-shore squadron, where he continued without intermission till the 5th of October, 1813, when he proceeded to Mahon to refit; and having performed that necessary duty, was ordered with his squadron to occupy a station off Cape St. Sebastian, the main body of the fleet remaining at Mahon for the winter.

On the 23d of January, 1814, he received his commission as rear-admiral, dated the 6th of the preceding month.   Having hoisted his flag in the Revenge, he was ordered on the 28th to proceed to the Adriatic, and take the command of the squadron in that sea: here he entered into a correspondence with the Austrian general, Bellegarde, and by a plan of co-operation with him, commenced the blockade of Venice, anchoring the ships off the town, while the boats watched the entrance of Chiazza; at the same time that a flotilla, equipped for the purpose, assisted and sustained the Austrian troops on the Adige.   During these conjoint operations, intelligence arrived of the success attending the allied armies in France, when Marshal Bellegarde, without consulting with, or even giving any intimation to, Admiral Gore, entered into a negociation with the French general, Eugene Beauharnois, for the surrender and occupation of Italy.   In the name of his royal master, Admiral Gore went to the head-quarters at Verona, and, with becoming spirit and dignity, remonstrated on the indignity thus offered to the British flag, demanding that the ships, naval arsenal, and all the naval stores therein should be placed in his hands; but not succeeding in this object, and having no troops to enforce his claims, he, on the 26th of April, withdrew his squadron from before Venice, explaining his conduct to his own government, and leaving it to them to assert the honour of the nation by remonstrating with the Austrian ministry on the unaccountable conduct of their general. Admiral Gore then proceeded to Corfu, and stated to the French governor-general, Donzelot, the great and important changes which had taken place in France, and requested him to deliver the island up to him in the name of the allies; but on the French general's declining to comply with this request, he repaired to Trieste, where he received instructions to proceed to Corfu, and aid General Campbell, his Majesty's commissioner for the Ionian circle, in taking possession of the island, ceded by treaty from the French; and on the 25th of June the English colours were hoisted on the citadel.

On the following day, the French squadron, with the transports furnished by Sir John Gore to convey their garrison, amounting to near 10,000 men, to France, sailed from the island; and on the 28th the British squadron left Corfu for England, agreeably to orders for that purpose. On the 16th of August they arrived at Spithead, and on the 18th Sir John struck his flag.

On the extension of the Order of the Bath, Sir John was created a K.C.B.; and we believe it will be readily granted, that but few had that honour conferred upon them who more richly deserved it than Sir John Gore. On the 28th of March, 1818, he was appointed commander-in-chief in the Medway, which he retained till June 1821; and during the time he held this command his Royal Highness the Duke of Clarence presented him with a handsome sword, as a mark of his friendship and esteem.

During the year 1826 Sir John Gore, Vice-Admiral Sir Benjamin Hallowell, Sir Edward Codrington, and Sir Thomas Hardy, were ordered to form a committee at the Admiralty, and examine all the various codes of signals that had been in use, or even proposed, and to form a new code of signals for the navy. They met daily during five months from ten till four, and often six o'clock; and on the 21st October, the anniversary of the victory of Trafalgar, presented their report to the Board, which was adopted for the service, and has since been continued without alteration. This fatiguing and important duty was executed without fee or reward!

In concluding the services of this able and distinguished officer, we have only to add, that, shortly after the information was received of the brilliant and decisive action at Navarin, Sir John was employed on a delicate and important mission to his friend, Sir Edward Codrington, at Malta, which was accomplished in the unexampled short period of six weeks; and so highly pleased was his Royal Highness the Lord High Admiral with the whole of his conduct on this occasion, that, on his return, his royal highness presented him with a superb sword, corresponding with his Majesty's order for the naval uniform.

Sir John married, in August 1808, the eldest daughter of Admiral Sir G. Montagu; and has one son and five daughters.

HISTORICAL MEMOIRS OF

ADMIRAL SIR THOMAS WILLIAMS, K.C.B.

DURING the progress of this work our principal object has been to display excellence, rather than demerit; to exhibit the bright parts of a man's character, rather than his faults; to seek after such incidents as are deserving praise, rather than pry into those casual lapses of judgment to which all men are liable, and the exposure of which casts a shade over the efforts of genuine merit, without carrying with it a corresponding benefit.   To the censorious we know this conduct is not agreeable ; they would prefer seeing a man's imperfections brought into view, and chastised by severe animadversion, rather than that his merits, his talents, and abilities should be held up for imitation.   But the plan we have adopted and pursued, we have the satisfaction of knowing has been sanctioned by the brave and the good.   It is not, however, improbable that we may have been misled in some parts of our information: if such be the case, if any one individual whom we have mentioned in the work should be considered as not meriting the degree of praise we have attributed to him, we shall be glad to be informed thereof, in order that we may, in a second edition, make the necessary emendations.

The life and services, however, of the officer who is the subject of the present Memoir will not, we are certain, be subject to any complaint: his professional career is beyond censure; while his private life has abounded with those acts of charity, kindness, and benevolence, which prove a real goodness of heart and disposition.   Mr. Williams first went to sea in the Active frigate, commanded by his father, who was second in command of the squadron under Sir Peter Parker, and led that squadron to the desperate attack made on the fort at Sullivan's Island, near Charlestown, South Carolina, in June 1776*.   On this service they were employed for ten successive hours, during which the Active expended the whole of her ammunition, and so close was she anchored to the fort, that, when casting off after dark to retire, she grounded, but was fortunately got off, and joined the squadron.   Mr. Williams subsequently joined the Prince of Wales, bearing the flag of Rear-Admiral

* See *Memoir of Sir* P. PARKER,

Barrington, and was present in the two indecisive actions with the French admiral, D'Estaing, and a superior force, in July 1778. He was also in Admiral Byron's action off Grenada in July 1779, when the Prince of Wales led into action, received the fire of the enemy's van ships, and consequently suffered greatly in killed and wounded. He continued in the Prince of Wales till 1780, when he was appointed lieutenant of the America, in which he served under the orders of Lord Rodney when he captured the Caraccas convoy, and was then placed in charge of one of the most valuable prizes, for the purpose of conveying her to the river Thames. Having rejoined the America, he proceeded to North America, and under the orders of Admiral Arbuthnot was present in the action with De Ternay in March 1781. In May following he removed to the Assurance, which he afterwards commanded for several months with an acting commission, and cruised with great success against the enemy in that quarter. At the termination of the American war he was promoted to the rank of commander, and appointed to the Rhinoceros, which he brought to England. In June 1789 he was appointed to the Otter sloop, and in November 1790 was promoted to post-rank.

In December 1792 Captain Williams was appointed to the Lizard frigate, and in February following he convoyed to Holland three batallions of the guards, and was afterwards actively employed in the North Seas, where he so effectually protected the commerce of the country by the capture and destruction of the enemy's cruisers, that the merchants of London voted him their thanks, and requested his acceptance of a piece of plate. In August 1794 he was appointed to the Dædalus, and during the winter, when the British army was closely pressed by the enemy near Embden, he was directed to take the Amphion frigate, thirty sail of revenue, and some transports, under his command, and proceed with them to the Ems, for the purpose of bringing away the sick and any portion of the army that it might be found expedient to embark. In consequence of the extreme severity of the winter, this was a service of considerable difficulty and hazard, more particularly on account of the dangerous state of the coast, and it was only by the greatest perseverance that he at last succeeded in getting his convoy through the ice into the Ems. But as the enemy at that time commanded one side of the river, it was still an arduous service to bring off the troops and shipping: nevertheless, the whole service was performed so much to the satisfaction of the Lords of the Admiralty, that Captain Williams was removed to the command of the Unicorn, as a mark of their approbation. He was then stationed on the coast of Ireland, and in October 1795, shortly after the commencement of the war with Holland, captured the Dutch sloop of war Comet, of 18 9-pounders. At the time the Comet was met with she had under her convoy two homeward-bound East India ships, one of them very large and valuable; they were both taken by the Diana and Seahorse, after the Unicorn had separated from them in chase of the Comet. On the arrival of Captain Williams with his prize at Cork, those two frigates had also arrived, but without their prizes; and Captain Williams was then ordered by Admiral Kingsmil to proceed to sea in search of them. Having run down the west and north-west coast of Ireland without success, he proceeded to the Hebrides, the Orkneys, Shetland, and Leith, without meeting or hearing any thing of them. He shaped his course for the coast of Norway, and at length, after much labour, anxiety, and danger, through an intricate navigation and an inclement season of the year, he fell in with the largest of the prize-ships, and fortunately saved her and her crew from perishing, she being in the greatest distress, with only one sail left, and her cargo shifted, so that she could sail only on one tack, while the people on board were worn out with fatigue and anxiety. Having conducted her to the mouth of the Thames, Captain Williams proceeded down the King's Channel to return through the Downs to his station. The other prize-ship was lost on the coast of Norway.

At two a. m. on the 8th of June, 1795, Captain Williams, having the Santa Margaretta under his orders, fell in with two French frigates and a corvette, under a commodore, which the two English ships instantly pursued. About one p. m. they arrived within gun-shot, when a running fight commenced, which continued till four p. m. when the Santa Margaretta having got along side of the Tribune, paired off*; whilst Captain Williams still continued in pursuit of the French commodore, whose skill and judgment, and the good use made of his stern chasers, by which the Unicorn's sails suffered severely and greatly retarded her sailing, enabled him to keep up a running engagement till ten p. m. when Captain Williams, by perseverance and great professional abilities, triumphed over the skill and judgment of his adversary, and, after a chase of 210 miles, got fairly along side of his opponent. Having obtained this long-wished for situation, the crew of the Unicorn immedi-

* See *Memoir of Sir B. Martin.*

ately gave three cheers in the true British style, and then began to ply their guns with destructive effect. The French commodore, however, proved that he was not an ordinary commander. Having sustained a close action of thirty-five minutes, in which many of his men were killed and wounded, he took advantage of the thickness of the smoke, and made a skilful attempt, close hauled, to cross the Unicorn's stern and gain the wind of her. To frustrate this manœuvre, the sails of the Unicorn were instantly thrown back, by which she dropped astern and regained her station, and the action was renewed with increased vigour. The fore, main, and mizen-top-masts of the enemy were soon after carried away; all hopes on his part now ceased, and he surrendered to an opponent inferior in size, number of guns, and amount of crew. The enemy's ship, La Tribune, mounted 44 guns, and had on board 339 men, out of whom she had 37 killed, her commander and 14 men wounded; while the Unicorn mounted only 38 guns, and had on board only 240 men, not one of whom was either killed or wounded. Commodore Moulston was an American, of very high reputation, of an active and enterprising disposition, and had proved himself a successful cruiser. By his capture, therefore, the commerce of Great Britain was greatly benefited; and accordingly the cities of London, Dublin, and Cork presented Captain Williams with their freedom, and the committee of the Patriotic Fund voted him a piece of plate, to express the high sense which they entertained of his merits and exertions.

In January 1796, Sir Thomas, when cruising in the Unicorn, obtained intelligence that the French fleet was at sea; and judging that they were destined for the invasion of Ireland, he immediately proceeded to Cork, to inform Admiral Kingsmil of the circumstance; and was then ordered again to sea to watch the enemy, taking under his orders any junior officer that he might fall in with, and to act according to circumstances. The good fortune which had hitherto attended Sir Thomas Williams still adhered to him; and the second day after his departure from Cork, he fell in with, and captured, a large ship *armée en flute*, having on board 450 French hussars and a cargo of military stores. On the following morning, however, he found himself in the midst of the enemy's fleet; notwithstanding which, by the most skilful manœuvres he not only extricated his own ship but also his prize. On the succeeding day he captured a French corvette of 20 guns; and having fallen in with Lord Bridport's fleet, communicated to him the position of the enemy.

In April 1797 Sir Thomas was removed to the Endymion frigate; and on the 13th of October fell in with a Dutch 74-gun ship, two brigs, and a schooner, and, notwithstanding their superiority, he immediately bore down upon them and brought them to action, the particulars of which are contained in the following letter addressed to Admiral Duncan, dated Endymion, at sea, October 13, 1797:

SIR,—After having received your orders yesterday on board the Venerable, I stood in to the rear of the fleet, and from thence discovered a line-of-battle ship making for the Texel, which on our nearer approach tacked and stood from us. We soon made her out to be an enemy, who not being able to weather the Hinder, anchored close to the sand, when he shewed himself to be a Dutch 74, bearing a rear-admiral's flag, supported by two brigs and a schooner, anchored ahead. They opened their fire upon us; we immediately closed with them, crossed the line-of-battle ship's bows at a small distance, and poured our raking fire into her on both tacks, I imagine with considerable effect.

The brigs and schooner cut and run in-shore as we advanced. I was unfortunately prevented from continuing this mode by the strong lee tide and swell, which carried us fast to leeward, insomuch that at one moment I was apprehensive we should not have cleared the enemy's bows, and he was anchored so close to the sand-head, that the pilot refused to bear up and pass under his stern.

Having to encounter a force so superior, a dark night and a lee shore, I was obliged to haul off, intending to renew my attack at daylight, and took a position during the night to prevent the enemy from running for the Texel unperceived. Before morning I was joined by the Beaulieu frigate; and at dawn of day, observing our antagonist to be still at anchor, we bore down upon him to engage, but were greatly disappointed to see him, as we approached, cast from his anchor and push into Goree. My pilots assure me, that his guns must have been thrown overboard and the ship much lightened to have enabled her to pass over the sands. I have the honour to be, &c. &c.   (Signed,)   T. WILLIAMS.

To which he had the satisfaction of receiving the following reply:

SHEERNESS, *October* 28, 1797.

SIR,—The Lords Commissioners of the Admiralty have this day transmitted me your letter of the 13th instant, giving an account of your proceedings with his Majesty's ship under your command, and of the attack on the Dutch ship Brutus, and have directed me to communicate to you their approbation of your conduct on the occasion. I am particularly satisfied and pleased at the spirited conduct you displayed in making the attack; and I am only sorry it was not attended with all the success you deserved. I am, sir, your very humble servant,

To Capt. Sir THOS. WILLIAMS, *Endymion.*   (Signed,)   ADAM DUNCAN.

On the day subsequent to his action with the Brutus, Sir Thomas fell in with the Jupiter of 74 guns, one of the prizes made in the action off Camperdown: she was at anchor on a lee shore, dismasted, with a signal of distress flying; but as it blew a hard gale of wind at the time, no immediate communication could be held with her: yet the Endymion kept as near to her as possible; and when the gale abated, Sir Thomas took her in tow, and, after thirty-four days' exertions and anxiety, partly occasioned by the advanced season and the difficulty of the navigation, he safely and triumphantly conducted her to the Nore. The conduct of Sir Thomas on this important and interesting occasion was duly estimated by the officers of Lord Duncan's fleet, who wrote him a letter of thanks, and presented him with a piece of plate, to mark the high opinion they entertained of his professional character. From Admiral Duncan he also received the following letter, dated Sheerness, November 9, 1797:

My DEAR SIR THOMAS,—I have just received a copy of your letter, and cannot refrain a moment in returning you, your officers and ship's company, my best thanks for your unremitting exertions in saving one of the Dutch ships; and I shall only say, that I have a most proper sense of it, and that I am, with much esteem and regard, (Signed,) ADAM DUNCAN.

At the request of Admiral Kingsmil, Sir Thomas was again attached to the squadron under his command; and during the rebellion in Ireland in 1798, he was placed in the command of a squadron consisting of six frigates, three sloops, and five cutters, with orders to cruise at the entrance of the Irish Channel, for the purpose of intercepting any ships of the enemy, as well as to co-operate with the British troops in their movements against the rebels in the vicinity of Wexford; and in the capture of which place the squadron rendered the most essential assistance, having taken a fort at the entrance of the harbour, the numerous vessels of which they had possession, and all their sea-commanders, one of whom, denominated an admiral, was, by the sentence of court-martial, hung on board the Endymion's barge, off the town of Wexford.

In August 1800, when the Endymion was escorting a valuable convoy to Gibraltar, a number of Spanish gun and mortar vessels, as usual, put out from Algeziras for the purpose of attacking the convoy: they were, however, immediately attacked by the Endymion, and driven back to their anchorage under the batteries, which opened a cannonade of shot and shells, but without effect. For his intrepid conduct on this occasion the masters of the convoy presented him with a letter of thanks, in

which they stated, " You have in a particular manner afforded us protection against the enemy, to whom we must all have become prizes but
for your gallant behaviour on the occasion."

In February 1801 Sir Thomas was appointed to the Vanguard of
74 guns, and ordered to join Lord Nelson off Copenhagen.   He afterwards continued in the Baltic under the orders of Sir Charles Pole, till
amicable arrangements were made with the northern powers, when he
returned with that admiral to England, and afterwards proceeded with
him off Cadiz, where he continued till the peace of Amiens.   On the renewal of the war, Sir Thomas was appointed to the Neptune of 98 guns,
and served in the Channel fleet till May 1806, when, in consequence of
ill health, he was obliged to resign the command of that ship.   In August 1807 he was again appointed to the Neptune; and after serving in
the Channel, accompanied Sir J. Duckworth to the coast of America
and the West Indies in quest of a French squadron.   In April 1808
he was made a colonel of marines; and in September following again
sailed to the West Indies, to strengthen the squadron under Sir A. Cochrane.   Having been promoted to the rank of rear-admiral in May 1810,
he hoisted his flag in the Venerable, and joined the fleet off the Scheldt,
of which he was left in command by Sir R. Strachan until the arrival
of Sir E. Pellew.   In September following he joined the Channel fleet,
of which he was second in command, with his flag in the Hannibal; and
in October he was ordered to proceed with a squadron to Lisbon, the
British army under Lord Wellington having retreated to the lines en-
compassing that capital.   On the 15th of November, the French army
having begun to move from those lines, Sir Thomas, on the same night,
proceeded up the Tagus with a flotilla, to co-operate with the British
army, and followed the enemy as far as Santarem, where they took up
their position.   He then conveyed across the Tagus General Hill's division, consisting of about 10,000 men; a service which was performed
with so much celerity and good order as to draw from General Hill a
strong letter of thanks.   While on this service Sir Thomas was in daily
communication with Lord Wellington, and owing to his activity and the
importance of his assistance, his name was favourably noticed by his
lordship in his official dispatch.

In January 1811 Sir Thomas sailed from the Tagus in command of
four sail of the line, a frigate, and sloop, to cruise off Cape St. Vincent,
for the purpose of intercepting any of the enemy's ships which might, as

was expected, attempt to afford any assistance to their army in Spain or Portugal. The French army having retreated from Santarem, he was ordered to England with his squadron; and on his arrival he shifted his flag to the Royal George, when he again joined the Channel fleet as second in command, which he retained till October 1811, when he was appointed commander-in-chief at the Nore. As, however, he was unwilling to quit active service at sea, he at first declined to accept this command; but Mr. Yorke, the First Lord of the Admiralty, having stated in a letter to Sir Thomas, that he "considered it an evil example for officers to refuse to undertake the performance of services to which they were appointed," he could not think of refusing to comply with the orders of the Board; and when he notified to the First Lord his acceptance of the offer, he had the satisfaction to receive from Mr. Yorke a letter, in which he was pleased thus to express himself:

" I have received your letter of yesterday with great satisfaction, informing me of your acceptance of the command at the Nore. I will frankly own to you, that I did feel much mortified at your refusing to accept of such a situation, and that not only on personal, but on public grounds; because I must say, that from the active state of affairs in the North and East seas, I should have been much concerned to have been deprived of your able and active services in superintending and directing the business at the mouths of the Thames and the Medway, including that of the equipments at Sheerness and Chatham; a concern of vital importance to the safety and even existence of the country."

Sir Thomas retained this command till the 30th of November, 1814, when he struck his flag, having been upwards of thirty-two years actually afloat, during which he had been in eight different actions with the enemy, besides various skirmishes on shore and in boats; and having, during the time he was a captain, captured twenty-five sail of the enemy's ships and vessels of war.

HISTORICAL MEMOIRS OF
Admiral Sir WILLIAM GEORGE FAIRFAX, Knt.

It affords us much satisfaction in being able to close this work with the Memoirs of an officer whose life was so fully and constantly devoted to the service of his king and country, and whose name, both in public and private, carried with it so high a degree of respect and veneration, as Sir William Fairfax's, who not only gained the admiration and regard of the officers and crews of those ships he commanded, but the good-will of all those who knew him even by hearsay. To an illustrious pedigree he added all those qualities which give dignity to any station; candour, sincerity, modesty, and a high sense of honour seemed inherent principles of his nature, and were the constant rules of his conduct. Having entered the naval service, and passed, with the highest reputation and credit to himself, through the different subordinate stations, he was commissioned as a lieutenant on the 20th December, 1757, and continued almost constantly employed during the remainder of the war, which did not cease for the space of five years. So long and meritorious a service might naturally have been expected to be productive of advancement. Such, however, was not the fate or fortune of Mr. Fairfax: he was employed, it is true; but the ancient and trite observation, that the services of the best men and most able officers frequently pass in obscurity a considerable period of time, till accident perhaps throws them into a situation where their abilities and bravery shine forth like meteors for the world to gaze at, was never on any occasion more fully exemplified than on this. The cessation of the war, and the promotions which generally follow a termination of hostilities, brought no advancement to Mr. Fairfax; and at the commencement of the war with the American colonies he was still on the list of lieutenants, and continued on it for some time after ; but his former services and his seniority on the list induced the Admiralty-Board not to employ him in the ordinary routine or line of service filled by officers of that rank, but to appoint him to command the Alert cutter. His means of exertion, and the consequent acquisition of fame, however, still continued very limited; but as the narrow seas became infested with a number of American privateers, his

prospects began to brighten. When convoying a fleet of coasters, he
fell in with one of those vessels, which, owing to their swiftness of sailing,
almost put at defiance the ships of war which usually accompanied the
trading vessels.   Notwithstanding a great apparent superiority on the
part of the enemy, he was brought to action by the Alert, and attacked
with such spirit, that he was in the end obliged to surrender.   The conduct of Lieutenant Fairfax on this occasion was duly appreciated by the
Lords of the Admiralty, who immediately raised him to the rank of commander, by commission bearing date 13th May, 1778; and, as if it were
considered injurious to remove him from a vessel in which he had acquired
so much honour, the Alert was converted into a sloop of war, an addition
being made to the number of her guns and crew. Captain Fairfax was afterwards placed under the orders of Admiral Keppel, and in the following
month of June had another opportunity to distinguish himself.   Being
ordered to accompany the Arethusa frigate in pursuit of a French frigate and a smaller vessel, they continued in chase till out of sight of the
fleet; and having come up with the French ships, an action commenced
between them, which, so far as relates to the Alert, was thus described
by Captain Marshall of the Arethusa: " I must not omit, in this relation, to acquaint their lordships that Captain Fairfax has had his share
in the business. He got along side of a schooner of 10 carriage-guns and
10 swivels, that attended the frigate which engaged the Arethusa. Upon
his requesting her commander to stand to the fleet, he made answer, that
he should do as the frigate did ; and upon the frigate's firing upon the
Arethusa, he fired his guns into the Alert. Captain Fairfax immediately
ran on board of him, and they continued in that situation, in close fight,
upwards of an hour, when the French vessel surrendered.   Captain
Fairfax killed him five men, and mortally wounded seven.   The Alert
had four wounded, two mortally."

Captain Fairfax continued in the Alert till the ensuing autumn, when
he fell in with La Junon, a French 40-gun frigate, by which he was unfortunately captured, and for a long time remained in captivity.   Being
at length exchanged, he was promoted, on the 12th January, 1782, to
post-rank, and appointed to the Tartar frigate of 28 guns, in which he
sailed to the West Indies, where he continued till the autumn of 1783,
when he returned to England.   The Tartar being then put out of commission, as the natural consequence of returned tranquillity, Captain
Fairfax is not known to have held any subsequent command till the war

with revolutionary France, when he was appointed to the Sheerness of 44 guns, and stationed in the North Sea. Towards the end of 1794 Rear-Admiral Sir Henry Harvey hoisted his flag on board the Sheerness, as the commander of a squadron ordered over to Flushing for the purpose of protecting that place against the depredations of the French, who were forcing their way into Holland. The Dutch, however, having made common cause with the French, a declaration of war was issued by the British government against that people; and Captain Fairfax was removed to the Repulse of 64 guns, the command of which he retained till October 1796, when Admiral Duncan, having been appointed to the chief command of the North-Sea fleet, selected Captain Fairfax to command his flag-ship, the Venerable of 74 guns. The situation of captain to the commander-in-chief is very important and honourable; and it is but a common act of justice to the memory of Sir William Fairfax to declare, that, by the uniform declaration of his admiral, added to the general suffrage of every one who was acquainted with his conduct and abilities, no person could have filled so delicate and difficult a station with greater ability and more general satisfaction. The encomium passed on his conduct in the Camperdown action by his gallant chief, forms, however, the most indisputable proof of his abilities and worth; and the honour conferred upon him by his sovereign sufficiently proves that such praise was not the effect of private attachment. With the official account of that brilliant victory Captain Fairfax was dispatched to England, and had the honour of knighthood conferred upon him by his Majesty. But as the Venerable was put out of commission, in consequence of the great damage she had sustained in the action, Sir William Fairfax did not again go to sea till April 1799, when the Venerable having undergone a thorough repair, he resumed the command of her. Previous, however, to this taking place, he received a farther proof of his sovereign's esteem, by being appointed a colonel of marines. He then joined the Channel fleet, where he remained till January 1801, when he attained the rank of rear-admiral, and consequently gave up the command of the Venerable.

Having thus closed his professional career, Sir William Fairfax returned to the bosom of his family, to share with them, and a small circle of friends by whom he was beloved, that happiness to which he so essentially contributed by his kindly nature and gentle manners. The warmth of feeling with which he entered into the pursuits and prosperity of others endeared him to all, and the evenness of his temper peculiarly fitted him for the enjoyment of social intercourse. Indeed it is not the least interesting trait in the character of our gallant countrymen who devote their lives to the toils and perils of the sea, that their social affections, instead of being diminished by the long absence resulting from professional duties, seem, on the contrary, to become more vivid. In recording the achievements of those illustrious men to whom our country owes so much, it has uniformly been our object to hold out examples worthy of the imitation of those who are to follow them in the path of glory; and we should consider our picture unfinished if we failed to avail ourselves of those circumstances which shew that the zealous discharge of the duties of the sailor are not incompatible with those of the husband, the father, and the friend, in all the relative situations of which the conduct of Sir William Fairfax was truly exemplary.

APPENDIX.

ADDENDA TO THE MEMOIR OF ADMIRAL SIR EDWARD CODRINGTON, G.C.B.

THE great and important victory obtained by Sir Edward Codrington since the publication of that part of the work which contained a Memoir of his professional life, induces us to add some *addenda* to the statement, for the purpose of recording the particulars of that glorious battle.

On the 1st November, 1826, Admiral Codrington was appointed commander-in-chief of his Majesty's ships and vessels in the Mediterranean; a command which had become most interesting and important on account of the hostilities which existed between the Greeks and the Turks, which had been for several years raging with the most deadly animosity, and to which there appeared no probability of a termination, except in the extermination of one party or the other. It is not for us to inquire into the right of any other power or powers to interfere, or put a period to the cruelties daily practised by both; we have only to record the fact that they did so, and the following are the reasons given:

" His Majesty the King of the United Kingdom of Great Britain and Ireland, his Majesty the King of France and Navarre, and his Majesty the Emperor of all the Russias, penetrated with the necessity of putting an end to the sanguinary contest, which, by delivering up the Greek provinces and the isles of the Archipelago to all the disorders of anarchy, produces daily fresh impediments to the commerce of the European states, and gives occasion to piracies, which not only expose the high contracting powers to considerable losses, but, besides, render necessary burdensome measures of protection and repression. His Majesty the King of Great Britain and Ireland, and his Majesty the King of France and Navarre, having, besides, received, on the part of the Greeks, a pressing request to interpose their mediation with the Ottoman Porte, and being, as well as his Majesty the Emperor of all the Russias, animated by the desire of stopping the effusion of blood, and of arresting the evils of all kinds which might arise from the continuance of such a state of things, have resolved to unite their efforts, and to regulate the operation thereof by a formal treaty, with the view of re-establishing peace between the contending parties, by means of an arrangement which is called for as much by humanity as by the interest of the repose of Europe."

The high contracting powers therefore nominated plenipotentiaries to discuss, agree upon, and sign a treaty, to effect the objects above named; and who, after having communicated their full powers, and found the same in good and due form, agreed upon certain articles, but of which we find it necessary to insert only the following:

"*Art.* 1. The high contracting powers will offer to the Ottoman Porte their mediation, with a view of bringing about a reconciliation between it and the Greeks.

"This offer of mediation shall be made to that power immediately after the ratification of the treaty, by means of a collective declaration signed by the plenipotentiaries of the allied courts at Constantinople; and there shall be made at the same time to the two contending parties, *a demand of an immediate armistice between them, as a preliminary condition indispensable to the opening of any negociation.*"

Additional and Secret Articles.

"In case that the Ottoman Porte does not accept within the space of one month the mediation which shall be proposed, the high contracting powers agree upon the following measures:

"1. It shall be declared, by their representatives at Constantinople, to the Porte, that the inconveniences and evils pointed out in the public treaty as inseparable from the state of things subsisting in the East for the last six years, and the termination of which, through the means at the disposal of the Sublime Porte, appears still remote, *impose upon the high contracting powers the necessity of taking immediate measures for an approximation with the Greeks.*

"It is to be understood that this approximation shall be brought about by establishing commercial relations with the Greeks, by sending to them for that purpose, and receiving from them, consular agents, so long as there shall exist among them authorities capable of maintaining such relations.

"2. If within the said term of one month the Porte do not accept the armistice proposed in the first article of the public treaty, or if the Greeks refuse to execute it, the high contracting powers shall declare to that one of the two contending parties which shall wish to continue hostilities, or to both, if such become necessary, that the said high contracting powers intend to exert all the means which circumstances may suggest to their prudence to obtain the immediate effect of the armistice, the execution of which they desire, by preventing, in as far as may be in their power, all collision between the contending parties; and in fact immediately after the aforesaid declaration, the high contracting powers will conjointly employ all their means in the accomplishment of the object thereof, without, however, taking any part in the hostilities between the two contending parties.

" In consequence the high contracting powers will, immediately after the signature of the present additional and secret articles, transmit eventual instructions, conformably to the provisions above set forth, to the admirals commanding their squadrons in the seas of the Levant."

Orders, conformably to these articles, were consequently forwarded to Sir Edward Codrington, who entered upon their execution with the utmost zeal and ability; and on the 8th September he issued the following orders to his squadron*:

Asia, *at Sea.*

Sir,—You are aware that a treaty has been signed between England, France, and Russia, for the pacification of Greece. A declaration of the decision of the powers has been presented to the Porte, and a similar declaration has been presented to the Greeks.

The armistice proposed to each in these declarations has been acceded to by the Greeks, whilst it has been refused by the Turks. It becomes therefore the duty of the allied naval forces to enter, in the first place, on friendly relations with the Greeks; and, next, to intercept every supply of men, arms, &c. destined against Greece, and coming either from Turkey or Africa in general.

The last measure is that which requires the greatest caution, and, above all, a complete understanding as to the operations of the allied naval forces.

Most particular care is to be taken that the measures adopted against the Ottoman navy do not degenerate into hostilities. The formal intention of the powers is, to interfere as conciliators, and to establish, in fact, at sea the armistice which the Porte would not concede as a right. Every hostile proceeding would be at variance with the pacific ground which they have chosen to take, and the display of forces which they have assembled is destined to cause that wish to be respected; but they must not be put into use, unless the Turks persist in forcing the passages which they have intercepted.

All possible means should be tried, in the first instance, to prevent the necessity of proceeding to extremities; but the prevention of supplies, as before mentioned, is to be enforced, if necessary, and when all other means are exhausted, by cannon-shot.

In giving you this instruction as to the duty which I am directed to perform, my intention is, to make you acquainted thoroughly with the object of our government, that you may not be taken by surprise as to whatever measures I may find it necessary to adopt. You will still look to me for farther instructions as to the carrying any such measures into effect. I am, &c.

(Signed,) Edward Codrington.

On the 25th September Admiral Codrington obtained an interview

* The Genoa, Albion, Dartmouth, Cambrian, Talbot, Glasgow, and Dryad.

with Ibrahim Pacha, commander of the Turkish fleet, when it was verbally agreed, that an armistice should take place between the forces under Ibrahim's command and the Greeks by sea and land, and that both troops and ships should remain inactive at Navarin until instructions should be received from Constantinople. As Sir Edward was informed that it was not usual for the Turks to enter into any written agreement, but that their words given in the presence of witnesses were held sacred, he demanded that the interview to which Ibrahim had agreed should take place in the presence of his chiefs; and on this account Sir Edward took with him several of his officers, among whom were Captain Curzon, Colonel Craddock, and his secretary; whilst Admiral de Rigny adopted the same course. The conversation took place in English, which the Pacha's dragoman proved that he well understood, by repeating the sense of what Sir Edward said to Admiral de Rigny in French, and then translating it to the Pacha and his chiefs in the Turkish language without the least hesitation. He was, moreover, always asked if he clearly understood the purport of what was said to him, to which he replied in the affirmative; and it was the conviction of all present that he did so, and that he faithfully translated the observations made to him, from the effect which they appeared to have on Ibrahim and his officers. Upon the dragoman being asked, if what passed was to be considered as binding as if committed to paper, he replied, that his highness's (Ibrahim) word was considered as his bond, and therefore it might be as much relied on as a written treaty. Nevertheless, Sir Edward, at the close of the conference, was desirous that that question should be put to Ibrahim; but the dragoman objected, thinking it an affront to his highness to doubt it. As Sir Edward, however, insisted, it was accordingly put, and the answer returned by Ibrahim was, " Most certainly." At this time the Turkish fleet was outside the harbour, which Sir Edward permitted, at Ibrahim's request, to enter, lest, as Ibrahim observed, suspicion of his inclinations and motives should arise from the circumstance of the Egyptian ships only being in the port. Every thing was now thought to be settled; but on the following day, when the Asia and Sirène were about to leave the harbour, between two and three o'clock p. m. Ibrahim's dragoman waited upon Sir Edward, to inform him that the Pacha had received information of Lord Cochrane having made a descent upon Patras (which, however, was not true), and requested permission to send a competent force to beat him off. But he was told, both by Sir Edward and Admiral de

Rigny, who was on board the Asia, that this could not be complied with, as it was directly contrary to their orders, and which orders they had read during the preceding day's conference to the Pacha. Sir Edward then inquired, if he was to consider the armistice as still binding. To which the dragoman in conclusion said, if the Pacha had any objection to urge, he would return to announce it; and that if he did not return in about an hour, it was to be concluded that the agreement remained as settled the preceding day. Having waited till the close of the evening, and the dragoman not having returned, Sir Edward, from the reputed honour of the Turks, naturally reposed the utmost confidence in the agreement, and of course expected that it would be kept with good faith; and as the squadron stood in want of stores and other articles, the Albion, Genoa, Cambrian, and some others, were dispatched to Malta for a supply; whilst Sir Edward, in the Asia, proceeded to Zante, supposing something might transpire to require his presence, leaving the Dartmouth, Captain Fellows, off Navarin, to watch the proceedings of the Turkish squadron; whilst the French squadron, under Admiral de Rigny, proceeded to Milo. But notwithstanding the confidence reposed in Turkish honour, it was very soon discovered that Ibrahim had not the same notion of an armistice which is usually attached to it, and that he was not disposed to observe it longer than he should find it convenient. Shortly after his arrival at Zante, Sir Edward was joined by the Dartmouth, with intelligence that a strong division of the Turkish fleet was steering out of Navarin to the N. W. towards Patras, where Ibrahim had an army. On this occasion Sir Edward displayed a strong proof of his bravery and decision: although the force he had with him consisted of only the Asia, Dartmouth, Talbot, and Zebra brig, and the Turks had two double-banked frigates, one large frigate, seven brigs, and eight corvettes, he immediately put to sea, and so astonished them by his presence, that, thinking he was at Malta, they at first considered it was another English admiral, but sent to know if Admiral Codrington would allow them to pass to Patras. He immediately sent a message to the commander to say, how much he was astonished at such a breach of faith, and that he would oppose force to the passage of the Ottoman squadron, as it was a violation of the armistice concluded with Ibrahim Pacha. The Turkish commander, Patrona Bey, replied, that he was acting under the orders of the Pacha; affected not to know that the proceeding was a violation of the armistice; and although he was present at the whole arrangement, when Admirals Codrington and de Rigny delivered to Ibrahim copies of a part of their orders, and it was stated to all present, that they were directed to proceed to the greatest extremities rather than allow any offensive operations in any part of Greece, he stated that he thought it was only objected that an expedition should be sent against Hydra. Sir Edward, however, told him, that they had broken their word of honour, and that he would not trust them again. At first he intimated to the Turkish commander, that as he had violated the armistice, he should not proceed to Patras, or return to Navarin: this, however, was not persisted in, and they then hauled their wind to beat back to Navarin, although it was fair for the gulf of Patras. In the evening, however, this division was joined by Ibrahim and a reinforcement of fifteen men of war; and after communicating with Patrona Bey on the following morning (the 3d October), and learning the determination of the British admiral, he, about two o'clock, made sail with his whole fleet, as if he intended to return to Navarin; but about nine p. m. during a dark squall, he again bore up for Patras, and anchored off the entrance of the gulf. As they were not seen by Sir Edward on the following morning, he immediately bore up for Patras also, where the Turks were of course discovered; and notwithstanding their superiority of force, he put the same bold front on his proceedings. He immediately cleared for action; and as several vessels belonging to the Turkish squadron did not shew their colours, he fired some shot across their bows, and subsequently into them: three or four, however, disregarded even this summons, when they were immediately boarded; and the remarkable circumstance transpired, that they were protected by Austrian papers and a Turkish firman conjointly. They were of course suffered to depart. This determined conduct intimidated the Pacha, and he returned to Navarin, without effecting his object. Admiral Codrington then returned to Zante to water, and on the 10th October heard of the Russian squadron being in sight of the island. In the mean time Admiral de Rigny having been informed that the Turks had quitted Navarin, steered from Milo; but between Cerigo and Cervi two of his line-of-battle ships, the Scipion and Provence, ran foul of each other in the night, and the bowsprit of the Provence going over the Scipion's gangway, the latter lost her main-mast, and the former her bowsprit. By this accident the French squadron was reduced by one ship of the line: the Provence, having given her main-mast to the Scipion, returned to

Toulon. Having completed his water and provisions, Sir Edward left Zante on the 12th, and on the following day fell in with the Russian squadron. Shortly after which two Turkish corvettes came along side, with a message from Ibrahim, asking permission to proceed to Patras; but which was positively refused. It was, however, curious to observe the fear and caution manifested by the Turks to keep clear of the Russians: when any of the latter got near them, they bore up and ran to the side of the English ships, and at last got close under their lee, as if for protection.

As it had become evident that the Turks did not intend to keep the armistice if they could find a favourable opportunity to break it, Admiral Codrington sent orders to Malta for the ships there to rejoin him without delay. On the 14th October he arrived off Navarin; and as a proof of the promptitude and energy displayed by all concerned, we must observe, that on that day he was joined by the Cambrian from Malta, where she had remained only four days, during which she had, although in quarantine, got in a new bowsprit and fore-mast, refitted, and took in fresh stores. In two days more he was rejoined by the Albion and Genoa; so that in six days from the receipt of his orders, the whole of the ships were again assembled under the flag of the admiral.

Disappointed in his object of relieving Patras, Ibrahim landed his troops in the Bay of Navarin, and wrecked his vengeance on the miserable Greek inhabitants of the Morea, butchering even the women and children, and endeavouring to reduce the whole country to a desert. A deputation of the Greeks accordingly waited upon Sir Edward, which, with other testimony, induced him to send the Cambrian frigate, Captain Hamilton, accompanied by a Russian frigate, to inquire into the particulars, with orders to stop any troops of Ibrahim's that might be proceeding from Navarin by the pass of Ancyro; and the following is an extract from Captain Hamilton's report:

" I have the honour of informing you that I arrived here yesterday morning, in company with the Russian frigate Constantine, the captain of which had placed himself under my orders. On entering the gulf, we observed, by clouds of fire and smoke, that the work of devastation was still going on. The ships were anchored off the pass of Ancyro, and a joint letter from myself and the Russian captain was dispatched to the Turkish commander. The Russian and English officers, the bearers of it, were not allowed to proceed to head-quarters, nor have we yet received any answer. In the afternoon we (the two captains) went on shore to the Greek quarters, and were received with the greatest enthusiasm. The distress of the inhabitants driven from the plain is shocking; women and children dying every moment of absolute starvation, and hardly any having better food than boiled grass. I have promised to send a small quantity of bread to the caves in the mountains, where these unfortunate wretches have taken refuge. It is supposed that if Ibrahim remain in Greece, more than a third of its inhabitants will die of starvation."

This conduct induced the three admirals to send in a strong letter of remonstrance to Ibrahim, which was carried in by Captain Fellows: but the answer returned was, that Ibrahim was not to be found; that no one knew where he was.

The allied admirals now held a consultation on the best means of carrying into effect the instructions under which they acted, and agreed upon the following:

"The admirals commanding the squadrons of the three powers which signed the treaty of London, having met before Navarin, for the purpose of concerting the means of effecting the object specified in the said treaty, viz. an armistice *de facto* between the Turks and the Greeks, have set forth in the present protocol the result of their conference.

"Considering that, after the provisional suspension of hostilities to which Ibrahim Pacha consented in his conference of the 25th September last with the English and French admirals, acting likewise in the name of the Russian admiral, the said Pacha did the very next day violate his engagement by causing his fleet to come out, with a view to its proceeding to another point in the Morea:

"Considering that, since the return of that fleet to Navarin, in consequence of a second requisition addressed to Ibrahim by Admiral Codrington, who had met him near Patras, the troops of the Pacha have not ceased carrying on a species of warfare more destructive and exterminating than before, putting women and children to the sword, burning their habitations, and tearing up trees by the roots, in order to complete the devastation of the country:

"Considering that, with a view of putting a stop to atrocities which exceed all that has hitherto taken place, the means of persuasion and conciliation, the representations made to the Turkish chiefs, and the advice given to Mehemit Ali and his son, have been treated as mockeries, whilst they might with one word have suspended the course of so many barbarities:

"Considering that there only remains to the commanders of the allied squadrons the choice between three modes of fulfilling the intentions of their respective courts; namely,

"1st. The continuing throughout the whole of the winter a blockade, difficult,

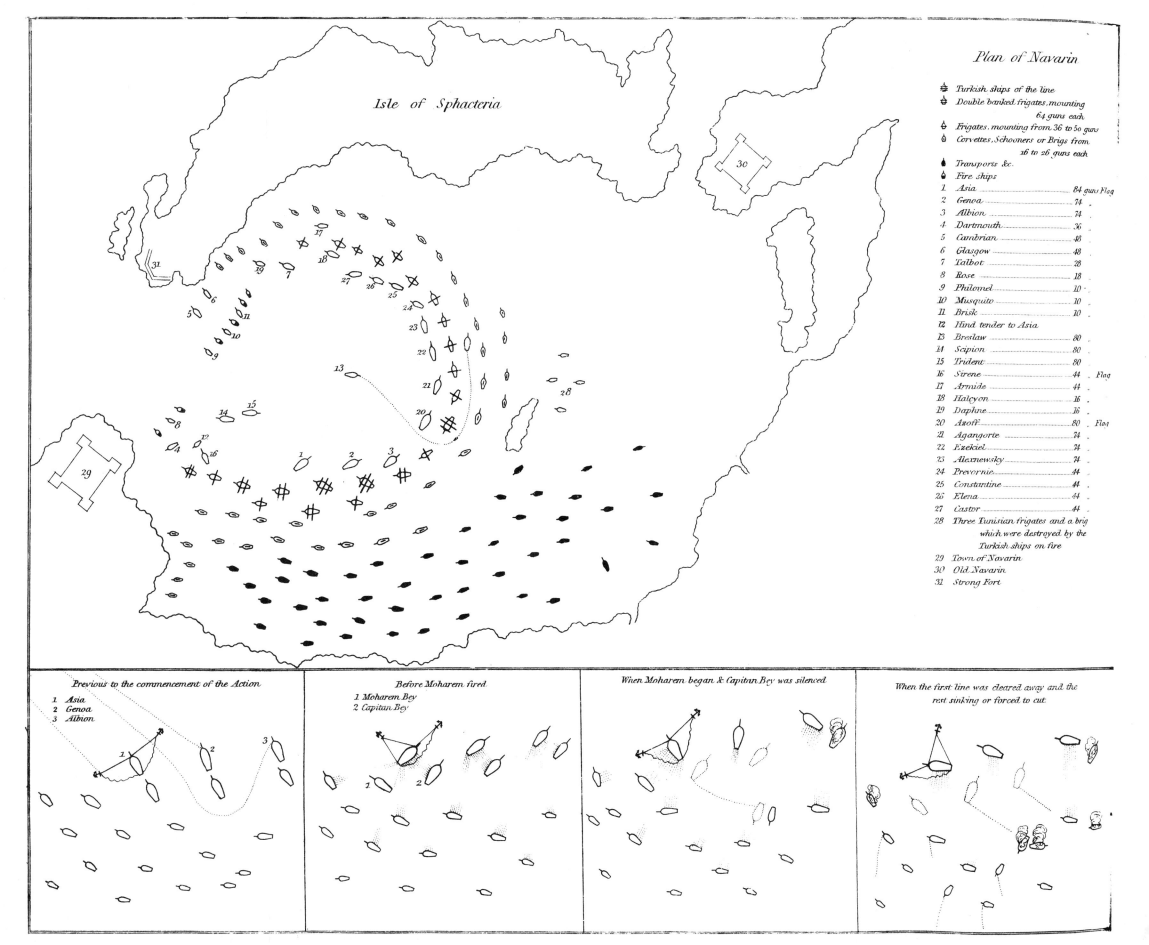

Plan of Navarin

Isle of Sphacteria

- Turkish ships of the line
- Double banked frigates, mounting 64 guns each
- Frigates, mounting from 36 to 50 guns
- Corvettes, Schooners or Brigs from 16 to 26 guns each
- Transports &c.
- Fire ships

1	Asia	84 guns Flag
2	Genoa	74
3	Albion	74
4	Dartmouth	36
5	Cambrian	48
6	Glasgow	48
7	Talbot	28
8	Rose	18
9	Philomel	10
10	Musquito	10
11	Brisk	10
12	Hind tender to Asia	
13	Breslaw	80
14	Scipion	80
15	Trident	80
16	Sirene	44 Flag
17	Armide	44
18	Halcyon	16
19	Daphne	16
20	Azoff	80 Flag
21	Agangorte	74
22	Ezekiel	74
23	Alexnewsky	74
24	Prevornie	44
25	Constantine	44
26	Elena	44
27	Castor	44
28	Three Tunisian frigates and a brig which were destroyed by the Turkish ships on fire	
29	Town of Navarin	
30	Old Navarin	
31	Strong Fort	

Previous to the commencement of the Action

1 Asia
2 Genoa
3 Albion

Before Moharem fired

1 Moharem Bey
2 Capitan Bey

When Moharem began & Capitan Bey was silenced

When the first line was cleared away and the rest sinking or forced to cut

expensive, and perhaps useless, since a storm may disperse the squadrons, and afford to Ibrahim the facility of conveying his destroying army to different points of the Morea and the islands:

" 2d. The uniting the allied squadrons in Navarin itself, and securing by their permanent presence the inaction of the Ottoman fleet: but which mode alone leads to no termination, since the Porte persists in not changing its resolution:

" 3d. The proceeding to take up a position with the squadrons in Navarin, in order to renew to Ibrahim propositions, which, *entering into the spirit of the treaty, were evidently to the advantage of the Porte itself:*

" After having taken these three modes into consideration, we have unanimously agreed, that this third mode may, without effusion of blood and without hostilities, produce a determination leading to the desired effect:

" We have in consequence adopted it, and set it forth in the present protocol."

Signed by the English, French, and Russian Admirals,

October 18, 1827.

Preparations were accordingly made to carry this resolution into immediate operation; but as the wind was variable, it was put off till the following day. In the mean time the following orders were issued:

INSTRUCTIONS *as to the manner of placing the Combined Fleet in the port of* NAVARIN.

ASIA, *off* NAVARIN, *19th October,* 1827.

It appears that the Egyptian ships in which the French officers are embarked are those most to the south-east; it is therefore my wish that H. E. Rear-Admiral Chevalier de Rigny should place his squadron abreast of them. As the next in succession appears to be a ship of the line, with a flag at the main, I propose placing the Asia abreast of her, with the Genoa and Albion next to the Asia; and I wish that H. E. Rear-Admiral Count Heiden will have the goodness to place his squadron next in succession to the British ships of the line.

The Russian frigates in this case can occupy the Turkish ships next in succession to the Russian ships of the line; the English frigates forming along side such Turkish vessels as may be on the western side of the harbour, abreast of the British ships of the line; and the French frigates forming in the same manner, so as to occupy the Turkish frigates, &c. abreast of the French ships of the line. If time permit before any hostility is committed by the Turkish fleet, the ships are to moor with springs on the rings of each anchor. No gun is to be fired from the combined fleet without a signal, unless shot be fired from any of the Turkish ships, in which case the ships so firing are to be destroyed immediately. The corvettes and brigs are, under the direction of Captain Fellows of the Dartmouth, to remove the fire-vessels into such a position as will prevent their being able to injure any of the combined fleet. In case of a regular battle ensuing, and creating that confusion which must naturally arise from it, it is to be observed, that, in the words of Lord Nelson, "no captain can do wrong who places his ship along side that of an enemy."   (Signed,)   EDWARD CODRINGTON.

Before detailing the particulars of the memorable action which ensued, we must make a few observations on the protocol signed by the three allied admirals, and point out the propriety and necessity of adopting the third and last mode of proceeding. Respecting the first-mentioned method, we have to observe, that the concurrent testimony of all the pilots and all the officers of the British fleet, whose local experience established the soundness of their opinion, proved that the blockade of Navarin is physically impossible during the winter. Even in the middle of September the squadron at one time was carried by a northerly current as far to the northward as the Strophadia Islands; and at another time, in a strong wind, aided by a southerly current, below the gulf of Coron. Moreover, there is no anchorage whatever upon any part of the neighbouring coast; nor is there any safety for any vessel larger than a sloop of war in Modon or under Sapienza. And so long as the allied forces remained outside the harbour, Ibrahim continued to practise, uninterruptedly, that barbarous and exterminating warfare which the treaty was framed to prevent: therefore the object of the allied powers could only be accomplished by their forces actually entering the bay, and by means of their imposing presence induce Ibrahim to desist. But it has been asked, if the second mode of proceeding had been adopted, would it not, on the one hand, have effectually obviated all the risks of the first? and, on the other hand, as effectually secured, so far as the naval forces in Navarin were concerned, the main object of Sir Edward's instructions, which were, to prevent all supplies of men, arms, and ammunition being sent to the Turkish forces in Greece, without incurring the same danger of collision as was to be apprehended from the third? If Sir Edward had known at the time that the Island of Sphacteria was in the circle of the Ionian Islands, it might have altered his proceedings; he could have taken up an anchorage along that island and within the bay. But even this must have led to a collision whenever he attempted to put his orders in force—prevent any supply of men, arms, or ammunition being sent to the Turkish forces in Greece. The third mode therefore, having in contemplation the renewing of propositions to Ibrahim for him to return to Alexandria or the Dardanelles with the whole of his forces, without undertaking any farther operations either in Greece or the islands, with a guarantee for his safe arrival, certainly appeared to be less likely to degenerate into hostilities than the second mode; and it was this expectation which induced Sir Edward to adopt it.

On the 20th, the weather being fine, with a moderate breeze from the south-east, the combined fleet stood towards Navarin at half-past one p. m. the Asia leading, followed by the Albion and Genoa; the Sirène frigate, bearing the flag of Admiral de Rigny, the Scipion, Trident, and Breslaw; then the Russian admiral, Count Heiden, followed by three ships of the line and four frigates; consisting of ten sail of the line, ten frigates, sixteen corvettes and brigs, in all twenty-six sail, and mounting 1324 guns. The Turkish force consisted of three sail of the line, four double-banked frigates of 64 guns each, nineteen frigates, forty-nine corvettes and brigs, besides several fire-ships, in all eighty-nine ships, besides forty transports, mounting 2240 guns; the whole of which were anchored in the Bay of Navarin in the form of a crescent, with springs on their cables, the larger ones presenting their broadsides towards the centre, the smaller ones, in succession within them, filling up the intervals. Their principal force was assembled to the right on entering, and consisted of one large and three double-banked frigates, two ships of the line, a double-banked frigate, and a ship of the line; frigates of various sizes finishing the line round to the left. Six fire-vessels were placed at the two extremities of the crescent, to be able to fall upon the combined squadron if an engagement should take place; the whole of which was adopted at the suggestion of a Frenchman named Letellier, who for several days had been employed in the arrangement.

On entering, the Asia beat to quarters, but every appearance of hostility not rendered necessary by this essential precaution was avoided; the ports of the fleet were not hauled flat aback against the side, but left square as at sea; and the ships were ordered not to anchor by the stern, which is the manner of ranging up in the presence of an enemy. At the time of entering the bay, the Turks were hauling on their springs, so as to bring their broadsides to bear on the centre. They were principally at quarters, the tompions of their guns were out, and their guns in some cases appeared filled up to their muzzles, the wadding being easily seen in them; and from some Englishmen whom they had detained on board, it was afterwards ascertained that they had used all kinds of things—broken bars, rusty nails, &c. At the moment the Asia was passing the entrance, a boat put off from under the fort, with a message from the commandant, to the effect that Ibrahim had not given any orders or permission for the allied fleet to enter; and it was consequently wished that they should remain outside. Sir Edward, however, was not to be shaken in his resolution, and he returned for answer, that *he was not come to receive orders, but to give them; that if any shot were fired at the allied fleet, the Turkish fleet would be destroyed; and that he would not be sorry should such an opportunity be given him.* The boat then pushed off from the ship, rowed in great haste to the landing-place, where the messenger got out, and ran up to the fort, where some bustle took place. A blank gun was fired to seaward just as the Asia was abreast of the battery: she, however, continued to stand on, passed close to the ship of Moharem Bey, rounded up under sail, and let go her small bower anchor, about a cable's length, on the Capitana's larboard bow, the first ship of the line, mounting 84 guns. Sixty fathoms of cable were run out from this first anchor, and then, being under sail, the best bower anchor was let go; then thirty fathoms were hauled on the small bower, and thirty were given out to the best bower. Springs, before letting them go, were put on both anchors, and the sails clued up and furled. The Genoa anchored close along side a ship of the line ahead of the Capitana Bey, and the Albion along side a double-banked frigate ahead of her, each having thus her proper opponent in the front line of the Turkish fleet. The ships to windward, or to the right on going in, part of the Egyptian squadron, including Moharem's, were allotted to the squadron under Admiral de Rigny. That part of the Turkish line in the bight of the crescent was to mark the stations of the Russian squadron, the ships of their line forming immediately ahead of the English, and followed up by their own frigates. The French frigate Armide was directed to place herself along side the outermost frigate on the left, and the Cambrian, Glasgow, and Talbot next to her; the Dartmouth, Musquito, Rose, Brisk, and Philomel were to look after the fire-vessels at the entrance of the harbour. Sir Edward gave particular directions that no gun should be fired unless the Turks should commence firing, which were strictly obeyed, and the three English ships of the line took their stations without any act of hostility. Indeed, every thing having been quietly carried on thus far, all idea of a fight on board the Asia was given up; the watch was called to square the yards, and the band was forming to play on the quarter-deck, when

a firing of musquetry took place into the boats belonging to the Dartmouth, under the orders of Lieutenant Smyth, which killed Lieutenant G.
W. H. Fitzroy. The Dartmouth then opened a fire of musquetry, to protect her boats. Almost at the same moment two shot were fired from the
Turkish vessels astern of the Sirène frigate, Admiral de Rigny's ship,
struck that ship, and wounded one of the crew, which of course brought
on a return, and the cannonade soon became general. Although the Asia
was along side the Capitana, she was still near to Moharem; but as the latter had sent a message to say he should not fire, the Asia was hove on her
larboard spring, and her broadside brought to bear on the Capitana's ship,
which was bringing her broadside to bear on the Asia, and fired her bow
guns into her. The Asia then opened with double-shotted guns; but whether
the Turk could not get his men to stand, or whether his spring was cut,
is uncertain, but he never brought his broadside fully to bear on the Asia.
The smoke soon became so thick that the guns were pointed by the flag
at the Capitana's mast-head, which was the only thing that could be perceived: the Asia's guns, however, occasionally ceased, to get a look at
her opponent's hull, when he often returned single guns, until his cable was cut or slipped, and he went to leeward a mere wreck. By the
annexed plan, it will be seen, that the Asia, in order to bring her broadside to bear on the Capitana, was obliged to expose her stern to the
raking fire of a frigate and a corvette or two in the inner line; and it was
from their fire, as much as from her immediate opponent's, that she received her damage.

During this conflict, Lieutenant Dilke was dispatched by Sir Edward
to Moharem, to assure him of his desire to avoid bloodshed, and that as
he had promised not to fire into the Asia, similar conduct should be observed towards him. But whilst Lieutenant Dilke was getting down the
Egyptian ship, and the pilot, Mitchell, was in the boat along side, the
latter was shot dead, but whether by Moharem's order was not known:
his ship, however, ultimately fired into the Asia. At a quarter-past three,
having settled the matter with the Turk, the Asia hove on her starboard
spring, and brought her larboard broadside to bear on Moharem's and
his second ahead, both of which were very soon destroyed. Moharem's
went to leeward, cut to pieces; and the other, burning to the water's
edge, at an anchor, soon after blew up.

As the smoke which arose completely concealed the Asia from the
rest of the fleet, and the explosion took place within a cable's length of her,

it was at first feared that she had blown up, and a momentary suspense took place; but on the smoke clearing off, and shewing the Asia still holding her proud and commanding situation, a cheer was given, which resounded from one extremity of the bay to the other, and the cannonade recommenced with the utmost vigour against whatever was opposed to them. This bloody and destructive battle was continued with unabated fury for about four hours, and the scene of wreck and destruction which presented itself at its termination was such as had been seldom before witnessed. As each of the Turkish ships became effectually disabled, such of her crew as could escape from her endeavoured to set her on fire; and by these means the greater part was totally destroyed. At a quarter-past five, the firing along the whole line ceased.

In this destructive but brilliant engagement, the mizen-mast of the Asia went by the board, in consequence of the raking fire of the Turkish second line, which also cut her rigging to pieces. Her main-mast was severely shattered with twenty-eight round shot, and was with difficulty saved. The fore-mast received eighteen shot, the bowsprit nine, and the hull 128. The main-yard was wounded, and having been got down on the deck, the main-mast was in itself so weak, that it was impossible to raise or remove it; consequently it was sawed in pieces and thrown overboard. The main-top-mast was lowered down to the main-mast, and made fast on it to strengthen it. In addition to which, she had 16 men killed, including Captain G. A. Bell, R. M.:—Mr. H. I. Codrington, the admiral's son, Mr. W. N. Lee, midshipmen; Mr. R. H. Bunbury, volunteer first class; Mr. C. Wakeham, supernumerary clerk; 26 seamen, and 2 marines, severely wounded:—Hon. Lieutenant-Colonel Craddock, passenger; Mr. H S. Dyer, admiral's secretary; 16 seamen, and 7 marines, slightly wounded. It was indeed almost miraculous how Sir Edward himself escaped; with the exception of going once or twice to the forecastle, and one short visit to his wounded son, he was on the poop the whole time, which was once or twice cleared during the action, once in particular, when there was no one to be seen on it but himself. A musket-ball passed through the sleeve of his coat at the wrist; his watch was smashed by a splinter; a cannon-ball passed through the rolled up awning under which he was standing, which just cleared his hat; he was twisted round several times and his coat was torn in several places by splinters.

To the whole of the officers and men under his command, Sir Edward bore the most unqualified testimony of approbation.

" The manner in which," said he, " the Genoa and Albion took their stations was beautiful; and the conduct of my brother admirals, Count Heiden and the Chevalier de Rigny, throughout, was admirable and highly exemplary. Captain Fellows in the Dartmouth executed the part allotted him perfectly, and with the able assistance of his little but brave detachment saved the Sirène from being burnt by the fire-vessels. The Cambrian and Glasgow, following the fine example of Captain Hugon of the Armide, who was opposed to the leading frigate of that line, effectually destroyed their opponents, and also silenced the batteries.

" It is impossible for me to say too much for the able and zealous conduct of Captain Curzon throughout this long and arduous contest; nor can I say more than it deserves for the conduct of Commander Baynes and the officers and crew of the Asia, for the perfection with which the fire of their guns was directed: each vessel, in turn, to which her broadside was presented became a complete wreck. His Royal Highness will be aware that so complete a victory by a few, however perfect, against an excessive number, however individually inferior, cannot be acquired but at a considerable sacrifice of life : accordingly I have to lament the loss of Captain Bathurst of the Genoa, whose example on this occasion is well worthy the imitation of his survivors. Captain Bell, commanding the royal marines of the Asia, an excellent officer, was killed early in the action, in the steady performance of his duty ; and I have to mourn the death of Mr. William Smith, the master, admired for the zeal and ability with which he executed his duty, and beloved by all for his private qualities as a man. Mr. Henry S. Dyer, my secretary, having received a severe contusion from a splinter, I am deprived temporarily of his valuable assistance in collecting and keeping up the general returns and communications of the squadron : I shall therefore retain in my office Mr. E. J. T. White, his first clerk, whom I have nominated to succeed the purser of the Brisk. I feel much personal obligation to Colonel Craddock for his readiness, during the heat of the battle, in carrying my orders and messages to the different quarters after my aides-de-camp were disabled. When I contemplate, as I do with extreme sorrow, the extent of our loss, I console myself with the reflection, that the measure which produced the battle was absolutely necessary for obtaining the results contemplated by the treaty, and that it was brought on entirely by our opponents. When I found that the boasted Ottoman's word of honour was made a sacrifice to wanton, savage devastation, and that a base advantage was taken of our reliance upon Ibrahim's good faith, I own I felt a desire to punish the offenders. But it was my duty to refrain, and refrain I did ; and I can assure his Royal Highness that I would still have avoided this disastrous extremity if other means had been open to me*."

We must now refer to the proceedings of the French squadron under Admiral de Rigny. That gallant officer took up his station athwart the hawse of the first Egyptian frigate, and his three line-of-battle ships were to occupy positions between him and the British admiral; but, owing to particular causes, they did not do so. A fire-ship got under the bows of the Scipion in coming in, to escape which she anchored, while the fire-ship was towed off by the boats of the Dartmouth and Rose. The Breslaw went to the end of the bay, and attacked the vessels in that quarter, where she rendered great assistance to the Russian squadron, the whole of which behaved in the most brave and gallant manner. Admiral de Rigny having set fire to his opponent, was in great danger of sharing the same fate when the Turk was cast loose from his anchor either by burning or slipping: to prevent this catastrophe, a man swam from the Sirène to the Dartmouth with a rope, and a hawser being made fast, the French frigate was enabled to get clear. Captain Davies of the Rose also relieved the French frigate Armide, commanded by an excellent officer, Hugon, from a disadvantageous and too perilous position; acts which Admiral de Rigny acknowledged in the following letter to Admiral Codrington, dated Sirène, October 23:

" SIR,—I hasten to do myself the honour to inform your excellency, from a detached report made by Captain Hugon of the Armide, that the excellent conduct of Captain Davies, when the Rose came and resolutely cast her anchor within pistol-shot of two Turkish corvettes, relieved the Armide in a few minutes from her unfavourable position; and it is my duty, and at the same time a great pleasure to me, to assure your excellency, that on this occasion Captain Davies did every thing that could be expected from a brave and experienced officer.

" Allow me also to take this opportunity of returning my thanks to Captain Fellows, for the assistance which the Sirène received from the boats of the Dartmouth, when, with much skill and bravery, they attacked and turned off the fireships ready to come down upon us."

These expressions of praise on the part of the French admiral were met by a corresponding warmth on the part of Sir Edward, who addressed the following letter to M. de Rigny, dated October 23:

" SIR,—When your excellency did me the honour of voluntarily placing yourself and the French squadron under my command, you gave me a right to judge in

* Official letter.

that situation, by making me in a great degree responsible for it. I take advantage then of that right to say, that I contemplated your way of leading your squadron into battle on the 20th with the greatest pleasure; that nothing can exceed the good management of the ships under your especial direction; and that my having had you under my orders in that bloody and destructive engagement will be one of the proudest events of my whole professional life. Although it was my wish to avoid entering into any particular detail, the general expression of the captains of the British ships who were near the Armide calls upon me to say, that the conduct of Captain Hugon entitles him to the marked consideration of your excellency."

A similar letter was addressed by Sir Edward to the Russian admiral, whose public and private conduct gained him the approbation of all the British officers whose duty led them into communication with him. The proceedings of the Albion, Captain Ommanney, were such as in every respect fully maintained the high character of the British navy; but it is unnecessary to enter into particulars on that head, as Sir Edward Codrington observed in his official letter, that the narration of the proceedings of the Asia would be applicable to most of the other ships of the fleet. She had 10 killed and 6 wounded: among the former was Captain C. J. Stevens, R.M.; and among the latter, W. Lloyd, mate, Mr. F. Gray, midshipman, severely; Commander J.N. Campbell, Lieutenant J. G. D. Urban, Rev. E. Winder, chaplain, and Mr. W. F. O'Kane, assistant-surgeon.

What has been said of the Asia and Albion may with great propriety be said of the Genoa, Captain Bathurst, who lost his life on the occasion. He was a meritorious and valuable officer, and the fall of such a man was to be greatly lamented. It was, however, some consolation to his friends to know, that his memory would long exist, and excite others to emulate his conduct, and obtain the same honourable place in public estimation. His death was glorious as his life was honourable, and he met it with all the resignation of a Christian and the spirit of a hero. When laid on his bed, after his wounds were dressed, he found his leg in an uneasy position; he therefore called to the surgeon, and requested him to move the limb, saying, in a tone of apology, " I'm a little fidgety just now, but I hope you will excuse it." Shortly afterwards Captain Moore, R. M. was brought down wounded, and Captain Bathurst, recognising his voice, exclaimed, " Ah! Moore, is that you?"—" Yes," said Captain Moore: " I am badly wounded."—" Ah!" replied Captain Bathurst, " c'est la *fortune de guerre.*" His spirit, however, **was** not sufficient to enable him to struggle with death, and he died happy in the reflection that he closed his career in the cause of suffering humanity. Besides her captain, the Genoa had 25 officers and men killed; Lieutenant H. R. Sturt, Mr. H. B. Gray, midshipman, Mr. J. Chambers, volunteer 2d class, and 30 men, wounded.

Several of the smaller vessels also acted a very prominent part in this tremendous conflict. That of the Talbot we have already alluded to: her gallant captain, relying on support from the ships astern, ran into a position where she had to sustain the fire of three Turkish frigates and a corvette, which she was opposed to for nearly twenty minutes, when the French frigate Armide came to her assistance, and by the intrepidity of her commander, Hugon, one of the Turkish frigates soon hauled down her colours; and then a circumstance occurred which proved the cordiality that existed between the allies. Captain Hugon took possession of the Turk, and hoisted, not the French flag only, but the French and English; thus modestly and generously admitting, that the vessel was conquered by the united efforts of the ships belonging to those two powers. The Talbot had 6 killed and 17 wounded: among the latter were Lieutenant R. S. Hay and Mr. A. C. College, midshipman.

The conduct of Captain Fellows of the Dartmouth was highly conspicuous, and Sir Edward Codrington and Admiral de Rigny bore ample testimony to his merits. He had 6 killed and 8 wounded: among the latter was Lieutenant Spencer Smyth.

The Glasgow had none killed, and only 2 wounded.

The Cambrian had Lieutenant Philip Sturgeon, R. M. killed, and 1 marine wounded.

The Philomel, which sunk a fire-ship, had 1 killed and 7 wounded.

The Rose had 3 killed and 15 wounded: among the latter were Lieutenant M. Lyons mortally, and Mr. D. Curry, midshipman. The circumstances under which Lieutenant Lyons received his wounds are so honourable to his memory and the profession to which he belonged, that we have a melancholy satisfaction in relating them. At that critical and awful moment when a Turkish fire-ship was drifting on board a French line-of-battle ship, the boats of the Rose pushed off, under the command of Lieutenant Lyons, and though exposed to a dreadful fire of grape, towed her clear. The services of the Rose on that memorable day were duly acknowledged, and will thus be handed down to posterity, by the

French admiral, De Rigny; and respecting Lieutenant Lyons, Captain Davies wrote the following letter to his brother, which was honourable to the feelings of both:

Rose, Malta, Nov. 29, 1827.

Dear Sir,—Your brother's loss is deplored by all who knew him, for his kindness of heart and evenness of temper; but he was chiefly admired for his cool self-possession in danger. He was often under fire from pirates when in command of the Rose's boats, and was always successful; but it was in the battle of Navarin that he pre-eminently distinguished himself in command of the Rose's boats, by towing a fire-ship clear of a French line-of-battle ship under a dreadful fire of grape, which must have ensured his promotion had he survived.

To Captain E. Lyons.   (Signed,)   E. L. Davies.

The Brisk, which also destroyed a fire-ship, had 3 wounded; and the Musquito 2 killed and 4 wounded.—Total 75 killed; 197 wounded.

We must also mention that the Hind cutter (tender to the Asia), commanded by Lieutenant Robb of that ship, unluckily fell on board a Turkish ship, the crew of which made several attempts to board her, but were effectually repulsed by Lieutenant Robb and his gallant little crew. She had 3 killed.

French Loss.

Sirène frigate, 21 killed, 32 wounded. Scipion, 2 killed, 36 wounded. Trident, 7 wounded. Breslaw, 1 killed, 14 wounded. Armide, 14 killed, 25 wounded.

Halcyone, 1 killed, 9 wounded. Daphné, 1 killed, 8 wounded. In addition to which there were 3 officers killed and 3 wounded.—Total, 34 killed, 144 wounded.

Russian Loss.

Azoff, 24 killed, 67 wounded. Hargood, 14 killed, 37 wounded. Ezekiel, 13 killed, 18 wounded. Alexander Newski, 5 killed, 7 wounded. Prevornie, 1 killed, 2 wounded. Constantine, 1 wounded. Elena, 5 wounded. Castor, none.—Total, 57 killed, 137 wounded.

After the battle Sir Edward Codrington sent the following notice to the Turkish commanders, which was also signed by the French and Russian admirals:

" As the squadrons of the allies did not enter Navarin with a hostile intention, but only to renew to the commanders of the Turkish fleet propositions which were to the advantage of the Grand Seignor himself, it is not our intention to destroy what ships of the Ottoman navy may yet remain, now that so signal a

3 T 2

vengeance has been taken for the first cannon-shot which has been ventured to be fired on the allied flags. We send therefore one of the Turkish captains, fallen into our hands as a prisoner*, to make known to Ibrahim Pacha, Moharem Pacha, Tahir Pacha, and Capitana Bey, as well as to all the other Turkish chiefs, that if *one single musket or cannon shot be again* fired on a ship or boat of the allied powers, we shall immediately destroy all the remaining vessels, as well as the forts of Navarin; and that we shall consider such new act of hostility *as a formal declaration of the Porte against the three allied powers, and of which the Grand Seignor and his Pachas must suffer the terrible consequences.* But if the Turkish chiefs, acknowledging the aggression they have committed by commencing the firing, abstain from any act of hostility, we shall resume those terms of good understanding which they have themselves interrupted. In this case they will have the white flag hoisted on all the forts before the end of this day. We demand a categorical answer, without evasions, before sunset."

No answer was, however, returned to this letter; but as the Turkish commanders did " abstain from any farther act of hostility," and as the allied admirals had taken signal vengeance for the insult which had been offered to them, they left Navarin on the 25th October, having employed the intermediate time in repairing their damages, and arrived at Malta on the 3d November.

Having now stated the particulars of that battle which put a period to those barbarities that had for years shocked humanity, we must notice the honours conferred upon Sir Edward and his brave companions. By his own sovereign, at the recommendation of his royal brother, the Lord High Admiral, Admiral Codrington was appointed a Grand Cross of the Order of the Bath; and Captains J. A. Ommanney, the Hon. J. A. Maude, Hon. F. Spencer, Edward Curzon†, and Commanders J. N. Campbell, Richard Dickenson, G. B. Martin, Lewis Davies, Hon. W. Anson, Viscount Ingestrie, and R. L. Baynes, were nominated Companions of the said Order. In addition to which all the commanders were promoted to post-rank, all the senior lieutenants to be commanders, and all the senior mates to be lieutenants. The King of France and Emperor of Russia were equally prompt in manifesting the high importance which they attached to the victory of Navarin, and their admiration of the conduct of those by whom it was achieved. The King of

---

* It was sent by Tahir Pacha, who came on board the Asia, and was asked to convey it to Ibrahim, which he consented to do, but would not answer for any effect being produced by it.

† Captain Fellows had the honour of knighthood conferred upon him on his arrival in London.

France conferred upon Sir Edward the Order of the Grand Cross of the Royal and Military Order of St. Louis*; and when the officer sent by him to return his Majesty thanks for this honour, arrived in Paris, his Majesty, still farther to testify his approbation of all that was done, conferred upon him an order of knighthood. The Emperor of Russia conferred upon Sir Edward the Military Order of St. George, which he made known to him by the following letter, written with his own hand:

Copie d'une lettre de sa Majesté l'Empereur de toutes les Russies à Monsieur le Vice-Amiral CODRINGTON.

MONSIEUR LE VICE-AMIRAL CODRINGTON,—Vous venez de remporter une victoire dont l'Europe civilisée doit vous être doublement reconnoissante. La mémorable bataille de Navarin, et les manœuvres hardies qui l'ont précédée, ne donnent pas seulement au monde la mesure du zèle de trois grandes puissances pour une cause dont leur désintéressement relève encore le noble caractère ; elles prouvent aussi ce que peut la fermeté contre le nombre, et une valeur habilement dirigée contre un courage aveugle quelles que soient les forces dont il s'appuie.

Votre nom appartient désormais à la postérité. Je croirois affaiblir par des éloges la gloire qui l'environne, mais j'éprouve le besoin de vous offrir une marque éclatante de la gratitude et de l'estime que vous inspirez à la Russie. C'est dans cette vue que je vous envoie ci-joint l'Ordre Militaire de St. George.

La marine Russe s'honore d'avoir obtenu votre suffrage devant Navarin, et pour moi j'ai le plus vif plaisir à vous assurer des sentimens de considération que je vous porte. (Signé), NICOLAS.

ST. PETERSBOURG, *le 8 Novembre*, 1827.

His Imperial Majesty also directed his minister, Count Nesselrode, to write another letter to Count Heiden, in which, after expressing his Majesty's favourable opinion of the battle, and of the admirable conduct of the allied forces engaged, he regrets the loss sustained by the Asia and two other British ships; and adds, that he should consider it an honour to the navy of Russia if Sir Edward Codrington would hoist his flag on board any of the Russian squadron; and for that purpose directed Count Heiden to place the whole, or any part, of that squadron that he might desire under his orders. In another letter, addressed by Count Nesselrode to Count Heiden, the latter was directed to point out how his Majesty could honour the son of Sir Edward, who was wounded in the battle, so as to prove his Majesty's regard for him.

After these manifestations of the sentiments of the allied kings, after

---

* Captain Fellows was nominated a Commander of the Legion of Honour, and the other captains were made Knights of the Order of St. Louis.

they had in terms of such generous feelings manifested their approbation of Sir Edward's conduct, and after those unequivocal demonstrations of regard by three of the principal crowned heads of Europe, it was with no little surprise that, at the opening of the British Parliament, the name of Sir Edward Codrington, contrary to all precedent in such cases, was not mentioned in the royal speech; that the battle itself was called an " untoward event;" while it was made known by the ministers, that it was not intended to propose the thanks of Parliament to those who had risked their lives in defending the reputation of the crown of England and the common interests of humanity; conduct which was loudly protested against by some of the most distinguished and honourable characters in both Houses of Parliament, where it appeared to be admitted on all sides, that Sir Edward had, under circumstances of the greatest difficulty and delicacy, acted with the plain straight forward talent of an unsophisticated British sailor, and had displayed wisdom in the management of the early part of the task committed to his hands, as well as shewn an instance of memorable valour in the celebrated battle which afterwards occurred; that he had gained a most glorious victory; and that there was no deed of arms which could be said to be superior in importance to that gained at Navarin, or redounded more to the honour of those who achieved it.

The Duke of Wellington declared that not the slightest charge could be made, or the most distant imputation cast, upon Sir Edward; that the gallant admiral had been placed in a difficult and peculiar situation; that he was in command of a squadron of ships in conjunction with admirals of foreign nations, and he so conducted himself as to acquire their confidence, they allowing him to lead them to victory. This service the noble duke admitted the gallant admiral had completed in a way which did credit alike to himself and his country; and then declared, that he should consider himself unworthy the office which he held, if he uttered a single word derogatory to that officer's character and services, admiring, as he did, the course which he had pursued in such a time of difficulty and danger.

The Marquis of Lansdowne declared, that if blame rested any where, it did not rest with Sir Edward Codrington. He agreed with those who said, that in some degree the battle of Navarin was an unfortunate circumstance, inasmuch as it occasioned the destruction of life and tended to hostilities; but at the same time, he said, he should be ashamed if he did not declare it would be childish to expect, that when an armed interference had been determined on by treaty, it could take place without the risk of war. He agreed with those who thought that war should not take place if the objects of the intervention could be effected without it; but the consequences of opposition must have been foreseen by those who framed the protocol and the treaty of London. There was no meaning in establishing a hostile intervention, unless we were ready to encounter all the consequences which must result from it, melancholy as they might be. He hoped it could be proved that blame did not rest any where; but if it did exist, it would be easy to prove that it was not with the gallant admiral: *it must be with those who had concluded those treaties* that had placed him in a situation from which he had extricated himself by the exercise of sound discretion and a sense of duty; and who was consequently entitled to the protection, not of his friends only, but of every person who was proud of British honour.

Lord Goderich entirely concurred in every thing that had been said by the Marquis of Lansdowne, both relating to the policy of the treaty and the conduct of Sir Edward Codrington; that, in his opinion, the gallant admiral had exercised a sound discretion; that he was placed in circumstances of no ordinary difficulty, and discharged his duty like a man of courage. He was prepared to support him, not only on the principle that it was the duty of a government to support those who executed their orders, but from a deliberate conviction that he was justified, under the circumstances, in the course which he took; and that, in taking that course, he neither tarnished his own previously acquired fame, nor sullied the honour or reputation of his country.

Lord Dudley said, that the admiral who commanded at Navarin, instead of being checked by the government for what he had done, had received large honours and rewards. The gallant admiral therefore stood in no need of a defence from his Majesty's ministers; and if his conduct had been censured by those who had no just ground for such a charge, that fact formed no reason why they should undertake it.

This, however, is laying down a principle in which we cannot agree: for if censure is thrown out where there is " no just ground for such a charge," the person to whom blame is attributed must be innocent; and it is the duty of every one to stand up in defence of injured innocence; more especially is it the duty of government to stand fairly by those officers whom they employ, and openly to justify their conduct when it meets with their approbation. And notwithstanding the high and pow-

erful testimonies which we have inserted, persons were still found to carp
at the conduct pursued by Sir Edward Codrington; and the foreign secretary himself, Lord Dudley, did not think he had made out such a case
as would justify the steps he had taken. Sir John Gore was sent out to the
admiral, to get his answers to a number of questions; and notwithstanding
they were fully and satisfactorily answered, no intimation was given that the
ministers intended to propose a vote of thanks in either House of Parliament to the hero of Navarin. Mr. Hobhouse accordingly gave notice
of his intention to submit such a motion to the House of Commons, and
in a very able speech proved the claims of Sir Edward Codrington to the
thanks of that House and the country at large. But although Mr. Huskisson admitted, that the queries which had been sent out had received
distinct and explicit answers, *which proved beyond a question that there
had been nothing precipitate or rash in the conduct of the admiral commanding the British fleet*, he refused his sanction to a vote of thanks, because there was no precedent for it! "We vote," he said, "the thanks of
Parliament for triumphs over our enemies; we vote them to mark our
satisfaction, that in a conflict which we have foreseen and directed, with
a power against which we have declared war, the skill and gallantry and
zeal of our officers have triumphed over the skill and gallantry and zeal
of our enemies, and that they have maintained by that skill, gallantry,
and zeal the ancient superiority of our country above all others." He
would not enter into the question whether Ibrahim Pacha had or had not
broken the terms of the armistice which had been made between him
and Sir Edward Codrington; he believed that he had. He would only
say, that Sir Edward did not enter the Bay of Navarin with a view of attacking a Turkish fleet, but with the view of obtaining by his position a
compliance with the terms of the armistice which he had settled with
Ibrahim. Upon entering that bay there ensued a scene in which the
greatest skill, seamanship, and gallantry were evinced by Sir Edward
Codrington, and every officer and man under his command. It was no
small addition to the praise which the gallant admiral obtained by his valour and skill, that he had effected that which it was not always easy to
effect when the forces of rival powers were employed together for a
joint object; that he had conciliated them by his conduct; and that he
had so produced a unity of purpose and a harmony of design, which
could not have been exceeded if the force employed had been entirely
British, and under the command of a British officer as much beloved,

as he understood Sir Edward had the happiness of being beloved by every man who sailed under his orders. But the affair in which he had so eminently distinguished himself was not a battle between enemies; it was an accident, a misfortune, which could not be foreseen, and perhaps, under the circumstances, could not be avoided.

Notwithstanding all these admissions, and notwithstanding all these praises, the vote of thanks was refused; because, forsooth, the victory was not gained over an " enemy;" because the victory arose out of an " accident;" and because " officers, looking at the signal benefit conferred on them by receiving such thanks, might be found prone to cherish too easy a disposition to create such accidents." It was, however, the first time, since the practice of thanking officers had prevailed, that the King of England opened his Parliament with a speech deploring such a victory; and it was the first time that the House of Commons ever hesitated, ever doubted the propriety of thanking men who had achieved so brilliant, so signal, and so important a victory. Notwithstanding the speciousness of this argument, a little plain sense and common understanding are sufficient to discover the flimsy foundation on which it rests. If there is any weight in the last reason given by Mr. Huskisson, it must be *in the absence of all honours and rewards;* but in the instance before us the three sovereigns most interested in the result of Sir Edward's conduct combined to express their satisfaction of his measures, conferred honours upon him, and congratulated him on his energy and decision; and the ministers of his own country declared, that he had acted with the greatest judgment, that his conduct was free from rashness or precipitancy, and his whole proceedings marked with zeal, valour, and ability. But when asked to put this acknowledgment into the form of a resolution (for the thanks of Parliament are nothing more), they refused, lest some other officer might be anxious to follow the steps of Admiral Codrington: this is splitting hairs. No doubt the thanks of Parliament regularly passed are duly estimated by all military men; but we will venture to say, that there is no one admiral in the British navy who will decline imitating the conduct of Sir Edward Codrington, should he ever be similarly situated. If he find that Parliament would not *in fact* vote their thanks to Sir Edward, he will find a sanction for his conduct in the recorded speeches of the principal members, including the ministers; and that its thanks were consequently virtually given. If this will not afford him consolation, he must turn to the conduct of the king, which cannot fail most amply to supply it. He will then see that the promptness of his Majesty to reward valour and abilities placed it out of the power of his ministers to cast the slightest censure on the admiral; and secure in the precedent thus set before them, all, we trust, will be anxious to cherish " a disposition to create such accidents," to prove the possession of equal abilities, and thus increase the honour and reputation of the British navy. If the action was " unexpected," if it did not arise out of any direct and positive orders for attack, if the victory was not " foreseen," then does it prove more fully the merits of the admiral and his fitness for command, inasmuch as it confirms the opinion entertained of him, that he was able to contend with unexpected difficulties; that he possesses those energies and resources within himself which enabled him to combat " unforeseen" and " unexpected" dangers with dauntless intrepidity, and to come forth from the encounter crowned with victory. But he did not triumph over an " enemy;" war was not declared against his opponent; he had no right to enter the harbour of Navarin in hostile array. Respecting this last assertion, we have only to observe, that the Island of Sphacteria* is in the circle of the Ionian Islands, and is therefore subject to the dominion of Britain; consequently he had as much right in the Bay of Navarin as Ibrahim Pacha. And if " war" was not actually declared against his opponent, is not that opponent to be treated as an " enemy" who shall presume to fire into a British man of war? Is the commander of an English fleet to stand tamely by and see his men killed, and not exert his utmost abilities to chastise, to revenge such an act of insult and of " war?" And having by a display of courage and nautical skill annihilated such a foe, is he to be met by the ministers of his own country, simply saying, we admire your resolution and professional conduct, but we cannot thank you, for fear some other admiral should " cherish a disposition to create such accidents?" Is not this condemning indirectly that which they affect to applaud? Well might it be said, that " it was reserved for the present times to see men triumph, and be afraid; to conquer, and to repine; to fight as heroes do the conquest of freedom, and still to tremble like slaves; to act gloriously, and repine bitterly; to win by brave men the battle of liberty in the East, and in the West to pluck from the valiant brow the laurels which it had so nobly earned, and plant the cypress there, because the conqueror had fought for religion and liberty."

One of the strongest parallel cases cited by Mr. Hobhouse, it appears

* See plan.

to us, was that of Algiers. Mr. Huskisson, however, said it bore no analogy to that of Navarin; because, in the former, there was an expedition fitted out for a specific purpose—of a *hostile nature*—and that purpose being executed, Parliament was called upon to praise the skill and gallantry of those who effected it. We, however, assert that this was not the case. Lord Exmouth's orders were, in the first place, *pacific,* and not hostile. He was sent there to effect the abolition of slavery; but this was to be done by negociation, if possible; he was furnished with proper authority for so doing, and a certain time was allowed for the determination of the Dey. "But if," say his orders, "the Dey of Algiers refuse to subscribe to the three conditions as proposed by your lordship, or if, having subscribed to them, he delay the execution of them, your lordship is instructed, in any one of these events, *immediately to commence hostilities,* by proceeding to destroy the Algerine fleet within the mole." And it is curious enough, that this was to be done because the Prince Regent was "*anxious to administer relief to the grievances which the maritime states of Europe experience in the Mediterranean.*" And Lord Exmouth, in his official letter, said, "thus has a provoked war of *two days' existence* been attended with complete victory." The treaty of July was formed to put an end to the sanguinary contest between the Greeks and the Turks, which was "*called for as much by humanity as by the interest of the repose of Europe;*" an immediate armistice between them was to be demanded; and if the Porte did not accept of the armistice within one month, the allies promised to exert all their means to obtain the effect of it, by preventing all collision between the contending parties; but it was certainly added, *without taking any part in the hostilities.* This was signed by Lord Dudley, and was evidently impracticable. Mr. Peel has declared, that Sir Edward Codrington's orders empowered him to blockade the Turkish fleet in any port in which they might be found: but what right have you to prevent the ingress or egress of the fleet of a friendly power into or from any of their own harbours? Surely this of itself is an act of " war."

Though we are not able to insert the orders sent to Sir Edward Codrington, we can state that *they were written in French—a very suspicious circumstance;* and that he was, in some degree, to regulate his conduct by the advice and opinion of the British ambassador at Constantinople; and finding that he could not prevent *all collision between the contending parties without taking part in the hostilities,* or lowering the honour and re-

putation of the British flag, he applied to the ambassador—fortunately he was not an Arbuthnot—who replied, "IF THE SPEAKING-TRUMPET WILL NOT ANSWER, YOU MUST USE CANNON-SHOT." This was speaking in a language which Sir Edward perfectly understood, as he had studied it from his infancy; and it therefore cannot be said that he had not orders to have recourse to hostilities.

Sir Edward certainly "did not enter the Bay of Navarin with a view of attacking the Turkish fleet, but with a view of obtaining by his position a compliance with the terms of the armistice," agreeably to the treaty. Neither did Lord Exmouth range his ships before Algiers "*with a view of attacking the Algerines, but with a view of obtaining by his position a compliance with the terms*" he was empowered by his orders to propose; both took up their positions without a shot being fired, and in both cases the firing was commenced by the—we must call them—enemies. Is not then the battle of Navarin a parallel case to that of Algiers? We must, however, pursue this subject a little farther, and place, we hope, the conduct of Sir Edward in the clearest possible point of view; and prove, we trust, that the mode adopted by Sir Edward of anchoring along side the Turkish fleet, was the only means he had of effecting the object of the treaty. That treaty certainly said he was not to take part in the hostilities, was not to come into collision with the Turks: but then his orders directed him to prevent any supplies of men, arms, or ammunition from being sent to the Turks in Greece. Seeing that these orders were in some degree opposed to the treaty, and duly weighing the probable effect of carrying them into execution, it appears he wrote to Mr. Stratford Canning, to know how he was by force to prevent the Turks, if obstinate, from pursuing any line of conduct which he was instructed to oppose, without committing hostility. And to which the ambassador replied, " I agree with you in thinking that any loss or imminent danger occurring to his highness's fleet is more likely to soften than to rivet his determination. In speaking of ' collision' in a former letter, I only meant, that the decisive moment as to war will be that in which he first learns by experience, that we mean to enforce, if necessary by cannon-shot, the armistice which it is the object of the treaty to establish, with or without him as the case may be. This I imagine to be the meaning of the second instructions addressed to you and your colleagues: You are not to take part with either of the belligerents, but you are to interpose your forces between them, and to keep the peace with your speaking-trumpet, if possible; but, in case of necessity, with that which is used for the maintenance of a blockade against friends as well as foes —I mean force." And in another letter he said, " On the subject of collision, we (the ambassadors) agree, that although the measures to be executed by you are not to be adopted in a hostile spirit, and although it is clearly the intention of the allied governments to avoid, if possible, any thing that may bring on war; yet the prevention of supplies, as stated in your instructions, is ultimately to be enforced, if necessary and when all the other means are exhausted, *by cannon-shot.*"

No doubt these documents shew that Sir Edward was to execute the treaty by persuasion if possible; but if that was impossible, then it was to be done by force, and that force is by the ambassador defined to be CANNON-SHOT. That Sir Edward used his utmost endeavours to avoid that alternative, we have made sufficiently clear: his anxiety on that point may, however, be seen when he met the Turkish division going to Patras, in breach of the armistice; and notwithstanding that favourable opportunity was afforded for professionally distinguishing himself, he refrained as much as possible from coming into actual collision with them. To do so, however, entirely was actually impossible; for if he had been enabled to keep up an effectual blockade of Navarin, he must have come to this extremity whenever a want of provisions would oblige the Ottoman fleet to put to sea: for if they had then refused to return upon his representations, he would have been obliged, according to his instructions, to have employed the forces under his command to effect it, without waiting, as he did in the bay, for the Ottomans to commence the attack. In the mean time, however, the whole Peloponnesus would have been ravaged by the revengeful Ibrahim and his army, and the unoffending and unopposing inhabitants reduced to that misery, to prevent which it was the principal object of the treaty of London to effect.

Unless therefore the treaty was to be a mere braggadocio, an idle menace, intended for no practical purpose, or to be followed by a display of diplomatic chicanery, whilst all practical proceedings were to be abstained from with fear and trembling, and the fleets of England, France, and Russia were assembled in the Mediterranean to witness their own degradation, the battle of Navarin must be considered as conferring an additional degree of splendour upon the British navy and nation; and that Sir Edward was fully deserving the same honours that had been conferred upon the destroyer of Algiers. This, however, was not done; and it forms the only instance upon record that a British House of Commons ever doubted, or even hesitated, about the propriety, much less refused, to bestow their thanks upon those who had increased the honour and reputation of their country, the glory and salvation of which depend upon justice being done to her defenders; but such as they experienced in this instance was certainly in general calculated to damp their ardour and enterprising spirit. They all naturally look up to that assembly for reward when they have done that which is deserving of it; and " a vigorous mind, baffled in the grand object of its pursuit, and despairing of better fortune, fatally impairs the body in which it is placed." Thanks, however, to the conduct of the King and the Lord High Admiral, it was not felt in the present instance; and upon this subject we are happy in being able to insert the following extract of a letter from an officer of the fleet : " Sir Edward is looking, and indeed is, remarkably well; and notwithstanding the rather *paltry conduct of some superiors at home, and all their questions,* is in excellent spirits : I might almost say that he is indifferent about the cause of Sir John Gore's coming here, so confident is he in his own mind of being justified on every point. But having seen the efforts of both body and mind that he has made to carry into effect the execution of the treaty, knowing how he has given up every thing to that object, one cannot help feeling hurt at the return. No one, however, can be more easy on the subject than he is; *he literally laughs at it and them.*"

Here we might close this addition to the Memoir of the gallant Sir Edward Codrington, in the confident expectation that it contains a faithful account of the whole proceedings relative to the important battle of Navarin; but as a matter of curiosity, we shall insert the following statement of Ibrahim Pacha to the French captain, Pujal, by whom it was forwarded to Admiral de Rigny, who sent it to Sir Edward Codrington, and by him it was transmitted to the Duke of Clarence :

Extrait d'un Rapport du Capitaine Pujal, *commandant la Goëlette de S. M.*
La Flèche.

" Navarin, *le 29 Octobre,* 1827.

" Ibrahim Pacha m'ayant fait dire qu'il désirait m'entretenir, je me rendis près de lui à six heures du soir, accompagné de deux de mes officiers. Peu après notre arrivée et ses complimens d'usage, il ordonna à ses officiers de se retirer, et me tient à peu près ce discours par l'intermediaire du dragoman :

" Monsieur le Capitaine, je vais avoir avec vous un entretien, que je desire que vous rapportiez aussi fidèlement et exactement que possible à l'Amiral de Rigny : je compte pour cela sur votre honneur.

" On me calomnie! Ibrahim a, dit on, manqué à sa parole; voici ce qui s'est passé: peu de temps avant la malheureuse affaire du 20, j'eus une conference avec Messieurs les Amiraux Anglois et François: plusieurs officiers etoient présents. Il a été convenu entre nous verbalement qu'il y aurait armistice entre les Grecs et les Turcs, jusqu'à la reception de la decision de la Porte en egard aux propositions des puissances. J'ai demandé si je pouvois approvisionner Patras, qui manquoit de vivres; on m'a repondu qu'il n'y avoit aucun empêchement. J'ai demandé dans le cas où les Grecs attaqueraient mon convoi, si on l'y opposerait; on a repondu que non: mais l'amiral Anglois m'a proposé une escorte ou un sauf-conduit, ce que j'ai refusé comme contraire à mon honneur. Peu de temps après le depart des escadres de devant Navarin, j'ai expedié un courier pour Patras, sous l'escorte de quelques bâtimens de guerre, ayant appris que les Grecs étoient de ce coté : devois-je en agir autrement, et laisser mourir de faim mes frères d'armes?

" Peu après, sur de nouveaux avis que Cochrane menaçoit Patras avec de forces considerables, je suis parti moi-même, accompagné d'une douzaine de frégates, pour aller assurer l'arrivée de mon convoi. Dans cette intervalle le convoi avoit été rencontré par les Anglois, et à la première sommation avoit retroussé chemin. Trouvant mon convoi à l'entrée du canal de Zante, après une conference avec mes principaux officiers, je me décidai à poursuivre ma première resolution d'approvisionner Patras, ne pensant pas violer mes engagemens, ma but n'étant pas d'entreprendre rien contre les Grecs, qui, d'ailleurs, de ce coté n'ont plus d'aucune possession.

" J'étois donc dans cette direction lorsque, rencontré de nouveau par les Anglois, je me decidai, sur une nouvelle sommation, à retourner à Navarin sans effectuer mon projet: j'étois de retour à Navarin et j'avois quitté cette place depuis quelque jours, lorsque les escadres Angloise, Françoise, et Russe se montrèrent. Une frégate et un brig Anglois entrent sans pavillon, et après avoir fait quelques bords dans la rade, en sortirent sans avoir hissé leurs couleurs; conduite que je ne saurois qualifier.

" Le 20 les alliés faisant route sur Navarin dans un ordre qui annonçoit des intentions hostiles; le Pacha qui commandoit en mon absence envoya une embarcation àbord de l'amiral Anglois, pour lui observer qu'il pouvoit entrer une partie de l'escadre si on le desiroit, et que si les alliés avoient quelques besoins, on y pourvoiroit—mais que, moi absent, il ne verroit pas avec plaisir entrer une armée aussi nombreuse.

" Je vous demande votre opinion, Monsieur le Capitaine, regardez-vous comme une offense une pareille demande? N'est-il pas naturel de ne pas désirer l'entrée dans un port, de forces quatre ou cinq fois supérieures, et qui inspirent de la dé-fiance? L'amiral Anglois envoya l'embarcation en repondant qu'il ne venoit pas recevoir des avis, mais pour donner des ordres, et continua à gouverner avec son escadre en ligne sur Navarin, où il entra à deux heures et demi de l'après midi, et fût de suite s'embosser à portée de pistolet devant l'armée Turque.

" Pendant ce temps une de ses frégates s'étoit détachée, et avoit mouillé par le travers de deux brûlots situés à l'entrée du port; et les François et les Russes, sui-vant de près l'amiral Anglois, imitaient sa manœuvre. L'amiral Turc ayant en-voyé une nouvelle embarcation àbord de l'Amiral Codrington pour demander des explications sur ces mesures hostiles, elle fut repoussée d'une manière outrageante; et dans le même moment la frégate embossée devant les brûlots, ayant envoyé des embarcations pour s'en emparer; alors commença une fusillade qui fut comme le signal du combat, qui ne finit qu'à la nuit, et effectua l'entière destruction de notre escadre, qui composé de trois vaisseaux de ligne, et nombre de frégates, et quan-tité d'avesons, et n'étant pas preparée au combat, avoit à faire à dix vaisseaux de ligne et nombre de frégates et corvettes. Les amiraux pensent-t-ils avoir fait une ample moisson de gloire en égorgeant ainsi, avec des forces aussi supérieures, ceux qui ne pouvoient s'attendre à une pareille attaque, qui n'y avoit point donné lieu, et qui, pour ainsi dire, n'avoient fait encore aucun preparatif de defense? Maintenant dire qui a commencé l'attaque et tiré le premier coup de canon, c'est ce dont chacun se defend. Ce qu'il y a de certain, c'est que la frégate Angloise à la première, et sans raisons, voulut s'emparer des brulôts, et que c'est la juste resistance de ce coté qui a occasionné le premier feu. Enfin, capitaine, ma con-science ne me reproche rien; j'avoue que j'ignore encore le veritable motif d'un pareil attentât. Les puissances ont voulu, disent-elles, faire cesser l'effusion de sang dans le Levant, et voici que leurs amiraux viennent de rougir la rade de Na-varin et de la couvrir de cadavres. On accuse, dit on, Ibrahim d'avoir manqué à sa parole; mais j'irai à Paris et à Londres, s'il le faut, faire connoitre la vérité; et ceux qui ont versé le sang innocent en porteront seuls la honte et le blâme. Les bâtimens sont faits pour devenir la proie du feu ou de la mer—ce n'est point ceux que je regrette; mais m'accuser d'avoir rompu mes engagemens, c'est une infame calomnie! Je compte sur votre honneur, Monsieur le Capitaine, pour répéter, mot pour mot, à votre amiral ce que viens de vous dire."

Although Ibrahim affects not to know on which side the firing com-menced, we will set that question at rest by the testimony of Captain Fellows:

H. M. S. Dartmouth, Malta, 10th December, 1827.

Sir,—Having been called on by you to furnish a statement of the immediate causes which led to the commencement of the action at Navarin on the 20th of October, 1827, I have the honour to state, for your information, that, in pursuance of your instruction of the 19th October, I anchored his Majesty's ship under my command betwixt the *brûlot* and the first ship (double-banked) on the eastern side of the harbour. While in the act of furling sails, a Turkish boat pulled past the Dartmouth in the greatest hurry, and went on board the *brûlot*. On perceiving them occupied in preparing the train, and from my being so very near, I felt it absolutely necessary that immediate steps should be taken to prevent the destruction of the fleet, which, from the manner of proceeding, seemed inevitable. I accordingly sent the pinnace with the first lieutenant, directing him to explain to them, that if they remained quiet no harm was intended; but as their position was one of great danger to us, I wished them to quit the vessel in their boats, or to remove her farther in-shore out of our way.

As the boat left the ship, perceiving one of the midshipmen with his sword drawn, I desired him to sheathe it; and that the men in the boat might perfectly understand, I called out from the gangway, in the hearing of the ship's company, "Recollect, sir, that no act of hostility is to be attempted by us on any account." When the boat reached the quarter of the vessel and was in the act of laying in the oars, the coxswain was shot dead, although the first lieutenant had made signs to the Turkish commander, that no act of violence was intended, which he even repeated after the man had been shot close by him. This shot was followed up by several others, fired through the after-ports, killing and wounding others of the boat's crew: at the same moment, we observed part of the Turkish crew ignite the train forward, upon which I dispatched Lieutenant Fitzroy in the cutter, for the purpose of towing her clear of this ship; in the execution of which he met a boat conveying the crew of the burning fire-vessel towards the shore, who immediately opened a fire of musquetry upon him, by which he was killed. On observing this, I ordered the marines to cover the retreat of the boats, which were again sent to tow the vessel, then in flames, clear of us. Almost at the same instant two shots were fired from an Egyptian corvette in-shore, one of which passed close over the gangway, and the other we observed strike the Sirène, bearing the flag of Rear-Admiral de Rigny, then in the act of anchoring. Thus, from the aggression on the part of the Turks, commenced the action; nor could forbearance on ours have been exceeded, or your particular instructions to avoid hostility more fully complied with.

(Signed,)   Thomas Fellows, *Captain.*

To Vice-Admiral Sir Edward Codrington.

Although we cannot insert the questions put to Sir Edward by "some of the superiors at home," yet, in their absence, the following, which were put to, and answered by, Captain Fellows, cannot fail of being highly satisfactory :

What proofs are there that the truce was broken ?

Leaving the port of Navarin on the 1st of October with part of his fleet, and proceeding to Cape Papas, when prevented by Sir Edward Codrington, and turned back on the 2d and again on the 4th of October, and afterwards committing all sorts of depredations in the Morea during the term of the said truce.

What attempt was made by Sir E. Codrington to obtain the assurance of the Pacha's intentions before the 20th of October?

Sir E. Codrington sent a frigate into Navarin on the 18th of October, with a letter to Ibrahim Pacha, by Colonel Craddock; but the pretence was, that the Pacha was not to be found, being absent with his army of 4 or 5,000 men, encamped at Modon, about seven or eight miles from Navarin. It was believed by the admiral that Ibraham was there, and the refusal to say where he was, only a subterfuge to gain time, particularly as the term of the truce was expired, and Ibrahim had engaged to acquaint Sir E. Codrington with the result of his dispatches to his two courts, and which we knew had been received some days, and no notice taken of it to the admiral. A person of high rank was seen reviewing his troops at Modon on the 16th of October, by one of the officers in the English squadron, which person was believed to be Ibrahim Pacha.

What must have been the situation of the combined fleets if Sir E. Codrington had forborne to enter the bay ?

Would it have been expedient or possible for the combined fleets to continue a blockade? and in case of tempestuous weather, had they any place of refuge but the harbour ? and would it have been consistent with the duty of the admirals to have quitted the blockade, and left the Turkish fleet in that position?

If the admiral had forborne to enter the harbour, it would have been impossible for him to have preserved the blockade with even an English force, much less with one composed of three nations, not having the same signals or rules of service, and speaking different languages, and no place nearer than Zante in which they could have taken shelter: consequently the blockade could no longer have existed, and the treaty could not have been enforced. Nor could they, under circumstances of bad weather, possibly have ventured into a port in which the Turco-Egyptian fleet were so hostilely arrayed, but by risking the whole of the combined fleets, as the *brûlots* could have done their work without a hope of relief from boats, which could not have acted in a sea ; and as the weather was then commencing, it became absolutely necessary for him to choose between two evils, and the one he adopted seemed to him to be the best and most likely to obtain the results contemplated by the treaty. Had he quitted the blockade, he would certainly have neglected his duty, as the Turks would then have effected their object.

Was it really the determination of the Turks to begin the contest? and was it not in the power of the combined fleets to have avoided it after they entered the harbour?

I have no doubt from all I saw, that it was the object of the Turk to gain time, knowing that the months of December, January, and February were unfavourable to any attempt at blockade of a coast iron-bound; and that feeling himself secure in his extraordinary position, he calculated on a division of the opinions of a force so formed against him, urged by a secret power to resist; and he did not believe we should enter the bay, and therefore pretended to keep out of the way; at the same time being perfectly prepared to resist any attack, having springs on the cables of all his ships, which were placed in a most warlike attitude; and the fire-ships also so placed that nothing but the greatest precaution could avert what appeared to them inevitable, had their plan not been prematurely exposed—by the evidence obtained from the Greeks who swam to the English ships during the action, that it was the intention of the Turks to set fire at night to their *brûlots*, and by that means destroy the whole of the combined fleets. Every precaution was taken, and the most positive orders given, not to fire; and as a proof how little the admiral expected an action, he had furled his sails, called the watch, and ordered the band to play on the poop; and he never formed the line, but entered only with the Dartmouth, the other ships following in the distance, when they (the Turks) began the action. As a farther proof of their intentions being hostile, when the Asia was at the entrance of the harbour, a Turkish boat went along side, and returned to the shore in a great hurry; and upon the officer reaching a certain point of the fort, a red flag was hoisted, and a gun fired, without shot, from that point which corresponded with the same signal made previous to the battle of Algiers; and immediately after a boat went from the Turkish admiral's ship to one of the fire-vessels, which was seen preparing her train: upon which a boat was sent to her, to say, that nothing hostile was intended from the combined fleets; but as their position was one of extreme danger to the fleets, we should be obliged to them to move her in-shore. But before the boat could reach her, and while in the act of laying in the oars, and notwithstanding the signs of peace made by the officer in the boat, he was fired at, and the coxswain behind him and another man killed; they at the same time igniting the train forward. At that moment one of the corvettes fired a round shot, which passed over the Dartmouth, and a second shot struck the French admiral's ship, passing under the stern, and a third cut his cable as he came to an anchor along side a double-banked ship of 62 guns, forming the advanced ship of the south-west horn of the crescent. After this the action became general; nor was it possible for the admiral to have prevented it, as the Turks themselves were the aggressors. On a former occasion, Admiral de Rigny called upon the French officers and men serving in the Egyptian fleet, on their allegiance, to quit the service of the Pacha, as in the event of an action, if found, they would suffer the penalty of the law. The fact of their having quitted the fleet the day before the action is surely another proof of the determination of the Turks to fight, if any more were wanting.

We now close this article with the earnest hope, that every British officer will, under similar circumstances, imitate the conduct of Sir Edward Codrington; and that he will be anxious to create such "accidents" as will redound to the honour of his king and country, "notwithstanding the paltry conduct of some superiors at home."

ADMIRAL ROBERT PLAMPIN.

ONE great advantage attending the publication of a periodical work is, the opportunity that is thereby afforded of noticing, at its close, any errors or mistakes that may have been committed in its progress, and which would not otherwise be discovered in time to enable the publisher to correct them in the same work. During the progress of the present publication, we have requested as a favour, that any gentleman who should discover in it any error or mistakes, would have the goodness to inform us thereof, in order that we might correct them in an appendix.

As the work will probably go to a second edition, we now repeat this request; and, farther, shall be infinitely obliged for any additional information on the subjects to which it relates.

The first error we have to notice occurs in the Memoir of Admiral Halkett; and respecting which we have received the following letter from Admiral Plampin, dated Admiralty-House, Cove, February 17, 1827:

DEAR SIR,—Late yesterday, I received by the Bristol steam-boat the seventeenth Number of the *Biography*, and seeing the name of my friend Admiral Halkett, I instantly began reading the Memoir respecting him; and was not a little surprised to see the very erroneous information you have been supplied with respecting the flotilla at Willemstadt. You state, that "as Captain Berkeley was not in commission, he could not take the command;" which is certainly a mistake, for although he was not in command of any ship, but at that time on his travels, he had been stopped at the Hague by Lord Aukland, the British ambassador, to attend the fitting out of the gun-boats at Rotterdam, in doing which he rendered great service; for such was the disaffection of many of the Dutch, and their habitual tardiness, that the flotilla which was fitting to be under the orders of Count Bentinck van Rohan, did not arrive at Willemstadt until after the French had raised the siege. That Captain Berkeley was, however, in command of our flotilla from first to last, I think I can satisfactorily prove. On my arrival at Helvoetsluys, I was directed by Captain Manby's (then in command of his Majesty's ship Sirène) order, dated 16th March, 1793, " to proceed forthwith to Dort, and put myself *under the orders of Captain Berkeley;* and this too in the name of the Lords Commissioners of the Admiralty, addressed to Lieutenant Plampin, of his Majesty's ship Princess Royal. His Royal Highness the Commander-in-Chief also gave directions, that I should be " permitted to pass without interruption to Streyensass, to join the gun-boats *under the command of Captain Berkeley.*" Again, in Lord Aukland's letter to me, dated 30th April, accompanying a gold chain and medal, he says, " for your services to this republic, *under our friend Captain Berkeley;*" and I beg to add, that Captain Berkeley was also presented with a gold chain and medal of superior value. Indeed, had not Captain Berkeley commanded, I must of necessity have done so, being eight years senior to Lieutenant Halkett, appointed to the Princess Royal on the 4th of March, and having been selected by the Lords of the Admiralty for that particular service in consequence of my knowledge of localities and the language of the country. All these circumstances considered, no one can possibly imagine that I could have condescended to act under the orders of Lieutenant Halkett. You are also wrong in stating, that the attack we made on the night of the 21st of March was upon Klundert. Klundert is a strongly fortified town, situate, as well as I remember, about five miles nearly S. E. from Willemstadt, and nearly due south about three miles and a half from the works we attacked, which were the enemy's advanced position on the east side of Willemstadt. Klundert was the head-quarters of the army besieging Willemstadt, and the village where the works in question were erected was, if I recollect right, called Noordschaans, which was in fact the landing-place on the great road to Klundert. The battery was erected on the top of the dyke, almost due east from Willemstadt, distant about two miles. You are no less in error in the particulars you have given of that attack. On my joining Captain Berkeley, he was lying with the whole of the flotilla at Streyensass; and I was immediately sent forward with a division to take up a position in the Hollands Diep, nearly opposite to Moerdyk, so as to observe any collecting of boats about that town, or any movement that might be made by Dumourier in that quarter. On the day in question our flotilla was all at anchor close in with Willemstadt; and we (that is to say, myself, Lieutenants Halkett and Western,) were dining with Captain Berkeley on board the yacht he lived in, when he proposed the attack; and as I was perfectly acquainted with the Dutch language, I was employed to examine the pilot belonging to my division; and in consequence of his information, it was determined to make an attack on the works in question that night. I started first with my division, that under Lieutenant Western immediately followed, and the one under Lieutenant Halkett, accompanied by Captain Berkeley, in a small rowing boat, I think a six-oared boat : on getting near the object of attack, I observed Lieutenant Halkett's division going to a different part of the dyke to that my pilot was directing me towards ; and on my noticing this to him, he assured me that we were going perfectly right, and that the other division was wrong. Lieutenant Halkett, shortly after this, rowed up along side of my boat, and, *in the name of Captain Berkeley*, asked what I was about. I replied that I was confident my pilot was correct, as he had been clear and distinct in all his conduct and observations ; which answer he carried to Captain Berkeley. After lying on our oars a very few minutes, we perceived that division coming after us, when we again pushed forward ; and very soon afterwards Lieutenant Western's boat and my own grounded, at the foot of the dyke, immediately under the battery. I had my hand on the gunwale of Western's boat, and was speaking to him in a low voice, when we were assailed by a tremendous shower of balls from musketry and wall-pieces, one of which entered the left eye of Western, and he dropped lifeless, without uttering a word. A brisk discharge of musketry and wall-pieces from the works, and grape and musketry from our boats, was then continued for some few minutes, when Lieutenant Halkett again came along side, and told me, " it *was Captain Berkeley's orders* that the boats should immediately retire." I then observed to Halkett, " I fear Western is dead."

By this time, however, the enemy's fire had ceased, or we must have suffered severely in retreating : we should indeed have suffered much more than we did in the first instance, had we not been so close in, which occasioned the greater part of the enemy's shot to go over our heads. You will perceive that your statement with regard to Lieutenant Western receiving a verbal order from Lieutenant Halkett at the time he was shot, is quite a mistake. The following morning the place was entered by a detachment sent by General Bottslaar from Willemstadt, who informed us, that there was every appearance of the place having been abandoned very precipitately, from the state in which they found the works and guard-house.

About this period the battle of Bois-le-Duc took place. Dumourier raised the siege of Willemstadt, abandoned his projected attack on Dort, and subsequent operations on Rotterdam and the Hague. On our return from Willemstadt, we met Lord Aukland and his family on board a Dutch government yacht near Dortrecht, when Captain Berkeley, Lieutenant Halkett, and myself were invited to dine with his lordship. Having assisted on the following day at the funeral of Lieutenant Western, in the church of Dort (in which a mural monument was erected to his memory by the gracious directions of his Royal Highness the much-lamented Duke of York), we proceeded to Rotterdam, and paid off the gun-boats, discharged the transports' men, and the Sirène's returned to their proper ship at Helvoet.

As the concluding paragraph of the advertisement, at the commencement of your work, requests your readers will inform you of any errors they may discover in it, I have troubled you with this, in justice both to you and myself. I remain, dear sir, your very obedient servant,

ROBERT PLAMPIN.

ADMIRAL SIR J. A. WOOD.

DURING the progress of this work our principal aim has been undeviatingly directed to truth, considering that to be the greatest recommendation an historical work can possess; and we can solemnly affirm, that we have not inserted a single sentence which we did not believe to be true. That it contains some trifling errors, some of which will be hereafter noticed, was to be expected; but we could not even hope that every opinion broached would meet with entire concurrence. It is now six years since we first commenced publishing this work; and during that time we have been favoured with the patronage and support of some of the most distinguished officers the country can boast of, whose private lives would add lustre to any profession, and who have expressed themselves in terms of the highest satisfaction with our exertions. We have sought for information from distant and various sources, and in most cases have applied to those who were in the highest degree interested in the correctness of our statements: some few have declined our invitations; but we take this opportunity to return our sincere and heartfelt thanks to all those to whom we are indebted for the slightest information. Amongst them is Rear-Admiral Sir James Athol Wood, who supplied us with various documents relating to his professional career, from which we drew up the Memoir of his services, and regret exceedingly that it should have given the slightest cause of complaint to any one. But although this is the only complaint we have received, we cannot even here plead guilty to the commission of any falsehood or incorrectness. Before, however, we offer a single observation, or endeavour to prove the truth of the statement, we must insert the following letter, which we have received from Rear-Admiral Sir Charles Brisbane:

GOVERNMENT-HOUSE, ST. VINCENT, *29th December*, 1827.

SIR,—By the last packet from England I received an extract from your *Naval Biography*, Part xx.; where, in giving the Memoir of Sir James Athol Wood, and speaking of the conquest of the Island of Curaçoa, I perceive you have glanced at, or rather derogated from, my character as an officer, by ascribing to another a large share of the merit of the plans of an enterprise, any part of the arrangements respecting which, until I saw the extract alluded to, I had believed there was not a man in the world who would claim, or even take to himself: for I here, at the outset, solemnly declare, that every scheme for the mode of attack as it was made was entered into by me on board the Arethusa, and communicated to the officers of that ship, before I ever consulted with either of the commanders of the three frigates who were to unite with me in the attempt. Painful, then, as it would be to me, under such circumstances, to allow this statement to go to the world through so important a publication as your work without contradiction; still, I think it probable I never should have addressed a letter to you on the subject, but have left the whole enterprise and its effects to be judged and spoken of by the many brave fellows who participated in the affair, had I not noticed in the Memoir a most shameful attack on the honour and courage of the daring Captain Bolton, now no longer amongst us; but than whom, whilst he lived and was known to me, there was not, in my opinion, to be found, either in his Majesty's land or sea forces, a more courageous or able officer. It is therefore due to his memory, and in a particular degree due from me, who was his friend, to deny, in the most forcible manner in my power, the authenticity of a conversation ascribed to Sir James (then Captain) Wood and myself respecting Captain Bolton; who, so far from coming into Curaçoa when there was nothing to be done, came in time, and in good time, to be very instrumental in the success of the attack. His frigate, although she accidentally grounded, was placed with her broadside to the face of a fortress at the entrance of the harbour, and by the judicious advantage taken of the situation, he prevented the enemy from coming down to man and work the guns, and thereby hindered a most destructive fire that could, and unquestionably would, have come from that battery.

I am fully sensible of the difficulty which an historian or biographer labours under in producing or compiling a work such as you are publishing, and am willing to make proper allowances for the imperfections it may contain; I am equally disposed to believe, that while you labour to give a proper history, you will be equally desirous to do justice to all, and prove yourself incapable of *knowingly* giving place to any production, from whatever quarter it may emanate, that could tend to detract from the honour of the two meritorious officers, Captains Bolton and Lydiard, who are both numbered with the dead. I therefore ascribe the error in your publication to misinformation; and as I entertain no doubt that you keep manuscripts, I call upon you, and I trust you will find no hesitation in referring to them, to favour me and the nation with the name of the party who furnished the Memoir in question. That you may feel the less reluctance in doing so, I pledge myself and my character as a British admiral, to the satisfactory refutation of every part of the statement that, either in substance or by implication, can be construed as casting a stigma on the character, or even a censure on the conduct, of those brave men; or of ascribing to any other individual than myself, then the commander of the squadron, whatever merit the suffrages of mankind have given to the plan which secured to his Majesty's arms a degree of success that could only have been contemplated by a sanguine man, and one who reposed unbounded confidence in the daring intrepidity of British seamen.

It is truly distressing to me, sir, to be placed in a situation which compels me to speak thus of myself; but the honest consideration of doing justice to the memory of two very deserving officers (one of whom was a most scientific man*), and of rescuing their fame from the unfair attempt that has been made on it, is, with me, of paramount importance; and when my king and my country ascribe to me, as I feel confident from their natural love of justice they will, the proper motives, I shall stand acquitted for what I have already said, as well as for that which I am now about to relate. It shall be a brief narrative of the circumstances connected with the conquest of Curaçoa; and if the detail goes farther to contradict parts of the Memoir in question, or should be found to fortify the remarks I have already made on it, I profess I am actuated by no other motives than those already assigned—a fondness for truth, and an ardent desire to preserve to the memory of two very deserving officers the fame to which it is so well entitled.

In the year 1806 I was in command of the Arethusa frigate, on the Jamaica station, under Admiral Dacres. About the beginning of December I received his orders to proceed in my ship, with the Latona, Fisgard, and Anson, commanded by Captains Wood, Bolton, and Lydiard, to Curaçoa. Besides my orders, having verbally from the admiral some discretion, I made up my mind without hesitation to the enterprise on that island, which eventually proved of so successful a nature. Immediately on leaving Jamaica I ordered scaling-ladders and every other preparation I thought necessary for the storming of Fort Amsterdam and the other fortifications of the town; and they were completed, and the officers of the Arethusa acquainted with my unalterable intention, before our arrival at the Island of Aruba, at which place I communicated a part of my plan to the

* Captain Bolton.

other three captains. I had resolved in my own mind to enter the harbour as soon after daylight as possible on the morning of the 1st January, knowing the previous one and that to be days of great festivity among the Dutch. This determination was *my own*, and it was never altered or shaken by any other person. In pursuance of this plan, I had Captains Wood, Bolton, and Lydiard on board the Arethusa on the 31st December, when, in conference with them, some objections were raised to the attack, for the reason that it was thought quite impracticable. My determination, as I before said, was previously taken; and before either of my brother captains left the Arethusa, I handed to each his orders. *They were written previous to the conference*, and were to this effect: That the squadron, to be led by the Arethusa, was to enter the harbour of Curaçoa at the approach of clear daylight on the following morning. The captains of the three ships, each in person, on entering, to head their respective ship's companies, either for the storming of the principal fortress, Fort Amsterdam, or of boarding any of the enemy's ships of war that might be found in the harbour for its defence; and that the *masters* of each ship, with thirty men each, were to be left on board, for the purpose, in the event of failure on our parts, of destroying them by fire; so that, in such a case, not a vestige of a British man-of-war should fall into the enemy's hands.

I never contemplated a thing so truly ridiculous as awaiting the " return of a flag of truce," as stated in your work. It is true, I wore a truce-flag; but not by the suggestion or advice of any other man. I entered with it flying; but being disregarded by the enemy opening a fire, it was hauled down. To have sent in and awaited the return of a flag of truce, would have defeated all my sanguine hopes; for such a proceeding would have secured to the enemy a defence, and my plan of succeeding by a surprise would have availed me nothing. To have attempted the conquest of Curaçoa with any chance of success, fortified as it was, by any other plan than a surprise, would have required many ships and several thousand men.

Here it may not be unnecessary to say, that the idle and puerile conversation ascribed to Captain Wood and myself about jumping over chains, &c. is too contemptible to require refutation, or even serious comment; as little recollection have I of the Latona's backing her main-top-sail to let the Arethusa enter first. The spirit of the Memoir forbids my thinking, as I otherwise should, that this was intended to be a satire on the captain of the Latona. The Arethusa was ahead all the time, and in such situation entered the harbour. It was from your book, the extract of which I saw only a week ago, that I derived the first intimation of the Dutch governor having, with a lady, gone along side of the Latona, and having been directed to come to me. If such had been the fact, the captain of that ship should certainly have sent him to me a prisoner, particularly as he must have known I was engaged in taking possession of the troops of the garrison, and that the enemy's flags were flying : indeed if there be one fact that I can relate with greater confidence than another, it is, that I took the governor prisoner while he was entering the fortress by a private door, and never let him out of my presence until the terms of the capitulation were agreed upon and signed.

Your work speaks also of some delay on the part of Captain Lydiard, to which I am utterly a stranger. I was the first person who entered the principal fort, to which I ascended by a scaling-ladder ; and can safely assert, that Captain Lydiard was the third. He was also in proper place on another important occasion ; for he *passed* the Latona, and laid the Anson on board a Dutch 20-gun ship, and hauled down her colours.

In justice to myself, I am bound also to deny the statement of my walking quietly with twenty or thirty men on the quay, and of hailing Captain Wood to know if the Dutch frigate had struck ; which I do with less hesitation, from the circumstance of having, before I went on shore at all, actually boarded that ship, and with my own hands hauled down her colours. It is true, her men forsook their guns before I reached her quarter-deck. I there directed her lieutenant to strike her colours ; he refused to do so, but surrendered to me his sword, which, so obtaining, I have ever since kept in my possession. When this was done I hailed Captain Wood, and directed him to take charge of the prisoners. I *then* landed on the quay, and instead of walking quietly with twenty or thirty men, as your work implies, I never found greater necessity for exertion than I did to arrive at the garrison, where I expected to encounter great difficulty ; but fortunately reached it in time to prevent about two hundred men, who, having partly recovered from their consternation, were clothing, and preparing to act against us. We succeeded in making prisoners the whole number.

On entering the embrasure of Fort Amsterdam, I found the major-commandant of the Dutch troops with his sword drawn : I took him prisoner. Proceeding farther on, at one of the angles of the fortress I encountered a black man, who bravely fired upon me, and the ball from his firelock passed through my coat. This man, by this time within my reach, might have been immediately cut down or shot by me, but seeing him a brave fellow, I let him pass ; and afterwards heard, with great regret, that he was killed ; but not until your Memoir of Sir James Wood appeared did I ever hear that any of the Latona's men took merit for *that* act.

These, sir, are some leading facts connected with the attack and conquest of Curaçoa, in which proceeding, and the correspondence consequent thereon, I have only one thing to regret—it is not necessary to state it here : it may, however, be wrested from me when I learn to whom the Memoir, now under discussion, is ascribable. In the present stage of the business I will say, the goodness of heart, ever inseparable from the characters of the two deceased captains, causes me to feel such regret.

Here, sir, I would stop, and refrain from adding any thing to this letter, already a very long one, had not your Memoir of Sir James Wood ascribed to me a mercenary selfishness, which I am well known, by those who know me at all, not to possess. Nothing was more foreign from my mind than a desire to make place or provision for my connections: I solemnly declare that I went into Curaçoa with an ardent desire to serve my country, and an inflexible determination to succeed or die in the conflict. Is it then fair to have such sordid motives ascribed to me? or is it expected that I am tamely to submit to the imputation? I thought not of pecuniary advantage. It is not true that I either offered place to Captain Wood, or proposed bargains respecting any, as will appear plainly from this fact— that in the terms of the capitulation I offered a guarantee of all situations and places to every functionary of the island, if they would take the oath of allegiance to my king. Not only did I not display any anxiety about the " good things," as in the Memoir you are pleased to term them, but I assert, without the fear of contradiction from any quarter, that I did not directly or indirectly make any provision in the colony for either myself or any one branch of my family; so far from doing so, I gave up the colonial emoluments of my government, amounting to more than a thousand sterling a year, to the charitable uses of the four religious sects of the island.

I have now to request that you will, in pursuance of the impartial plan of your work, give place and very early publicity to this letter, and as speedily as possible favour me with a reply. I am, sir, your most obedient, humble servant,

CHARLES BRISBANE,
Rear-Admiral of his Majesty's Red Squadron.

To J. RALFE, *Esq.*
Author of a *Naval Biography of Great Britain,*
No. 6, Charing-Cross, London.

In acknowledging the receipt of this letter, we stated to Sir Charles, that the particulars of the capture of Curaçoa were inserted on the authority of Sir James Wood himself, and that we had his permission to state the fact: that we should, agreeably to his request, insert his letter in the work; but that justice to Sir James and ourselves would demand our offering such observations upon it as additional information and the nature of the case demanded.

In the above letter it will be seen, that Sir Charles denies *every particular* which we have stated respecting the capture of Curaçoa; but we must repeat some of his words in order to a complete understanding of the different points. He says, " I here at the outset solemnly declare, that every scheme for the mode of attack, *as it was made,* was entered into by me on board the Arethusa, and communicated to the officers of that ship before I consulted with either of the commanders of the other three frigates who were to unite with me in the attempt." We have stated in the Memoir, that Sir Charles declared he would attack the Island of Curaçoa, if it were not surrendered to him *on his sending in a flag of truce:* Sir Charles says in the above letter, " I never *contemplated* a thing so truly ridiculous." This then is the grand point at issue, which may indeed be called the foundation upon which every other point rests; and if we can clearly establish the truth of our assertion in this instance, we might, though we shall not do so, leave every other point unnoticed.

In the collection of papers belonging to Sir James Wood we find an original document, *in the hand-writing of Sir Charles Brisbane,* of which the following is a copy:

His Majesty's Ship ARETHUSA, — *day of December,* 1806.

WHEN THE FLAG OF TRUCE LEAVES THE ARETHUSA, boats of every description are to be hoisted out and towed on each quarter.

To JAMES ATHOL WOOD, *Esq.* (Signed,) C. BRISBANE.
Capt. of H. M. S. LATONA.

Now if this order does not prove that Sir Charles not only *contemplated,* but had *actually decided* on, sending in a flag of truce, we really do not know what would. However, he did not send it in: what was the reason? We have already said, that he was induced to abstain from so doing by the representations of Sir James Wood, who went on board the Arethusa on the evening of the 30th for that purpose, accompanied by his pilot, a native of Curaçoa, and of course acquainted with the manners and customs of his countrymen. Sir Charles says, that he decided on the mode of attack " *as it was made*" from the very first, and that " this determination was my own, and it was never altered or shaken by any other person." As Mr. Bislake, the pilot, in whose presence the conversation we have inserted is said to have taken place, is dead, we cannot of course add his testimony to that of Sir James Wood; but surely the unsupported assertion of Sir James is equal to that of Sir Charles. However, Sir James has referred us to three gentlemen who belonged to the Latona—the present Captain W. Grint, Lieutenant Brown, and Mr. Foggo, the latter of whom was his clerk, and is now secretary to the

Naval Club in Bond-street; and to whom the following question has been put: " Do you recollect, that on the evening of the 30th December, 1806, about sunset, after the signal was made for seeing the land in the N. E. known to be Curaçoa, which was answered by the Arethusa, that the latter made the signal to prepare to tack; that Sir James Wood then made the signal to speak with the Arethusa; and that, on her bringing-to, he went on board that ship in company with his Dutch pilot?" To this question Captain Grint has replied, " I recollect the signals; and I understood quite well what Sir James took the pilot on board for—*to advise Captain Brisbane to change his plan of sending in a flag of truce*, as that would knock every thing on the head; and to stand over during the night to the Spanish main, work up that coast all day of the 31st, and be ready to enter the harbour of Curaçoa at dawn of day on the first of the new year, when we should find the Dutchmen drunk and off their guard. Bislake informed me, that ' *the commodore had consented to do so*,' and it proved a most excellent plan." Lieutenant Brown states, that the intention of Sir Charles Brisbane to *send in a flag of truce* was publicly talked of, and that he has not the smallest doubt but he changed it in consequence of Sir James Wood's representations. Mr. Foggo says, that he does not remember the signals, but has a perfect recollection of Sir James going on board the Arethusa with the pilot; and after their return, heard it openly stated, that the commodore had consented to change his own plan, and adopt that of Sir James Wood. After such testimony, it must be unnecessary to offer another observation on this point; we therefore proceed to the remainder.

Sir Charles says, that he has " no recollection of the Latona backing her main-top-sail to let the Arethusa enter first." That he should have no recollection of this comparatively trifling circumstance is not at all surprising, when he could forget who was the projector of the plan under which he was acting. Sir James Wood, however, has a perfect recollection of it, and the following question has been put to the three gentlemen above-named: " Do you recollect, on entering the harbour of Curaçoa, that the Arethusa was to leeward of the Latona and very close to the lee point of the harbour; that the Latona was shooting ahead of, and taking the wind out of the Arethusa's sails; and that Sir James, being under the fire of all the enemy's batteries, ordered the Latona's sails to be backed, to enable the Arethusa to enter first?" Mr. Foggo says, " Yes;"—Lieutenant Brown's recollection on the point is equally clear and satisfactory;—and Captain Grint says, " I do, *as part of that duty was performed by myself*."

It is really painful to us to pursue this subject farther; but there are still two or three points which we must notice. Sir Charles says, " It was from your book that I derived the first intimation of the Dutch governor having, with a lady, gone along side of the Latona, and having been directed to come to me." Neither Captain Grint nor Mr. Foggo recollect this circumstance; but Lieutenant Brown remembers it perfectly well, and that Sir James told him the commodore was in the government-house, whither he was directed to proceed. Sir Charles indeed says, " if such had been the fact," it was the duty of Captain Wood to have sent him a prisoner to the government-house. If there had been any hostilities going forward, or the smallest appearance of danger, no doubt that would have been done; but as every thing was as quiet as in a drawing-room, such a measure was totally useless.

Sir Charles also says, " In justice to myself, I am bound to deny the statement of my walking with twenty or thirty men on the quay, and of hailing Captain Wood, to know if the Dutch frigate had struck; which I do with less hesitation, from the circumstance of having, before I went on shore at all, actually boarded that ship, and with my own hands hauled down her colours." All that we have to observe upon that point is, that Captain Grint declares he went on board the Dutch frigate, agreeably to the orders of Captain Wood, and that *it was himself who hauled down the enemy's colours*. And in answer to the following question, " Do you recollect Sir Charles Brisbane asking Captain Wood, from the wharf, and before he went on board the Dutch frigate, if she had surrendered; and if he was informed that she had long since, but that her colours were foul; and that owing to the Latona having kept up an occasional fire over her, and up the street, to prevent any one passing from the town to the fort, her people could not keep the deck?" Captain Grint says, " I do recollect this conversation taking place *when Captain Brisbane was on his way to the fort*." Mr. Foggo says, " I remember Sir Charles Brisbane hailing the Latona, *when he was on the wharf, on his way to the fort*, and conversing with Sir James Wood, but I do not recollect the particulars of it." Lieutenant Brown declares most positively, that Sir Charles went from the wharf to the Dutch frigate, and did not go on board of her previous to his landing from his own ship.

Sir Charles farther states, that " instead of walking quietly along the quay, I never found greater necessity for exertion than I did to arrive at the garrison; but fortunately reached it in time to prevent about two hundred men, who, having partly recovered from their consternation, were *clothing*, and preparing to act against us." What the necessity for exertion was, Sir Charles does not state; but if any existed, it surely was a waste of time to go on board the Dutch frigate, which was completely subdued. He does not say that he encountered the smallest resistance or opposition, except what arose from the conduct of one man, who fired at him, and though he was within reach, and might have cut him down, he let him pass, *seeing he was a brave fellow.* The fact is as we have stated it, and which we re-assert upon the authority of the above three gentlemen—that owing to the admirable plan of Sir James Wood, the enemy was so taken by surprise, that he had not time to take the slightest means for resisting the force brought against him; and farther, that owing to the masterly position taken up by Sir James Wood, the Latona not only raked and subdued the Dutch frigate and 20-gun ship, but her guns enfiladed the whole of the forts towards the harbour, and by which the enemy's fire was silenced in half an hour.

Respecting the Anson, Sir Charles says, " Your work speaks also of some delay on the part of Captain Lydiard, to which I am utterly a stranger. I was the first person who entered the principal fort, to which I ascended by a scaling-ladder; and can safely assert, that Captain Lydiard was the third. He was also in his place on another important occasion; for *he passed the Latona*, and laid the Anson on board the Dutch 20-gun ship, and hauled down her colours." Notwithstanding the confidence with which this assertion is made, we are authorized by Sir James Wood, Captain Grint, Lieutenant Brown, and Mr. Foggo, to contradict it; and to re-assert, that after the Anson entered the harbour, she ran on board the Latona, carried away her driver-boom, and swung round along side the Dutch 20-gun ship. That Captain Lydiard, or some of his crew, hauled down the colours of the latter, is probable, but it was after she had been completely subdued by the Latona: but if Captain Lydiard had *passed the Latona*, he must also have passed the enemy's ship, as she was lying with her head directly to the beam of the Latona. That Captain Lydiard may also have been the third to mount the scaling-ladder is also possible, as there was plenty of time for him to land and join Sir Charles on the wharf on his way to the fort. We must, however, observe, that though we mentioned a delay on the part of Captain Lydiard, we by no means wished to impute any blame to him; having stated in the Memoir, that it was owing to an accident.

With regard to the conversation which we have stated to have taken place between the commodore and Captain Wood respecting the Fisgard, we shall not add a single word; we feel confident as to its correctness, and it is perfectly unnecessary to enforce it. But when Sir Charles Brisbane says, that Captain Bolton, "so far from coming into Curaçoa when there was nothing to be done, came in time, and in good time, to be very instrumental in the success of the attack;" that "his frigate, although she accidentally grounded, *was placed* with her broadside to the face of a fortress at the entrance of the harbour, and by the judicious advantage taken of the situation, he prevented the enemy from coming down to man and work the guns, and thereby hindered a most destructive fire that could, and unquestionably would, have come from that battery," it is making an assertion which we cannot allow so easily to pass. Sir James still feels confident, that it was above an hour *after the Anson entered* that the Fisgard came in; an opinion in which he is fully borne out by the testimony of Lieutenant Brown. Captain Grint does not exactly recollect how long it was, but says it must have been some time, as she was greatly astern. But Mr. Foggo will not hazard an opinion about the time, as he has no clear recollection on the subject. All, however, agree that the forts had ceased firing before she entered: but notwithstanding that circumstance, she commenced firing upon the government-house, until her commander was directed by Captain Wood to cease; and both Captain Grint and Lieutenant Brown perfectly recollect Sir James giving that order. In his anxiety to defend the character of Captain Bolton, the zeal of Sir Charles has outstripped his judgment: for in stating that the Fisgard "prevented the enemy from coming down to man and work the guns" of the battery at the entrance of the harbour, he appears to have forgotten, that *those guns were fired at his own ship and the Latona as they passed along;* and, consequently, if the Fisgard had been exactly in her proper station, *she could not* have " prevented the enemy from coming down to man and work the guns," as "the enemy" was already there. We, however, take this as a proof of the correctness of our own account. Sir Charles admits by this, that the enemy's batteries were not manned when the Fisgard came in; but he knows that they were manned when he entered the harbour: then why did the enemy leave them? Because they were driven from them by the guns of the Latona, which enfiladed the whole.

We have now gone through Sir Charles's letter, and we hope without giving him the smallest pain; at all events, we can safely say, that we have not the slightest wish or inclination to cause him an unpleasant feeling of any description. We can assure him, that our being obliged to enter into, *not a refutation of his statement*, but *a justification of our own*, is the most unpleasant circumstance which has attended the publication of the work; and were not a third person so intimately interested in our account being fully and substantially proved to be correct, we rather think we should have inserted Sir Charles's letter without comment or observation: as it was, we had no other alternative.

In conclusion, we beg to assure Sir Charles, that in making use of the term " good things," we by no means wished to attach to it any invidious meaning; we merely stated the fact, without wishing it to be thought that he had done more than is usual on such occasions. We wish also to observe, that we cannot agree with Sir Charles in the opinion, that in ascribing to an officer who was second in command a large share of the merits of the enterprise, was derogating from his character; on the contrary, we are ready to admit, that, as the commander of the squadron, he was entitled to the greatest praise; and have stated in the Memoir, that Sir James Wood acknowledged he had done that which would do him " immortal honour." Surely this is not derogating from his character.

We have been favoured with the following:

DUNKIRK, *October 28, 1827.*

SIR,—I herewith have the honour to inclose to you a letter I received from Admiral Rolles, who has taken great offence at the article in your Life of Sir R. Otway, as communicated to you by me. When Admiral Rolles first wrote to me, I requested him, if what I stated was not correct, to favour me with the particulars of the mutiny, in order that you, in any future edition of your valuable *Biography*, might correct my statement. I confess I was no little astonished on reading his account of it, which falsifies mine in almost every particular. In reply to the admiral, I could only state, in my own justification, that what I heard concerning that mutiny, every other officer of the Trent heard; and that when I heard it, I had no reason to doubt it, for it was characteristic of Sir R. Otway, who, in either mutiny or battle, possessed a presence of mind that the best of us might well envy. I, however, assured Admiral Rolles, that, in giving it to you for insertion, I had not the slightest intention of casting any imputation on either his conduct or that of any other officer of the Renommée; that I spoke of Sir R. Otway's conduct in that affair as I should have spoken of it in a general action, as it applied to himself as an individual. It is impossible for me to recommend what ought to be done: all I can say is, that I cannot set my memory against Admiral Rolles' statement; but I have no doubt that before this can reach you, Sir R. Otway will have noticed my incorrectness. I am, sir, your most obedient, humble servant,   T. Ussher.

WICKHAM, *near* FAREHAM, HANTS, *9th October*, 1827.

MY DEAR CAPTAIN USSHER,—I acknowledge the receipt of your letter of the 20th ult. with that of the 16th of June, within a few days after we met in town; and I have delayed answering your last till I could hear from one of the officers of the Renommée, who fully corroborates the account I shall give of the *meditated* mutiny. He says, " the statement (Ralfe's) is wholly incorrect, and I think must give offence to such an officer as Sir R. Otway, should it meet his observation." I cannot allow myself to suppose that in making the statement you did to Mr. Ralfe relative to the matter in question, that you *intended* to cast any reflection on my conduct; but it certainly appears to me, that in your zeal to exalt the character of Sir R. Otway, you did not sufficiently consider those who were more deeply concerned. I have no desire to provoke an angry discussion; but in justice to myself, as well as the officers of the ship I commanded, I must repeat, that your information has been incorrect in almost every particular. It must be obvious, that Captain Otway's being with me, his boat along side, and his ship almost within hail at the time the plot was discovered, were of themselves circumstances sufficient to discourage, if not to defeat, the plan of the mutineers, who did not amount to more than about forty. I ever have, and ever will, acknowledge, with every proper feeling, that I received every assistance from Captain Otway which a brother officer could give upon so trying an occasion; but I deny most positively, that the ship was saved by the presence of mind or the act of Sir R. Otway, or any other individual whatever. The following are the particulars: On the evening in question, a man (and not a boy) sent in, wishing to speak with me in the cabin; and upon his coming in, with considerable agitation of manner, he said that the ship's company were about to mutiny, murder all the officers, and carry the ship into the Havannah; but, from fear of personal danger, he hesitated telling who were the ringleaders. At last, by persuasion and threats, he gave the names of several, one of whom was sent for; and while he was interrogated, the accuser (at the suggestion of Captain Otway) was put into the quarter-gallery. The accused denied all knowledge of the business, and the accuser was brought face to face before him, when he repeated enough of what he had said before to convince us that there was foundation for the report; and the accused was put into confinement immediately. The first lieutenant, who had been present during this examination, was then directed to order all the officers and petty officers (who had previously been desired to arm themselves privately) to repair to the quarter-deck; and I proposed turning all hands up, which Captain Otway rather objected to, as a dangerous measure: but as I considered it almost impossible that more than a small portion of a ship's company could be privy to so horrid an act, they were turned up; and after Captain Otway and I had briefly addressed them, one man muttered something by way of complaint, and not in the most orderly manner. This took place near where Captain Otway stood, who noticed, and I believe took hold of him. Many of the petty officers and best men came forward, declaring their ignorance of what had been meditated, and their determination to stand by and support the officers. No other disposition to mutiny or resistance was manifested, and consequently no occasion for coercive measures were necessary, and they were dismissed in an orderly manner. The marines were all true, I believe, to a man; and the report of sending to the carpenter to turn the cocks and let water in, and give out that the ship had sprung a leak, and all hands being ordered to the pumps, is all without any foundation whatever. The report from the lieutenant (now post-captain) is a long one, or I would transcribe it for your perusal, which I will do at any time, if you wish it. I remain, my dear sir, yours very truly,　　　　ROBERT ROLLES.

We are requested by Vice-Admiral Foote to state, that it was not owing to the Niger being "a small frigate" that she could not keep to windward with the Emerald and Minerva, as we have stated in the Memoir of Sir George Cockburn, but to *the small quantity of stores, provisions, and water she had on board—of the latter, not more than two tons;* and that, in consequence of her casks having been put on shore, by permission of Lord St. Vincent, she could not fill them with salt water. Her inefficient state was indeed known to the commander-in-chief, but as the Trinidad was reported to be near Cape St. Mary a perfect wreck, it was necessary that the ships should immediately sail in quest of her.

We are also requested by Rear-Admiral Thomas Harvey to contradict the assertion we have made at page 180, vol. IV. in stating that the Arethusa and Pelican were directed to make an attack on the Spanish frigate then lying in the gulf of Paria; and in proof of his correctness in this respect, has sent us a copy of the orders delivered to Captain Wolley of the Arethusa on the occasion, which certainly do not make any allusion to hostile operations, but direct him to cruise between Tobago and Grenada for the protection of the trade, to look frequently into the gulf of Paria, attend to the proceedings of the Spanish squadron, and to send to the admiral immediate notice of any movement they might make, or any reinforcement that might join them. Admiral Harvey admits that great credit was due to Captain Wood for the information which he gave to the commander-in-chief; but assures us, that the latter was not undecided in his plans of attacking the island.

These are the whole of the errors of importance that have been pointed out to us; and when the extent of the work is considered, and the various sources of information we have been obliged to have recourse to, and that we are quite "unprofessional," we do hope that they are such as may be very readily pardoned.

We now take our leave of the work, with heartfelt thanks to the Bestower of all blessings for granting us health and strength to bring it to a termination; and with feelings of great obligation to those officers who have favoured us with information, and supported us with their patronage and subscriptions. We must, however, make a few parting observations. Addison says, that "a true critic ought to dwell rather upon excellences than imperfections; to endeavour to discover the concealed beauties of a writer, and communicate such things to the world as are worth observation, rather than those which detract from his reputation." This principle we have endeavoured to follow in treating of the conduct of the officers of the British navy. Entertaining the highest admiration of their conduct, our exertions have been directed to place their characters in the most conspicuous point of view; and if it be objected that we have been too lenient in our remarks, and have searched for incidents whereon to rest a measure of praise rather than censure or complaint, we must in some degree plead guilty: but we must observe, that we have endeavoured to make the voice of praise the voice of truth; and, farther, that the work consists of a selection of the most meritorious and distinguished, and who, with all their blemishes, are still ornaments to their country. We certainly have not been anxious to inquire into their faults, much less to bring them into light; but, on the contrary, where we could with propriety throw a shadow over their defects, we have not failed to do so.

THE END.

Printed by L. Harrison, 5, Prince's-street, Leicester-square.

ERRATA.

Vol. I. p. 187, line 21, for *chests*, read *charts.*

II. p. 56, line 22, for *lunavian*, read *lunarian.*

— p. 63, line 24, for *Demarara*, read *Dominica.*

— p. 367, line 3, for *nephew*, read *cousin.*

— p. 389, line 21, for *hoisted blue-lights*, read *burnt blue-lights.*

— p. 501, line 19, for 1825, read 1805.

III. p. 20, line 15, for *eastward*, read *westward.*

— p. 31, line 14, for " appointed to the chief command at the Nore," read " appointed to succeed Sir R. G. Keats in the Baltic; and while lying in the Downs, assumed the chief command on that station, in the absence of Sir G. Campbell (absent on leave); and also directed the arrangements of the North-Sea cruisers at the same time, in the absence of Sir R. Strachan, then in London, and to whom he made his reports, by order of the Admiralty-Board.—Line 31, for " lugger," read " dogger."

— p. 124, line 4, for *we may say*, read *you may say;* and at the end of the Memoir, for *all of whom*, read *two of whom.*

— p. 202, line 24, for *stern*, read *stem.*

IV. p. 117, line 27, for *conveyed*, read *convoyed.*

— p. 121, line 17, after " she lost sight of them in the evening," add " of the 19th."

— p. 324, line 1, after *Lockhart Ross*, read *Admiral Duff and Captain (afterwards Admiral) Sawyer.*—Line 21, after " on the return of Sir John Laforey in 1795," read " he found a number of small vessels, which had been purchased in America for the purpose of cruising in the hurricane months for the protection of the trade among the islands, to be manned from the line-of-battle ships ; but which were useless, from the impossibility of sparing a sufficient number of officers properly qualified to command them, in consequence of the great mortality prevailing in the squadron ; but being acquainted with Mr. Anderson's services, and his perfect knowledge of the navigation among the islands, acquired from long experience there, induced him," &c.

— p. 325, line 8, after " was appointed to the Atlas," read " on the particular application of Captain (now Vice-Admiral) Sir W. Johnstone Hope."

— p. 333, line 25, read " Rinaldo and Redpole, however, pursued the next praam ahead, and attacked her with such vigour and effect, that they soon drove all her crew from their quarters, and continued the contest with the whole of the praams, now closing round them, with the greatest," &c.

— p. 337, line 12, for *tick*, read *teak.*

— — line 23, after " guns on shore," read " although heavy ordnance was most particularly wanted for the Lake service," &c.

— p. 459, line 32, for *James* Smyth, read *Isaac.*

RALFE'S

Naval Chronology

OF

GREAT BRITAIN;

OR, AN

HISTORICAL ACCOUNT

OF

NAVAL AND MARITIME EVENTS:

INCLUDING THE

Official Letters of every Action which occurred from the Commencement of the War in 1803, *to the End of the Year* 1816:

ALSO,

Narratives of Shipwrecks, Particulars of the most important Courts-Martial, Votes of Parliament, List of Flag-Officers in Commission and of Promotions for each Year.

The whole forming a complete Naval History of the above Period.

ILLUSTRATED WITH

SIXTY PLAIN AND SIXTY COLOURED ENGRAVINGS

OF THE MOST DISTINGUISHED ACTIONS,

Taken from original Sketches made by Officers present, and whose Names are attached to them.

Price SIX GUINEAS; or with *Sixty plain Prints* only, FOUR GUINEAS.

PUBLISHED BY WHITMORE AND FENN, CHARING-CROSS.